W9-ADF-653

EARLIER AMERICAN MUSIC

EDITED BY H. WILEY HITCHCOCK
for the *Music Library Association*

5

GOSPEL HYMNS NOS. 1 TO 6 COMPLETE

GOSPEL HYMNS NOS. 1 TO 6 COMPLETE

BY

IRA D. SANKEY
JAMES MCGRANAHAN
GEORGE C. STEBBINS
PHILIP P. BLISS

NEW INTRODUCTION BY H. WILEY HITCHCOCK
Director, Institute for Studies in American Music,
Brooklyn College, CUNY

DA CAPO PRESS • NEW YORK • 1972

This Da Capo Press edition of *Gospel Hymns Nos. 1 to 6 Complete* is an unabridged republication of the "Excelsior Edition" published originally in 1895.

Library of Congress Catalog Card Number 70-171076

ISBN 0-306-77305-8

Published by Da Capo Press, Inc.
A Subsidiary of Plenum Publishing Corporation
227 West 17th Street
New York, New York 10011

Manufactured in the United States of America.

EDITOR'S FOREWORD

American musical culture, from Colonial and Federal Era days on, has been reflected in an astonishing production of printed music of all kinds: by 1820, for instance, more than fifteen thousand musical publications had issued from American presses. Fads, fashions, and tastes have changed so rapidly in our history, however, that comparatively little earlier American music has remained in print. On the other hand, the past few decades have seen an explosion of interest in earlier American culture, including earlier American music. College and university courses in American civilization and American music have proliferated; recording companies have found a surprising response to earlier American composers and their music; a wave of interest in folk and popular music of past eras has opened up byways of musical experience unimagined only a short time ago.

It seems an opportune moment, therefore, to make available for study and enjoyment—and as an aid to furthering performance of earlier American music—works of significance that exist today only in a few scattered copies of publications long out of print, and works that may be well known only in later editions or arrangements having little relationship to the original compositions.

Earlier American Music is planned around several types of musical scores to be reprinted from early editions of the eighteenth, nineteenth, and early twentieth centuries. The categories are as follows:

Songs and other solo vocal music
Choral music and part-songs
Solo keyboard music
Chamber music
Orchestral music and concertos
Dance music and marches for band
Theater music

The idea of *Earlier American Music* originated in a paper read before the Music Library Association in February, 1968, and published under the title "A Monumenta Americana?" in the Association's journal, *Notes* (September, 1968). It seems most appropriate, therefore, for the Music Library Association to sponsor this series. We hope *Earlier American Music* will stimulate further study and performance of musical Americana.

H. Wiley Hitchcock

INTRODUCTION

In 1875, the year he returned from a two-year revival tour of Great Britain as organist and song-leader for the charismatic evangelist Dwight L. Moody, Ira D. Sankey collaborated with a fellow hymnodist, Philip P. Bliss, to publish a collection called *Gospel Hymns.* Almost twenty years and five hymnbooks later, Sankey, together with two different collaborators (Bliss had died in 1876), issued a cumulation of the six earlier books under the title *Gospel Hymns Nos. 1 to 6 Complete.* With its 704 hymns in choral settings, plus texts for some thirty-five more, the book not only symbolizes the gospel-hymn movement of the later nineteenth century, but virtually embodies it between two covers.

To the mid-twentieth century, "gospel music" connotes the religious song of black Americans. But originally, the gospel hymn was a product of the northern urban revivals, organized and attended mostly by whites, that succeeded the earlier camp meetings and tent revivals of the back country and the frontier. Gospel hymnodists like Bliss and Sankey, James McGranahan, George C. Stebbins, and the Rev. Robert Lowry cannily adopted the early revival hymn's infectious pattern of a verse followed by a catchy, and usually thunderous, refrain. To it they adapted the predictable, and thus easily singable, melodic contours and smooth, simple harmony of the school of Lowell Mason and Thomas Hastings (lacing it often, however, with that kind of mild chromaticism we know from "Sweet Adeline"). The result, at its best, was a kind of religious pop art almost irresistible in its visceral appeal; at its worst, an embarrassingly trivial sacred counterpart of the sentimental "songs of hearth and home" of the same era.

Tastemakers of the twentieth century tended to reject gospel hymns as "a slough of sentimental music-hall sloppiness . . .

flabby and futile" (to quote Erik Routley, a British historian of hymnody). But in fact gospel hymns live on in some quarters of American society, although, as has so often happened in American popular music, their locus has shifted, in this case from urban to rural environment, and from north to south. In the meantime, some of their melodies and at least some phrases from their texts have become universally known, part of the American vernacular. The tune everyone recognizes as "How dry I am!" had an earlier incarnation as the gospel hymn *Happy Day* (No. 543); Bliss's *Hallelujah, 'tis Done* (No. 5) was secularized as "Hallelujah, I'm a bum." Many of us have unconsciously quoted bits of gospel hymn texts in such phrases, now become clichés, as "arise and shine" (see No. 103), "hold the fort" (No. 11), "where is my wandering boy tonight" (No. 631), and "throw out the lifeline" (No. 441).

If Sankey and Bliss wrote a new chapter in American popular hymnody, they did not entirely reject the past. *Gospel Hymns* includes pages from virtually every earlier chapter in the history of Protestant congregational song, from Luther and the Huguenots (Nos. 414 and 1, respectively) on to adaptations of Handel and Haydn (Nos. 606 and 442), eighteenth-century Yankee tunesmiths like Daniel Read and Oliver Holden (Nos. 728 and 729), and the "scientific" nineteenth-century hymnody of Mason and Hastings (Nos. 733 and 31, among others). Whenever tunes or texts, or both, struck their fancy (and served their purpose, that of providing the musical material for massive cathartic hymnfests), they cheerfully turned them into gospel hymns.

H.W.H.

The present edition of *Gospel Hymns Nos. 1 to 6 Complete* reproduces the so-called "Excelsior Edition" (1895). Type for this edition was newly set, reducing the length of the book to 512 pages from the mammoth 688 page "Diamond Edition" of 1894. Otherwise, the two editions are the same.

GOSPEL HYMNS
NOS. 1 TO 6 COMPLETE

GOSPEL HYMNS

Nos. 1 to 6

BY

IRA D. SANKEY

JAMES MCGRANAHAN AND GEO. C. STEBBINS

(EXCELSIOR EDITION)

PUBLISHED BY

THE BIGLOW & MAIN CO.
NEW YORK
CHICAGO

THE JOHN CHURCH CO.
CINCINNATI NEW YORK
CHICAGO

PREFACE.

GOSPEL HYMNS Nos. 1 and 2, by P. P. BLISS and IRA D. SANKEY; Nos. 3, 4, 5, and 6, by IRA D. SANKEY, JAMES McGRANAHAN, and GEO. C. STEBBINS, are now compiled in this volume under the title of

GOSPEL HYMNS NOS. 1 TO 6.

All duplicate pieces have been omitted and the Hymns re-numbered in consecutive order from 1 to 739.

In addition to the large number of Gospel Hymns and Sacred Songs in this collection there will also be found over 125 of the most useful and popular STANDARD HYMNS AND TUNES OF THE CHURCH.

GOSPEL HYMNS

NOS. 1 TO 6 COMPLETE.

No. 1. All People that on Earth.

"Come before his presence with singing."—PSA. 100: 2.

Rev. WM. KETHE. (OLD HUNDRED. L. M.) L. BOURGEOIS.

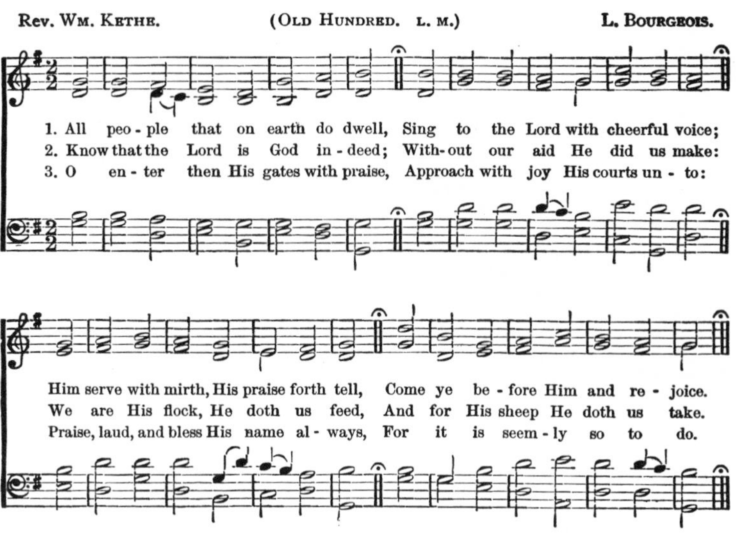

1. All peo - ple that on earth do dwell, Sing to the Lord with cheerful voice;
2. Know that the Lord is God in - deed; With- out our aid He did us make:
3. O en - ter then His gates with praise, Approach with joy His courts un - to:
Him serve with mirth, His praise forth tell, Come ye be - fore Him and re - joice.
We are His flock, He doth us feed, And for His sheep He doth us take.
Praise, laud, and bless His name al - ways, For it is seem - ly so to do.

4 For why? the Lord our God is good,
His mercy is for ever sure;
His truth at all times firmly stood,
And shall from age to age endure.

No. 2. Doxology. L. M.

Praise God, from whom all blessings flow;
Praise Him, all creatures here below;
Praise Him above, ye heavenly host;
Praise Father, Son, and Holy Ghost.

Thos. Ken.

Grace.

May be sung before and after meat.

No. 3. BLESSING INVOKED.

Be present at our table, Lord,
Be here and every where adored;
These mercies bless, and grant that we
May feast in Paradise with Thee.

No. 4. THANKS RETURNED.

We thank Thee, Lord, for this our food,
For life, and health, and every good:
Let manna to our souls be given,—
The Bread of Life sent down from heaven.

No. 5.

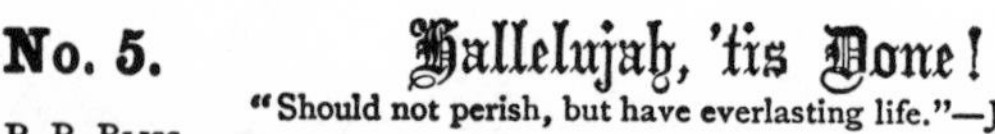

Hallelujah, 'tis Done!

"Should not perish, but have everlasting life."—JOHN 3: 10.

P. P. BLISS. P. P. BLISS.

1. 'Tis the prom-ise of God, full sal - va- tion to give Un - to him who on Je - sus, his Son, will be- lieve.
2. Tho' the path-way be lone- ly, and dan- ger - ous too, Sure-ly Je - sus is a - ble to car - ry me through.
3. Ma - ny loved ones have I in yon heav- en - ly throng, They are safe now in glo - ry, and this is their song:
4. Lit - tle chil- dren I see stand - ing close by their King, And He smiles as their song of sal - va - tion they sing:
Hal - le - lu - jah, 'tis done! I be- lieve on the Son; I am saved by the blood of the cru - ci - fied One; cru - ci - fied One.
1
2
Copyright property of The John Church Co.

5 There are prophets and kings in that throng I behold,
And they sing as they march through the streets of pure gold;
Hallelujah, 'tis done! etc.

6 There's a part in that chorus for you and for me,
And the theme of our praises forever will be:
Hallelujah, 'tis done! etc.

No. 6. Safe in the Arms of Jesus.

"Underneath are the everlasting arms."—DEUT. 33: 27.

FANNY J. CROSBY. W. H. DOANE.

1. Safe in the arms of Je - sus, Safe on His gen- tle breast, There by His love o'er- shad - ed, Sweet- ly my soul shall rest.
2. Safe in the arms of Je - sus, Safe from cor- rod- ing care, Safe from the world's temp- ta - tions, Sin can- not harm me there.
3. Je - sus, my heart's dear ref - uge, Je - sus has died for me; Firm on the Rock of A - ges Ev - er my trust shall be.
CHO.—Safe in the arms of Je - sus, Safe on His gen- tle breast, There by His love o'er-
rit.
FINE.
Hark! 'tis the voice of an - gels,
Free from the blight of sor - row,
Here let me wait with pa- tience,
Copyright property of The Biglow & Main Co.

shad - ed, Sweet - ly my soul shall rest.

Safe in the Arms of Jesus.
D.C. Chorus.
Borne in a song to me, O - ver the fields of glo - ry, O - ver the Jas-per sea..........
Free from my doubts and fears; On - ly a few more tri - als, On - ly a few more tears!......
Wait till the night is o'er; Wait till I see the morn-ing Break on the golden shore. .....
No. 7. The Lord will Provide.
"Casting all your care upon him, for he careth for you."—1 Peter 5: 7.
Mrs. M. A. W. Cook.
Philip Phillips.
1. In some way or oth - er the Lord will pro- vide: It may not be my way, It may not be thy way; And yet, in His own way, "The Lord will pro - vide."
2. At some time or oth - er the Lord will pro- vide: It may not be my time, It may not be thy time; And yet, in His own time, "The Lord will pro - vide."
3. De - spond then no lon - ger: the Lord will pro- vide; And this be the to - ken—No word He hath spo - ken Was ev - er yet bro - ken: "The Lord will pro - vide."
4. March on then right bold-ly; the sea shall di - vide The path-way made glorious, With shoutings vic - to - rious, We'll join in the cho - rus, "The Lord will pro - vide."
Copyright property of The Biglow & Main Co.
Chorus.
Then, we'll trust in the Lord, And He will provide; Yes, we'll trust in the Lord, and He will pro - vide.
No. 8. Where are the Nine?
P. P. Bliss.
Read Luke 17: 12–19.
P. P. Bliss.
Moderato.
1. Wand'ring a - far from the dwellings of men, Hear the sad cry of the lep - ers—the ten;
2. Loud - ly the stranger sang praise to the Lord, Knowing the cure had been wrought by His word,
3. "Who is this Naz - a - rene?" Phari - sees say; "Is He the Christ? tell us plain - ly, we pray."
4. Je - sus on tri - al to-day we can see, Thousands de - rid - ing - ly ask, "Who is He?"

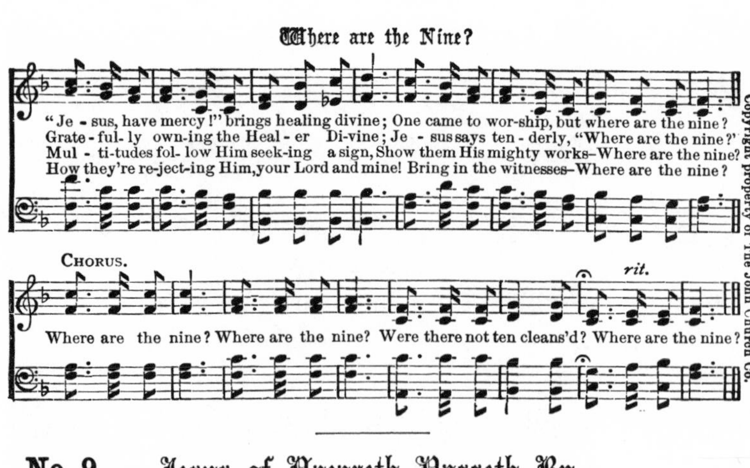
Where are the Nine?
"Je - sus, have mercy!" brings healing divine; One came to wor-ship, but where are the nine?
Grate - ful- ly own-ing the Heal - er Di-vine; Je - sus says ten - derly, "Where are the nine?"
Mul - ti-tudes fol- low Him seek-ing a sign, Show them His mighty works-Where are the nine?
How they're re-ject-ing Him, your Lord and mine! Bring in the witnesses-Where are the nine?
Chorus.
rit.
Where are the nine? Where are the nine? Were there not ten cleans'd? Where are the nine?
Copyright property of The John Church Co.

No. 9. Jesus of Nazareth Passeth By.

"He heard that it was Jesus of Nazareth."—Mark 10: 47.

Emma Campbell. Theo. E. Perkins.

1. What means this ea - ger, anxious throng, Which moves with bus - y haste a - long,
2. Who is this Je - sus? Why should He The cit - y move so might - i - ly?

These won - drous gath-'rings day by day? What means this strange com-mo - tion pray?
A pass - ing stran - ger, has He skill To move the mul - ti - tude at will?

In ac - cents hush'd the throng re - ply: "Je - sus of Naz - a - reth pass - eth by."
A - gain the stir - ring tones re - ply: "Je - sus of Naz - a - reth pass - eth by."

In ac-cents hush'd the throng re - ply: "Je - sus of Naz - a - reth pass - eth by."
A - gain the stir - ring notes re - ply: "Je - sus of Naz - a - reth pass - eth by."

Used by per.

Jesus of Nazareth.

3 Jesus! 'tis He who once below
Man's pathway trod, 'mid pain and woe;
And burdened ones, where'er He came,
Brought out the sick, and deaf, and lame,
The blind rejoiced to hear the cry:
"Jesus of Nazareth passeth by."

4 Again He comes! From place to place
His holy footprints we can trace.
He pauseth at our threshold—nay,
He enters—condescends to stay.
Shall we not gladly raise the cry—
"Jesus of Nazareth passeth by?"

5 Ho! all ye heavy-laden, come!
Here's pardon, comfort, rest, and home.
Ye wanderers from a Father's face,
Return, accept His proffered grace.
Ye tempted ones, there's refuge nigh,
"Jesus of Nazareth passeth by."

6 But if you still this call refuse,
And all His wondrous love abuse,
Soon will He sadly from you turn,
Your bitter prayer for pardon spurn.
"Too late! too late!" will be the cry—
"Jesus of Nazareth *has passed by*."

No. 10. Calling Now.

"To-day if ye will hear his voice, harden not your hearts."—Heb. 3: 15.

P. P. Bliss. P. P. Bliss.

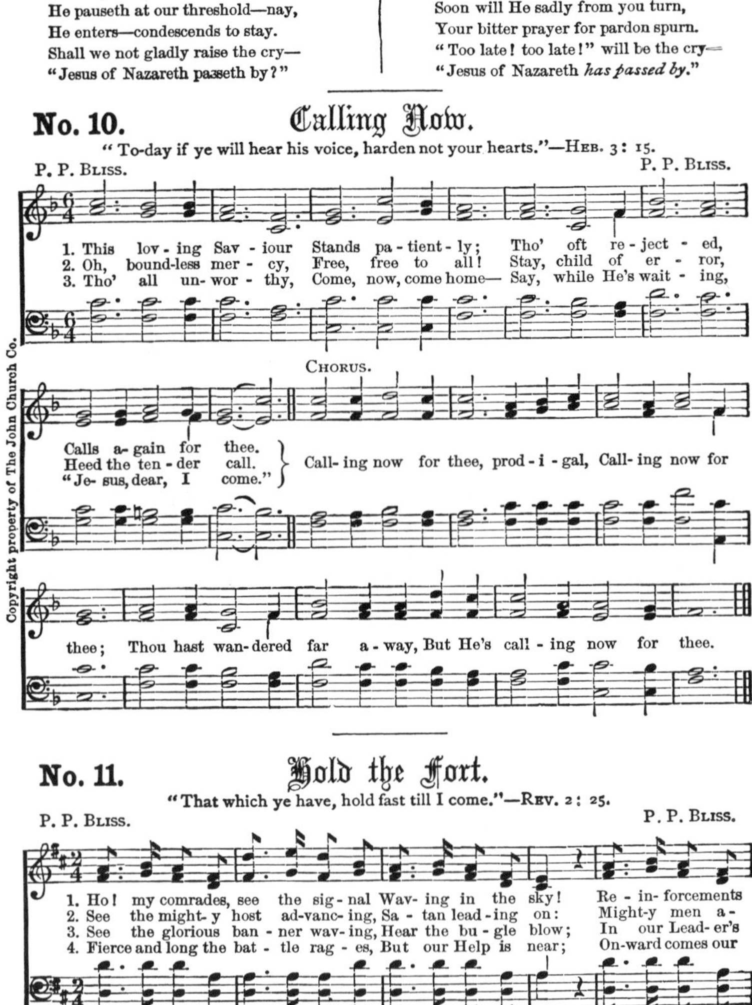

1. This lov-ing Sav-iour Stands pa-tient-ly; Tho' oft re-ject-ed, Calls a-gain for thee.
2. Oh, bound-less mer-cy, Free, free to all! Stay, child of er-ror, Heed the ten-der call.
3. Tho' all un-wor-thy, Come, now, come home— Say, while He's wait-ing, "Je-sus, dear, I come."
Chorus.
Call-ing now for thee, prod-i-gal, Call-ing now for thee; Thou hast wan-dered far a-way, But He's call-ing now for thee.

No. 11. Hold the Fort.

"That which ye have, hold fast till I come."—Rev. 2: 25.

P. P. Bliss. P. P. Bliss.

1. Ho! my comrades, see the sig-nal Wav-ing in the sky! Re-in-forcements
2. See the might-y host ad-vanc-ing, Sa-tan lead-ing on: Might-y men a-
3. See the glorious ban-ner wav-ing, Hear the bu-gle blow; In our Lead-er's
4. Fierce and long the bat-tle rag-es, But our Help is near; On-ward comes our

Hold the Fort.

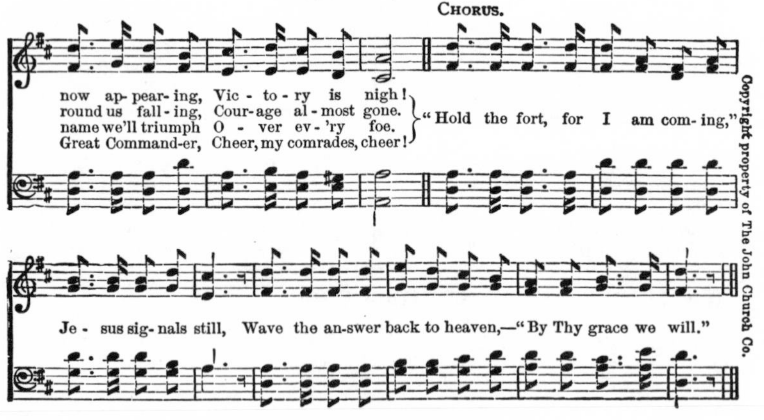
CHORUS.
now ap- pear- ing, Vic - to - ry is nigh!
round us fall - ing, Cour- age al - most gone.
name we'll triumph O - ver ev - 'ry foe.
Great Command- er, Cheer, my comrades, cheer!
"Hold the fort, for I am com- ing,"
Je - sus sig- nals still, Wave the an- swer back to heaven,—"By Thy grace we will."
Copyright property of The John Church Co.

No. 12. The Gate Ajar for Me.

"The gates of it shall not be shut at all by day; for there shall be no night there."
REV. 21: 25.

MRS. LYDIA BAXTER. S. J. VAIL.

1. There is a gate that stands a - jar, And thro' its por- tals gleaming, A radiance from the Cross a - far, The Saviour's love re - veal- ing.
2. That gate a - jar stands free for all Who seek thro' it sal - va - tion; The rich and poor, the great and small, Of ev - 'ry tribe and na - tion.
3. Press onward then, tho' foes may frown, While mercy's gate is o - pen: Ac- cept the cross, and win the crown, Love's ev - er- last - ing to - ken.
4. Be - yond the river's brink we'll lay The cross that here is giv - en, And bear the crown of life a- way, And love Him more in heav- en.

REFRAIN.

Oh, depth of mer - cy! can it be That gate was left a - jar for me? For me,...... for me?........ Was left a - jar for me?

For me, for me?

No. 13. Once for All.

"Justified by his grace, through the redemption that is in Christ Jesus."—ROMANS 3: 24.

P. P. BLISS. P. P. BLISS.

1. Free from the law, oh, hap - py con - di - tion, Je - sus hath bled, and *there* is re - mis - sion, Curs'd by the law and bruised by the fall, Grace hath redeemed us once for all.

2. Now are we free— there's no con - dem - na - tion, Je - sus pro - vides a per - fect sal - va - tion; "Come un - to *Me*," oh, hear His sweet call, Come, and He saves us once for all.

3. "Chil-dren of God," oh, glo - ri - ous call - ing, Sure - ly His grace will keep us from fall - ing; Pass - ing from death to life at His call, Bless - ed sal - va - tion once for all.

CHORUS.

Once for all, oh, sin-ner re - ceive it, Once for all, oh, broth - er, be - lieve it; Cling to the Cross, the bur - den will fall, Christ hath re - deemed us once for all.

No. 14. Work, for the Night is Coming.

ANNIE L. WALKER. DR. LOWELL MASON.

1. Work, for the night is com-ing, Work thro' the morning hours; Work while the dew is sparkling,
Work 'mid springing flow'rs; Work, when the day grows brighter, Work in the glow-ing sun;
D.S.—Work, for the night is com - ing,
When man's work is done.
FINE.
cres.
D.S.
By per. O. Ditson & Co., owners of the copyright.

2 Work, for the night is coming,
Work through the sunny noon;
Fill brightest hours with labor,
Rest comes sure and soon,
Give every flying minute,
Something to keep in store;
Work, for the night is coming,
When man works no more.

3 Work, for the night is coming,
Under the sunset skies;
While their bright tints are glowing,
Work, for daylight flies,
Work till the last beam fadeth,
Fadeth to shine no more;
Work while the night is darkening,
When man's work is o'er.

No. 15. Home of the Soul.

"In my Father's house are many mansions."—John 14: 2.

MRS. ELLEN H. GATES. PHILIP PHILLIPS.

1. I will sing you a song of that beau - ti - ful land, The far a - way
home of the soul, Where no storms ev - er beat on the glit - ter-ing strand, While the
years of e - ter - ni - ty roll. While the years of e - ter - ni - ty roll; Where no
storms ev - er beat on the glit - tering strand, While the years of e - ter - ni - ty roll.
Copyright property of The Biglow & Main Co.

Home of the Soul.

2 Oh, that home of the soul in my visions and dreams,
Its bright, jasper walls I can see;
Till I fancy but thinly the vail intervenes
‖: Between the fair city and me. :‖
Till I fancy, etc.

3 That unchangeable home is for you and for me,
Where Jesus of Nazareth stands,
The King of all kingdoms forever, is He,
‖: And He holdeth our crowns in His hands. :‖
The King of, etc.

4 Oh, how sweet it will be in that beautiful land,
So free from all sorrow and pain; [hands,
With songs on our lips and with harps in our
‖: To meet one another again. :‖
With songs on, etc.

No. 16. There is a Land.

"Thine eyes shall behold the land that is very far off."—Isa. 33: 17.

Isaac Watts. (Varina. C. M. D.) Geo. F. Root.

1. {There is a land of pure de- light, Where saints im- mor - tal reign;}
{E - ter - nal day ex - cludes the night, And pleas- ures ban - ish pain.}
2. {Sweet fields be- yond the swell- ing flood, Stand dressed in liv - ing green,}
{So to the Jews old Ca - naan stood, While Jor - dan rolled be - tween.}
There ev - er - last - ing spring a - bides, And nev - er- with - 'ring flowers;
Could we but climb where Mo - ses stood, And view the land - scape o'er,
Death, like a nar - row sea, di- vides This heaven - ly land from ours.
Not Jor-dan's stream, nor death's cold flood, Should fright us from the shore.

No. 17. We're Going Home To-morrow.

"Willing rather to be absent from the body, and to be present with the Lord."—2 Cor. 5: 8.

Mrs. E. W. Griswold. P. P. Bliss.

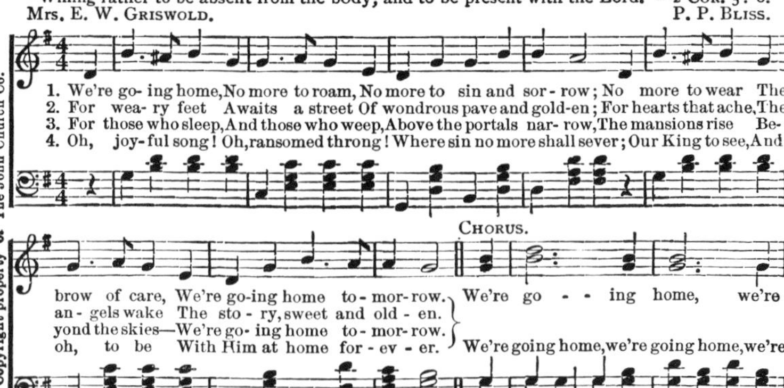

1. We're go- ing home, No more to roam, No more to sin and sor - row; No more to wear The
2. For wea - ry feet Awaits a street Of wondrous pave and gold-en; For hearts that ache, The
3. For those who sleep, And those who weep, Above the portals nar - row, The mansions rise Be-
4. Oh, joy- ful song! Oh, ransomed throng! Where sin no more shall sever; Our King to see, And
brow of care, We're go-ing home to - mor- row.
an - gels wake The sto - ry, sweet and old - en.
yond the skies—We're go- ing home to - mor- row.
oh, to be With Him at home for - ev - er.
Chorus.
We're go - - ing home, we're
We're going home, we're going home, we're

We're Going Home To-morrow.

going home to-morrow; We're go - - ing home, We're going home to-morrow.
going home to-morrow; We're going home, we're going home, We're going home to-morrow.

No. 18. Jesus Loves Even Me.

"God is love."—1 John 4: 8.

P. P. Bliss. P. P. Bliss.

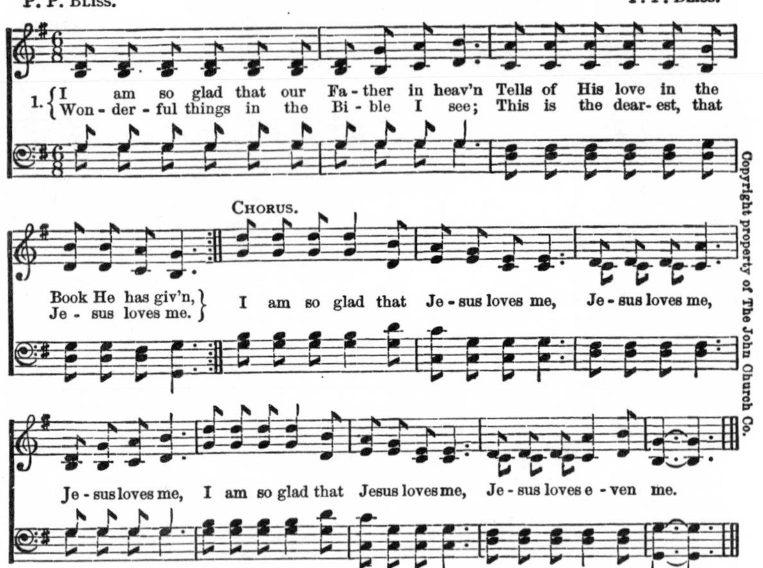
1. { I am so glad that our Fa - ther in heav'n Tells of His love in the Book He has giv'n,
Won - der - ful things in the Bi - ble I see; This is the dear - est, that Je - sus loves me. }
Chorus.
I am so glad that Je - sus loves me, Je - sus loves me, Je - sus loves me,
I am so glad that Jesus loves me, Je - sus loves e - ven me.
Copyright property of The John Church Co.

2 Though I forget Him and wander away,
Still He doth love me wherever I stray;
Back to His dear loving arms would I flee,
When I remember that Jesus loves me.
I am so glad, etc.

3 Oh, if there's only one song I can sing,
When in His beauty I see the Great King,
This shall my song in eternity be:
"Oh, what a wonder that Jesus loves me."
I am so glad, etc.

---

1 Jesus loves me, and I know I love Him,
Love brought Him down my poor soul to redeem:
Yes, it was love made Him die on the tree,
Oh, I am certain that Jesus loves me.
I am so glad, etc.

2 If one should ask of me, how could I tell?
Glory to Jesus, I know very well:
God's Holy Spirit with mine doth agree,
Constantly witnessing—Jesus loves me.
I am so glad, etc.

3 In this assurance I find sweetest rest,
Trusting in Jesus, I know I am blest;
Satan dismayed, from my soul now doth flee,
When I just tell him that Jesus loves me. I am so glad, etc.

S. W.

No. 19. Rejoice and be Glad.

The poor among men shall rejoice in the Holy One of Israel."—Isa. 29: 19.

Rev. Horatius Bonar. John J. Husband.

1. Re - joice and be glad! The Re-deem - er has come! Go look on His
2. Re - joice and be glad! It is sun-shine at last! The clouds have de-
3. Re - joice and be glad! For the blood hath been shed; Re - demp- tion is
4. Re - joice and be glad! Now the par - don is free! The Just for the
5. Re - joice and be glad! For the Lamb that was slain O'er death is tri-
6. Re - joice and be glad! For our King is on high, He plead - eth for
7. Re - joice and be glad! For He com- eth a - gain; He com - eth in
Chorus.
cra - dle, His cross, and His tomb. Sound His prais - es, tell the Sto - ry Of......
part- ed, the shad- ows are past.
fin- ished, the price hath been paid.
un - just has died on the tree.
umphant, and liv - eth a - gain.
us on His throne in the sky.
(Cho. for 7th verse.)
glo - ry, the Lamb that was slain. Sound His prais - es, tell the Sto - ry Of........
Him who was slain; Sound His prais-es, tell with gladness, He liv-eth a - gain.
Him who was slain; Sound His prais-es, tell with gladness, He com-eth a - gain.

No. 20. Revive us Again.

"O Lord, revive thy work."—Hab. 3: 2.

1 We praise Thee, O God! for the Son of Thy love,
For Jesus who died, and is now gone above.

Cho.—Hallelujah! Thine the glory, Hallelujah! amen.
Hallelujah! Thine the glory, revive us again.

2 We praise Thee, O God! for Thy Spirit of light,
Who has shown us our Saviour, and scattered our night.—*Cho.*

3 All glory and praise to the Lamb that was slain,
Who has borne all our sins, and hath cleansed every stain.—*Cho.*

4 All glory and praise to the God of all grace,
Who has bought us; and sought us, and guided our ways.—*Cho.*

5 Revive us again; fill each heart with Thy love;
May each soul be rekindled with fire from above.—*Cho.*

Rev. Wm. Paton Mackay.

No. 21. Rock of Ages.
"The Lord is my defence, and my God is the Rock of my refuge."—Psa. 94 : 22.
Rev. A. M. Toplady.
(Toplady 7s. 6 lines.)
Dr. Thos. Hastings.
1. Rock of A - ges, cleft for me, Let me hide myself in Thee; Let the wa - ter and the blood,
2. Not the la - bor of my hands Can fulfil Thy law's demands; Could my zeal no respite know,
3. Nothing in my hand I bring, Sim-ply to Thy cross I cling; Naked, come to Thee for dress,
4. While I draw this fleeting breath, While mine eyes shall close in death, When I soar to worlds unknown,
From Thy riven side which flowed, Be of sin the doub-le cure, Save me from its guilt and power.
Could my tears for-ev - er flow, All for sin could not atone; Thou must save, and Thou alone.
Help-less look to Thee for grace; Foul, I to the fountain fly, Wash me, Sav-iour, or I die.
See Thee on Thy judgment throne, Rock of A - ges, cleft for me, Let me hide my-self in Thee.
No. 22. "More to Follow."
P. P. Bliss.
"Bring me yet a vessel."—2 Kings 4 : 6.
Bliss.
1. Have you on the Lord believed? Still there's more to follow; Of His grace have you received?
2. Have you felt the Saviour near? Still there's more to follow; Does His blessed presence cheer?
3. Have you felt the Spirit's pow'r? Still there's more to follow; Fall - ing like the gentle show'r?
Still there's more to fol-low; Oh, the grace the Father shows! Still there's more to follow,
Still there's more to fol-low; Oh, the love that Je-sus shows! Still there's more to follow,
Still there's more to fol-low; Oh, the pow'r the Spir - it shows! Still there's more to follow,
Copyright property of The John Church Co.
Chorus.
Free-ly He His grace bestows, Still there's more to follow.
Free-ly He His love bestows, Still there's more to follow.
Free-ly He His pow'r bestows, Still there's more to follow.
More and more, more and more,
Always more to fol - low, Oh, His matchless, boundless love! Still there's more to follow.

No. 23. Bless Me Now.

"Behold, now is the accepted time; behold, now is the day of salvation."—2 Cor. 6: 2.

Rev. Alexander Clark. Rev. Robert Lowry.

1. Heavenly Father, bless me now; At the cross of Christ I bow; Take my guilt and grief a-way;
Hear and heal me now, I pray. Bless me now, bless me now, Heavenly Fa-ther, bless me now.
Refrain.

2 Now, O Lord! this very hour,
Send Thy grace and show Thy power;
While I rest upon Thy word,
Come and bless me now, O Lord!—*Ref.*

3 Now, just now, for Jesus' sake,
Lift the clouds, the fetters break;
While I look, and as I cry,
Touch and cleanse me ere I die.—*Ref.*

4 Never did I so adore
Jesus Christ, Thy Son, before;
Now the time! and this the place!
Gracious Father, show Thy grace—*Ref.*

No. 24. Where Hast Thou Gleaned To-Day?

"The field is the world * * * and the reapers are the angels."—Matt. 13: 38.

P. P. Bliss. P. P. Bliss.

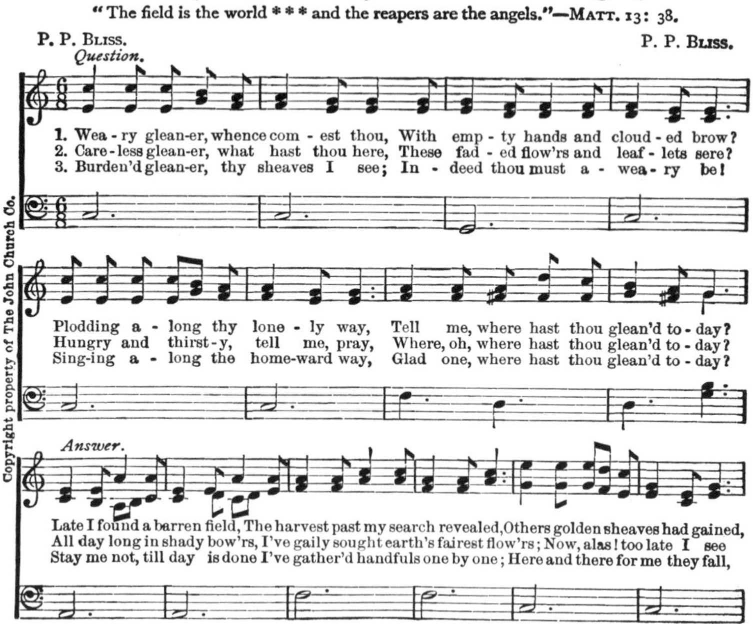
Question.
1. Wea-ry glean-er, whence com-est thou, With emp-ty hands and cloud-ed brow?
2. Care-less glean-er, what hast thou here, These fad-ed flow'rs and leaf-lets sere?
3. Burden'd glean-er, thy sheaves I see; In-deed thou must a-wea-ry be!
Plodding a-long thy lone-ly way, Tell me, where hast thou glean'd to-day?
Hungry and thirst-y, tell me, pray, Where, oh, where hast thou glean'd to-day?
Sing-ing a-long the home-ward way, Glad one, where hast thou glean'd to-day?
Answer.
Late I found a barren field, The harvest past my search revealed, Others golden sheaves had gained,
All day long in shady bow'rs, I've gaily sought earth's fairest flow'rs; Now, alas! too late I see
Stay me not, till day is done I've gather'd handfuls one by one; Here and there for me they fall,

Where Hast Thou Gleaned To-Day?
CHORUS.
On - ly stub-ble for me remained.
All I've gather'd is van - i - ty.
Close by the reap'rs I've found them all.
Forth to the harvest field a-way! Gather your handfuls
while you may; All day long in the field a - bide, Gleaning close by the reap-ers' side.
No. 25. Ah, My Heart.
"Come unto me, all ye that labor and are heavy laden."—MATT. 11: 28.
Tr. JOHN M. NEALE.
P. P. BLISS.
1st SOLO.
2d SOLO.
1. Ah, my heart is heav-y la - den, Wea-ry and oppressed! "Come to Me," saith One, "and
2. Hath He marks to lead me to Him, If He be my Guide? "In His feet and hands are
CHORUS. Repeat last two lines of each verse. rit. p
com - ing, Be at rest!" "Come to Me," saith One, "and com-ing, Be at rest!"
wound-prints, And His side." "In His feet and hands are wound-prints, And His side."
Copyright property of The John Church Co.
3 Is there diadem, as monarch,
That His brow adorns?
"Yes, a crown in very surety,
But of thorns!"—Cho.
4 If I find Him, if I follow,
What's my portion here?
"Many a sorrow, many a conflict,
Many a tear."—Cho.
5 If I still hold closely to Him,
What have I at last?
"Sorrow vanquished, labor ended,
Jordan past!"—Cho.
6 If I ask Him to receive me,
Will He say me nay?
"Not till earth and not till heaven
Pass away!"—Cho.
No. 26. One more Days's Work for Jesus.
"I must work the works of him that sent me, while it is day."—JOHN 9: 4.
Miss ANNA WARNER.
Rev. ROBERT LOWRY.
1. One more day's work for Je - sus; One less of life for me! But heav'n is near-er,
2. One more day's work for Je - sus; How glo-rious is my King! 'Tis joy, not du - ty,
3. One more day's work for Je - sus; How sweet the work has been, To tell the sto - ry,
4. One more day's work for Je - sus—Oh, yes, a wea - ry day; But heav'n shines clearer,
16

One more Day's Work for Jesus.

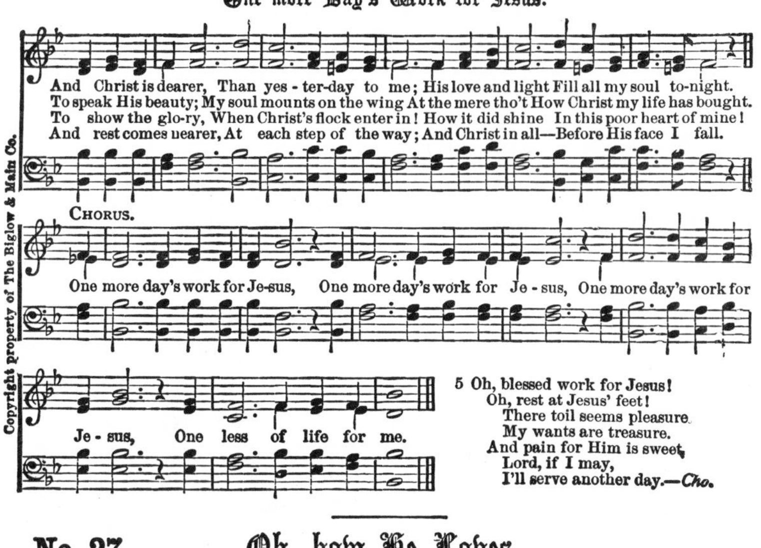
And Christ is dearer, Than yes - ter-day to me; His love and light Fill all my soul to-night.
To speak His beauty; My soul mounts on the wing At the mere tho't How Christ my life has bought.
To show the glo-ry, When Christ's flock enter in! How it did shine In this poor heart of mine!
And rest comes nearer, At each step of the way; And Christ in all—Before His face I fall.
CHORUS.
One more day's work for Je-sus, One more day's work for Je - sus, One more day's work for
Je - sus, One less of life for me.
5 Oh, blessed work for Jesus!
Oh, rest at Jesus' feet!
There toil seems pleasure,
My wants are treasure,
And pain for Him is sweet.
Lord, if I may,
I'll serve another day.—Cho.
Copyright property of The Biglow & Main Co.

No. 27. Oh, how He Loves.

"A friend that sticketh closer than a brother."—PROV. 18: 24.

Adp. by Miss MARIANNE NUNN. HUBERT P. MAIN.

1. One there is a - bove all oth - ers, Oh, how He loves! His is love be-
2. 'Tis e - ter - nal life to know Him, Oh, how He loves! Think, oh, think how
3. Bless - ed Je - sus! would you know Him, Oh, how He loves! Give yourselves en-
4. All your sins shall be for-giv - en, Oh, how He loves! Back-ward shall your
yond a brother's, Oh, how He loves! Earth-ly friends may fail or leave us, One day
much we owe Him, Oh, how He loves! With His precious blood He bought us, In the
tire - ly to Him, Oh, how He loves! Think no long-er of the mor-row, From the
foes be driv-en, Oh, how He loves! Best of bless-ings He'll provide you, Nought but
soothe, the next day grieve us; But this Friend will ne'er de-ceive us, Oh, how He loves!
wil - der-ness He sought us, To His fold He safe - ly brought us, Oh, how He loves!
past new courage bor - row, Je - sus car - ries all your sor - row, Oh, how He loves!
good shall e'er be-tide you, Safe to glo - ry He will guide you, Oh, how He loves!
Copyright, 1872, by Hubert P. Main.

No. 28. Tell Me the Old, Old Story.

"Tell them how great things the Lord hath done."—MARK 5: 19.

MISS KATE HANKEY. W. H. DOANE.

1. Tell me the Old, Old Sto - ry, Of un - seen things a - bove, Of
2. Tell me the Sto - ry slow - ly, That I may take it in— That
3. Tell me the Sto - ry soft - ly, With earn - est tones, and grave; Re -
4. Tell me the same old Sto - ry, When you have cause to fear That
Je - sus and His glo - ry, Of Je - sus and His love. Tell me the Sto - ry
won - der - ful re - demption, God's rem - e - dy for sin. Tell me the Sto - ry
member! I'm the sin - ner Whom Je - sus came to save; Tell me the Sto - ry
this world's emp - ty glo - ry Is cost - ing me too dear. Yes, and when that world's
sim - ply, As to a lit - tle child, For I am weak and wea - ry, And
oft - en, For I for - get so soon, The "ear - ly dew" of morn - ing Has
al - ways, If you would real - ly be, In a - ny time of troub - le, A
glo - ry Is dawn-ing on my soul, Tell me the old, old Sto - ry: "Christ
help - less and de - filed.
passed a - way at noon.
com - fort - er to me.
Je - sus makes thee whole."
CHORUS.
Tell me the Old, Old Sto - ry, Tell me the Old, Old
Sto - ry, Tell me the Old, Old Sto - ry Of Je - sus and His love.
Copyright property of The Biglow & Main Co.

No. 29. The Holy Spirit.

Three warnings: Resist not, Grieve not, Quench n

P. P. Bliss. P. Bliss.

1. The Spir - it, oh, sin - ner, In mer - cy doth move, Thy heart, so long
2. Oh, child of the king-dom, From sin ser-vice cease: Be filled with the
3. De - filed is the tem - ple, Its beau - ty laid low, On God's ho - ly
hard - ened, Of sin to re - prove; *Re - sist* not the Spir - it, Nor
Spir - it, With com - fort and peace. Oh, *grieve* not the Spir - it, Thy
al - tar The em - bers faint glow. By love yet re - kin - dled, A
long - er de - lay; God's gra-cious en-trea - ties, May end with to - day.
Teach - er is He, That Je - sus, thy Sav - iour, May glo - ri - fied be.
flame may be fanned; Oh, *quench* not the Spir - it, *The Lord is at hand.*

Copyright property of The John Church Co.

No. 30. I Love to Tell the Story.

"I will speak of thy wondrous work."—Psalm 145: 5.

Miss Kate Hankey. W. G. Fischer.

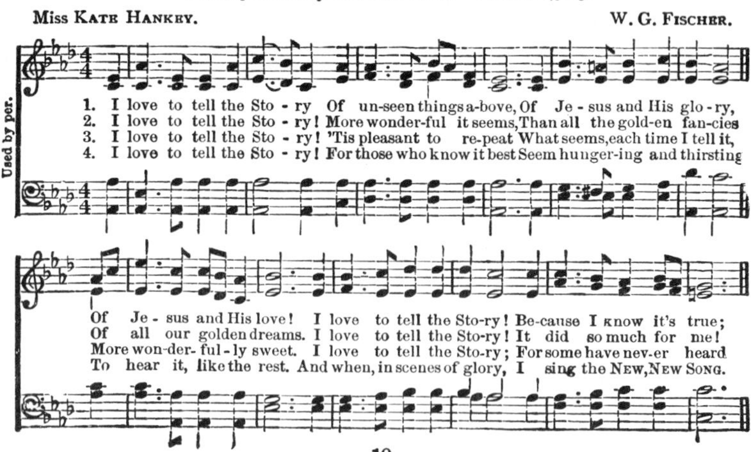

1. I love to tell the Sto - ry Of un-seen things a-bove, Of Je - sus and His glo - ry,
2. I love to tell the Sto - ry! More wonder-ful it seems, Than all the gold-en fan-cies
3. I love to tell the Sto - ry! 'Tis pleasant to re-peat What seems, each time I tell it,
4. I love to tell the Sto - ry! For those who know it best Seem hunger-ing and thirsting
Of Je - sus and His love! I love to tell the Sto-ry! Be-cause I know it's true;
Of all our golden dreams. I love to tell the Sto-ry! It did so much for me!
More won-der- ful - ly sweet. I love to tell the Sto-ry; For some have nev-er heard
To hear it, like the rest. And when, in scenes of glory, I sing the New, New Song.

Used by per.

I Love to Tell the Story.
Chorus.
It sat - is- fies my longings, As noth-ing else would do.
And that is just the rea- son, I tell it now to thee.
The message of sal- va- tion From God's own Holy Word.
'Twill be—the Old, Old Story That I have loved so long.
I love to tell the Sto- ry!
'Twill be my theme in glo- ry, To tell the Old, Old Sto- ry, Of Je- sus and His love.
No. 31. Holy Spirit, Faithful Guide.
" I will guide thee with mine eye."—Psalm 32 : 8.
M. M. Wells.
M. M. Wells.
1. Ho- ly Spir-it, faith-ful guide, Ever near the Christian's side; Gently lead us by the hand,
Used by per.
D.S.—Whisp'ring softly, " Wanderer, come!
Fine.
D.S.
Pilgrims in a des - ert land; Wea-ry souls for e'er rejoice, While they hear that sweetest voice
Follow me, I'll guide thee home."
2 Ever present, truest Friend,
Ever near Thine aid to lend,
Leave us not to doubt and fear,
Groping on in darkness drear,
When the storms are raging sore,
Hearts grow faint, and hopes give o'er,
Whispering softly, " Wanderer, come!
Follow me, I'll guide thee home."
3 When our days of toil shall cease,
Waiting still for sweet release,
Nothing left but heaven and prayer,
Wond'ring if our names were there;
Wading deep the dismal flood,
Pleading nought but Jesus' blood;
Whispering softly, " Wanderer, come!
Follow me, I'll guide thee home."
No. 32. The Cross of Jesus.
" His children shall have a place of refuge."—Prov. 14: 26.
Miss E. C. Clephane.
Ira D. Sankey.
1. Be-neath the Cross of Je - sus I fain would take my stand—The sha - dow of a

The Cross of Jesus.

Copyright property of The Biglow & Main Co.
might - y Rock, With- in a wea - ry land. A home with- in the wil - der-ness, A
rest up - on the way, From the burning of the noontide heat, And the burden of the day.
Copyright property of The John Church Co.
Allegretto.
1. With harps and with vi - ols, there stands a great throng In the pre - sence of
Je - sus, and sing this new song:— Un - to Him who hath loved us and
Chorus.
washed us from sin, Un - to Him be the glo - ry for - ev - er, A - men.

2 O safe and happy shelter,
O refuge tried and sweet,
O trysting-place where Heaven's love,
And Heaven's justice meet!
As to the Holy Patriarch
That wondrous dream was given,
So seems my Saviour's Cross to me,
A ladder up to heaven.

3 There lies beneath its shadow,
But on the further side,
The darkness of an awful grave
That gapes both deep and wide;
And there between us stands the Cross,
Two arms outstretched to save,
Like a watchman set to guard the way
From that eternal grave.

4 Upon that Cross of Jesus,
Mine eye at times can see
The very dying form of One,
Who suffered there for me;
And from my smitten heart with tears,
Two wonders I confess,—
The wonders of His glorious love,
And my own worthlessness.

5 I take, O Cross, thy shadow,
For my abiding place;
I ask no other sunshine
Than the sunshine of His face:
Content to let the world go by,
To know no gain nor loss,—
My sinful self, my only shame,—
My glory all the Cross.

No. 33. The New Song.

"And they sung as it were a new song before the throne."—Rev. 14: 3.

Rev. A. T. Pierson. P. P. Bliss.

2 All these once were sinners, defiled in His sight,
Now arrayed in pure garments in praise they unite.—*Cho.*

3 He maketh the rebel a priest and a king,
He hath bought us and taught us this new song to sing.—*Cho.*

4 How helpless and hopeless we sinners had been,
If He never had loved us till cleansed from our sin.—*Cho.*

5 Aloud in His praises our voices shall ring,
So that others believing, this new song shall sing.—*Cho.*

No. 34. Oh, Sing of His Mighty Love.

"Mighty to save."—ISAIAH 63: 1.
Rev. FRANK BOTTOME, D.D.
WM. B. BRADBURY.
1. Oh, bliss of the pu - ri - fied, bliss of the free, I plunge in the crim-son-tide o - pen'd for me; O'er sin and un-clean-ness ex - ult - ing I stand, And point to the print of the nails in His hand.
2. Oh, bliss of the pu - ri - fied, Je - sus is mine, No long - er in dread con-dem - na - tion I pine; In con - scious sal - va - tion I sing of His grace, Who lift - eth up - on me the light of His face.
3. Oh, bliss of the pu - ri - fied! bliss of the pure! No wound hath the soul that His blood can - not cure; No sor - row-bowed head but may sweet - ly find rest, No tears but may dry them on Je - sus' breast.
4. O Je - sus the cru - ci - fied! Thee will I sing, My bless - ed Re-deem - er, my God and my King; My soul, filled with rap - ture, shall shout o'er the grave, And tri - umph in death in the "Might-y to Save."
CHORUS.
Oh, sing of His might-y love, Sing of His might - y love, Sing of His might-y love, Might - y to save.
rit.
Copyright property of The Biglow & Main Co.
No. 35. The Wondrous Gift.
"By grace are ye saved."—EPH. 2: 8.
Dr. PHILIP DODDRIDGE.
IRA D. SANKEY.
1. Grace! 'tis a charming sound, Har - mo - nious to the ear; Heaven with the ech - o
2. Grace first contrived a way To save re - bell-ious man; And all the steps that
3. Grace taught my rov - ing feet To tread the heavenly road; And new supplies each
4. Grace all the work shall crown, Thro' ev - er - last - ing days; It lays in heaven the

The Wondrous Gift.
Refrain.
shall re-sound, And all the earth shall hear.
grace dis-play, Which drew the wondrous plan.
hour I meet, While press-ing on to God.
top-most stone, And well de-serves our praise.
Saved by grace a-lone,
This is all my plea; Je-sus died for all mankind, And Je-sus died for me.
Copyright, 1875, by Biglow & Main.
No. 36.
Precious Promise.
"Whereby are given unto us exceeding great and precious promises."—2 Pet. 1: 4.
Nathaniel Niles.
P. P. Bliss.
1. Pre-cious prom-ise God hath giv-en To the wea-ry pass-er by,
2. When temp-ta-tions al-most win thee, And thy trust-ed watch-ers fly,
3. When thy se-cret hopes have per-ished, In the grave of years gone by,
4. When the shades of life are fall-ing, And the hour has come to die,
On the way from earth to heav-en, "I will guide thee with mine eye."
Let this prom-ise ring with-in thee, "I will guide thee with mine eye."
Let this prom-ise still be cher-ished, "I will guide thee with mine eye."
Hear thy trust-y Pi-lot call-ing, "I will guide thee with mine eye."
Refrain.
I will guide thee, I will guide thee, I will guide thee with mine eye;
On the way from earth to heav-en, I will guide thee with mine eye.
Copyright property of The John Church Co.

No. 37. When Jesus Comes.

"Unto them that look for him shall he appear the second time, without sin, unto salvation."—Heb. 9: 28.

P. P. Bliss. P. P. Bliss.

1. Down life's dark vale we wan-der, Till Je-sus comes; We watch and wait and won-der, Till Je-sus comes.
2. Oh, let my lamp be burn-ing When Je-sus comes; For Him my soul be yearning, When Je-sus comes.
3. No more heart-pangs nor sad-ness, When Je-sus comes; All peace and joy and glad-ness, When Je-sus comes.
4. All doubts and fears will van-ish, When Je-sus comes; All gloom His face will ban-ish, When Je-sus comes.

Chorus.

All joy His loved ones bringing, When Je-sus comes; All praise thro' heav-en ring-ing, When Je-sus comes. All beau-ty bright and ver-nal, When Je-sus comes; All glo-ry, grand, e-ter-nal, When Je-sus comes.

5 He'll know the way was dreary,
When Jesus comes;
He'll know the feet grew weary,
When Jesus comes.—*Cho.*

6 He'll know what griefs oppressed me,
When Jesus comes;
Oh, how His arms will rest me!
When Jesus comes.—*Cho.*

No. 38. White as Snow.

"Come now, and let us reason together, saith the Lord: though your sins be as scarlet, they shall be as white as snow."—Isa. 1: 18.

H. Bonar, arr. by L. N. P. P. Bliss.

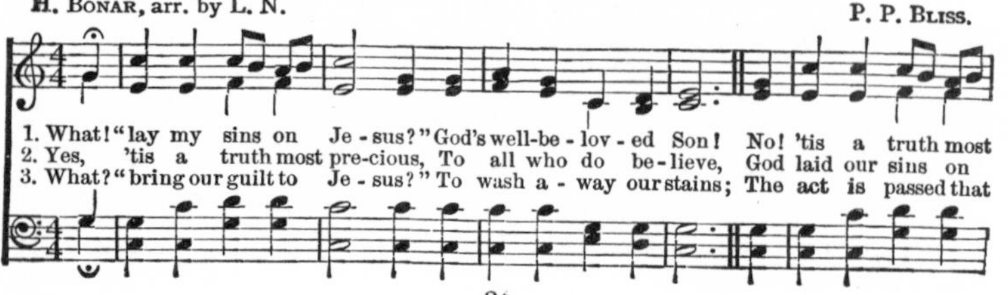
1. What! "lay my sins on Je-sus?" God's well-be-lov-ed Son! No! 'tis a truth most
2. Yes, 'tis a truth most pre-cious, To all who do be-lieve, God laid our sins on
3. What? "bring our guilt to Je-sus?" To wash a-way our stains; The act is passed that

White as Snow.

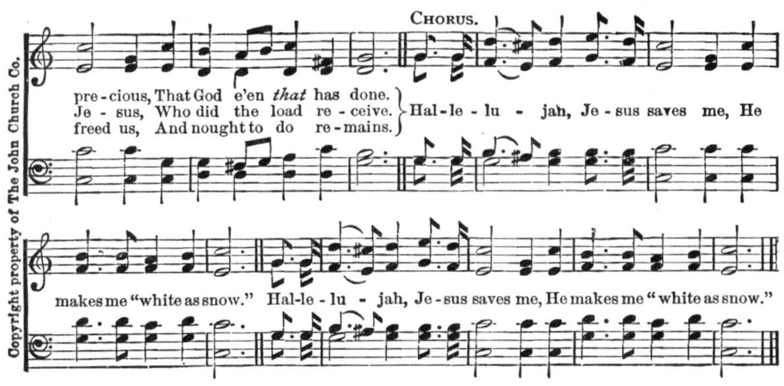

Chorus.
pre - cious, That God e'en *that* has done.
Je - sus, Who did the load re - ceive.
freed us, And nought to do re - mains.
Hal - le - lu - jah, Je - sus saves me, He
makes me "white as snow." Hal - le - lu - jah, Je - sus saves me, He makes me "white as snow."
Copyright property of The John Church Co.

No. 39. Substitution.

"He was wounded for our transgressions."—Isaiah 53.

Mrs. A. R. Cousin. Ira D. Sankey.

1. O Christ, what bur - dens bowed Thy head! Our load was laid on Thee; Thou
2. Death and the curse were in our cup— O Christ, 'twas full for Thee; But
3. Je - ho - vah lift - ed up His rod— O Christ, it fell on Thee! Thou
4. The tem - pest's aw - ful voice was heard—O Christ, it broke on Thee! Thy

stood - est in the sin - ner's stead, Didst bear all ill for me. A
Thou hast drained the last dark drop— 'Tis emp - ty now for me. That
wast sore strick - en of Thy God; There's not one stroke for me. Thy
o - pen bo - som was my ward, It braved the storm for me. Thy

Vic - tim led, Thy blood was shed; Now there's no load for me.
bit - ter cup— love drank it up; Now bless - ings' draught for me.
tears, Thy blood, be - neath it flowed; Thy bruis - ing heal - eth me.
form was scarred, Thy vis - age marred; Now cloud - less peace for me.

5 Jehovah bade His sword awake—
O Christ, it woke 'gainst Thee!
Thy blood the flaming blade must slake;
Thy heart its sheath must be—
All for my sake, my peace to make;
Now sleeps that sword for me.

6 For me, Lord Jesus, Thou hast died,
And I have died in Thee;
Thou'rt risen: my bands are all untied,
And now Thou liv'st in me.
When purified, made white, and tried,
Thy Glory then for me.

No. 40. In the Presence of the King.

"In thy presence is fulness of joy; at thy right hand there are pleasures for evermore."—PSALM 16: 11.

Miss FLORENCE C. ARMSTRONG. English.

Moderato.
1. Oh, to be o - ver yon - der! In that land of wond - der, Where the an - gel voic - es min - gle, and the an - gel harp - ers ring; To be free from pain and sor - row, And the anx - ious, dread to - mor - row, To rest in light and sun - shine in the pres - ence of the King.
2. Oh, to be o - ver yon - der! My yearn-ing heart grows fonder Of look - ing to the east, to see the bless - ed day - star bring Some tid - ings of the wak - ing, The cloud - less, pure day break - ing; My heart is yearn - ing—yearn - ing for the com - ing of the King.
3. Oh, to be o - ver yon - der! Alas! I sigh and won - der Why clings my poor, weak, sin - ful heart to a - ny earth - ly thing; Each tie of earth must sev - er, And pass a - way for - ev - er; But there's no more sep - a - ra - tion in the pres - ence of the King.
4. Oh, when shall I be dwell - ing Where angel voic-es, swell - ing In tri - umphant hal - le - lu - jahs, make the vault - ed heav - ens ring? Where the pearl - y gates are gleam - ing, And the morn - ing star is beam - ing? Oh, when shall I be yon - der in the pres - ence of the King.
p
cres.
f
rit.
tempo.

5 Oh, when shall I be yonder?
The longing groweth stronger
To join in all the praises the redeemed ones do sing
Within those heavenly places,
Where the angels vail their faces,
In awe and adoration in the presence of the King.

6 Oh I shall soon be yonder,
And lonely as I wander,
Yearning for the welcome summer—longing for the bird's fleet wing,
The midnight may be dreary,
And the heart be worn and weary,
But there's no more shadow yonder, in the presence of the King.

No. 41. Missionary Hymn. 7s, & 6s.

"Come over.........and help us."—Acts 16: 9.

R. Heber. Dr. Lowell Mason.

1. From Greenland's i-cy mountains, From In-dia's cor-al strand, Where Af-ric's sun-ny fount-ains Roll down their gold-en sand, From many an an-cient riv-er, From many a palm-y plain, They call us to de-liv-er Their land from er-ror's chain.
2. What tho' the spi-cy breez-es Blow soft o'er Ceylon's isle, Tho' ev-'ry prospect pleas-es And on-ly man is vile? In vain, with lav-ish kind-ness, The gifts of God are strown: The heathen, in his blind-ness, Bows down to wood and stone.
3. Shall we, whose souls are light-ed By wis-dom from on high, Shall we to men be-night-ed The light of life de-ny? Sal-va-tion! oh, sal-va-tion! The joy-ful sound pro-claim, Till earth's re-mot-est na-tion Has learned Mes-si-ah's name.
4. Waft, waft, ye winds, His sto-ry, And you, ye wa-ters, roll, Till, like a sea of glo-ry, It spreads from pole to pole; Till o'er our ransom'd na-ture, The Lamb, for sin-ners slain, Re-deem-er, King, Cre-a-tor, In bliss re-turns to reign.

No. 42. All the Way My Saviour Leads Me.

"The Lord alone did lead him."—Deut. 32: 12.

Fanny J. Crosby.
Rev. R. Lowry.
1. All the way my Sav-iour leads me; What have I to ask be-side? Can I doubt His ten-der mer-cy, Who thro' life has been my guide? Heav'nly peace, di-vin-est
2. All the way my Sav-iour leads me; Cheers each winding path I tread; Gives me grace for ev-'ry tri-al, Feeds me with the liv-ing bread; Tho' my wea-ry steps may
3. All the way my Sav-iour leads me; Oh, the full-ness of His love! Per-fect rest to me is promised In my Father's house a-bove; When my spir-it, cloth'd im-
Copyright, 1875, by Biglow & Main.

All the Way My Saviour Leads Me.

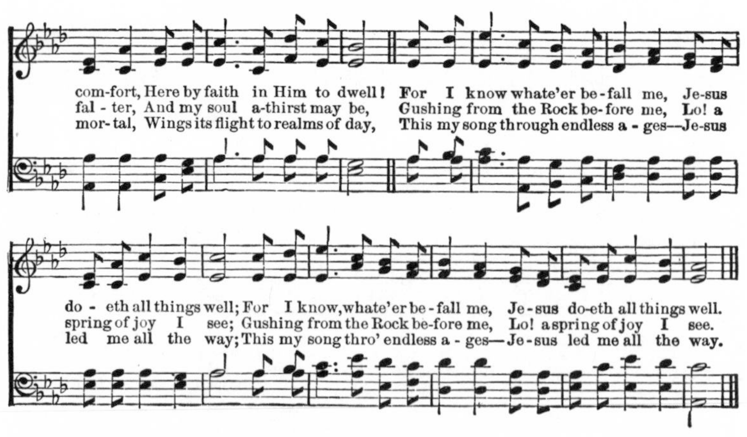

com-fort, Here by faith in Him to dwell! For I know whate'er be-fall me, Je-sus
fal - ter, And my soul a-thirst may be, Gushing from the Rock be-fore me, Lo! a
mor-tal, Wings its flight to realms of day, This my song through endless a - ges—Je-sus
do - eth all things well; For I know, whate'er be - fall me, Je-sus do-eth all things well.
spring of joy I see; Gushing from the Rock be-fore me, Lo! a spring of joy I see.
led me all the way; This my song thro' endless a - ges— Je-sus led me all the way.

No. 43. Go Bury thy Sorrow.

"They shall obtain joy and gladness, and sorrow and sighing shall flee away."—Isaiah 35: 10.

Mary A. Bachelor. P. P. Bliss.

1. Go bur - y thy sor - row, The world hath its share;
2. Go tell it to Je - sus, He know - eth thy grief;
3. Hearts grow-ing a - wea - ry With heav - i - er woe
Go bur - y it deep - ly, Go hide it with care, Go think of it calm - ly,
Go tell it to Je - sus, He'll send thee re - lief, Go gath - er the sun - shine
Now droop 'mid the darkness—Go com - fort them, go! Go bur - y thy sor - rows,
rit.
When cur-tain'd by night, Go tell it to Je - sus, And all will be right.
He sheds on the way; He'll lighten thy bur - den, Go, wea-ry one, pray.
Let oth - ers be blest; Go give them the sun-shine; Tell Je-sus the rest.
Copyright property of The John Church Co.

No. 44. A Sinner Forgiven.

"He said unto her, thy sins are forgiven."—LUKE 7: 48.

JEREMIAH J. CALLAHAN. Arr. by I. B. WOODBURY.

1. To the hall of the feast came the sin-ful and fair; She heard in the cit - y that
2. The frown and the murmur went round thro' them all, That one so un-hallowed should
3. She heard but the Saviour; she spoke but with sighs; She dare not look up to the
4. In the sky, aft - er tem - pest, as shin-eth the bow,—In the glance of the sunbeam, as

Je - sus was there; Un-heed- ing the splendor that blazed on the board, She si - lent-ly
tread in that hall; And some said the poor would be ob-jects more meet, As the wealth of her
heav'n of His eyes; And the hot tears gush'd forth at each heave of her breast, As her lips to his
melt- eth the snow He looked on that lost one: "her sins were forgiv'n," And the sinner went

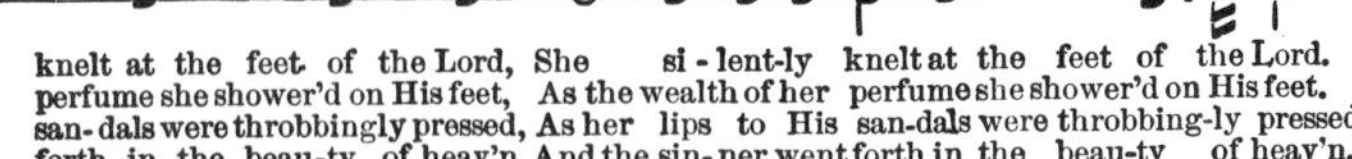

knelt at the feet of the Lord, She si - lent-ly knelt at the feet of the Lord.
perfume she shower'd on His feet, As the wealth of her perfume she shower'd on His feet.
san- dals were throbbingly pressed, As her lips to His san-dals were throbbing-ly pressed.
forth in the beau-ty of heav'n, And the sin- ner went forth in the beau-ty of heav'n.

No. 45. Let the Lower Lights be Burning.

"Let your light so shine before men, that they may see your good works, and glorify your Father which is in heaven."—MATT. 5: 16.

P. P. BLISS. P. P. BLISS.

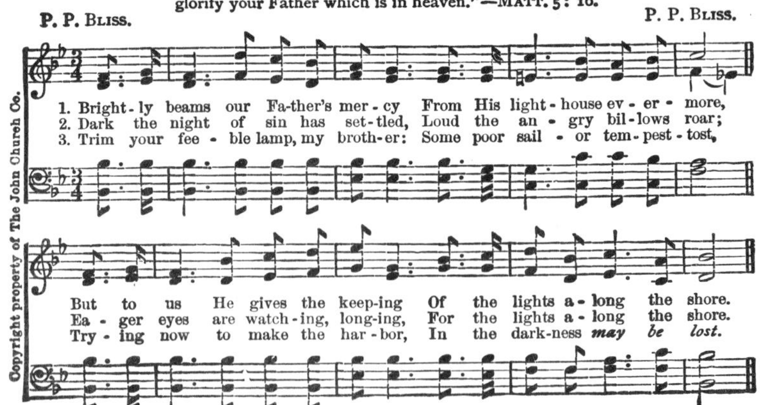

1. Bright- ly beams our Fa-ther's mer - cy From His light - house ev - er - more,
2. Dark the night of sin has set-tled, Loud the an - gry bil-lows roar;
3. Trim your fee - ble lamp, my broth-er: Some poor sail - or tem - pest - tost,
But to us He gives the keep-ing Of the lights a - long the shore.
Ea - ger eyes are watch - ing, long-ing, For the lights a - long the shore.
Try - ing now to make the har - bor, In the dark-ness *may be lost.*

Let the Lower Lights be Burning.
Chorus.
Let the low - er lights be burn-ing! Send a gleam a - cross the wave!
Some poor faint - ing, struggling sea-man; You may res - cue, you may save.
No. 46. Wishing, Hoping, Knowing.
"My beloved is mine, and I am his."—Songs of Solomon 2: 16.
P. P. Bliss.
P. P. Bliss.
1. A long time I wan-dered in dark - ness and sin, And won-dered if ev - er the
2. I heard the glad gos - pel of "good will to men;" I read "who-so - ev - er" a-
3. Oh, mer - cy sur-pris - ing, He saves e - ven me! "Thy por-tion for - ev - er," He
light would shine in; I heard Christian friends tell of rap - ture di - vine, And
gain and a - gain; I said to my soul, "Can that prom - ise be thine?" And
says, "will I be," On His word I'm rest - ing—as - sur - ance di - vine— I'm
wish'd, how I wish'd, that their Sav-iour were mine.
then be - gan hop - ing that Je - sus was mine.
"hop - ing" no long - er— I know He is mine!
Chorus.
I wish'd He were mine, yes, I
I hoped He was mine, yes, I
I know He is mine, yes, I
wish'd He were mine; I wish'd, how I wish'd, that their Sav-iour were mine.
hoped He was mine; I then be - gan hop - ing that Je - sus was mine.
know He is mine; I'm "hop - ing" no long - er— I know He is mine!
Copyright property of The John Church Co.

No. 47. The Precious Name.

"And blessed be his glorious name for ever."—Psa. 72: 19.

Mrs. Lydia Baxter. W. H. Doane.

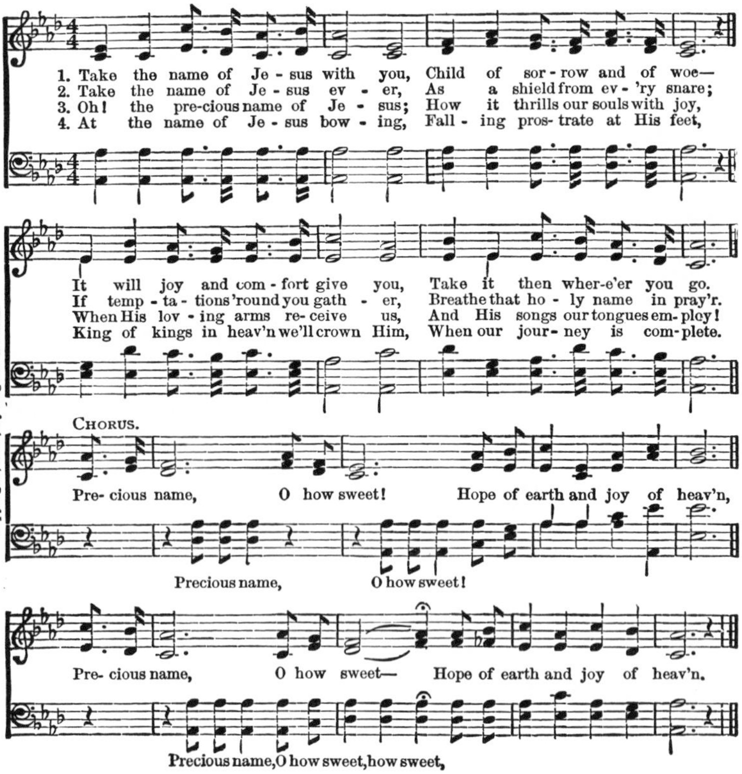

1. Take the name of Je - sus with you, Child of sor - row and of woe—
2. Take the name of Je - sus ev - er, As a shield from ev - 'ry snare;
3. Oh! the pre-cious name of Je - sus; How it thrills our souls with joy,
4. At the name of Je - sus bow - ing, Fall - ing pros- trate at His feet,
It will joy and com - fort give you, Take it then wher-e'er you go.
If temp - ta - tions 'round you gath - er, Breathe that ho - ly name in pray'r.
When His lov - ing arms re - ceive us, And His songs our tongues em - ploy!
King of kings in heav'n we'll crown Him, When our jour - ney is com - plete.
Chorus.
Pre- cious name, O how sweet! Hope of earth and joy of heav'n,
Precious name, O how sweet!
Pre- cious name, O how sweet— Hope of earth and joy of heav'n.
Precious name, O how sweet, how sweet,

No. 48. Oh, to be Nothing.

"Neither is he that planteth anything, neither he that watereth."—1 Cor. 3: 7.

Georgiana M. Taylor. R. Geo. Halls. Arr. by P. P. Bliss.

Very slow.
1. Oh, to be noth - ing, noth - ing, On - ly to lie at His feet,......
2. Oh, to be noth - ing, noth - ing, On - ly as led by His hand;.....
3. Oh, to be noth - ing, noth - ing, Pain-ful the humbling may be,......
Cho.—Oh, to be noth - ing, noth - ing, On - ly to lie at His feet,......

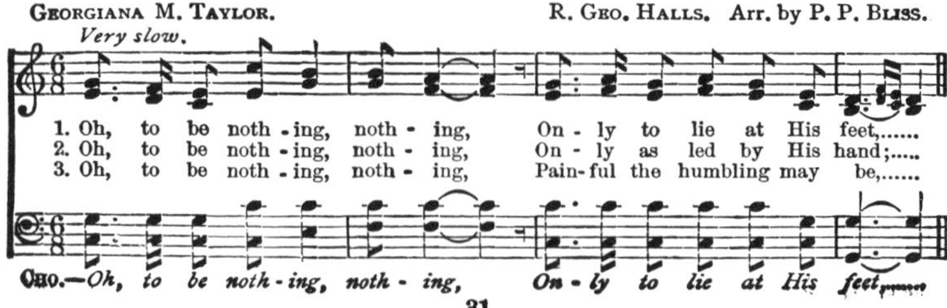

Oh, to be Nothing.
Fine.
A broken and emptied vessel, For the Master's use made meet.
A messenger at His gateway, Only waiting for His command,
Yet low in the dust I'd lay me That the world might my Saviour see,
A broken and emptied vessel, For the Master's use made meet.
Emptied that He might fill me As forth to His service I go;
Only an instrument ready His praises to sound at His will,
Rather be nothing, nothing, To Him let our voices be raised,
D.C. Chorus.
Broken, that so unhindered, His life through me might flow..........
Willing, should he not require me, In silence to wait on Him still..........
He is the Fountain of blessing, He only is meet to be praised.......
Copyright property of The John Church Co.
No. 49. Fully Persuaded.
"Believe on the Lord Jesus Christ and thou shalt be saved."—Acts 16: 31.
Rev. J. B. Atchinson.
Wm. F. Sherwin.
1. Fully persuaded, Lord, I believe! Fully persuaded, Thy Spirit give;
2. Fully persuaded—Lord, hear my cry! Fully persuaded—pass me not by;
3. Fully persuaded, no more oppress, Fully persuaded, now I am blest:
4. Fully persuaded, Jesus is mine; Fully persuaded, Lord, I am Thine!
rit.
I will obey Thy call; Low at Thy feet I fall; Now I surrender all, Christ to receive.
Just as I am I come, I will no longer roam, O make my heart Thy home; Save, or I die!
Jesus is now my Guide, I will in Christ abide; My soul is satisfied In Him to rest!
O make my love to Thee Like Thine own love to me, So rich, so full and free, Saviour divine!
Copyright, 1875, by Biglow & Main.

No. 50. Only an Armour-Bearer.

"Now it came to pass upon a day, that Jonathan the son of Saul said unto the young man that bare his armour, Come, and let us go over to the Philistines' garrison that *is* on the other side; it may be that the LORD will work for us: for *there is* no restraint to the LORD to save by many or by few. And his armour-bearer said unto him, Do all that *is* in thine heart: turn thee; behold, I *am* with thee according to thine heart. And Jonathan climed up upon his hands and upon his feet, and his armour-bearer after him: and they fell before Jonathan; and his armour-bearer slew after him. So the LORD saved Israel that day; and the battle passed over unto Beth-aven." —1 SAM. 14: 1, 6, 7, 13, 23.

P. P. BLISS. P. P. BLISS.

1. On - ly an armour-bearer, proudly I stand, Waiting to follow at the King's command;
2. On - ly an armour-bearer, now in the field, Guarding a shining helmet, sword, and shield,
3. On - ly an armour-bearer, yet may I share, Glo - ry immortal, and a bright crown wear:
Marching if "onward" shall the or-der be, Standing by my Captain, serving faithful-ly.
Wait- ing to hear the thrilling bat - tle cry, Ready then to an-swer, "Master, here am I."
If, in the bat- tle, to my trust I'm true, Mine shall be the honors in the Grand Review.
CHORUS.
Hear ye the battle cry! "Forward," the call! See! see the falt'ring ones! backward they fall.
Sure- ly the Captain may depend on me, Tho' but an armour-bearer I may be.
Sure-ly the Captain may depend on me, Tho' but an armour-bearer I may be.

Copyright property of The John Church Co.

No. 51. Pull for the Shore

"Therefore, if any man be in Christ, he is a new creature; old things are passed away, behold, all things are become NEW."—2 COR. 5: 17.

"Therefore, my beloved, * * ork out your own salvation with fear and trembling."—PHIL. 2: 12.

P. P. BLISS.
P. P. BLISS.
1. Light in the darkness, sailor, day is at hand! See o'er the foaming billows fair Haven's land,
2. Trust in the life-boat, sailor, all else will fail, Stronger the surges dash and fierc- er the gale,
3. Bright gleams the morning, sailor, up lift the eye; Clouds and darkness disappearing, glory is nigh!
Drear was the voyage, sailor, now almost o'er, Safe within the life-boat, sailor, pull for the shore.
Heed not the stormy winds, tho' loudly they roar, Watch the "bright and morning star," and pull for the shore.
Safe in the life-boat, sailor, sing ev- er- more, "Glo-ry, glo- ry, hal-le-lujah!" pull for the shore.
Copyright property of The John Church Co.
CHORUS.
Pull for the shore, sail - or, pull for the shore! Heed not the roll- ing waves, but
bend to the oar, Safe in the life - boat, sail - or, cling to self no more!
Leave the poor old strand - ed wreck, and pull for the shore.

No. 52. No Other Name.

"Neither is there salvation in any other."—ACTS 4 : 12.

P. P. BLISS. P. P. BLISS.

1. One of - fer of sal - va - tion, To all the world make known; The on - ly sure foun-
2. One on - ly door of heav-en Stands o - pen wide to - day, One sac - ri - fice is
3. My on - ly song and sto - ry Is— Je - sus died for me; My on - ly hope of
da - tion Is Christ, the Cor - ner-Stone.
giv - en, 'Tis Christ, the liv - ing way.
glo - ry, The Cross of Cal - va - ry.
CHORUS.
No oth - er name is giv - en, No
oth - er way is known, 'Tis Je- sus Christ, the First and Last, He saves, and He a - lone.

No. 53. I Left it All with Jesus.

"Casting all your care upon him; for he careth for you."—1 PETER 5 : 7.

Miss ELLEN H. WILLIS. Miss H. M. WARNER.

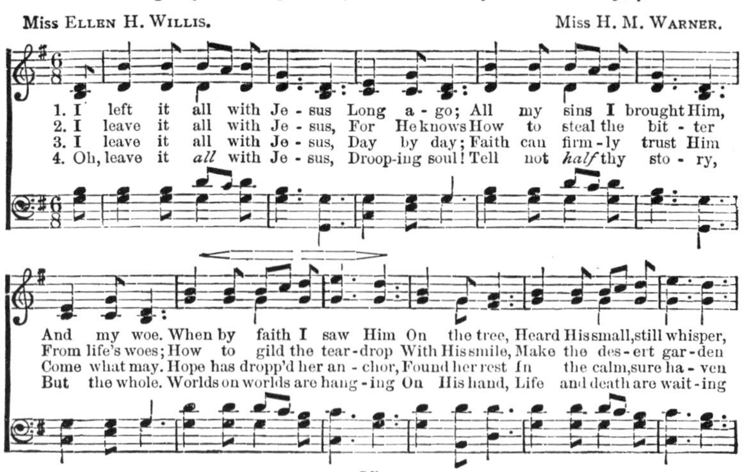
1. I left it all with Je - sus Long a - go; All my sins I brought Him,
2. I leave it all with Je - sus, For He knows How to steal the bit - ter
3. I leave it all with Je - sus, Day by day; Faith can firm - ly trust Him
4. Oh, leave it *all* with Je - sus, Droop-ing soul! Tell not *half* thy sto - ry,
And my woe. When by faith I saw Him On the tree, Heard His small, still whisper,
From life's woes; How to gild the tear - drop With His smile, Make the des - ert gar - den
Come what may. Hope has dropp'd her an - chor, Found her rest In the calm, sure ha - ven
But the whole. Worlds on worlds are hang - ing On His hand, Life and death are wait - ing

I Left it All with Jesus.

"'Tis for thee,' From my heart the bur - den Rolled a - way—Hap - py day!
Bloom a-while: When my weak-ness lean - eth On His might, All seems light.
Of His breast: Love es - teems it heav - en To a - bide At his side.
His com-mand; Yet His ten - der bos - om Makes *thee* room—Oh, come home!
cres.
rit.
From my heart the bur - den Rolled a - way— Hap - py day!
When my weak - ness lean - eth On His might, All seems light.
Love es - teems it heav - en To a - bide At His side.
Yet His ten - der bos - om Makes *thee* room— Oh, come home!

No. 54. The Home Over There.

"Oh that I had wings like a dove, for then would I fly away and be at rest."—Psalm 55: 6.

Rev. D. W. C. Huntington. Tullius C. O'Kane.

1. Oh, think of the home o - ver there, By the side of the riv - er of light. o - ver there, Where the saints, all im - mor - tal and fair, Are robed in their gar-ments of white, o - ver there.
2. Oh, think of the friends o - ver there, Who be - fore us the jour - ney have trod, o - ver there, Of the songs that they breathe on the air, In their home in the pal - ace of God, o - ver there.
3. My Sav - iour is now o - ver there, There my kin - dred and friends are at rest; o - ver there, Then a - way from my sor - row and care, Let me fly to the land of the blest. o - ver there.
4. I'll soon be at home o - ver there, For the end of my jour - ney I see; o - ver there, Ma - ny dear to my heart, o - ver there, Are watch-ing and wait - ing for me. o - ver there.
Refrain.
O - ver there, o - ver there, O - ver

The Home Over There.
there, o - ver there, Oh, think of the home o - ver there, o - ver there; O - ver
there, o - ver there, Oh, think of the friends o - ver there, o - ver there; O - ver
there, o - ver there, My Sav - iour is now o - ver there, o - ver there; O - ver
there, o - ver there, I'll soon be at home o - ver there, o - ver there; O - ver
there, o - ver there, o - ver there, o - ver there, Oh, think of the home o - ver there.
there, o - ver there, o - ver there, o - ver there, Oh, think of the friends o - ver there.
there, o - ver there, o - ver there, o - ver there, My Sav - iour is now o - ver there.
there, o - ver there, o - ver there, o - ver there, I'll soon be at home o - ver there.
No. 55. Yes, There is Pardon for You.
"He will abundantly pardon."—Isa. 55: 17.
Fanny J. Crosby.
Hubert P. Main.
Slowly.
1. Oh, come to the Sav-iour, believe in His name, And ask Him your heart to re - new;
2. The way of trans-gression that leads un-to death, Oh, why will you long-er pur - sue?
3. Be warned of your dan-ger; es-cape to the cross; Your on - ly sal - va-tion is there;
He waits to be gracious, O turn not a - way, For now there is par-don for you.
How can you re - ject the sweet message of love That of - fers full par-don for you?
Be-lieve, and that moment the Spir - it of grace Will an - swer your pen - i - tent prayer.
Chorus.
Yes, there is par - don for you,.......... Yes, there is par-don for you;..........
for you, for you,
For Je - sus has died to re-deem you, And of - fers full par - don to you.
Copyright, 1875, by Biglow & Main.

No. 56. Go Work in My Vineyard.

"Go work to-day in my vineyard."—MATT. 21 : 28.

T. C. O'KANE. T. C. O'KANE.

1. "Go work in My vineyard," there's plenty to do, The har-vest is great and the lab-rer's are few; There's weeding and fenc-ing and clear-ing of roots, And ploughing, and sow-ing, and gath'ring the fruits. There are fox-es to take, there are wolves to de-stroy, All a-ges and ranks I can ful-ly em-ploy.
D.S.—I've sheep to be tend-ed, and lambs to be fed, The lost must be gathered, the wea-ry ones led. [Go to Chorus.]
2. "Go work in My vineyard," I claim thee as Mine, With blood did I buy thee, and all that is thine; Thy time and thy tal-ents, thy loft-iest pow-ers, Thy warm-est af-fec-tions, thy sun-ni-est hours. I will-ing-ly yield-ed My king-dom for thee, The song of arch-an-gels—to hang on the tree;
D.S.—In pain and temp-ta-tion, in an-guish and shame, I paid thy full ran-som; My purchase I claim. [Go to Chorus.]
D.S.
CHORUS.
work,........................ go work,........................
Go work in My vineyard, go work in My vineyard, go work in My vineyard; there's plen-ty to do,
Go work,.......... go work,
Go work, work, work, work, The harvest is great and the lab'rers are few.
Copyright property of The Biglow & Main Co.

Go Work in My Vineyard.

3 "Go work in My vineyard;" oh, "work while 'tis day,"
The bright hours of sunshine are hastening away;
And night's gloomy shadows are gathering fast;
Then the time for our labor shall ever be past.
Begin in the morning, and toil all the day,
Thy strength I'll supply and thy wages I'll pay;
And blessed, thrice blessed the diligent few,
Who finish the labor I've given them to do.

No. 57. Seymour. 7s.

"A broken and a contrite heart, O God, thou wilt not despise."—Ps. 51: 17.

Rev. Chas. Wesley. C. M. Von Weber.

No. 58. When the Comforter Came.

William Moore. "He shall give you another Comforter."—John 14: 16. Rev. R. Lowry.

1. Depth of mer-cy! can there be Mer-cy still re-served for me?
2. I have long with-stood His grace; Long pro-voked Him to His face;
3. Now, in-cline me to re-pent; Let me now my sins la-ment;
Can my God His wrath for-bear? Me, the chief of sin-ners, spare?
Would not heark-en to His calls, Grieved Him by a thous-and falls.
Now my foul re-volt de-plore, Weep, be-lieve, and sin no more.
1. My heart, that was heav-y and sad, Was made to re-joice and be glad,
2. To sin and to e-vil in-clined, With darkness per-vad-ing my mind,
3. The voice of thanksgiv-ing I raised, The Lord, my Re-deem-er, I praised;
And peace with-out meas-ure I had, When the Com-fort-er came.
No rest I could an-y-where find, Till the Com-fort-er came.
I was at His mer-cy a-maz'd, When the Com-fort-er came.
Refrain.
Peace, sweet peace, Peace when the Com-fort-er came! My
Copyright, 1875, by Biglow & Main.

When the Comforter Came.

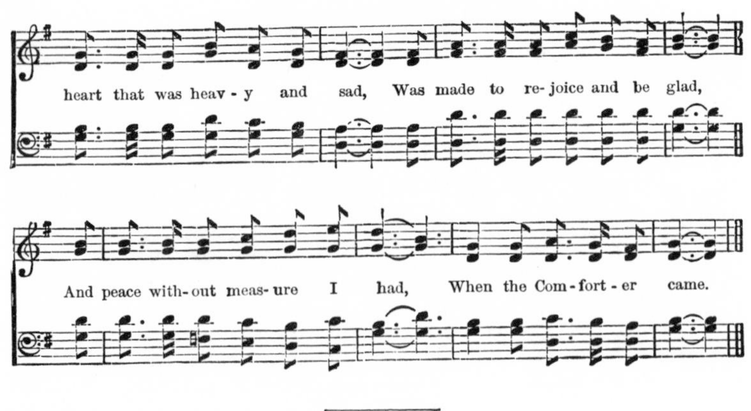

No. 59. Salvation.

"For the grace of God that bringeth salvation to all men hath appeared."—Titus 2 : 11.

P. P. Bliss. P. P. Bliss.

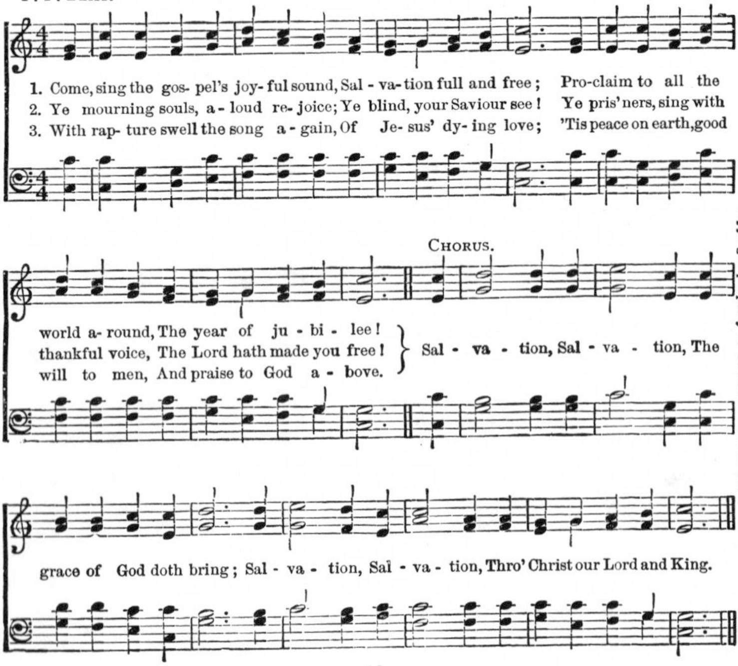

1. Come, sing the gos- pel's joy- ful sound, Sal - va- tion full and free; Pro-claim to all the world a- round, The year of ju - bi - lee!
2. Ye mourning souls, a- loud re- joice; Ye blind, your Saviour see! Ye pris'ners, sing with thankful voice, The Lord hath made you free!
3. With rap- ture swell the song a - gain, Of Je- sus' dy- ing love; 'Tis peace on earth, good will to men, And praise to God a - bove.

Chorus.

Sal - va - tion, Sal - va - tion, The grace of God doth bring; Sal - va - tion, Sal - va - tion, Thro' Christ our Lord and King.

No. 60. Onward, Upward.

"Hold that fast which thou hast, that no man take thy crown."—Rev. 3: 11.

Fanny J. Crosby.
Ira D. Sankey.
1. On-ward! up-ward! Christian sol-dier, Turn not back nor sheath thy sword, Let its
2. On-ward! up-ward! do - ing, dar - ing All for Him who died for thee; Face the
3. On-ward! till thy course is fin-ished, Like the ran-somed ones be - fore; Keep the
blade be sharp for con-quest, In the bat - tle for the Lord. From the great white throne e-
foe and meet with bold-ness Danger what-so-e'er it be. From the bat-tlements of
faith thro' per - se - cu - tion, Nev-er give the bat - tle o'er. On-ward! up-ward! till vic-
ter - nal, God him-self is look-ing down; He it is who now commands thee, Take the
glo - ry, Ho - ly ones are look-ing down, Thou canst almost hear them shouting: "On! let
to - rious, Thou shalt lay thy ar-mor down, And thy lov-ing Sav-iour bids thee At His
cross and win the crown. He it is who now commands thee, Take the cross and win the crown.
no one take thy crown." Thou canst almost hear them shouting: "On! let no one take thy crown."
hand receive thy crown. And thy lov-ing Saviour bids thee At His hand receive thy crown.
cres.

No. 61. More Love to Thee, O Christ.

"Continue ye in my love."—John 15: 9.

Mrs. Elizabeth Prentiss. W. H. Doane.

1. More love to Thee, O Christ! More love to Thee; Hear Thou the pray'r I make On bended knee;
2. Once earthly joy I craved, Sought peace and rest; Now Thee alone I seek, Give what is best:
3. Let sorrow do its work, Send grief or pain; Sweet are Thy messengers, Sweet their refrain,
4. Then shall my latest breath, Whisper Thy praise, This be the parting cry My heart shall raise;

More Love to Thee, O Christ.
This is my earnest plea, More love, O Christ, to Thee, More love to Thee! More love to Thee!
This all my pray'r shall be, More love, O Christ, to Thee, More love to Thee! More love to Thee!
When they can sing with me,—More love, O Christ, to Thee, More love to Thee! More love to Thee!
This still its pray'r shall be: More love, O Christ, to Thee, More love to Thee! More love to Thee!
No. 62.
Wholly Thine.
"The God of peace sanctify you wholly."—Thes. 5: 23.
Mrs. Annie S. Hawks.
Rev. Robert Lowry.
1. Thine, most gra - cious Lord, O make me whol - ly Thine— Thine in thought, in word, and deed, For Thou, O Christ, art mine.
2. Whol - ly Thine, my Lord, To go when Thou dost call; Thine to yield my ver - y self In all things, great and small.
3. Whol - ly Thine, O Lord, In ev - 'ry pass - ing hour; Thine in si - lence, Thine to speak, As Thou dost grant the power.
4. Whol - ly Thine, O Lord, To fash - ion as Thou wilt,— Strengthen, bless, and keep the soul Which Thou hast saved from guilt.
5. Thine, Lord, whol - ly Thine, For ev - er one with Thee— Root - ed, ground - ed in Thy love, A - bid - ing, sure, and free.
Refrain.
Whol - ly Thine, whol - ly Thine; Thou hast bought me, I am Thine; Blessed Saviour, Thou art mine; Make me wholly Thine.
Copyright, 1875, by Biglow & Main.
No. 63.
Fully Trusting.
"Fully I trust in thy word."—Ps. 119: 42.
J. C. Morgan.
Geo. C. Stebbins.
Slowly.
1. All my doubts I give to Je - sus! I've His gracious promise heard—"I shall nev - er be con -
2. All my sin I lay on Je - sus! He doth wash me in His blood: He will keep me pure and
3. All my fears I give to Je - sus! Rests my wea - ry soul on Him; Tho' my way be hid in
4. All my joys I give to Je - sus! He is all I want of bliss: He of all the world is
5. All I am I give to Je - sus! All my bod - y, all my soul, All I have, and all I

Fully Trusting.
CHORUS.
found - ed"—I am trust-ing in that word.
ho - ly, He will bring me home to God.
dark - ness, Nev-er can His light grow dim.
Mas - ter— He has all I need in this.
hope for, While e-ter - nal a - ges roll.
I am trust-ing, ful - ly trusting, Sweetly
trusting in His word; I am trusting, Ful-ly trusting, Sweetly trusting in His word.
Copyright, 1876, by Ira D. Sankey.
No. 64.
Jesus Shall Reign.
"The Lord is King forever and ever."—Ps. 10: 16.
ISAAC WATTS.
KARL WILHELM. Arr.
1. Je - sus shall reign wher - e'er the sun Does his suc-cess - ive journeys run; His
2. To Him shall end - less prayer be made And end - less prais-es crown His head; His
king-dom spread from shore to shore, Till moons shall wax and wane no more. From
name like sweet per-fume shall rise With ev - 'ry morn-ing sac - ri - fice. Peo-
north to south the princ - es meet, To pay their hom-age at His feet; While west-ern
ple and realms of ev - 'ry tongue Dwell on His love with sweetest song, And in-fant
em - pires own their Lord, And sav-age tribes at - tend His word.
voic - es shall pro - claim Their ear-ly bless - ings on His Name.

No. 65. My Song shall be of Jesus.

"His praise shall continually be in my mouth."—Ps. 34: 1.

Mrs. Van Alstyne. W. H. Doane.

1. My song shall be of Je - sus,His mer - cy crowns my days, He fills my cup with
2. My song shall be of Je - sus,When,sit- ting at His feet, I call to mind His
3. My song shall be of Je - sus,While pressing on my way To reach the bliss - ful

bless - ings, And tunes my heart to praise; My song shall be of Je - sus, The
good - ness, In med - i - ta- tion sweet; My song shall be of Je - sus, What-
re - gion Of pure and per - fect day. And when my soul shall en - ter The

ritard.

pre-cious Lamb of God, Who gave Himself my ran - som,And bought me with His blood.
ev - er ill be - tide; I'll sing the grace that saves me, And keeps me at His side.
gate of E - den fair, A song of praise to Je - sus I'll sing for - ev - er there.

No. 66. Only a Step to Jesus.

"Then come thou, for there is peace."—1 Sam. 20: 21.

Fanny J. Crosby. W. H. Doane.

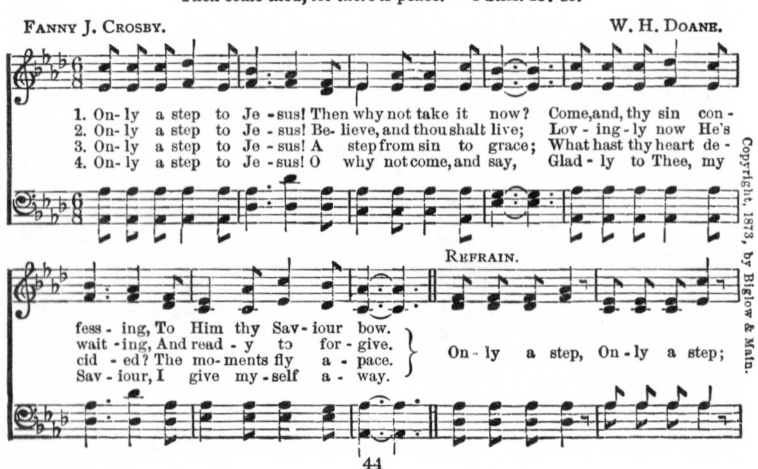
1. On- ly a step to Je - sus! Then why not take it now? Come,and, thy sin con -
2. On- ly a step to Je - sus! Be- lieve, and thou shalt live; Lov - ing - ly now He's
3. On- ly a step to Je - sus! A step from sin to grace; What hast thy heart de -
4. On- ly a step to Je - sus! O why not come, and say, Glad - ly to Thee, my
Refrain.
fess - ing, To Him thy Sav - iour bow.
wait - ing, And read - y to for - give.
cid - ed? The mo- ments fly a - pace.
Sav - iour, I give my - self a - way.
On - ly a step, On - ly a step;
Copyright, 1873, by Biglow & Main.

Only a Step to Jesus.

Come, He waits for thee; Come, and, thy sin con - fess - ing, Thou shalt re-ceive a
bless - ing; Do not re - ject the mer - cy He free - ly of - fers thee.

No. 67 Immanuel's Land.

"And there shall be no night there."—Rev. 22: 5.

Annie R. Cousin. C. M. Wyman.

Earnestly.
1. The sands of time are sink-ing, The dawn of heaven breaks, The sum-mer morn I've sighed for— The fair, sweet morn a - wakes. Dark, dark hath been the mid-night, But day- spring is at hand, And glo - ry—glo - ry dwelleth In Im-man-uel's land.
2. I've wres - tled on t'ward heaven, 'Gainst storm and wind and tide, Now, like a wea - ry trav' - ler That lean - eth on His guide, A - mid the shades of eve - ning, While sinks life's lingering sand, I hail the glo - ry dawning, From Im-man- uel's land.
3. Deep waters crossed life's pathway, The hedge of thorns was sharp; Now these lie all be - hind me— O! for a well-tuned harp! O! to join the hal - le - lu - jah With yon triumphant band! Who sing where glo - ry dwelleth, In Im-man- uel's land.

No. 68. Dark is the Night.

"Thou shalt compass me about with songs of deliverance."—Ps. 32 : 7.

FANNY J. CROSBY. T. E. PERKINS.

1. { Dark is the night, and cold the wind is blow - ing, Near - er and nearer comes the breaker's roar; }
{ Where shall I go, or whith - er fly for ref - uge? Hide me, my Father, till the storm is o'er; }
CHORUS.
{ With His lov - ing hand to guide, let the clouds a - bove me roll, And the bil - lows in their fu - ry dash a - round me. }
{ I can brave the wild - est storm, with His glo - ry in my soul, I can (Omit.........) sing amidst the tempest—Praise the Lord! }
Used by per.

2 Dark is the night, but cheering is the promise;
He will go with me o'er the troubled wave;
Safe He will lead me through the pathless waters,
Jesus, the mighty one, and strong to save.

3 Dark is the night, but lo! the day is breaking,
Onward my bark, unfurl thy every sail;
Now at the helm I see my Father standing,
Soon will my anchor drop within the vail.

No. 69. Hear the Call.

"Put on the whole armour of God."—EPH. 6: 11.

W. F. S. WM. F. SHERWIN.

March movement.

1. Lo! the day of God is break-ing; See the gleam-ing from a - far! Sons of earth from slum - ber wak - ing, Hail the Bright and Morn - ing Star.
2. Trust in Him who is your Cap - tain; Let no heart in ter - ror quail; Je - sus leads the gath - 'ring le - gions, In His name we shall pre - vail.
3. On - ward march-ing, firm and stead - y, Faint not, fear not Sa - tan's frown, For the Lord is with you al - ways, Till you wear the vic - tor's crown.
4. Conq-'ring hosts with ban - ners wav - ing, Sweep-ing on o'er hill and plain, Ne'er shall halt till swells the an - them, "Christ o'er all the world doth reign!"

Hear the Call.
CHORUS.
Hear the call! O gird your ar-mour on, Grasp the Spir - it's might - y Sword:
Take the hel - met of sal - va - tion, Press - ing on to bat - tle for the Lord!
No. 70. Joy in Sorrow.
"Your sorrow shall be turned into joy."—JOHN 16 : 20.
Mrs. JANE CREWDSON.
IRA D. SANKEY.
1. I've found a joy in sor - row, A se - cret balm for pain, A beau - ti - ful to -
2. I've found a glad ho - san - na For ev - 'ry woe and wail; A hand - ful of sweet
3. An E - lim with its cool - ness, Its fountains and its shade; A bless - ing in its
4. My Saviour, Thee pos - sess - ing, I have the joy, the balm, The heal - ing and the
mor - row Of sun - shine af - ter rain; I've found a branch of heal - ing Near
man - na When grapes of Esh - col fail; I've found a Rock of A - ges When
ful - ness, When buds of prom - ise fade. O'er tears of soft con - tri - tion I've
bless - ing, The sun - shine and the psalm; The prom - ise for the fear - ful, The
ev - ery bit - ter spring, A whis - pered prom - ise steal - ing O'er ev - ery bro - ken
des - ert wells are dry; And af - ter wea - ry sta - ges, I've found an E - lim
seen a rain - bow light; A glo - ry and fru - i - tion, So near!—yet out of
E - lim for the faint; The rain - bow for the tear - ful, The glo - ry for the
string, A whis - pered prom - ise steal - ing, O'er ev - ery bro - ken string.
nigh. And af - ter wea - ry sta - ges, I've found an E - lim nigh.
sight. A glo - ry and fru - i - tion, So near!—yet out of sight.
saint! The rain - bow for the tear - ful, The glo - ry for the saint!
Copyright property of The Biglow & Main Co.
57

No. 71. The Heavenly Land.

"A better country, that is an heavenly."—Heb. 11: 16.

Rev. Lewis Hartsough. Wm. B. Bradbury.

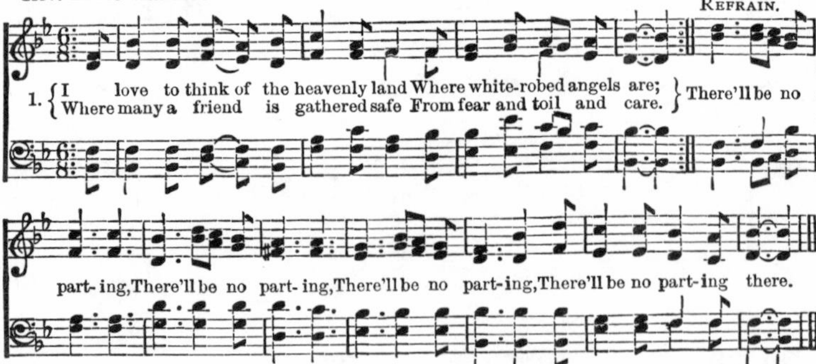

Refrain.
1. { I love to think of the heavenly land Where white-robed angels are;
Where many a friend is gathered safe From fear and toil and care. } There'll be no
part-ing, There'll be no part-ing, There'll be no part-ing, There'll be no part-ing there.

Copyright, 1861, by Wm. B. Bradbury.

2 I love to think of the heavenly land,
Where my Redeemer reigns,
Where rapturous songs of triumph rise,
In endless, joyous strains.—*Ref.*

3 I love to think of the heavenly land,
The saints eternal home,
Where palms, and robes, and crowns ne'er fade,
And all our joys are one.—*Ref.*

4 I love to think of the heavenly land,
The greetings there we'll meet,
The harps—the songs forever ours—
The walks—the golden streets.—*Ref.*

5 I love to think of the heavenly land,
That promised land so fair,
Oh, how my raptured spirit longs,
To be forever there.—*Ref.*

No. 72. Call Them in.

"Go out into the highways and hedges, and compel them to come in."—Luke 14: 23.

Miss Anna Shipton. Ira D. Sankey.

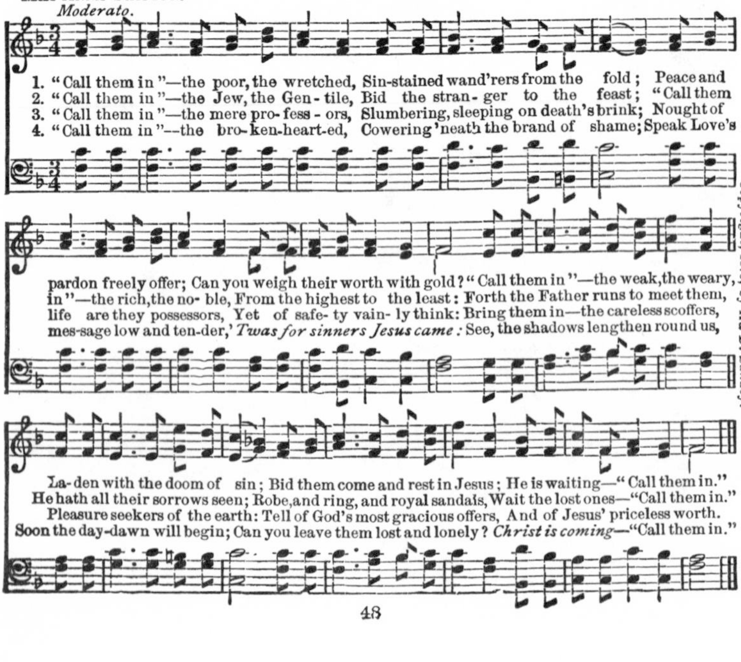

Moderato.
1. "Call them in"—the poor, the wretched, Sin-stained wand'rers from the fold; Peace and
2. "Call them in"—the Jew, the Gen-tile, Bid the stran-ger to the feast; "Call them
3. "Call them in"—the mere pro-fess-ors, Slumbering, sleeping on death's brink; Nought of
4. "Call them in"—the bro-ken-heart-ed, Cowering 'neath the brand of shame; Speak Love's
pardon freely offer; Can you weigh their worth with gold? "Call them in"—the weak, the weary,
in"—the rich, the no-ble, From the highest to the least: Forth the Father runs to meet them,
life are they possessors, Yet of safe-ty vain-ly think: Bring them in—the careless scoffers,
mes-sage low and ten-der, 'Twas for sinners Jesus came: See, the shadows lengthen round us,
La-den with the doom of sin; Bid them come and rest in Jesus; He is waiting—"Call them in."
He hath all their sorrows seen; Robe, and ring, and royal sandals, Wait the lost ones—"Call them in."
Pleasure seekers of the earth: Tell of God's most gracious offers, And of Jesus' priceless worth.
Soon the day-dawn will begin; Can you leave them lost and lonely? Christ is coming—"Call them in."

Copyright, 1876, by Ira D. Sankey.

No. 73.

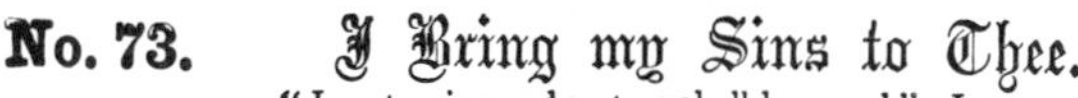
I Bring my Sins to Thee.

"In returning and rest ye shall be saved."—Isa. 30 : 15.

Frances Ridley Havergal. P. P. Bliss.

1. I bring my *sins* to Thee, The sins I can-not count, That all may cleansed be In Thy once o-pened Fount; I bring them Sav-iour, all to Thee; The bur-den is too great for me, The bur-den is too great for me.
2. I bring my *grief* to Thee, The grief I can-not tell; No words shall need-ed be, Thou knowest all so well; I bring the sor-row laid on me, O suff'ring Sav-iour, all to Thee, O suff'ring Sav-iour, all to Thee.
3. My *joys* to Thee I bring, The joys Thy love has given, That each may be a wing To lift me near-er heaven, I bring them, Sav-iour, all to Thee, Who hast procured them all for me, Who hast procured them all for me.
4. My *life* I bring to Thee, I would not be my own; O Sa-viour, let me be Thine ev-er, Thine a-lone, My heart, my life, my all I bring To Thee, my Sav-iour and my King, To Thee, my Sav-iour and my King.

No. 74. Song of Salvation.

"Come unto me all ye that labor and are heavy laden, and I will give you rest."—Matt. 11 : 28.

Anon. Philip Phillips.

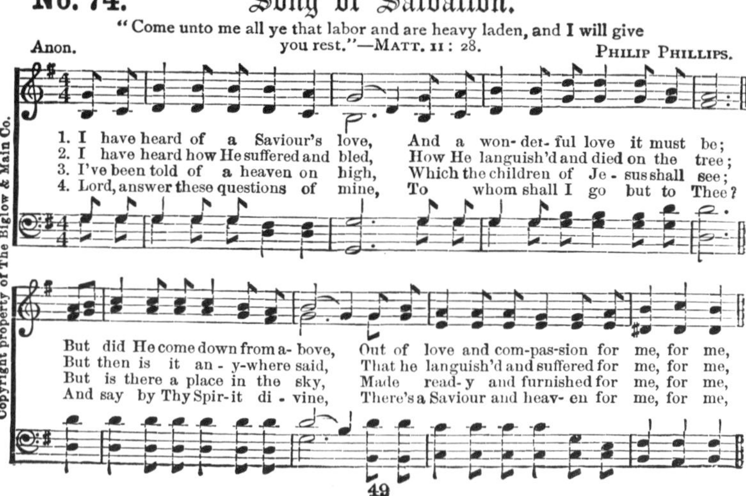
1. I have heard of a Saviour's love, And a won-der-ful love it must be; But did He come down from a-bove, Out of love and com-pas-sion for me, for me,
2. I have heard how He suffered and bled, How He languish'd and died on the tree; But then is it an-y-where said, That he languish'd and suffered for me, for me,
3. I've been told of a heaven on high, Which the children of Je-sus shall see; But is there a place in the sky, Made read-y and furnished for me, for me,
4. Lord, answer these questions of mine, To whom shall I go but to Thee? And say by Thy Spir-it di-vine, There's a Saviour and heav-en for me, for me,

CHORUS.
Out of love and compassion for me?
That He languish'd and suffered for me!
Made ready and furnished for me?
There's a Saviour and heaven for me.
Response.*
Yes, yes, yes, for me, for me, Yes, yes, yes, for me;
rit.
Our Lord from above in His infinite love, On the cross died to save you and me.
No. 75. At the Feet of Jesus.
"Mary which also sat at Jesus' feet, and heard his word."—LUKE 10: 39.
P. P. B.
P. P. BLISS.
Moderato.
1. At the feet of Jesus, List'ning to His word: Learning wisdom's lesson From her loving Lord: Mary, led by heav'nly grace, Chose the meek disciple's place.
2. At the feet of Jesus, Pouring perfume rare, Mary did her Saviour, For the grave prepare: And, from love the "good work" done, She her Lord's approval won.
3. At the feet of Jesus, In that morning hour, Loving hearts receiving Resurrection power: Haste with joy to preach the Word: "Christ is risen, Praise the Lord!"
CHORUS.
At the feet of Jesus is the place for me, There a humble learner would I choose to be.
At the feet of Jesus is the place for me, There in sweetest service would I ever be.
At the feet of Jesus, risen now for me, I shall sing His praises through eternity.
Copyright property of The John Church Co.

No. 76. A Little While.

"What is this that he saith a little while."—John 16 : 17.

Mrs. Jane Crewdson. Ira D. Sankey.

Slowly.

1. Oh, for the peace that floweth as a riv - er, Making life's desert places bloom and smile;
2. "A lit- tle while" for patient vig-il-keeping, To face the storm and wrestle with the strong;
3. "A lit- tle while" the earthen pitcher taking, To wayside brooks, from far off fountains fed;
4. "A little while" to keep the oil from failing, "A little while" faith's flickering lamp to trim;

rit.

Oh, for the faith to grasp "Heav'n's bright forever," A-mid the shadows of earth's "little while."
"A little while" to sow the seed with weeping, Then bind the sheaves and sing the harvest song.
Then the parched lip its thirst forev-er slaking Beside the fulness of the Fountain-head.
And then the Bridegroom's coming footsteps hailing, We'll haste to meet Him with the bridal hymn.

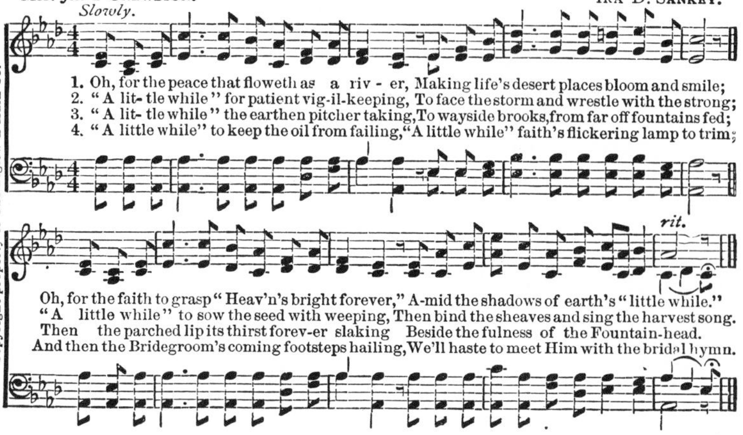

No. 77. Just a Word for Jesus.

"Wilt thou not tell."—Ezek. 24 : 19.

Fanny J. Crosby. W. H. Doane.

1. Now just a word for Je - sus; Your dear-est Friend so true, Come, cheer our hearts and tell us What He has done for you.
2. Now just a word for Je - sus; You feel your sins for-given, And by His grace are striv- ing To reach a home in heaven.
3. Now just a word for Je - sus; A cross it can - not be To say, "I love my Sav - iour Who gave His life for me."

Refrain.

Now just a word for Je - sus—'Twill help us on our way; One lit - tle word for Je - sus, O speak, or sing, or pray.

4 Now just a word for Jesus;
Let not the time be lost;
The heart's neglected duty
Brings sorrow to its cost.—*Ref.*

5 Now just a word for Jesus;
And if your faith be dim,
Arise in all your weakness,
And leave the rest to Him.—*Ref.*

No. 78. Who's on the Lord's Side?

"Who is on the Lord's side."—Ex. 32: 26.

Mrs. E. W. Griswold. P. P. Bliss.

1. We're march-ing to Ca - naan with ban - ner and song, We're sol - diers en -
2. The sword may be burn - ished, the ar - mor be bright, For Sa - tan ap -
3. Who is there a - mong us yet un - der the rod, Who knows not the
4. Oh, heed not the sor - row, the pain and the wrong, For soon shall our
list - ed to fight 'gainst the wrong; But, lest in the con - flict our
pears as an an - gel of light; Yet dark - ly the bo - som may
par - don - ing mer - cy of God? Oh, bring to Him hum - bly the
sigh - ing be changed in - to song; So, bear - ing the cross of our
strength should di - vide, We ask, who a - mong us is on the Lord's side?
treach - er - y hide, While lips are pro - fess - ing, "I'm on the Lord's side."
heart in its pride; Oh, haste, while He's wait - ing and seek the Lord's side.
cov - e - nant Guide, We'll shout, as we tri - umph, "I'm on the Lord's side."
Chorus.
Oh, who is there a - mong us, the true and the tried, Who'll stand by his
col - ors— who's on the Lord's side? Oh, who is there a - mong us, the
true and the tried, Who'll stand by his col - ors— who's on the Lord's side?
Copyright property of The John Church Co.

No. 79.

Remember Me.

"O Lord, thou knowest; remember."—JER. 15: 15.

ISAAC WATTS. ASA HULL.

Used by per.

1. A - las! and did my Sav - iour bleed? And did my Sovereign die?
2. Was it for crimes that I had done He groaned up - on the tree?
3. Well might the sun in dark - ness hide, And shut his glo - ries in,
CHO.—Help me, dear Sav - iour, Thee to own, And ev - er faith-ful be;
Would He de - vote that sa - cred head For such a worm as I?
A - maz - ing pit - y! grace un-known! And love be - yond de - gree.
When Christ, the might - y Mak - er died For man, the crea-ture's sin.
And when Thou sit - test on Thy throne, O Lord, re - mem - ber me.

4 Thus might I hide my blushing face,
Whilst His dear cross appears,
Dissolve my heart in thankfulness,
And melt mine eyes to tears.—*Cho.*

5 But drops of grief can ne'er repay
The debt of love I owe;
Here, Lord, I give myself away;
'Tis all that I can do.—*Cho.*

No. 80. Look Away to Jesus.

Rev. HENRY BURTON. "Looking unto Jesus."—HEB. 12: 2. P. P. BLISS.

Copyright property of The John Church Co.

1. Look a - way to Je - sus, Soul by woe op - press'd; 'Twas for thee He
2. Look a - way to Je - sus, Sol - dier in the fight; When the bat - tle
3. Look a - way to Je - sus, When the skies are fair; Calm seas have their
4. Look a - way to Je - sus, 'Mid the toil and heat; Soon will come the
5. When, a - mid the mu - sic Of the end - less feast, Saints will sing His
suf - fer'd, Come to Him and rest, All thy griefs He car - ried,
thick - ens Keep thine arm - or bright; Though thy foes be ma - ny,
dan - gers; Mar - in - er, be - ware! Earth - ly joys are fleet - ing,
rest - ing At the Mas - ter's feet; For the guests are bid - den,
prais - es, Thine shall not be least; Then, a - mid the glo - ries
All thy sins He bore; Look a - way to Je - sus; Trust Him ev - er - more.
Tho' thy strength be small, Look a - way to Je - sus; He shall con - quer all.
Go - ing as they came, Look a - way to Je - sus; Ev - er - more the same.
And the feast is spread; Look a - way to Je - sus; In His foot - steps tread.
Of the crys - tal sea, Look a - way to Je - sus; Through e - ter - ni - ty.

No. 81. Behold, the Bridegroom Cometh.

"At midnight there was a cry made, behold the Bridegroom cometh."—MATT. 25: 6.

G. F. R. GEO. F. ROOT.

1. Our lamps are trimm'd and burn-ing, Our robes are white and clean, We've
2. Go forth, go forth to meet Him, The way is o - pen now, All
3. We see the mar - riage splen-dor With - in the o - pen door; We
tar - ried for the Bridegroom, Oh, may we en - ter in? We know we've nothing
light-ed with the glo - ry That's streaming from His brow. Ac - cept the in - vi -
know that those who en - ter Are blest for - ev - er - more. We see He is more
wor-thy That we can call our own— The light, the oil, the robes we wear,
ta - tion Be - yond de - serv - ing kind; Make no de - lay, but take your lamps,
love-ly Than all the sons of men, But still we know the door once shut,
Are all from Him a - lone.
And joy e - ter - nal find.
Will nev - er ope a - gain.
CHORUS.
Be-hold the Bridegroom cometh! And all may
en - ter in, Whose lamps are trimm'd and burning, Whose robes are white and clean.
Copyright property of The John Church Co.

No. 82. Whiter than Snow.

"Wash me, and I shall be whiter than snow."—Ps. 51: 7.

JAMES NICHOLSON. WM. G. FISCHER.

1. Lord Je - sus, I long to be per - fect - ly whole; I want Thee for-
2. Lord Je - sus, look down from Thy throne in the skies, And help me to
3. Lord Je - sus, for this I most hum - bly en - treat; I wait, bless - ed
4. Lord Je - sus, Thou seest I pa - tient - ly wait; Come now, and with
ev - er, to live in my soul; Break down ev - 'ry i - dol, cast
make a com - plete sac - ri - fice; I give up my - self, and what-
Lord, at Thy cru - ci - fied feet, By faith, for my cleansing, I
in me a new heart cre - ate; To those who have sought Thee, Thou
out ev - 'ry foe; Now wash me, and I shall be whit - er than snow.
ev - er I know—Now wash me, and I shall be whit - er than snow.
see Thy blood flow— Now wash me, and I shall be whit - er than snow.
nev - er said'st No— Now wash me, and I shall be whit - er than snow.
Used by per.
CHORUS.
Whit - er than snow, yes, whit - er than snow;
Now wash me, and I shall be whit - er than snow.

No. 83. Blessed River.

"And he shewed me a pure river of water of life."—Rev. 22 : 1.

Horatius Bonar, D.D. — Rev. Robert Lowry.

1. Fresh from the throne of glo - ry Bright in its crys - tal gleam, Bursts out the liv - ing fount - ain, Swells on the liv - ing stream; Bless - ed Riv - er, Let me ev - er Feast my eyes on thee, Bless - ed Riv - er, Let me ev - er Feast my eyes on thee.
2. Stream full of life and glad - ness, Spring of all health and peace, No harps by thee hang si - lent, Nor hap - py voic - es cease; Tran - quil Riv - er, Let me ev - er Sit and sing by thee, Tran - quil Riv - er, Let me ev - er Sit and sing by thee.
3. Riv - er of God, I greet thee, Not now a - far, but near; My soul to thy still wa - ters Hastes in its thirstings here; Ho - ly Riv - er, Let me ev - er Drink of on - ly thee, Ho - ly Riv - er, Let me ev - er Drink of on - ly thee.
Copyright, 1871, by Biglow & Main.

No. 84. My High Tower.

"The Lord is my Rock.........and my high Tower."—Ps. 18 : 2.

P. P. B. — P. P. Bliss.

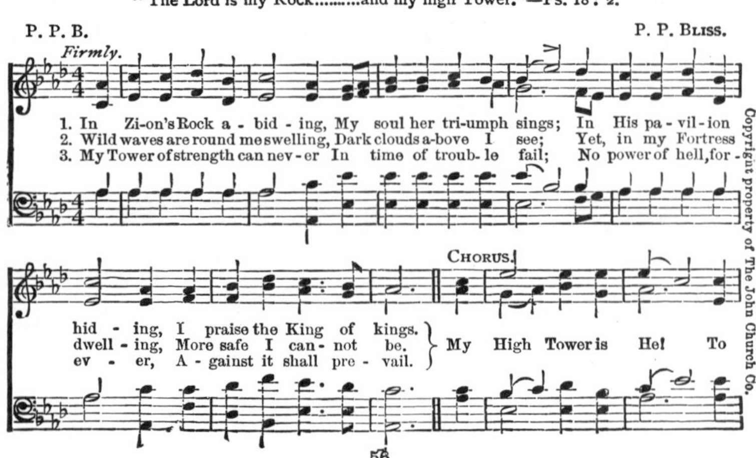
Firmly.
1. In Zi - on's Rock a - bid - ing, My soul her tri - umph sings; In His pa - vil - ion hid - ing, I praise the King of kings.
2. Wild waves are round me swelling, Dark clouds a - bove I see; Yet, in my Fortress dwell - ing, More safe I can - not be.
3. My Tower of strength can nev - er In time of troub - le fail; No power of hell, for - ev - er, A - gainst it shall pre - vail.
CHORUS.
My High Tower is He! To
Copyright property of The John Church Co.

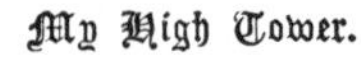
My High Tower.

Him will I flee; In Him con-fide, In Him a-bide; My High Tower is He!

No. 85. I Stood Outside the Gate.

"Enter ye in at the strait gate."—MATT. 7: 13.

Miss JOSEPHINE POLLARD. HUBERT P. MAIN.

1. I stood out - side the gate, A poor, way - far - ing child; With
2. Oh, "Mer - cy!" loud I cried, "Now give me rest from sin!" "I
3. In Mer - cy's guise I knew The Sav - iour long a - bused, Who

in my heart there beat A tem - pest loud and wild; A fear oppressed my
will," a voice re - plied; And Mer - cy let me in; She bound my bleed-ing
oft - en sought my heart, And wept when I re - fused; Oh! what a blest re -

soul, That I might be *too late*; And oh, I trem-bled sore, And
wounds, And soothed my heart op - prest; She washed a - way my guilt And
turn For all my years of sin; I stood out - side the gate, And

prayed out - side the gate, And prayed out - side......... the gate.
gave me peace and rest, And gave me peace ...... and rest.
Je - sus let me in, And Je - sus let .... me in.

No. 86. Scatter Seeds of Kindness.

"Be kindly affectioned one to another."—ROM. 12 : 10.

Mrs. ALBERT SMITH.
S. J. VAIL.
1. Let us gath - er up the sunbeams, Ly - ing all a - round our path; Let us
2. Strange we nev - er prize the mu - sic Till the sweet-voiced bird is flown! Strange that
3. If we knew the ba - by fin - gers, Pressed a - gainst the win-dow pane, Would be
4. Ah! those lit - tle ice-cold fin - gers, How they point our mem'ries back To the
keep the wheat and ros - es, Cast - ing out the thorns and chaff, Let us find our sweet-est
we should slight the vio-lets Till the love - ly flowers are gone! Strange that summer skies and
cold and stiff to-mor-row—Nev - er troub - le us a - gain—Would the bright eyes of our
hast - y words and ac-tions Strewn a - long our backward track! How those lit - tle hands re-
com - fort In the bless-ings of to - day, With a pa-tient hand re-mov-ing All the
sun - shine Nev - er seem one half so fair, As when win-ter's snow - y pin-ions Shake the
dar - ling Catch the frown up - on our brow?—Would the prints of ro - sy fin-gers Vex us
mind us, As in snow - y grace they lie, Not to scat-ter thorns—but ros - es— For our
bri - ers from the way.
white down in the air.
then as they do now?
reap - ing by and by.
CHORUS.
Then scat-ter seeds of kindness, Then scat-ter seeds of
kind-ness, Then scat - ter seeds of kind-ness, For our reap-ing by and by.
ad lib.
Copyright property of The Biglow & Main Co.

No. 87. Onward, Christian Soldiers.
"Take unto you the whole armor of God."—Eph. 6: 13.
Rev. S. Baring-Gould.
Jos. Haydn, arr.
1. On - ward, Christian sol - diers! Marching as to war, With the cross of Je - sus Go - ing on be - fore. Christ the Roy - al Mas - ter Leads a-gainst the foe, For-ward in - to bat - tle, See His ban - ners go.
2. Like a might - y ar - my Moves the Church of God; Broth-ers, we are tread - ing Where the saints have trod; We are not di - vid - ed, All one bod - y we; One in hope and doc - trine, One in char - i - ty.
3. Crowns and thrones may per-ish, Kingdoms rise and wane But the Church of Je - sus Con - stant will re - main: Gates of hell can nev - er 'Gainst that Church pre - vail; We have Christ's own prom-ise— And that can - not fail.
4. On - ward, then, ye faith - ful, Join the hap - py throng, Blend with ours your voic - es In the tri-umph song; Glo - ry, laud, and hon - or, Un - to Christ the King. This thro' countless a - ges Men and an - gels sing.
Chorus.
On-ward, Christian sol - diers! March-ing as to war, With the Cross of Je - sus Go - ing on be - fore.
No. 88. Hold Fast till I Come.
"That which ye have already, hold fast till I come."—Rev. 2: 25.
Mrs. E. W. Griswold.
P. P. Bliss.
1. Oh, spirit, o'erwhelmed by thy failures and fears, Look up to thy Lord, tho' with trembling and tears: Weak Faith, to thy call seem the heav'ns only dumb? To thee is the message, "Hold fast till I come."
2. Hold fast when the world would allure thee to sin; Hold fast when the tempter assails from within; In sunshine or sadness, in gain or in loss, To falter were madness; Oh, cling to the cross.
3. Thy Sav-iour is com-ing in ten-der-est love, To make up His jew-els and bear them a-bove: Oh, child, in thine anguish, despairing or dumb, Remember the message, "Hold fast till I come."
Copyright property of The John Church Co.

Hold Fast till I Come.
Chorus.
Hold fast till I come, Hold fast till I come; A bright crown awaits thee; Hold fast till I come.
No. 89. Seeking to Save.
"For the Son of Man is come to seek and to save that which was lost."—Luke 19: 10.
P. P. B.
P. P. Bliss.
1. Tenderly the Shepherd, O'er the mountains cold, Goes to bring His lost one Back to the fold.
2. Patient-ly the own-er Seeks with earnest care, In the dust and darkness Her treasure rare.
3. Lovingly the Father Sends the news around: "He once dead now liveth—Once lost is found."
Chorus.
Seek-ing to save, Seek-ing to save, Lost one, 'tis Je - sus Seek-ing to save.
Seek-ing to save, Seek-ing to save, Lost one, 'tis Je - sus Seek-ing to save.
Copyright property of The John Church Co.
No. 90. Hallelujah, He is Risen!
"He is not here; for he is risen, as he said."—Matt. 23: 6.
P. P. B.
P. P. Bliss.
1. Hal - le - lu - jah, He is ris - en! Je - sus is gone up on high!
2. Hal - le - lu - jah, He is ris - en! Our ex - alt - ed Head to be;
3. Hal - le - lu - jah, He is ris - en! Death for aye hath lost his sting,
Burst the bars of death a - sun - der, An - gels shout and men re - ply:
Sends the wit - ness of the Spir - it That our ad - vo - cate is He:
Christ, Him - self the Res - ur - rec - tion, From the grave His own will bring:
Copyright property of The John Church Co.

Hallelujah, He is Risen!
He is ris-en, He is ris-en, Liv-ing now, no more to die. now, no more to die.
He is ris-en, He is ris-en, Jus-ti-fied in Him are we. fied in Him are we.
He is ris-en, He is ris-en, Liv-ing Lord and coming King. Lord and coming King.
No. 91. O Crown of Rejoicing.
"Henceforth there is laid up for me a crown of righteousness."—2 Tim. 4: 8.
Rev. J. B. Atchinson.
P. P. Bliss.
Duet.
1. O crown of re-joic-ing that's wait-ing for me, When fin-ished my course, and when Je-sus I see, And when from my Lord comes the sweet sounding word: "Re-ceive, faith-ful serv-ant, the joy of thy Lord."
2. O won-der-ful song that in glo-ry I'll sing, To Him who re-deemed me, to Je-sus my King; All glo-ry and hon-or to Him shall be given, And prais-es un-ceas-ing for-ev-er in heaven.
3. O joy ev-er-last-ing when heav-en is won, For-ev-er in glo-ry to shine as the sun; No sor-row nor sigh-ing—these all flee a-way, No night there, no shad-ows—'tis one end-less day.
4. O won-der-ful name which the glo-ri-fied bear, The new name which Je-sus bestows on us there; To him that o'er-com-eth 'twill on-ly be given, Blest sign of ap-prov-al, our wel-come to heaven.
Chorus.
O crown of re-joic-ing, O won-der-ful song;.......... O joy ev-er-last-ing, O glo-ri-fied throng;............ O beau-ti-ful home,......... my home can it be? O glo-ry reserved for me!
Crown of re-joic-ing, O won-der-ful, won-der-ful song;
Joy ev-er-last-ing, O glo-ri-fied, glo-ri-fied throng;
Beau-ti-ful home,
Copyright property of The John Church Co.

No. 92. His Word a Tower.
" As thy days, so shall thy strength be?"—Deut. 33: 25.
Anon.
P. P. Bliss.
1. While foes are strong and dan-ger near, A voice falls gent - ly on my ear:
2. With such a prom - ise need I fear, For all that now I hold most dear?
3. And when at last I'm called to die, Still on Thy prom-ise I'll re - ly;
My Sav- iour speaks, He says to me, That as my days my strength shall be.
No, I will nev - er anx- ious be, For as my days my strength shall be.
Yes, Lord, I then will trust in Thee, That as my days my strength shall be.
Copyright property of The John Church Co.
Chorus.
His word a Tower to which I flee, For as my days my strength shall be.
His word a Tower to which I flee, For as my days my strength shall be.
No. 93. In the Silent Midnight Watches.
"Behold I stand at the door and knock."—Rev. 3: 20.
Rev. A. C. Coxe, D.D.
Geo. F. Root.
Piano e Marcato.
1. In the si - lent midnight watches, List—thy bos-om's door! How it knocketh,
2. Death comes down with reckless footsteps, To the hall and hut; Think you death will
3. Then 'tis time to stand en-treat-ing Christ to let thee in; At the gate of
Used by per.
knock-eth, knocketh, Knocketh ev - er - more! Say not 'tis thy puls - e's beat- ing,
tar - ry knocking, When the door is shut? Je - sus wait-eth, wait-eth, wait-eth,
heav - en beat- ing, Wail-ing for thy sin? Nay! a - las, thou guilt - y crea-ture!

In the Silent Midnight Watches.

'Tis thy heart of sin; 'Tis thy Saviour knocks, and cri-eth, "Rise, and let me in!"
But the door is fast; Grieved, away thy Sav- iour go- eth, Death breaks in at last.
Hast thou, then, for- got? Je - sus wait- ed long to know thee, Now He knows thee not!
No. 94. We shall Sleep, but not Forever.
" Sown in corruption......raised in incorruption."—1 Cor. 15: 42.
Mrs. M. A. Kidder.
S. J. Vail.
1. We shall sleep, but not for - ev - er, There will be a glo- rious dawn! We shall meet to part, no, nev - er, On the res - ur - rec- tion morn! From the deep- est caves of o - cean, From the des - ert and the plain, From the val - ley and the mountain, Countless throngs shall rise again.
2. When we see a pre- cious blos - som That we tend - ed with such care, Rude - ly tak - en from our bo - som, How our ach - ing hearts de-spair! Round its lit - tle grave we lin - ger, Till the set - ting sun is low, Feel - ing all our hopes have per- ished With the flow'r we cherished so.
3. We shall sleep, but not for - ev - er, In the lone and si - lent grave; Bless - ed be the Lord that tak- eth, Bless - ed be the Lord that gave. In the bright, e - ter- nal cit - y Death can nev - er, nev - er come! In His own good time He'll call us From our rest, to Home, sweet Home.
p Chorus.
cres.
We shall sleep, but not for - ev - er, There will be a glorious dawn; We shall meet to part, no, nev- er, On the res - ur- rection morn!
Copyright property of The Biglow & Main Co.

No. 95. Watchman, Tell Me.
"Watchman, what of the night."—Isa. 21 : 11.
Rev. Sidney S. Brewer.
Arr. by Wm. B. Bradbury.
Fine.
1. Watchman, tell me, does the morn-ing Of fair Zi - on's glo - ry dawn;
Have the signs that mark His com-ing, Yet up - on my pathway shone?
2. See the glo - rious light as - cend-ing Of the grand Sa - bat - ic year,
Hark! the voi - ces loud pro - claim-ing The Mes - si - ah's king-dom near;
D.C.—Spurn the un - be - lief that bound thee, Morning dawns, a - rise, a - rise!
D.C.—Sa - lem, too, ap-pears in grandeur, Tow'ring 'neath her sun - lit skies!
D.C.
Pil - grim, yes, a - rise, look round thee, Light is break - ing in the skies;
Watchman, yes; I see just yon - der, Ca - naan's glo - rious heights a - rise;
3 Pilgrim in that golden city,
Seated in the jasper throne,
Zion's King, arrayed in beauty,
Reigns in peace from zone to zone;
There, on verdant hills and mountains,
Where the golden sunbeams play,
Purling streams, and crystal fountains,
Sparkle in th' eternal day.
4 Pilgrim, see! the light is beaming
Brighter still upon thy way;
Signs thro' all the earth are gleaming,
Omens of the coming day,
When the last loud trumpet sounding,
Shall awake from earth to sea,
All the saints of God now sleeping,
Clad in immortality.
No. 96. Give me the Wings of Faith.
"Here we have no continuing city."—Heb. 13: 14.
Rev. I. Watts.
Arr. by Walter Kittredge.
Solo.
1. Give me the wings of faith to rise, With - in the vail, and see
2. Once they were mourn - ers here be - low, And pour'd out cries and tears;
3. I asked them whence their vic - t'ry came: They, with u - ni - ted breath,
The saints a - bove, how great their joys, How bright their glo - ries be.
They wres- tled hard, as we do now, With sins, and doubts, and fears.
A - scribe their con - quest to the Lamb, Their tri - umph to His death.
Chorus.
Ma - ny are the friends who are wait-ing to-day, Hap-py on the gold - en strand,
Used by arr. with Oliver Ditson Co., owners of copyright.

Give me the Wings of Faith.

Ma-ny are the voi-ces call-ing us a-way, To join their glo-rious band.
Repeat pp.
Call-ing us a-way, Call-ing us a-way, Call-ing to the bet-ter land.

No. 97. The Land of Beulah.

" Thou shalt be called Beulah, for the Lord delighteth in thee."—Isa. 62 : 4.
Rev. Jefferson Hascall.
Wm. B. Bradbury.
1. {My lat-est sun is sink-ing fast, My race is near-ly run; / My strong-est tri-als now are past, My tri-umph is be-gun.}
2. {I know I'm nearing the ho-ly ranks Of friends and kin-dred dear, / For I brush the dews on Jor-dan's banks, The cross-ing must be near.}
Chorus.
f
O come, an-gel band, Come and around me stand, O, bear me a-way on your snowy wings To my im-mor-tal home. O, bear me a-way on your snowy wings To my im-mor-tal home.
Copyright property of The Biglow & Main Co.

3 I've almost gained my heavenly home,
My spirit loudly sings;
Thy holy ones, behold, they come!
I hear the noise of wings.

4 O, bear my longing heart to Him
Who bled and died for me;
Whose blood now cleanses from all sin,
And gives me victory.

No. 98. Room for Thee.

"There was no room for them in the inn."—LUKE 2 : 7.

EMILY S. ELLIOTT. IRA D. SANKEY.

Slow.
1. Thou didst leave Thy throne, and Thy king- ly crown, When Thou camest to earth for
2. Heav'n's arch - es rang when the an - gels sang, Of Thy birth, and Thy roy- al de-
3. Fox - es found their rest, and the birds had their nests, In the shade of the ce - dar
4. Thou cam-est, O Lord, with Thy liv - ing word, That should set Thy peo - ple
5. Heaven's arch-es shall ring, and its choirs shall sing, At Thy com - ing to vic- to-
me; But in Bethlehem's home there was found no room, For Thy ho - ly na- tiv - i - ty.
gree; But in low - ly birth didst Thou come to earth, And in greatest hu- mil - i - ty.
tree; But Thy couch was the sod, O Thou Son of God, In the des- erts of Gal - i - lee.
free; But with mocking and scorn and with crown of thorn, Did they bear Thee to Calva- ry.
ry; Thou wilt call me home, saying, "yet there is room," There is room at My side for thee.
REFRAIN.
Oh, come to my heart, Lord Je - sus! There is room in my heart for Thee.
Oh, come to my heart, Lord Je - sus, come! There is room in my heart for Thee.

No. 99. Home at Last.

"In my Father's house are many mansions—I go to prepare a place for you."—JOHN 14 : 2.
"And there shall be no more death, neither sorrow nor crying."—REV. 21 : 4.

Mrs. MARIA P. A. CROZIER. IRA D. SANKEY.

1. "Home at last" on heavenly mountains, Heard the "Come and enter in;" Saved by life's fair
2. Free at last from all temp-ta- tion, No more need of watchful care; Joy - ful in com-
3. Saved to greet on hills of glo - ry Loved ones we have missed so long; Saved to tell the
4. Wel- comed at the pearl - y por - tal, Ev- er more a welcome guest; Welcomed to the

Home at Last.
Refrain.
flow- ing fountains, Saved from earthly taint and sin.
plete sal - va- tion, Given the victor's crown to wear.
sin - ner's sto - ry, Saved to sing redemption's song.
life im - mor - tal, In the mansions of the blest.
"Home, sweet home," our home forever;
Slow.
All the pilgrim-journey past; Welcomed home to wander, never, Saved thro' Jesus—"Home at last."
Copyright, 1876, by Biglow & Main.
No. 100. The Mistakes of my Life.
"Behold, I have set before thee an open door."—Rev. 3: 8.
Mrs. Urania Locke Bailey.
Rev. Robert Lowry.
Tenderly.
1. The mistakes of my life have been ma- ny, The sins of my heart have been more, And I scarce can see for weep- ing, But I'll knock at the o - pen door.
2. I am low - est of those who love Him, I am weak- est of those who pray; But I come as He has bid- den, And He will not say me nay.
3. My mistakes His free grace will cov - er, My sins He will wash a- way, And the feet that shrink and fal - ter, Shall walk thro' the gates of day.
4. The mistakes of my life have been ma- ny, And my spir - it is sick with sin, And I scarce can see for weep- ing, But the Sav- iour will let me in.
Chorus.
I know I am weak and sin - ful, It comes to me more and more; But when the dear Sav- iour shall bid me come in, I'll en - ter the o - pen door.
Copyright, 1871, by Biglow & Main.

No. 101. Come; for the Feast is Spread.
"Come; for all things are now ready."—LUKE 14: 17.
Rev. HENRY BURTON.
P. P. BLISS.
1. Come, for the feast is spread; Hark to the call! Come to the
2. Come where the fount-ain flows—Riv - er of life— Heal - ing for
3. Come to the throne of grace, Bold - ly draw near; He who would
4. Come to the Bet - ter Land, Pil - grim, make haste! Earth is a
5. Je - sus, we come to Thee, Oh, take us in! Set Thou our
Liv - ing Bread, Bro - ken for all; Come to His house of wine,
all thy woes, Doubt - ing and strife; Mill - ions have been sup - plied,
win the race Must tar - ry here; What - e'er thy want may be,
for - eign strand—Wil - der - ness waste! Here are the harps of gold,
spir - its free; Cleanse us from sin! Then, in yon land of light,
Low on His breast re - cline, All that He hath is thine; Come, sin - ner, come.
No one was e'er de - nied; Come to the crim-son tide, Come, sin - ner, come.
Here is the grace for thee, Je - sus thy on - ly plea, Come, Christian, come.
Here are the joys un - told—Crowns for the young and old; Come, pil - grim, come.
Clothed in our robes of white Rest - ing not day nor night, Thee will we sing.
Copyright property of The John Church Co.
No. 102. One Sweetly Solemn Thought.
"Now they desire a better country that is, an heavenly."—HEB. 11: 16.
Miss PHOEBE CAREY.
PHILIP PHILLIPS.
1. One sweet-ly sol - emn thought Comes to me o'er and o'er; I'm near - er home to -
2. Near - er my Fa - ther's house, Where ma - ny mansions be; Near - er the great white
3. Near - er the bound of life, Where burdens are laid down; Near - er to leave the
4. Be near me when my feet Are slip - ping o'er the brink; For I am near - er
CHORUS.
day, to - day, Than I have been be - fore.
throne to - day, Near - er the crys - tal sea.
cross to - day, And near - er to the crown.
home to - day, Per - haps, than now I think.
Near-er my home, Near-er my home,
Copyright property of The Biglow & Main Co.

One Sweetly Solemn Thought.

Near - er my home to - day, to - day, Than I have been be - fore.

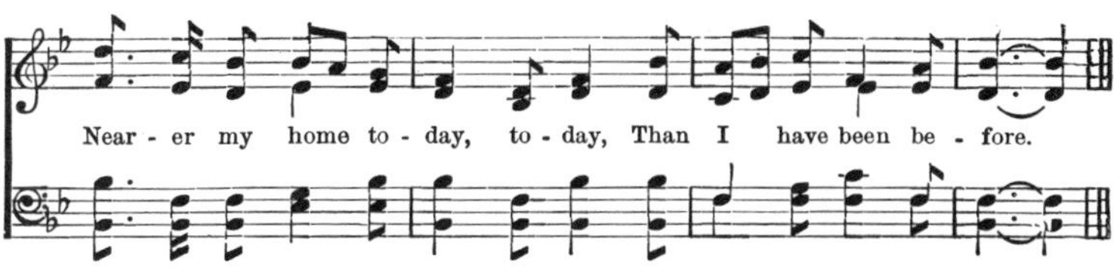

No. 103. Arise and Shine.

"Arise, shine, for thy light is come."—Isa. 60: 1.

Mary A. Lathbury. P. P. Bliss.

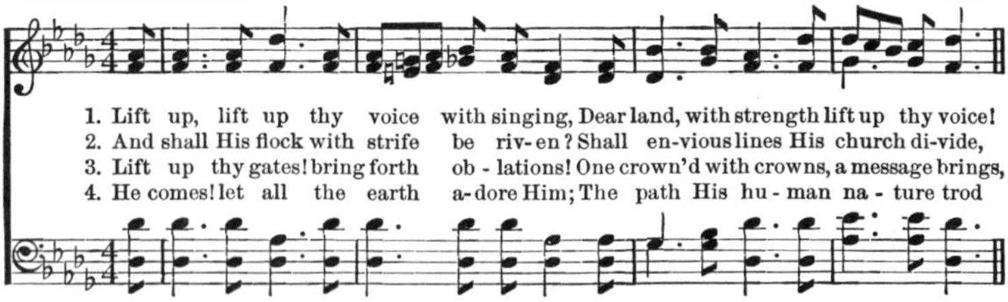

1. Lift up, lift up thy voice with singing, Dear land, with strength lift up thy voice!
2. And shall His flock with strife be riv-en? Shall en-vious lines His church di-vide,
3. Lift up thy gates! bring forth ob - lations! One crown'd with crowns, a message brings,
4. He comes! let all the earth a-dore Him; The path His hu - man na - ture trod

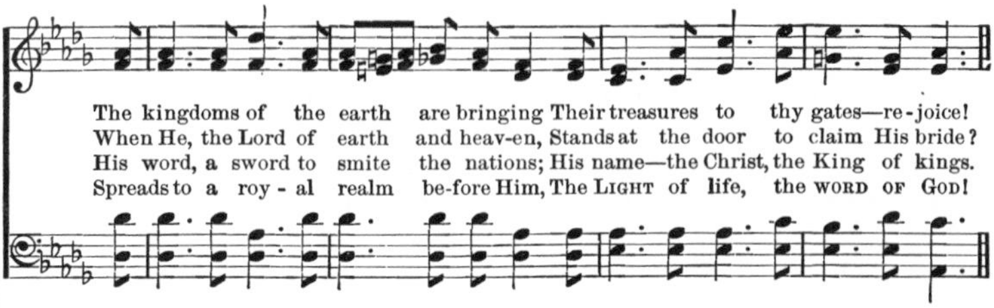

The kingdoms of the earth are bringing Their treasures to thy gates—re-joice!
When He, the Lord of earth and heav-en, Stands at the door to claim His bride?
His word, a sword to smite the nations; His name—the Christ, the King of kings.
Spreads to a roy - al realm be-fore Him, The Light of life, the Word of God!

Chorus.

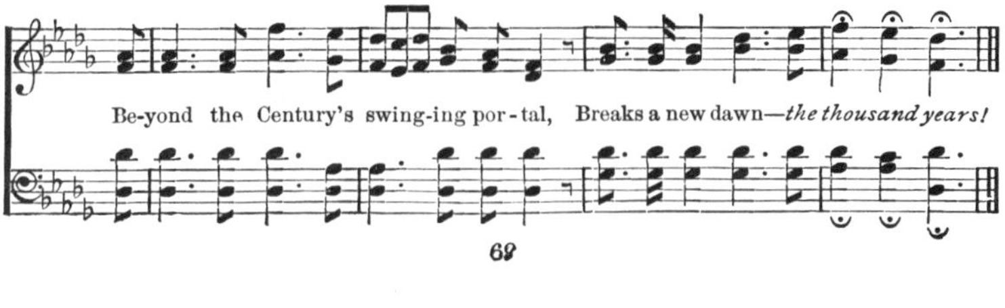

A - rise and shine in youth im-mor-tal, Thy light is come, thy King ap-pears!

Be-yond the Century's swing-ing por - tal, Breaks a new dawn—*the thousand years!*

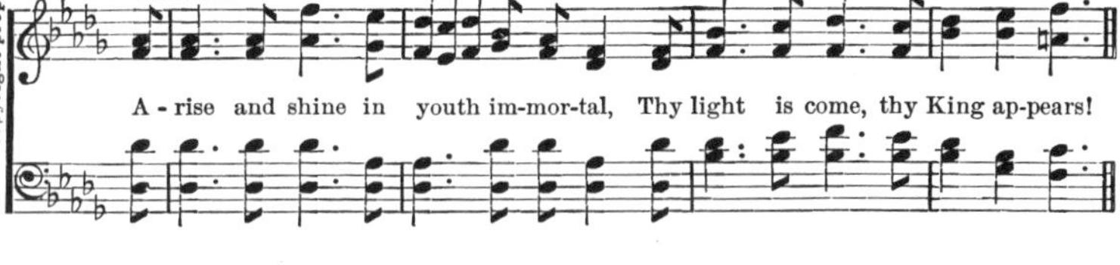

No. 104. The Valley of Blessing.

"The valley of Berachah."—2 Chr. 20: 26.

Mrs. Annie Wittenmyer. Wm. G. Fischer.

1 I have entered the val-ley of blessing so sweet, And Je-sus a-bides with me there;
2. There is peace in the val-ley of blessing so sweet, And plen-ty the land doth im-part,
3. These is love in the val-ley of blessing so sweet, Such as none but the blood-wash'd may feel,
4. There's a song in the val-ley of blessing so sweet, That an-gels would fain join the strain,
And His spirit and blood make my cleansing complete, And His perfect love cast-eth out fear.
And there's rest for the weary-worn trav-el-er's feet, And joy for the sor-row-ing heart.
When heaven comes down redeemed spir-its to greet, And Christ sets His cov-e-nant seal.
As with rap-tur-ous prais-es we bow at His feet, Crying, Worthy the Lamb that was slain.
Used by per.
Chorus.
blessing
Oh, come to this val-ley of blessing so sweet, Where Je-sus will fullness be-stow—
And be-lieve, and re-ceive, and con-fess Him, That all His sal-va-tion may know.

No. 105. I'm a Pilgrim.

Mrs. M. S. B. D. Shindler. Italian Air.

1. I'm a pil-grim, and I'm a stranger; I can tar-ry, I can tar-ry but a
2. Of that cit-y, to which I jour-ney; My Re-deemer, my Redeemer is the
3. There the sun-beams are ev-er shin-ing, Oh, my longing heart, my longing heart is

night! Do not de-tain me, for I am go-ing To where the streamlets are ev-er flowing.
light; There is no sor-row, nor an-y sigh-ing, Nor an-y tears there, nor an-y dy-ing:
there; Here in this country, so dark and drear-y, I long have wandered forlorn and wea-ry:

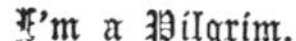
I'm a Pilgrim.

Chorus.
I'm a pil-grim, and I'm a stran-ger; I can tar-ry, I can tar-ry but a night!

No. 106. Oh, what are You Going to Do?

"How long halt ye between two opinions."—1 Kings 18: 21.

Fanny J. Crosby. Philip Phillips.

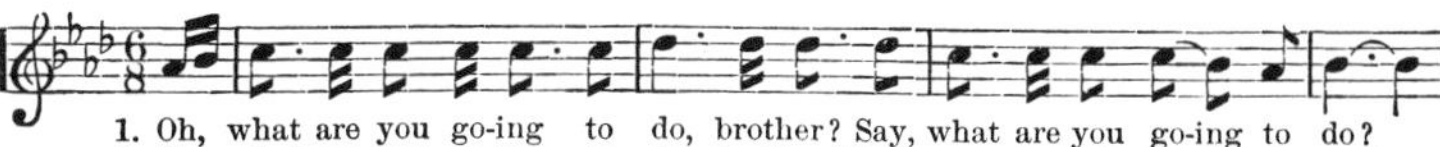

1. Oh, what are you go-ing to do, brother? Say, what are you go-ing to do?
2. Oh, what are you go-ing to do, brother? The morn-ing of youth is past;
3. Oh, what are you go-ing to do, brother? Your sun at its noon is high;
4. Oh, what are you go-ing to do, brother? The twi-light ap-proach-es now;—

You have thought of some use-ful la-bor, But what is the end in view?
The vig-or and strength of man-hood, My broth-er, are yours at last:
It shines in me-rid-ian splen-dor, And rides through a cloud-less sky:
Al-read-y your locks are sil-vered, And win-ter is on your brow:

You are fresh from the home of your boy-hood, And just in the bloom of youth!
You are ris-ing in world-ly pros-pects, And prospered in world-ly things;—
You are hold-ing a high po-si-tion, Of hon-or, and trust, and fame;—
Your tal-ents, your time and your rich-es, To Je-sus, your Mas-ter, give;

Have you tast-ed the spark-ling wa-ter That flows from the fount of truth?
A........ du-ty to those less fa-vored, The smile of your for-tune brings.
Are you will-ing to give the glo-ry And praise to your Sav-iour's Name?
Then ask if the world a-round you Is bet-ter be-cause you live.

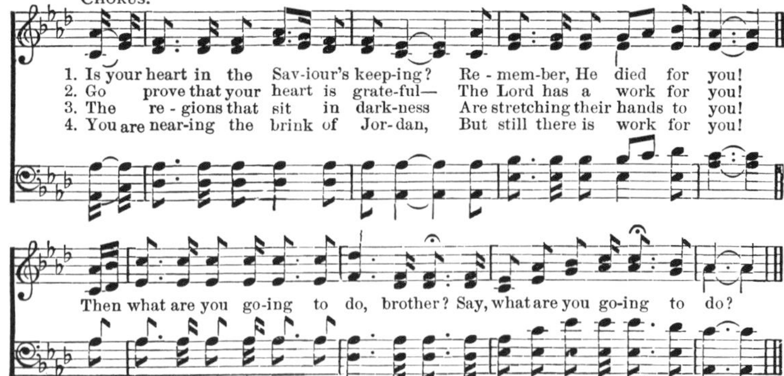
Chorus.
1. Is your heart in the Sav-iour's keep-ing? Re-mem-ber, He died for you!
2. Go prove that your heart is grate-ful— The Lord has a work for you!
3. The re-gions that sit in dark-ness Are stretching their hands to you!
4. You are near-ing the brink of Jor-dan, But still there is work for you!
Then what are you go-ing to do, brother? Say, what are you go-ing to do?

No. 107. Art Thou Weary?

"Come unto me, and I will give you rest."—Matt. 11 : 28.

Rev. J. M. Neale, trans. Rev. Henry W. Baker.

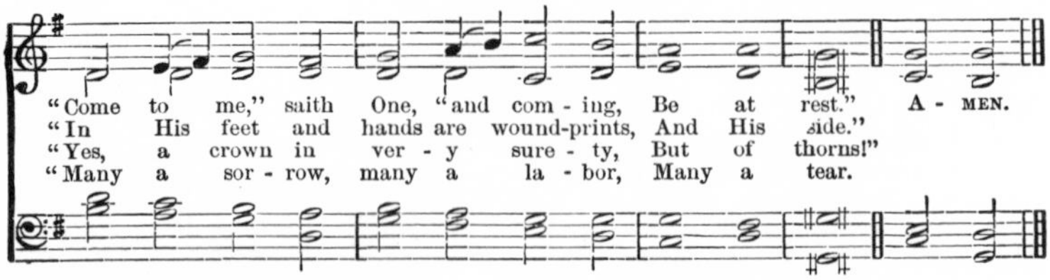

1. Art thou wea - ry, art thou lan - guid? Art thou sore dis - tress'd? "Come to me," saith One, "and com - ing, Be at rest."
2. Hath He marks to lead me to Him If He be my guide? "In His feet and hands are wound-prints, And His side."
3. Is there di - a - dem as mon - arch, That His brow a - dorns? "Yes, a crown in ver - y sure - ty, But of thorns!"
4. If I find Him, if I fol - low, What my fu - ture here? "Many a sor - row, many a la - bor, Many a tear.

A - men.

5 If I still hold closely to Him,
What hath He at last?
"Sorrow vanquished, labor ended,
Jordan past."

6 If I ask Him to receive me,
Will He say me nay?
"Not till earth and not till heaven
Pass away."

No. 108. Shall we Meet?

"The ransomed of the Lord shall return and come to Zion with songs and everlasting joy upon their heads."—Isa. 30 : 10.

Horace L. Hastings. Elihu S. Rice.

Moderato.
1. Shall we meet be - yond the riv - er, Where the sur - ges cease to roll?
2. Shall we meet in that blest har - bor, When our storm - y voyage is o'er?
3. Shall we meet in yon - der cit - y, Where the tow'rs of crys - tal shine?
4. Shall we meet with Christ our Sav - iour, When He comes to claim His own?
Where in all the bright for - ev - er, Sor - row ne'er shall press the soul?
Shall we meet and cast the an - chor By the fair, ce - les - tial shore?
Where the walls are all of jas - per, Built by work - man - ship di - vine?
Shall we know His bless - ed fa - vor, And sit down up - on His throne?
Chorus.
Shall we meet, shall we meet, Shall we meet be - yond the riv - er?
Used by per

No. 109. Jesus is Mighty To Save.

"Mighty to save."—Isa. 63: 1.

Mrs. Annie Wittenmyer. Wm. G. Fischer.

Moderato.

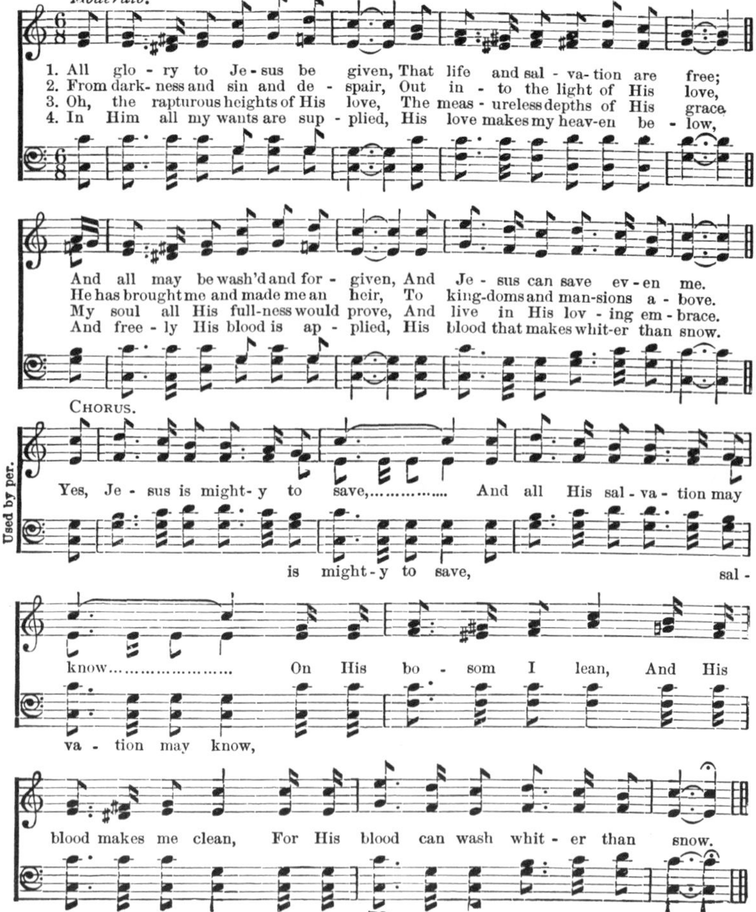

1. All glo-ry to Je-sus be given, That life and sal-va-tion are free;
And all may be wash'd and for-given, And Je-sus can save ev-en me.
2. From dark-ness and sin and de-spair, Out in-to the light of His love,
He has brought me and made me an heir, To king-doms and man-sions a-bove.
3. Oh, the rapturous heights of His love, The meas-ureless depths of His grace,
My soul all His full-ness would prove, And live in His lov-ing em-brace.
4. In Him all my wants are sup-plied, His love makes my heav-en be-low,
And free-ly His blood is ap-plied, His blood that makes whit-er than snow.

Chorus.

Yes, Je-sus is might-y to save,........ And all His sal-va-tion may know.....................
is might-y to save, sal-va-tion may know,
On His bo-som I lean, And His blood makes me clean, For His blood can wash whit-er than snow.

Used by per.

No. 110. Sweet By-and-By.

"The ransomed of the Lord shall return and come to Zion with songs and everlasting joy upon their heads."—ISA. 35: 10.

S. FILLMORE BENNETT.
JOS. P. WEBSTER.
1. There's a land that is fair - er than day, And by faith we can see it a -
2. We shall sing on that beau - ti - ful shore The mel - o - di - ous songs of the
3. To our boun - ti - ful Fa - ther a - bove, We will of - fer our trib - ute of
far; For the Fa - ther waits o - ver the way, To pre - pare us a
blest, And our spir - its shall sor - row no more, Not a sigh for the
praise, For the glo - ri - ous gift of His love, And the bless - ings that
dwell - ing place there.
bless - ing of rest.
hal - low our days.
CHORUS.
In the sweet by - and - by, We shall
In the sweet by and by,
meet on that beau - ti - ful shore, In the sweet by - and -
by-and-by, by-and-by, by-and
by, We shall meet on that beau - ti - ful shore.
by, by - and - by,
Used by arr. with Oliver Ditson Co., owners of Copyright.

No. 111. Expostulation.

"Turn ye, turn ye—for why will ye die?"—Ezek. 33: 11.

J. H. Rev. Josiah Hopkins.

1. Oh, turn ye, oh, turn ye, for why will ye die? When God in great
2. How vain the de - lu - sion, that while you de - lay, Your hearts may grow
3. The con - trite in heart He will free - ly re - ceive, Oh! why will you

mer - cy is com - ing so nigh? Now Je - sus in - vites you, the
bet - ter your chains melt a - way; Come guilt - y, come wretch - ed, come
not the glad mes - sage be - lieve? If sin be your bur - den, why

Spir - it says, "Come," And an - gels are wait - ing to wel - come you home.
just as you are All help - less and dy - ing, to Je - sus re - pair.
will you not come? 'Tis you He makes wel - come; He bids you come home.

No. 112. Cross and Crown.

"And he bearing his cross, went forth."—John 19: 17.

Thos. Shepherd. Geo. N. Allen.

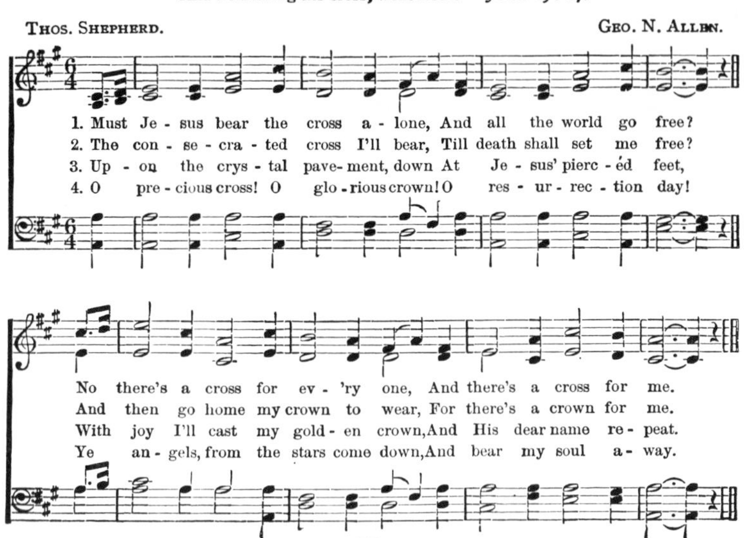
1. Must Je - sus bear the cross a - lone, And all the world go free?
2. The con - se - cra - ted cross I'll bear, Till death shall set me free?
3. Up - on the crys - tal pave- ment, down At Je - sus' pierc - ed feet,
4. O pre - cious cross! O glo - rious crown! O res - ur - rec - tion day!
No there's a cross for ev - 'ry one, And there's a cross for me.
And then go home my crown to wear, For there's a crown for me.
With joy I'll cast my gold - en crown, And His dear name re - peat.
Ye an - gels, from the stars come down, And bear my soul a - way.

No. 113. There's a Light in the Valley.

" Though I walk through the valley * * * I will fear no evil."—Psa. 23 : 4.

P. P. B.
P. P. Bliss.
With expression.
1. Thro' the val-ley of the shadow I must go, Where the cold waves of Jor - dan roll;
2. Now the roll-ing of the billows I can hear, As they beat on the turf-bound shore;
But the promise of my Shepherd will I know, Be the rod and the staff to my soul.
But the beacon light of love so bright and clear, Guides my bark, frail and lone safely o'er.
Slower.
E- ven now down the val - ley as I glide, I can hear my Saviour say, "Follow me!"
I shall find down the val - ley no a - larms, For my Saviour's blessed smile I can see;
a tempo.
And with Him I'm not afraid to cross the tide, There's a light in the val - ley for me.
He will bear me in His lov-ing, mighty arms, There's a light in the val - ley for me.
Chorus.
p
f
p
There's a light in the valley, There's a light in the valley, There's a light in the valley for me,......
for me,
Repeat pp.
And no evil will I fear, While my Shepherd is so near, There's a light in the valley for me, for me.
Copyright property of The John Church Co.

No. 114. The Palace of the King.
"With gladness—they shall enter into the King's palace"—Ps. 48: 15.
Arr by Fanny J. Crosby.
S. J. Vail.
1. 'Tis a good-ly pleasant land that we pilgrims journey thro', And our Father's constant
2. Our Redeem-er is the King; what a sac-ri-fice He made, When He purchased our re-
bless-ings fall a-round us like the dew; But its sunshine and its beau-ty to our
demption, and His blood the ran-som paid; In His cross shall be our glo-ry, to that
hearts no joy can bring, Like the splendors that a-wait us in the pal-ace of the King.
bless-ed cross we'll cling, Till we reach the gates that o-pen to the pal-ace of the King.
Refrain.
In this goodly pleasant land on-ly strangers now are we, For we seek a bet-te
We shall see Him bye and bye, hal-le-lu-jah to His name! Thro' the blood of His a
D.C.—O the pal-ace of the King, roy-al palace of the King; Where our Father in His
coun-try, and 'tis there we long to be; Yes, we long to swell the an-them that for-
tonement, life e-ter-nal we may claim; We shall cast our crowns be-fore Him and our
mer-cy all the ransomed ones will bring; Where our sorrows and our tri-als like a
rit. D.C. for Refrain.
ev-er-more shall ring, From the pure in heart made perfect in the pal-ace of the King.
songs of vic-t'ry sing, When we en-ter in triumph-ant to the pal-ace of the King.
dream will pass away, And our souls shall dwell forever in the realms of endless day.
Copyright, 1876, by Biglow & Main.

No. 115. Out of the Ark.

"Come thou and all thy house into the ark,"—GEN. 7: 1.

KATE HARRINGTON.
P. P. BLISS.
1. They dream'd not of danger, those sinners of old, Whom No-ah was cho-sen to warn;
2. He could not arouse them, unheeding they stood, Un-mov'd by his warning and prayer;
3. O sin-ners, the her-alds of mer-cy implore, They cry like the pa-triarch, "Come;"
rit.
By frequent transgressions their hearts had grown cold, They laugh'd his entreaties to scorn:
The prophet passed in from the on-com-ing flood, And left them to hope-less de-spair:
The Ark of sal-va-tion is moored to your shore, Oh, en-ter while yet there is room!
Yet dai-ly he called them, "Oh, come, sinners, come, Be-lieve and pre-pare to em-bark!
The flood-gates were opened, the del-uge came on, The heavens as midnight grew dark,
The storm-cloud of Justice rolls dark o-ver head, And when by its fu-ry you're tossed,
rit.
Re-ceive ye the message, and know there is room For all who will come to the Ark!"
Too late, then they turned, ev'ry foothold was gone, They perished in sight of the Ark.
A-las, of your per-ish-ing souls 'twill be said, "They heard—they refused—and were lost!
p CHORUS.
Then come, come, oh, come; There's ref-uge a-lone in the Ark, Re-
p
rit.
ceive ye the mes-sage, and know there is room For all who will come to the Ark.
Copyright property of The John Church Co.

No. 116. Waiting and Watching for Me.

"I shall go to him * * * he shall not return to me."—2 Sam. 12: 23.

Marianne Hearn. P. P. Bliss.

No. 117. What shall I do to be Saved?

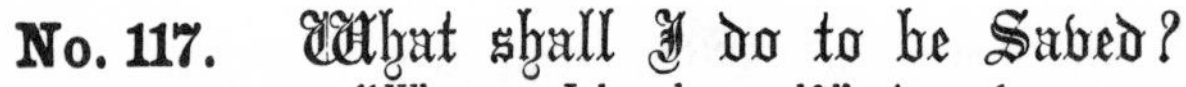

"What must I do to be saved?"—ACTS 16: 30.

J. W. HOLMAN. WM. B. BRADBURY.

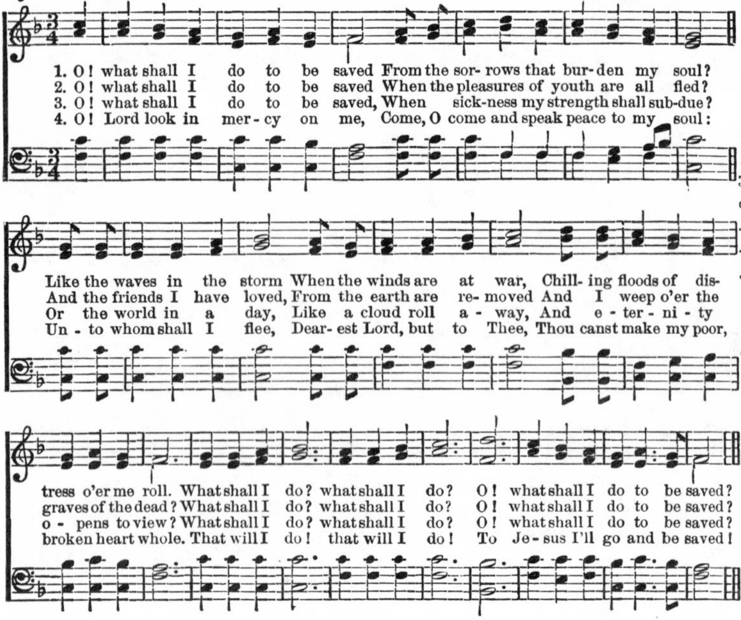

1. O! what shall I do to be saved From the sor- rows that bur- den my soul?
2. O! what shall I do to be saved When the pleasures of youth are all fled?
3. O! what shall I do to be saved, When sick-ness my strength shall sub-due?
4. O! Lord look in mer - cy on me, Come, O come and speak peace to my soul:
Like the waves in the storm When the winds are at war, Chill- ing floods of dis-
And the friends I have loved, From the earth are re- moved And I weep o'er the
Or the world in a day, Like a cloud roll a - way, And e - ter - ni - ty
Un - to whom shall I flee, Dear- est Lord, but to Thee, Thou canst make my poor,
tress o'er me roll. What shall I do? what shall I do? O! what shall I do to be saved?
graves of the dead? What shall I do? what shall I do? O! what shall I do to be saved?
o - pens to view? What shall I do? what shall I do? O! what shall I do to be saved?
broken heart whole. That will I do! that will I do! To Je - sus I'll go and be saved!

No. 118. Holy, Holy! Lord God Almighty!

"They rest not day nor night, saying, Holy, Holy, Holy, Lord God Almighty, which was, and is, and is to come."—REV. 4: 8.

REGINALD HEBER, D.D. REV. JOHN B. DYKES.

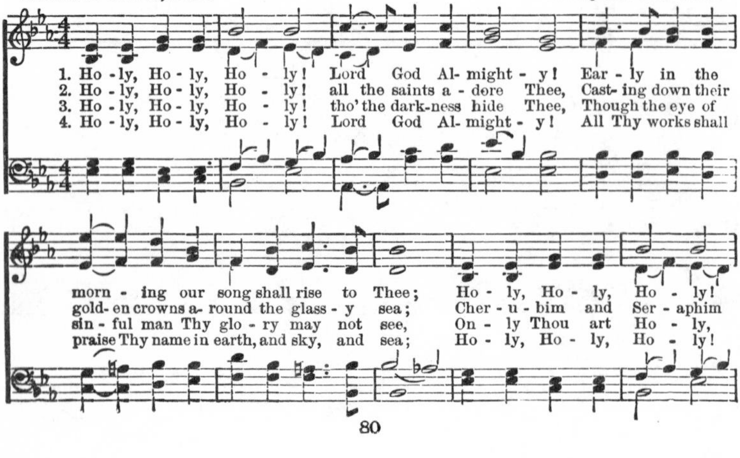

1. Ho - ly, Ho - ly, Ho - ly! Lord God Al- might - y! Ear - ly in the
2. Ho - ly, Ho - ly, Ho - ly! all the saints a - dore Thee, Cast- ing down their
3. Ho - ly, Ho - ly, Ho - ly! tho' the dark-ness hide Thee, Though the eye of
4. Ho - ly, Ho - ly, Ho - ly! Lord God Al- might - y! All Thy works shall
morn - ing our song shall rise to Thee; Ho - ly, Ho - ly, Ho - ly!
gold- en crowns a- round the glass - y sea; Cher - u - bim and Ser - aphim
sin - ful man Thy glo - ry may not see, On - ly Thou art Ho - ly,
praise Thy name in earth, and sky, and sea; Ho - ly, Ho - ly, Ho - ly!

Holy, Holy! Lord God Almighty!
Mer - ci - ful and Might-y! God in three Per - sons, bless-ed Trin -i - ty!
fall - ing down be-fore Thee, Which wert and art, and ev - ermore shall be.
there is none be-side Thee, Per - fect in pow'r, in love, and pur - i - ty.
Mer - ci - ful and Might-y! God in three Per - sons, bless-ed Trin - i - ty! A - MEN.

No. 119. He will Hide Me.

"In the shadow of his hand hath he hid me."—ISA. 49: 2.

Miss M. E. SERVOSS. JAMES McGRANAHAN.

1. When the storms of life are rag - ing, Tempests wild on sea and land.
2. Though He may send some af - flic - tion, 'Twill but make me long for home;
3. En - e - mies may strive to in - jure, Sa - tan all his arts em - ploy;
4. So, while here the cross I'm bear - ing, Meeting storms and bil-lows wild,

I will seek a place of ref - uge In the shad - ow of God's hand.
For in love and not in an - ger, All His chast - en - ings will come.
He will turn what seems to harm me In - to ev - er - last - ing joy.
Je - sus, for my soul is car - ing, Naught can harm His Fa - ther's child.

CHORUS.

He will hide me, He will hide me, Where no harm......... can e'er be-tide me;
He will hide me, He will hide me, Where no harm can e'er be-tide me;

He will hide me, safe-ly hide me, In the shad - ow of His hand.
He will hide me, safe - ly hide me In the shadow of His hand.

No. 120. 
Thine, Jesus, Thine.

"I am thine."—Ps. 119: 94.

ENGLISH. P. P. BLISS.

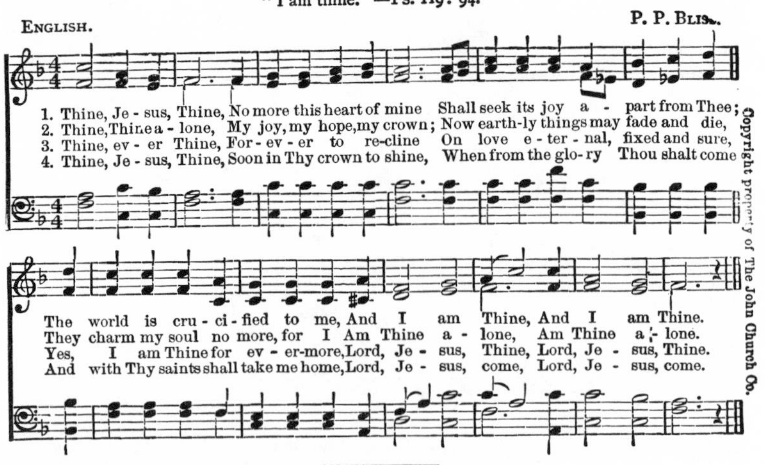
1. Thine, Je - sus, Thine, No more this heart of mine Shall seek its joy a - part from Thee;
2. Thine, Thine a - lone, My joy, my hope, my crown; Now earth-ly things may fade and die,
3. Thine, ev - er Thine, For - ev - er to re-cline On love e - ter - nal, fixed and sure,
4. Thine, Je - sus, Thine, Soon in Thy crown to shine, When from the glo - ry Thou shalt come
The world is cru - ci - fied to me, And I am Thine, And I am Thine.
They charm my soul no more, for I Am Thine a - lone, Am Thine a - lone.
Yes, I am Thine for ev - er-more, Lord, Je - sus, Thine, Lord, Je - sus, Thine.
And with Thy saints shall take me home, Lord, Je - sus, come, Lord, Je - sus, come.

No. 121. Out of Darkness into Light.

"I am the light of the world, he that followeth me shall not walk in darkness."—JOHN 8: 12.

W. O. LATTIMORE.* (TEMPERANCE HYMN.) IRA D. SANKEY.

1. Long in dark - ness we have wait - ed, For the shin - ing of the Light;
2. Now, at last, the Light ap - pear - eth, Je - sus stands up - on the shore;
3. Noth-ing have we, but our weak - ness, Naught but sor - row, sin and care;
4. All our tal - ents we have wast - ed, All Thy laws have dis - o - beyed;
5. Thou hast saved us— do Thou keep us, Guide us by Thine eye di - vine;
Long have felt the things we ha - ted, Sink us still in deep - er night.
And, with ten - der voice, He call - eth, "Come to me and sin no more!"
All with - in, is loath-some vile - ness, All with - out, is dark de - spair.
But Thy good - ness now we've tast - ed, In Thy robes we stand ar - rayed.
Let the Ho - ly Spir - it teach us, That our light may ev - er shine.
CHORUS.
Bless - ed Je - sus, lov - ing Sav - iour! Ten - der, faith - ful, strong and true,

* Written by one rescued from strong drink.

Out of Darkness into Light.

Final Chorus.—Blessēd Jesus, be Thou near us,
Give us of Thy grace to-day;
While we're calling, do Thou hear us,
Send us, now, Thy peace, we pray.

No. 122. Jesus Calls Thee.

"I the Lord have called thee."—Isa. 42 : 6.

Mrs. S. A. Collins. W. H. Doane.

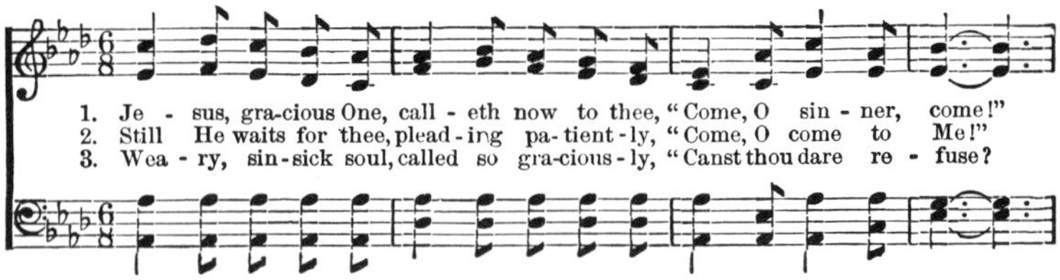

1. Je - sus, gra-cious One, call - eth now to thee, "Come, O sin - ner, come!"
2. Still He waits for thee, plead - ing pa - tient - ly, "Come, O come to Me!"
3. Wea - ry, sin-sick soul, called so gra-cious - ly, "Canst thou dare re - fuse?

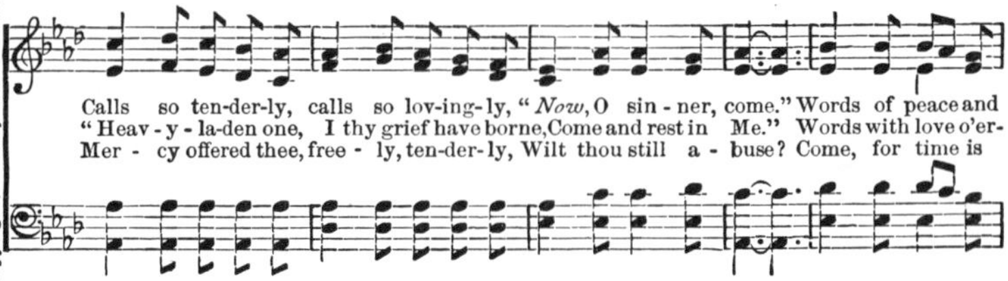

Calls so ten-der-ly, calls so lov-ing-ly, "*Now*, O sin - ner, come." Words of peace and
"Heav - y - la-den one, I thy grief have borne, Come and rest in Me." Words with love o'er-
Mer - cy offered thee, free - ly, ten-der-ly, Wilt thou still a - buse? Come, for time is

bless - ing, Christ's own love con - fess - ing;
flow - ing, Life and bliss be - stow - ing;
fly - ing, Haste, thy lamp is dy - ing;

Refrain.

Hear the sweet voice of Je - sus, Full, full of love; Call - ing tender - ly, call-ing lov-ing-ly, "Come, O sin-ner, come."

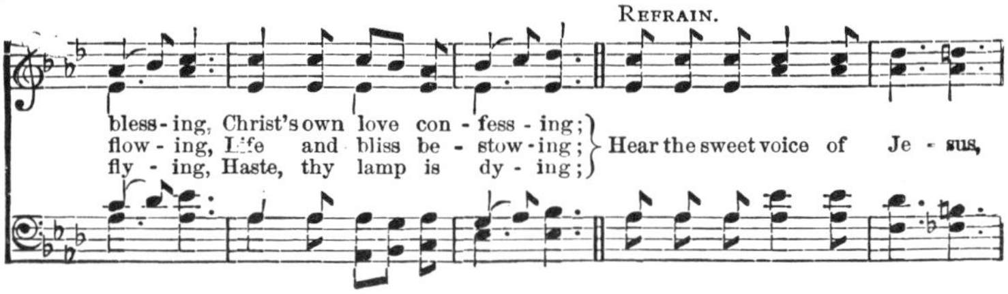

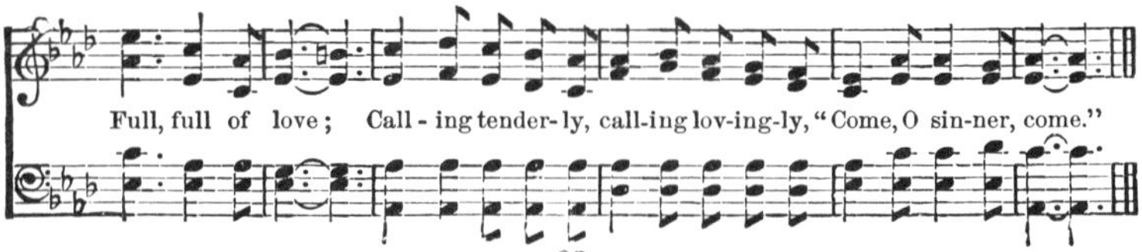

No. 123. A Light upon the Shore.

"No night there."—Rev. 21 : 25.

Rev. Henry Burton, M.A.
James McGranahan.
1. We've journey'd many a day Up - on an o - cean wide, A -
2. We've had our storms of doubt, Our rains of bit - ter tears, Our
3. O land of calm - est rest, Where suns no more go down! O
mid the mist and spray Of many a surg - ing tide; But,
fight-ings fierce with - out, With - in our anx - ious fears; But,
hav - en of the blest, With bliss and glo - ry crown'd! No
lo! the land is near! For just be - yond the foam I
lo! the storms are past, They can - not reach us more; We've
more the storm, the dark, The break - ers and the foam, No
see it bright and clear, The light of home, sweet home.
sight - ed land at last, The bless - ed storm - less shore.
more the wail, for hark! We hear the songs of home.
Refrain.
There's a light up - on the shore, broth - er, It flash - es from the
strand; The night is al - most o'er, broth - er, The ha - ven's just at hand.
Copyright, 1877, by James McGranahan.

No. 124. Consecration.

"Ye are not your own."—1 Cor. 6: 19.

Miss Frances R. Havergal.
P. P. Bliss.
1. Take my life and let it be Con - se - cra - ted, Lord, to Thee;
2. Take my feet and let them be Swift and beau - ti - ful for Thee;
3. Take my lips and let them be Fill'd with mes - sa - ges from Thee;
4. Take my mo-ments and my days, Let them flow in end - less praise;
5. Take my will and make it Thine, It shall be no lon - ger mine;
6. Take my love, my God, I pour At Thy feet its treas-ure store;
Copyright property of The John Church Co.
Take my hands and let them move At the im - pulse of Thy love.
Take my voice and let me sing Al - ways— on - ly— for my King.
Take my sil - ver and my gold, Not a mite would I with - hold.
Take my in - tel - lect and use Ev - 'ry pow'r as Thou shalt choose.
Take my heart, it is Thine own, It shall be Thy roy - al throne.
Take my - self, and I will be Ev - er, on - ly, all for Thee.
Chorus, after each stanza.
All to Thee, all to Thee, Con - se - cra - ted, Lord, to Thee.
No. 125. The Gospel Bells.
"For God so loved the world, that he gave his only begotten Son."—John 3: 16.
S. W. M.
S. Wesley Martin.
1. The Gos - pel bells are ring - ing, O - ver land, from sea to sea: Bless-ed news of
2. The Gos - pel bells in - vite us To a feast prepared for all; Do not slight the
3. The Gos - pel bells give warning, As they sound from day to day, Of the fate which
4. The Gos - pel bells are joy - ful, As they ech - o far and wide, Bringing notes of
Used by per.
free sal - va - tion Do they of - fer you and me. "For God so loved the world That His
in - vi - ta - tion, Nor re-ject the gra-cious call. "I am the bread of life; Eat of
doth a-wait them Who for-ev - er will de - lay. "Es - cape ye, for thy life; Tar - ry
per-fect par - don, Thro' a Sav-iour cru - ci - fied. "Good tid - ings of great joy To all

on - ly Son He gave, Who-so-e'er be-liev-eth in Him Ev - er - last - ing life shall have."
Me, thou hungry soul, Tho' your sins be red as crim-son, They shall be as white as wool."
not in all the plain, Nor behind thee look, oh, nev - er, Lest thou be consumed in pain."
peo-ple do I bring, Un - to you is born a Sav-iour, Which is Christ the Lord" and King.
Chorus.
Gos - pel bells, how they ring; Gos - pel
Gos-pel bells, how they ring; O - ver land from sea to sea;
bells free - ly bring
Gos - pel bells free - ly bring Bless-ed news to you and me.
No. 126. Joy to the World.
"The mighty God, the everlasting Father, the Prince of Peace."—Isa. 9: 6.
Rev. Isaac Watts, arr.
Geo. F. Root.
Joyfully.
Reverently.
1. Joy to the world! the Lord is come; The might - y God, the Ev - er - last - ing
2. Joy to the world! the Sav - iour reigns, The might - y God, the Ev - er - last - ing
3. He rules the world with truth and grace, The might - y God, the Ev - er - last - ing
Fa - ther, and the Prince of Peace. Let every heart pre - - - pare Him room,
Fa - ther, and the Prince of Peace. O praise Him, floods, rocks, hills and plains,
Fa - ther, and the Prince of Peace. And saves us by His righteous - ness,
The might - y God, the Ev - er - last-ing Fa - ther, and the Prince of Peace.
Copyright property of The John Church Co.

No. 127. Ye Must be Born Again.

"Verily, verily, I say unto thee, except a man be born again, he cannot see the kingdom of God."—JOHN 3: 3.

W. T. SLEEPER. GEO. C. STEBBINS.

1. A rul - er once came to Je - sus by night, To
2. Ye chil - dren of men, at - tend to the word So
3. O ye who would en - ter that glo - ri - ous rest, And
4. A dear one in heav - en thy heart yearns to see, At the
ask Him the way of sal - va - tion and light; The Mas - ter made an-swer in
sol - emn - ly ut - tered by Je - sus, the Lord, And let not this message to
sing with the ran-som'd the song of the blest; The life ev - er - last-ing if
beau - ti - ful gate may be watch-ing for thee; Then list to the note of this
a - gain..............
words true and plain, "Ye must be born a - gain, a - gain."
you be in vain, "Ye must be born a - gain, a - gain."
ye would ob - tain, "Ye must be born a - gain, a - gain."
sol - emn re - frain, "Ye must be born a - gain, a - gain."
CHORUS.
a - gain,.......... a - gain,.........
"Ye must be born a - gain, a - gain," Ye must be born a - gain, a - gain, I
a - gain............
ver - i - ly, ver - i - ly, say un - to thee, Ye must be born a - gain, a - gain.
Copyright, 1877, by F. H. Revell.

No. 128. Cut it Down.

"Cut it down, why cumbereth it the ground."—LUKE 13: 7.

P. P. BLISS.
P. P. BLISS.
Slow.
1. Justice. Cut it down, cut it down, Spare not the fruit - less tree!
2. Mercy. One year more, one year more, Oh, spare the fruit - less tree!
3. Justice. Cut it down, cut it down, And burn the worth - less tree!
4. Mercy. One year more, one year more, For mer - cy spare the tree!
5. Still it stands, still it stands, A fair, but fruit - less tree!
It spreads a harm - ful shade a - round, It spoils what else were use - ful ground,
Be - hold its branch-es broad and green, Its spread-ing leaves have hope - ful been,
For oth - er use the soil pre - pare, Some oth - er tree will flour - ish there,
An - oth - er year of care be - stow, On its fair form some fruit may grow,
The Mas - ter, seek - ing fruit there-on Has come—but, griev'd at find - ing none,
No fruit for years on it I've found, Cut it down, cut it down.
Some fruit there - on may yet be seen, One year more, one year more.
And in my vine - yard much fruit bear, Cut it down, cut it down.
If not—then lay the cum - b'rer low, One year more, one year more.
Now speaks to Jus - tice—Mer - cy flown—Cut it down, cut it down.
Copyright property of The John Church Co.
No. 129. Come near Me.
"The Lord is nigh unto them that are of a broken heart; and saveth such as be of a contrite spirit."—Ps. 34: 18.
Rev. G. G. LLOYD.
J. W. BISCHOFF.
Tenderly.
1. Come near me, O my Sav - iour; Thy ten - der - ness re - veal;
2. Come near me, my Re - deem - er, And nev - er leave my side;
3. Come near me, bless - ed Je - sus, I need Thee in my joy,
4. Be near me, might - y Sav - iour, When comes the lat - est strife;
O, let me know the sym - pa - thy Which Thou for me dost feel,
My bark, when toss'd on troub - le's sea, The storm can - not out - ride,
No less than when the dir - est ills My hap - pi - ness de - stroy;
For Thou hast thro' death's shad - ows pass'd, And ope'd the gates of life;
Used by per.

Come near Me.
I need Thee ev - 'ry mo - ment; Thine ab - sence brings dis - may;
Un - less Thy word of pow - er Ar - rest the surg - ing wave;
For when the sun shines o'er me And flow - ers strew my way,
And when a - mong the ran - som'd I stand with crown and palm,
But when the tempt - er hurls his darts, 'Twere death with Thee a - way.
No voice but Thine its rage can quell, No arm but Thine can save.
With - out Thy wise and guid - ing hand More eas - i - ly I stray.
To Thee, Di - vine, un - fail - ing Friend, I'll raise e - ter - nal psalm.
No. 130. Why do You Wait?
"Arise, he calleth thee."—Mark 10: 49.
G. F. R.
Geo. F. Root.
1. Why do you wait, dear broth-er, Oh, why do you tar - ry so long? Your
2. What do you hope, dear broth-er, To gain by a fur-ther de - lay? There's
3. Do you not feel, dear broth-er, His Spir - it now striv-ing with - in? Oh,
4. Why do you wait, dear broth-er, The har-vest is pass-ing a - way, Your
Sav-iour is wait-ing to give you A place in His sanc - ti - fied throng.
no one to save you but Je - sus, There's no oth - er way but His way.
why not ac - cept His sal - va - tion, And throw off thy bur - den of sin.
Sav-iour is long-ing to bless you, There's dan-ger and death in de - lay.
Chorus.
Why not? why not? Why not come to Him now? Why not? why not? Why not come to Him now?
Copyright property of The John Church Co.

No. 131. Is Jesus able to Redeem?

"Come unto me all ye that labor."—MATT. 11: 28.

MRS. A. R. COUSIN. IRA D. SANKEY.

1. Is Je-sus a-ble to re-deem A sin-ner lost, like me? My sins so great, so ma-ny seem! O sin-ner, "come and see."
2. Is Je-sus will-ing to for-give A reb-el child, like me? Who would not in His fa-vor live? O reb-el, "come and see."
3. Is Je-sus wait-ing to re-lieve A wan-der-er, like me, Who chose the Father's House to leave? O wanderer, "come and see."
4. Is Je-sus read-y now to save A guilt-y one, like me, Who brought him to the cross and grave? Come, guilty one, and see.
REFRAIN.
The blood that Je-sus shed of old, Was shed for you and me: And there is room with-in the fold—O "come to Him and see."

No. 132. Verily, Verily.

"He that believeth on me hath everlasting life."—JOHN 6: 47.

JAMES MCGRANAHAN. JAMES MCGRANAHAN.

1. O what a Sav-iour that He died for me! From con-dem-na-tion He hath made me free; "He that be-liev-eth on the Son" saith He, "*Hath* ev-er-last-ing life."
2. All my in-iq-ui-ties on Him were laid, All my in-debt-ed-ness by Him was paid; All who believe on Him, the Lord hath said, "*Have* ev-er-last-ing life."
3. Tho' poor and need-y I can trust my Lord, Tho' weak and sin-ful I be-lieve His word; O glad message! ev-'ry child of God, "*Hath* ev-er-last-ing life."
4. Tho' all un-worth-y, yet I will not doubt, For him that com-eth, He will not cast out, "He that be-lieveth," O the good news shout, "HATH ev-er-last-ing life."

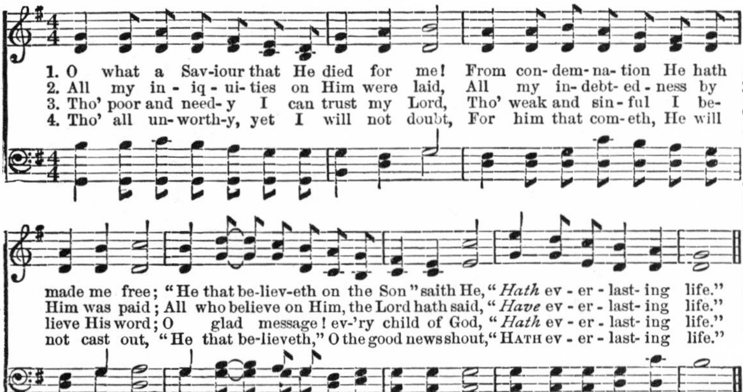

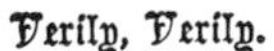

CHORUS.

"Ver - i - ly, ver - i - ly, I say un - to you, Ver - i - ly, ver - i - ly"

message ev- er new; "He that be - lieveth on the Son" 'tis true," *Hath* ev- er- last- ing life."

No. 133. The Lamb is the Light thereof.

"And the Lamb is the light thereof."—REV. 21 : 23.

Mrs. E. W. GRISWOLD. GEO. C. STEBBINS.

1. If nev - er the gaze of sun and moon, On the bless-ed home a - bove, From whence, are its rays of won-drous noon? Oh! "The LAMB is the light there- of."
2. And thus saith the page of Ho - ly Writ Of the land of song and love, "The glo - ry of God did light - en it, And the LAMB is the light there- of."
3. Then fol - low Him, till the eye grows dim, And the soul, as ark-freed dove, Shall speed a - way to realms of day, Where "The LAMB is the light there- of."

CHORUS.

They shall walk in white, there shall be no night In the fade- less home a - bove; And the shout shall ring as the ran-somed sing, Oh! "The LAMB is the light there - of.

No. 134. How Happy are We.

"He that keepeth the law, happy is he."—Prov. 29 : 18.

P. P. B. — P. P. Bliss.

1. Oh, how hap-py are we, Who in Je - sus a-gree, And expect His re- turn from a-bove ;
2. When u- nit- ed to Him, We partake of the stream, Ev - er flowing in peace from the throne,
3. We remember the word Of our cru- ci-fied Lord, When He went to prepare us a place,
4. Come, Lord, from the skies And command us to rise To the mansions of glo- ry a- bove ;
We sit 'neath His vine, and delight-ful- ly join In the praise of His ex - cellent love.
We in Je - sus be- lieve, and the Spir-it re-ceive, That proceeds from the Father and Son.
"I will come in that day and will take you a- way, And ad- mit to a sight of my face."
With Thee to as- cend and e - ter - ni-ty spend, In a rap-ture of heav- en - ly love.
Chorus.
Oh, how hap-py are we Who in Je - sus a- gree, How hap- py, how hap- py are we.
Copyright property of The John Church Co.
No. 135. Blessed Hope.
"That ye sorrow not even as others which have no hope."—1 Thess. 4 : 13.
W. W. D.
James McGranahan.
1. Bless-ed hope that in Je - sus is giv - en, In our sor- row to cheer and sus - tain,
2. Bless-ed hope in the word God has spo - ken, All our peace by that word we ob - tain,
3. Bless-ed hope ! how it shines in our sor - row, Like the star o - ver Beth-lehem's plain,
4. Bless-ed hope ! the bright star of the morning, That shall herald His com- ing to reign ;
That soon in the mansions of Heav - en, We shall meet with our lov'd ones a- gain.
And as sure as God's word was ne'er bro-ken, We shall meet with our lov'd ones a- gain.
That it may be, with Him, ere the mor- row, We shall meet with our lov'd ones a- gain.
Oh, the glo- ry that waits its fair dawn-ing, When we meet with our lov'd ones a- gain.
Copyright, 1877, by James McGranahan.

Blessed Hope.
Chorus.
Bless-ed hope,......... blessed hope,......... We shall meet with our lov'd ones a - gain,
Blessed hope, blessed hope,
Bless-ed hope,......... blessed hope,......... We shall meet with our lov'd ones a - gain.
Blessed hope, blessed hope,
No. 136. Tempted and Tried.
" Knowing this that the trial of your faith worketh patience."—Jas. 1 : 3.
Frances R. Havergal.
James McGranahan.
Copyright, 1878, by James McGranahan.
1. Tempted and tried! Oh ! the ter - ri - ble tide May be rag - ing and deep, may be wrath-ful and wide! Yet its fu - ry is vain, For the Lord shall re-strain, And for-ev - er and ev - er Je - ho-vah shall reign.
2. Tempted and tried There is One at thy side, And nev - er in vain shall His chil - dren con - fide! He shall save and de - fend, For He loves to the end, A - dor - a - ble Mas - ter and glo - ri-ous Friend!
3. Tempted and tried What - e'er may be - tide, In His se - cret pa - vil - ion His chil - dren shall hide, 'Neath the shadow - ing wing, Of E - ter - ni - ty's King, His children shall trust, and His servants shall sing.
4. Tempted and tried! Yet the Lord will a - bide, Thy faith - ful Re - deem - er, thy Keep - er, and Guide, Thy Shield and thy Sword, Thine exceed - ing Re - ward, Then e - nough for the ser - vant to be as his Lord.
Chorus.
Tempted and tried, Yet the Lord at thy side, Shall guide thee, and keep thee, Tho' tempted and tried.
5 Tempted and tried,
The Saviour who died,
Hath called thee to suffer and reign by His side;
His cross thou shalt bear,
And His crown thou shalt wear,
And forever and ever His glory shalt share.

No. 137. I Cannot Tell how Precious.

"Unto you therefore which believe he is precious."—1 PETER 2:7.

CHAS. H. GABRIEL. JAMES McGRANAHAN.

1. I can-not tell how pre-cious The Sav-iour is to me, Since I have Him ac-cept-ed, And He hath made me free; I can-not tell His goodness, E-nough to sat-is-fy; And if you'll on-ly take Him, You'll see the rea-son why.

2. I can-not do for Je-sus As much as I should like; But I will e'er en-deav-or To work with all my might; For, was not my dear Sav-iour For sin-ners cru-ci-fied? For me, then, surely, Je-sus Hung on the cross and died.

3. Whene'er I think of Je-sus, I can-not but re-joice; To me He's ev-er pre-cious, For Him I raise my voice; I know He has in glo-ry A home pre-par'd for me, Where I shall live for-ev-er So hap-py, and so free.

CHORUS.

I cannot tell how pre-cious The Sav-iour is to me; I on-ly can en-treat you To come, and taste and see.

No. 138. Beautiful Valley of Eden.

REV. W. O. CUSHING. "A rest to the people of God."—HEB. 4:9. WM. F. SHERWIN.

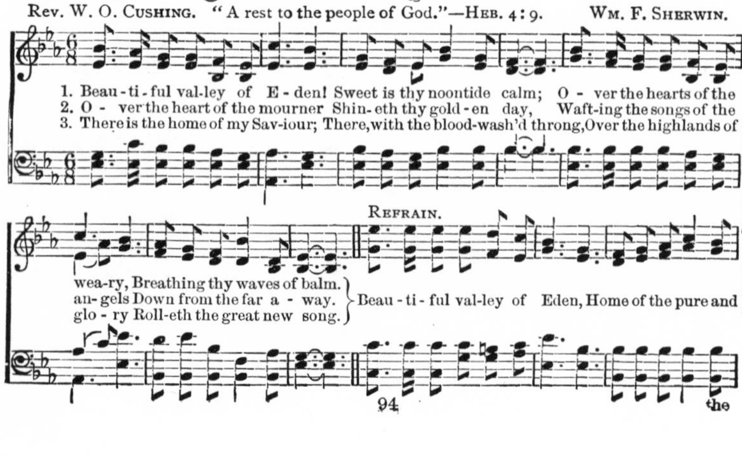

1. Beau-ti-ful val-ley of E-den! Sweet is thy noontide calm; O-ver the hearts of the wea-ry, Breathing thy waves of balm.

2. O-ver the heart of the mourner Shin-eth thy gold-en day, Waft-ing the songs of the an-gels Down from the far a-way.

3. There is the home of my Sav-iour; There, with the blood-wash'd throng, Over the highlands of glo-ry Roll-eth the great new song.

REFRAIN.

Beau-ti-ful val-ley of Eden, Home of the pure and the

Beautiful Valley of Eden.

Rit.
blest,...... How oft - en a - mid the wild bil - lows I dream of thy rest–sweet rest!
pure and blest,

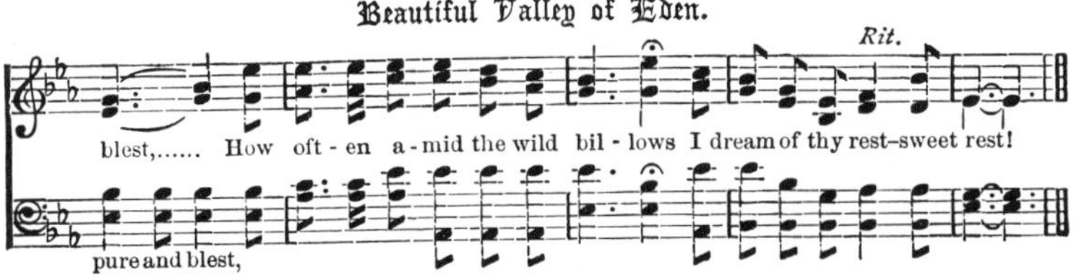

No. 139. I'll Stand by You.

This song was suggested by a thrilling incident of a wreck and rescue at sea.

W. W. D. JAMES McGRANAHAN.

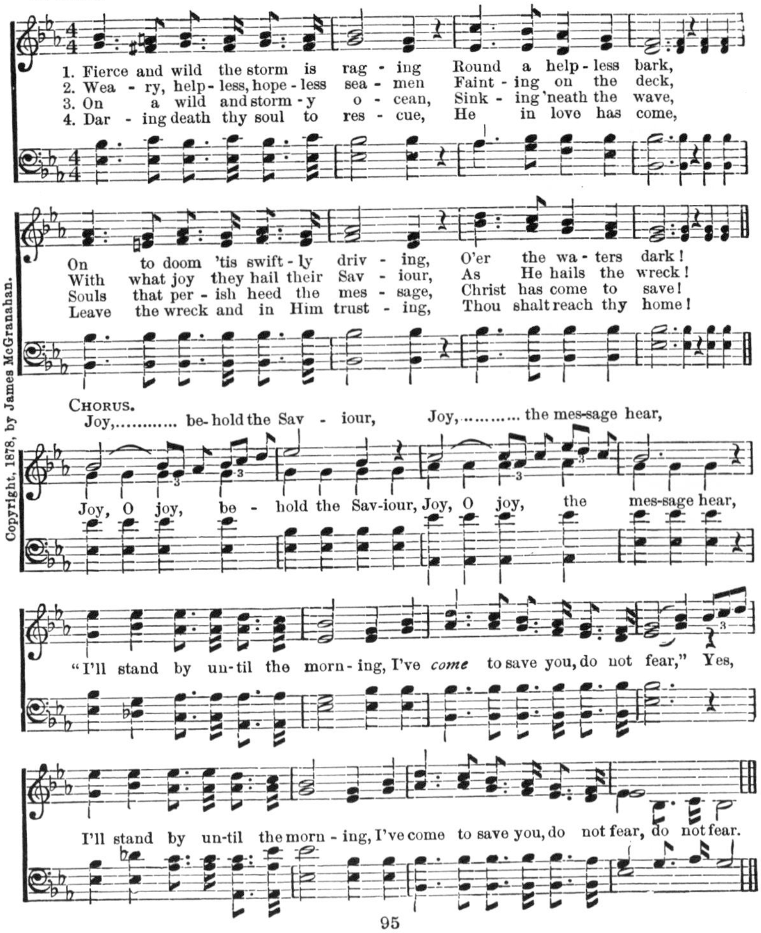

1. Fierce and wild the storm is rag - ing Round a help - less bark,
2. Wea - ry, help - less, hope - less sea - men Faint - ing on the deck,
3. On a wild and storm - y o - cean, Sink - ing 'neath the wave,
4. Dar - ing death thy soul to res - cue, He in love has come,
On to doom 'tis swift - ly driv - ing, O'er the wa - ters dark!
With what joy they hail their Sav - iour, As He hails the wreck!
Souls that per - ish heed the mes - sage, Christ has come to save!
Leave the wreck and in Him trust - ing, Thou shalt reach thy home!
CHORUS.
Joy,........... be - hold the Sav - iour, Joy,........... the mes-sage hear,
Joy, O joy, be - hold the Sav-iour, Joy, O joy, the mes-sage hear,
"I'll stand by un-til the morn - ing, I've *come* to save you, do not fear," Yes,
I'll stand by un-til the morn - ing, I've come to save you, do not fear, do not fear.

No. 140. Saved by the Blood.

"The blood of Christ cleanseth us from all sin."—1 JOHN 1 : 7.

FANNY J. CROSBY. W. H. DOANE.

1. We're saved by the blood That was drawn from the side Of Je - sus our
2. O yes, 'tis the blood Of the Lamb that was slain; He con-quered the
3. We're saved by the blood, We are sealed by its power; 'Tis life to the
4. That blood is a fount Where the vil - est may go, And wash till their
5. We're saved by the blood, Hal - le - lu - jah a - gain; We're saved by the
REFRAIN.
Lord, When He lan-guished and died.
grave, And He liv - eth a - gain.
soul, And its hope ev - 'ry hour.
souls Shall be whit - er than snow.
blood, Hal - le - lu - jah, A - men.
Hal - le - lu - jah to God, For re - demp-tion so free; Hal - le - lu - jah, Hal - le - lu - jah, Dear Sav- iour, to Thee.
Copyright, 1875, by Biglow & Main.
1. What tho' clouds are hov-'ring o'er me, And I seem to walk a - lone—
2. What tho' all my earth - ly jour - ney Bringeth naught but wea - ry hours,
3. What tho' all my heart is yearn-ing For the lov'd of long a - go—
4. When I soar to realms of glo - ry, And an en - trance I a - wait,
Long-ing 'mid my cares and cross-es, For the joys that now are flown—
And, in grasp - ing for life's ros - es, Thorns I find in-stead of flow'rs—
Bit - ter les - sons sad - ly learn-ing, From the shad - owy page of woe—
If I whis - per, "Je - sus on - ly!" Wide will ope the pearl - y gate;
Copyright, 1876, by Robert Lowry.

No. 141. Jesus Only.

"They saw no man, save Jesus only."—MATT. 17 : 8.

HATTIE M. CONREY. REV. R. LOWRY.

Jesus Only.
If I've Je - sus, "Je - sus on - ly," Then my sky will have a gem;
If I've Je - sus, "Je - sus on - ly," I pos - sess a clus - ter rare;
If I've Je - sus, "Je - sus on - ly," He'll be with me to the end;
When I join the heavenly cho - rus, And the an - gel hosts I see,
He's a Sun of bright-est splen-dor, And the Star of Beth - le - hem.
He's the "Lil - y of the Val - ley," And the "Rose of Sha - ron" fair.
And, un - seen by mor - tal vis - ion, An - gel bands will o'er me bend.
Pre - cious Je - sus, "Je - sus on - ly," Will my theme of rap - ture be.
No. 142.
Christ for Me.
"The Lord is my helper."—Heb. 13: 6.
R. G. H.
R. Geo. Halls.
Moderato—bold.
1. Whom have I, Lord, in heav'n but Thee? None but Thee! None but Thee! And this my song thro' life shall be, Christ for me! Christ for me! He hath for me the wine-press trod, He hath re - deemed me "by His blood," And rec-onciled my soul to God, Christ for me! Christ for me!
2. I en - vy not the rich their joys, Christ for me! Christ for me! I cov - et not earth's glitt'ring toys, Christ for me! Christ for me! Earth can no last - ing bliss be - stow, "Fading" is stamped on all be - low; Mine is a joy no end can know, Christ for me! Christ for me!
3. Tho' with the poor be cast my lot, Christ for me! Christ for me! "He knoweth best,"–I mur - mur not, Christ for me! Christ for me! Tho' "Vine and Fig-tree" blight assail, The "la - bor of the Olive fail," And death o'er flocks and herds prevail, Christ for me! Christ for me!
mf

4 Tho' I am now on hostile ground,
Christ for me! Christ for me!
And sin beset me all around,
Christ for me! Christ for me!
Let earth her fiercest battles wage,
And foes against my soul engage,
Strong in His strength I scorn their rage,
Christ for me! Christ for me!

5 And when my life draws to its close,
Christ for me! Christ for me!
Safe in His arms I shall repose,
Christ for me! Christ for me!
When sharpest pains my frame pervade,
And all the powers of nature fade,
Still will I sing thro' death's cold shade.
Christ for me! Christ for me!

No. 143. To be There.

"Having a desire to depart, and to be with Christ."—Phil. 1: 23.

Rev. W O. Cushing.
Ira D. Sankey.
1. I have heard of a land far a - way, And its glo- ries no tongue can de - clare;
2. There are fore-tastes of heav- en be - low, There are mo-ments like joys of the blest;
3. In that noon-tide of glo - ry so fair, In the gleam of the riv - er of life,
4. There the ransomed with Je - sus a - bide In the shade of the shel-ter - ing fold;
But its beau - ty hangs o - ver the way, And with Je - sus I long to be there.
But the splen-dors no mor - tal can know, Of the land where the wea - ry shall rest.
There are joys that the faithful shall share; O how sweet-ly they rest from the strife!
Ev - er-more by Im - man - u - el's side, They shall dwell in the glo - ry un - told.
Copyright, 1877, by Biglow & Main.
Refrain.
To be there, to be there, And with Je - sus I long to be
To be there, to be there,
there; To be there, to be there,........ And with Je-sus I long to be there.
to be there; To be there, to be there,
No. 144. Blessed Home-Land.
"There remaineth therefore a rest."—Heb. 4: 9.
Fanny J. Crosby.
Hubert P. Main.
1. Glid- ing o'er life's fit - ful wa - ters, Heav - y surg - es sometimes roll; And we
2. Oft we catch a faint re - flec - tion Of its bright and ver - nal hills; And, tho'
3 To our Fa - ther, and our Sav - iour, To the Spir - it, Three in One, We shall
4. 'Tis the wea - ry pilgrim's Home-land, Where each throbbing care shall cease, And our

Blessed Home-Land.

Refrain.
cres.
sigh for yonder ha- ven, For the Home-land of the soul.
distant, how we hail it! How each heart with rapture thrills!
sing glad songs of triumph When our harvest work is done.
longings and our yearnings, Like a wave, he hushed to peace.
Bless- ed Home-land, ev-er fair!
dim.
cres.
dim.
Sin can nev- er en- ter there; But the soul, to life a- waking, Ev- erlasting bloom shall wear.
Copyright, 1877, by Biglow & Main.

No. 145. Fix your Eyes upon Jesus.

"Look unto me and be ye saved."—Isa. 45 : 22.

W. W. D. JAMES McGRANAHAN.

1. Would you lose your load of sin? Fix your eyes upon Jesus; Would you know God's peace within?
2. Would you calmly walk the wave? Fix your eyes upon Jesus; Would you know His pow'r to save?
3. Would you have your cares grow light? Fix your eyes upon Jesus; Would you songs have in the night?
4. Grieving, would you comfort know? Fix your eyes upon Jesus; Humble be when blessings flow?
5. Would you strength in weakness have? Fix your eyes upon Jesus; See a light beyond the grave?
Chorus.
Fix your eyes up- on Je- sus; Je- sus who on the cross did die, Je- sus who *lives* and *reigns* on high, He a- lone can jus- ti- fy; Fix your eyes up- on Je- sus.
Copyright, 1877, by James McGranahan.

No. 146. The Heavenly Canaan.

"Thine eyes shall behold the land that is very far off."—ISA. 33: 17.

REV. ISAAC WATTS. WILLIAM HENRY OAKLEY.

1. There is a land of pure de- light, Where saints immor-tal reign; E - ter- nal day ex-
2. Sweet fields, beyond the swelling flood, Stand dress'd in liv- ing green; So to the Jews fair
3. O could we make our doubts remove,—Those gloomy doubts that rise,—And see the Ca- naan

cludes the night, And pleas-ures ban- ish pain. There ev - er- last - ing spring a- bides, And
Ca - naan stood, While Jor- dan rolled be-tween. But tim'rous mor- tals start and shrink To
that we love, With un - be- cloud- ed eyes,—Could we but climb where Moses stood, And

nev- er - fad-ing flow'rs; Death, like a nar- row sea, di-vides That heavenly land from ours.
cross this narrow sea, And lin-ger, trembling on the brink, And fear to launch a-way.
view the landscape o'er,–Not Jordan's stream, nor death's cold flood, Should fright us from the shore.

No. 147. Oh, I am so Happy in Jesus.

"Happy are thy men, happy are these thy servants."—I KINGS 10: 8.

ARTHUR T. PIERSON. JAMES MCGRANAHAN.

1. Oh, I am so hap - py in Je - sus, His blood has redeem'd me from sin,
2. Oh, I am so hap - py in Je - sus, He taught me the *se- cret of faith,*
3. Oh, I am so hap - py in Je - sus, I lay my whole soul at His feet;
4. Oh, I am so hap - py in Je - sus, If earth in His love is so blest,
I weep and I sing in my glad - ness, To know He is dwell-ing with - in.
To rest in be - liev- ing His prom - ise, And *trust whatso - ev - er He saith.*
The love He has kin- dled with- in me Makes service and suf- fer - ing sweet.
What joy in His glo - ri- fied pres - ence, To sit at His feet as His guest.

Oh, I am so Happy in Jesus.

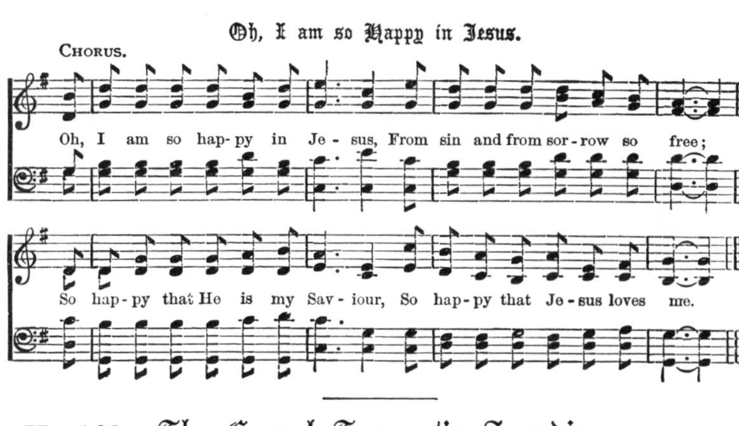
CHORUS.
Oh, I am so hap-py in Je - sus, From sin and from sor-row so free;
So hap-py that He is my Sav - iour, So hap-py that Je - sus loves me.

No. 148. The Gospel Trumpet's Sounding.

LEV. 25: 8–13.

ENGLISH. R. S. THAIN.

1. The gos - pel trum-pet's sound - ing The year of ju - bi - lee, And grace is all a-bound-ing, To set the bond-men free.
2. For-sake your wretch-ed ser - vice, Your mas-ter's claims are o'er; A-vail yourselves of free - dom, Be Sa-tan's slaves no more.
3. A bet - ter Mas - ter's call - ing, In ac - cents true and kind; He asks a lov - ing ser - vice, And claims a will-ing mind.
4. He of - fers you sal - va - tion, And points to joys a - bove; And, long-ing, waits to make you The ob-jects of His love.
5. In liv - ing faith ac - cept Him, Give up all else be - side; While grace is loud-ly call - ing, Look to the cru - ci - fied.

CHORUS.

Re-turn, re-turn, ye cap-tives, Re-turn un - to your home, The gos - pel trumpet's sound - ing, The ju - bi - lee is come! The gos-pel trumpet's sound-ing, The ju - bi - lee is come!

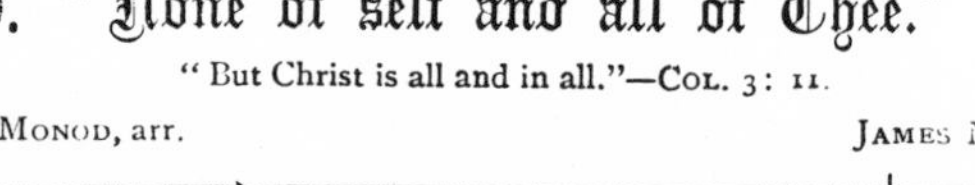

No. 149. "None of self and all of Thee."

"But Christ is all and in all."—Col. 3: 11.

Rev. Theo. Monod, arr. JAMES McGRANAHAN.

1. Oh, the bit - ter pain and sor - row That a time could ev - er
2. Yet He found me; I be - held Him Bleed - ing on th'ac - curs - ed
3. Day by day His ten - der mer - cy Heal - ing, help - ing, full and
4. High - er than the high - est heav - ens, Deep - er than the deep - est

be, When I proud - ly said to Je - sus "All of self, and none of
tree, And my wist - ful heart said faint - ly, "Some of self, and some of
free, Bro't me low - er, while I whis - pered "Less of self, and more of
sea, Lord, Thy love at last has con - quered "*None* of self, and *all* of

Thee," All of self and none of Thee, All of self and none of
Thee," Some of self and some of Thee, Some of self and some of
Thee," Less of self and more of Thee, Less of self and more of
Thee," *None* of self and *all* of Thee, *None* of self and *all* of

Thee, When I proud - ly said to Je - sus "All of self and none of Thee."
Thee, And my wist - ful heart said faint - ly "Some of self and some of Thee."
Thee, Bro't me low - er while I whis-pered "Less of self and more of Thee."
Thee, Lord, Thy love at last has conquered "*None* of self and *all* of Thee."

No. 150. Can it be Right?

"Wherefore didst thou doubt?"—Matt. 14: 31.

Rev. A. T. Pierson. P. P. Bliss.

1. Can it be right for me to go On in this dark, un - cer-tain way?
2. Can it be right in doubt to wait, Wait for the day that tries the heart,
3. Can it be right such loads to bear, While He says "Come, I'll give you rest?"
4. Can it be right to doubt His pow'r, Both to for - give and vanquish sin?

Can it be Right?
Say, "I be-lieve," and yet not know Wheth-er my sins are put a - way?
Ere I shall learn what is my state, Fear - ing the Judge should say de - part?
Bid-ding me cast on Him my care, Lean - ing in love, up - on His breast.
E - ven in trials of dark-est hour, Can not His love give peace with-in?
Chorus.
I will no long-er doubt Thee, O Lord! I will for - ev - er rest in Thy word.
Copyright property of The John Church Co.
5 Can it be right no soul to seek,
Lest I should prove unfit to guide?
Can He not teach my tongue to speak,
Will He not ample strength provide?
6 Can it be right with such a Lord,
Even to dread the hour of death?
Waiting in faith the great reward,
Calmly I'll yield my dying breath.
No. 151. The Smitten Rock.
"They drank of that spiritual rock that followed them, and that rock was Christ."—1 Cor. 10: 4.
Geo. C. Needham.
Ira D. Sankey.
1. From the riv - en Rock there flow - eth, Liv - ing wa - ter ev - er clear;
2. "With - out mon - ey, with - out mer - it," Je - sus calls, "Come un - to me,"
3. Faint - ing in the des - ert, drear - y, Guilt - y sin - ner, hark! 'tis He!
Wea - ry pil - grim, journey-ing on - ward, Know you not that Fount is near?
Thirst - y trav - 'ler, be en - cour - aged, Know you not the Fount is free?
'Tis the Sav - iour still en - treat - ing, Know you not He call - eth thee?
Chorus.
Je - sus is the Rock of A - ges—Smit - ten, strick - en, lo! He dies;
From His side a liv - ing fount - ain, Know you not it sat - is - fies?
Copyright, 1877, by Biglow & Main.

No. 152. Thou art Coming!

"Looking for that blessed hope, and the glorious appearing of the great God and our Saviour, Jesus Christ."—Titus 2: 13.

Arr. from Frances R. Havergal.
James McGranahan.
1. Thou art com-ing, O my Sav-iour, Thou art com-ing! O my King,
2. Thou art com-ing, not a shad-ow, Not a mist and not a tear,
3. Thou art com-ing, we are wait-ing With a hope that can - not fail,
Ev - 'ry tongue Thy name con-fess-ing, Well may we re - joice and sing;
Not a sin and not a sor-row, On that sun - rise grand and clear;
Ask - ing not the day or hour, An - chored safe with - in the veil;
Thou art com-ing! rays of glo - ry, Thro' the veil Thy death has rent,
Thou art com-ing! Je - sus Sav-iour, Noth - ing else seems worth a thought,
Thou art com-ing! at Thy ta - ble We are wit - ness - es for this,
D.S.-Thou art com-ing! Thou art com-ing! Je - sus our be - lov - ed Lord,
Fine.
Glad-den now our pil - grim path-way, Glo - ry from Thy pres - ence sent.
Oh, how mar - vel - ous the glo - ry, And the bliss Thy pain hath bought.
As we meet Thee in com-mun-ion, Earn - est of our com - ing bliss.
O the joy to see Thee reign-ing, Worship'd, glo - ri - fied, a - dored.
Chorus.
D.S.
Thou art com-ing, Thou art com-ing, We shall meet Thee on Thy way,
Thou art com-ing, we shall see Thee, And be like Thee on that day.
Copyright, 1878, by James McGranahan.

No. 153. Only Trusting in my Saviour.

"Jesus Christ and him crucified."—1 Cor. 2: 2.

Fanny J. Crosby. Wm. F. Sherwin.

1. On - ly trust - ing in my Sav - iour, All to Him my soul would leave;
2. On - ly trust - ing, noth - ing doubt - ing, This is all that I can do;
3. There are break - ers in the dis - tance, Yet no dan - ger will I fear;
4. On - ly trust - ing, on - ly trust - ing, This is joy and life to me;

He has suf - fered to re-deem me, And His word I now be - lieve.
Ev - 'ry tri - al that be - falls me He will safe - ly bring me thro'.
On the Rock my feet are rest - ing, Naught of harm can reach me here.
Thou wilt nev - er leave me friend-less While I cling, O Christ, to Thee.

Refrain.

Now to Christ a - lone I'm cling-ing, Tho' the tem - pest round me blow;
Heed - ing not the clouds a - bove me, Dread - ing not the waves be - low.

No. 154. Forever with Jesus There.

"In my Father's house are many mansions."—John 14: 2.

Rev. Arthur T. Pierson. James McGranahan.

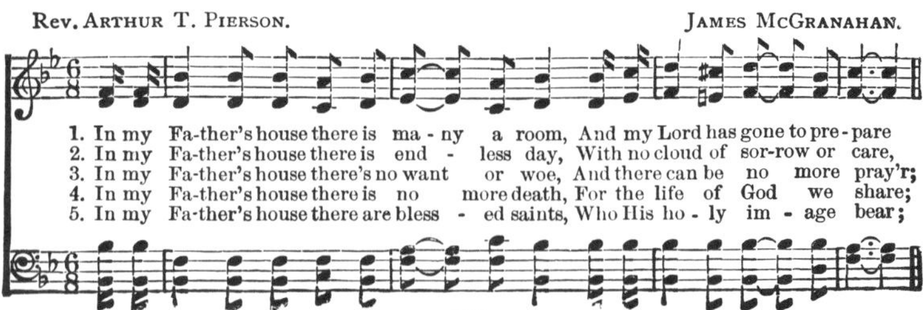
1. In my Fa-ther's house there is ma - ny a room, And my Lord has gone to pre - pare
2. In my Fa-ther's house there is end - less day, With no cloud of sor-row or care,
3. In my Fa-ther's house there's no want or woe, And there can be no more pray'r;
4. In my Fa-ther's house there is no more death, For the life of God we share;
5. In my Fa-ther's house there are bless - ed saints, Who His ho - ly im - age bear;

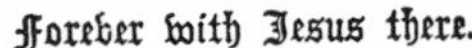
Forever with Jesus there.

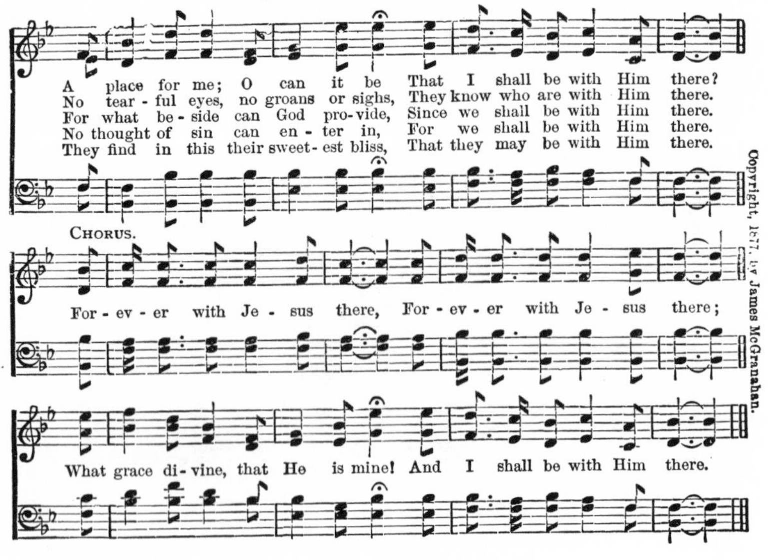
A place for me; O can it be That I shall be with Him there?
No tear - ful eyes, no groans or sighs, They know who are with Him there.
For what be - side can God pro - vide, Since we shall be with Him there.
No thought of sin can en - ter in, For we shall be with Him there.
They find in this their sweet - est bliss, That they may be with Him there.
CHORUS.
For - ev - er with Je - sus there, For - ev - er with Je - sus there;
What grace di - vine, that He is mine! And I shall be with Him there.

Copyright, 1877, by James McGranahan.

No. 155. Ten Thousand Times.

"The number of them was ten thousand times ten thousand."—Rev. 5 : 11.

Henry Alford, D.D. Ira D. Sankey.

1. Ten thousand times ten thous - and, In sparkling raiment bright, The ar - mies of the
2. What rush of hal - le - lu - jahs Fill all the earth and sky! What ringing of a
3. O, then what raptured greet - ings On Canaan's hap - py shore! What knitting severed
ransom'd saints Throng up the steeps of light; 'Tis fin - ished, all is fin - ished, Their
thousand harps Be - speaks the triumphs nigh! O day, for which cre - a - tion And
friendships up, Where partings are no more! Then eyes with joy shall spark - le, That
fight with death and sin; Fling o - pen wide the gold - en gates, And let the vic - tors in.
all its tribes were made! O joy, for all its form - er woes A thousand-fold re - paid!
brimm'd with tears of late; Or - phans no lon - ger fa - ther - less, Nor wid - ows des - o - late.

Copyright, 1877, by Biglow & Main.

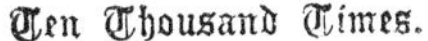

No. 156. Singing all the Time.

"Then was our mouth filled with singing."—Ps. 126 : 2.

Rev. E. P. HAMMOND. GEO. C. STEBBINS.

1. I feel like sing - ing all the time, My tears are wiped a - way;
For Je - sus is a friend of mine, I'll serve Him ev - 'ry day.

2. When on the cross my Lord I saw, Nail'd there by sins of mine;
Fast fell the burn - ing tears; but now, I'm sing - ing all the time.

3. When fierce temp - ta - tions try my heart, I sing, Je - sus is mine;
And so, though tears at times may start, I'm sing - ing all the time.

4. The won - drous sto - ry of the Lamb, Tell with that voice of thine,
Till oth - ers, with the glad new song Go sing - ing all the time.

CHORUS.

I'm sing - ing, sing - ing, Singing all the time; Sing - ing, sing - ing, Singing all the time.

I'll praise Him, &c.

No. 157. Mine!

"And all mine are thine, and thine are mine."—JOHN 17: 10.

E. L. B. *Alt.* JAMES McGRANAHAN.

1. Mine! what rays of glo-ry bright Now up-on the prom-ise shine! I have found the Lord my light; I am His, and He is mine.
2. Mine! the prom-ise oft-en read, *Now* in liv-ing truth im-press'd, Once ac-knowleg'd in the head, Now a fire with-in the breast.
3. Mine! the prom-ise can-not change, Mine! tho' oft my eyes are dim; Naught can from His love es-trange, Those who place their trust in Him.
4. Mine! tho' oft my hand may fail, *He* is strong and holds me fast; By His blood I shall pre-vail, He shall lead me home at last.
5. Mine! when death the bars shall break, 'Mid those glo-ries all di-vine. "Sat-is-fied" I shall a-wake, Clasp His feet, and call Him *mine.*

CHORUS.

Mine, oh, mine, mine, oh, mine, Je-sus Christ, my Lord and Sav-iour, I am His and He is mine!

No. 158. "Sing and Pray!"

Last words of a faithful minister of Christ, who recently died in the hope of the gospel.

MARY S. WHEELER. P. P. BLISS.

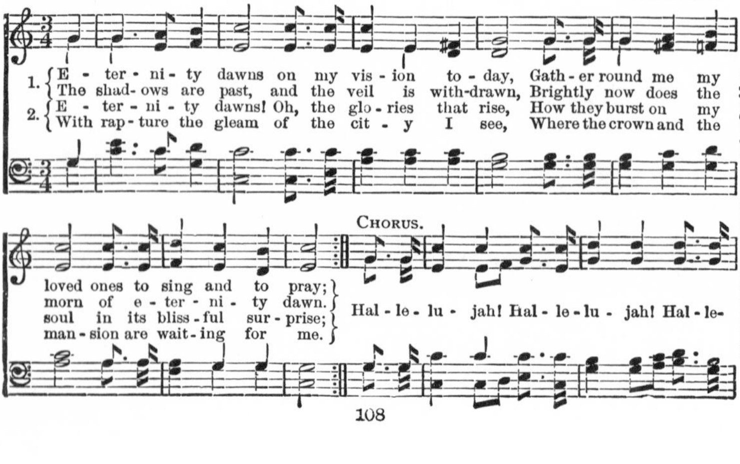

1. { E-ter-ni-ty dawns on my vis-ion to-day, Gath-er round me my loved ones to sing and to pray;
The shad-ows are past, and the veil is with-drawn, Brightly now does the morn of e-ter-ni-ty dawn. }
2. { E-ter-ni-ty dawns! Oh, the glo-ries that rise, How they burst on my soul in its bliss-ful sur-prise;
With rap-ture the gleam of the cit-y I see, Where the crown and the man-sion are wait-ing for me. }

CHORUS.

Hal-le-lu-jah! Hal-le-lu-jah! Hal-le-

lu-jah, we sing! Je - sus conquered the grave, robbing death of its sting; Ho -
san-na! a - gain let the glad anthem ring, "Sing and pray! E - ter - ni - ty dawns!"

3 "Eternity dawns!" There will be no more night,
I am nearing the gates of the city of light;
The shadows of time are passing away,
Tarry not, O my Saviour, come quickly, I pray.

4 "Eternity dawns!" Earth recedes from my view;
Weeping friends, now farewell, I must bid you adieu;
I'm resting in Jesus, His merits I plead,
Fear ye not, "for my God shall supply all your need."

5 "Eternity dawns!" 'Tis a source of content,
That in preaching salvation my life has been spent;
'Tis "Jesus my All," and the Saviour of men,
May His grace be upon you forever. Amen.

No. 159. It is Finished!

"What shall I do to inherit eternal life?"—Luke 18: 18.

Rev. James Proctor. Ira D. Sankey.

1. Noth-ing, eith-er great or small—Noth-ing, sin-ner, no; Je - sus died and paid it all, Long, long a - go.
2. When He, from His loft - y throne, Stooped to do and die, Ev - 'ry-thing was ful - ly done: Hearken to His cry.
3. Wea - ry, working, burdened one, Wherefore toil you so? Cease your do - ing; all was done Long, long a - go.
4. Till to Je - sus' work you cling By a sim - ple faith, "Do-ing" is a dead - ly thing—"Do-ing" ends in death.
5. Cast your dead - ly "do-ing" down—Down at Je - sus' feet; Stand in Him, in Him a - lone, Glo - rious - ly com - plete.

Chorus.

"It is fin-ished!" yes, in - deed, Finished ev - 'ry jot; Sin - ner, this is all you need, Tell me, is it not?

No. 160. What must it be to be There?
"There shall be no more death, neither sorrow, nor crying."—Rev. 21: 4.
Mrs. Elizabeth Mills.
Geo. C. Stebbins.
Duet.
1. We speak of the land of the blest, A coun - try so bright and so fair,
2. We speak of its path-ways of gold, Its walls deck'd with jew - els so rare,
3. We speak of its peace and its love, The robes which the glo - ri - fied wear,
4. We speak of its free-dom from sin, From sor - row, temp-ta - tion and care,
5. Do Thou, Lord, midst pleasure or woe, For heav - en our spi'r - its pre - pare,
And oft are its glo - ries con - fest, But what must it be to be there?
Its won - ders and pleas - ures un - told, But what must it be to be there?
The songs of the bless - ed a - bove, But what must it be to be there?
From tri - als with-out and with - in, But what must it be to be there?
Then short - ly we al - so shall know, And feel what it is to be there!
Copyright, 1878, by Geo. C. Stebbins.
Refrain.
To be there, to be there, Oh, what must it be to be there?
To be there, to be there, to be there?
To be there, to be there, Oh, what must it be to be there?
To be there, to be there, to be there?
No. 161. There's a Work for each of Us.
"For the Son of man is as a man taking a far journey, who left his home, and gave authority to his servants, and to every man his work."—Mark 13: 34.
A. A. A.
James McGranahan.
1. Our Mas-ter has tak - en His jour - ney To a coun - try that's far a - way,
2. In this "lit-tle while," doth it mat- ter, As we work, and we watch, and we wait,
3. There's on - ly one thing should concern us, To find just the task that is ours;
4. Our Mas - ter is com-ing most sure - ly, To reck-on with ev - 'ry one;
And has left us the care of the vine - yard, To work for Him day by day.
If we're fill-ing the place He as - signs us, Be its ser - vice small or great.
And then, hav-ing found it, to do it With all our God-giv - en pow'rs.
Shall we then, count our toil or our sor - row, If His sen - tence be, "Well done."
Copyright, 1878, by James McGranahan.

There's a Work for each of Us.
Chorus.
There's a work for me and a work for you, Something for each of us now to do;
Yes, a work for me and a work for you, Something for each of us now to do.
No. 162.
Jesus, only Jesus.
"They saw no man, save Jesus only."—Matt. 17: 8.
Selina P. Pierce.
Geo. C. Stebbins.
1. Be our joy - ful song to - day, Je - sus, on - ly Je - sus; He who took our
2. Once we wan-der'd far from God, Know-ing not of Je - sus, Tread-ing still the
3. Be our trust thro' years to come, Je - sus, on - ly Je - sus; Pass-word to the
sins a - way, Je - sus, on - ly Je - sus. Name with ev - 'ry bless - ing rife,
down-ward road, Lead-ing far from Je - sus; Till the Spir - it taught us how,
heav'n-ly home, Je - sus, on - ly Je - sus. When from sin and sor - row free,
Be our joy and hope thro' life, Be our strength in ev - 'ry strife, Je - sus, on - ly Je - sus.
'Neath the Saviour's yoke to bow, And we fain would fol-low now, Je - sus, on - ly Je - sus.
On thro' all e - ter - ni - ty, This our theme and song shall be, Je - sus, on - ly Je - sus.
Copyright, 1878, by Geo. C. Stebbins.

No. 163. Paradise.

"And Jesus said unto him, Verily I say unto thee, To-day thou shalt be with me in Paradise."—LUKE 23: 43.

W. W. D. JAMES McGRANAHAN.

1. How sweet the word of Christ the Lord, While on the cross He dies, A word to all who on Him call For life in par - a - dise.
2. The dy-ing thief, in full be-lief, On Je-sus fixed his eyes; His on-ly plea, "Re-mem-ber me, O Lord, in par - a - dise."
3. By man condemn'd, without a friend, Will Je-sus heed his cries? O bless-ed Lord, how quick Thy word, "To-day in par - a - dise.
4. Tho' vile as he, O sin-ner, flee While Je-sus calls, be wise; His word be-lieve, and now re-ceive A life in par - a - dise.

CHORUS.

From the cross the Saviour cries, Come with Me to par - a-dise; Look to Me, be-lieve and live. Ac-cept the life I free - ly give.

No. 164. Rejoice with Me.

"Rejoice in the Lord alway."—PHIL. 4: 4.

REV. J. B. ATCHINSON. P. P. BLISS.

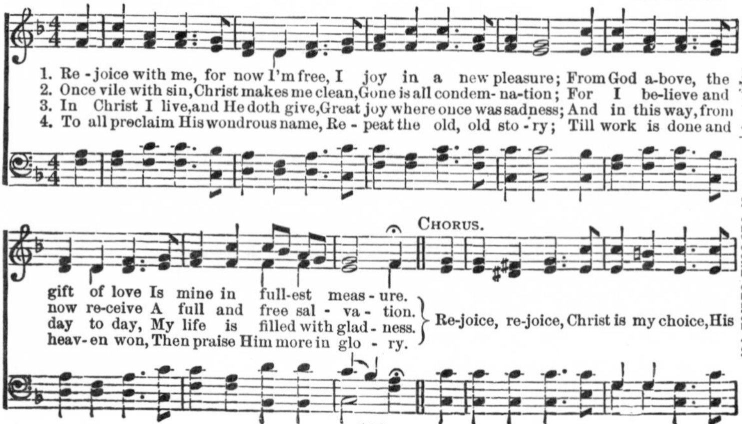

1. Re-joice with me, for now I'm free, I joy in a new pleasure; From God a-bove, the gift of love Is mine in full-est meas - ure.
2. Once vile with sin, Christ makes me clean, Gone is all condem-na-tion; For I be-lieve and now re-ceive A full and free sal - va - tion.
3. In Christ I live, and He doth give, Great joy where once was sadness; And in this way, from day to day, My life is filled with glad - ness.
4. To all proclaim His wondrous name, Re-peat the old, old sto-ry; Till work is done and heav-en won, Then praise Him more in glo - ry.

CHORUS.

Re-joice, re-joice, Christ is my choice, His

Rejoice with Me.

cross alone my glo-ry; While life shall last, when death is past, I'll sing the joyful sto - ry.
No. 165. Triumph By and By.
"I press toward the mark."—Phil. 3 : 14.
Dr. C. R. Blackall.
H. R. Palmer.
1. The prize is set be-fore us, To win, His words im-plore us, The eye of God is o'er us From on high, from on high; His lov - ing tones are call - ing While sin is dark, ap - pall - ing, 'Tis Je - sus gen - tly call - ing, He is nigh, He is nigh.
2. We'll fol - low where He lead - eth, We'll pas - ture where He feed - eth, We'll yield to Him who plead - eth From on high, from on high; Then naught from Him shall sev - er, Our hope shall bright - en ev - er, And faith shall fail us nev - er, He is nigh, He is nigh.
3. Our home is bright a - bove us, No tri - als dark to move us, But Je - sus dear to love us There on high, there on high; We'll give Him best en - deav - or, And praise His name for - ev - er, His pre - cious words can nev - er, Nev - er die, nev - er die.
Used by per.

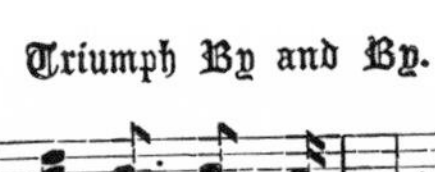
Triumph By and By.

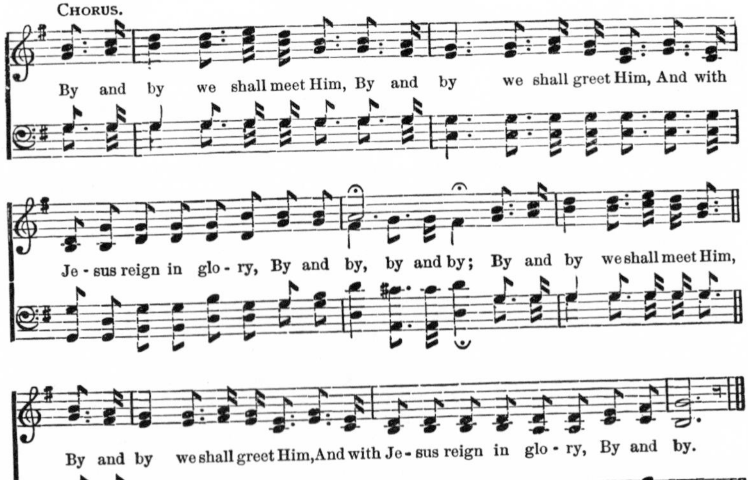
Chorus.
By and by we shall meet Him, By and by we shall greet Him, And with
Je - sus reign in glo - ry, By and by, by and by; By and by we shall meet Him,
By and by we shall greet Him, And with Je - sus reign in glo - ry, By and by.

No. 166. I am Trusting Thee.

"Trusting in the Lord."—Ps. 112 : 7.

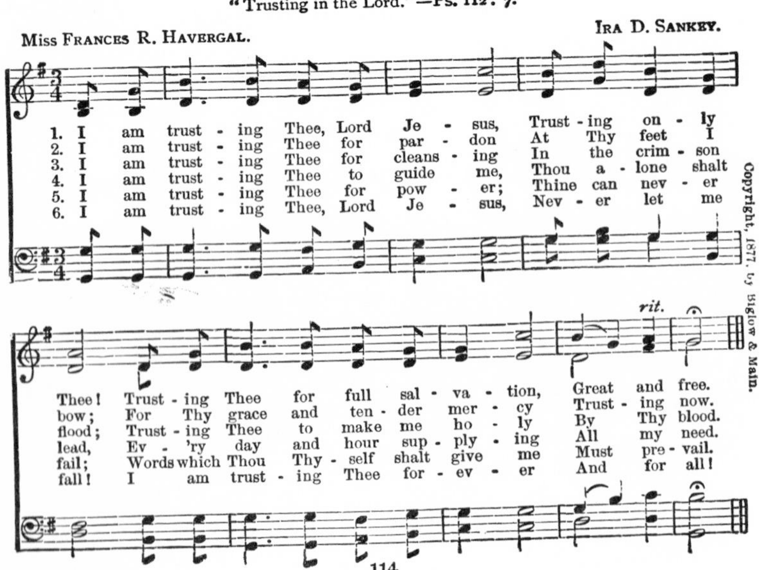
Miss Frances R. Havergal.
Ira D. Sankey.
1. I am trust - ing Thee, Lord Je - sus, Trust - ing on - ly Thee! Trust - ing Thee for full sal - va - tion, Great and free.
2. I am trust - ing Thee for par - don At Thy feet I bow; For Thy grace and ten - der mer - cy Trust - ing now.
3. I am trust - ing Thee for cleans - ing In the crim - son flood; Trust - ing Thee to make me ho - ly By Thy blood.
4. I am trust - ing Thee to guide me, Thou a - lone shalt lead, Ev - 'ry day and hour sup - ply - ing All my need.
5. I am trust - ing Thee for pow - er; Thine can nev - er fail; Words which Thou Thy - self shalt give me Must pre - vail.
6. I am trust - ing Thee, Lord Je - sus, Nev - er let me fall! I am trust - ing Thee for - ev - er And for all!
rit.
Copyright, 1877, by Biglow & Main.

No. 167. Good News.

"The glorious gospel of the blessed God."—1 TIM. 1 : 11.

Rev. J. C. RYLE. JAMES MCGRANAHAN.

1. Good news from heav'n, good news for thee, There flows a par- don, full and free, To guilt-y sin-ners, thro' the blood Of the In- carnate Son of God; He paid the debt that thou didst owe, He suf-fered death for thee be - low, He bore the wrath di - vine for thee, He groan'd and bled on Cal - va - ry.
2. Good news from heav'n, good news for thee, The Saviour cries," Come un-to Me All ye who toil, with fears oppress; Come, weary one, oh, come and rest:" He loves thee with o'er- flowing love, He hears thy pray'r in heav'n a - bove, He all thy pas - ture shall pre - pare, And lead thee with a shepherd's care.
3. Good news from heav'n, good news for thee, Has ech-oed from e - ter- ni - ty; And loud shall our hosannas ring, When with the ransom'd throng we sing. "Worthy the Lamb," whose precious blood Has made us kings and priests to God; Our harps we'll tune to no- blest strains, And glo- ry give to Him who reigns.
CHORUS.
Good news from heav'n, good news for thee, There flows a par-don, full and free, To guilt-y sinners thro' the blood Of the In- carnate Son of God.

No. 168. Evening Prayer.

"Bless me—O my Father."—Gen. 27: 38.

J. Edmeston. Geo. C. Stebbins.

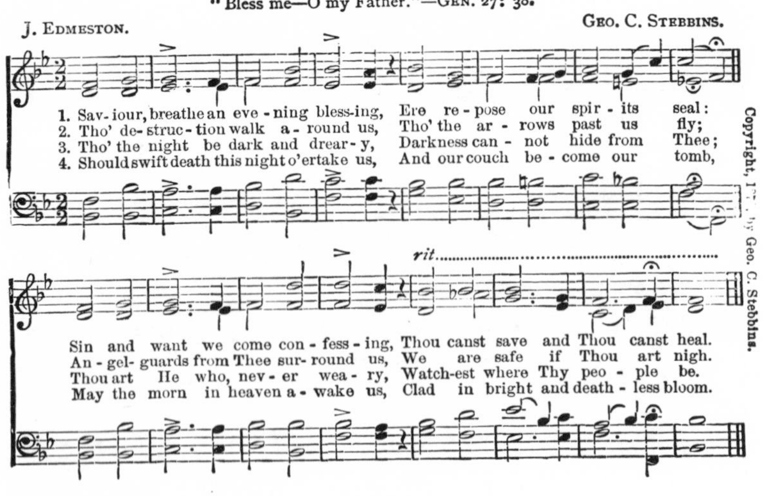

1. Sav- iour, breathe an eve - ning bless-ing, Ere re - pose our spir - its seal:
2. Tho' de- struc - tion walk a - round us, Tho' the ar - rows past us fly;
3. Tho' the night be dark and drear - y, Darkness can - not hide from Thee;
4. Should swift death this night o'ertake us, And our couch be - come our tomb,
rit.
Sin and want we come con - fess - ing, Thou canst save and Thou canst heal.
An - gel- guards from Thee sur- round us, We are safe if Thou art nigh.
Thou art He who, nev - er wea - ry, Watch-est where Thy peo - ple be.
May the morn in heaven a - wake us, Clad in bright and death - less bloom.
Copyright, 187[illegible], by Geo. C. Stebbins.

No. 169. Sound the High Praises.

"Worthy is the Lamb that was slain to receive power, and riches, and wisdom, and strength, and honor, and glory, and blessing."—Rev. 5: 12.

Rev. J. C. Ryle. James McGranahan.

1. Sound the high prais - es of Je - sus our King, He came and He conquer'd, His
2. Praise to the Con- quer - or! Praise to the Lord, The en - e - my quail'd at the
vic - to - ry sing; Sing, for the pow'r of the ty - rant is bro - ken, The
might of His word; In heav'n He as - cends and un - folds the glad sto - ry, The
tri - umph's complete o - ver death and the grave; Vain is their boast-ing, Je-
hosts of the bless - ed ex - ult in His fame: In love He looks down from the
Copyright, 1878, by James McGranahan.

Sound the High Praises.

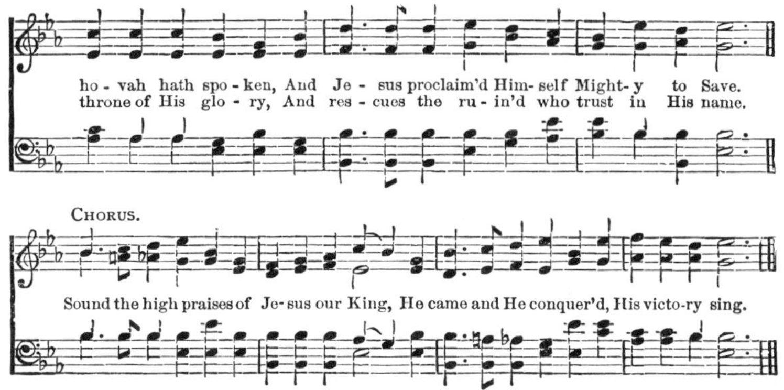
ho - vah hath spo - ken, And Je - sus proclaim'd Him- self Might- y to Save.
throne of His glo - ry, And res - cues the ru - in'd who trust in His name.
CHORUS.
Sound the high praises of Je- sus our King, He came and He conquer'd, His victo-ry sing.

No. 170. Pressing On.

"There remaineth therefore a rest."—HEB. 4: 9.

HORATIUS BONAR, D.D. GEO. C. STEBBINS.

1. This is the day of toil Be- neath earth's sultry noon, This is the day of ser - vice true, But rest- ing com- eth soon.
2. Spend and be spent would we, While last-eth time's brief day; No turn - ing back in cow- ard fear, No lingering by the way.
3. On - ward we press in haste, Up- ward our jour- ney still; Ours is the path the Mas- ter trod Thro' good re - port and ill.
4. The way may rough-er grow, The wea - ri - ness in-crease, We gird our loins and hast- en on,—The end, the end is peace.
CHORUS.
Hal- le - lu - jah! Hal- le- lu - jah! There re- mains a rest for us. Hal- le- lu - jah! Hal- le - lu - jah! There remains a rest for us.
Used by per.

No. 171. There is Joy among the Angels.

"There is joy in the presence of the angels of God over one sinner that repenteth."—LUKE 15: 10.

EDWARD A. BARNES. C. C. CASE.

1. There is joy a-mong the an-gels, Sing-ing round the throne a-bove, When re-pent-ant tears are flow-ing, While the ris-en Lord is show-ing All the rich-es of His love, All the rich-es of His love, All the rich-es of His love.
2. There is joy a-mong the an-gels, When a sin-ner heeds the call; When he turns to Christ be-liev-ing, And from Him is love re-ceiv-ing, Grace that saves us one and all, Grace that saves us one and all, Grace that saves us one and all.
3. There is joy a-mong the an-gels, When His cause is speed-ing on; When the notes of praise are ring-ing, That the gos-pel work is bring-ing, Pre-cious sheaves for harvest morn, Precious sheaves for harvest morn, Precious sheaves for harvest morn.
Copyright, 1878, by C. C. Case.
CHORUS.
There is joy,......... oh, there is joy, Joy that nev-er can be told,
glad joy, there is joy, glad joy, nev-er can be told,
When a soul...... that long has wan-der'd, Comes within the Sav-iour's fold.
When a soul that long has wander'd, long has wander'd,

No. 172. Over the Ocean Wave.

"I will give thee the heathen for thine inheritance."—Ps. 2: 8.

JULIA SAMPSON HASKELL. (MISSIONARY.) WM. B. BRADBURY.

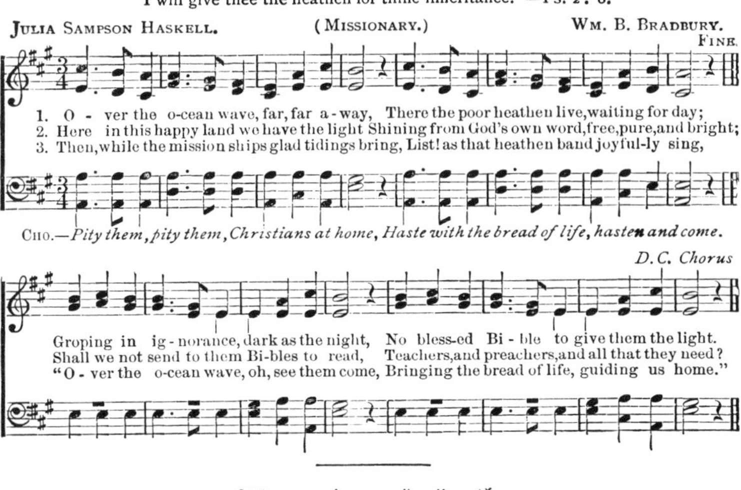

FINE.
1. O - ver the o-cean wave, far, far a-way, There the poor heathen live, waiting for day;
2. Here in this happy land we have the light Shining from God's own word, free, pure, and bright;
3. Then, while the mission ships glad tidings bring, List! as that heathen band joyful-ly sing,
CHO.—Pity them, pity them, Christians at home, Haste with the bread of life, hasten and come.
D.C. Chorus
Groping in ig-norance, dark as the night, No bless-ed Bi-ble to give them the light.
Shall we not send to them Bi-bles to read, Teachers, and preachers, and all that they need?
"O - ver the o-cean wave, oh, see them come, Bringing the bread of life, guiding us home."

No. 173. Memories of Earth.

"These are they which came out of great tribulation."—REV. 7: 14.

W. P. MACKAY, M. D. JAMES MCGRANAHAN.

1. When we reach our Fa-ther's dwell-ing, On the Strong e-ter-nal hills,
2. When the paths of pray'r and du-ty, And af-flic-tion all are trod,
3. And the way by which He brought us, All the griev-ings that He bore,
And our praise to Him is swell-ing Who the vast cre-a-tion fills,
And we wake and see the beau-ty Of our Sav-iour and our God,
All the pa-tient love that taught us, We'll re-mem-ber ev-er-more,
Shall we then re-call the sad-ness, And the clouds that hung so dim,
Shall we then re-call the sto-ry Of our mor-tal griefs and tears,
And His rest will be the dear-er, As we think of wea-ry ways,

When our hearts were turn'd from hard-ness, And our feet from paths of sin?
When on earth we sought the glo - ry Wrestling oft with doubts and fears?
And His light will be the clear-er As we muse on cloud - y days.
CHORUS.
Yes, we sure - ly shall re - mem - ber, And His grace we'll free - ly
own; For the love so strong and ten - der, That redeem'd and bro't us home.

No. 174. Must I Go and Empty Handed?

After a month only of Christian life, nearly all of it upon a sick bed, a young man of nearly 30 years lay dying. Suddenly a look of sadness crossed his face, and to the query of a friend he exclaimed: "No, I am not afraid, Jesus saves me now; but oh, *must I go and empty handed?*"

C. C. LUTHER. (DAN. 12: 3.) GEO. C. STEBBINS.

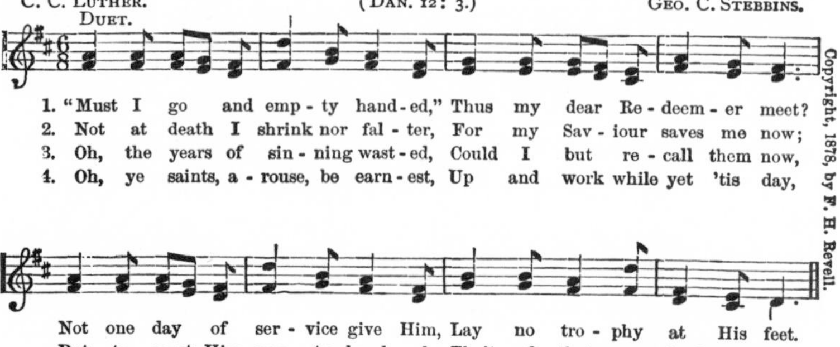
DUET.
1. "Must I go and emp - ty hand - ed," Thus my dear Re - deem - er meet?
2. Not at death I shrink nor fal - ter, For my Sav - iour saves me now;
3. Oh, the years of sin - ning wast - ed, Could I but re - call them now,
4. Oh, ye saints, a - rouse, be earn - est, Up and work while yet 'tis day,
Not one day of ser - vice give Him, Lay no tro - phy at His feet.
But to meet Him emp - ty hand - ed, Tho't of that now clouds my brow.
I would give them to my Sav - iour, To His will I'd glad - ly bow.
Ere the night of death o'er-takes thee, Strive for souls while still you may.
Copyright, 1878, by F. H. Revell.

Must I Go and Empty Handed?
Chorus.
"Must I go and emp - ty hand - ed," Must I meet my Sav - iour so?
Not one soul with which to greet Him, Must I emp - ty hand - ed go?
No. 175. My Faith still Clings.
"Watch, stand fast in the faith."—Rom. 14: 1.
Rev. H. F. Colby.
W. H. Doane.
1. My sin is great, my strength is weak, My path be - set with snares,
2. The world is dark with - out Thee, Lord, I turn me from its strife
3. Temp - ta - tions lure and fears as - sail My frail, in - con - stant heart;
4. Un - fold Thy pre - cepts to my mind, And cleanse my blind - ed eyes;
But Thou, O Christ, hast died for me, And Thou wilt hear my prayers.
To find Thy love a sweet re - lief; Thou art the light of life.
But pre - cious are Thy prom - is - es, And they new strength im - part.
Grant me to work for Thee on earth, Then praise Thee in the skies.
Copyright, 1876, by Wm. H. Doane.
Refrain.
To Thee, to Thee, the Cru - ci - fied, The sin - ner's on - ly plea,
Re - ly - ing on Thy prom - ised grace, My faith still clings to Thee.

No. 176. The Pearl of Greatest Price.

"One pearl of great price."—MATT. 13: 46.

Rev. JOHN MASON. P. P. BLISS.

1. I've found the pearl of great - est price! My heart doth sing for joy; And sing I must, for Christ is mine! Christ shall my song employ.
2. Christ is my Proph - et, Priest, and King; My Proph - et full of light, My great High Priest be - fore the throne, My King of heav'nly might.
3. For He in - deed is Lord of lords, And He the King of kings; He is the Sun of Righteous - ness, With heal - ing in His wings.
4. Christ is my peace; He died for me, For me He shed His blood; And as my won - d'rous Sac - ri - fice, Of - fered Himself to God.
5. Christ Je - sus is my all in all, My com - fort and my love; My life be - low, and He shall be My joy and crown a - bove.
CHORUS.
I've found the pearl of greatest price! My heart doth sing for joy; And sing I must, for Christ is mine! Christ shall my song employ.
Copyright property of The John Church Co.
No. 177. Faint, yet Pursuing.
Mrs. E. W. GRISWOLD. (JUDGES 8: 4.) GEO. C. STEBBINS.
1. "Faint, yet pur - su - ing," we press our way Up to the glo - ri - ous gates of day; Fol - low - ing Him who has gone be - fore, O - ver the path to the bright - er shore.
2. "Faint, yet pur - su - ing," whate'er be - fall, He who has died for us, died for all; So should they come, as a might - y throng Bearing His ban - ner a - loft with song.
3. "Faint, yet pur - su - ing," till e - ven - tide, Un - der the cross of the Cru - ci - fied; Knowing, when dark - ly are skies o'er - cast, Sor - row and sigh - ing will end at last.
4. "Faint, yet pur - su - ing," the eye a - far Sees thro' the darkness the Morn - ing Star, Shed - ding its ray for the wea - ry feet, Keeping the way, to the gold - en street.
by F. H. Revell.

Faint, yet Pursuing.
Chorus.
"Faint, yet pur-su - ing," from day to day, O - ver the sure and the blood-marked way;
Strengthen and keep us, O Sav-iour, Friend, Ev - er pur-su - ing, un - to life's end.
No. 178. Ho, every One that Thirsteth.
"Come ye, buy and eat."—Isa. 55: 1.
Anon.
P. P. Bliss.
Duet.
1. Be - side the well at noon-time, I hear a sad one say: "I want that liv - ing
2. Be - side the pool Be-thes - da, I hear a mournful cry: "No help, no hope is
3. While seated on the hill - side, The hungry ones were fed By Him who said most
wa - ter, Give me to drink, I pray; The well is deep, O pil - grim, But
of - fered To one so weak as I;" Oh, cease thy sad com-plain-ing, The
tru - ly: "I am the liv - ing bread;" 'Tis He, the heavenly man - na, Who
deep-er is my need, I thirst for life e - ter - nal, The 'Gift of God' in - deed."
gos - pel gives thee cheer; Come to the house of mer - cy, For Christ the pool is here.
doth our souls re - store; By faith of Him par-tak - ing We live for-ev - er - more.
Chorus.
Ho, ev - 'ry one that thirst - eth, The liv - ing wa - ter buy!
'Tis He, the great Phy - si - cian, Can cure the sin - sick soul;
Ho, ev - 'ry one that thirst - eth, The liv - ing wa - ter buy!
Ye bless - ed ones that hun - ger, Take, eat and nev - er die.
"Rise up and walk," He bids thee, "Thy faith hath made thee whole."
Ye bless - ed ones that hun - ger, Take, eat and nev - er die.
Copyright property of The John Church Co.

No. 179. On Jordan's Stormy Banks.

"Thine eyes shall behold the land."—Isa. 33: 17.

Rev. Samuel Stennett. T. C. O'Kane.

1. On Jor - dan's storm - y banks I stand, And cast a wish - ful eye
2. O'er all those wide - ex - tend - ed plains Shines one e - ter - nal day;
3. When shall I reach that hap - py place, And be for - ev - er blest?
4. Filled with de-light, my rap - tured soul Would here no long - er stay;
To Ca - naan's fair and hap - py land, Where my pos - ses - sions lie.
There God the Son for - ev - er reigns, And scat - ters night a - way.
When shall I see my Fa - ther's face, And in His bo - som rest?
Though Jor-dan's waves a - round me roll, Fear - less I'd launch a - way.
Chorus.
We will rest in the fair and hap - py land, by and by, Just a - cross on the ev - er - green shore,...................... Sing the song of Mo - ses and the
ev - er - green shore,
Lamb, by and by, And dwell with Je - sus ev - er - more.

No. 180. We'll Work till Jesus comes.

"Thy work shall be rewarded."—Jer. 31 : 16.

Mrs. Elizabeth Mills. Dr. Wm. Miller.

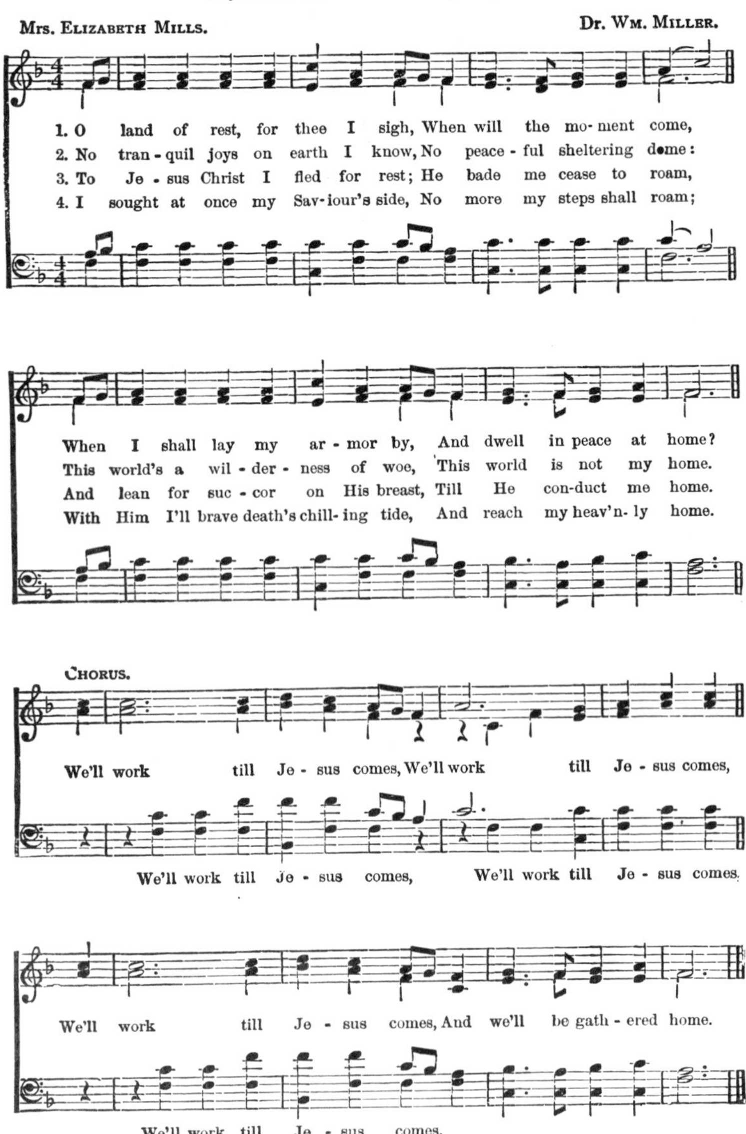

1. O land of rest, for thee I sigh, When will the mo-ment come,
2. No tran-quil joys on earth I know, No peace-ful sheltering dome:
3. To Je-sus Christ I fled for rest; He bade me cease to roam,
4. I sought at once my Sav-iour's side, No more my steps shall roam;
When I shall lay my ar-mor by, And dwell in peace at home?
This world's a wil-der-ness of woe, This world is not my home.
And lean for suc-cor on His breast, Till He con-duct me home.
With Him I'll brave death's chill-ing tide, And reach my heav'n-ly home.
Chorus.
We'll work till Je-sus comes, We'll work till Je-sus comes,
We'll work till Je-sus comes, We'll work till Je-sus comes.
We'll work till Je-sus comes, And we'll be gath-ered home.
We'll work till Je-sus comes,

No. 181. He Knows.

MARY G. BRAINARD. Words arranged by P. P. BLISS. P. P. BLISS.

1. I know not what a-waits me, God kind-ly veils mine eyes,
2. One step I see be-fore me, 'Tis all I need to see,
3. O bliss-ful lack of wis-dom, 'Tis bless-ed not to know;
4. So on I go not know-ing, I would not if I might;
And o'er each step of my on-ward way He makes new scenes to rise;
The light of heav'n more bright-ly shines, When earth's il-lu-sions flee;
He holds me with His own right hand, And will not let me go,
I'd rath-er walk in the dark with God Than go a-lone in the light;
And ev-'ry joy He sends me, comes A sweet and glad sur-prise.
And sweet-ly through the si-lence, came His lov-ing "Fol-low me."
And lulls my troub-led soul to rest In Him who loves me so.
I'd rath-er walk by faith with Him Than go a-lone by sight.
CHORUS.
Where He may lead I'll fol-low, My trust in Him re-pose; And ev-'ry hour in
per-fect peace I'll sing, He knows, He knows; And ev-'ry hour in per-fect peace I'll
sing, He knows, He knows.
After last verse only.
He knows, He knows, He knows.......................
He knows.
Copyright property of The John Church Co.

No. 182. When we get Home.

"Eye hath not seen, nor ear heard, neither have entered into the heart of man, the things which God hath prepared for them that love him."—1 Cor. 2 : 9.

Chas. H. Gabriel.
James McGranahan.
1. When we get home from our sor - row and care, And we stand with the
2. When we get home to the man-sions a - bove, With the loved ones gone
3. When we get home, when the morn-ing is come, And forth from the
an - gels of light, Oh, what a meet-ing in heav - en there'll be, In that
o - ver be - fore, Oh, who can tell what a joy that will be There, to
cit - y of gold An - gels of God, com-ing down, shall call home All of
land without shad-ow or night; Sor-row and care, trib - u - la - tion and pain We'll
live and re-joice ev - er-more: An-gels will praise, the Re-deem - er will smile, And
those who be-long to His fold; Will you be there, brother, loved ones to greet, Or
leave, when we pass thro' the tomb Clouds of de-spair, storms of tri - al and care We shall
loved ones we'll clasp by the hand; Free from all pain, far be-yond earth-ly stain, We shall
will you for - ev - er be lost? What is thy choice, fleeting pleasures of earth, Or a
leave for that beau-ti - ful home.
dwell in that beau-ti - ful land.
home when death's river is cross'd?
Chorus.
When we get home, oh, when we get home, Get home to
glo - ry land, Prais-es we'll sing to Je-sus, our King, A ransomed, a glo - ri - fied band.
Copyright, 1877, by James McGranahan.

No. 183. Not Half has ever been Told.

"And the building of the wall of it was of jasper; and the city was pure gold, like unto clear glass."—Rev. 21 : 18.

Rev. J. B. Atchinson. O. F. Presbrey.

1. I have read of a beau - ti - ful cit - y, Far a - way in the king-dom of
2. I have read of bright mansions in Heav - en, Which the Saviour has gone to pre-
3. I have read of white robes for the right- eous, Of bright crowns which the glo-ri-fied
4. I have read of a Christ so for - giv - ing, That vile sin- ners may ask and re-
God; I have read how its walls are of jas - per, How its streets are all gold- en and
pare; And the saints who on earth have been faith-ful, Rest for- ev - er with Christ o - ver
wear, When our Father shall bid them "Come, en- ter, And my glo - ry e - ter- nal - ly
ceive Peace and par- don from ev- 'ry trans- gres-sion, If when ask - ing they on - ly be-
broad. In the midst of the street is life's riv - er, Clear as crys- tal and pure to be-
there; There no sin ev - er en- ters, nor sor- row, The in- hab - i - tants nev- er grow
share;" How the righteous are ev - er-more bless - ed As they walk thro' the streets of pure
lieve. I have read how He'll guide and protect us, If for safe - ty we en - ter His
hold; But not half of that cit- y's bright glo- ry To mor-tals has ev - er been told.
old; But not half of the joys that a- wait them To mor-tals has ev - er been told.
gold; But not half of the won-der- ful sto - ry To mor-tals has ev - er been told.
fold; But not half of His goodness and mer- cy To mor-tals has ev - er been told.
Used by per.

Not Half has ever been Told.

CHORUS.
Not half has ev - er been told;......... Not half has ev- er been told;.........
been told;
been told;
Repeat the Chorus p.
Not half of that cit - y's bright glo - ry To mortals has ev - er been told.

No. 184. Are you coming Home to-night?

"All things are ready, come."—MATT. 22: 4.

Arranged. JAMES MCGRANAHAN.

1. Are you coming Home, ye wand'rers, Whom Jesus died to win, All footsore, lame and wea - ry, Your garments stain'd with sin; Will you seek the blood of Je - sus To wash your garments white; Will you trust His precious promise, Are you coming Home to-night?
2. Are you coming Home, ye lost ones? Behold your Lord doth wait: Come, then no long-er lin - ger, Come ere it be too late; Will you come and let Him save you, O trust his love and might; Will you come while He is calling, Are you coming Home to-night?
3. Are you coming Home, ye guilt - y, Who bear the load of sin; Outside you've long been stand-ing, Come now and ven - ture in; Will you heed the Saviour's prom - ise, And dare to trust Him quite; "Come un-to me," saith Je- sus, Are you coming Home to-night?
rit.........

Are you coming Home to-night?

Chorus.
Are you coming Home to-night, Are you coming Home to-night, Are you coming Home to
Je - sus, Out of darkness in - to light? Are you com-ing Home to-night, Are you
coming Home to-night To your lov-ing, heav'nly Fa-ther, Are you coming Home to-night?

No. 185. Where is Thy Refuge?

"What is a man profited, if he shall gain the whole world, and lose his own soul."—Matt. 16: 26.

Fanny J. Crosby. Silas J. Vail.

1. Say, where is thy ref- uge, poor sin - ner, And what is thy pros- pect to - day?
2. The Mas- ter is call - ing thee, sin - ner, In tones of com- pas- sion and love,
3. As summer is wan- ing, poor sin - ner, Re - pent, ere the sea- son is past;

Why toil for the wealth that will per - ish, The treas-ures that rust and de - cay?
To feel that sweet rap- ture of par - don, And lay up thy treas-ure a - bove:
God's goodness to thee is ex- tend - ed, As long as the day-beam shall last;

Oh! think of thy soul, that for - ev - er Must live on e - ter - ni - ty's shore,
Oh! kneel at the cross where He suf- fered, To ran- som thy soul from the grave;
Then slight not the warn- ing re- peat - ed With all the bright moments that roll,

When thou, in the dust art for- got - ten, When pleasure can charm thee no more.
The arm of His mer - cy will hold thee, The arm that is might - y to save.
Nor say, when the har- vest is end - ed, That no one hath cared for thy soul.

Where is Thy Refuge?
Chorus.
'Twill prof- it thee nothing, but fear- ful the cost, To gain the whole world if thy
soul should be lost! To gain the whole world if thy soul should be lost.
No. 186. Brightly Gleams our Banner.
" Lift ye up a banner upon the high mountains."—Isa. 13 : 2.
Rev. Thomas J. Potter.
Sir Arthur S. Sullivan.
1. Brightly gleams our ban- ner, Point-ing to the sky, Wav-ing wand'rers homeward,
2. Je - sus, Lord and Mas - ter, At Thy sa - cred feet, Here with hearts re-joic - ing,
3. All our days di - rect us, In the way we go, Lead us on vic - to - rious
4. Then with Saints and An-gels May we join a - bove, Off'- ring end-less prais - es
To their home on high; Journeying o'er the des - ert, Glad- ly thus we pray,
See Thy chil- dren meet; Oft - en have we left Thee, Oft - en gone a - stray,
O - ver ev - 'ry foe; Bid Thine an- gels shield us, When the storm-clouds lower,
At Thy throne of love; When the toil is o - ver, Then comes rest and peace,—
And with hearts u - nit - ed, Take our heav'nward way.
Keep us, might-y Sav - iour, In the nar- row way.
Par- don Thou and save us In the last dread hour.
Je - sus, in His beau - ty;— Songs that nev - er cease.
Chorus.
Brightly gleams our
ban - ner, Pointing to the sky, Waving wand'rers on-ward To their home on high.

No. 187. He that Believeth.
"He that believeth on me hath everlasting life."—John 6: 47.
P. P. B.
P. P. Bliss.
1. Hear ye the glad Good News from heav'n? Life to a death-doomed race is given!
2. When we were lost, the Son of God Made an a-tone-ment by His blood:
3. Why not be-lieve the glad Good News? Why still the voice of God re-fuse?
Christ on the cross for you and me Pur-chased a par-don full and free.
When we the glad Good News be-lieve, Then the a-tone-ment we re-ceive.
Why not be-lieve, when God hath said, All, all our guilt "on Him" was laid.
Copyright property of The John Church Co.
Chorus.
He that be-liev-eth, he that be-liev-eth, He that be-liev-eth hath
ev-er-last-ing life; He that be-liev-eth hath ev-er-last-ing life.
No. 188. Father, Take my Hand.
"For thy name's sake lead me, and guide me."—Ps. 31: 3.
Rev. H. N. Cobb.
S. J. Vail.
1. The way is dark my Fa-ther! Cloud upon cloud is gathering thickly o'er my head, and loud The thunders
roar a-bove me, Yet see, I stand like one bewildered! Father, take my hand, And thro' the gloom lead
Used by per.

Father, Take my Hand.

safe - ly home, safe - ly home, Safe - ly home, Lead safe - ly home Thy child!

2 The day declines, my Father! ‖ and the night
Is drawing darkly down. My faithless sight
Sees | ghostly | visions. ‖ Fears like a spectral band
Encompass me. O Father, | take my | hand,
And from the night lead up to light,
Up to light, up to light,
Lead up to light Thy child!

3 The way is long, my Father! ‖ and my soul
Longs for the rest and quiet | of the | goal; ‖
While yet I journey through this weary land,
Keep me from wandering. Father, | take my | hand,
And in the way to endless day,
Endless day, endless day,
Lead safely on Thy child!

4 The path is rough, my Father! ‖ Many a thorn
Has pierced me! and my feet, all torn
And bleeding, | mark the | way. ‖ Yet Thy command
Bids me press forward. Father, | take my | hand;
Then safe and blest, O lead to rest,
Lead to rest, lead to rest,
O lead to rest Thy child!

5 The throng is great, my Father! ‖ Many a doubt
And fear of danger compass me about;
And foes op- | press me | sore. ‖ I cannot stand
Or go, alone. O Father! | take my | hand;
And through the throng, lead safe along,
Safe along, safe along,
Lead safe along Thy child.

6 The cross is heavy, Father! ‖ I have borne
It long, and | still do | bear it. ‖ Let my worn
And fainting spirit, rise to that bright land
Where crowns are given. Father, | take my | hand;
And, reaching down, lead to the crown,
To the crown, to the crown,
Lead to the crown Thy child.

No. 189. Parting Hymn.

"The blessing of the Lord be upon you."—Ps. 129: 8.

FANNY J. CROSBY. REV. R. LOWRY.

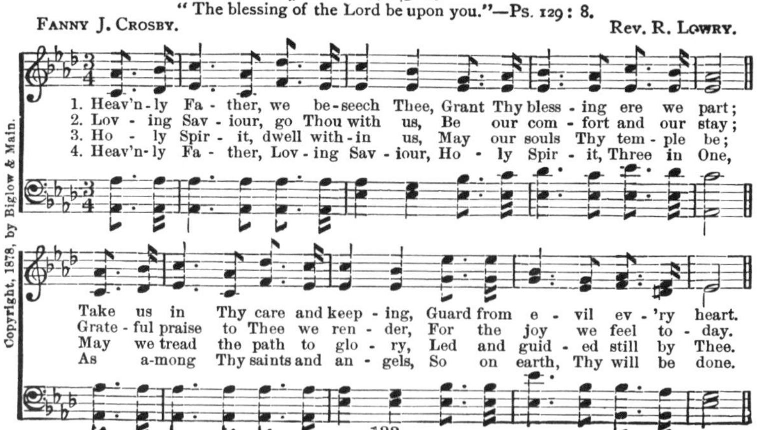
1. Heav'n-ly Fa - ther, we be-seech Thee, Grant Thy bless - ing ere we part;
2. Lov - ing Sav - iour, go Thou with us, Be our com - fort and our stay;
3. Ho - ly Spir - it, dwell with - in us, May our souls Thy tem - ple be;
4. Heav'n-ly Fa - ther, Lov - ing Sav - iour, Ho - ly Spir - it, Three in One,
Take us in Thy care and keep - ing, Guard from e - vil ev - 'ry heart.
Grate - ful praise to Thee we ren - der, For the joy we feel to - day.
May we tread the path to glo - ry, Led and guid - ed still by Thee.
As a-mong Thy saints and an - gels, So on earth, Thy will be done.

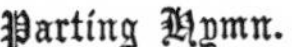
Parting Hymn.

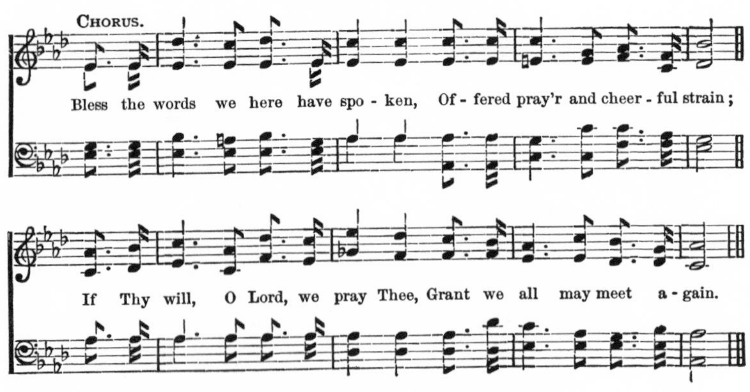
Chorus.
Bless the words we here have spo - ken, Of - fered pray'r and cheer - ful strain;
If Thy will, O Lord, we pray Thee, Grant we all may meet a - gain.

No. 190. The Gospel of Thy Grace.

"God so loved the world that he gave his only-begotten Son."—John 3 : 16.

Rev. A. T. Pierson. James McGranahan.

1. The gos - pel of Thy grace My stubborn heart has won, "For God so loved the world He gave His on - ly Son, That
2. The ser - pent "lift - ed up" Could life and heal - ing give, So Je - sus on the cross Bids me to look and live; For
3. "The soul that sin - neth dies:" My aw - ful doom I heard; I was for - ev - er lost, But for Thy gra - cious word That
4. "Not to con-demn the world" The "Man of sor-rows" came; But that the world might have Sal - va - tion thro' His name; For
5. "Lord, help my un - be - lief!" Give me the peace of faith, To rest with child-like trust On what Thy gos - pel saith, That

"Who - so - ev - er will believe, shall ev - er - last - ing life receive!" Shall ev - er - last - ing life re - ceive!"

No. 191.
Gloria Patri.
Anon.
Glory be to the Father, and to the Son, and to the Ho - ly Ghost.
As it was in the beginning, is now, and................. ev - er shall be, world with - out end. A - MEN.
No. 192.
Tell it Out.
"The Lord is King for ever and ever."—Ps. 10: 16.
FRANCES R. HAVERGAL.
Arr. by IRA D. SANKEY.
1. Tell it out among the na-tions that the Lord is King; Tell it out! Tell it out! Tell it out a-mong the na-tions, bid them shout and sing; Tell it out! Tell it out! Tell it out with ad - o - ra-tion that He shall in - crease, That the might - y King of glo - ry is the King of Peace; Tell it out with ju - bi - la - tion, let the song ne'er cease; Tell it out! Tell it out!
2. Tell it out among the peo-ple that the Sav-iour reigns; Tell it out! Tell it out! Tell it out a-mong the heath-en, bid them break their chains; Tell it out! Tell it out! Tell it out a-mong the weep-ing ones that Je - sus lives, Tell it out a-mong the wea - ry ones what rest He gives, Tell it out a-mong the sin-ners that He came to save; Tell it out! Tell it out!
3. Tell it out among the peo-ple, Je-sus reigns a - bove; Tell it out! Tell it out! Tell it out a-mong the na-tions that His reign is love; Tell it out! Tell it out! Tell it out a-mong the highways and the lanes at home, Let it ring a-cross the mountains and the o - cean's foam, That the wea - ry, heav-y - la - den, need no lon - ger roam; Tell it out! Tell it out!
ff CHORUS
Copyright, 1881, by Ira D. Sankey.

No. 193. Light after Darkness.

"Sorrow and sighing shall flee away."—Isa. 35: 10.

Frances R. Havergal.
Ira D. Sankey.
1. Light aft - er dark - ness, Gain aft- er loss, Strength after weak-ness, Crown aft-er cross;
2. Sheaves aft-er sow - ing, Sun aft- er rain, Sight aft- er myster- y, Peace aft- er pain;
3. Near aft - er dis - tant, Gleam after gloom, Love aft- er loneli-ness, Life aft- er tomb;
Sweet aft - er bit - ter, Hope aft- er fears, Home aft-er wand'ring, Praise aft-er tears.
Joy aft - er sor - row, Calm aft- er blast, Rest aft-er weariness, Sweet rest at last.
Aft - er long ag - o- ny, Rap- ture of bliss, Right was the pathway, Lead- ing to this.
Copyright, 1881, by Ira D. Sankey.
No. 194. Glory be to Jesus' Name.
"Lift up your heads, O ye gates; * * * and the King of glory shall come in."—Ps. 24: 7.
Anon.
Geo. C. Stebbins.
1. Glo - ry, glo - ry be to Je - sus, Glo - ry to His pre- cious name;
2. In the place of His re - jec - tion, Where He suf- fered, where He died,
3. Here was marred His bless - ed vis - age, Here His brow was wreathed with thorn,
4. Yes, tri- umph- ant hal - le - lu - jahs Still a- rise to greet His name;
Sweet it is to sound His prais- es, Blest it is to spread His fame.
Bursts of ho - ly praise as- cend- ing, Greets the glo- rious Cru - ci - fied.
Here the ob - ject of de - ris - ion, Bit - ter taunt and mock- ing scorn.
Sweet it is to sound His prais - es, Blest it is to spread His fame.
Copyright, 1879, by Geo. C. Stebbins.
Chorus.
Glo - ry, glo - ry, hal - le - lu - jah! Glo - ry be to Je - sus' name,

Glory be to Jesus' Name.

Sweet it is to sound His prais - es, Blest it is to spread His fame.

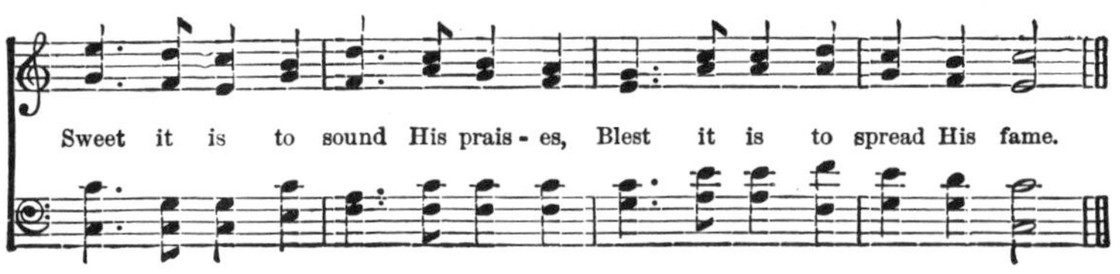

No. 195. Nothing but the Blood of Jesus.

"Without shedding of blood is no remission."—Heb. 9 : 22.

Rev. Robert Lowry. Rev. Robert Lowry.

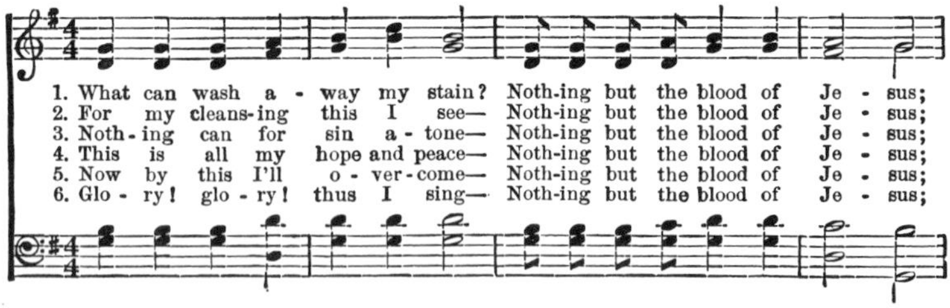

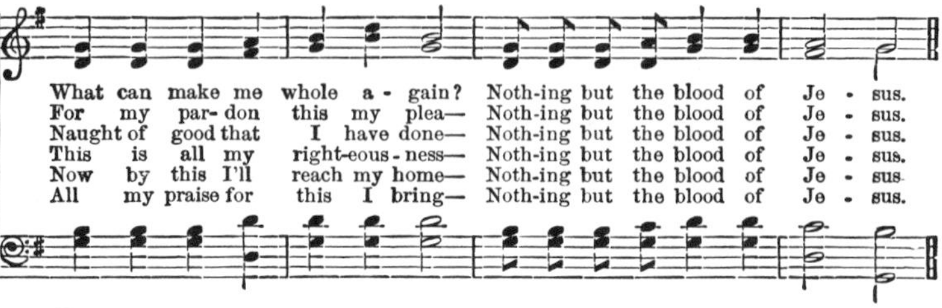

1. What can wash a - way my stain? Noth-ing but the blood of Je - sus;
2. For my cleans-ing this I see— Noth-ing but the blood of Je - sus;
3. Noth - ing can for sin a - tone— Noth-ing but the blood of Je - sus;
4. This is all my hope and peace— Noth-ing but the blood of Je - sus;
5. Now by this I'll o - ver - come— Noth-ing but the blood of Je - sus;
6. Glo - ry! glo - ry! thus I sing— Noth-ing but the blood of Je - sus;

What can make me whole a - gain? Noth-ing but the blood of Je - sus.
For my par- don this my plea— Noth-ing but the blood of Je - sus.
Naught of good that I have done— Noth-ing but the blood of Je - sus.
This is all my right-eous - ness— Noth-ing but the blood of Je - sus.
Now by this I'll reach my home— Noth-ing but the blood of Je - sus
All my praise for this I bring— Noth-ing but the blood of Je - sus.

Refrain.

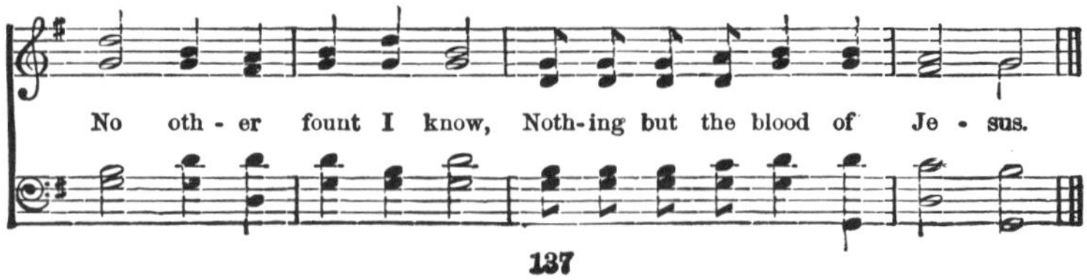

Oh, pre - cious is the flow That makes me white as snow;

No oth - er fount I know, Noth-ing but the blood of Je - sus.

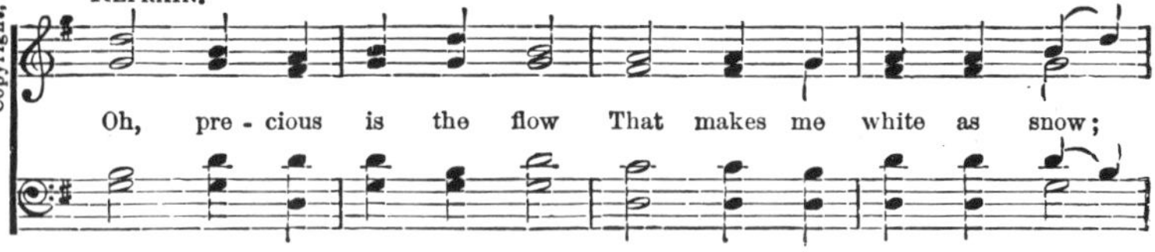

No. 196. None but Christ can Satisfy.

"We also joy in God, through our Lord Jesus Christ, by whom we have now received the atonement."—Rom. 5: 118.

B. E. Arr.
James McGranahan.
1. O Christ in Thee my soul hath found, And found in Thee a - lone, The peace, the joy I sought so long, The bliss till now un - known.
2. I sighed for rest and hap- pi-ness, I yearned for them, not Thee; But while I passed my Sav- iour by, His love laid hold on me.
3. I tried the bro-ken cis-terns, Lord, But ah! the wa- ters failed! E'en as I stooped to drink they fled, And mock'd me as I wailed.
4. The pleasures lost I out sadly mourn'd, But nev- er wept for Thee, Till grace my sightless eyes received, Thy lov- li- ness to see.
Chorus.
Now none but Christ can sat - is - fy, None oth - er name for me, There's love, and life, and lasting joy, Lord Jesus, found in Thee.
for me,
Copyright, 1879, by James McGranahan.
No. 197. Come, Prodigal, Come.
"I will arise and go to my Father."—Luke 15: 18.
Mabel C. Frost.
Ira D. Sankey.
1. O soul in the far a - way coun-try, A - wea- ry, and famished, and sad, There's rest in the home of thy Fa - ther, His welcome will make thy heart glad.
2. A - rise! and come back to thy Fa- ther, He'll meet thee while yet on the way; As - sured of His ten- der com- pas - sion, O why wilt thou long-er de - lay.
3. Although thou hast sinned against heav- en, And weak and un- wor- thy may be; He of- fers thee full res - to - ra - tion, And par- don a- bundant and free.
Copyright, 1881, by Ira D. Sankey.

Come, Prodigal, Come.
Chorus.
Come, come, prod - i - gal, come, And wan - der no long - er a - far from home;
Come, come, prod - i - gal, come, A wel - come a - waits in thy Fa - ther's home.
No. 198. We shall Reign.
"If we suffer, we shall also reign with him."—2 Tim. 2: 12.
Geo. C. Needham.
C. C. Case.
1. When the Lord from heav'n ap - pears, When are ban - ished all our fears,
2. When our eyes the King shall see, In His glo - rious Ma - jes - ty,
3. Debt - ors to His match - less grace, At His feet our crowns will place,
4. Let this hope now pu - ri - fy Those who on Thy word re - ly;
When the sleep - ers from the tomb, With the watch - ers reach their home.
When to Him we're call'd a - bove, Part - ners of His joy and love.
And as a - ges roll a - long, Still will sing the glad new song.
Com - fort to our hearts af - ford, 'Till the com - ing of the Lord.
Copyright, 1880, by C. C. Case.
Chorus.
Then en - throned our Lord with Thee, We shall reign...... E - ter - nal - ly,..............
Then enthroned our Lord with Thee, We shall reign E - ter - nally,
Then en - throned our Lord with thee,............ We shall reign e - ter - nal - ly.
Then enthroned our Lord with Thee, We shall reign e - ter - nal - ly.

No. 199. Redemption Ground.

"The redemption of their soul is precious."—Ps. 49: 8.

El. Nathan.
James McGranahan.
1. Come, sing, my soul, and praise the Lord, Who hath re-deem'd thee by His blood;
2. Once from my God I wandered far, And with His ho - ly will made war:
3. O joy-ous hour when God to me A vis-ion gave of Cal - va - ry:
4. No works of mer - it now I plead, But Je - sus take for all my need;
5. Come, wea-ry soul, and here find rest; Ac - cept re-demp-tion, and be blest:
De - liv-ered thee from chains that bound, And bro't thee to re-demp-tion ground.
But now my songs to God a - bound; I'm stand-ing on re-demp-tion ground.
My bonds were loosed, my soul un - bound; I sang up - on re-demp-tion ground.
No right-eous-ness in me is found, Ex - cept up - on re-demp-tion ground.
The Christ who died, by God is crown'd To par - don on re-demp-tion ground.
Chorus.
Re-demp-tion ground, the ground of peace, Re - demp-tion ground, O won-drous grace;
Here let our praise to God a - bound, Who saves us on re-demp-tion ground.

No. 200. Rise Up and Hasten.

"Rise up, my love, my fair one, and come away."—Song of Sol. 2: 10.

J. Denham Smith. Arr. Arr. by James McGranahan.

1. Rise up, and hast - en! my soul, haste a - long! And speed on thy jour - ney with hope and with song;
Home, home is near - ing, 'tis com - ing in - to view, A lit - tle more of toil - ing and then to earth a - dieu.
2. Why should we lin - ger when heav - en lies be - fore! While earth's fast re - ced - ing, and soon will be no more;
Pleas - ures and treas - ures which once here we knew, No more can they charm us with such a goal in view.
Chorus.
Come then, come, and raise the joy - ful song! Ye chil - dren of the wil - der-ness, our time can - not be long. Home, home, home, oh, why should we de lay? The morn of heav'n is dawn - ing, we're near the break of day.

3 Loved ones in Jesus they've passed on before,
Now resting in glory, they weary are no more;
Toils all are ended, and nothing now but joy,
And praises, ascending their ever glad employ.
Come then, come, &c.

4 No condemnation! how blessed is the word,
And no separation! forever with the Lord;
He will be with us who loved us long before,
And Jesus, our Jesus, is ours for evermore.
Come then, come, &c.

No. 201. The Sweet Story of Old.

"And he took them up in his arms, put his hands upon them, and blessed them."—Mark 10: 16.
Mrs. Jemima Luke.
J. C. Englebrecht.
1. I think when I read that sweet sto - ry of old, When Je - sus was here a-mong men, How He called lit-tle children as lambs to His fold, I should like to have been with them then.
2. I wish that His hands had been placed on my head, That His arm had been thrown a-round me, And that I might have seen His kind look when He said, "Let the lit - tle ones come un - to Me."
3. Yet still to His foot-stool in prayer I may go, And ask for a share in His love; And if I now earn-est - ly seek Him be - low, I shall see Him and hear Him a - bove,
4. In that beau-ti-ful place He is gone to pre - pare, For all that are washed and for - given; And ma - ny dear children are gath - er - ing there, For "Of such is the king-dom of heaven."
Fine. Refrain.
I should like to have been with them then.
"Let the lit - tle ones come un - to Me."
I shall see Him and hear Him a - bove.
For "Of such is the kingdom of heaven."
D.S.
By per. O. Ditson & Co.
No. 202. Jesus, I will Trust Thee.
"I will trust in thee."—Ps. 55: 23.
Mary J. Walker.
Ira D. Sankey.
1. Je-sus, I will trust Thee, trust Thee with my soul; Guilt - y, lost, and help - less, Thou canst make me whole. There is none in heav - en or on earth like Thee:
2. Je-sus, I can trust Thee, trust Thy written word, Since Thy voice of mer - cy I have oft-en heard, When Thy Spir - it teach - eth, to my taste how sweet—
3. Je-sus, I do trust Thee, trust Thee without doubt: "Who-so - ev - er com - eth, Thou wilt not cast out," Faith-ful is Thy prom - ise, precious is Thy blood—
Copyright, 1881, by Ira D. Sankey.
D.S.—Je - sus, I will trust Thee, trust Thee with my soul;

Jesus, I will Trust Thee.
Fine. Chorus.
Thou hast died for sin-ners—therefore Lord for me.
On - ly may I hearken, sit-ting at Thy feet.
These my soul's sal - va - tion, Thou my Sav - iour God!
In Thy love con-fid - ing
Guilt-y, lost, and help-less, Thou canst make me whole.
D.S.
I will seek Thy face, Wor-ship and a - dore Thee, for Thy wondrous grace.
No. 203. Not My Own.
"Ye are not your own, for ye are bought with a price."—1 Cor. 6: 19, 20.
El. Nathan.
James McGranahan.
1. "Not my own," but saved by Je - sus, Who re-deemed me by His blood,
2. "Not my own!" to Christ, my Sav - iour, I be - liev - ing, trust my soul;
3. "Not my own!" my time, my tal - ent, Free - ly all to Christ I bring,
4. "Not my own!" the Lord ac - cepts me, One a - mong the ransomed throng,
Glad - ly I ac - cept the mes - sage, I be - long to Christ the Lord.
Ev - 'ry - thing to Him com - mit - ted, While e - ter - nal a - ges roll.
To be used in joy - ful serv - ice For the glo - ry of my King.
Who in heav'n shall see His glo - ry, And to Je - sus Christ be - long.
Copyright, 1878, by James McGranahan.
Chorus.
"Not my own!" Oh, "not my own!" Je - sus, I........... be-long to
be-
Oh, no! Oh, no! Je - sus, I be - long, be -
long to Thee!
Thee!......... All I have, and all I hope for, Thine for all e - ter - ni - ty.
long to Thee!

No. 204. Over Jordan.

(Read Deut. 11: 31. 8: 7, 8.)

Mrs. M. B. C. Slade. J. R. Murray.

1. With His dear and lov - ing care, Will the Sav - iour lead us on, To the
2. Through the rock - y wil - der - ness, Will the Sav - iour lead us on, To the
2. With His strong and might - y hand, Will the Sav - iour lead us on, To that
4. In the Prom - ised Land to be, Will the Sav - iour lead us on, Till fair

hills and val - leys fair, O - ver Jor - dan? Yes, we'll rest our wea - ry feet
land we shall pos - sess, O - ver Jor - dan? Yes, by night the won-drous ray,
good and pleas - ant land, O - ver Jor - dan? Yes, where vine and ol - ive grow,
Ca - naan's shore we see, O - ver Jor - dan? Yes, to dwell with Thee, at last,

By the crys - tal wa - ters, sweet, When the peace - ful shore we greet,
Cloud - y pil - lar by the day, They shall guide us on our way,
And the brooks and fount - ains flow, Thirst nor hun - ger shall we know,
Guide and lead us, as Thou hast, Till the part - ed wave be passed,

O - ver Jor - dan.

CHORUS.

O - ver Jor - dan! O - ver Jor - dan! Yes, we'll rest our wea - ry feet, By the crys - tal wa - ters sweet, O - ver Jor - dan,

From "Pure Diamonds," by per. Brainard & Sons.

Over Jordan.

O - ver Jor - dan, When the peace - ful shore we'll greet, O - ver Jor - dan.

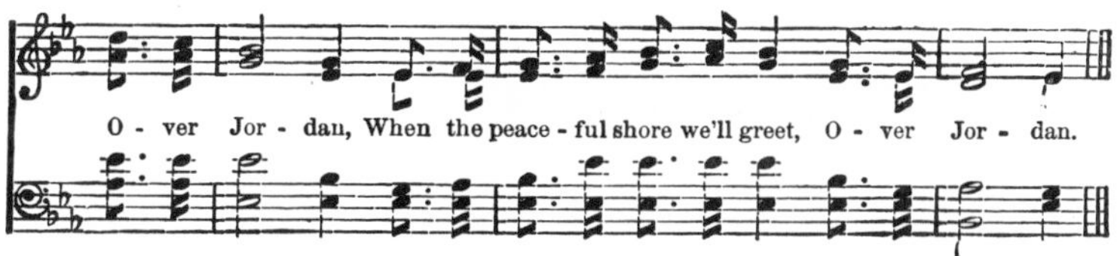

No. 205. Praise Ye the Lord.

"It is good to sing praises unto our God; he healeth the broken in heart * * he telleth the number of the stars."—Ps. 147: 1, 3, 4.

Rous' Version. C. E. Pollock.

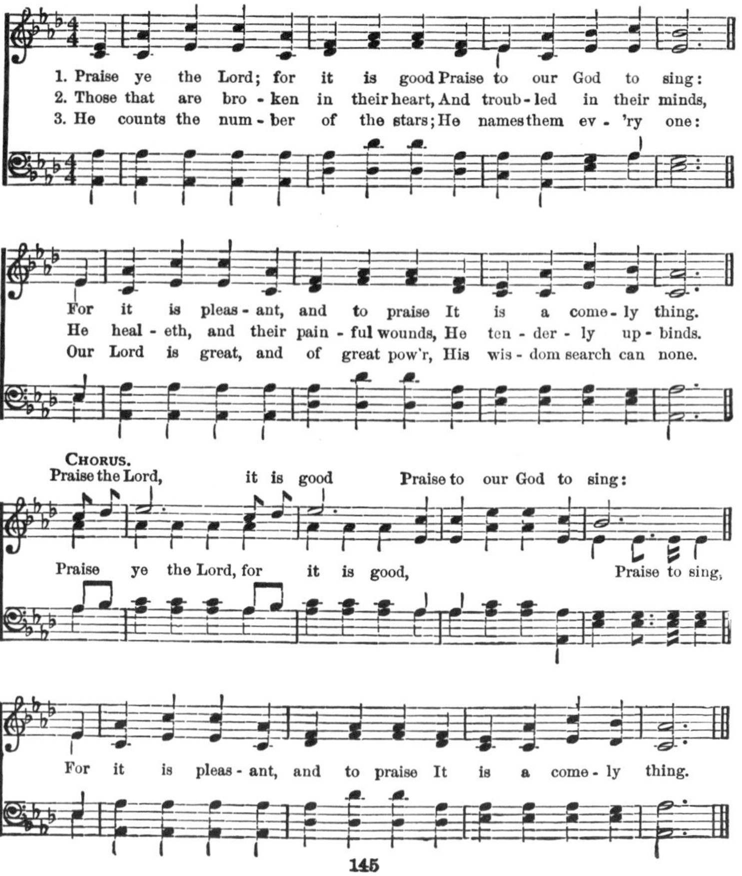

1. Praise ye the Lord; for it is good Praise to our God to sing:
2. Those that are bro - ken in their heart, And troub - led in their minds,
3. He counts the num - ber of the stars; He names them ev - 'ry one:
For it is pleas - ant, and to praise It is a come - ly thing.
He heal - eth, and their pain - ful wounds, He ten - der - ly up - binds.
Our Lord is great, and of great pow'r, His wis - dom search can none.
Chorus.
Praise the Lord, it is good Praise to our God to sing:
Praise ye the Lord, for it is good, Praise to sing,
For it is pleas - ant, and to praise It is a come - ly thing.

Used by per.

No. 206. I Left it all with Jesus.

"Casting all your care upon him, for he careth for you."—1 Pet. 5: 7.

Mrs. E. H. Willis. Arr. James McGranahan.

1. Oh, I left it all with Je-sus, long a-go; long a-go; All my sins I bro't Him and my woe; and my woe; When by faith I saw Him bleeding on the tree; on the tree; Heard His still small whis-per, "'Tis for thee!" "'Tis for thee!"
2. Oh, I leave it all with Je-sus, for He knows, for He knows, How to steal the bitter from life's woes; from life's woes; How to gild the tear of sorrow with His smile, with His smile, Make the des-ert gar-den bloom a-while, bloom a-while,
3. Oh, I leave it all with Je-sus, day by day; day by day; Faith can firmly trust Him, come what may; come what may; Hope has dropp'd for aye her anchor, found her rest; found her rest; In the calm, sure ha-ven of His breast, of His breast,
4. Leave, oh, leave it all with Je-sus, droop-ing soul; droop-ing soul; Tell not half thy sto-ry but the whole; but the whole; Worlds on worlds are hanging ever on His hand, on His hand, Life and death are wait-ing His com-mand, His com-mand,

Chorus.

From my wea-ry heart the bur-den rolled a-way: Hap-py day! hap-py day!
From my weary heart the burden rolled away; rolled a-way; Hap-py day! hap-py day!

Then with all my weakness leaning on His might, All is light! all is light!
Then with all my weakness leaning on His might, on His might, All is light! all is light!

Love es-teems it joy of heav-en to a-bide At His side! at His side!
Love es-teems it joy of heaven to a-bide, to a-bide, At His side! at His side!

Yet His ten-der, lov-ing mer-cy makes thee room: Oh, come home! oh, come home!
Yes, His ten-der loving mercy makes thee room, makes thee room, Oh, come home! oh, come home!

No. 207. Depth of Mercy.

"God is love."—1 JOHN 4: 8.

CHARLES WESLEY. From J. STEVENSON.

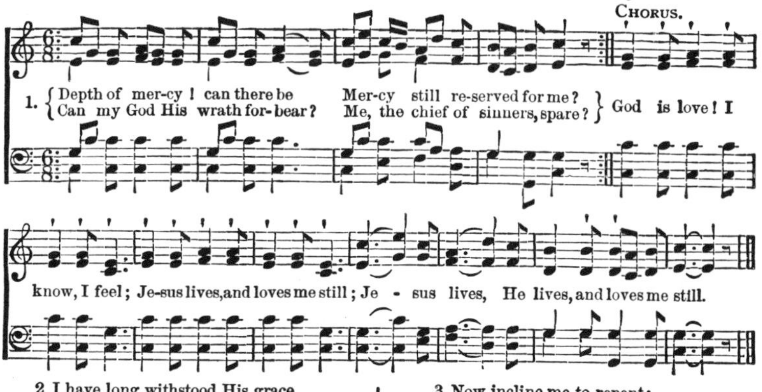

1. { Depth of mer-cy! can there be Mer-cy still re-served for me?
Can my God His wrath for-bear? Me, the chief of sinners, spare? }

CHORUS.

God is love! I know, I feel; Je-sus lives, and loves me still; Je - sus lives, He lives, and loves me still.

2 I have long withstood His grace
Long provoked Him to His face:
Would not hearken to His calls;
Grieved Him by a thousand falls.

3 Now incline me to repent;
Let me now my sins lament;
Now my foul revolt deplore,
Weep, believe, and sin no more.

No. 208. Precious Blood.

"Ye know that ye were not redeemed with corruptible things as silver and gold * * * but with the precious blood of Christ."—1 PET. 1: 18, 19.

MACLEOD WYLIE. GEO. C. STEBBINS.

1. The blood has al-ways precious been, 'Tis precious now to me; Thro' it a-lone my soul has rest, From fear and doubt set free.
2. I will re-member now no more, God's faithful Word has said, The fol-lies and the sins of him For whom my Son has bled.
3. Not all my well-remembered sins Can star-tle or dis-may; The precious blood a-tones for all And bears my guilt a-way.
4. Per-haps this fee-ble frame of mine Will soon in sick-ness lie But rest-ing on the pre-cious blood How peace-ful-ly I'll die.

CHORUS.

Oh, wondrous is the crimson tide Which from my Sav-iour flowed; And still in heav'n my song shall be, The precious, precious blood.

No. 209. Is my Name written There?

"Rejoice because your names are written in heaven."—LUKE 10: 20.

Mrs. MARY A. KIDDER.
FRANK M. DAVIS.
1. Lord, I care not for rich - es, Neith-er sil - ver nor gold; I would make sure of
2. Lord, my sins they are ma - ny, Like the sands of the sea, But Thy blood, oh, my
3. Oh! that beau - ti - ful cit - y, With its man-sions of light, With its glo - ri - fied
heav - en, I would en - ter the fold. In the book of Thy king-dom, With its
Sav - iour! Is suf - fi - cient for me; For Thy prom-ise is writ-ten, In bright
be - ings, In pure gar-ments of white; Where no e - vil thing com-eth, To de -
pa - ges so fair, Tell me, Je - sus, my Sav-iour, Is my name writ-ten there?
let - ters that glow, "Tho' your sins be as scar - let, I will make them like snow."
spoil what is fair; Where the an - gels are watch-ing, Yes, my name's written there.
Used by per.
CHORUS.
Is my name writ - ten there, On the page white and fair?
CHORUS for 2d & 3d Verses. Yes, my name's, &c.
In the book of Thy king - dom, Is my name writ - ten there?
2d & 3d V.—Yes, my name's, &c.

No. 210. My Soul will Overcome.

"They overcame him by the blood of the Lamb."—Rev. 12: 11.

Rev. R. Lowry.
Rev. R. Lowry.
Moderato.
1. Help - less I come to Je - sus' blood, And all my - self re - sign;
2. 'Tis Je - sus gives me life with - in, And nerves me for the fray;
3. Tho' clouds of con - flict hide my view, And foes are fierce and strong,
I lose my weak - ness in that flood, And gath - er strength di - vine.
He spoiled the hosts of death and sin, And took their pow'r a - way.
In Je - sus' name I'll strug - gle thro', And en - ter heav'n with song.
Refrain.
My soul will o - ver - come by the blood of the Lamb, My soul will o - ver - come by the blood of the Lamb; O - ver - come, o - ver - come, O - ver - come by the blood of the Lamb.
O - ver - come, My soul will o - ver - come.
Copyright, 1876, by Rev. R. Lowry.

No. 211. We Worship Thee.
"Whom having not seen, ye love."—1 Pet. 1: 8.
Frances R. Havergal.
James McGranahan.
Fine.
1. O Saviour, precious Saviour, Whom, yet unseen, we love;
2. O Bringer of salvation, Who wondrously hast wrought
3. In Thee all fulness dwelleth, All grace and pow'r divine;
4. Oh, grant the consummation Of this our song, above,
D.C.—We praise Thee and confess Thee, Our Saviour and our King!
Last v.-And evermore confess Thee, Our Saviour and our King!
O Name of might and favor, All other names above.
Thyself the revelation Of love beyond our thought.
The glory that excelleth, O Son of God, is Thine.
In endless adoration And everlasting love.
Chorus.
D.C.
We worship Thee! we bless Thee! To Thee alone we sing!......
Last v. Then shall we praise and bless Thee! Where perfect praises ring!......
Copyright, 1879, by James McGranahan.
No. 212. Trust On!
"Trust in the Lord with all thine heart."—Prov. 3: 5.
Anon.
Geo. C. Stebbins.
1. Trust on! trust on believer! Tho' long the conflict be, Thou yet shalt prove vic-
2. Trust on! trust on; thy failings May bow thee to the dust, But in thy deepest
3. Trust on! the danger presses; Temptation strong is near, Yet o'er life's dangerous
4. O Christ is strong to save us, He is a faithful Friend, Trust on! trust on! be-
torious; Thy God shall fight for thee.
sorrow, O give not up thy trust.
rapids, He shall thy passage steer.
liever, O trust Him to the end.
Chorus.
Trust on! (trust on!) Trust on! (trust on!) Tho'
Copyright, 1881, by Geo. C. Stebbins.

Trust On!

dark the night and drear; Trust on! (trust on!) trust on! (trust on!) The morning dawn is near.

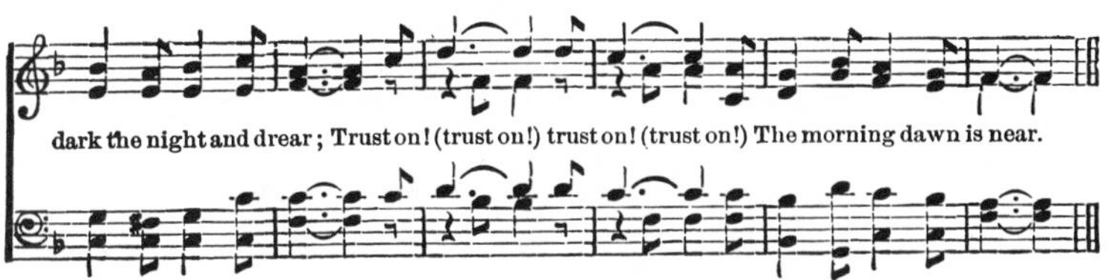

No. 213. Say, are You Ready?

"Therefore be ye also ready."—Matt. 24: 44.

A. S. Kieffer. T. C. O'Kane.

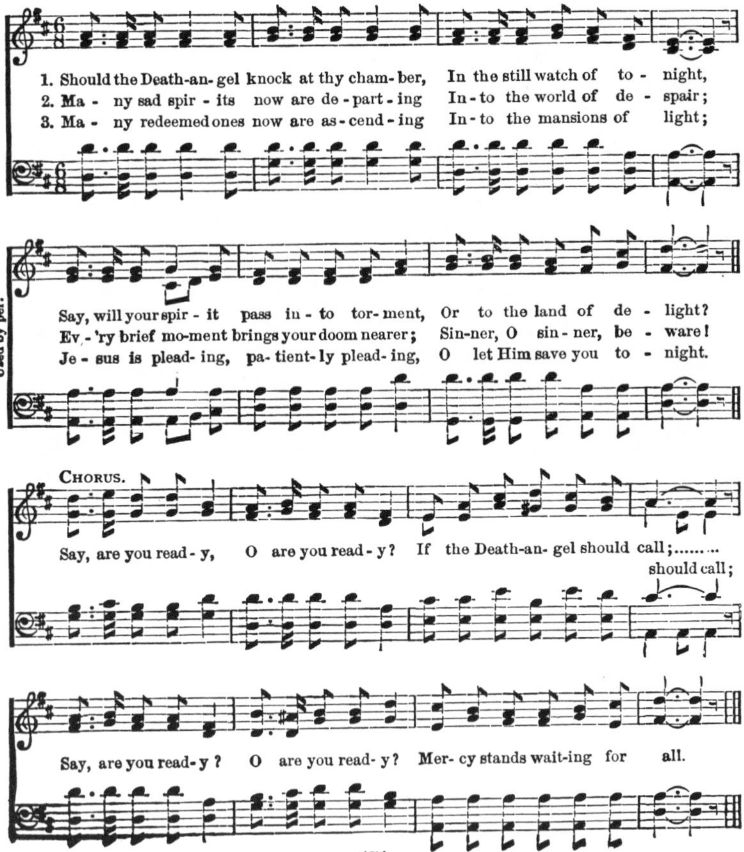

1. Should the Death-an-gel knock at thy cham-ber, In the still watch of to - night,
2. Ma - ny sad spir - its now are de - part - ing In - to the world of de - spair;
3. Ma - ny redeemed ones now are as - cend - ing In - to the mansions of light;
Say, will your spir - it pass in - to tor-ment, Or to the land of de - light?
Ev - 'ry brief mo-ment brings your doom nearer; Sin-ner, O sin - ner, be - ware!
Je - sus is plead - ing, pa - tient - ly plead - ing, O let Him save you to - night.
Chorus.
Say, are you read - y, O are you read - y? If the Death-an - gel should call;........
should call;
Say, are you read - y? O are you read - y? Mer - cy stands wait - ing for all.

Used by per.

No. 214. Onward Go!

"Forgetting those things which are behind, and reaching forth unto those things which are before."—PHIL. 3 : 13.

E. B. Arr. JAMES McGRANAHAN.

1. Trust - ing in the Lord thy God, On - ward go! on - ward go!
2. Has He call'd thee to the plough? On - ward go! on - ward go!
3. Has He giv'n thee gold - en grain? On - ward go! on - ward go!
4. Has He said the end is near? On - ward go! on - ward go!
5. In this lit - tle mo - ment then, On - ward go! on - ward go!
Hold - ing fast His prom - ised word,
Night is com - ing, serve Him now;
Sow, and thou shalt reap a - gain;
Serv - ing Him with ho - ly fear,
In thy ways ac - knowledge Him;
On - ward go!
On-ward! on-ward go!
On-ward! on-ward!
On - ward! On-ward! on-ward!
Ne'er de - ny His worth - y Name, Tho' it bring re - proach and shame;
Faith and love in ser - vice blend; On His might - y arm de - pend;
To thy Mas - ter's gate re - pair, Watching be and wait - ing there;
Christ thy por - tion, Christ thy stay, Heav'n-ly bread up - on the way,
Let His mind be found in thee: Let His will thy pleas - ure be;
Spread - ing still His won - drous fame,
Stand - ing fast un - til the end,
He will hear and an - swer prayer;
Lead - ing on to glo - rious day;
Thus in life and lib - er - ty,
On - ward go!
On-ward, on-ward! On-ward go!
On-ward go!
On-ward, on-ward go!
Copyright, 1879, by James McGranahan.

No. 215. More than Tongue can Tell.
"Greater love hath no man than this."—1 John 15 : 13.
J. E. Hall. Arr.
J. E. Hall.
1. The love that Je - sus had for me, To suf - fer on the cru - el tree,
2. The ma - ny sor - rows that He bore, And oh, that crown of thorns He wore,
3. The peace I have in Him, my Lord, Who pleads be - fore the throne of God
4. The joy that comes when He is near, The rest He gives, so free from fear,
That I a ran-somed soul might be, Is more than tongue can tell.
That I might live for ev - er - more, Is more than tongue can tell.
The mer - it of His pre - cious blood, Is more than tongue can tell.
The hope in Him so bright and clear, Is more than tongue can tell.
By permission of F. A. North & Co.
Chorus.
His love is more than tongue can tell; than tongue can tell; His love is more than tongue can tell; than tongue can tell;
The love that Je - sus had for me Is more than tongue can tell.
No. 216. Hear Thou my Prayer.
"Hear my prayer, O Lord, give ear to my supplications."—Ps. 143 : 1.
Rev. Henry C. Graves.
Geo. C. Stebbins.
1. All - see - ing, gra-cious Lord— My heart be - fore Thee lies; All sin of thought and
2. Thou knowest all my need, My in-most thought dost see; Ah, Lord! from all al-
3. Thou ho - ly bless - ed One, To me, I pray, draw near; My spir - it fill, O
4. Bind Thou my life to Thine, To me Thy life is given; While I my all to

Hear Thou my Prayer.

Chorus.
life abhorred, My soul to Thee would rise.
lurements freed, Like Thee transformed I'd be.
heavenly Son, With lov-ing, God - ly fear.
Thee re- sign, Thou art my all in heaven.
Hear Thou my prayer, O God, U-
rit.
nite my heart to Thee; Beneath Thy love, beneath Thy rod, From sin de- liv - er me.
Copyright, 1879, by F. H. Revell.

No. 217. Is your Lamp Burning?

"Let your light so shine before men, that they may see your good works, and glorify your Father which is in heaven."—Matt. 5 : 16.

Mrs. E. M. H. Gates.
C. C. Williams.
1. Say, is your lamp burn - ing, my broth - er? I pray you look
2. Up - on the dark moun- tains they stum - ble, They are bruised on the
3. If once all the lamps that are light - ed Should stead - i - ly
quick- ly and see; For if it were burn - ing, then sure - ly, Some
rocks and they lie With white plead- ing fa - ces turn'd up- ward, To the
blaze in a line, Wide o - ver the land and the o - cean, What a
beam would fall bright- ly on me. There are ma - ny and ma - ny a-
clouds and the pit - i - ful sky. There is ma - ny a lamp that is
gir - dle of glo - ry would shine! How all the dark pla - ces would
D.S.—Say, is your lamp burn-ing, my
Copyright, 1880, by James McGranahan.

Is your Lamp Burning?
round you, Who fol - low wher - ev - er you go,......... If you
light - ed— We be - hold them a - near and a - far;........ But not
bright - en! How the mists would roll up and a - way!...... How the
broth - er? I pray you look quick - ly and see; For
D.S. for Chorus
thought that they walk'd in the shad - ow, Your lamp would burn brighter, I know.
ma - ny a-mong them, my broth - er, Shine stead - i - ly on like a star.
earth would laugh out in her glad-ness, To hail the mil - len - ni - al day!
if it were burning, then sure - ly Some beam would fall brightly on me!
No. 218. We are Going Home.
"And so shall we ever be with the Lord."—1 Thess. 5: 17.
El. Nathan.
James McGranahan.
1. Our way is oft - en rug - ged While here on earth we roam, And thorns are in the
2. To Ma - rah's bit - ter wa - ters We oft have murm'ring come, But God the cup has
3. When of the des - ert wea - ry, Our God His grace has shown, By rest - ing us at
4. With hun - ger oft - en faint - ing, We've made complain - ing moan; But, fed by heavenly
5. Some stand to - day on Ne - bo, The jour - ney near - ly done, And some are in the
Copyright, 1881, by James McGranahan.
Chorus.
We're go - ing, go - ing,
path - way, But we are go - ing home.
sweet - ened; And so we're go - ing home.
E - lim, With sweet fore - tastes of home.
man - na, We still are go - ing home.
val - ley; But all are go - ing home.
go - ing, we are go - ing, Yes,
we are go - ing home; We soon shall cross the riv - er, And be with Christ at home.
going home;

No. 219. Come unto Me, and Rest.

"Come unto me, all ye that labor and are heavy-laden, and I will give you rest."—MATT. 11 : 28.

EL. NATHAN. JAMES McGRANAHAN.

1. Broth-er, art thou worn and wea-ry, Tempt-ed, tried, and sore op-press'd? List-en to the word of Je-sus, "Come un-to me, and rest!"
2. Oh, He knows the dark fore-bod-ings Of the con-science-troub-led breast; And to such His word is giv-en, "Come un-to me, and rest!"
3. To the Lord bring all your bur-den, Put the prom-ise to the test; Hear Him say, your Bur-den-Bear-er, "Come un-to me, and rest!"
4. If in sor-row thou art weep-ing, Griev-ing for the loved ones missed, Sure-ly then to you He whis-pers, "Come un-to me, and rest!"
5. Trust to Him for all thy fu-ture, He will give thee what is best; Why then fear when He is say-ing, "Come un-to me, and rest!"

REFRAIN.

"Come un-to me, and rest!" "Come un-to me, and rest!"

Come, Oh, come and rest! Come, Oh, come and rest!

Come, ye wea-ry, heav-y-la-den, "Come un-to me, and rest!"

No. 220. Gathering Home.

"Ye shall be gathered one by one O ye children of Israel."—Ps. 27: 12.

MARY LESLIE. W. A. OGDEN.

1. They're gath'ring homeward from ev-'ry land, One by one! one by one!
2. Be-fore they rest they pass thro' the strife, One by one! one by one!
3. We too must come to the riv-er-side, One by one! one by one!
4. Oh, Jesus, Re-deem-er, we look to Thee, One by one! one by one!

Gathering Home.

As their wea - ry feet touch the shin - ing strand, Yes, one by one!
Thro' the wa - ters of death they en - ter life, Yes, one by one!
We are near - er its wa - ters each e - ven - tide, Yes, one by one!
We lift up our voi - ces tremb - ling - ly, Yes, one by one!
They rest with the Sav - iour, they wait their crown, Their trav - el-stained
To some are the floods of the riv - er still, As they ford on their
We can hear the noise of the dash - ing stream, Oft now and a -
The waves of the riv - er are dark and cold, But we know the
gar-ments are all laid down; They wait the white rai-ment the Lord shall pre-pare
way to the heaven - ly hill; The waves to oth - ers run fierce - ly and wild
gain, thro' our life's deep dream; Some-times the dark floods all the banks o - ver-flow,
place where our feet shall hold; O Thou who didst pass thro' the deep - est mid-night,
For all who the glo - ry with Him shall share.
Yet they reach the home of the un - de - filed.
Some - times in rip - ples and small waves go.
Now guide us, and send us the staff and light.
Refrain.
Gath'ring home! gath'ring home
Ford-ing the riv - er one by one! Gath'ring home! gath'ring home, Yes, one by one!
By permission of W. W. Whitney, Toledo, O.

No. 221. Only a Little While.

"Weeping may endure for a night, but joy cometh in the morning."—Ps. 30: 5.

Mrs. M. P. A. Crozier. Geo. C. Stebbins.

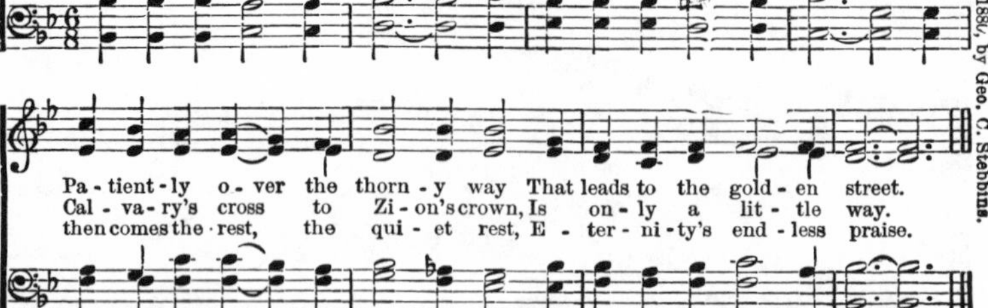
1. On - ly a lit - tle while Of walk-ing with wea - ry feet,
2. Suf - fer if God shall will, And work for Him while we may, From
3. On - ly a lit - tle while, For toil - ing a few short days, And
Pa - tient - ly o - ver the thorn - y way That leads to the gold - en street.
Cal - va - ry's cross to Zi - on's crown, Is on - ly a lit - tle way.
then comes the rest, the qui - et rest, E - ter - ni - ty's end - less praise.
Copyright, 1884, by Geo. C. Stebbins.

No. 222. I hear the Words of Jesus.

"Christ is all, and in all."—Col. 3: 2.

Geo. C. Needham. C. C. Case.

1. I hear the words of Je - sus, They speak of peace with God;
2. His word di - vine - ly bless - ed, It shows me what I am;
3. Oh! hear the words of Je - sus, The tid - ings are for thee;
I see the Lamb, Christ Je - sus, Who bore my heav - y load;
His cross it brings sal - va - tion, The vic - tim was the Lamb;
Oh, clasp the cross of Je - sus, And there for ref - uge flee;
I trust the blood of Je - sus, From sin it sets me free,
His blood pro - cur - eth par - don, And jus - ti - fies the soul,
Oh! trust the blood of Je - sus, Be saved this ver - y hour;
Copyright, 1881, by C. C. Case.

I hear the Words of Jesus.

I love the name of Je - sus, Who gave Him - self for me.
His name, how sweet and pre - cious, It makes the sin - ner whole.
Oh! love the name of Je - sus, Blest name of won - drous pow'r.
No. 223. Jesus is my Saviour.
"—went on his way rejoicing."—Acts 8 : 39.
Rev. R. Lowry.
Rev. R. Lowry.
1. My soul is hap - py all day long— Je - sus is my Sav - iour;
2. My heav - y load of sin is gone— Je - sus is my Sav - iour;
3. I heard the voice of mer - cy call— Je - sus is my Sav - iour;
4. Now will I tell it all a - round—Je - sus is my Sav - iour;
And all my life is full of song— Je - sus died for me.
At His dear cross I laid it down— Je - sus died for me.
I sim - ply trust - ed, that was all— Je - sus died for me.
How sweet a bless - ing I have found— Je - sus died for me.
Copyright, 1878, by Robert Lowry.
Chorus.
Hal - le - lu - jah! Hal - le - lu - jah! To the lov - ing Lamb for sin - ners slain;
Hal - le - lu - jah! Hal - le - lu - jah! To the Lamb who lives a - gain.

No. 224. I am Coming.

"Come unto me all ye that labor and are heavy laden, and I will give you rest."—MATT. 9: 28.
HELEN R. YOUNG.
IRA D. SANKEY.
1. Sad and wea - ry, lone and drear - y, Lord, I would Thy call o - bey;
2. Thou, the Ho - ly, meek and low - ly, Je - sus, un - to Thee I come;
3. Here a - bid - ing, in Thee hid - ing, Seeks my wea - ry soul to rest,
4. Be Thou near me, keep and cheer me, Thro' life's dark and storm - y way;
Thee be - liev - ing, Christ re - ceiv - ing, I would come to Thee to - day.
Keep me ev - er, let me nev - er From Thy bless - ed keep-ing roam.
Till the dawn - ing of the morn - ing, When I wake a - mong the blest.
Turn my sad - ness in - to glad - ness, Turn my dark - ness in - to day.
Copyright, 1881, by Ira D. Sankey.
CHORUS.
I am com - ing, I am com - ing, Com - ing, Sav - iour to be blessed;
I am com - ing, I am com - ing, Com - ing, Lord, to Thee for rest.
No. 225. Deliverance will Come.
"We are journeying unto the place of which the Lord said, I will give you."—NUM. 10: 29.
J. B. M.
REV. JNO. B. MATTHIAS.
1. I saw a way - worn trav' - ler In tat - ter'd gar - ments clad,
His back was la - den heav - y, His strength was al - most gone,
2. The sum - mer sun was shin - ing, The sweat was on his brow,
But he kept press - ing on - ward, For he was wend - ing home;
3. The song - sters in the ar - bor, That stood be - side the way,
His watch - word be - ing "On - ward!" He stopped his ears and ran,

Deliverance will Come.
And strug-gling up the moun-tain, It seem'd that He was sad;
Yet he shout-ed as he journeyed, De-liv-er-ance will come.
His gar-ments worn and dust-y, His step seemed ver-y slow:
Still shout-ing as he journeyed, De-liv-er-ance will come.
At-tract-ed his at-ten-tion, In-vit-ing his de-lay:
Still shout-ing as he journeyed, De-liv-er-ance will come.
CHORUS.
Then palms of vic-to-ry, crowns of glo-ry, Palms of vic-to-ry I shall bear.
4 I saw him in the evening,
The sun was bending low,
He'd overtopped the mountain,
And reached the vale below:
He saw the golden city,—
His everlasting home,—
And shouted loud, Hosanna,
Deliverance will come!
5 While gazing on that city,
Just o'er the narrow flood,
A band of holy angels
Came from the throne of God:
They bore him on their pinions
Safe o'er the dashing foam;
And joined him in his triumph,—
Deliverance had come!
6 I heard the song of triumph
They sang upon that shore,
Saying, Jesus has redeemed us
To suffer nevermore:
Then, casting his eyes backward
On the race which he had run,
He shouted loud, Hosanna,
Deliverance has come!
No. 226. Take me as I am.
"Hear my prayer, O Lord, and let my cry come unto thee."—Ps. 102: 1.
ELIZA H. HAMILTON.
GEO. C. STEBBINS.
Copyright, 1881, by Geo. C. Stebbins.
1. Je-sus, my Lord, to Thee I cry, Un-less Thou help me I must die; Oh, bring Thy free sal-va-tion nigh, And take me as I am.
2. Help-less I am and full of guilt, But yet for me Thy blood was spilt; And Thou canst make me what thou wilt, And take me as I am.
3. I bow be-fore Thy mer-cy-seat, Be-hold me, Sav-iour, at Thy feet; Thy work begin, Thy work complete, And take me as I am.
4. If Thou hast work for me to do, In-spire my will, my heart re-new; And work both in, and by me too, And take me as I am.
5. And when at last the work is done, The bat-tle fought, the victory won; Still, still my cry shall be a-lone, Oh, take me as I am.
CHORUS.
Take me as I am,

Take me as I am.

Take me as I am; Lord, I give myself to Thee, Oh, take me as I am.

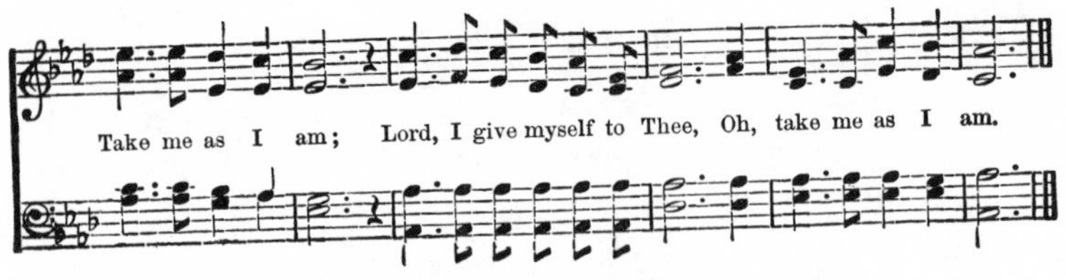

No. 227. Doers of the Word.

"Be ye doers of the word, and not hearers only, deceiving your own selves."—JAMES I: 22.

EL. NATHAN. JAMES MCGRANAHAN.

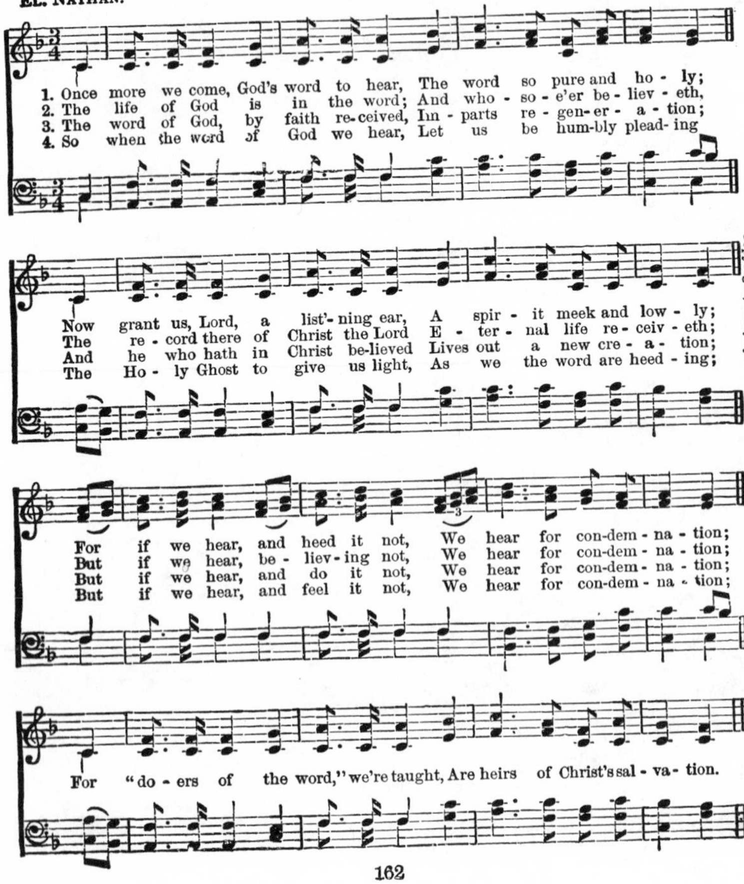

1. Once more we come, God's word to hear, The word so pure and ho - ly;
2. The life of God is in the word; And who - so - e'er be - liev - eth,
3. The word of God, by faith re-ceived, Im - parts re - gen - er - a - tion;
4. So when the word of God we hear, Let us be hum-bly plead- ing
Now grant us, Lord, a list'- ning ear, A spir - it meek and low - ly;
The re - cord there of Christ the Lord E - ter - nal life re - ceiv - eth;
And he who hath in Christ be-lieved Lives out a new cre - a - tion;
The Ho - ly Ghost to give us light, As we the word are heed - ing;
For if we hear, and heed it not, We hear for con-dem - na - tion;
But if we hear, be - liev - ing not, We hear for con-dem - na - tion;
But if we hear, and do it not, We hear for con-dem - na - tion;
But if we hear, and feel it not, We hear for con-dem - na - tion;
For "do - ers of the word," we're taught, Are heirs of Christ's sal - va - tion.

No. 228. We Praise Thee and Bless Thee.

"Oh ye servants of the Lord, praise the name of the Lord."—Ps. 113: 1.

EL. NATHAN. JAMES MCGRANAHAN.

1. We praise Thee and bless Thee, Our Fa-ther in heaven, For the joy of sal-va-tion Thy gos-pel hath given.
2. We praise Thee and bless Thee: Once sin-ful and sad, By the word thou hast giv-en, To Christ we were led.
3. We praise Thee and bless Thee: The Spir-it hath come To dwell with, and teach us, And guide us safe home.
CHORUS.
Hal-le-lu-jah! we praise Thee Thro' Je-sus our Lord; Hal-le-lu-jah! we bless Thee For the gift of Thy word!

4 We praise Thee and bless Thee,
For food by the way;
The manna from heaven
Provided each day.

5 We praise Thee and bless Thee;
Thy word hath gone forth,
That Christ shall be King and
Reign over the earth.

6 We praise Thee and bless Thee,
And wait His return
To fulfil every promise
He made to His own.

7 We praise Thee and bless Thee:
We'll reign with Him then,
To praise Thee and bless Thee
For ever. Amen.

No. 229. Thy Will be Done!

"Thy will be done in earth, as it is in heaven."—MATT. 6: 10.

CHARLOTTE ELLIOTT. JAMES MCGRANAHAN.

1. My God and Fa-ther, while I stray Far from my home, on life's rough way, Oh, teach me from my heart to say, "Thy will be done!"
2. What tho' in lone-ly grief I sigh For friends be-loved, no lon-ger nigh, Sub-mis-sive still would I re-ply, "Thy will be done!"
3. Let but my faint-ing heart be blest With Thy sweet Spir-it for its guest, My God, to Thee I leave the rest, "Thy will be done!"
4. Re-new my will from day to day; Blend it with Thine; and take a-way All now that makes it hard to say, "Thy will be done!"
5. Then when on earth I breathe no more The prayer oft mixed with tears be-fore, I'll sing up-on a hap-pier shore, "Thy will be done!"

REFRAIN.
Thy will be done! Thy will be done!
Thy will— Thy will be done! Thy will— Thy will be done!
Oh, teach me from my heart to say, "Thy will be done!"
Sub - mis - sive still would I re - ply, "Thy will be done!"
My God, to Thee I leave the rest, "Thy will be done!"
All now that makes it hard to say, "Thy will be done!"
I'll sing up - on a hap - pier shore, "Thy will be done!"
No. 230.
Hide Thou Me.
"Thou art my hiding place."—Ps. 32: 7.
FANNY J. CROSBY.
REV. ROBERT LOWRY.
1. In Thy cleft, O Rock of A - ges, Hide Thou me; When the fit - ful tempest ra - ges, Hide Thou me; Where no mor - tal arm can sev - er From my heart Thy love for - ev - er, Hide me, O Thou Rock of A - ges, Safe in Thee.
2. From the snare of sin - ful pleas-ure, Hide Thou me; Thou, my Soul's e - ter - nal treas - ure, Hide Thou me; When the world its power is wield - ing, And my heart is al - most yielding, Hide me, O Thou Rock of A - ges, Safe in Thee.
3. In the lone - ly night of sor - row, Hide Thou me; Till in glo - ry dawns the mor - row, Hide Thou me; In the sight of Jor - dan's bil - low, Let Thy bo - som be my pil - low; Hide me, O Thou Rock of A - ges, Safe in Thee.
Copyright, 1880, by Biglow & Main.

No. 231. I Never Knew You.

"I never knew you: depart from me."—Matt. 7: 23.

Mrs. G. C. Needham.
C. C. Case.
1. When the King in His beau - ty shall come to His throne, And a - round Him are gath-er'd His lov'd ones, His own; There be some who will knock at His fair pal - ace door, To be an-swered with - in "There is mer - cy no more."
2. They had known whence He came, and the grace which He brought; In their pres - ence He heal'd, in their streets He had taught; They had mention'd His name and their friend-ship pro-fess'd; But they nev - er be - lieved, for of them He con - fess'd;
3. Now the right - eous are reign - ing with A - bra - ham there; But for these is ap-point-ed an end - less de - spair; It is vain that they call: He once knock'd at their gate, But they wel-com'd Him not; so now this is their fate:
4. O sin - ner, give heed to this sto - ry of gloom, For the hour is fast near-ing that fix - es your doom: Will you still re - ject mer - cy? still hard - en your heart? Oh, then, what will you do as the King cries?—"De-part!"
Chorus.
"I have nev - er known you," "I have nev - er known you," "I have nev - er, I have nev - er, I have nev - er known you."
Copyright, 1881, by C. C. Case.

No. 232. Only Waiting.

"The Lord direct your hearts into......the patient waiting for Christ."—2 Thess. 3: 5.

W. G. Irvin. J. H. Fillmore.

1. I am wait-ing for the morn-ing Of the bless-ed day to dawn,
2. I am wait-ing; worn and wea-ry With the bat-tle and the strife,
3. Wait-ing, hop-ing, trust-ing ev - er, For a home of boundless love;
4. Hop-ing soon to meet the lov'd ones Where the "ma-ny mansions" be;
When the sor-row and the sad-ness Of this change-ful life are gone.
Hop-ing when the war-fare's o-ver To re-ceive a crown of life.
Like a pil-grim, look-ing for-ward To the land of bliss a-bove.
List-'ning for the hap-py wel-come Of my Sav-iour call-ing me.
Used by per.
Chorus.
I am wait - - - ing, on-ly wait-ing, Till this
I am wait-ing, wait-ing, wait-ing, on-ly wait-ing, on-ly wait-ing, Till this
wea - - ry life is o'er; On-ly wait - - ing for my
wea-ry, wea-ry, weary—Till this weary life is o'er; On-ly waiting, waiting, waiting for my
wel-come,
welcome, for my welcome, From my Sav-iour on the oth - er shore.

No. 233. Oh, Revive Us by Thy Word.

"I will cause the shower to come down in his season. There shall be showers of blessing."—EZEK. 34: 26.

EL. NATHAN. JAMES MCGRANAHAN.

1. Heav'-nly Fa - ther, we Thy chil - dren, Gath-er'd round our ris - en Lord,
2. Gra - cious gales of heav'nly bless - ing In Thy love to us af - ford;
3. Weak and wea - ry in the con - flict, "Wrestling not with flesh and blood,"
4. With Thy strength, O Mas-ter, gird us: Be our Guide and be our Guard:

Lift our hearts in earn - est plead - ing: Oh, re - vive us by Thy word!
Let us feel Thy Spir - it's pres - ence, Oh, re - vive us by Thy word!
Help us, Lord, as faint we fal - ter; Oh, re - vive us by Thy word!
Fill us with Thy ho - ly Spir - it, Oh, re - vive us by Thy word!

CHORUS.

Send re - fresh-ing, send re - fresh-ing From Thy pres - ence, gra-cious Lord!
Send re - fresh - ing, send re - fresh - ing, And re - vive us by Thy word!

No. 234. Jesus is Coming.

"The Lord himself shall descend from heaven."—1 THESS. 4: 16.

EL. NATHAN. JAMES MCGRANAHAN.

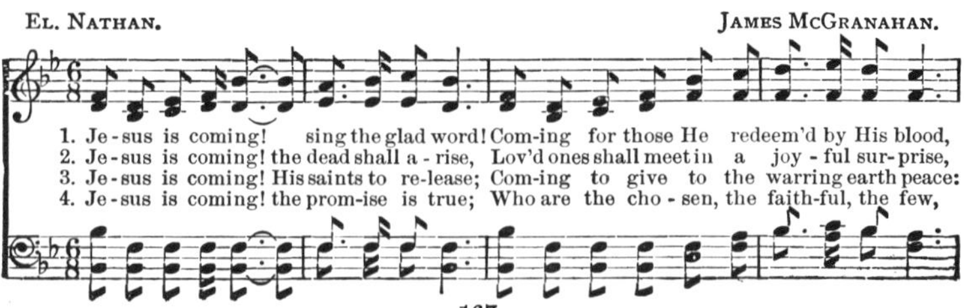
1. Je - sus is coming! sing the glad word! Com-ing for those He redeem'd by His blood,
2. Je - sus is coming! the dead shall a - rise, Lov'd ones shall meet in a joy - ful sur-prise,
3. Je - sus is coming! His saints to re-lease; Com-ing to give to the warring earth peace:
4. Je - sus is coming! the prom-ise is true; Who are the cho - sen, the faith-ful, the few,

Jesus is Coming.
Com - ing to reign as the glo - ri - fied Lord! Je - sus is com-ing a - gain!
Caught up to - geth - er to Him in the skies. Je - sus is com-ing a - gain!
Sin - ning, and sigh-ing, and sor - row, shall cease. Je - sus is com-ing a - gain!
Wait - ing and watching, pre - pared for re - view? Je - sus is com-ing a - gain!
Copyright, 1880, by James McGranahan.
CHORUS.
Je - sus is coming, is coming a-gain! Je - sus is com-ing a - gain!
Yes, Je - sus is coming! Oh,
Shout the glad tid - ings o'er mountain and plain! Je - sus is com-ing a - gain!
No. 235.
Singing as we Journey.
"Then was our mouth filled with singing."—Ps. 126: 2.
LUCY J. RIDER.
LUCY J. RIDER.
1. We are chil-dren of a King, Heav'nly King, Heav'nly King, We are children
2. We are trav'ling to our home, Bless - ed home, Bless - ed home, We are trav'ling
3. Full of joy we on-ward go, Heav'nward go, Homeward go, Full of joy we
of a King, Sing - ing as we jour - ney; Je - sus Christ our Guard and Guide, Bids us,
to our home, Sing - ing as we jour - ney; Tow'rd a cit - y out of sight Where will
on-ward go Sing - ing as we jour - ney; Sing - ing all the jour - ney thro'—Singing
Copyright, 1878, by F. H. Revell.
noth - ing ter - ri - fied, Fol - low close - ly at His side, Sing - ing as we jour - ney.
fall no shade of night, For our Sav - iour is its light, Sing - ing as we jour - ney.
hearts are brave and true—Singing till our home we view, Sing - ing as we jour - ney.

No. 236. Who is on the Lord's Side?

"Thine are we, David, and on thy side, thou son of Jesse."—1 CHRON. 12: 18.

FRANCES R. HAVERGAL.
IRA D. SANKEY.
Spirited.
Copyright, 1881, by Ira D. Sankey.
1. Who is on the Lord's side? Who will serve the King? Who will be His
2. Not for weight of glo - ry, Not for crown and palm, En - ter we the
3. Je - sus, Thou hast bought us, Not with gold or gem, But with Thine own
4. Fierce may be the con - flict, Strong may be the foe, But the King's own
help - ers, Oth - er lives to bring? Who will leave the world's side?
ar - my, Raise the war - rior - psalm; But for love that claim - eth
life - blood, For Thy di - a - dem; With Thy bless - ing fill - ing
ar - my, None can o - ver - throw; Round His stan - dard rang - ing,
Who will face the foe? Who is on the Lord's side? Who for Him will go?
Lives for whom He died, He whom Je - sus nam - eth Must be on His side.
All who come to Thee, Thou hast made us will - ing, Thou hast made us free.
Vic - t'ry is se - cure, For His truth un - chang - ing, Makes the tri - umph sure.
CHORUS.
Who is on the Lord's side? Who will serve the King? Who will be His
help - ers, Oth - er lives to bring? By Thy grand re - demp - tion,
By Thy grace di - vine, We are on the Lord's side; Sav - iour, we are Thine.

No. 237. Lead me on.

"For thy name's sake lead me and guide me."—Ps. 31 : 3.

C. C. Converse.

1. Trav - 'ling to the bet - ter land, O'er the des - ert's scorch-ing sand,
2. When at Ma - rah, parched with heat, I the spark - ling fount - ain greet,
3. When the wil - der - ness is drear, Show me E - lim's palm-groves near,

Fa - ther! let me grasp Thy hand! Lead me on, lead me on!
Make the bit - ter wa - ters sweet; Lead me on, lead me on!
And her wells as crys - tal clear; Lead me on, lead me on!

Used by per.

4 Through the water, through the fire,
Never let me fall or tire,
Every step brings Canaan nigher:
Lead me on!

5 Bid me stand on Nebo's height,
Gaze upon the land of light,
Then transported with the sight,
Lead me on!

6 When I stand on Jordan's brink,
Never let me fear or shrink;
Hold me, Father, lest I sink;
Lead me on!

7 When the victory is won,
And eternal life begun,
Up to glory lead me on!
Lead me on, lead me on!

No. 238. I've Passed the Cross.

"Passed from death unto life."—John 5 : 24.

P. P. Bliss. James McGranahan.

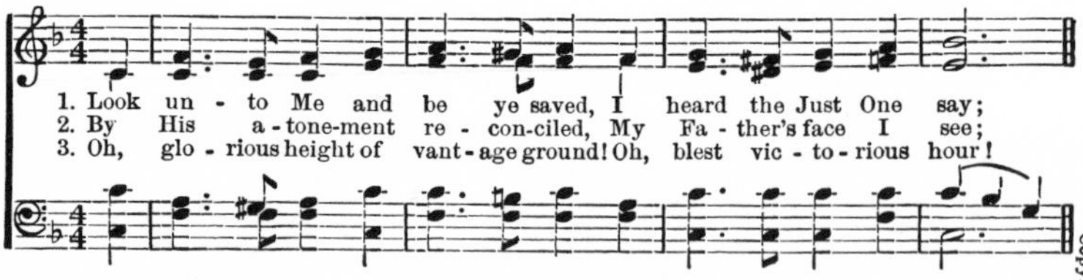

1. Look un - to Me and be ye saved, I heard the Just One say;
2. By His a - tone-ment re - con-ciled, My Fa - ther's face I see;
3. Oh, glo - rious height of vant - age ground! Oh, blest vic - to - rious hour!

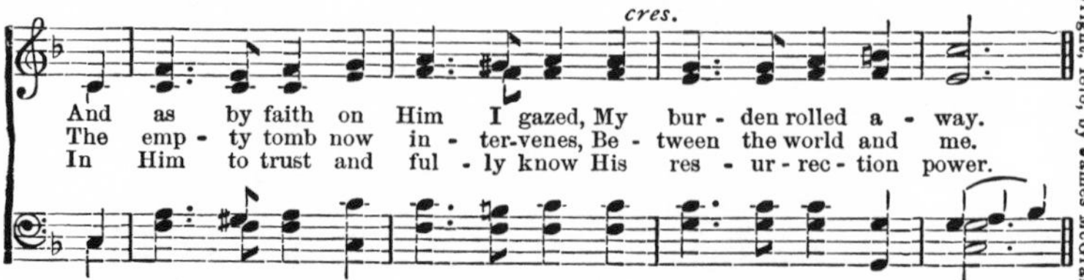

cres.

And as by faith on Him I gazed, My bur - den rolled a - way.
The emp - ty tomb now in - ter-venes, Be - tween the world and me.
In Him to trust and ful - ly know His res - ur - rec - tion power.

Chorus.

I've passed the cross at Cal - va - ry, I'm on the Heav-en side;

I've Passed the Cross.

The world is cru - ci - fied to me, Since Christ my ran - som died;
The world is cru - ci - fied to me, Since Christ my ran - som died.

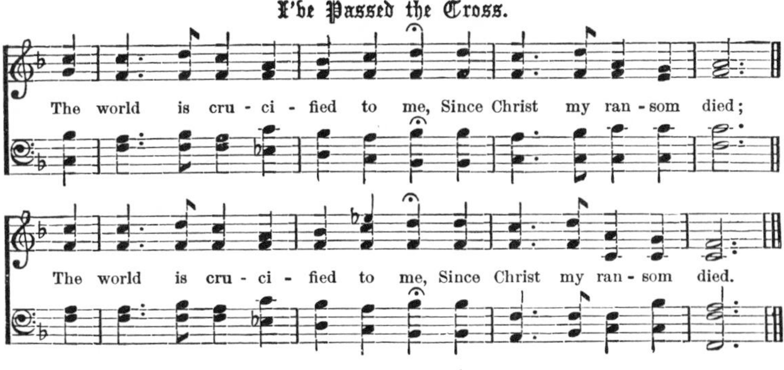

No. 239. We Take the Guilty Sinner's Name.

"These things have I written unto you that ye may know that ye have eternal life."—1 John 5: 13.

Rev. W. P. Mackay. H. F. Williams.

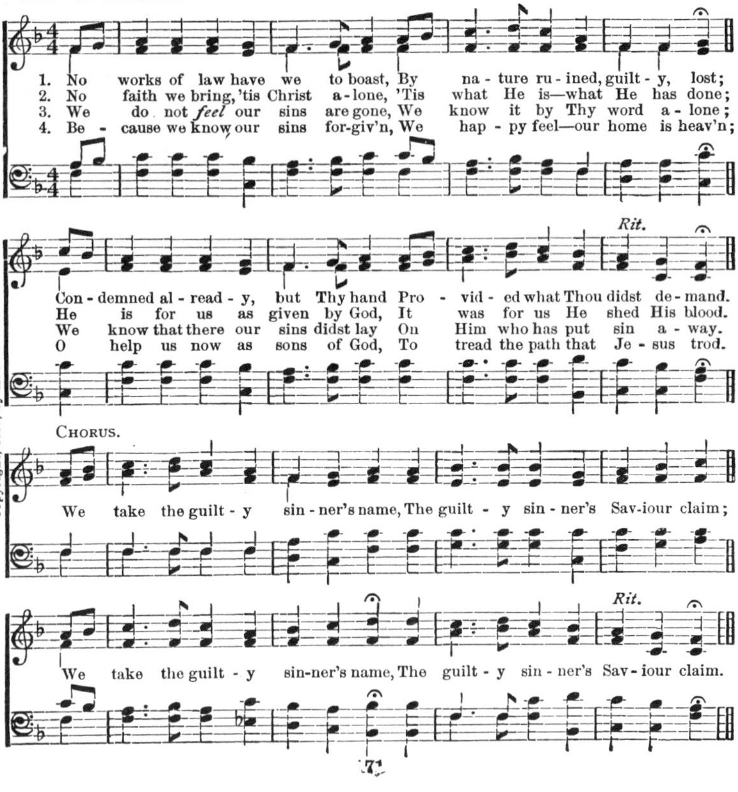

1. No works of law have we to boast, By na - ture ru - ined, guilt - y, lost;
2. No faith we bring, 'tis Christ a - lone, 'Tis what He is—what He has done;
3. We do not *feel* our sins are gone, We know it by Thy word a - lone;
4. Be - cause we know our sins for-giv'n, We hap - py feel—our home is heav'n;
Rit.
Con - demned al - read - y, but Thy hand Pro - vid - ed what Thou didst de - mand.
He is for us as given by God, It was for us He shed His blood.
We know that there our sins didst lay On Him who has put sin a - way.
O help us now as sons of God, To tread the path that Je - sus trod.
Chorus.
We take the guilt - y sin - ner's name, The guilt - y sin - ner's Sav-iour claim;
Rit.
We take the guilt - y sin-ner's name, The guilt - y sin - ner's Sav - iour claim.

No. 240. He Came to Bethany.

"Then Jesus came to Bethany."—1 JOHN 12 : 1.

P. P. BLISS. JAMES MCGRANAHAN.

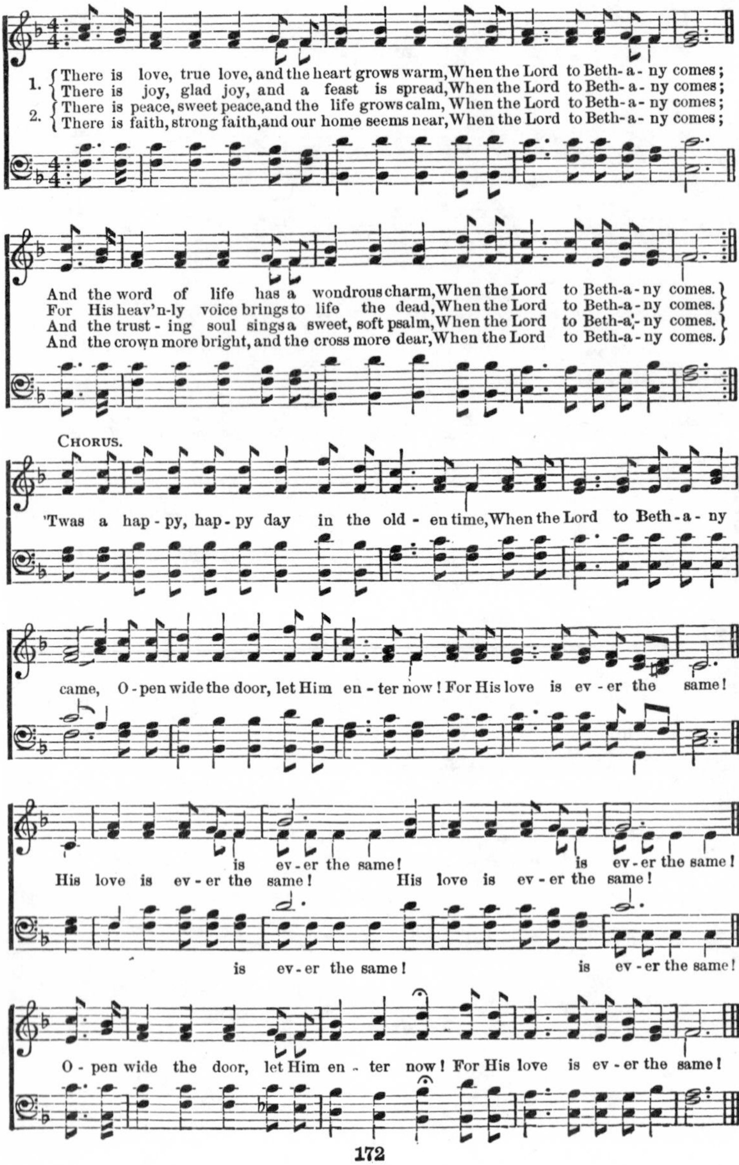

1. { There is love, true love, and the heart grows warm, When the Lord to Beth-a-ny comes;
And the word of life has a wondrous charm, When the Lord to Beth-a-ny comes.
There is joy, glad joy, and a feast is spread, When the Lord to Beth-a-ny comes;
For His heav'n-ly voice brings to life the dead, When the Lord to Beth-a-ny comes. }

2. { There is peace, sweet peace, and the life grows calm, When the Lord to Beth-a-ny comes;
And the trust-ing soul sings a sweet, soft psalm, When the Lord to Beth-a-ny comes.
There is faith, strong faith, and our home seems near, When the Lord to Beth-a-ny comes;
And the crown more bright, and the cross more dear, When the Lord to Beth-a-ny comes. }

CHORUS.

'Twas a hap-py, hap-py day in the old-en time, When the Lord to Beth-a-ny came, O-pen wide the door, let Him en-ter now! For His love is ev-er the same! His love is ev-er the same! is ev-er the same! His love is ev-er the same! is ev-er the same! O-pen wide the door, let Him en-ter now! For His love is ev-er the same!

No. 241. Child of Sin and Sorrow.

"Come, for all things are now ready."—Luke 14 : 17.

Th. Hastings. Thomas Hastings.

1. Child of sin and sor - row, Fill'd with dis - may,
Wait not for to - mor - row, Yield thee to - day:
Heav'n bids thee come,
While yet there's room; Child of sin and sor - row, Hear and o - bey.
2. Child of sin and sor - row, Why wilt thou die?
Come while thou canst bor - row Help from on high;
Grieve not that love
Which from a - bove, Child of sin and sor - row, Would bring thee nigh.

No. 242. This I Know.

"I know whom I have believed."—2 Tim. 1 : 12.

Fanny J. Crosby. W. H. Doane.

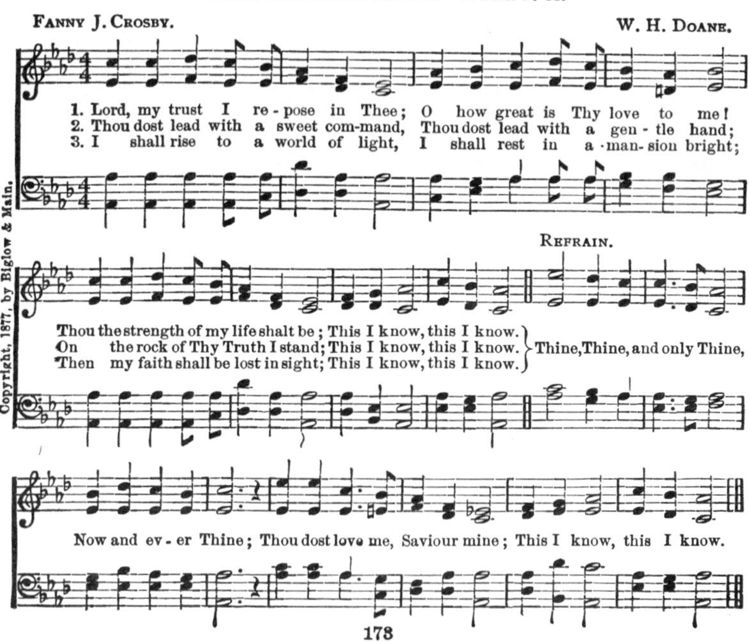

1. Lord, my trust I re - pose in Thee; O how great is Thy love to me!
Thou the strength of my life shalt be; This I know, this I know.
2. Thou dost lead with a sweet com-mand, Thou dost lead with a gen - tle hand;
On the rock of Thy Truth I stand; This I know, this I know.
3. I shall rise to a world of light, I shall rest in a man- sion bright;
Then my faith shall be lost in sight; This I know, this I know.
Refrain.
Thine, Thine, and only Thine,
Now and ev - er Thine; Thou dost love me, Saviour mine; This I know, this I know.

No. 243. Not what these Hands have Done.

"Having made peace through the blood of his cross."—Col. 1 : 20.
Horatius Bonar, D.D.
James McGranahan.
1. Not what these hands have done, Can save this guilt-y soul; Not what this toil-ing flesh has borne, Can make my spir-it whole.
2. Not what I feel or do, Can give me peace with God; Not all my pray'rs, nor sighs, nor tears, Can ease my aw-ful load.
3. Thy love to me, O God, Not mine, O Lord, to Thee, Can rid me of this dark un-rest, And set my spir-it free.
4. No oth-er work save Thine, No mean-er blood, will do; No strength, save that which is di-vine, Can bear me safely through.
5. I praise the God of grace, I trust His love and might; He calls me His, I call Him mine; My God, my joy, my light!
Refrain.
Thy work a-lone, my Sav-iour, Can ease this weight of sin; Thy blood a-lone, O Lamb of God, Can give me peace with-in.
Copyright, 1879, by James McGranahan.
No. 244. How can I Keep from Singing?
"I will sing praises unto my God while I have my being."—Ps. 146 : 2.
Anon.
Ira D. Sankey.
1. My life flows on in end-less song; A-bove earth's lamen-ta-tion, I hear the sweet tho' far-off hymn That hails a new cre-a-tion; Thro' all the tu-mult and the strife I
2. What tho' my joys and comforts die? The Lord my Sav-iour liv-eth What tho' the dark-ness gather round? Songs in the night He giv-eth; No storm can shake my in-most calm While
3. I lift my eyes; the cloud grows thin; I see the blue a-bove it; And day by day this pathway smooths, Since first I learned to love it; The peace of Christ makes fresh my heart, A
Copyright, 1881, by Ira D. Sankey.

How can I Keep from Singing?

hear the mu-sic ringing; It finds an ech - o in my soul—How can I keep from singing?
to that refuge clinging; Since Christ is Lord of heav'n and earth, How can I keep from singing?
fountain ever springing; All things are mine since I am His—How can I keep from singing?
No. 245.
Come Believing!
"Him that cometh to me I will in no wise cast out."—John 6 : 37.
El. Nathan.
James McGranahan.
1. Once a- gain the Gos - pel mes - sage From the Sav - iour you have heard;
2. Ma - ny sum- mers you have wast - ed, Ri - pened har - vests you have seen;
3. Je - sus for your choice is wait - ing; Tar - ry not: at once de - cide!
4. Cease of fit - ness to be think ing; Do not long - er try to feel;
5. Let your will to God be giv - en, Trust in Christ's a - ton- ing blood;
Will you heed the in - vi - ta - tion? Will you turn and seek the Lord?
Win- ter snows by Spring have melt - ed, Yet you lin - ger in your sin.
While the Spir - it now is striv - ing, Yield, and seek the Sav- iour's side.
It is trust - ing, and not feel - ing, That will give the Spir - it's seal.
Look to Je - sus now in heav - en, Rest on His un-chang- ing word.
Chorus.
Come be-liev- ing! come be- liev- ing! Come to Je - sus! look and live!
come! come! look! Oh, look and live!
look! Oh, look and live!
Come be - liev- ing! come be - liev- ing! Come to Je - sus! look and live!
come! come!
Copyright, 1879, by James McGranahan.

No. 246. Sound the Alarm!
Fanny J. Crosby.
"Sound an alarm!"—Joel 2: 1.
W. H. Doane.
1. Sound the a-larm! let the watchman cry!— "Up! for the day of the Lord is nigh;
2. Sound the a-larm! let the cry go forth, Swift as the wind, o'er the realms of earth;
3. Sound the a-larm on the mountain's brow! Plead with the lost by the way-side now;
4. Sound the a-larm in the youth-ful ear, Sound it a-loud that the old may hear;
Who will es-cape from the wrath to come? Who have a place in the soul's bright home?"
Flee to the Rock where the soul may hide! Flee to the Rock! in its cleft a-bide.
Warn them to come and the truth em-brace; Urge them to come and be saved by grace.
Blow ye the trump while the day-beams last! Blow ye the trump till the light is past!
Copyright, 1880, by Biglow & Main.
Refrain.
Sound the alarm, watchman, Sound the alarm! For the Lord will come with a conq'ring arm;
And the hosts of sin, as their ranks advance, Shall with-er and fall at His glance.
No. 247. Beautiful Morning.
Anon.
"He is not here but is risen."—Luke 24: 6.
Lucy J. Rider.
1. Beau-ti-ful morn-ing! Day of hope, Dawn of a bet-ter life;
2. Beau-ti-ful morn-ing! All the week Wait-eth thy wel-come light,
3. Beau-ti-ful morn-ing! Grief and pain, Weep-ing be-fore the tomb,
Now in thy peace-ful hours we rest, Far from earth's noise and strife.
Since thy first dawn-ing, calm and clear, Out of the dark-est night.
Fly at thy dawn-ing, Je-sus rose, Je-sus dis-pelled the gloom.
Copyright, 1879, by F. H. Revell.

Beautiful Morning.
Chorus.
Morn - ing of res - ur - rec - tion joy, Day when the Sav - iour rose,
Sing - ing shall greet thy open - ing hour, Sing - ing shall mark thy close.
No. 248. 'Twill not be Long.
" We are journeying unto a place of which the Lord said I will give it you."—Num. 10: 29.
Fanny J. Crosby.
W. H. Doane.
1. 'Twill not be long our jour - ney here, Each bro - ken sigh and fall - ing tear, Will soon be gone, and all will be A cloud - less sky, a wave - less sea.
2. 'Twill not be long the yearn - ing heart May feel its ev - 'ry hope de - part, And grief be min - gled with its song; We'll meet a - gain, 'twill not be long.
3. Though sad we mark the clos - ing eye, Of those we lov'd in days gone by, Yet sweet in death their lat - est song— We'll meet a - gain, 'twill not be long.
4. These check - ered wilds, with thorns o'er-spread, Thro' which our way so oft is led— This march of time, with truth so strong, Will end in bliss, 'twill not be long.
rit.
Refrain.
Roll on, dark stream, We dread not thy foam; The Pil - grim is long - ing For home, sweet home.
Roll on, roll on, dark stream, roll on, We
rit.
Copyrighted in "Silver Spray," 1868, by W. H. Doane.

No. 249. Tell me more about Jesus.

"That I may know him."—PHIL. 3: 10.

P. P. BLISS. JAMES MCGRANAHAN.

1. 'Tis known on earth, in heav - en too, 'Tis sweet to me be - cause 'tis true;
2. Earth's fair - est flowers will droop and die, Dark clouds o'er-spread yon a - zure sky;
3. When o - verwhelmed with un - be - lief, When bur - dened with a blind-ing grief,
4. And when the Glo - ry - land I see, And take the "place pre-pared" for me,

The "old, old story" is ev - er new; Tell me more a - bout Je - sus.
Life's dear - est joys flit fleet - est by; Tell me more a - bout Je - sus.
Come kind - ly then to my re - lief; Tell me more a - bout Je - sus.
Thro' end - less years my song shall be— "Tell me more a - bout Je - sus."

CHORUS.

"Tell me more a - bout Je - sus!" "Tell me more a - bout Je - sus!"
Him would I know who loved me so; "Tell me more a - bout Je - sus!"

No. 250. We'll gather there in Glory by and by.

"When Christ, who is our life, shall appear, then shall ye also appear with him in glory."—COL. 3: 4.

EL. NATHAN. JAMES MCGRANAHAN.

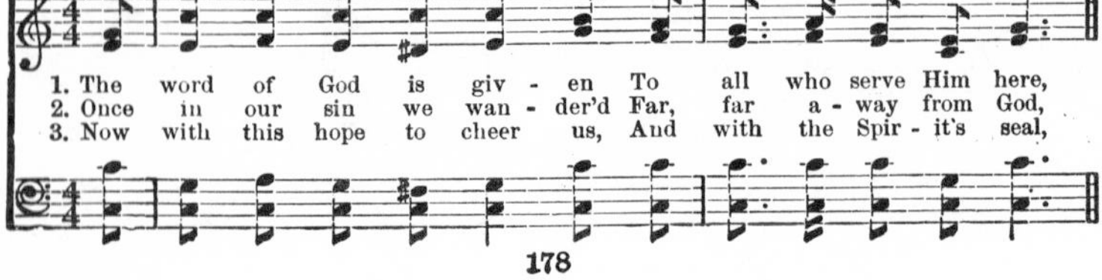

1. The word of God is giv - en To all who serve Him here,
2. Once in our sin we wan - der'd Far, far a - way from God,
3. Now with this hope to cheer us, And with the Spir - it's seal,

We'll gather there in Glory by and by.

That when the Lord from heav - en In glo - ry shall ap - pear,
And pre - cious hours we squan - der'd Up - on the down - ward road;
That all our sins were par - doned, Thro' Him whose stripes did heal;
We then shall be de - liv - ered From sor - row, sin, and pain;
But God in grace hath call'd us, And giv - en us to share
As "stran - gers" and as "pil - grims," No place on earth we own,
And if for Christ we suf - fer, With Him we then shall reign.
The pur - chase of our Sav - iour, A man - sion bright and fair.
But work and watch as "ser - vants," Un - til our Lord shall come.
Chorus.
We are go-ing home to Je - sus! Go-ing home to Je - sus! Go - ing to the
man-sions He's pre - par - ing there on high! We are go - ing home to Je - sus!
Go-ing home to Jesus! And we'll gath-er there in glo - ry, By and by! by and by!

No. 251. To Him be Glory Evermore.

"Thou hast redeemed us to God by thy blood."—Rev. 5: 9.

El. Nathan.
James McGranahan.
1. To Him who for our sins was slain, To Him for all His dy-ing pain.
2. To Him, the Lamb, our Sac-ri-fice, Who gave His life the ransomed price.
3. To Him who died that we might die To sin and live with Him on high.
4. To Him who rose that we might rise, And reign with Him be-yond the skies.
5. To Him who now for us doth plead, And help-eth us in all our need.
6. To Him who doth pre-pare on high, Our home in im-mor-tal-i-ty.
7. To Him be glo-ry ev-er-more! Ye heaven-ly hosts, your Lord a-dore.
Refrain.
Hal-le-lu-jah! hal-le-lu-jah, Hal-le-lu-jah to His name.
Copyright, 1879, by James McGranahan.
No. 252. The Sands of Time.
"Thine eyes shall behold the land that is very far off."—Isa. 33: 17.
Mrs. A. R. Cousin.
Ira D. Sankey.
Moderato.
1. The sands of time are sink-ing, The dawn of heav-en breaks, The summer morn I've
2. I've wres-tled on t'ward heav-en, 'Gainst storm and wind and tide, Now, like a wea-ry
3. Deep waters crossed life's pathway, The hedge of thorns was sharp; Now these lie all be-
sighed for—The fair, sweet morn a-wakes: Dark, dark hath been the mid-night, But
trav-'ler That lean-eth on his guide; A-mid the shades of ev'-ning, While
hind me—O! for a well tuned harp! O, to join the hal-le-lu-jah With
day-spring is at hand, And glo-ry, glo-ry dwell-eth In Im-man-uel's land.
sinks life's ling'ring sand, I hail the glo-ry dawn-ing From Im-man-uel's land.
yon tri-umphant band! Who sing where glo-ry dwell-eth In Im-man-uel's land.
Copyright, 1879, by Biglow & Main.

No. 253. I know that my Redeemer Lives.

"I know that my Redeemer lives."—Job 19: 25.

Rev. Sam. Medley. James McGranahan.

1. I know that my Re-deem-er lives! What com-fort this sweet mes-sage gives!
2. He lives, to bless me with His love; He lives, to plead for me a-bove,
3. He lives, tri-umphant from the grave; He lives, e-ter-nal-ly to save;
4. He lives, my man-sion to pre-pare; He lives to bring me safe-ly there;
He lives, who once was dead; He lives, all glo-rious in the sky;
My hun-gry soul to feed; He lives, to grant me rich sup-ply;
And while He lives I'll sing; He lives, my ev-er faith-ful Friend;
My Je-sus still the same: What joy this blest as-sur-ance gives!—
He lives, ex-alt-ed there on high, My ev-er-last-ing Head.
He lives, to guide me with His eye, To help in time of need.
He lives, and loves me to the end, My Proph-et, Priest, and King!
"I know that my Re-deem-er lives:" All glo-ry to His name!
Chorus.
He lives! He lives! I know that my Re-deem-er lives!
He lives! He lives!
He lives! He lives! I know that my Re-deem-er lives.
He lives! He lives!

No. 254. A Little While.

"Yet a little while; and he that shall come will come, and will not tarry."—HEB. 10: 37.

EL. NATHAN. JAMES MCGRANAHAN.

1. "A lit - tle while!" and He shall come; The hour draws on a - pace, The bless-ed
2. "A lit - tle while!" with patience, Lord, I fain would ask "How long?" For how can
3. Yet peace, my heart! and hush, my tongue! Be calm, my troubled breast! Each pass-ing
hour, the glorious morn, When we shall see His face: How light our tri - als then will
I with such a hope Of glo - ry and of home, With such a joy a - wait- ing
hour is hast'ning on The ev - er - last- ing rest: Thou knowest well—the time thy
seem! How short our pil- grim way! Our life on earth a fit - ful dream, Dis-
me, Not wish the hour were come? How can I keep the long - ing back, And
God Ap- points for thee is best: The morning star will soon a - rise; The
CHORUS.
pelled by dawning day!
how sup-press the groan?
glow is in the East.
Then come, Lord Jesus, quickly come, In glo - ry and in
light! Come take thy long - ing chil- dren home, And end earth's wea - ry night!
rit.
Copyright, 1879, by James McGranahan.

No. 255. Only for Thee.

"For me to live is Christ."—PHIL. 1: 21.

ELIZA ANN WALKER. JAMES MCGRANAHAN.

1. { Pre- cious Sav - iour, may I live, On - ly for Thee! Spend the pow - ers Thou dost give On - ly for Thee! }
{ Be my spir - it's deep de - sire On - ly for Thee! May my in - tel- lect as - pire On - ly for Thee! }

2. { In my joys may I re - joice, On - ly for Thee! In my choos-ing make my choice On - ly for Thee! }
{ Meek-ly may I suf - fer grief, On - ly for Thee! Grate- ful - ly ac- cept re - lief, On - ly for Thee! }

3. { Be my smiles and be my tears, On - ly for Thee! Be my young and rip - er years, On - ly for Thee! }
{ Be my peace and be my strife On - ly for Thee! Be my love and be my life, On - ly for Thee! }

CHORUS.

On - ly Christ who died for me Paid the price and made me free, Now, and thro' e - ter - ni - ty, On - ly for Thee!

No. 256. Waiting.

"Waiting for the coming of our Lord Jesus Christ."—1 COR. 1: 7.

MRS. FRANCES L. MACE. IRA D. SANKEY.

1. On - ly wait - ing till the shad - ows Are a lit - tle long - er grown; On - ly wait - ing till the glim - mer Of the day's last beam is flown;
2. On - ly wait - ing till the reap - ers Have the last sheaf gath - er'd home; For the sum - mer - time has fad - ed And the au - tumn winds have come.
3. On - ly wait - ing till the an - gels O - pen wide the pearl - y gate, At whose por - tals long I've lin - gered, Wea - ry, poor, and des - o - late:
4. Wait-ing for a bright - er dwell - ing Than I ev - er yet have seen, Where the tree of life is bloom - ing, And the fields are ev - er green;

No. 257. I Will!

"I will trust, and not be afraid."—ISAIAH 12 : 2.

(Suggested by the responses of the young men of Limerick to Mr. Moody's question, "Will you trust Christ?" at the Meetings in that City, October, 1883.)

EL. NATHAN. JAMES MCGRANAHAN.

I Will!

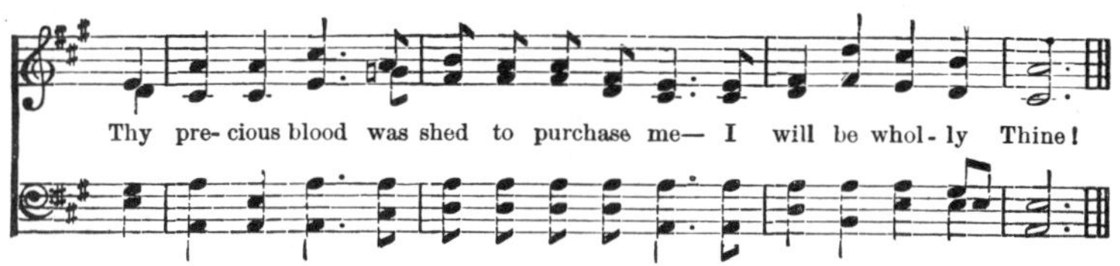

No. 258. The Palace o' the King.

"In thy presence is fulness of joy."—Ps. 16: 11.

WILLIAM MITCHELL. GEO. C. STEBBINS.

1. It's a bon - nie, bon - nie war - l' that we're liv - in' in the noo',
2. Then a - gain, I've juist been think- in' that when a' - thing here's sae bricht,
3. Oh! its hon - or heaped on hon - or that His cour- tiers should be ta'en
4. Then let us trust Him bet - ter than we've ev - er dune a - fore,
5. Nae nicht shall be in Heav - en, an' nae des - o - la - tin' sea,

An' sun - ny is the lan' that noo we aft - en traiv - 'll throo;
The sun in a' its grand- eur, an' the mune wi' quiver - in' licht,
Frae the wan'd- rin' anes He died for i' this warl' o' sin an' pain,
For the King will feed His ser- vants frae His ev - er bounteous store:
And nae ty - rant hoofs shall tram - ple i' the cit - y o' the free;

But in vain we look for some-thing here to which oor hearts may cling,
The o - cean i' the sim - mer; or the wood- land i' the spring,
An' its fu' - est love an' ser - vice that the Christ- ians aye should bring,
Lat us keep a clo - ser grip o' Him, for time is on the wing,
There's an ev - er - last - in' day- licht, an' a ev - er - fad - in' spring,

For its beau - ty is as nae- thing tae the pal - ace o' the King.
What maun it be up yon- ner i' the pal - ace o' the King.
To the feet o' Him wha reign-eth i' the pal - ace o' the King.
An' sune He'll come an' tak' us tae the pal - ace o' the King.
Where the Lamb is a' the glo - ry i' the pal - ace o' the King.

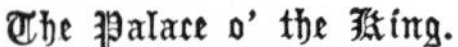

We like the gild - ed sim - mer, wi' its mer - ry, mer - ry tread,
It's here we hae oor tri - als, an' it's here that He pre - pares
The time for saw - in' seed, it is a wear - in', wear - in' dune;
It's iv - 'ry halls are bon - nie up - on which the rain - bows shine,
We see oor freen's a - wait us o - wer yon - ner at His gate;

An' we sigh when hoar - y win - ter lays its beau - ties wi' the dead;
His cho - sen for the rai - ment which the ran - somed sin - ner wears.
An' the time for win - nin' souls will be o - wer ver - ra sune.
An' its E - den bow'rs are trel - lised wi' a nev - er fad - in' Vine;
Then lat us a' be read - y, for ye ken it's get - tin' late;

For tho' bon - nie are the snaw-flakes, an' the doon on Win - ter's wing,
An' its here that He wad hear us 'mid oor trib - u - la - tions sing,
Then lat us a' be ac - tive, if a fruit - fu' sheaf we'd bring
An' the pearl - y gates o' Heav - en, do a glo - rious ra - diance fling,
Let oor lamps be bricht - ly burn - in'; let us raise oor voice and sing,

It's fine to ken it daur - na touch the pal - ace o' the King.
"We'll trust oor God wha' reign - eth i' the pal - ace o' the King.
To a - dorn the Roy - al ta - ble i' the pal - ace o' the King.
On the star - ry floor that shim - mers i' the pal - ace o' the King.
For sune we'll meet, to pairt nae mair, i' the pal - ace o' the King.

No. 259. Redeemed.

"Let the redeemed of the Lord say so."—Ps. 107: 2.

El. Nathan. James McGranahan.

1. "Re - deemed!" "re - deemed!" Oh, sing the joy - ful strain! Give praise; give
2. What grace! what grace! That He who calmed the wave, Should stoop, my
3. "Re - deemed!" "re - deemed!" The word has brought re - pose, And joy, and
4. "Re - deemed!" "re - deemed!" O joy, that I should be In Christ, in

"Redeemed!" "redeemed!" Give praise!
What grace! what grace! Should stoop,

Redeemed.

praise and glo-ry to His name; Who gave His blood our souls to save, And purchased freedom for the slave! And pur-chased free-dom for the slave!
soul, my guilt-y soul to save! That He the curse should bear for me, A sin-ful wretch, His en-e-my! A sin-ful wretch His en-e-my!
joy that each redeemed one knows, Who sees his sins on Je-sus laid, And knows His blood the ran-som paid, And knows His blood the ran-som paid.
Christ, from sin for-ev-er free! For-ev-er free to praise His name, Who bore for me the guilt and shame, Who bore for me the guilt and shame!
give praise!
my soul!
And purchased freedom, purchased freedom for the slave!
A sin-ful wretch, His en-e-my, His en-e-my!
And knows His blood the ransom paid, the ran-som paid.
Who bore for me the guilt and shame, the guilt and shame!
Copyright, 1879, by James McGranahan.
CHORUS.
* "Re-deemed!" "re-deemed!" from sin and all its woe!" "Re-deemed!" "re-deemed" e-ter-nal life to know! "Re-deemed!" "Re-deemed!" by Je-sus' blood, "Re-deemed!" "Re-deemed!" Oh, praise........ the Lord!

* The CHORUS may be omitted if desired.

No. 260. Grace before Meals.

"The eyes of all wait upon thee, and thou givest them their meat in due season."—Ps. 145: 15.

P. P. Bliss.

No. 261. Peace! Be Still!

"Jesus rebuked the wind, and said unto the sea, Peace! be still!"—Mark 4: 39.

Miss M. A. Baker. H. R. Palmer.

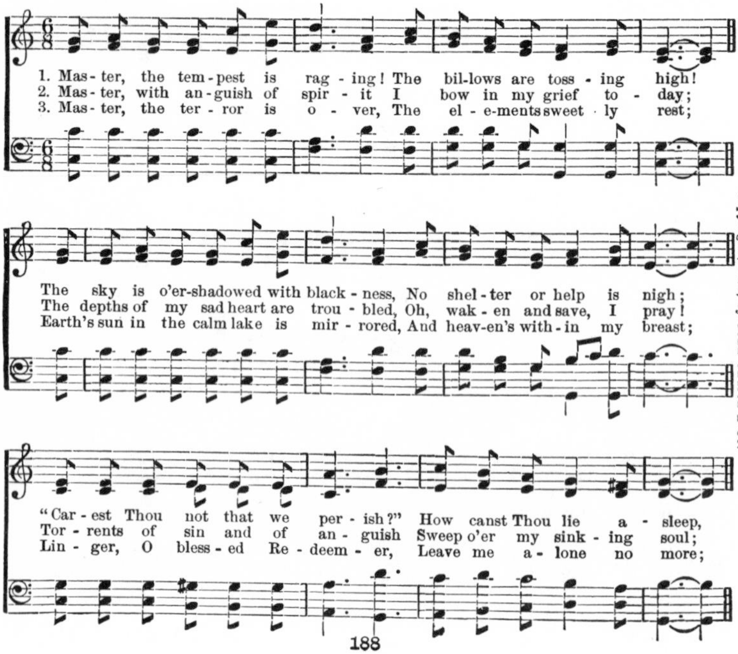

1. Mas - ter, the tem - pest is rag - ing! The bil - lows are toss - ing high!
2. Mas - ter, with an - guish of spir - it I bow in my grief to - day;
3. Mas - ter, the ter - ror is o - ver, The el - e - ments sweet - ly rest;

The sky is o'er-shadowed with black - ness, No shel - ter or help is nigh;
The depths of my sad heart are trou - bled, Oh, wak - en and save, I pray!
Earth's sun in the calm lake is mir - rored, And heav-en's with - in my breast;

"Car - est Thou not that we per - ish?" How canst Thou lie a - sleep,
Tor - rents of sin and of an - guish Sweep o'er my sink - ing soul;
Lin - ger, O bless - ed Re - deem - er, Leave me a - lone no more;

Peace! Be Still!

When each moment so mad-ly is threat-'ning A grave in the an-gry deep?
And I per-ish! I per-ish! dear Mas-ter; Oh! has-ten, and take con-trol.
And with joy I shall make the blest har-bor, And rest on the bliss-ful shore.
Chorus.
p
pp
"The winds and the waves shall o-bey My will, Peace,...... be still!........
Peace, be still! peace, be still!
Wheth-er the wrath of the storm-tossed sea, Or de-mons, or men, or what-
cres
cen
ev-er it be, No wa-ter can swal-low the ship where lies The
do.
ff
Mas-ter of o-cean and earth and skies; They all shall sweet-ly o-bey My will;
p
p
pp
Peace, be still! Peace, be still! They all shall sweetly o-bey My will; Peace, peace, be still!"

No. 262. I am the Door.

"I am the door: by me if any man enter in he shall be saved."—JOHN 10: 9.

EL. NATHAN. JAMES MCGRANAHAN.

Moderato.

1. O what shall I do to be saved? The gath-'ring storm I be - hold,
2. O what shall I do to be saved? No light, no hope can I see,
3. O what shall I do to be saved? So vile, so burdened with sin,
4. I en - ter the wide o - pen door, In Christ I *now* have be - lieved;

Ex - posed to the wrath of my God; Is there no shel - ter - ing fold,
No help in my - self can I find; Is there no mer - cy for me,
O how to the fold may I come, How may I en - ter there - in,
I'm cleans'd from my sins by His blood; I trust and *now* I am saved,

cres.

Is there no shel - ter - ing fold?
Is there no mer - cy for me?
How may I en - ter there - in?
I trust and *now* I am saved?

CHORUS.

I am the door, by Me if an - y man en - ter in, he shall be saved, he shall be saved, I am the door.

f

by Me if an - y man en - ter in, He shall be saved, he shall be saved.

ff *ad lib.*

"Behold, we have forsaken all, and followed thee."—MATT, 19 : 27.

Rev. H. F. LYTE. F. H. BARTHELEMON.

1. Je - sus, I my cross have ta - ken, All to leave and fol - low Thee,
2. Let the world de - spise and leave me, They have left my Sav - iour, too;
3. Haste thee on from grace to glo - ry, Arm'd by faith, and wing'd by pray'r!

Na - ked, poor, despised, for - sak - en, Thou from hence my all shalt be,
Hu - man hearts and looks de - ceive me— Thou art not, like them, un - true;
Heaven's e - ter - nal day's be - fore thee; God's own hand shall guide thee there:

FINE

D.S.—Yet how rich is my con - di - tion, God and heav'n are still my own.
D.S.—Foes may hate, and friends dis-own me, Show Thy face, and all is bright.
D.S.—Hope shall change to glad fru - i - tion, Faith to sight, and pray'r to praise.

Per - ish ev - 'ry fond am - bi - tion, All I've sought, or hoped, or known,
Oh! while Thou dost smile up - on me, God of wis - dom, love, and might,
Soon shall close thy earth - ly mis - sion, Soon shall pass thy pil - grim days,

D.S.

No. 264. Along the River of Time.

"Remember how short time is."—Ps. 89 : 47.

GEO. F. ROOT. GEO. F. ROOT.

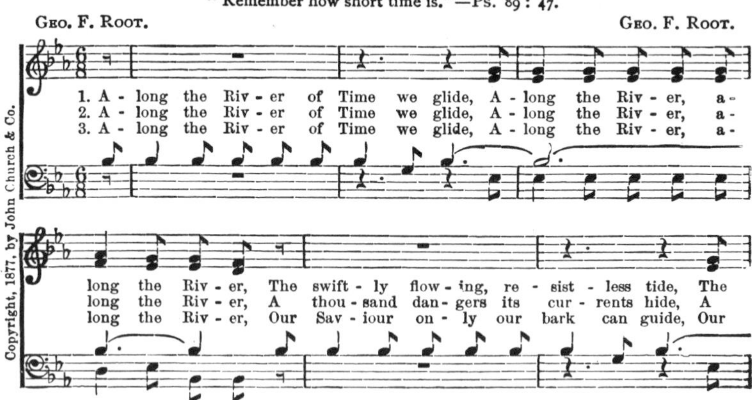

If a single voice sings this, let it change from the Tenor lines to the Soprano.

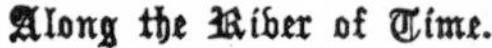

swift - ly flow - ing, the swift - ly flow - ing, Ah, soon, ah, soon, the
thou - sand dan - gers, a thou - sand dan - gers, And near our course the
Sav - iour on - ly, our Sav - iour on - ly, But with Him we se-

end we'll see, Yes, soon 'twill come and we will be
rocks we see, Oh, dread - ful thought! a wreck to be,
cure may be, No fear, no doubt, but joy to be

p

Float - ing, Float - ing, Out on the sea of e - ter - ni - ty!

pp *rit.*

Float - ing, float - ing, Out on the sea of e - ter - ni - ty!

No. 265. Till He Come.

" For yet a little while and he that shall come will come, and will not tarry."—Heb. 10 : 37.

Rev. E. H. Bickersteth. Dr. Lowell Mason.

1. " *Till He come!*"—Oh, let the words Lin - ger on the trem - bling chords;
2. When the wea - ry ones we love En - ter on their rest a - bove,
3. Clouds and dark - ness round us press; Would we have one sor - row less?
4. See the feast of love is spread, Drink the wine and eat the bread;

Till He Come.

Let "the lit - tle while" be - tween In their gold - en light be seen:
When the words of love and cheer Fall no long - er on our ear,
All the sharp-ness of the cross, All that tells the world is loss.
Sweet me- mo - rials, till the Lord Call us round His heaven-ly board;
Let us think, how heav'n and home Lie be - yond that "Till He come!"
Hush! be ev - ery mur - mur dumb, It is on - ly "Till He come!"
Death, and dark - ness, and the tomb, Pain us on - ly "Till He come!"
Some from earth, from glo - ry some, Sev - ered on - ly "Till He come!"
No. 266. Oh! to be over Yonder.
"In thy presence is fulness of joy."—Ps. 16: 11.
Miss Florence C. Armstrong.
Geo. C. Stebbins.
1. Oh, to be o - ver yon - der! In that land of won - der,
2. Oh, to be o - ver yon - der! My yearn - ing heart grows fond - er
3. Oh, to be o - ver yon - der! A - las! I sigh and won - der
4. Oh, when shall I be dwell - ing Where an - gel voi - ces swell - ing
5. Oh, I shall soon be yon - der, Tho' lone - ly here I wan - der,
Where the an - gel voi - ces min - gle, and the an - gel harp - ers ring;
Of look - ing to the east, to see the bless - ed day - star bring
Why clings my poor, weak, sin - ful heart to an - y earth - ly thing:
In tri - ump - ant hal - le - lu - jahs, make the vault - ed heav'ns ring?
Yearn - ing for the wel - come sum - mer—longing for the bird's fleet wing;
To be free from pain and sor - row, And the anx - ious, dread to - mor - row,
Some tid - ings of the wak - ing, The cloud - less, pure day break - ing;
Each tie of earth must sev - er, And pass a - way for - ev - er;
Where the pearl - y gates are gleam - ing, And the morn - ing star is beam - ing?
The mid - night may be drear - y, And the heart be worn and wea - ry,
Copyright, 1881, by Geo. C. Stebbins.

To rest in light and sun-shine In the pres-ence of the King.
My heart is yearn-ing—yearn-ing For the com-ing of the King.
But there's no more sep-a-ra-tion In the pres-ence of the King.
Oh, when shall I be yon-der In the pres-ence of the King.
But there's no more shad-ow yon-der In the pres-ence of the King.

CHORUS.

Oh!.......... to be o-ver yon-der, In........... that land of won-der,
Oh! to be o-ver yonder, yonder, In that land, that land of wonder,

There............ to be for-ev-er In the pres-ence of the King.
There to be for-ev-er

No. 267. Come, thou Weary.

"I will give you rest."—MATT. 11 : 28.

Rev. S. C. MORGAN. IRA D. SANKEY.

1. Come, thou wea-ry, Je-sus calls thee To His wound-ed side;
2. Seek-ing Je-sus? Je-sus seeks thee— Wants thee as thou art;
3. If thou let Him, He will save thee— Make thee all His own;
4. Wilt thou still re-fuse His of-fer? Wilt thou say Him nay?
5. Dost thou feel thy life is wea-ry? Is thy soul dis-tressed?

"Come to me," saith He, "and ev-er Safe a-bide."
He is knock-ing, ev-er knock-ing At thy heart.
Guide thee, keep thee, take thee, dy-ing, To His throne.
Wilt thou let Him, grieved, re-ject-ed, Go a-way?
Take His of-fer, wait no long-er; Be at rest!

No. 268. Every Day Will I Bless Thee.

Ps. 145: 2.

J. E. A. JAMES McGRANAHAN.

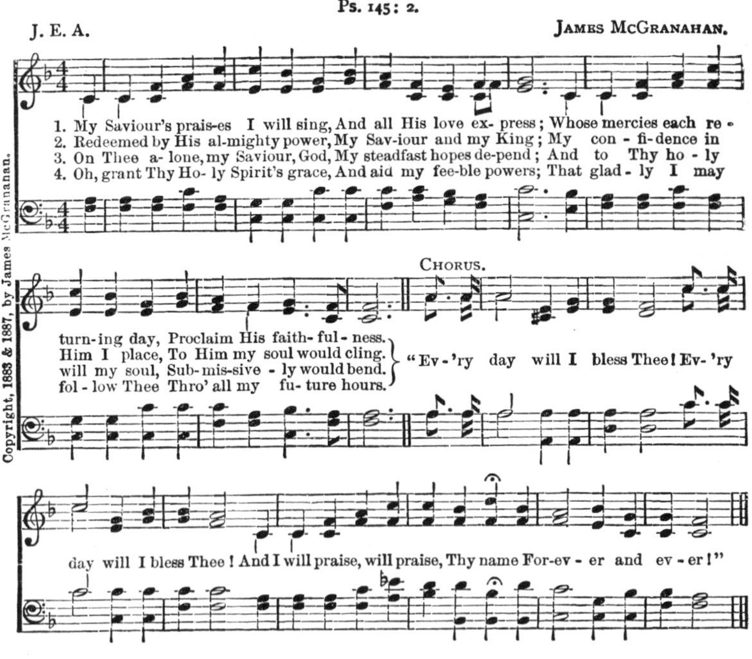
1. My Saviour's prais-es I will sing, And all His love ex- press; Whose mercies each re - turn-ing day, Proclaim His faith- ful - ness.
2. Redeemed by His al-mighty power, My Sav-iour and my King; My con - fi-dence in Him I place, To Him my soul would cling.
3. On Thee a- lone, my Saviour, God, My steadfast hopes de-pend; And to Thy ho - ly will my soul, Sub-mis-sive - ly would bend.
4. Oh, grant Thy Ho- ly Spirit's grace, And aid my fee-ble powers; That glad - ly I may fol - low Thee Thro' all my fu- ture hours.
CHORUS.
"Ev - 'ry day will I bless Thee! Ev- 'ry day will I bless Thee! And I will praise, will praise, Thy name For-ev - er and ev - er!"

No. 269. Onward, Upward, Homeward!

"I press toward the mark."—PHIL. 3: 16.

ALBERT MIDLANE. IRA D. SANKEY.

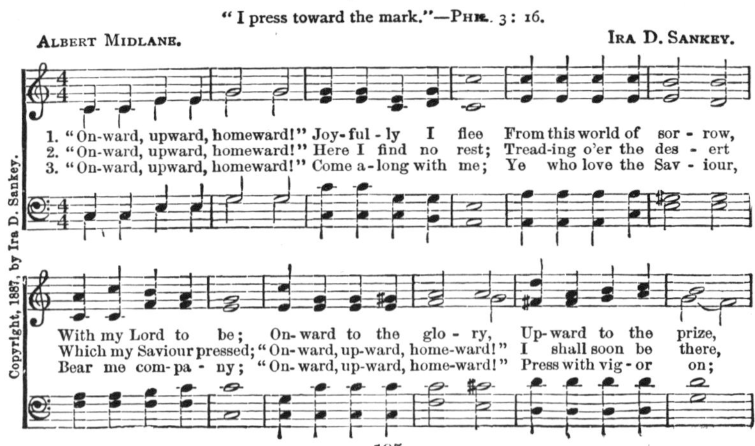
1. "On-ward, upward, homeward!" Joy- ful - ly I flee From this world of sor - row, With my Lord to be; On- ward to the glo - ry, Up- ward to the prize,
2. "On-ward, upward, homeward!" Here I find no rest; Tread-ing o'er the des - ert Which my Saviour pressed; "On- ward, up-ward, home-ward!" I shall soon be there,
3. "On-ward, upward, homeward!" Come a - long with me; Ye who love the Sav - iour, Bear me com- pa - ny; "On- ward, up-ward, home-ward!" Press with vig - or on;

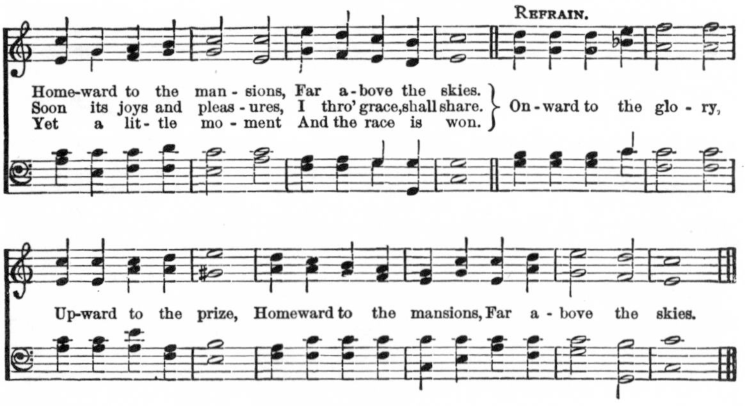

Refrain.
Home-ward to the man - sions, Far a-bove the skies.
Soon its joys and pleas - ures, I thro' grace, shall share.
Yet a lit- tle mo - ment And the race is won.
On - ward to the glo - ry,
Up-ward to the prize, Homeward to the mansions, Far a - bove the skies.

No. 270. In The Hollow of His Hand.

"Neither shall any man pluck them out of my hand."—John 10: 28.

Louise J. Kirkwood, alt. Geo. C. Stebbins.

1. Oh, soul toss'd on the bil - lows, a - far from friend-ly land,
2. Tho' rag - ing winds may drive thee, a wreck up - on the strand,
3. When strength is spent in toil - ing, and wea - ri - ly you stand,
4. When by the swell - ing Jor - dan, your feet in sink - ing sand,
5. And when at last we're gath - ered, with all the ran - somed band,

Look up to Him who holds thee in "The hol - low of His hand."
Still cling to Him who holds thee in "The hol - low of His hand."
Then rest in Him who holds thee in "The hol - low of His hand."
Re - mem - ber still He holds thee in "The hol - low of His hand."
We'll praise our God who holds us in "The hol - low of His hand."

Chorus.

In "The hol - low of His hand," In the hol - low of His hand,

In The Hollow of His Hand.

No. 271. Praise Him! Praise Him!

"I will sing praises unto my God."—Ps. 146: 2.

FANNY J. CROSBY. CHESTER G. ALLEN.

1. Praise Him! praise Him! Je-sus, our blessed Re-deem-er! Sing, O earth—His
2. Praise Him! praise Him! Je-sus, our blessed Re-deem-er! For our sins He
3. Praise Him! praise Him! Je-sus, our blessed Re-deem-er! Heav'n-ly por-tals,

won-der-ful love pro-claim! Hail Him! hail Him! highest arch-an-gels in
suf-fered, and bled, and died; He our rock, our hope of e-ter-nal sal-
loud with ho-san-nas ring! Je-sus, Sav-iour, reigneth for-ev-er and

D.S.—Praise Him! praise Him! tell of His ex-cel-lent

glo-ry; Strength and hon-or give to His ho-ly name! Like a shep-herd,
va-tion, Hail Him! hail Him! Je-sus, the cru-ci-fied. Sound His prais-es!
ev-er: Crown Him! crown Him! Prophet, and Priest, and King! Christ is com-ing!

great-ness, Praise Him! praise Him! ev-er in joy-ful song!

FINE.

Je-sus will guard His chil-dren, In His arms He car-ries them all day long;
Je-sus who bore our sor-rows, Love un-bound-ed, won-der-ful, deep and strong;
o-ver the world vic-to-rious, Pow'r and glo-ry un-to the Lord be-long;

D.S.

No. 272. I Know Whom I Have Believed.

2 TIM. 1: 12.
EL. NATHAN.
JAMES MCGRANAHAN.
Moderato.
1. I know not why God's won-drous grace To me He hath made known,
2. I know not how this sav - ing faith To me He did im - part,
3. I know not how the Spir - it moves, Con - vinc - ing men of sin,
4. I know not what of good or ill May be re - served for me,
5. I know not when my Lord may come, At night or noon-day fair
Nor why— un - wor - thy—Christ in love Re - deemed me for His own.
Nor how be - liev - ing in His word Wrought peace within my heart.
Re - veal - ing Je - sus through the word, Cre - at - ing faith in Him.
Of wea - ry ways or gold - en days, Be - fore His face I see.
Nor if I'll walk the vale with Him, Or "meet Him in the air."
Copyright, 1883 & 1887, by James McGranahan.
CHORUS.
But "I know whom I have be - liev - ed, And am per - suad-ed that He is a - ble
To keep that which I've com - mit - ted Un - to Him a-gainst that day."
No. 273. The Cleansing Fountain.
"A fountain opened for sin and for uncleanness."—ZECH. 13: 1.
RIAN A. DYKES.
IRA D. SANKEY.
1. Be - hold a Fountain deep and wide, Be - hold its on - ward flow; 'Twas
2. From Calvary's cross, where Je - sus died In sor - row, pain, and woe, Burst
3. O may we all the heal - ing power Of that bless'd Fountain know; Trust
4. And when at last the mes -'sage comes, And we are called to go, Our

The Cleansing Fountain.

o - pened in the Sav - iour's side, And cleans - eth "white as snow, And
forth the won - drous crim - son tide That cleans - eth "white as snow, That
on - ly in the pre - cious blood That cleans - eth "white as snow, That
trust shall still be in the blood That cleans - eth "white as snow, That
Chorus.
cleans- eth white as snow."
cleans- eth white as snow."
cleans- eth white as snow."
cleans- eth white as snow."
Come to this Fount - ain, 'Tis flow - ing to -
day; And all who will may free - ly come, And wash their sins a - way.
Copyright, 1887, by Ira

No. 274. Come to the Fountain.

"For with thee is the fountain of life."—Ps. 36 : 9.

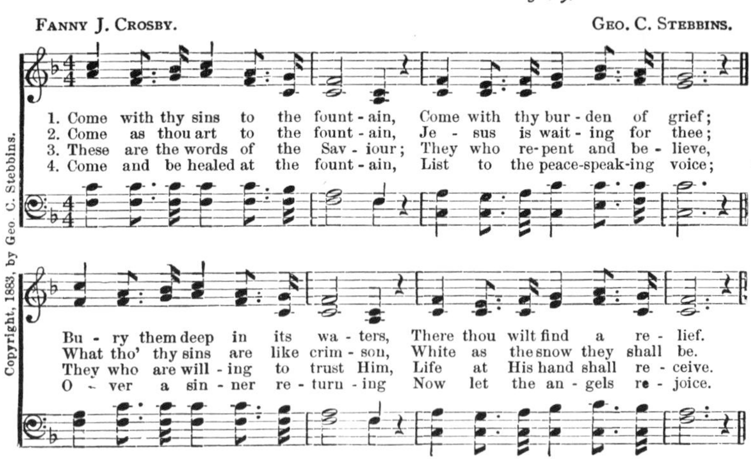

Fanny J. Crosby.
Geo. C. Stebbins.
1. Come with thy sins to the fount - ain, Come with thy bur - den of grief;
2. Come as thou art to the fount - ain, Je - sus is wait - ing for thee;
3. These are the words of the Sav - iour; They who re - pent and be - lieve,
4. Come and be healed at the fount - ain, List to the peace-speak-ing voice;
Bu - ry them deep in its wa - ters, There thou wilt find a re - lief.
What tho' thy sins are like crim - son, White as the snow they shall be.
They who are will - ing to trust Him, Life at His hand shall re - ceive.
O - ver a sin - ner re - turn - ing Now let the an - gels re - joice.
Copyright, 1883, by Geo. C. Stebbins.

Come to the Fountain.

CHORUS.
Haste thee a-way, why wilt thou stay? Risk not thy soul on a mo-ment's de-lay;
Je - sus is wait - ing to save thee, Mer - cy is plead - ing to - day.
No. 275. O Child of God.
"Joy cometh in the morning."—Ps. 30: 5.
F. J. CROSBY.
IRA D. SANKEY.
1. O child of God, wait pa-tient-ly When dark thy path may be, And let thy faith lean trust-ing - ly On Him who cares for thee; And though the clouds hang drear-i - ly Up - on the brow of night, Yet in the morning joy will come, And fill thy soul with light.
2. O child of God, He lov-eth thee, And thou art all His own; With gen-tle hand He lead - eth thee, Thou dost not walk a - lone; And though thou watchest wea - ri - ly The long and storm - y night, Yet in the morning joy will come, And fill thy soul with light.
3. O child of God, how peace-ful - ly He calms thy fears to rest, And draws thee up-ward ten - der - ly, Where dwell the pure and blest; And He who bend - eth si - lent-ly A - bove the gloom of night, Will take thee home where endless joy Shall fill thy soul with light.
Copyright, 1886, by Ira D. Sankey.

No. 276. Redemption.

"In whom we have redemption through his blood."—EPH. 1: 7.

F. J. CROSBY.
PETER BILHORN.
1. O won - der - ful words of the gos - pel! O won - der - ful mes-sage they bring, Pro - claim - ing a blessed re - demp-tion Thro' Je - sus our Sav - iour and King.
2. He came from the throne of His glo - ry, And left the bright mansions a - bove, The world to re - deem from its bond - age; So great His com - pas - sion and love.
3. O come to this won - der - ful Sav - iour, Come wea - ry and sor - row - op - pressed; Be - hold on the cross how He suf - fered, That you in His kingdom might rest.
4. There's no oth - er ref - uge but Je - sus, No shel - ter where lost ones may fly; And now, while He's ten - der - ly call - ing: O "turn ye," "for why will ye die?"
CHORUS.
Be - lieve, oh, be - lieve in His mer - cy That flows like a fountain so free; Be - lieve, and re ceive the re - demp - tion He of - fers to you and to me.
Rit.
Copyright, 1887, by Ira D. Sankey.

No. 277. Closer, Lord, to Thee.

"It is good for me to draw near to God."—Ps. 73: 28.
E. G. Taylor, D.D. Alt.
Geo. C. Stebbins.
1. Clos - er, Lord, to Thee I cling, Clos - er still to Thee; Safe beneath Thy
2. Clos - er yet, O Lord, my Rock, Ref - uge of my soul; Dread I not the
3. Clos - er still, my Help, my Stay, Clos - er, clos - er still; Meek - ly there I
4. Clos - er, Lord, to Thee I come, Light of life Di - vine; Thro' the ev - er
sheltering wing I would ev - er be; Rude the blast of doubt and sin, Fierce as -
tem - pest-shock, Tho' the bil-lows roll. Wild - est storm can - not a - larm, For, to
learn to say, "Fa - ther, not my will;" Learn that in af - flic-tion's hour, When the
Bless - ed Son, Joy and peace are mine; Let me in Thy love a - bide, Keep me
saults without, with - in, Help me, Lord, the bat - tle win;—Clos - er, Lord, to Thee.
me, can come no harm, Lean-ing on Thy lov - ing arm;—Clos - er, Lord, to Thee.
clouds of sor - row lower, Love di - rects Thy hand of power;—Clos - er, Lord, to Thee.
ev - er near Thy side, In the "Rock of A - ges" hide,—Clos - er, Lord, to Thee.
Copyright, 1887, by Ira D. Sankey.
No. 278. If God be For Us.
G. M. J.
Rom. 8: 13.
James McGranahan.
1. Re - joice in the Lord, O let His mer-cy, cheer, He sun - ders the bands that en-thrall;
2. Be strong in the Lord, re - joic-ing in His might, Be loy - al and true, day by day;
3. Con-fide in His word, His promis - es so sure, In Christ, they are "yea, and a - men;"
4. A - bide in the Lord, se - cure in His con-trol, 'Tis life ev - er - last - ing be - gun;
Redeemed by His blood, why should we ev - er fear, Since Je - sus is our 'all in all.'
When e - vils as - sail, be val-iant for the right, And He will be our strength, our stay.
Tho' earth pass a - way, they ev - er shall en-dure, 'Tis writ-ten o'er and o'er a - gain.
To pluck from His hand the weakest, trembling soul, It nev - er, nev - er can be done.
Copyright, 1886, by James McGranahan.

CHORUS.
If God be for us, if God be for us, if God be for us, Who can be a-
If God be for us, if God be for us,
gainst us, who, who, who............ Who can be against us, a-gainst us?
Who, who, Who can be against us?
No. 279.
God is Love!
"He that loveth not, knoweth not God; for God is love."—1 JOHN 4: 8.
RIAN A. DYKES.
IRA D. SANKEY.
1. "God is Love!"—His word pro-claims it, Day by day the truth we prove;
2. "God is Love!"—Oh, tell it glad-ly, How the Sav-iour from a-bove
3. "God is Love!"—Oh, boundless mer-cy—May we all its full-ness prove!
Heav'n and earth with joy are tell-ing, Ev-er tell-ing, "God is Love!"
Came to seek and save the lost ones, Show-ing thus the Fa-ther's love.
Tell-ing those who sit in dark-ness, "God is Light, and God is Love!"
CHORUS.
Hal-le-lu-jah! tell the sto-ry, Sung by an-gel choirs a-bove;
Sound-ing forth the might-y cho-rus—"God is Light, and God is Love!"

No. 280. Seeking for Me.

"I will both search my sheep, and seek them out."—Ezek. 34: 11.

A. N. E. E. Hasty.

1. Je-sus, my Saviour, to Beth-le-hem came, Born in a manger to sor-row and shame;
2. Je-sus, my Saviour, on Cal-va-ry's tree, Paid the great debt, and my soul He set free;
3. Je-sus, my Saviour, the same as of old, While I was wand'ring a-far from the fold,
4. Je-sus, my Saviour, shall come from on high—Sweet is the promise as wea-ry years fly;

Oh, it was won-der-ful—blest be His name! Seek-ing for me, for me!
Oh, it was won-der-ful—how could it be? Dy-ing for me, for me!
Gen-tly and long did He plead with my soul, Call-ing for me, for me!
Oh, I shall see Him de-scend-ing the sky, Com-ing for me, for me!

Used by per.

Refrain. For me!.............. For me!..............

Seek-ing for me! Seek-ing for me! Seek-ing for me! Seek-ing for me!
Dy-ing for me! Dy-ing for me! Dy-ing for me! Dy-ing for me!
Call-ing for me! Call-ing for me! Call-ing for me! Call-ing for me!
Com-ing for me! Com-ing for me! Com-ing for me! Com-ing for me!

Oh, it was won-der-ful—blest be His name! Seek-ing for me, for me!
Oh, it was won-der-ful—how could it be? Dy-ing for me, for me!
Gen-tly and long did He plead with my soul, Call-ing for me, for me!
Oh, I shall see Him de-scend-ing the sky, Com-ing for me, for me!

No. 281. Jesus, I Come.

"Deliver me, O my God."—Ps. 71: 4.

W. T. Sleeper. Geo. C. Stebbins.

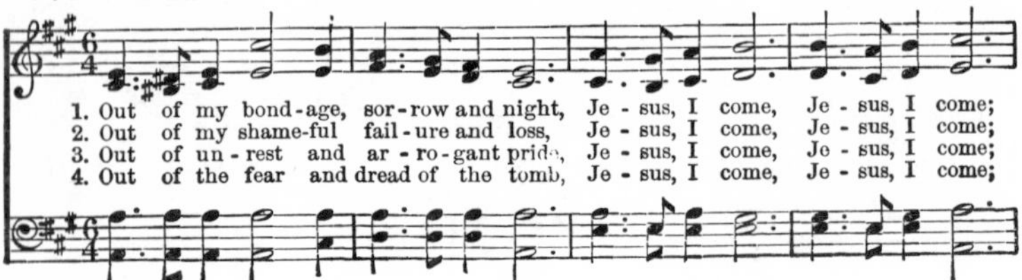

1. Out of my bond-age, sor-row and night, Je-sus, I come, Je-sus, I come;
2. Out of my shame-ful fail-ure and loss, Je-sus, I come, Je-sus, I come;
3. Out of un-rest and ar-ro-gant pride, Je-sus, I come, Je-sus, I come;
4. Out of the fear and dread of the tomb, Je-sus, I come, Je-sus, I come;

Jesus, I Come.

In - to Thy free - dom, glad- ness and light, Je - sus, I come to Thee;
In - to the glo - rious gain of Thy cross, Je - sus, I come to Thee;
In - to Thy bless - ed will to a - bide, Je - sus, I come to Thee;
In - to the joy and light of Thy home, Je - sus, I come to Thee;
Out of my sick- ness in - to Thy health, Out of my want and in - to Thy wealth,
Out of earth's sorrows in - to Thy balm, Out of life's storms and in - to Thy calm,
Out of my- self to dwell in Thy love, Out of de- spair in- to rap-tures a - bove,
Out of the depths of ru - in un - told, In - to the peace of Thy shel-ter- ing fold,
Out of my sin and in - to Thy- self, Je - sus, I come to Thee.
Out of dis- tress to ju - bi- lant psalm, Je - sus, I come to Thee.
Up - ward for aye on wings like a dove, Je - sus, I come to Thee.
Ev - er Thy glo - rious face to be- hold, Je - sus, I come to Thee.
Copyright, 1887, by Ira D. Sankey.

No. 282. Glory Ever be to Jesus.

"Give unto the Lord glory and strength."—Ps. 96: 7.

Rian A. Dykes. Ira D. Sankey.

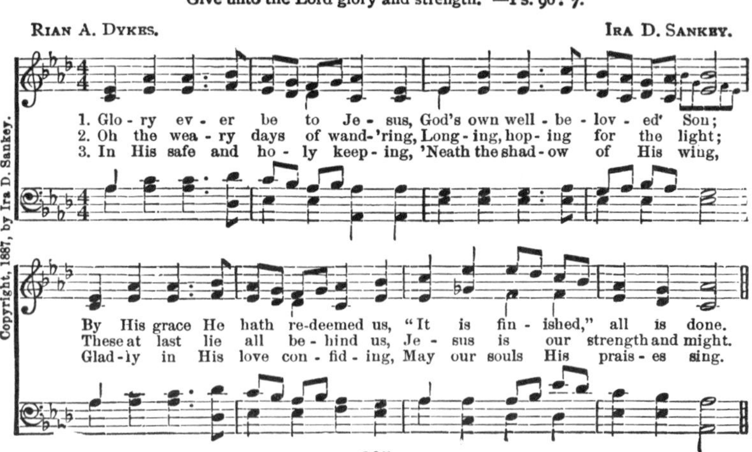
1. Glo - ry ev - er be to Je - sus, God's own well - be - lov - ed Son;
2. Oh the wea - ry days of wand-'ring, Long - ing, hop - ing for the light;
3. In His safe and ho - ly keep - ing, 'Neath the shad - ow of His wing,
By His grace He hath re-deemed us, "It is fin - ished," all is done.
These at last lie all be - hind us, Je - sus is our strength and might.
Glad - ly in His love con - fid - ing, May our souls His prais - es sing.
Copyright, 1887, by Ira D. Sankey.

CHORUS.
Saved by grace thro' faith in Je - sus, Saved by His own pre - cious blood,
May we in His love a - bid - ing, Fol - low on to know the Lord.

No. 283. Jesus Christ our Saviour.

"This is indeed the Christ the Saviour of the world."—JOHN 4: 42.

EL. NATHAN. JAMES McGRANAHAN.

CHOIR.
ALL.
CHOIR.
1. Who came down from heav'n to earth? Je - sus Christ our Sav - iour; Came a child of
2. Who was lift - ed on the tree? Je - sus Christ our Sav - iour; There to ran- som
3. Who hath promised to for- give? Je - sus Christ our Sav - iour; Who hath said, 'Be-
4. Who is now en-throned a- bove? Je - sus Christ our Sav - iour; Whom should we o-
5. Who a- gain from heav'n shall come? Je - sus Christ our Sav - iour; Take to glo - ry
ALL.
CHORUS.
low - ly birth? Je - sus Christ our Sav - iour.
you and me? Je - sus Christ our Sav - iour.
lieve and live?' Je - sus Christ our Sav - iour.
bey and love? Je - sus Christ our Sav - iour.
all His own? Je - sus Christ our Sav - iour.
Sound the cho - rus loud and clear,
He hath brought salvation near; None so precious, none so dear; Jesus Christ our Sav- iour.
Copyright, 1886, by James McGranahan.

No. 284.
Jesus Saves!
"Believe on the Lord Jesus Christ, and thou shalt be saved."—Acts 16: 31.
Priscilla J. Owens.
Wm. J. Kirkpatrick.
1. We have heard the joy-ful sound: Je - sus saves! Je - sus saves! Spread the tidings all a-
2. Waft it on the roll-ing tide: Je - sus saves! Je - sus saves! Tell to sin- ners far and
3. Sing a- bove the bat- tle strife, Je - sus saves! Je - sus saves! By His death and end-less
4. Give the winds a might-y voice: Je - sus saves! Je - sus saves! Let the na- tions now re-
round: Je - sus saves! Je - sus saves! Bear the news to ev - 'ry land, Climb the
wide: Je - sus saves! Je - sus saves! Sing, ye is - lands of the sea, Ech - o
life, Je - sus saves! Je - sus saves! Sing it soft - ly thro' the gloom, When the
joice,— Je - sus saves! Je - sus saves! Shout sal - va - tion full and free, High- est
steeps and cross the waves; Onward!—'tis our Lord's command: Je- sus saves! Je - sus saves!
back, ye o - cean caves; Earth shall keep her ju- bi- lee: Je- sus saves! Je - sus saves!
heart for mer- cy craves; Sing in tri-umph o'er the tomb,— Je- sus saves! Je- sus saves!
hills and deep-est caves; This our song of vic - to - ry,— Je- sus saves! Je- sus saves!
From "Royal Fountain," by per. John J. Hood.
No. 285.
He is Coming.
"I will come again."—John 14: 3.
Alice Monteith.
Ira D. Sankey.
1. He is com - ing, the "Man of Sor-rows," Now ex - alt - ed on high;
2. He is com - ing, our lov- ing Sav- iour, Bless-ed Lamb that was slain;
3. He is com - ing, our Lord and Mas - ter, Our Re - deem - er and King;
4. He shall gath - er His cho- sen peo - ple, Who are called by His name;
He is com- ing with loud ho - san - nas, In the clouds of the sky.
In the glo - ry of God the Fa - ther, On the earth He shall reign.
We shall see Him in all His beau - ty, And His praise we shall sing.
And the ran- somed of ev - 'ry na - tion, For His own He shall claim.
Copyright, 1886, by Ira D. Sankey.

He is Coming.
Chorus.
Hal - le - lu - jah! Hal - le - lu - jah! He is com - ing a - gain;
And with joy we shall gath - er round Him, At His com - ing to reign.
No. 286. Give Me Thine Heart!
"My son, give me thine heart."—Proverbs 23 : 26.
E. R. Latta.
A. J. Abbey, arr.
1. Wher - ev - er we may go, by night or day, A lov - ing voice with - in doth gent - ly say: My son, from ev - 'ry way of sin de - part; Be Sa - tan's slave no more, "Give Me thy heart!"
2. Slight not that voice so kind, but glad - ly hear, And choose the Lord to - day, while He is near; He will His pard'ning love to thee im - part; Oh, hear Him call - ing still, "Give Me thy heart!"
3. We may have cho - sen long from Him to roam, Yet He will wel - come us, if we but come; Oh, may we not de - lay, but quick - ly start— While Je - sus say - eth still, "Give Me thy heart!"
Chorus.
"Give Me thy heart, give Me thy heart; O wea - ry, wand - 'ring child, give Me thy heart."
Copyright, 1886, by Ira D. Sankey.

No. 287. They that be Wise.

"They that be wise shall shine as the firmament."—DAN. 12: 3

F. J. CROSBY.
IRA D. SANKEY.
1. O list to the voice of the Proph - et of old, Pro -
2. Tho' rug - ged the path where our du - ty may lead, O!
3. The grand - eur of wealth, and the tem - ples of fame, Where
4. Then let us go forth to the work yet to do, With
claim - ing in lan - guage di - vine, The won - der - ful, won - der - ful
why should we ev - er re - pine? When faith - ful and true, is the
beau - ty and splen - dor com - bine, Will per - ish, for - got - ten and
zeal that shall nev - er de - cline, Be strong in the Lord, and the
mes - sage of truth That "They that be wise shall shine."
prom - ise to all, That "They that be wise shall shine."
crum - ble to dust, But "They that be wise shall shine."
prom - ise be - lieve That "They that be wise shall shine."
CHORUS.
They shall shine as bright as the stars, In the fir - ma - ment jeweled with light;
Rit.
And they that turn ma - ny to right-eous-ness As the stars for - ev - er bright.

No. 288. Believe, and Keep on Believing.

"He that believeth on the Son hath everlasting life."—JNO. 3: 36.

Arr. from W. L. by EL. NATHAN.
JAMES MCGRANAHAN.
1. I be - lieved in God's won-der - ful mer - cy and grace, Be-lieved in the smile of His
2. I be - lieved in the work of my cru - ci - fied Lord, Be-lieved in re-demption a -
3. I be - lieved in the heart that was o-pened for me, Be-lieved in the love flow-ing
4. I be - lieved in Him-self, as the true Liv - ing One, Be-lieved in His presence on
rec - on-ciled face, Be-lieved in His mes-sage of par - don and peace; I be -
lone thro' His blood, Be-lieved in my Sav-iour by trust - ing His word; I be -
bless - ed and free, Be-lieved that my sins were all nailed to the tree; I be -
high on the throne, Be-lieved in His com - ing in glo - ry full soon; I be -
lieved, and I keep on be - liev - ing.
CHORUS.
Be - lieve! and the feel - ing may
come or may go, Be - lieve in the word, that was writ - ten to show That
all who be-lieve, their sal - va-tion may know; Be-lieve, and keep right on be - liev-ing.
Copyright, 1887, by James McGranahan.

No. 289. Meet me There!

"Where I am there ye may be also."—John 14 : 3.

E. G. Taylor. Geo. C. Stebbins.

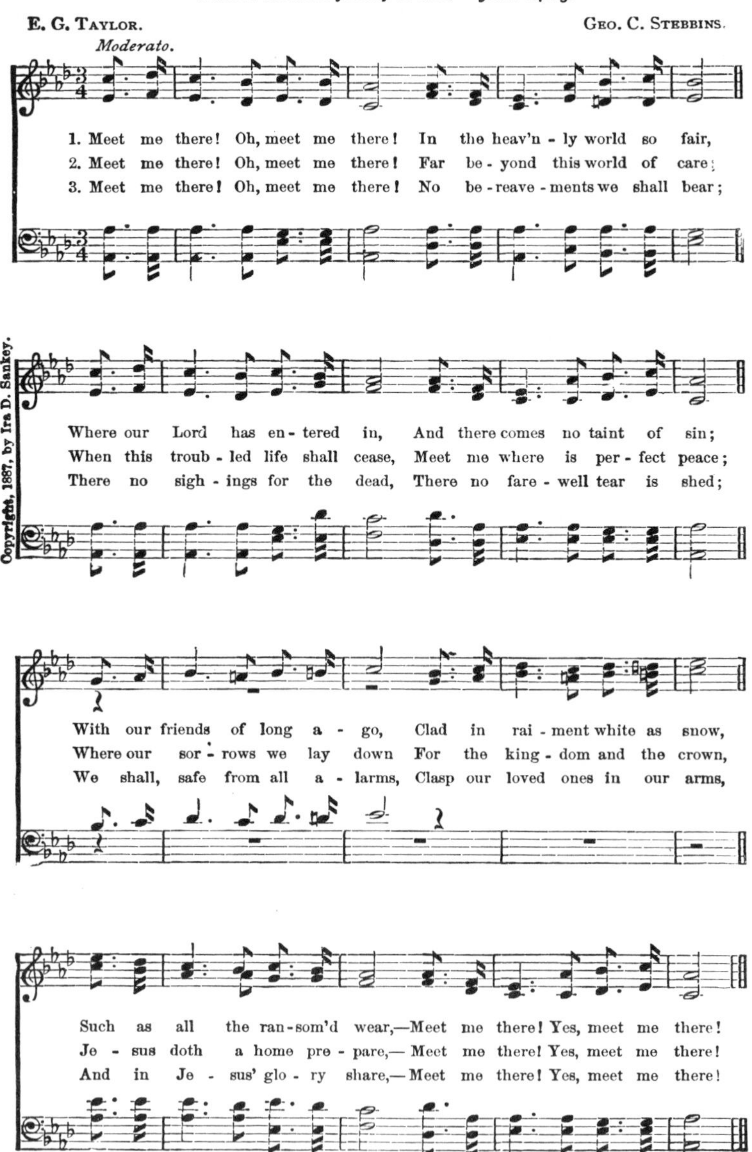
Moderato.
1. Meet me there! Oh, meet me there! In the heav'n - ly world so fair,
2. Meet me there! Oh, meet me there! Far be - yond this world of care;
3. Meet me there! Oh, meet me there! No be - reave - ments we shall bear;
Where our Lord has en - tered in, And there comes no taint of sin;
When this troub - led life shall cease, Meet me where is per - fect peace;
There no sigh - ings for the dead, There no fare - well tear is shed;
With our friends of long a - go, Clad in rai - ment white as snow,
Where our sor - rows we lay down For the king - dom and the crown,
We shall, safe from all a - larms, Clasp our loved ones in our arms,
Such as all the ran - som'd wear,—Meet me there! Yes, meet me there!
Je - sus doth a home pre - pare,—Meet me there! Yes, meet me there!
And in Je - sus' glo - ry share,—Meet me there! Yes, meet me there!
Copyright, 1887, by Ira D. Sankey.

No. 290. Be Ye also Ready.

MATT. 24: 44.

Geo. R. Clark. | James McGranahan.

1. Are you read-y, are you read-y for the com-ing of the Lord? Are you liv-ing as He bids you in His word? Are you walk-ing in the light? Is your hope of heav-en bright? Could you wel-come Him to-night? Are you read-y?......

2. Are you wait-ing, are you wait-ing for the com-ing of the King? Have yon bundles of the gold-en grain to bring? Can you lay at Je-su:' feet An-y gath-er'd sheaves of wheat, There your bless-ed Lord to greet? Are you read-y?......

3. Have you ris-en, have you ris-en from the heav-y midnight sleep? Have you ris-en from your slum-ber long and deep? Are your garments wash'd from sin, Are you cleansed and pure within? Are you read-y for the King? Are you read-y?......

CHORUS.

There-fore be ye al-so read-y, (there-fore) be ye al-so read-y, there-fore be ye al-so, be ye al-so read-y, (read-y............................) for in such an hour, such an hour as ye think not, the Son of man com-eth.

No. 291. Praise the Saviour.
T. Kelly.
Heb. 13: 15.
German Melody.
1. Praise the Sav - iour, ye who know Him; Who can tell how much we owe Him? Glad - ly let us ren - der to Him All we are and have.
2. Je - sus is the name that charms us; He for con - flict fits and arms us; Noth - ing moves and noth - ing harms us, When we trust in Him.
3. Trust in Him, ye saints, for ev - er; He is faith - ful, changing nev - er; Nei - ther force nor guile can sev - er Those He loves from Him.
4. Keep us, Lord, oh, keep us cleav - ing To Thy - self, and still be - liev - ing, Till the hour of our re - ceiv - ing Prom-ised joys in heaven.
5. Then we shall be where we would be, Then we shall be what we should be; Things which are not now, nor could be, Then shall be our own.
No. 292. Shine on, O Star!
"The bright and morning Star."—Rev. 22: 16.
Victoria Stuart.
Ira D. Sankey.
1. Shine on, O Star of beau - ty, Thou Christ enthroned a - bove; Re - flect - ing in Thy brightness, Our Father's look of love.
2. Shine on, O Star of glo - ry, We lift our eyes to Thee; Be - yond the clouds that gath - er, Thy ra - diant light we see.
3. Shine on, O Star un - chang - ing, And guide our pil - grim way, Un - til we see the dawn - ing Of heav'n's e - ter - nal day.
4. And when, with Thy redeem'd ones, We reach the heav'nly shore, May we with Thee in glo - ry Shine on for - ev - er - more.
Chorus.
Shine on,......... shine on, shine on, Thou bright and beautiful Star, shine on; Shine on, shine on, shine on, Thou bright and beautiful Star, shine on.
shine on, ...
Shine on, shine on,
Star,........
shine on,..........
Beauti-ful Star.........
shine on; Shine on, shine on,
rit.
Copyright, 1886, by Ira D. Sankey.

No. 293. Go Ye Into all the World.

MATT. 28: 18. MARK 16: 15.

G. M. J.

JAMES MCGRANAHAN.

1. Far, far away in heathen darkness dwelling, Millions of souls for ever may be lost; Who, who will go salvation's story telling, Looking to Jesus, heeding not the cost?
2. See o'er the world the open doors inviting, Soldiers of Christ, arise and enter in! Breth'ren, awake! our forces all uniting, Send forth the gospel, break the chains of sin.
3. "Why will ye die?" the voice of God is calling, "Why will ye die?" re-echo in His Name; Jesus hath died to save from death appalling, Life and salvation therefore go proclaim.
4. God speed the day when those of ev'ry nation "Glory to God" triumphantly shall sing; Ransomed, redeemed, rejoicing in salvation, Shout "Hallelujah for the Lord is King."

CHORUS.

"All power is given unto me, All power is given unto me, Go ye into all the world and preach the gospel, and lo, I am with you alway."

No. 294. I know I love Thee better, Lord.

"Behold, the half was not told."—1 Kings 10: 7.

Frances R. Havergal. R. E. Hudson.

1. I know I love Thee bet - ter, Lord, Than an - y earth - ly joy;
For Thou hast giv - en me the peace Which noth - ing can de - stroy.

2. I know that Thou art near - er still Than an - y earth - ly throng;
And sweet - er is the thought of Thee Than an - y love - ly song.

3. Thou hast put glad - ness in my heart; Then may I well be glad!
With - out the se - cret of Thy love I could not but be sad.

4. O Sav - iour, pre - cious Sav - iour, mine! What will Thy pres - ence be,
If such a life of joy can crown Our walk on earth with Thee?

Chorus.

The half has nev - er yet been told, yet been told, Of love so full and free!
The half has nev - er yet been told, yet been told, The blood—it cleanseth me! *rit.* cleanseth me!

No. 295. O Precious Word.

"Him that cometh unto me I will in no wise cast out."—John 6: 37.

Fanny J. Crosby. Ira D. Sankey.

1. O pre - cious word that Je - sus said! The soul that comes to Me,
2. O pre - cious word that Je - sus said! Be - hold, I am the Door;
3. O pre - cious word that Je - sus said! Come, wea - ry souls op - pressed,
4. O pre - cious word that Je - sus said! The world I o - ver - came;

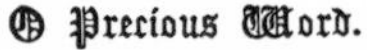
O Precious Word.

I will in no wise cast him out, Who-ev-er he may be.
And all who en-ter in by Me Have life for ev-er-more.
Come take My yoke and learn of Me, And I will give you rest.
And they who fol-low where I lead Shall con-quer in My name.
REFRAIN.
Who-ev-er he may be, Who-ev-er he may be, I
Have life for ev-er-more, Have life for ev-er-more, And
And I will give you rest, And I will give you rest, Come
Shall con-quer in My Name, Shall con-quer in My Name, And
will in no wise cast him out, Who-ev-er he may be.
all who en-ter in by Me Have life for ev-er-more.
take my yoke and learn of Me, And I will give you rest.
they who fol-low where I lead Shall con-quer in My Name.
Copyright, 1886, by Ira D. Sankey.

No. 296. O the Crown, the Glory-Crown.

"When the chief Shepherd shall appear, ye shall receive a crown of glory that fadeth not away."—1 PETER 5: 4.

G. M. J. JAMES MCGRANAHAN.

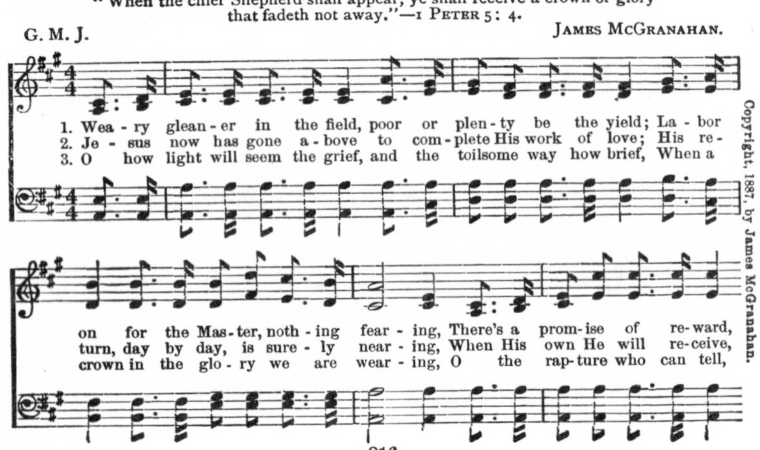
1. Wea-ry glean-er in the field, poor or plen-ty be the yield; La-bor
2. Je-sus now has gone a-bove to com-plete His work of love; His re-
3. O how light will seem the grief, and the toilsome way how brief, When a
on for the Mas-ter, noth-ing fear-ing, There's a prom-ise of re-ward,
turn, day by day, is sure-ly near-ing, When His own He will re-ceive,
crown in the glo-ry we are wear-ing, O the rap-ture who can tell,
Copyright, 1887, by James McGranahan.

O the Crown, the Glory-Crown.
at the com-ing of the Lord, Un - to all them that love His ap - pear - ing.
and a welcome He will give, Un - to all them that love His ap - pear - ing.
as for ev- er there we dwell, With re-deem'd ones that lov'd His ap - pear - ing.
Chorus.
O the crown,.................... the glo - ry crown, O the
The glo - ry crown, the glo - ry crown,
day the hap - py day is near-ing, When the crown of rich re - ward shall be
giv - en by the Lord, Un - to all them that love His ap - pear - ing.
No. 297. We lift our Songs to Thee.
"Ye are not your own."—1 Cor. 6: 19.
N. J. Squires.
H. H. McGranahan.
1. We lift our songs to Thee, Our Sav - iour and our guide;
2. We lift our pray'rs to Thee, Who on - ly hear - eth pray'r;
3. We lift our faith to Thee, In - creased by grace di - vine;
4. We lift our all to Thee, For all things, Lord, are Thine;
O make us from our bur - dens free, And keep us near Thy side.
They who on earth do thus a - gree, Shall find Thy bless - ing there.
Help us, O Lord, Thy foot - steps see, And on Thy help re - cline.
Take us, and all we have, and see Thy like - ness in us shine.
Copyright, 1886, by H. H. McGranahan.

No. 298. I Know that my Redeemer Lives.

"For I know that my Redeemer liveth."—Job 19 : 25.

Rev. H. A. Merrill, alt. Arr. by Geo. C. Stebbins.

1. I know that my Re-deem-er lives, And has pre-pared a place for me,
2. I'm trust-ing Je-sus Christ for all, I know His blood now speaks for me;
3. I'm now en-rap-tur'd with the thought, I stand and won-der at His love—
4. I know that Je-sus soon will come, I know the time will not be long,

D.C.—For I am on-ly wait-ing here To hear the summons: "child, come home,"

Fine.

And crowns of vic-to-ry He gives To those who would His chil-dren be.
I'm list-'ning for the wel-come call, To say: "The Mas-ter wait-eth thee!"
That He from heav'n to earth was brought, To die, that I may live a-bove.
'Till I shall reach my heavenly home, And join the ev-er-last-ing song.

For I am on-ly wait-ing here To hear the summons: "Child, come home!"

Chorus. D.C.

Then ask me not to lin-ger long A-mid the gay and thoughtless throng,

No. 299. Not far from the Kingdom.

"Thou art not far from the kingdom of God."—Mark 12 : 34.

Words arr. Ira D. Sankey.

1. Not far, not far from the King-dom, Yet in the shad-ow of sin;
2. Not far, not far from the King-dom, Where voi-ces whis-per and wait;
3. A-way in the dark and the dan-ger, Far out in the night and the cold;
4. Not far, not far from the King-dom, 'Tis on-ly a lit-tle space;

How ma-ny are com-ing and go-ing!—How few there are en-ter-ing in!
Too tim-id to en-ter in bold-ly, So lin-ger still out-side the gate.
There Je-sus is wait-ing to lead you So ten-der-ly in-to His fold.
But oh, you may still be for-ev-er Shut out from yon heaven-ly place!

Not far from the Kingdom.
Refrain.
How few there are en - ter - ing in! How few there are en - ter - ing in!
How ma - ny are com - ing and go - ing!—How few there are en - ter - ing in!
No. 300. Only a Beam of Sunshine.
"Be kindly affectioned one to another."—Rom. 12: 10.
Fanny J. Crosby.
Jno. R. Sweney.
1. On - ly a beam of sun - shine, But oh, it was warm and bright; The
2. On - ly a beam of sun - shine That in - to a dwell - ing crept, Where,
3. On - ly a word for Je - sus! Oh, speak it in His dear name; To
heart of a wea - ry trav - 'ler Was cheer'd by its wel - come sight.
o - ver a fad - ing rose - bud, A moth - er her vig - il kept.
per - ish-ing souls a - round you The mes - sage of love pro - claim.
On - ly a beam of sun - shine That fell from the arch a - bove, And
On - ly a beam of sun - shine That smil'd thro' her fall - ing tears, And
Go, like the faith - ful sun - beam, Your mis - sion of joy ful - fil; Re -
ten - der - ly, soft - ly whis - per'd A mes - sage of peace and love.
show'd her the bow of prom - ise, For - got - ten per - haps for years.
mem - ber the Sav - iour's prom - ise, That He will be with you still.
From "Melodious Sonnets," by per. John J. Hood.

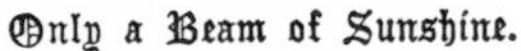

CHORUS.

On - ly a word for Je - sus, On - ly a whis - per'd pray'r
O - ver some grief-worn spir - it May rest like a sun - beam fair.

No. 301. Awake, my Soul.

JOEL BARLOW. (ST. PETER. C. M.) A. R. REINAGLE.

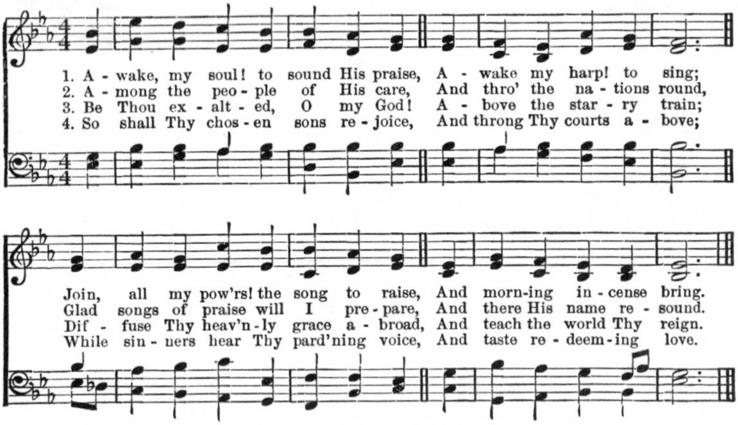

1. A - wake, my soul! to sound His praise, A - wake my harp! to sing;
Join, all my pow'rs! the song to raise, And morn-ing in - cense bring.

2. A - mong the peo - ple of His care, And thro' the na - tions round,
Glad songs of praise will I pre - pare, And there His name re - sound.

3. Be Thou ex - alt - ed, O my God! A - bove the star - ry train;
Dif - fuse Thy heav'n - ly grace a - broad, And teach the world Thy reign.

4. So shall Thy chos - en sons re - joice, And throng Thy courts a - bove;
While sin - ners hear Thy pard'ning voice, And taste re - deem - ing love.

No. 302. The Child of a King!

"Heirs of the kingdom."—JAMES. 2: 5.

HATTIE E BUELL. JOHN B. SUMNER, arr.

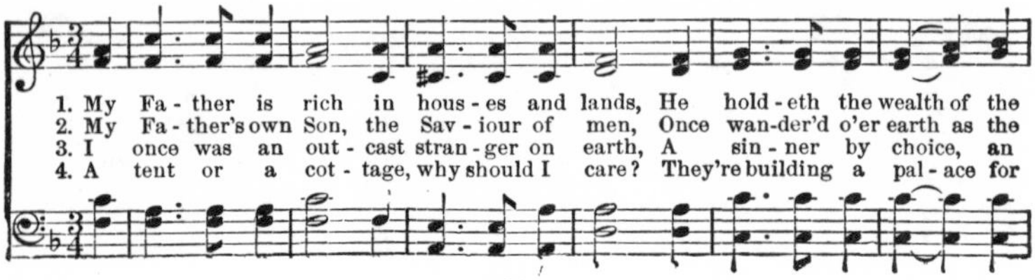

1. My Fa - ther is rich in hous - es and lands, He hold - eth the wealth of the
2. My Fa - ther's own Son, the Sav - iour of men, Once wan-der'd o'er earth as the
3. I once was an out - cast stran - ger on earth, A sin - ner by choice, an
4. A tent or a cot - tage, why should I care? They're building a pal - ace for

The Child of a King!

world in His hands! Of ru - bies and diamonds, of sil - ver and gold, His
poor - est of them; But now He is reigning for ev - er on high, And will
a - lien by birth! But I've been a - dopt-ed, my name's writ-ten down,—An
me o - ver there! Tho' ex - iled from home, yet still I may sing: All
Chorus.
cof - fers are full,—He has rich - es un - told.
give me a home in heav'n by and by.
heir to a mansion, a robe, and a crown!
glo - ry to God, I'm the child of a King!
I'm the child of a King! The
ad lib.
child of a King! With Je - sus my Sav-iour, I'm the child of a King!
Copyright, 1882, by Biglow & Main.

No. 303. Songs of Gladness.

"In thy presence is fulness of joy; at thy right hand there are pleasures forever more."—Ps. 16: 11.

HORATIUS BONAR. Alt. IRA D. SANKEY.

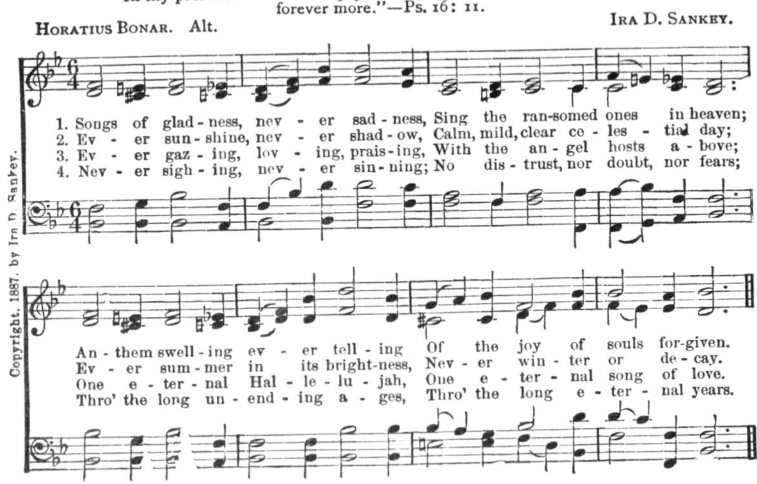

1. Songs of glad - ness, nev - er sad - ness, Sing the ran-somed ones in heaven;
2. Ev - er sun - shine, nev - er shad - ow, Calm, mild, clear ce - les - tial day;
3. Ev - er gaz - ing, lov - ing, prais - ing, With the an - gel hosts a - bove;
4. Nev - er sigh - ing, nev - er sin - ning; No dis - trust, nor doubt, nor fears;
An - them swell - ing ev - er tell - ing Of the joy of souls for-given.
Ev - er sum - mer in its bright-ness, Nev - er win - ter or de - cay.
One e - ter - nal Hal - le - lu - jah, One e - ter - nal song of love.
Thro' the long un - end - ing a - ges, Thro' the long e - ter - nal years.
Copyright, 1887, by Ira D. Sankey.

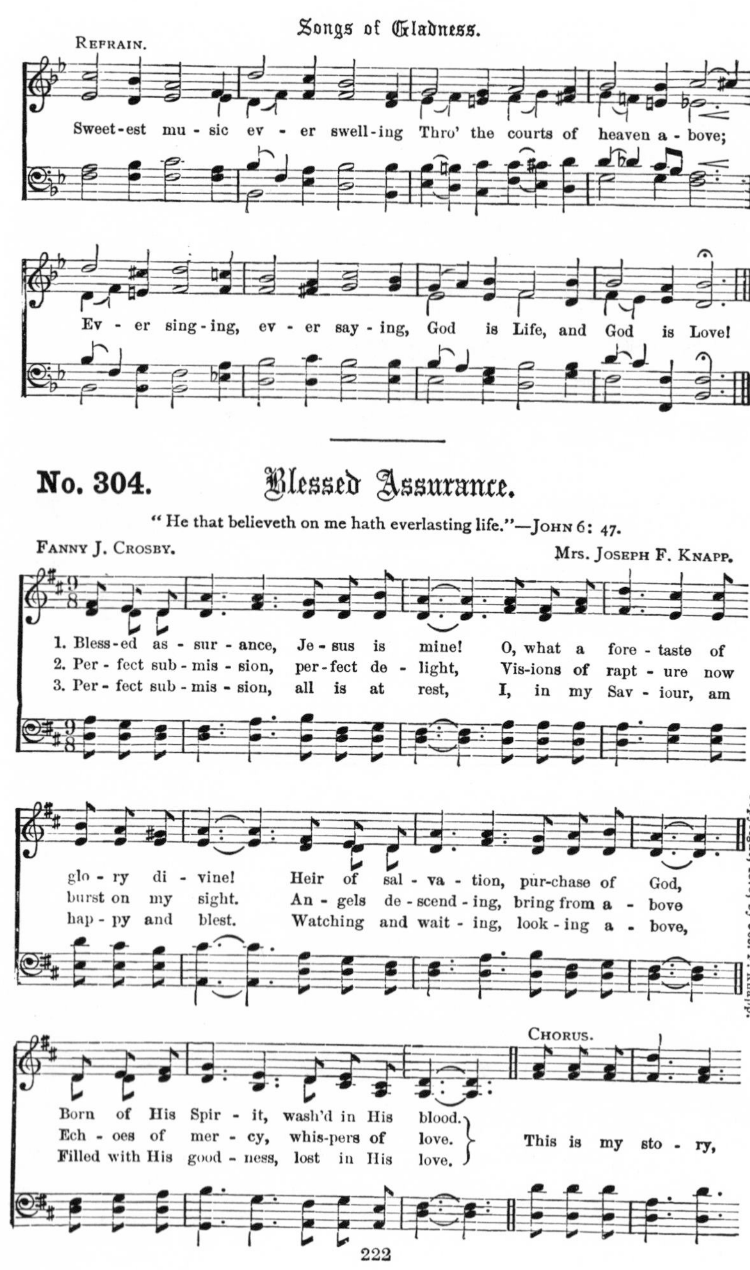
Refrain.
Sweet-est mu - sic ev - er swell-ing Thro' the courts of heaven a - bove;
Ev - er sing-ing, ev - er say - ing, God is Life, and God is Love!
No. 304. Blessed Assurance.
"He that believeth on me hath everlasting life."—John 6: 47.
Fanny J. Crosby.
Mrs. Joseph F. Knapp.
1. Bless-ed as - sur - ance, Je - sus is mine! O, what a fore - taste of glo - ry di - vine! Heir of sal - va - tion, pur-chase of God, Born of His Spir - it, wash'd in His blood.
2. Per - fect sub - mis - sion, per-fect de - light, Vis-ions of rapt - ure now burst on my sight. An - gels de - scend - ing, bring from a - bove Ech - oes of mer - cy, whis-pers of love.
3. Per - fect sub - mis - sion, all is at rest, I, in my Sav - iour, am hap - py and blest. Watching and wait - ing, look - ing a - bove, Filled with His good - ness, lost in His love.
Chorus.
This is my sto - ry,
Copyright, 1873, by Jos. F. Knapp.

Blessed Assurance.
this is my song, Praising my Saviour all the day long; This is my
sto - ry, this is my song, Prais-ing my Sav - iour all the day long.
No. 305.
At the Cross.
"Look unto me, and be ye saved."—Isa. 45: 22.
I. Watts.
R. E. Hudson.
1. A - las! and did my Saviour bleed, And did my Sovereign die? Would He devote that
2. Was it for crimes that I have done, He groaned up-on the tree? A - maz - ing pit - y,
3. But drops of grief can ne'er re - pay The debt of love I owe; Here, Lord, I give my -
sa - cred head For such a worm as I?
grace unknown, And love be-yond de - gree!
self a - way, 'Tis all that I can do!
Chorus.
At the cross, at the cross, where I
first saw the light, And the bur-den of my heart rolled a - way,
rolled a-way,
It was
there by faith I re-ceived my sight, And now I am hap-py all the day.
Copyright, 1885, by R. E. Hudson.

No. 306. In the Shadow of His Wings.

" Hide me under the shadow of thy wings."—Ps. 17: 8.

Rev. J. B. Atchinson. E. O. Excell.

1. In the shad-ow of His wings There is rest, sweet rest; There is rest from care and
2. In the shad-ow of His wings There is peace, sweet peace, Peace that pass-eth un-der-
3. In the shad-ow of His wings There is joy, glad joy, There is joy to tell the
la-bor, There is rest for friend and neigh-bor; In the shad-ow of His wings,
standing, Peace, sweet peace that knows no end-ing; In the shad-ow of His wings,
sto-ry, Joy ex-ceed-ing, full of glo-ry; In the shad-ow of His wings,
There is rest, sweet rest, In the shad-ow of His wings There is rest, *sweet rest.*
There is peace, sweet peace, In the shad-ow of His wings There is peace, *sweet peace.*
There is joy, glad joy, In the shad-ow of His wings There is joy, *glad joy.*
Chorus.
There is rest, There is peace, There is joy In the shadow of His wings:
sweet rest, sweet peace, glad joy,
There is rest, There is peace, There is joy, In the shad-ow of His wings.
Sweet rest, sweet peace, glad joy,
From " Sacred Echoes and Songs of My Redeemer," by per.

No. 307. Jesus, Thy Name I Love.
J. G. Deck.
(Lyte. 6s. & 4s.)
J. P. Holbrook.
1. Je - sus, Thy name I love, All oth - er names a-bove, Je - sus, my Lord! Oh, Thou art
2. Thou, blessed Son of God, Hast bought me with Thy blood, Je - sus, my Lord! Oh, how great
3. When un - to Thee I flee, Thou wilt my Ref - uge be, Je - sus, my Lord! What need I
4. Soon Thou wilt come again! I shall be hap - py then, Je - sus, my Lord! Then Thine own
Used by per.
all to me! Noth-ing to please I see, Noth - ing a-part from Thee, Je - sus, my Lord!
is Thy love, All oth-er loves a-bove, Love that I dai - ly prove, Je - sus, my Lord!
now to fear? What earthly grief or care, Since Thou art ev - er near, Je - sus, my Lord!
face I'll see, Then I shall like Thee be, Then ev - er-more with Thee, Je - sus, my Lord!
No. 308. Jesus is Calling.
"Arise, he calleth thee."—John 11: 28.
Fanny J. Crosby.
Geo. C. Stebbins.
1. Je - sus is ten - der - ly call - ing thee home—Call - ing to - day, call - ing to - day;
2. Je - sus is call - ing the wea - ry to rest—Call - ing to - day, call - ing to - day;
3. Je - sus is wait - ing, oh, come to Him now—Waiting to - day, wait - ing to - day;
4. Je - sus is plead - ing, oh, list to His voice—Hear Him to - day, hear Him to - day;
Why from the sun-shine of love wilt thou roam Far - ther and far - ther a - way?
Bring Him thy bur - den, and thou shalt be blest; He will not turn thee a - way.
Come with thy sins, at His feet low - ly bow; Come, and no long - er de - lay.
They who be - lieve on His name shall re - joice; Quick - ly a - rise and a - way.
Copyright, 1883, by Geo. C. Stebbins.
Refrain.
Call - - ing to - day,............ call - - ing to - day;............
Call - ing, call - ing to - day, to - day; Call - ing, call - ing to - day, to - day;
Je - - - sus is call - - - ing, is ten - der - ly call - ing to - day.
Je - sus is ten - der - ly call - ing to - day,

No. 309. Shall you? Shall I?

Luke 13: 24.

G. M. J.
(Subject from M. E. I.)
James McGranahan.
f
pp
1. Some one will en - ter the pearl - y gate By and by, by and by,
2. Some one will glad - ly his cross lay down By and by, by and by,
3. Some one will knock when the door is shut By and by, by and by,
4. Some one will sing the tri - umph - ant song By and by, by and by,
f
repeat pp.
Taste of the glo - ries that there a - wait, Shall you? shall I?.........
Faith - ful, ap-proved, shall re - ceive a crown, Shall you? shall I?.........
Hear a voice say - ing, "I know you not," Shall you? shall I?.........
Join in the praise with the blood-bought throng, Shall you? shall I?.........
Copyright, 1887, by James McGranahan.
Some one will trav - el the streets of gold, Beau - ti - ful vis - ions will
Some one the glo - ri - ous King will see, Ev - er from sor - row of
Some one will call and shall not be heard, Vain - ly will strive when the
Some one will greet on the gold - en shore Loved ones of earth who have
f
repeat pp.
there be - hold, Feast on the pleasures so long fore-told: Shall you? shall I?.......
earth be free, Hap - py with Him thro' e - ter - ni - ty: Shall you? shall I?.......
door is barred, Some one will fail of the saint's re - ward: Shall you? shall I?.......
gone be - fore, Safe in the glo - ry for ev - er - more: Shall you? shall I?.......
No. 310. Oh, Wondrous Name!
"Wonderful, Counsellor, The mighty God."—Isaiah 9: 6.
Victoria Frances.
Ira D. Sankey.
1. Oh, wondrous Name, by prophets heard Long years before His birth; They saw Him com-ing
2. Oh, glorious Name, the angels praise, And ransomed saints a - dore,—The Name a-bove all
3. Oh, precious Name, ex - alt - ed high, To Him all pow'r is given; Thro' Him we tri-umph

Oh, Wondrous Name!
CHORUS.
from a-far, The Prince of Peace on earth.
oth-er names, Our Ref-uge ev-er-more.
o-ver sin, By Him we en-ter heaven.
The Won-der-ful! The Coun-sel-lor! The
Great and Might-y Lord! The ev-er-last-ing Prince of Peace! The King, the Son of God!
Copyright, 1886, by Ira D. Sankey.
No. 311. The Love that gave Jesus to Die.
EL. NATHAN.
JNO. 3: 16.
JAMES MCGRANAHAN.
1. Let us sing of the love of the Lord, As now to the cross we draw nigh; Let us
2. O how great was the love that was shown To us—we can nev-er tell why—Not to
3. Now this love un-to all God com-mends, Not one would His mer-cy pass by: "Whoso-
4. Who is he that can sep-a-rate those Whom God doth in love jus-ti-fy; What-so-
sing to the praise of the God of all grace, For the love that gave Je-sus to die.
an-gels, but men; let us praise Him a-gain For the love that gave Je-sus to die.
ev-er shall call," there is par-don for all In the love that gave Je-sus to die.
ev-er we need He in-cludes in the deed, In the love that gave Je-sus to die.
Copyright, 1887, by James McGranahan.
REFRAIN.
O the love that gave Je-sus to die, The love that gave Je-sus to die;
Praise God, it is mine, this love so di-vine, The love that gave Je-sus to die.

No. 312. O Brother, Life's Journey Beginning.

"Resist the devil, and he will flee from you."—James 4: 7.

Rian J. Sterling. Ira D. Sankey.

1. O broth-er, life's jour-ney be-gin-ning, With courage and firmness a-rise;
2. O broth-er, yield not the tempt-er, No mat-ter what oth-ers may do;
3. O broth-er, the Sav-iour is call-ing; Be-ware of the dan-ger of sin;
Look well to the course thou art choos-ing, Be earn-est, be watchful, and wise;
Stand firm in the strength of the Mas-ter, Be loy-al, be faith-ful, and true;
Re-sist not the voice of the Spir-it, That whispers so gen-tly with-in;
Re-mem-ber, two paths are be-fore thee, And both, thy at-ten-tion in-vite;
Each tri-al will make you the strong-er, If you, in the name of the Lord,
God calls you to en-ter His serv-ice,— To live for Him here, day by day,
But one leadeth on to de-struc-tion,— The oth-er to joy and de-light.
Fight man-ful-ly un-der your Lead-er, O-bey-ing the voice of His word.
And share by and by in the glo-ry That nev-er shall van-ish a-way.
Chorus.
God help you to fol-low His ban-ner, And serve Him wherev-er you go;
And when you are tempted, my broth-er, God give you the grace to say "No."

No. 313. O God, our Help.
(Bemerton. C. M.)
Isaac Watts.
H. W. Greatorex.
1. O God, our help in a - ges past, Our hope for years to come,
2. Un - der the shad - ow of Thy throne Still may we dwell se - cure;
3. Be - fore the hills in or - der stood, Or earth re - ceived her frame,
4. A thou - sand a - ges, in Thy sight, Are like an eve - ning gone;
Our shel - ter from the storm - y blast, And our e - ter - nal home:—
Suf - fi - cient is Thine arm a - lone, And our de - fence is sure.
From ev - er - last - ing Thou art God, To end - less years the same.
Short as the watch that ends the night, Be - fore the ris - ing sun.
No. 314. Fear Not!
"I am thy shield, and thy exceeding great reward."—Gen. 15: 1.
E. G. Taylor.
Geo. C. Stebbins.
1. Fear not! God is thy shield, And He thy great re - ward; His might has won the field:........ Thy strength is in the Lord!
2. Fear not! for God has heard The cry of thy dis - tress; The wa - ter of His word......... Thy faint - ing soul shall bless.
3. Fear not! be not dis - mayed! He ev - er - more will be With thee, to give His aid,........... And He will strengthen thee.
4. Fear not! ye lit - tle flock; Your Shepherd soon will come, Give wa - ter from the rock,......... And bring you to His home!
Refrain.
Fear not! 'tis God's own voice That speaks to thee this word; Lift up your head: re - joice...... In Je - sus Christ thy Lord!
Copyright, 1882, by Geo. C. Stebbins.

No. 315. There shall be Showers of Blessing.

Ezek. 34: 26.
El. Nathan.
James McGranahan.
1. "There shall be showers of blessing:" This is the promise of love: There shall be seasons refreshing, Sent from the Saviour above.
2. "There shall be showers of blessing"—Precious reviving again; O - ver the hills and the valleys, Sound of abundance of rain.
3. "There shall be showers of blessing:" Send them up - on us, O Lord; Grant to us now a refreshing, Come, and now honor Thy Word.
4. "There shall be showers of blessing:" Oh, that to - day they might fall, Now as to God we're confessing, Now as on Je - sus we call!
Chorus.
Show - ers of bless-ing, Showers, showers of bless-ing,
Showers of blessing we need; Mercy-drops round us are falling, But for the showers we plead.
Copyright, 1883, by James McGranahan.
No. 316. Numberless as the Sands.
"The number shall be as the sand of the sea."—Hosea 1: 10.
F. A. B., arr.
F. A. Blackmer, arr.
1. When we gath - er at last o - ver Jor - dan, And the ransomed in glo - ry we see, As the numberless sands of the sea-shore—What a won-der-ful sight that will be!
2. When we see all the saved of the a - ges, Who from sorrow and tri - als are free, Meet-ing there with a heav-en - ly greet-ing—What a won-der-ful sight that will be!
3. When we stand by the beau - ti - ful riv - er, 'Neath the shade of the life-giv-ing tree, Gaz - ing o - ver the fair land of prom - ise—What a won-der-ful sight that will be!
4. When at last we be - hold our Re-deem - er, And His glo - ry transcendent we see, While as King of all kingdoms He reign - eth—What a won-der-ful sight that will be!
Copyright, 1887, by Ira D. Sankey

Numberless as the Sands.
CHORUS.
Num-ber-less as the sands of the sea - shore! Num-ber-less as the
sands of the shore! (of the shore!) Oh, what a sight 'twill be, When the
ran-som'd host we see, As num-ber-less as the sands of the sea - shore!
No. 317. Abide with Me.
"Abide with us, for it is toward evening."—LUKE 24: 29.
H. F. LYTE.
WM. H. MONK.
1. A - bide with me! Fast falls the e - ven - tide, The dark - ness
2. Swift to its close ebbs out life's lit - tle day; Earth's joys grow
3. I need Thy pres - ence ev - 'ry pass - ing hour, What but Thy
4. Hold Thou Thy cross be - fore my clos - ing eyes; Shine thro' the
deep - ens— Lord, with me a - bide! When oth - er help - ers
dim, its glo - ries pass a - way; Change and de - cay in
grace can foil the tempt - er's pow'r? Who, like Thy - self, my
gloom, and point me to the skies; Heav'n's morning breaks and
fail, and com-forts flee, Help of the help-less, oh, a - bide with me!
all a - round I see; O Thou, who changest not, a - bide with me!
guide and stay can be? Thro' cloud and sunshine, oh, a - bide with me!
earth's vain shadows flee! In life, in death, O Lord, a - bide with me!

No. 318. Rejoice in the Lord Alway.
Wilbur F. Crafts.
Phil. 4: 4.
James McGranahan.
1. O praise the Lord with heart and voice, With God's own word your doubts de - stroy,
2. My life is hid with Thine, O Lord, And shel-tered from the world's a - larm;
3. For noth - ing anx - ious I shall be, But trust - ing Thee in ev - 'ry - thing,
4. The joys that mem-'ry turns to pain, I leave for joys that nev - er end;
Let those that trust in Him re - joice, Yea, let them shout for joy.
Why should I sink be - neath my load, When lean - ing on Thine arm.
With thanks for ev - 'ry gift from Thee, My troub - les all take wing.
My loss I count my rich - est gain, For Christ His joy doth send.
Copyright, 1887, by James McGranahan.
f Chorus.
p
mf
Re - joice, re - joice in the Lord, re - joice in the Lord al - way;
f
p
mf
f
p
f
Re - joice, re - joice in the Lord, and a - gain I say, Re - joice!
f
p
f
Re - joice in the Lord, re - joice in the Lord,
No. 319. O, Land of the Blessed!
"Come, ye blessed of my Father, inherit the kingdom."—Matt. 25: 34.
Emily H. Miller.
Ira D. Sankey.
Moderato.
1. O Land of the bless-ed! thy shad-owless skies Sometimes in my dreaming I see;
Copyright, 1886, by Ira D. Sankey.
rit. . . . .
Fine.
I hear the glad songs that the glo - ri - fied sing, Steal o - ver E - ter - ni - ty's sea;
D.S.—I catch but a glimpse of thy glory and light, And whisper: "Would God I were there!"

O, Land of the Blessed!

D.S.
Though dark are the shadows that gather between, I know that thy morning is fair;......

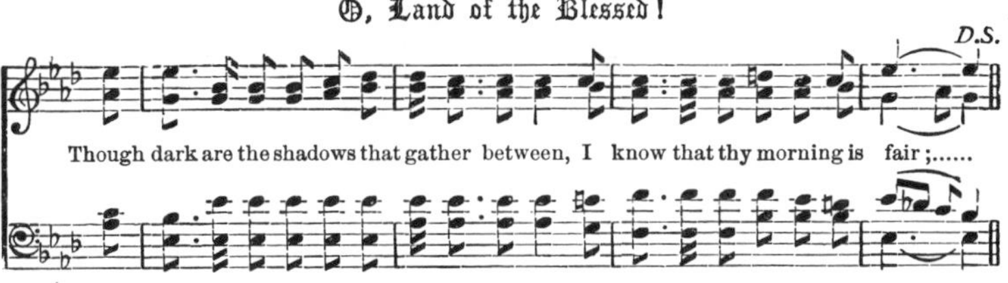

2 O Land of the blessed! thy hills of delight
Sometimes to my vision unfold;
Thy mansions celestial, thy palaces bright,
Thy bulwarks of jasper and gold;
Dear voices are chanting thy chorus of praise,
Their forms in thy sunlight are fair;
I look from the valley of shadows below,
And whisper: "Would God I were there!"

3 Dear home of my Father, thou City of peace,
No shadow of changing can mar;
How glad are the souls that have tasted thy joy
How blest thine inhabitants are!
When weary of toiling, I think of the day—
Who knows if its dawning be near?—
When He who doth love me shall call me away
From all that hath burdened me here?

No. 320. Nearer the Cross.

"The cross of our Lord Jesus Christ."—Galatians 6: 14.

F. J. Crosby. Mrs. J. F. Knapp.

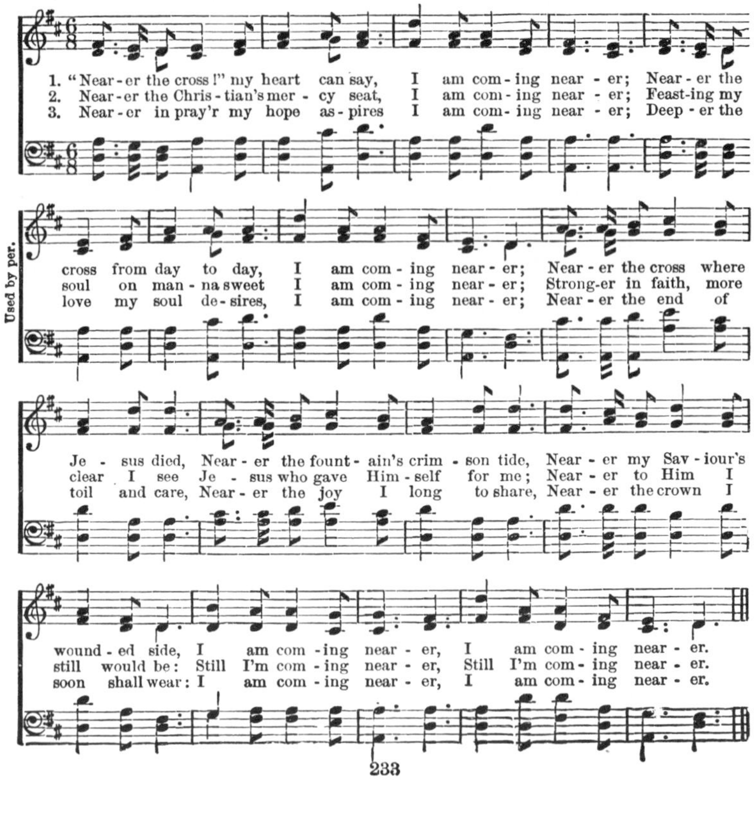

1. "Near-er the cross!" my heart can say, I am com-ing near-er; Near-er the
2. Near-er the Chris-tian's mer-cy seat, I am com-ing near-er; Feast-ing my
3. Near-er in pray'r my hope as-pires I am com-ing near-er; Deep-er the
cross from day to day, I am com-ing near-er; Near-er the cross where
soul on man-na sweet I am com-ing near-er; Strong-er in faith, more
love my soul de-sires, I am com-ing near-er; Near-er the end of
Je-sus died, Near-er the fount-ain's crim-son tide, Near-er my Sav-iour's
clear I see Je-sus who gave Him-self for me; Near-er to Him I
toil and care, Near-er the joy I long to share, Near-er the crown I
wound-ed side, I am com-ing near-er, I am com-ing near-er.
still would be: Still I'm com-ing near-er, Still I'm com-ing near-er.
soon shall wear: I am com-ing near-er, I am com-ing near-er.
Used by per.

No. 321. A Shelter in the Time of Storm.
Words arr.
"My God is the Rock of my refuge."—Ps. 94: 22.
Ira D. Sankey.
1. The Lord's our Rock, in Him we hide, A shel-ter in the time of storm;
2. A shade by day, de-fence by night, A shel-ter in the time of storm;
3. The rag-ing storms may round us beat, A shel-ter in the time of storm;
4. O Rock di-vine, O Ref-uge dear, A shel-ter in the time of storm;
Se-cure what-ev-er ill be-tide, A shel-ter in the time of storm.
No fears a-larm, no foes af-fright, A shel-ter in the time of storm.
We'll nev-er leave our safe re-treat, A shel-ter in the time of storm.
Be Thou our help-er ev-er near, A shel-ter in the time of storm.
Chorus.
Oh, Je-sus is a Rock in a wea-ry land, A wea-ry land, a wea-ry land; Oh,
Je-sus is a Rock in a wea-ry land, A shel-ter in the time of storm.
Copyright, 1885, by Ira D. Sankey.
No. 322. Mighty to Save.
"I that speak in righteousness, mighty to save."—Isaiah 63:1.
Rev. R. W. Todd.
Geo. C. Stebbins.
1. Oh, who is this that com-eth From E-dom's crim-son plain, With wounded side; with
2. Oh, why is Thine ap-par-el So ver-y deep-ly dyed?—Like them that tread the
3. O bleed-ing Lamb, my Sav-iour, How couldst Thou bear this shame? With mer-cy fraught, Thine
gar-ments dyed? Oh, tell me now Thy name. "I that saw thy soul's dis-tress,
wine-press red? Oh, why this crim-son tide? "I the wine-press trod a-lone,
arm has brought Sal-va-tion in Thy name! "I the vic-to-ry have won,
Copyright, 1887, by Ira D. Sankey.

Mighty to Save.
FINE.
A ran-som gave; I that speak in righteousness, Might-y to save!"
'Neath sorrow's wave; Of the peo-ple there was none Might-y to save!"
Con-quered the grave: Now the year of joy has come, Might-y to save!"
D.S.—Lord, I'll trust Thy wondrous love, "Mighty to save!"
CHORUS.
D.S.
Might-y to save! (to save!) Might-y to save! (to save!)
No. 323.
Christ Arose!
"He is not here, but is risen."—LUKE 24: 6.
R. L.
ROBERT LOWRY.
Slow.
1. Low in the grave He lay- Je-sus, my Sav-iour! Wait-ing the coming day—Je-sus, my Lord!
2. Vain-ly they watch His bed-Je-sus, my Sav-iour! Vain-ly they seal the dead—Je-sus, my Lord!
3. Death cannot keep his prey-Je-sus, my Sav-iour! He tore the bars a-way—Je-sus, my Lord!
CHORUS. faster.
Up from the grave He a-rose, With a might-y triumph o'er His foes;
He a-rose, He a-rose!
He a-rose a Vic-tor from the dark do-main, And He lives for-ev-er with His
rit.
saints to reign; He a-rose! He a-rose! Hal-le-lu-jah! Christ a-rose!
He a-rose! He a-rose!
Copyright, 1874, by Biglow & Main.

No. 324. Softly and Tenderly.

"Come unto me."—Matt. 11 : 28.

W. L. T. | Will L. Thompson.

Slow.

1. Soft-ly and ten-der-ly Je-sus is call-ing, Call-ing for you and for me;
See on the por-tals He's wait-ing and watching, Watching for you and for me.

2. Why should we tar-ry when Je-sus is pleading, Pleading for you and for me?
Why should we lin-ger and heed not His mer-cies, Mer-cies for you and for me?

3. Time is now fleet-ing, the moments are passing, Pass-ing from you and from me;
Shadows are gath-er-ing, death-beds are com-ing, Com-ing for you and for me.

4. Oh, for the won-der-ful love He has promis'd, Promis'd for you and for me;
Tho' we have sinn'd He has mer-cy and par-don, Par-don for you and for me.

Chorus.

Come home,...... Come home,....... Ye who are wea-ry, come home;.........
Come home, Come home,
Earn-est-ly, ten-der-ly, Je-sus is call-ing, Calling, O sinner, come home!

By permission of Will L. Thompson & Co., E. Liverpool, O.

No. 325. Whoever Will.

"Whosoever will, let him take of the water of life freely."—Rev. 22: 17.

A. Montieth. | Ira D. Sankey.

1. O wan-d'ring souls, why will you roam A-way from God, a-way from home;
2. Be-hold His hands ex-tend-ed now, The dews of night are on His brow;
3. In sim-ple faith His word be-lieve, And His a-bun-dant grace re-ceive;
4. The "Spir-it and the Bride say, Come!" And find in Him sweet rest, and home;

Whoever Will.

The Sav - iour calls, O hear Him say, Who - ev - er will may come to - day.
He knocks, He calls, He wait - eth still; Oh, come to Him, who - ev - er will.
No love like His the heart can fill, Oh, come to Him, who - ev - er will.
Let him that hear - eth, ech - o still, The bless - ed who - so - ev - er will.
Refrain.
Who - ev - er will, who - ev - er will, Who - ev - er will may come to - day;
Who - ev - er will may come to - day, And drink of the wa - ter of life.
Copyright, 1887, by Ira. D. Sankey.

No. 326. The Prodigal's Return.

"I will arise, and go to my Father."—Luke 15:,18.

John Newton. Arr. by Ira D. Sankey.

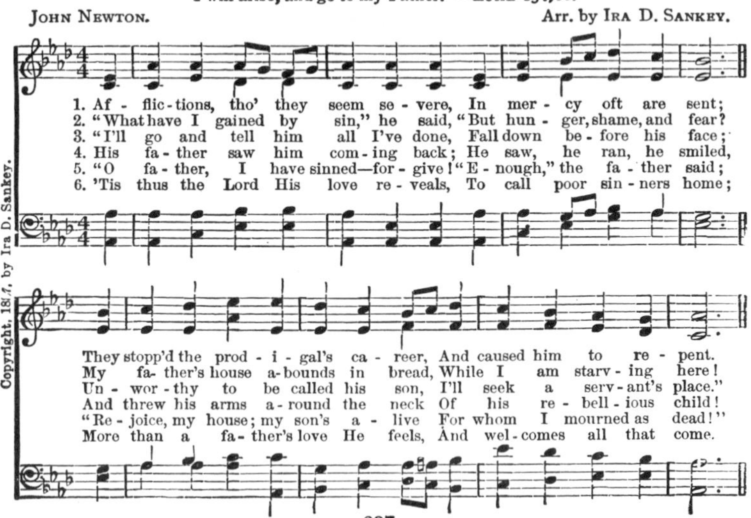
1. Af - flic - tions, tho' they seem se - vere, In mer - cy oft are sent;
2. "What have I gained by sin," he said, "But hun - ger, shame, and fear?
3. "I'll go and tell him all I've done, Fall down be - fore his face;
4. His fa - ther saw him com - ing back; He saw, he ran, he smiled,
5. "O fa - ther, I have sinned—for - give!" "E - nough," the fa - ther said;
6. 'Tis thus the Lord His love re - veals, To call poor sin - ners home;
They stopp'd the prod - i - gal's ca - reer, And caused him to re - pent.
My fa - ther's house a - bounds in bread, While I am starv - ing here!
Un - wor - thy to be called his son, I'll seek a serv - ant's place."
And threw his arms a - round the neck Of his re - bell - ious child!
"Re - joice, my house; my son's a - live For whom I mourned as dead!"
More than a fa - ther's love He feels, And wel - comes all that come.
Copyright, 18?, by Ira D. Sankey.

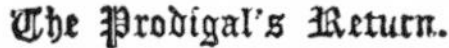
The Prodigal's Return.

CHORUS.
"I'll not die here for bread, "I'll not die here for bread," he cries; "Nor starve in
for - eign lands; My father's house has large sup-plies, And bounteous are his hands."

No. 327. Casting all your Care upon Him.

1 Pet. 5: 7.

From Cæsar Malan, by J. E. A. — James McGranahan.

1. How sweet, my Sav - iour, to re - pose On Thine al-might - y pow'r!
To feel Thy strength up - hold - ing me, Thro' ev - 'ry try - ing hour!

2. It is Thy will that I should cast My ev - 'ry care on Thee;
To Thee re - fer each ris - ing grief, Each new per - plex - i - ty;

3. That I should trust Thy lov - ing care, And look to Thee a - lone,
To calm each troub - led thought to rest, In prayer be - fore Thy throne.

4. Why should my heart then be dis-trest By dread of fu - ture ill?
Or why should un - be - liev - ing fear My tremb - ling spir - it fill?

CHORUS.

Cast - ing all .... your care up - on Him,.......................... Cast - ing
Cast - ing all your care, all your care up - on Him,

all........ your care up-on Him,................... Cast-ing all................ your care up-on
all your care, all your care upon Him, your care,
Him,................................ For He car - eth, He car - eth for you."
All your care up - on Him,
No. 328. Labor On.
"The harvest truly is plenteous; but the laborers are few."—Matt. 9: 37.
C. R. Blackall.
W. H. Doane.
Spirited.
1. In the har-vest field there is work to do, For the grain is ripe, and the reap-ers few;
2. Crowd the garner well with its sheaves all bright, Let the song be glad, and the heart be light;
3. In the gleaner's path may be rich re-ward, Tho' the time seems long, and the labor hard;
4. Lo! the Harvest Home in the realms a-bove Shall be gained by each who has toiled and strove;
And the Master's voice bids the workers true Heed the call that He gives to - day.
Fill the pre-cious hours, ere the shades of night Take the place of the gold - en day.
For the Master's joy, with His chosen shared, Drives the gloom from the dark-est day.
When the Master's voice, in its tones of love, Calls a - way to e - ter - nal day.
Copyright, 1870, by W. H. Doane.
Chorus.
La - bor on! la - bor on! Keep the bright re - ward in view;
La-bor on! la - bor on!
For the Mas - ter has said, He will strength renew; La-bor on till the close of day.

No. 329. Glory to God the Father.

"Every tongue should confess that Jesus Christ is Lord to the Glory of God the Father."—Phil. 2: 11.

El. Nathan. James McGranahan.

1. "For God so loved!" Oh, wondrous theme! Oh! wondrous key to wondrous scheme! A Saviour sent to sin-ful men— Glo-ry to God the Fa-ther!
2. In love God gave, in love Christ came, That man might know the Fa-ther's name, And in the Son sal-va-tion claim— Glo-ry to God the Fa-ther!
3. As man He tar-ried here be-low, The pow'r and love of God to show; To help and heal all hu-man woe— Glo-ry to God the Fa-ther!
4. Up-on the cross His life He gave, His peo-ple from their sins to save; For them de-scend-ed to the grave— Glo-ry to God the Fa-ther!
5. By God ex-alt-ed from the dead, He reigns on high the liv-ing head Of ev-'ry soul for whom He bled— Glo-ry to God the Fa-ther!

Chorus.

Glo-ry to God the Fa-ther! Glo-ry to God the Fa-ther!

Glo-ry, Glo-ry, *Glo-ry to the Fa-ther!* Glo-ry, Glo-ry, *Glo-ry to the Fa-ther!*

Glo-ry, Glo-ry, Glo-ry to God the Fa-ther!

No. 330. Wait, and Murmur Not.

"It is good that a man hope and quietly wait."—Sam. 3: 26.

W. H. Bellamy. Wm. J. Kirkpatrick.

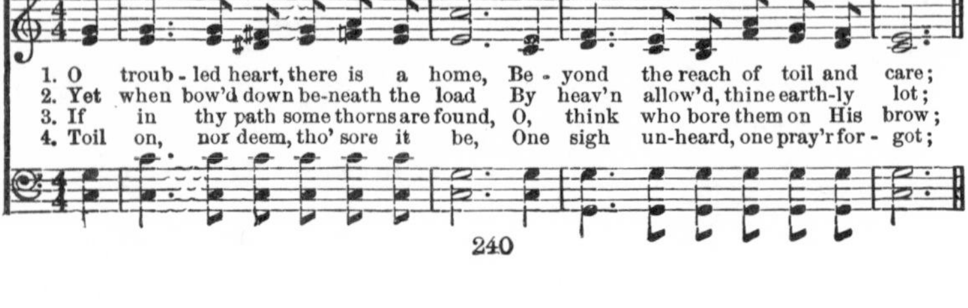

1. O troub-led heart, there is a home, Be-yond the reach of toil and care;
2. Yet when bow'd down be-neath the load By heav'n allow'd, thine earth-ly lot;
3. If in thy path some thorns are found, O, think who bore them on His brow;
4. Toil on, nor deem, tho' sore it be, One sigh un-heard, one pray'r for-got;

Wait, and Murmur Not.

A home where changes nev - er come; Who would not fain be rest -ing there?
Look up! thou'l't reach that blest a - bode, Wait, meek - ly wait, and mur-mur not.
If grief thy sorrowing heart has found, It reached a ho - li - er than thou.
The day of rest will dawn for thee; Wait, meek - ly wait, and mur-mur not.

CHORUS.

O, wait, meek - ly wait, meek - ly wait, and mur - mur not, O,
wait, meek - ly wait, meek-ly wait, and mur-mur not; O wait, meek-ly wait,
O, wait, meek - ly wait, O wait, and mur - mur not. O, mur-mur not.

From "Leaflet Gems," by per. John J. Hood.

No. 331. Christ Receiveth Sinful Men.

"They that are whole need not a physician, but they that are sick."—MATT. 9: 12.

Arr. from NEUMASTER. JAMES MCGRANAHAN.

1. Sin - ners Je - sus will re - ceive: Sound this word of grace to all
2. Come, and He will give you rest; Trust Him, for His word is plain;
3. Now my heart con-demns me not, Pure be - fore the law I stand;
4. Christ re - ceiv - eth sin - ful men, E - ven me with all my sin;

Christ Receiveth Sinful Men.

Who the heav'n - ly path - way leave, All who lin - ger, all who fall.
He will take the sin - ful - est; Christ re - ceiv - eth sin - ful men.
He who cleansed me from all spot, Sat - is - fied its last de - mand.
Purged from ev - 'ry spot and stain, Heav'n with Him I en - ter in.
Refrain.
Sing it o'er........................... and o'er a - gain:...................... Christ re -
Sing it o'er a - gain, Sing it o'er a - gain:
ceiv - - eth sin - ful men;..................... Make the mes - - sage
ceiv - eth sin - ful men, Christ re - ceiv - eth sin - ful men; Make the message plain,
clear and plain:........................ Christ re - ceiv - eth sin - ful men.
Make the mes - sage plain:
Copyright, 1882, by James McGranahan.
No. 332. Let the Saviour in!
"If any man hear my voice, and open the door, I will come in to him."—Rev. 3: 20.
J. B. Atchinson.
E. O. Excell.
1. There's a Stran - ger at the door; Let Him in!
2. O - pen now to Him your heart; Let Him in!
3. Hear you now His lov - ing voice? Let Him in!
4. Now ad - mit the heav'nly Guest; Let Him in!
Let the Saviour in! Let the Saviour in!

He has been there oft be - fore; Let Him in!
If you wait He will de - part; Let Him in!
Now, oh, now make Him your choice; Let Him in!
He will make for you a feast; Let Him in!
Let the Saviour in! Let the Saviour in!

Let Him in ere He is gone; Let Him in, the Ho - ly One,
Let Him in; He is your Friend; And your soul He will de - fend,
He is stand - ing at the door; Joy to you He will re - store,
He will speak your sins for - giv'n, And when earth - ties all are riv'n,

Je - sus Christ, the Fa - ther's Son; Let Him in!
He will keep you to the end; Let Him in!
And His name you will a - dore; Let Him in!
He will take you home to heav'n; Let Him in!
Let the Saviour in! Let the Saviour in!

No. 333. I Looked to Jesus.

"I looked to him, he looked on me, and we were one for ever."—C. H. SPURGEON.

EL. NATHAN. JAMES MCGRANAHAN.

Moderato.

1. I looked to Je - sus in my sin, My woe and want con - fess - ing;
2. I looked to Je - sus on the cross, For me I saw Him dy - ing;
3. I looked to Je - sus there on high, From death up-raised to glo - ry;
4. He looked on me! O look of love! My heart by it was bro - ken;
5. Now one with Christ, I find my peace In Him to be a - bid - ing,

Un - done and lost, I came to Him, I sought and found a bless - ing.
God's word be-lieved, that all my sins Were there up - on Him ly - ing.
I trust - ed in His power to save, Be - lieved the old, old sto - ry.
And, with that look of love, He gave The Ho - ly Spir - it's to - ken.
And in His love for all my need, In child - like faith con - fid - ing.

No. 334. Let us Crown Him.

"O Lord, our Lord, how excellent is thy name."—Ps. 8: 9.

Rev. E. PERRONET. JAMES McGRANAHAN.

Allegretto moderato.

1. All hail the pow'r of Je - sus' name! Let an - gels pros - trate fall;......
2. Let ev - 'ry kin - dred, ev - 'ry tribe, On this ter - res - trial ball,........
3. O that with yon - der sa - cred throng We at His feet may fall;........

Bring forth the roy - al di - a - dem, And crown Him Lord of all.
To Him all maj - es - ty as - cribe, And crown Him Lord of all.
We'll join the ev - er - last - ing song, And crown Him Lord of all.

CHORUS.
Let us crown Him, let us crown Him, Let us
Let us crown Him Lord of all, Let us crown Him Lord of all, Let us

Let us Crown Him.

crown the Great Re-deem - er Lord of all;......... Let us crown Him,
· Let us crown Him Lord of al.
Let us crown Him, Let us crown.................. Him Lord of all.
Let us crown Him Lord of all, Let us crown the Great Redeem-er Lord of all.

No. 335. Take Me as I Am.

"Him that cometh to me, I will in no wise cast out."—John 6: 37.

Eliza H. Hamilton. Ira D. Sankey.

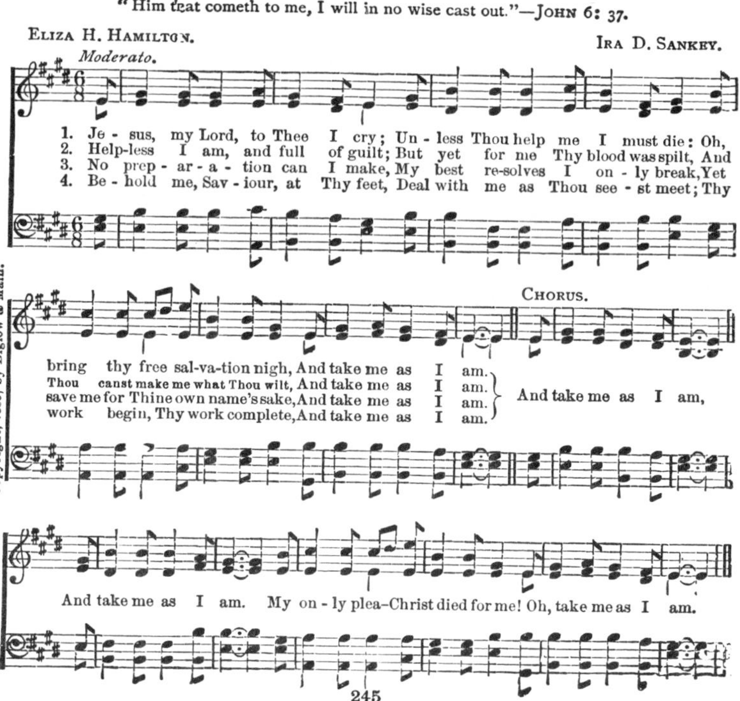

Moderato.
1. Je - sus, my Lord, to Thee I cry; Un - less Thou help me I must die: Oh,
2. Help-less I am, and full of guilt; But yet for me Thy blood was spilt, And
3. No prep - ar - a - tion can I make, My best re-solves I on - ly break, Yet
4. Be - hold me, Sav - iour, at Thy feet, Deal with me as Thou see - st meet; Thy
bring thy free sal-va-tion nigh, And take me as I am.
Thou canst make me what Thou wilt, And take me as I am.
save me for Thine own name's sake, And take me as I am.
work begin, Thy work complete, And take me as I am.
Chorus.
And take me as I am,
And take me as I am. My on - ly plea–Christ died for me! Oh, take me as I am.
Copyright, 1880, by Biglow & Main.

No. 336. Souls of Men, why will ye Scatter?

"All we like sheep have gone astray."—Isa. 53 : 6.

F. W. Faber. Wm. B. Bradbury.

1. Souls of men, why will ye scat - ter Like a crowd of fright-en'd sheep?
2. It is God! His love *looks* might - y, But *is* might - ier than it seems:
3. There is no place where earth's sorrows Are more felt than up in heaven;
Fool - ish hearts! why will ye wan - der From a love so true and deep?
'Tis our Fa - ther, and His fond - ness Goes far out be - yond our dreams.
There is no place where earth's fail-ings Have such kind - ly judgment given.
Was there ev - er kind - er Shep-herd, Half so gen - tle, half so sweet,
There's a wide - ness in God's mer - cy, Like the wide - ness of the sea;
There is wel - come for the sin - ner, And more gra - ces for the good;
As the Sav - iour who would have us Come and gath - er round His feet?
There's a kind - ness in His jus - tice, Which is more than lib - er - ty.
There is mer - cy with the Sav - iour; There is heal - ing in His blood.
rall.
Copyright, 1861. In "Golden Chain," by Wm. B. Bradbury.

4 But we make His love too narrow,
By false limits of our own;
And we magnify His strictness
With a zeal He will not own.
There is plentiful redemption
In the blood that has been shed;
There is joy for all the members
In the sorrows of the Head.

5 If our love were but more simple,
We should take Him at His word;
And our lives would all be sunshine
In the sweetness of our Lord.
For the love of God is broader
Than the measures of man's mind;
And the heart of the Eternal
Is most wonderfully kind.

No. 337. Welcome! Wanderer, Welcome!

"This my son was dead, and is alive again; he was lost, and is found."—Luke 15 : 24.

Horatius Bonar. Ira D. Sankey.

1. In the land of strangers, Wither thou art gone, Hear a far voice calling, "My son! my son!"
2. "From the land of hunger, Fainting, famished lone, Come to love and gladness, "My son! my son!"
3. "Leave the haunts of riot, Wasted, woe-begone, Sick at heart and weary, "My son! my son!"

Welcome! Wanderer, Welcome!
Copyright, 1884, by Ira D. Sankey.
Chorus.
"Welcome! wand'rer, welcome! Welcome back to home! Thou hast wandered far away: Come home! come home!"
4 "See the door still open!
Thou art still my own;
Eyes of love are on thee,
My son! my son!"
5 "Far off thou hast wandered;
Wilt thou farther roam?
Come, and all is pardoned,
My son! my son!"
6 "See the well-spread table,
Unforgotten one!
Here is rest and plenty,
My son! my son!"
7 "Thou art friendless, homeless,
Hopeless, and undone;
Mine is love unchanging,
My son! my son!"
No. 338. What a Gathering!
"Sorrow and sighing shall flee away."—Isa. 35: 10.
F. J. Crosby.
Ira D. Sankey.
Copyright, 1887, by Ira D. Sankey.
1. On that bright and gold - en morn - ing, when the Son of man shall come, And the radiance of His glo - ry we shall see; When from ev - 'ry clime and na - tion He shall call His peo - ple home, What a gath'-ring of the ran-somed that will be.
2. When the blest who sleep in Je - sus, at His bid - ding shall a - rise From the si - lence of the grave, and from the sea, And with bod - ies all ce - les - tial they shall meet Him in the skies, What a gath'-ring and re - joic - ing there will be.
3. When our eyes be - hold the cit - y, with its ma - ny mansions bright And its riv - er, calm and rest - ful, flow - ing free; When the friends that death has part - ed shall in bliss a - gain u - nite, What a gath'-ring and a greet - ing there will be.
4. O the King is sure - ly com - ing, and the time is draw - ing nigh, When the blessed day of promise, we shall see; Then the changing "in a moment," "in the twinkling of an eye," And for - ev - er in His pres - ence we shall be.
Chorus.
What a gath' - - ring, what a gath' - - ring, What a
What a gath'ring, what a gath'ring, gath'ring, what a gath'ring,

What a Gathering!
gath'ring of the ransomed in the summer land of love; What a gath' - - ring,
gath'ring, what a gath'ring
what a gath' - ring, Of the ran-somed in that hap-py home a - bove.
No. 339. Come, Great Deliverer, Come.
"Thou art my help and my deliverer."—Ps. 40: 17.
Fanny J. Crosby.
W. H. Doane.
1. O hear my cry, be gra-cious now to me, Come, Great De-liv' - rer, come;
2. I have no place, no shel-ter from the night, Come, Great De-liv' - rer, come;
3. My path is lone, and wea-ry are my feet, Come, Great De-liv' - rer, come;
4. Thou wilt not spurn con-tri-tion's bro-ken sigh, Come, Great De-liv' - rer, come;
My soul bowed down is long-ing now for Thee, Come, Great De-liv' - rer, come.
One look from Thee would give me life and light, Come, Great De-liv' - rer, come.
Mine eyes look up Thy lov-ing smile to meet, Come, Great De-liv' - rer, come.
Re - gard my prayer, and hear my hum-ble cry, Come, Great De-liv' - rer, come.
Copyright, 1877, by Biglow & Main.
Refrain.
I've wandered far a-way o'er mountains cold, I've wandered far a-way from home;
O take me now, and bring me to Thy fold, Come, Great De-liv' - rer, come.

No. 340. God be with You!

"The grace of our Lord Jesus Christ be with you."—ROMANS 16: 20.

J. E. RANKIN. W. G. TOMER.

1. God be with you till we meet a-gain!—By His counsels guide, up-hold you,
2. God be with you till we meet a-gain!—'Neath His wings protecting hide you,
3. God be with you till we meet a-gain!—When life's per-ils thick confound you,
4. God be with you till we meet a-gain!—Keep love's banner float-ing o'er you,

With His sheep se-cure-ly fold you; God be with you till we meet a-gain!
Dai-ly man-na still di-vide you; God be with you, till we meet a-gain!
Put His arms un-fail-ing round you; God be with you till we meet a-gain!
Smite death's threat'ning wave before you; God be with you till we meet a-gain!

CHORUS.

Till we meet!......... Till we meet! Till we meet at Je-sus' feet;
Till we meet! Till we meet a-gain! Till we meet!
Till we meet!......... Till we meet! God be with you till we meet a-gain!
Till we meet! Till we meet a-gain!

By per. of J. E. Rankin.

No. 341. Through the Valley and the Shadow.

"Yea, though I walk through the valley and the shadow."—PSA. 23: 4.

.IAN A. DYKES. IRA D. SANKEY.

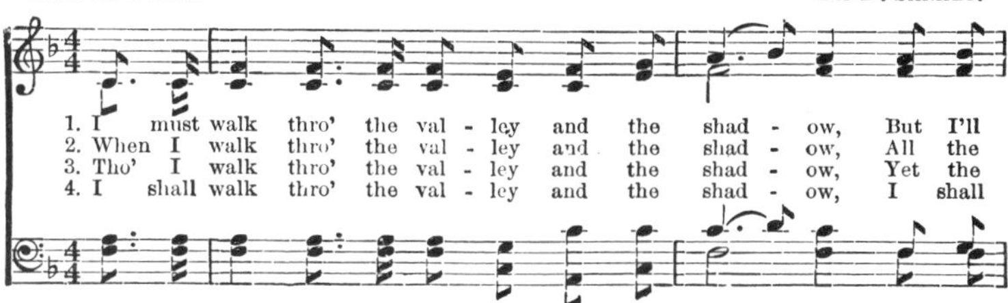

1. I must walk thro' the val-ley and the shad-ow, But I'll
2. When I walk thro' the val-ley and the shad-ow, All the
3. Tho' I walk thro' the val-ley and the shad-ow, Yet the
4. I shall walk thro' the val-ley and the shad-ow, I shall

Through the Valley and the Shadow.

jour - ney in a lov - ing Sav - iour's care; He hath said He will
wea - ry days of toil - ing will be o'er; For the strong arms of
glo - ry of the dawn - ing I shall see; I shall join in the
fol - low where my Lord has gone be - fore; Thro' the mists of the
D.S.—But the dark waves of
Fine.
nev - er, nev - er leave me, With His Staff He will com - fort me there.
Je - sus will en - fold me, And with Him I shall sor - row no more.
an - thems o - ver Jor - dan, Where the loved ones are wait - ing for me.
val - ley He will lead me, Till I rest on the ev - er - green Shore.
Jor - dan will not harm me, There is peace in the val - ley, I know.
Copyright, 1887, by Ira D. Sankey.
Chorus.
D.S.
Thro' the val - ley, thro' the val - ley, Thro' the val - ley and the shadow I must go,
No. 342.
Peace, Peace is Mine.
"He is our peace."—Eph. 2: 14.
J. Denham Smith.
James McGranahan.
1. God's almight - y arms are round me, Peace, peace is mine; Judgment scenes need not con-
2. While I hear life's rug - ged bil - lows, Peace, peace is mine; Why suspend my harp on
3. Ev - 'ry tri - al draws Him near - er, Peace, peace is mine; All His strokes but make him
4. Wel - come ev - 'ry ris - ing sunlight, Peace, peace is mine; Near - er home each roll - ing
Copyright, 1887, by James McGranahan.
found me, Peace, peace is mine. Je - sus came Him - self and sought me! Sold to Death, He
wil - lows? Peace, peace is mine. I may sing with Christ be - side me, Tho' a thousand
dear - er, Peace, peace is mine. Bless I then the hand that smit - eth, Gen - tly, and to
midnight, Peace, peace is mine. Death and hell can - not ap - pal me; Safe in Christ what-

Peace, Peace is Mine.

found and bought me! Then my bless-ed freedom taught me, Peace, peace is mine.
ills be-tide me; Safe-ly He hath sworn to guide me, Peace, peace is mine.
heal de-light-eth; 'Tis a-gainst my sins He fight-eth, Peace, peace is mine.
e'er be-fall me; Calm-ly wait I till He call me, Peace, peace is mine.

No. 343. Look Unto Me.

Isa. 45: 22.

El. Nathan. James McGranahan.

1. "Look un-to me, and be ye saved," O hear the blest command, Sal-va-tion full! sal-va-tion free! Proclaim thro' ev-'ry land.
2. "Look un-to me," up-on the cross, O wea-ry, burdened soul, 'Twas there on Me thy sins were laid, Be-lieve and be made whole.
3. "Look un-to me," thy ris-en Lord, In dark temp-ta-tion's hour, The need-ful grace I'll free-ly give, To keep from Satan's pow'r.
4. "Look un-to me," and not *with-in*, No help is *there* for thee; For par-don peace and all thy need, Look on-ly un-to Me.

Chorus.

"Look un-to me,............ and be ye saved,
"Look unto me, and be ye saved,
all the ends of the earth,.................. for I am God,........
all the ends, all the ends of the earth, for I am
God, I am God, there is none else............ Look un-to me, and be ye saved."...............
there is none else, and be ye saved."

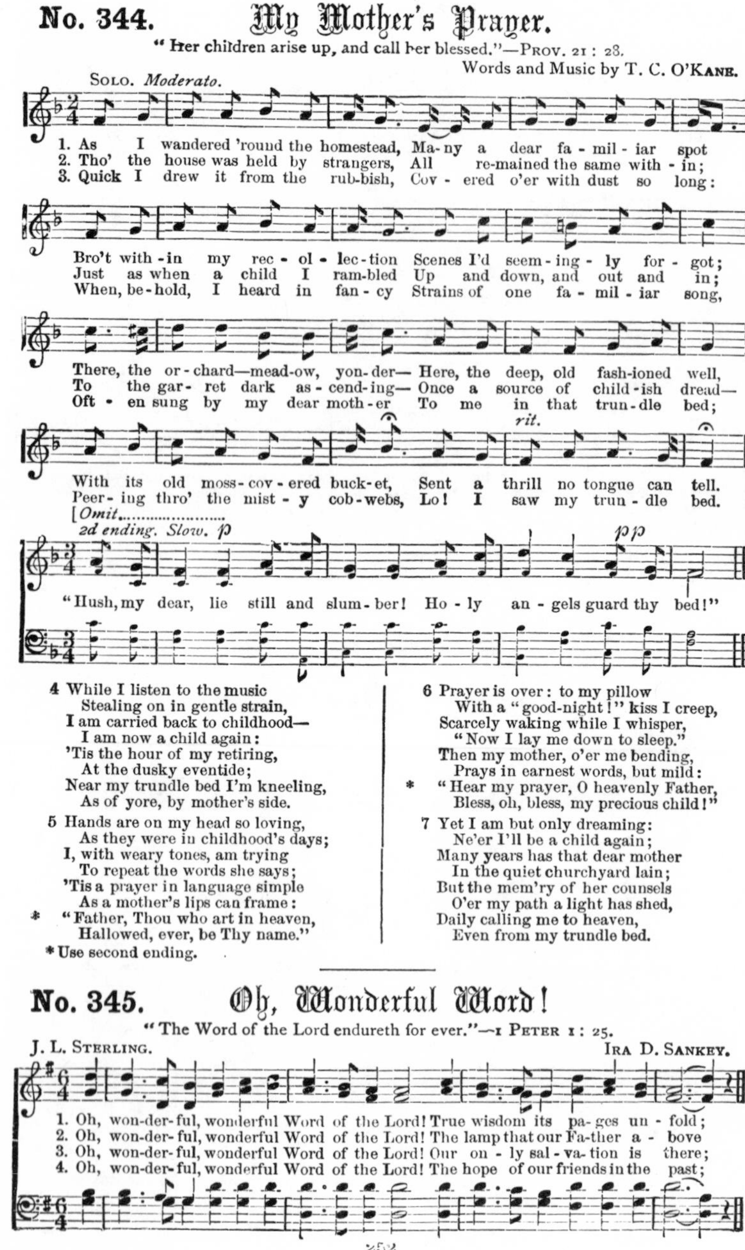
No. 344. My Mother's Prayer.
"Her children arise up, and call her blessed."—Prov. 21 : 28.
Words and Music by T. C. O'Kane.
Solo. Moderato.
1. As I wandered 'round the homestead, Ma-ny a dear fa-mil-iar spot
2. Tho' the house was held by strangers, All re-mained the same with-in;
3. Quick I drew it from the rub-bish, Cov-ered o'er with dust so long:
Bro't with-in my rec-ol-lec-tion Scenes I'd seem-ing-ly for-got;
Just as when a child I ram-bled Up and down, and out and in;
When, be-hold, I heard in fan-cy Strains of one fa-mil-iar song,
There, the or-chard—mead-ow, yon-der— Here, the deep, old fash-ioned well,
To the gar-ret dark as-cend-ing— Once a source of child-ish dread—
Oft-en sung by my dear moth-er To me in that trun-dle bed;
rit.
With its old moss-cov-ered buck-et, Sent a thrill no tongue can tell.
Peer-ing thro' the mist-y cob-webs, Lo! I saw my trun-dle bed.
[Omit.......................
2d ending. Slow. p pp
"Hush, my dear, lie still and slum-ber! Ho-ly an-gels guard thy bed!"
By per. of Ira D. Sankey, owner of copyright.
4 While I listen to the music
Stealing on in gentle strain,
I am carried back to childhood—
I am now a child again:
'Tis the hour of my retiring,
At the dusky eventide;
Near my trundle bed I'm kneeling,
As of yore, by mother's side.
5 Hands are on my head so loving,
As they were in childhood's days;
I, with weary tones, am trying
To repeat the words she says;
'Tis a prayer in language simple
As a mother's lips can frame:
* "Father, Thou who art in heaven,
Hallowed, ever, be Thy name."
* Use second ending.
6 Prayer is over: to my pillow
With a "good-night!" kiss I creep,
Scarcely waking while I whisper,
"Now I lay me down to sleep."
Then my mother, o'er me bending,
Prays in earnest words, but mild:
* "Hear my prayer, O heavenly Father,
Bless, oh, bless, my precious child!"
7 Yet I am but only dreaming:
Ne'er I'll be a child again;
Many years has that dear mother
In the quiet churchyard lain;
But the mem'ry of her counsels
O'er my path a light has shed,
Daily calling me to heaven,
Even from my trundle bed.
No. 345. Oh, Wonderful Word!
"The Word of the Lord endureth for ever."—1 Peter 1 : 25.
J. L. Sterling. Ira D. Sankey.
1. Oh, won-der-ful, wonderful Word of the Lord! True wisdom its pa-ges un-fold;
2. Oh, won-der-ful, wonderful Word of the Lord! The lamp that our Fa-ther a-bove
3. Oh, won-der-ful, wonderful Word of the Lord! Our on-ly sal-va-tion is there;
4. Oh, won-der-ful, wonderful Word of the Lord! The hope of our friends in the past;

Oh, Wonderful Word!

And tho' we may read them a thousand times o'er, They nev-er, no nev-er, grow old!
So kind-ly has light-ed to teach us the way That leads to the arms of His love:
It car-ries con-vic-tion down deep in the heart, And shows us ourselves as we are.
Its truth, where so firmly they anchored their trust, Thro' a-ges e-ter-nal shall last.
Each line hath a treasure, each promise a pearl, That all if they will may se-cure; And we
Its warnings, its counsels, are faithful and just; Its judgments are perfect and pure; And we
It tells of a Saviour, and points to the cross, Where pardon we now may se-cure; For we
Oh, won-der-ful, wonder-ful Word of the Lord! Unchang-ing, a-bid-ing and sure; For we
know that when time and the world pass a-way, God's Word shall for-ev-er en-dure.
Copyright, 1886, by Ira D. Sankey.

No. 346. The Sweetest Name.

"Thou shalt call his name Jesus; for he shall save his people from their sins."—Matt. 1: 21.

Geo. W. Bethune. Wm. B. Bradbury.

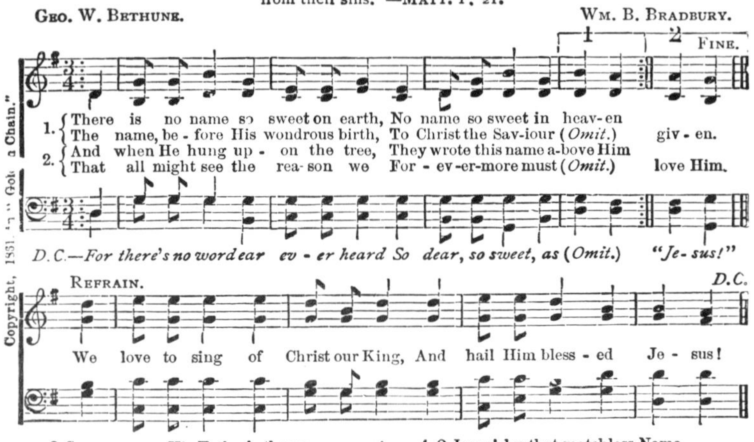

1 2 Fine.
1. {There is no name so sweet on earth, No name so sweet in heav-en
{The name, be-fore His wondrous birth, To Christ the Sav-iour (Omit.) giv-en.
2. {And when He hung up-on the tree, They wrote this name a-bove Him
{That all might see the rea-son we For-ev-er-more must (Omit.) love Him.
D.C.—For there's no word ear ev-er heard So dear, so sweet, as (Omit.) "Je-sus!"
Refrain. D.C.
We love to sing of Christ our King, And hail Him bless-ed Je-sus!
Copyright, 1881, in "Golden Chain."

3 So now, upon His Father's throne—
Almighty to release us
From sin and pain—He ever reigns,
The Prince and Saviour, Jesus.

4 O Jesus! by that matchless Name
Thy grace shall fail us never
To-day as yesterday the same,
Thou art the same for ever!

No. 347. The Harbor Bell.

"We were nearing a dangerous coast, and night was drawing near; suddenly a heavy fog settled down upon us; no lights had been sighted, the pilot seemed anxious and troubled, not knowing how soon we might be dashed to pieces on the hidden rocks along the shore; The whistle was blown loud and long, but no response was heard; the Captain ordered the engines to be stopped and for some time we drifted about on the waves; Suddenly the pilot cried,—Hark! and far away in the distance, we heard the welcome tones of the Harbor bell, which seemed to say, This way,—this way,— Again the engines were started, and guided by the welcome sound we entered the port in safety."

JOHN H. YATES.
(SOLO AND CHORUS.)
IRA D. SANKEY.
1. Our life is like a storm-y sea Swept by the gales of sin and grief, While on the windward and the lee Hang heavy clouds of un-be-lief; But o'er the deep a call we hear, Like har-bor bell's in-vit-ing voice; It tells the lost that hope is near, And bids the trembling soul re-joice.
2. O let us now the call o-bey, And steer our bark for yon-der shore, Where still that voice di-rects the way, In plead-ing tones for ev-er more; A thousand life wrecks strew the sea; They're going down at ev-'ry swell; "Come unto me," Come un-to me," Rings out th' assur-ing Har-bor bell.
3. O tempt-ed one, look up, be strong; The prom-ise of the Lord is sure, That they shall sing the vic-tor's song, Who faithful to the end en-dure; God's Ho-ly Spir-it comes to thee, Of His a-bid-ing love to tell; To bliss-ful port, o'er stormy sea, Calls heav'n's in-vit-ing Har-bor bell.
4. Come, gracious Lord, and in thy love Conduct us o'er life's stormy wave; O guide us to the home a-bove, The bliss-ful home beyond the grave; There safe from rock, and storm, and flood, Our song of praise shall nev-er cease, To Him who bought us with His blood, And brought us to the port of peace.
CHORUS.
This way, this way, O heart oppress'd, So long by storm and tem-pest driv'n; This way, this way, lo, here is rest, Rings out the Har-bor bell of heaven.
rit.
Copyright, MDCCCXCI, by The Biglow & Main Co.

No. 348. No Hope in Jesus.

"Having no hope, and without God in the world."—EPH. 2: 12.

Rev. W. O. CUSHING. Rev. ROBERT LOWRY.

1. Oh, to have no Christ, no Saviour! No Rock, no Ref - uge nigh! When the dark days 'round thee gath-er, When the storms sweep o'er the sky!
2. Oh, to have no Christ, no Sav-iour! How lone - ly life must be! Like a sail - or, lost and driv - en, On a wide and shoreless sea.
3. Oh, to have no Christ, no Sav-iour! No hand to clasp thine own! Thro' the dark, dark vale of shadows, Thou must press thy way a - lone.
4. Now, we pray thee, come to Je - sus; His pard'ning love re - ceive; For the Sav - iour now is call - ing, And He bids thee turn and live.

CHORUS.

Oh, to have no hope in Je - sus! No Friend, no Light in Jesus! Oh, to have no hope in Je - sus! How dark this world must be!
*Come to Je - sus, He will save you; He is the Friend of sinners; Then, when thou hast found the Saviour, How bright this world will be!

* For last verse only.

No. 349. There is a Land.

"A better country, that is a heavenly."—HEB. 11: 16.

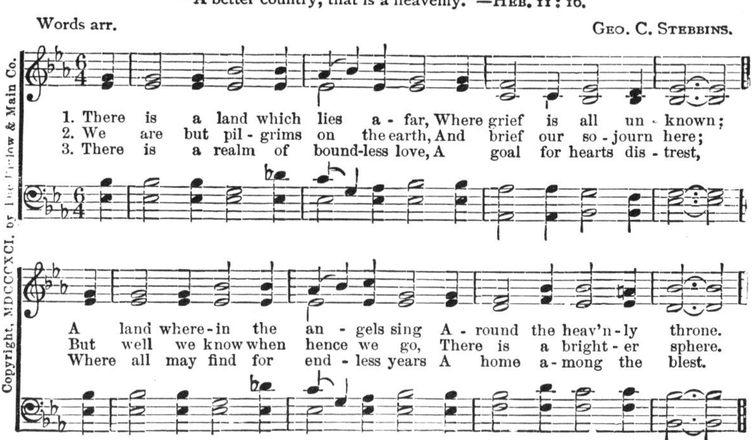
Words arr.
GEO. C. STEBBINS.
1. There is a land which lies a - far, Where grief is all un - known; A land where-in the an - gels sing A - round the heav'n-ly throne.
2. We are but pil - grims on the earth, And brief our so - journ here; But well we know when hence we go, There is a bright - er sphere.
3. There is a realm of bound-less love, A goal for hearts dis - trest, Where all may find for end - less years A home a - mong the blest.
Copyright, MDCCCXCI, by The Biglow & Main Co.

There is a Land.
Refrain.
O 'twill be sweet when we shall meet Up-on that dis-tant shore, Where-on the glo-rious
sun ne'er sets, But shines for-ev-er-more, But shines for-ev-er-more.
No. 350. "I am He that Liveth."
"And was dead; and behold I am alive forever more."—Rev. 1: 18.
C. R. H.
J. H. Burke.
1. He dies! He dies! the low-ly Man of sor-rows, On whom were laid our many griefs and
2. He lives! He lives! what glorious conso-la-tion! Ex-alt-ed at His Father's own right
3. He comes! He comes! O blest an-tic-i-pa-tion! In keep-ing with His true and faithful
woes; Our sins He bore, be-neath God's awful bil-lows, And He hath triumph'd o-ver
hand, He pleads for us, and by His in-ter-ces-sion, En-a-bles all His saints by
word; To call us to our heav'nly con-sum-ma-tion–Caught up, to be "for-ev-er
all our foes.
grace to stand.
with the Lord."
Chorus.
"I am he that liv-eth, that liv-eth and was dead,
I am he that liv-eth, that liv-eth and was dead; And be-hold,...... I am a-
I am, I
Copyright, MDCCCXCI, by The Biglow & Main Co.

live............ for - ev - er - more, Be - hold,............ I am a-
am a - live for - ev - er - more, I am, I
live......... for-ev-er - more;..... I am he that liv - eth, that liv - eth and was
am a-live for - ev-er-more;
dead, And be - hold,........... I am a - live for - ev - - er - more."
I am, I am a - live for - ev - er, ev - er - more."

No. 351. Joy Cometh in the Morning!

"Weeping may endure for a night, but joy cometh in the morning."—Ps. 30: 5.

M. M. Wienland. E. S. Lorenz, (Arr.)

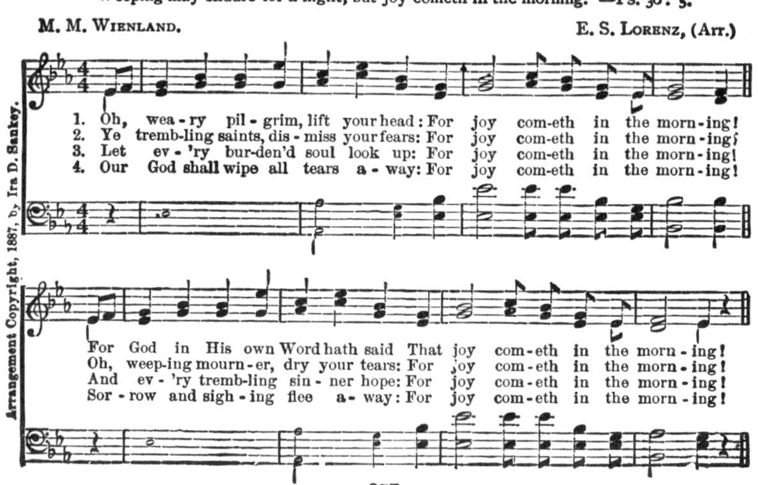
1. Oh, wea - ry pil - grim, lift your head: For joy com-eth in the morn-ing!
2. Ye tremb-ling saints, dis - miss your fears: For joy com-eth in the morn-ing!
3. Let ev - 'ry bur-den'd soul look up: For joy com-eth in the morn-ing!
4. Our God shall wipe all tears a - way: For joy com-eth in the morn-ing!
For God in His own Word hath said That joy com-eth in the morn - ing!
Oh, weep-ing mourn-er, dry your tears: For joy com-eth in the morn - ing!
And ev - 'ry tremb-ling sin - ner hope: For joy com-eth in the morn - ing!
Sor - row and sigh - ing flee a - way: For joy com-eth in the morn - ing!

Joy Cometh in the Morning!
Chorus.
Joy com - eth in the morn - ing! Joy com - eth in the morn - ing!
Weep - ing may en - dure for a night; But joy com - eth in the morn - ing!
No. 352. Rejoice, Rejoice Believer.
"Rejoice in the Lord alway."—Phil. 4: 4.
Grace J. Frances.
Hubert P. Main.
1. Re - joice, re-joice be - liev - er, And let thy joy and glo - ry ev - er be
2. Re - joice, in thy Re - deem - er, Thou hast a place that noth - ing can re-move;
3. Re - joice, re-joice be - liev - er, A home on high is wait - ing now for thee;
4. Re - joice, re-joice be - liev - er, Press on to join the hap - py, hap - py throng;
In Him, the Great De - liv - 'rer, Who gave Him-self a sac - ri - fice for thee.
He bids thee dwell in safe - ty, And rest be-neath the shad - ow of His love.
And there, in all His beau - ty, The King of saints with won - der thou shalt see.
Where soon thy Lord will call thee To realms of joy and ev - er - last - ing song.
Copyright, 1887, by Ira D. Sankey.
Chorus.
Re - joice, O re - joice, be - liev - er, Re - joice........ O re - joice, and sing Of
Him who lives for - ev - er, Thy great High Priest and King.

No. 353. Come unto Me.

"Come unto me all ye that labor, and I will give you rest."—MATT. 11 : 28.

NATH. NORTON.
GEO. C. STEBBINS.
1. "Come un - to Me," It is the Sav-iour's voice, The Lord of life, who bids thy heart re-joice; O wea - ry heart, with heav - y cares op-press'd, "Come un - to Me," and I will give you rest.
2. Wea - ry with life's long strug-gle full of pain, O doubt-ing soul, thy Sav - iour calls a - gain; Thy doubts shall van - ish and thy sor-rows cease, "Come un - to Me," and I will give you peace.
3. Oh, dy - ing man, with guilt and sin dis-mayed, With con-science wak - ened, of thy God a - fraid; Twixt hopes and fears— oh, end the anx-ious strife, "Come un - to Me," and I will give you life.
4. Rest, peace, and life, the flow'rs of death-less bloom, The Sav - iour gives us, not be-yond the tomb— But here, and now, on earth, some glimpse is giv'n Of joys which wait us thro' the gates of heav'n.
Copyright, 1887, by Ira D. Sankey.
REFRAIN.
"Come un-to me," "come un-to me," "Come un-to me, and I will give you rest," I will give you rest,...... I will give you rest........
"Come un - to me," oh, come un - to me, Come un - to me,
will give you rest, will give you rest.
ritard...............

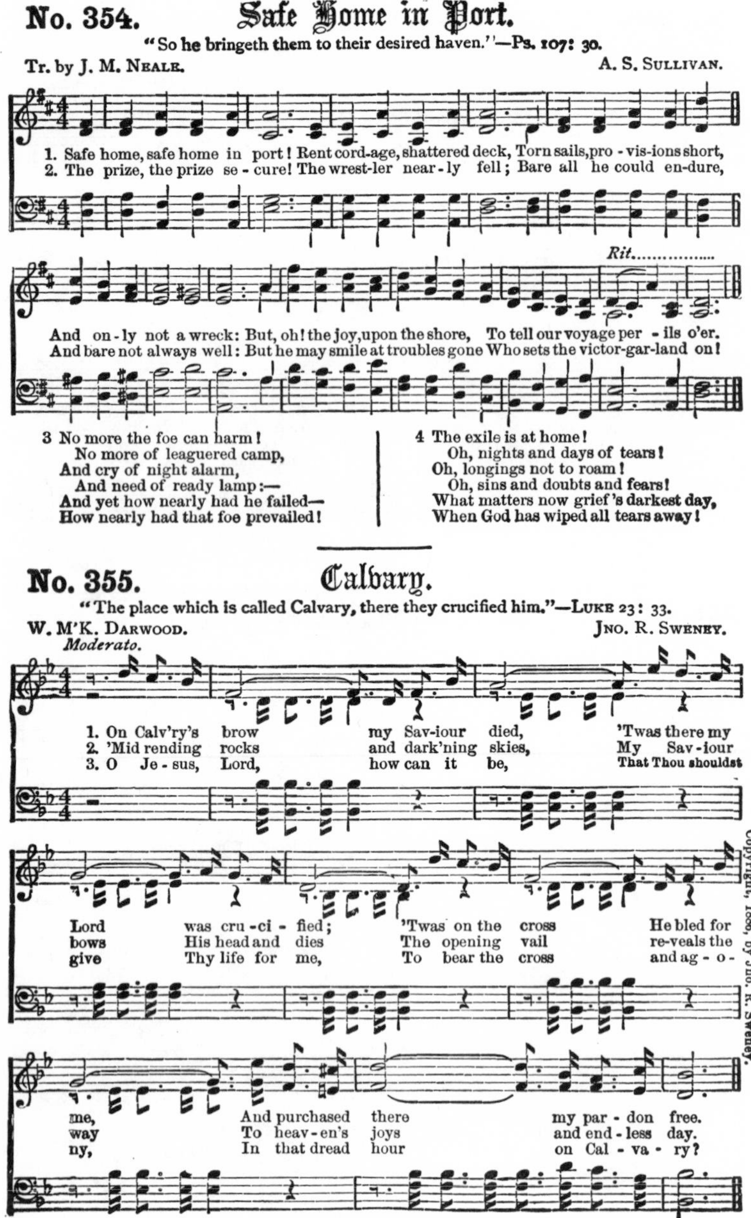
No. 354. Safe Home in Port.
"So he bringeth them to their desired haven."—Ps. 107: 30.
Tr. by J. M. Neale.
A. S. Sullivan.
1. Safe home, safe home in port! Rent cord-age, shattered deck, Torn sails, pro - vis-ions short,
2. The prize, the prize se - cure! The wrest-ler near - ly fell; Bare all he could en-dure,
Rit.
And on - ly not a wreck: But, oh! the joy, upon the shore, To tell our voyage per - ils o'er.
And bare not always well: But he may smile at troubles gone Who sets the victor-gar-land on!
3 No more the foe can harm!
No more of leaguered camp,
And cry of night alarm,
And need of ready lamp:—
And yet how nearly had he failed—
How nearly had that foe prevailed!
4 The exile is at home!
Oh, nights and days of tears!
Oh, longings not to roam!
Oh, sins and doubts and fears!
What matters now grief's darkest day,
When God has wiped all tears away!
No. 355. Calvary.
"The place which is called Calvary, there they crucified him."—Luke 23: 33.
W. M'K. Darwood.
Jno. R. Sweney.
Moderato.
1. On Calv'ry's brow my Sav-iour died, 'Twas there my Lord was cru - ci - fied; 'Twas on the cross He bled for me, And purchased there my par - don free.
2. 'Mid rending rocks and dark'ning skies, My Sav - iour bows His head and dies The opening vail re-veals the way To heav - en's joys and end - less day.
3. O Je - sus, Lord, how can it be, That Thou shouldst give Thy life for me, To bear the cross and ag - o - ny, In that dread hour on Cal - va - ry?
Copyright, 1886, by Jno. R. Sweney.

Calvary.
Chorus.
O Cal - va - ry! dark Cal - va - ry! Where Je - sus shed His blood for me, for me;
O Cal - va - ry! blest Cal - va - ry! 'Twas there my Sav - iour died for me.
rit.
p
No. 356. Hold Thou my Hand.
"I the Lord have called thee......and will hold thine hand."—Isaiah 42: 6.
Grace J. Frances.
Hubert P. Main.
Moderato.
1. Hold Thou my hand; so weak I am, and help - less, I dare not
2. Hold Thou my hand; and clos - er, clos - er draw me To Thy dear
3. Hold Thou my hand; the way is dark be - fore me With - out the
4. Hold Thou my hand, that when I reach the mar - gin Of that lone
take one step without Thy aid; Hold Thou my hand; for then, O lov - ing
self— my hope, my joy, my all; Hold Thou my hand, lest hap - ly I should
sun - light of Thy face di - vine; But when by faith I catch its ra - diant
riv - er Thou didst cross for me, A heaven - ly light may flash a - long its
Sav - iour, No dread of ill shall make my soul a - fraid.
wan - der, And, miss - ing Thee, my tremb - ling feet should fall.
glo - ry, What heights of joy, what rapt - urous songs are mine!
wa - ters, And ev - 'ry wave like crys - tal bright shall be.
Copyright, 1880, by Biglow & Main.

No. 357. Be ye Strong in the Lord.

"Be strong in the Lord, and in the power of his might."—EPH. 6. : 10.

EL. NATHAN.
IRA D. SANKEY.
1. "Be ye strong in the Lord and the pow - er of His might," Firm - ly
2. "Be ye strong in the Lord and the pow - er of His might," Nev - er
3. "Be ye strong in the Lord and the pow - er of His might," For His
standing for the truth of His word; He shall lead you safe - ly through the
turn-ing from the face of the foe; He will sure - ly by you stand, as you
prom - is - es shall nev - er, nev - er fail; By thy right hand He'll hold thee while
thick-est of the fight, You shall con - quer in the name of the Lord.
bat - tle for the right, In the pow - er of His might on - ward go.
bat - tling for the right, Trusting Him thou shalt for ev - er - more pre - vail.
Copyright, 1887, by Ira D. Sankey.
CHORUS.
Firm - ly stand for the right, On to
Firm - ly stand for the right,
vic - t'ry at the King's com-mand; For the hon - or of the Lord, and the
tri - umph of His word, In the strength of the Lord firm - ly stand.

No. 358. Resurrection Morn.

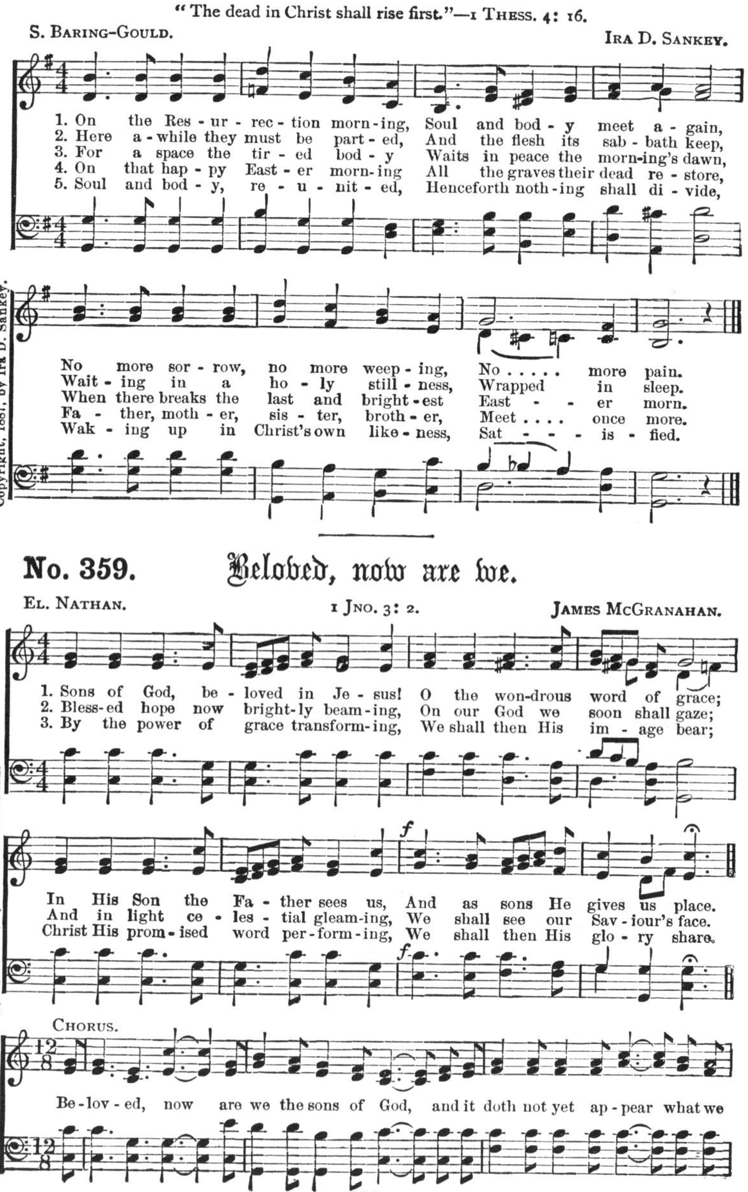
"The dead in Christ shall rise first."—1 Thess. 4: 16.
S. Baring-Gould.
Ira D. Sankey.
1. On the Res - ur - rec - tion morn - ing, Soul and bod - y meet a - gain,
2. Here a - while they must be part - ed, And the flesh its sab - bath keep,
3. For a space the tir - ed bod - y Waits in peace the morn-ing's dawn,
4. On that hap - py East - er morn - ing All the graves their dead re - store,
5. Soul and bod - y, re - u - nit - ed, Henceforth noth - ing shall di - vide,
No . . . . . more sor - row, no more weep - ing, No . . . . . more pain.
Wait - ing in a ho - ly still - ness, Wrapped in sleep.
When there breaks the last and bright - est East - - er morn.
Fa - ther, moth - er, sis - ter, broth - er, Meet . . . . once more.
Wak - ing up in Christ's own like - ness, Sat - - - is - fied.
Copyright, 1887, by Ira D. Sankey.
No. 359. Beloved, now are we.
El. Nathan.
1 Jno. 3: 2.
James McGranahan.
1. Sons of God, be - loved in Je - sus! O the won-drous word of grace;
2. Bless-ed hope now bright-ly beam-ing, On our God we soon shall gaze;
3. By the power of grace transform-ing, We shall then His im - age bear;
In His Son the Fa - ther sees us, And as sons He gives us place.
And in light ce - les - tial gleam-ing, We shall see our Sav - iour's face.
Christ His prom - ised word per - form - ing, We shall then His glo - ry share.
Copyright, 1883, by James McGranahan.
Chorus.
Be - lov - ed, now are we the sons of God, and it doth not yet ap - pear what we

but we know . . . . that when He shall ap-pear, ...
shall be: but we know, we know, we know that when He shall ap-pear, we
know . . . . that when He shall ap - pear, ... we shall be
know, we know, we know that when He shall ap-pear,
f
Rit.
like Him; we shall be like Him, for we shall see . . . Him as . . . He is. . . . . .
No. 360. There is a Name I Love.
F. Whitfield.
(Geer. C. M.)
H. W. Greatorex.
1. There is a name I love to hear; I love to sing its worth;
2. It tells me of a Sav - iour's love Who died to set me free;
3. It tells of One whose lov - ing heart Can feel my small - est woe—
4. It bids my tremb - ling soul re - joice, And dries each ris - ing tear;
It sounds like mu - sic in mine ear— The sweet - est Name on earth.
It tells me of His pre - cious blood—The sin - ner's per - fect plea.
Who in each sor - row bears a part That none can bear be - low.
It tells me in a "still small voice," To trust, and not to fear.

No. 361. Blessed be the Fountain.
"Wash me, and I shall be whiter than snow."—Psalm 51 : 7.
E. R. Latta.
H. S. Perkins.
Moderato.
1. Bless-ed be the Fount-ain of blood, To a world of sin-ners re-vealed;
2. Thorn-y was the crown that He wore, And the cross His bod-y o'er-came;
3. Fa-ther, I have wan-dered from Thee, Oft-en has my heart gone a-stray;
Bless-ed be the dear Son of God: On-ly by His stripes we are healed.
Grievous were the sor-rows He bore, But He suf-fered thus not in vain.
Crim-son do my sins seem to me— Wa-ter can-not wash them a-way.
Tho' I've wandered far from His fold, Bring-ing to my heart pain and woe,
May I to that Foun-tain be led, Made to cleanse my sins here be-low;
Je-sus to that Foun-tain of Thine, Lean-ing on Thy prom-ise I go;
Wash me in the Blood of the Lamb, And I shall be whit-er than snow.
Wash me in the Blood that He shed, And I shall be whit-er than snow.
Cleanse me by Thy wash-ing di-vine, And I shall be whit-er than snow.
Copyright. Used by per. Oliver Ditson & Co.
Chorus.
Whit - - - er than the snow, ... Whit - - - er than the snow; . . . .
Whiter than the snow, whiter than the snow, Whiter than the snow, whiter than the snow;
Wash me in the Blood of the Lamb, ... And I shall be whit-er than snow. . . .
rit. . . . .
Wash me in the Blood of the Lamb, of the Lamb, And I shall be whiter than snow, than snow.

No. 362. Now the Day is Over.

"For the shadows of the evening are stretched out."—JER. 6: 4.

SABINE BARING-GOULD. JOSEPH BARNBY.

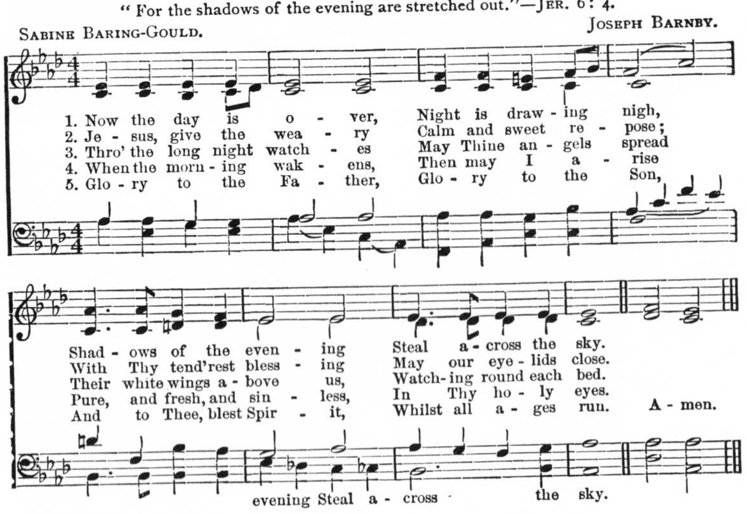

1. Now the day is o - ver, Night is draw - ing nigh,
2. Je - sus, give the wea - ry Calm and sweet re - pose;
3. Thro' the long night watch - es May Thine an - gels spread
4. When the morn - ing wak - ens, Then may I a - rise
5. Glo - ry to the Fa - ther, Glo - ry to the Son,
Shad - ows of the even - ing Steal a - cross the sky.
With Thy tend'rest bless - ing May our eye - lids close.
Their white wings a - bove us, Watch - ing round each bed.
Pure, and fresh, and sin - less, In Thy ho - ly eyes.
And to Thee, blest Spir - it, Whilst all a - ges run. A - men.
evening Steal a - cross the sky.

No. 363. In the Secret of His Presence.

"Thou shalt hide them in the secret of thy presence."—PSALM 31: 20.

ELLEN LAKSHMI GOREH, of India. GEO. C. STEBBINS.

Slowly.
1. In the se - cret of His pres - ence how my soul de - lights to hide!
2. When my soul is faint and thirst - y, 'neath the shad - ow of His wing
3. On - ly this I know: I tell Him all my doubts, my griefs and fears;
4. Would you like to know the sweet - ness of the se - cret of the Lord?
Slowly.
Oh, how pre - cious are the les - sons which I learn at Je - sus' side! Earth - ly
There is cool and pleas - ant shel - ter, and a fresh and crys - tal spring; And my
Oh, how pa - tient - ly He list - ens! and my droop - ing soul He cheers: Do you
Go and hide be - neath His shad - ow: this shall then be your re - ward; And when -
Copyright, 1885, by Ira D. Sankey.

In the Secret of His Presence.

cares can nev - er vex me, neither tri - als lay me low; For when Sa - tan comes to
Sav - iour rests be - side me, as we hold commu - nion sweet: If I tried, I could not
think He ne'er re - proves me? what a false friend He would be, If He nev - er, nev - er
e'er you leave the si - lence of that hap - py meeting place, You must find and bear the
rit.
tempt me, to the se - cret place I go, to the se - cret place I go.
ut - ter what He says when thus we meet, what He says when thus we meet.
told me of the sins which He must see, of the sins which He must see.
im - age of the Mas - ter in your face, of the Mas - ter in your face.
rit.

No. 364. Till He Come.

"For yet a little while and he that shall come will come, and will not tarry."—Heb. 10: 37.

Henry Alford. P. P. Bliss.

Moderato.
Fine.
1. "*Till He come!*"—Oh, let the words Lin - ger on the trem - bling chords,
2. When the wea - ry ones we love En - ter on their rest a - bove,
D.C.—Let us think how heav'n and home Lie be - yond that, "Till He come."
D.C.—Hush! be ev - 'ry mur - mur dumb! It is on - ly "Till He come."
D.C.
Let the "lit - tle while" be - tween In their gold - en light be seen;
When their words of love and cheer Fall no long - er on our ear,
Used by per. The John Church Co., owners of the Copyright.

3 Clouds and darkness round us press;
Would we have one sorrow less?
All the sharpness of the cross,
All that tells the world is loss,
Death, and darkness, and the tomb,
Pain us only "*Till He come.*"

4 See, the feast of love is spread,
Drink the wine and eat the bread:
Sweet memorials, till the Lord
Call us round His heavenly board,
Some from earth, from glory some,
Severed only "*Till He come.*"

No. 365. Onward, Christian Soldiers.

"Be strong and of a good courage."—Deut. 31: 6.
S. Baring-Gould.
A. S. Sullivan.
Presto.
1. On-ward, Christian sol - diers! Marching as to war, With the cross of Je - sus Go - ing on be - fore. Christ, the Roy - al Mas - ter, Leads a - gainst the foe; Forward in - to bat - tle, See His banners go.
2. Like a might - y ar - my Moves the Church of God: Brothers, we are tread - ing Where the saints have trod. We are not di - vi - ded, All one bod - y we— One in hope and doc - trine, One in char - i - ty.
3. Crowns and thrones may perish, Kingdoms rise and wane; But the Church of Je - sus Constant will re - main: Gates of hell can nev - er 'Gainst that Church prevail: We have Christ's own promise— And that can-not fail.
4. On-ward, then, ye faith - ful, Join our hap - py throng, Blend with ours your voi - ces, In the tri-umph song: Glo - ry, laud, and hon - or, Un - to Christ the King: This thro' countless a - ges Men and an-gels sing.
Chorus.
Onward, Christian sol - diers! Marching as to war, With the cross of Je - sus, Go - ing on be - fore.
With the cross of
No. 366. Jesus, Saviour, Pilot Me.
(Pilot. 7s. 6 lines.)
Rev. Edward Hopper.
J. E. Gould.
1. Je - sus, Sav - iour, pi - lot me, O - ver life's tem - pest - ous sea;
2. As a moth - er stills her child, Thou canst hush the o - cean wild;
3. When at last I near the shore, And the fear - ful break - ers roar

Jesus, Saviour, Pilot Me.

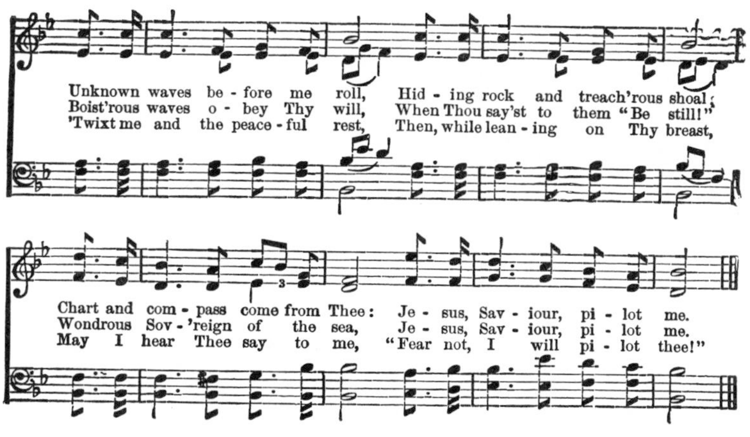
Unknown waves be - fore me roll, Hid - ing rock and treach'rous shoal;
Boist'rous waves o - bey Thy will, When Thou say'st to them "Be still!"
'Twixt me and the peace - ful rest, Then, while lean - ing on Thy breast,
Chart and com - pass come from Thee: Je - sus, Sav - iour, pi - lot me.
Wondrous Sov - 'reign of the sea, Je - sus, Sav - iour, pi - lot me.
May I hear Thee say to me, "Fear not, I will pi - lot thee!"

No. 367. The Lily of the Valley.

"I am the rose of Sharon, and the lily of the valleys."—Song of Solomon 2: 1.

C. W. Fry. Arr. from J. R. Murray by I. D. Sankey.

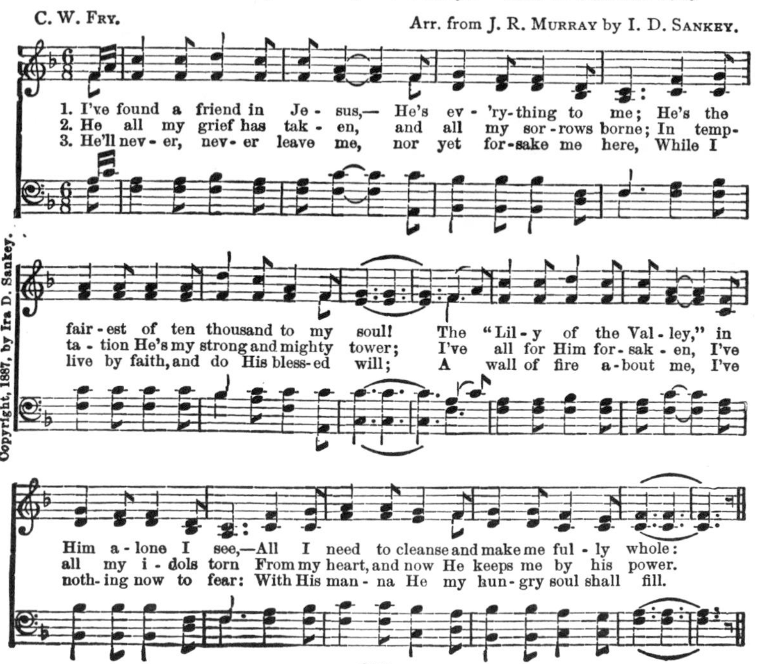
1. I've found a friend in Je - sus,— He's ev - 'ry-thing to me; He's the
2. He all my grief has tak - en, and all my sor - rows borne; In temp-
3. He'll nev - er, nev - er leave me, nor yet for-sake me here, While I
fair - est of ten thousand to my soul! The "Lil - y of the Val - ley," in
ta - tion He's my strong and mighty tower; I've all for Him for - sak - en, I've
live by faith, and do His bless - ed will; A wall of fire a - bout me, I've
Him a - lone I see,—All I need to cleanse and make me ful - ly whole:
all my i - dols torn From my heart, and now He keeps me by his power.
noth - ing now to fear: With His man - na He my hun - gry soul shall fill.

The Lily of the Valley.
In sor-row He's my com-fort, in troub-le He's my stay; He
Tho' all the world for-sake me, and Sa-tan tempts me sore, Thro'
When crown'd at last in glo-ry, I'll see His bless-ed face, Where
D.S.—In sor-row He's my com-fort, in troub-le He's my stay: He
tells me ev-'ry care on Him to roll; He's the "Lil-y of the Val-ley," the
Je-sus I shall safe-ly reach the goal; He's the "Lil-y of the Val-ley," the
riv-ers of de-light shall ev-er roll; He's the "Lil-y of the Val-ley," the
tells me ev-'ry care on Him to roll; He's the "Lil-y of the Val-ley," the
D.S. for Chorus.
Bright and Morning Star; He's the fair-est of ten thousand to my soul!
Bright and Morning Star; He's the fair-est of ten thousand to my soul!
No. 368. Jesus, the very Thought.
(St. Agnes. C. M.)
E. Caswall, tr.
John B. Dykes.
1. Je-sus, the ver-y tho't of Thee, With sweetness fills my breast;
2. Nor voice can sing, nor heart can frame, Nor can the mem-'ry find.
3. Oh, hope of ev-'ry con-trite heart! Oh, joy of all the meek!
But sweet-er far Thy face to see, And in Thy pres-ence rest.
A sweet-er sound than Thy blest name, O Sav-iour of man-kind!
To those who fall, how kind Thou art! How good to those who seek.

4 And those who find Thee, find a bliss
Nor tongue nor pen can show;
The love of Jesus, what it is
None but His loved ones know.

5 Jesus! our only joy be Thou,
As Thou our prize wilt be;
Jesus! be Thou our glory now,
And through eternity.

No. 369. I Am the Way.

Jno. 14: 6.

G. M. J. — James McGranahan.

1. Like wand-'ring sheep o'er mount-ains cold, Since all have gone a - stray;'
2. Be - wil-dered oft with doubt and care, To God I fain would go;
3. To Christ the Way, the Truth, the Life, I come, no more to roam;
To "Life" and peace with-in the fold, How may I find the way?.........
While ma - ny cry "Lo here! lo there!" The Truth how may I know?..........
He'll guide me to my "Father's house," To my E - ter - nal home.........
Chorus.
I...................... am the way,...................... the truth,................ and the
I am the way, I am the way, I am the way, the
life;............ no man com - eth un - to the Fa - ther, but by me.
truth, and the life:
I......................... am the way,......................... the truth,................. and the
I am the way, I am the way, I am the way, the
I......................... am the way,......................... the truth,................. and the
life;................
truth, and the life: no man com-eth un - to the Fa - ther, but by me."
life;..........
Copyright, 1887, by James McGranahan.

No. 370. Have Faith in God.

MARK 11: 22.

EL. NATHAN. JAMES MCGRANAHAN.

1. Have faith in God; what can there be For Him too hard to do for thee?
2. Have faith thy par - don to be - lieve, Let God's own word thy fears re - lieve;
3. Have faith in God, and trust His might That He will con - quer as you fight,
4. Have faith in God; press near His side; Thy troubled soul trust Him to guide;
He gave His Son; now all is free; Have faith, have faith in God.
Have faith the Spir - it to re - ceive; Have faith, have faith in God.
And give the tri - umph to the right; Have faith, have faith in God.
In life, in death, what - e'er be - tide, Have faith, have faith in God.
Copyright, 1887, by James McGranahan.

No. 371. Some Sweet Day, By and By.

"Then I shall know."—1 COR. 13: 12.

F. J. CROSBY. W. H. DOANE.

1. We shall reach the sum-mer-land, Some sweet day, by and by; We shall
2. At the crys - tal riv - er's brink, Some sweet day, by and by; We shall
3. Oh, these part - ing scenes will end, Some sweet day, by and by; We shall
press the gold - en strand, Some sweet day, by and by; Oh, the
find each brok - en link, Some sweet day, by and by; Then the
gath - er friend with friend, Some sweet day, by and by; There be -
loved ones watch-ing there, By the tree of life so fair, Till we
star that, fad - ing here, Left our hearts and homes so drear, We shall
fore our Fa - ther's throne, When the mists and clouds have flown, We shall
Copyright, 1884, by Biglow & Main.

Some Sweet Day By and By.

Refrain.
come their joy to share, Some sweet day, by and by.
see more bright and clear, Some sweet day, by and by.
know as we are known, Some sweet day, by and by.
By and by,
By and by, yes, by and by,
Some sweet day, We shall meet our lov'd ones gone, Some sweet day, by and by.
No. 372. My Jesus, as Thou Wilt.
(Jewett. 6s. D.)
Jane Borthwick, tr.
Weber, arr. by H. P. Main.
1. My Je - sus, as Thou wilt; Oh, may Thy will be mine; In - to Thy
2. My Je - sus, as Thou wilt; Tho' seen thro' many a tear, Let not my
3. My Je - sus, as Thou wilt; All shall be well for me; Each changing
hand of love I would my all re - sign: Thro' sor - row or thro' joy,
star of hope Grow dim or dis-ap - pear: Since Thou on earth hast wept
fu - ture scene I glad - ly trust with Thee: Straight to my home a - bove
Rit.
Con - duct me as Thine own, And help me still to say, My Lord, Thy will be done.
And sor - rowed oft a - lone, If I must weep with Thee, My Lord, Thy will be done.
I trav - el calm - ly on, And sing, in life or death, - My Lord, Thy will be done.

No. 373. What will you do with Jesus?

"What shall I do with Jesus, which is called Christ?"—MATT. 27: 22.

NATHANIEL NORTON. GEO. C. STEBBINS.

1. Oh, what will you do with Je - sus? The call comes low and sweet;
2. Oh, what will you do with Je - sus? The call comes loud and clear;
3. Oh, think of the King of Glo - ry From heav'n to earth come down,
As ten - der - ly He bids you Your bur - dens lay at His feet;
The sol - emn words are sound - ing In ev - 'ry list - 'ning ear;
His life so pure and ho - ly, His death, His cross, His crown;
Oh, soul so sad and wea - ry, That sweet voice speaks to thee;
Im - mor - tal life's in the ques - tion, And joy thro' e - ter - ni - ty;
Of His di - vine com - pas - sion, His sac - ri - fice for thee;
Then what will you do with Je - sus? Oh, what shall the an - swer be?
REFRAIN.
What shall the an - swer be? What shall the an - swer be?
What will you do with Je - sus? Oh, what shall the an - swer be?
Copyright, 1887, by Ira. D. Sankey.

No. 374. Laborers of Christ, Arise.

(AHIRA. S. M.)

Mrs. L. H. SIGOURNEY. H. W. GREATOREX.

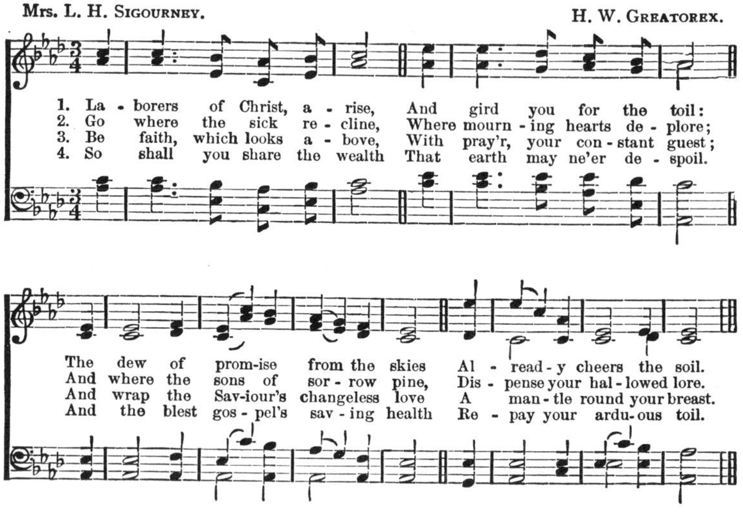
1. La - borers of Christ, a - rise, And gird you for the toil:
2. Go where the sick re - cline, Where mourn - ing hearts de - plore;
3. Be faith, which looks a - bove, With pray'r, your con - stant guest;
4. So shall you share the wealth That earth may ne'er de - spoil.
The dew of prom-ise from the skies Al - read - y cheers the soil.
And where the sons of sor - row pine, Dis - pense your hal - lowed lore.
And wrap the Sav-iour's changeless love A man - tle round your breast.
And the blest gos - pel's sav - ing health Re - pay your ardu - ous toil.

No. 375. God is Calling Yet.

"My spirit shall not always strive with man."—GEN. 6: 3.

GERHARDT TERSTEEGEN. E. O. EXCELL.

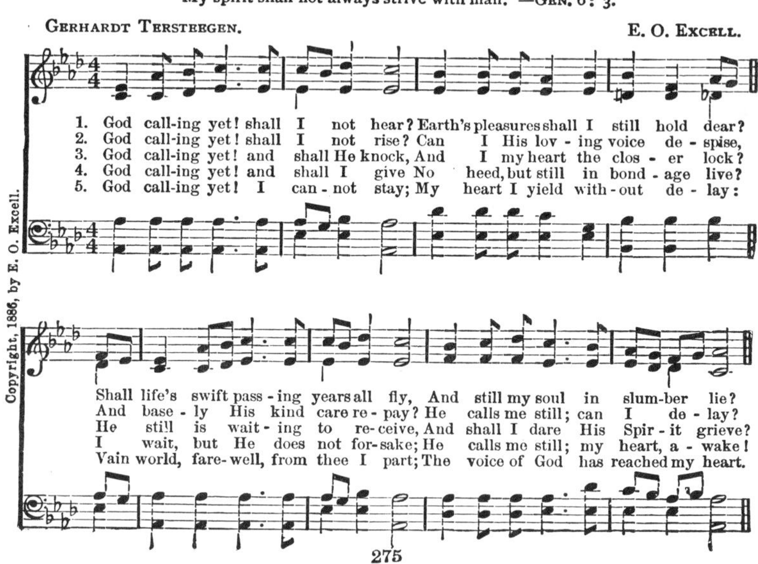
1. God call-ing yet! shall I not hear? Earth's pleasures shall I still hold dear?
2. God call-ing yet! shall I not rise? Can I His lov - ing voice de - spise,
3. God call-ing yet! and shall He knock, And I my heart the clos - er lock?
4. God call-ing yet! and shall I give No heed, but still in bond - age live?
5. God call-ing yet! I can - not stay; My heart I yield with - out de - lay:
Shall life's swift pass - ing years all fly, And still my soul in slum - ber lie?
And base - ly His kind care re - pay? He calls me still; can I de - lay?
He still is wait - ing to re - ceive, And shall I dare His Spir - it grieve?
I wait, but He does not for - sake; He calls me still; my heart, a - wake!
Vain world, fare - well, from thee I part; The voice of God has reached my heart.

God is Calling Yet.

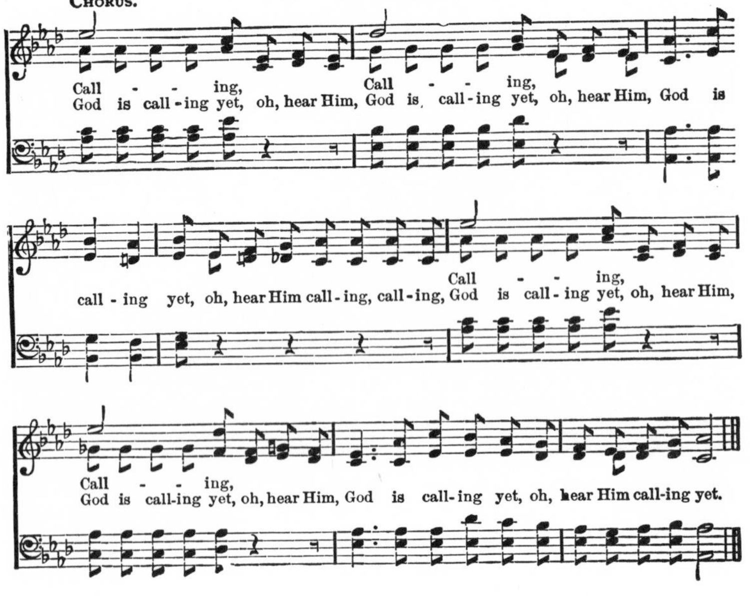
CHORUS.
Call - - ing, Call - - ing,
God is call-ing yet, oh, hear Him, God is call-ing yet, oh, hear Him, God is
call-ing yet, oh, hear Him call-ing, call-ing, God is call-ing yet, oh, hear Him,
Call - - ing,
Call - - ing,
God is call-ing yet, oh, hear Him, God is call-ing yet, oh, hear Him call-ing yet.

No. 376. Oh Cease, my Wandering Soul.

(ADRIAN. S. M.)

W. A. MUHLENBERG. J. E. GOULD.

1. Oh, cease, my wand-'ring soul, On rest - less wing to roam;
2. Be - hold the ark of God! Be - hold the o - pen door!
3. There safe thou shalt a - bide, There sweet shall be thy rest;
4. Ah, yes! I all for - sake, My all to thee re - sign;
All this wide world, to eith - er pole, Hath not for thee a home.
Oh, haste to gain that dear a - bode, And rove, my soul, no more.
And ev - 'ry long - ing sat - is - fied, With full sal - va - tion blest.
Gra - cious Re - deem - er, take, oh take And seal me ev - er Thine!
Used by permission O. Ditson & Co., owners of Copyright.

No. 377.
How Shall we Escape?
HEB. 2: 3.
G. M. J.
JAME GRANAHAN.
1. God loved a world of sin-ners, For them He gave His Son;
2. Be-hold the bleed-ing Sav-iour Up-on the cru-el tree,—
3. God loves the vil-est sin-ner, But hates the small-est sin;
4. Re-turn to God, O wand-'rer, Thy pur-chased par-don take;
And who-so-e'er re-ceives Him, He saves them, ev-'ry one;
The Just, con-demned, for-sak-en— He dies for you and me;
Then who shall see His King-dom? Or who can en-ter in?
Thy sins He'll not re-mem-ber, For thy Re-deem-er's sake;
He came to bring sal-va-tion, To bear our sins a-way,
The "Son of God" be-lov-ed, For us a curse was made;
'The pre-cious blood of Je-sus'—Let ev-'ry creat-ure know—
He'll cast them all be-hind Him, Or 'neath the deep-est sea,
That we with Him in glo-ry Might live thro' end-less day.
That we might have re-demp-tion, The aw-ful price He paid.
Can make the "chief of sin-ners" Full whit-er than the snow.
And love us ev-er free-ly Thro'-out E-ter-ni-ty.
Copyright, 1887, by James McGranahan.
CHORUS.
"How shall we es-cape if we ne-glect so great sal-va-tion? How shall we es-
cape if we ne-glect so great sal-va-tion, ne-glect so great sal-va-tion?"
cres.

No. 378. Come to Jesus! Come Away!

John 6: 37.

1. Come to Je - sus! come a - way! For - sake thy sins—oh, why de - lay?
2. Come to Je - sus! all is free; Hark! how He calls, "Come un - to Me!
3. Come to Je - sus! cling to Him; He'll keep thee far from paths of sin;
4. Come to Je - sus!—Lord, I come! Wea - ry of sin, no more I'd roam.
His arms are o - pen night and day; He waits to wel - come thee!
I cast out none, I'll par - don thee," Oh, thou shalt wel - come be!
Thou shalt at last a vic - t'ry win, And He will wel - come thee!
But with my Sav - iour be at home; I know He'll wel - come me!

No. 379. The Handwriting on the Wall.

"And the king saw the part of the hand that wrote."—Daniel 5: 5.

Words and Music by Knowles Shaw. Arr. by Ira D. Sankey.

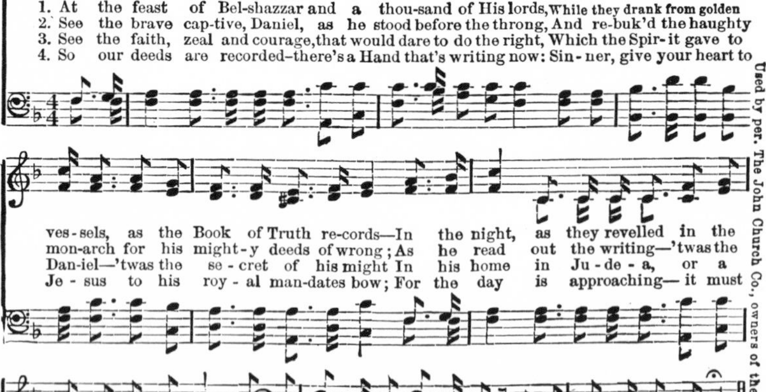
1. At the feast of Bel-shazzar and a thou-sand of His lords, While they drank from golden ves-sels, as the Book of Truth re-cords—In the night, as they revelled in the roy - al pal - ace hall, They were seized with consternation,—'twas the Hand upon the wall!
2. See the brave cap-tive, Daniel, as he stood before the throng, And re-buk'd the haughty mon-arch for his might-y deeds of wrong; As he read out the writing—'twas the doom of one and all, For the kingdom now was finished—said the Hand up-on the wall!
3. See the faith, zeal and courage, that would dare to do the right, Which the Spir-it gave to Dan-iel—'twas the se - cret of his might In his home in Ju - de - a, or a cap - tive in the hall, He un-der-stood the writing of his God up-on the wall!
4. So our deeds are recorded—there's a Hand that's writing now: Sin - ner, give your heart to Je - sus to his roy - al man-dates bow; For the day is approaching— it must come to one and all, When the sin-ners' condem-na-tion will be writ-ten on the wall!

CHORUS.
'Tis the hand of God on the wall! 'Tis the
writ-ing on the wall!
hand of God on the wall! Shall the rec-ord be "Found wanting!" or
writ-ing on the wall!
shall it be "Found trusting!" While that hand is writing on the wall?
rit.
writing on the wall!

No. 380. Jerusalem my Happy Home.

(MANOAH. C. M.)

Anon. F. J. HAYDN.

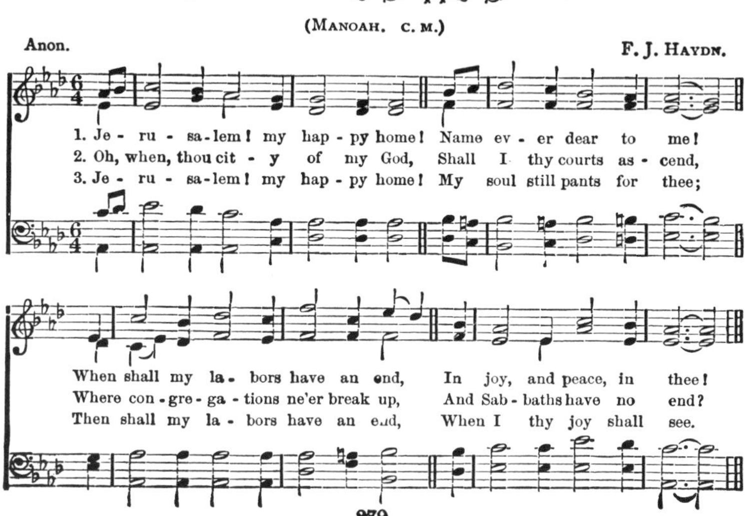
1. Je - ru - sa-lem! my hap - py home! Name ev - er dear to me!
2. Oh, when, thou cit - y of my God, Shall I thy courts as - cend,
3. Je - ru - sa-lem! my hap - py home! My soul still pants for thee;
When shall my la - bors have an end, In joy, and peace, in thee!
Where con-gre - ga - tions ne'er break up, And Sab - baths have no end?
Then shall my la - bors have an end, When I thy joy shall see.

No. 381. The Banner of the Cross.

"Thou hast given a banner to them that fear thee, that it may be displayed because of the truth."—Ps. 60: 4

El. Nathan. James McGranahan.

1. There's a royal banner given for display To the soldiers of the King; As an ensign fair we lift it up today, While as ransomed ones we sing.
2. Tho' the foe may rage and gather as the flood, Let the standard be displayed; And beneath its folds, as soldiers of the Lord, For the truth be not dismayed!
3. Over land and sea, wherever man may dwell, Make the glorious tidings known; Of the crimson banner now the story tell, While the Lord shall claim His own!
4. When the glory dawns—'tis drawing very near— It is hast'ning day by day— Then before our King the foe shall disappear, And the Cross the world shall sway.
Chorus.
Marching on!............ Marching on!........... For Christ count ev'rything but loss;.............................. And to crown Him King, toil and sing, 'Neath the banner of the cross.
Marching on! on! on! Marching on! on! on! For Christ count ev'rything, ev'rything but loss; And to crown Him King, we'll toil and sing, Beneath the banner of the cross.

No. 382. A Sinner like Me!

"Christ Jesus came into the world to save sinners."—1 Tim. 1: 15

C. J. B. C. J. Butler.

Slow.
1. I was once far a - way from the Sav - iour, And as
2. I wan - der'd on in the dark - ness, Not a
3. And then, in that dark lone - ly hour,............ A
vile as a sin - ner could be; And I won - der'd if
ray of light could I see; And the tho't filled my
voice sweet - ly whis-pered to me, Say - ing, Christ the Re -
rit.
Christ the Re - deem - er Could save a poor sin - ner like me.
heart with sad - ness, There's no hope for a sin - ner like me.
deem - er has pow - er To save a poor sin - ner like me.

4 I listened: and lo! 'twas the Saviour
That was speaking so kindly to me;
I cried, "I'm the chief of sinners,
Thou canst save a poor sinner like me!"

5 I then fully trusted in Jesus;
And oh, what a joy came to me!
My heart was filled with His praises,
For saving a sinner like me.

6 No longer in darkness I'm walking,
For the light is now shining on me;
And now unto others I'm telling
How He saved a poor sinner like me.

7 And when life's journey is over,
And I the dear Saviour shall see,
I'll praise Him for ever and ever,
For saving a sinner like me.

No. 383. There is a Calm.

"There remaineth a rest to the people of God."—Heb. 4: 9.

Ernest Rickman. Geo. C. Stebbins.

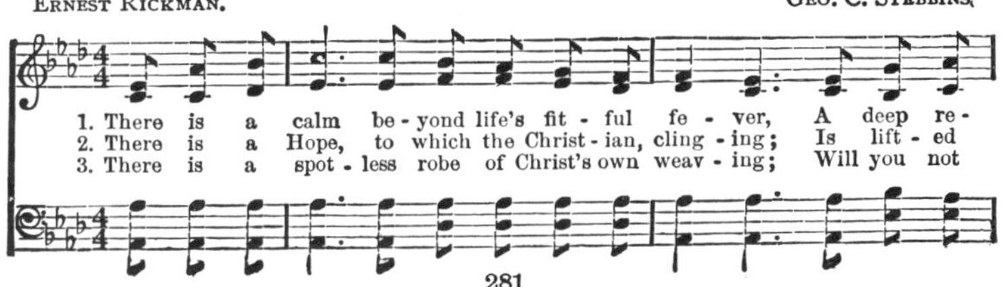
1. There is a calm be - yond life's fit - ful fe - ver, A deep re -
2. There is a Hope, to which the Christ - ian, cling - ing; Is lift - ed
3. There is a spot - less robe of Christ's own weav - ing; Will you not

There is a Calm.

pose, an ev - er-last-ing rest; Where white-robed angels welcome the be - liev- er
high a- bove life's surging wave; Finds life in death, and fadeless flowers springing
wrap it round your sin-stained soul? Poor wand'ring child, up-on thy past life griev-ing,
rit.
A - mong the blest, a - mong the blest. There is a Home, where all the soul's deep
From the dark grave, from the dark grave. There is a Crown pre-pared for those who
Christ makes thee whole! Christ makes thee whole! There is a Home, a Harp, a Crown in
yearn-ings, And si - lent pray'rs shall be at last ful - filled; Where strife and
love Him; The Christ-ian sees it in the dis-tance shine, Like a bright
Heav - en;—A - las! that an - y should Thy gift re - fuse!—The aw - ful
rit.
sor - row, murm'rings and heart burnings At last are stilled, at last are stilled.
bea - con glit - ter - ing a - bove Him, And whispers, "Mine!" and whispers, "Mine!"
choice of life and death is giv - en— Which wilt thou choose? which wilt thou choose?
Copyright, 1887, by Ira D. Sankey.
No. 384. There is a Stream.
(Ward. L. M.)
Isaac Watts.
Lowell Mason.
1. There is a stream, whose gentle flow Supplies the cit - y of our God;
2. That sacred stream, Thy ho - ly Word, Supports our faith, our fears con - trols;
3. Loud may the troubled o - cean roar; In sa - cred peace our souls a - bide;

There is a Stream.
Life, love, and joy, still glid - ing thro', And wat'ring our di - vine a - bode.
Sweet peace Thy promis - es af - ford, And give new strength to faint-ing souls.
While ev-'ry na - tion, ev - 'ry shore, Trembles, and dreads the swell-ing tide.
No. 385. There is None Righteous.
Rom. 3: 10, 23.
G. M. J.
James McGranahan.
Allegretto.
1. A guilt - y soul, by Phar - i - sees of old, Was brought accused, a - lone,
2. A learn - ed Mas - ter, Rul - er of the Jews, God's king - dom could not gain,
3. "Good Mas-ter," pray can aught be lack-ing yet? Thy laws I do o - bey;
But Je - sus said, "Let him without a sin, Be first to cast a stone."
With all the lore and cult - ure of the age, He "must be born a - gain."
"Go tell and give, then come and fol - low me," But sad he turned a - way.
Chorus.
"There is none righteous, no, but one, all, all have sinned," There is none righteous, for
all have sinned,
all have sinned, and come short of the glo - ry, the glo - ry of God, come
short of the glo - ry, Come short of the glo - ry, of the glo - - - ry of God.
ad lib.
the glo - ry of God.
Copyright, 1887, by James McGranahan.

No. 386. Little Lights.

Anna B. Warner, by per. | James McGranahan.

1. Je - sus bids us shine with a clear, pure light, Like a lit - tle can - dle burn-ing in the night; In the world is dark - ness; so we must shine, You in your cor - ner and I in mine.
2. Je - sus bids us shine first of all for Him, Well He sees and knows it if our light is dim; He looks down from heav - en, He sees us shine, You in your cor - ner and I in mine.
3. Je - sus bids us shine then for all a - round, Ma - ny kinds of dark - ness in the world are found; Sin and want and sor - row; so we must shine, You in your cor - ner and I in mine.
Used by per. The John Church Co., owners of the Copyright.

No. 387. Abundantly Able to Save.

"He will abundantly pardon."—Isa. 55: 7.

E. A. Hoffman. | P. P. Bliss.

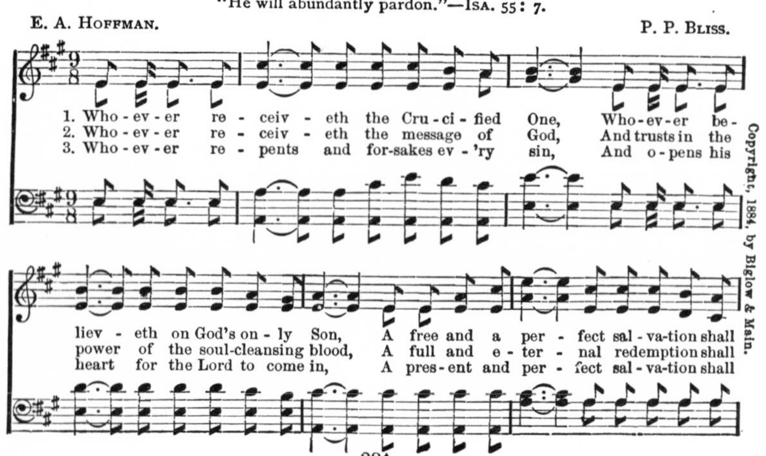
1. Who - ev - er re - ceiv - eth the Cru - ci - fied One, Who - ev - er be - liev - eth on God's on - ly Son, A free and a per - fect sal - va-tion shall
2. Who - ev - er re - ceiv - eth the message of God, And trusts in the power of the soul-cleansing blood, A full and e - ter - nal redemption shall
3. Who - ev - er re - pents and for-sakes ev - 'ry sin, And o - pens his heart for the Lord to come in, A pres - ent and per - fect sal - va-tion shall
Copyright, 1884, by Biglow & Main.

Abundantly Able to Save.

have: For He is a - bun - dant - ly a - ble to save.
have: For He is both a - ble and will - ing to save.
have: For Je - sus is read - y this mo - ment to save.
CHORUS.
My broth-er, the Mas - - ter is call - ing for thee;
Broth-er, the Mas - ter is come, and is call-ing for thee;
His grace and His mer - - - cy are won-drous-ly free;
Broth-er, His grace and His mer - cy are won-drous - ly free;
His blood as a ran - - - - som for sin - ners He gave,
Broth-er, His blood as a ran - som for sin-ners He gave,
rit.
And He is a - bund - - - ant - ly a - ble to save.
And He is a - bund- ant - ly a - ble to save.

No. 388. Come, Come to Jesus.
"Come unto me."—Matt. 11: 28.
Geo. B. Peck.
Hubert P. Main.
1. Come, come to Je - sus! He waits to wel - come thee
2. Come, come to Je - sus! He waits to ran - som thee
3. Come, come to Je - sus! He waits to light - en thee
4. Come, come to Je - sus! He waits to give to thee
O wand'rer, ea - ger - ly Come, come to Je - sus!
O slave! so will - ing - ly; Come, come to Je - sus!
O burdened! trust - ing - ly Come, come to Je - sus!
O blind! a vis - ion free; Come, come to Je - sus!
Copyright, 1864.
5 Come, come to Jesus!
He waits to shelter thee
O weary! blessedly
Come, come to Jesus!
6 Come, come to Jesus!
He waits to carry thee
O lamb! so lovingly,
Come, come to Jesus!
No. 389. Carried by the Angels.
Luke 16: 22.
El. Nathan.
James McGranahan.
1. Sit - ting by the gate - way of a pal - ace fair, Once a child of
2. What shall be the end - ing of this life of care? Oft the ques - tion
3. Fol - low - er of Je - sus, scant - y tho' thy store, Treasures, pre - cious
4. Up - ward, then, and on - ward! on - ward for the Lord; Time and tal - ent
God was left to die; By the world neg - lect - ed, wealth would nothing share;
com - eth to us all; Here up - on the path - way hard the bur - dens bear,
treas - ures wait on high; Count the tri - als joy - ful, soon they'll all be o'er;
all in His em - ploy; Small may seem the serv - ice, sure the great re - ward;
Copyright, 1887, by James McGranahan.
See the change awaiting there on high.
And the burning tears of sor - row fall.
O the change that's coming bye and bye.
Here the cross, but there the crown of joy.
Chorus.
Carried by the an - gels to the land of rest,

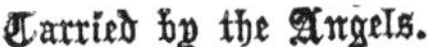

Mu - sic sweet - ly sound - ing thro' the skies;............. Wel-comed by the

Sav - iour to the heav'n-ly feast, Gath-ered with the loved in Par - a - dise.

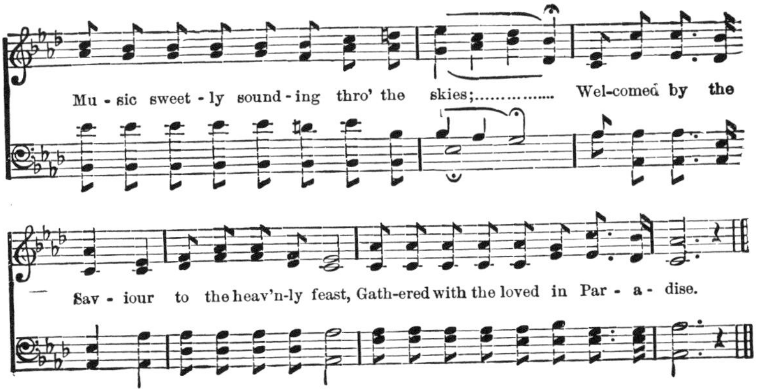

No. 390. Fear Thou Not.

J. E. A.
Trans. from Dr. MALAN.

ISA. 41: 10.

JAMES McGRANAHAN.

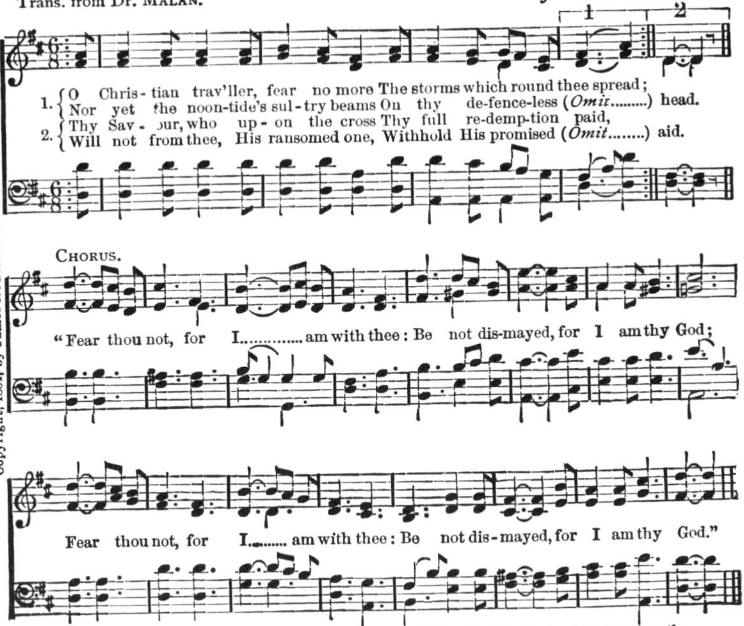

1. { O Chris - tian trav'ller, fear no more The storms which round thee spread;
   { Nor yet the noon-tide's sul - try beams On thy de-fence-less (*Omit*.........) head.

2. { Thy Sav - iour, who up - on the cross Thy full re-demp-tion paid,
   { Will not from thee, His ransomed one, Withhold His promised (*Omit*........) aid.

CHORUS.

"Fear thou not, for I............. am with thee: Be not dis-mayed, for I am thy God;

Fear thou not, for I........ am with thee: Be not dis-mayed, for I am thy God."

3 A safe retreat and hiding-place
Thy Saviour will provide;
And sorrow cannot fill thy heart,
While sheltered at His side.

4 No; in thy darkest days on earth,
When every joy seems flown,
Believer, thou shalt never tread
The toilsome way alone.

No. 391. Repent Ye.
Matt. 3: 2.
G. M. J.
James McGranahan.
1. Have our hearts grown cold since the days of old? Have we left our souls' "first love?" Nei- ther cold nor hot, God commends us not, Nor our luke-warm ways ap- prove.
2. Has the God a - bove our su - preme true love? Have we bowed to Him al - way? Do we own His claim and re - vere His name, And ob- serve His ho - ly day?
3. Do we hon - or those who have soothed our woes? Have we ren - dered good for ill? Are we pure in heart, do - ing *all* our part To ful - fil the Saviour's will?
4. Are we al - ways tru in the thing we do, In our words, our works, our ways? Are we quite con- tent with the bless-ings sent, Giv - ing God a - lone the praise?
5. Dare a mor - tal say— for a sin - gle day—"I have kept Thy law, O God! Un - de - filed by sin, I am pure with - in, And I need no cleansing blood?"
Copyright, 1887, by James McGranahan.
Chorus.
Re - pent ye, re - pent ye, re - pent ye! 'Tis the call of God to ev - 'ry land;
Re - pent ye, re - pent ye, re - pent ye! For the king - dom of heav - en is at hand.
No. 392. Cling to the Bible.
Ps. 119: 105.
M J. Smith.
J. R. Murray.
1. Cling to the Bi - ble, tho' all else be tak - en; Lose not its prom - is - es
2. Cling to the Bi - ble, this jew - el, this treas - ure Brings to us hon - or and
3. Lamp for the feet that in by - ways have wander'd, Guide for the youth that would

Cling to the Bible.

pre - cious and sure; Souls that are sleep - ing its ech - oes a - wak - en,
saves fall - en man; Pearl whose great val - ue no mor - tal can meas - ure,
oth - er - wise fall; Hope for the sin - ner whose best days are squan-der'd,

CHORUS.

Drink from the fount - ain, so peace - ful, so pure.
Seek and se - cure it, O soul, while you can.
Staff for the a - ged, and best book of all.
Cling to the Bi - ble!

Cling to the Bi - ble! Cling to the Bi - ble, Our Lamp and Guide.

No. 393. Hark! Hark, my Soul!

"Are they not all ministering spirits."—HEB. 1: 14.

F. W. FABER. C. C. CONVERSE. Arr. by I. D. S.

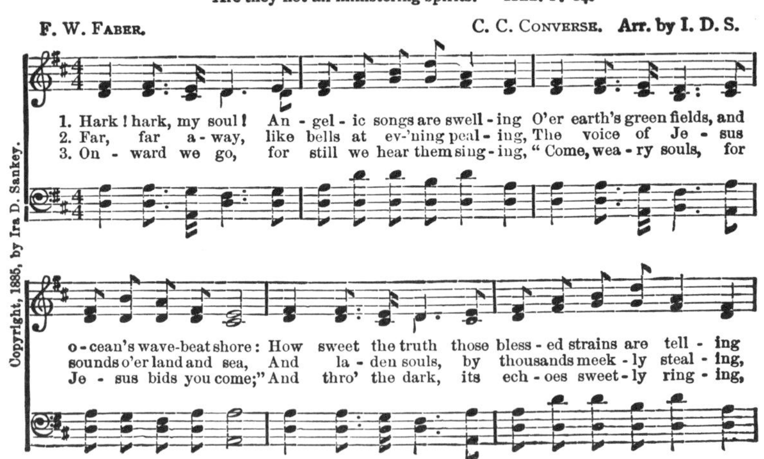
1. Hark! hark, my soul! An - gel - ic songs are swell - ing O'er earth's green fields, and
2. Far, far a - way, like bells at ev-'ning peal - ing, The voice of Je - sus
3. On - ward we go, for still we hear them sing - ing, "Come, wea - ry souls, for
o - cean's wave-beat shore: How sweet the truth those bless - ed strains are tell - ing
sounds o'er land and sea, And la - den souls, by thousands meek - ly steal - ing,
Je - sus bids you come;" And thro' the dark, its ech - oes sweet - ly ring - ing,

Hark! Hark, my Soul!
CHORUS.
Of that new life when sin shall be no more.
Kind Shep-herd, turn their wea - ry steps to Thee.
The mu - sic of the Gos - pel leads us home.
An - gels, sing on! your
faith-ful watches keep-ing; Sing us sweet fragments of the songs a - bove, Till morning's
joy shall end the night of weep - ing, And life's long shadows break in cloud - less love.
No. 394.
Guide Me.
"For thy name's sake, lead me, and guide me."—PSALM 31: 3.
W. WILLIAMS.
WM. L. VINER.
FINE.
1. Guide me, O Thou great Je - ho - vah, Pil - grim thro' this bar - ren land;
Bread of heav - en, Bread of heav - en, Feed me till I want no more.
D.C.
I am weak, but Thou art might - y; Hold me with Thy powerful hand:

2 Open now the crystal fountain,
Whence the healing waters flow;
Let the fiery, cloudy pillar
Lead me all my journey thro':
Strong Deliv'rer, Strong Deliv'rer,
Be Thou still my strength and shield.

3 When I tread the verge of Jordan,
Bid my anxious fears subside;
Bear me through the swelling current,
Land me safe on Canaan's side:
Songs of praises, Songs of praises
I will ever give to Thee.

No. 395. Waiting for the Promise.

LUKE 24: 49.

WILBUR F. CRAFTS. JAMES MCGRANAHAN.

1. We bow our knees un - to the Fa - ther Of Christ the Lord of earth and heaven,
2. O fill the in - ward man with pow - er, As Christ with-in our hearts doth dwell;
3. The love that pass - eth knowledge give us, Its height and depth and breadth and length;
4. Thy pow'r it is that work-eth in us, O mul - ti - ply it here to - day,
That rich - es of His grace and glo - ry And pow'r for serv - ice may be given.
Our root in Him, tho' storms may low - er, Vic - to - rious love we still shall tell.
A - bun - dant - ly be - yond our ask - ing, Be - yond our thought give us Thy strength.
And Christ, our Lord, shall have the glo - ry With - in His church thro' endless day.
CHORUS, not too fast.
We are waiting for the promise of the Fa - ther—For the Ho - ly Spir - it's power;
O our Father, for Thy Spirit we are wait - ing, e - ven now, this ver - y hour.
(May end here.)
We are waiting for His coming, We are waiting for His coming, For the Ho - ly Spir - it's
power; O our Father, for Thy Spirit we are wait - ing, e - ven now, this ver - y hour.

No. 396.
Come, Praise the Lord.
A. Mc. G.
Con spirito.
1. Come, praise the Lord, ex - alt His name, Our Sav - iour and our King;
2. How great, how pre - cious is His name, How poor the praise we bring;
3. A day will come, its dawn we greet, When heav'n it - self shall ring,
'Tis meet we should His praise pro - claim, And hal - le - lu - jah sing.
His peo - ple still should own His claim, And hal - le - lu - jah sing.
And all the saints with joy shall meet, And hal - le - lu - jah sing.
Used by per. The John Church Co., owners of the Copyright.
No. 397.
But is that All?
"Christ is all, and in all."—Col. 3: 11.
Horatius Bonar.
Mrs. C. Barnard, arr.
1. Some-times I catch sweet glimpses of His face, But that is all, Some -
2. And is this all He meant when first He said, "Come un - to me?" Is
3. Nay, do not wrong Him by thy heav - y tho'ts, But love His love; Do
4. Christ and His love shall be thy bless-ed all For ev - er-more; Christ
times He looks on me and seems to smile, But that is all;
there no deep - er, more en - dur - ing rest In Him for thee?
thou full jus - tice to His ten - der - ness, His mer - cy prove;
and His light shall shine on all thy ways For ev - er - more;
Arrangement Copyright, 1887, by Ira D. Sankey.

But is that All?

Sometimes He speaks a pass-ing word of peace, But that is all:
Is there no stead-ier light for thee in Him? O come and see;
Take Him for what He is, O take Him all, And look a-bove;
Christ and His peace shall keep thy troub-led soul For-ev-er-more;
Sometimes I think I hear His lov-ing voice Up-on me call;
Is there no deep-er, more en-dur-ing rest In Him for thee?
And do not wrong Him by thy heavy thoughts, But love His love.
Christ and His love shall be thy bless-ed all For-ev-er-more.

No. 398. Christian, Walk Carefully.

"Walk worthy of the vocation wherewith you are called."—EPH. 4: 1.

Words arr. GEO. C. STEBBINS.

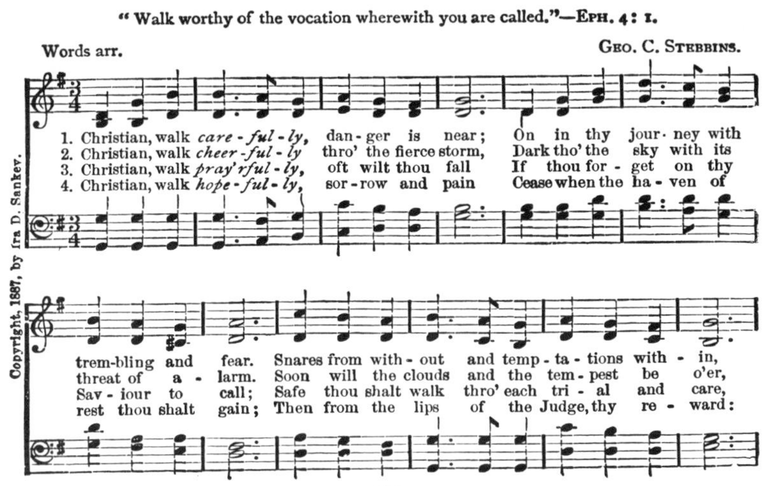
1. Christian, walk *care-ful-ly,* dan-ger is near; On in thy jour-ney with trem-bling and fear. Snares from with-out and temp-ta-tions with-in,
2. Christian, walk *cheer-ful-ly* thro' the fierce storm, Dark tho' the sky with its threat of a-larm. Soon will the clouds and the tem-pest be o'er,
3. Christian, walk *pray'rful-ly,* oft wilt thou fall If thou for-get on thy Sav-iour to call; Safe thou shalt walk thro' each tri-al and care,
4. Christian, walk *hope-ful-ly,* sor-row and pain Cease when the ha-ven of rest thou shalt gain; Then from the lips of the Judge, thy re-ward:

Christian, Walk Carefully.

CHORUS.
Seek to en - tice thee once more in - to sin. Christian, walk care - ful - ly,
Then with thy Sav - iour thou'lt rest ev - er more. Christian, walk cheer-ful - ly,
If thou art clad in the ar - mor of pray'r. Christian, walk pray'r-ful - ly,
"En - ter thou in - to the joy of thy Lord." Christian, walk hope - ful - ly,
Christian, walk care - ful - ly, Christian, walk care - ful - ly, dan - ger is near.
Christian, walk cheer-ful - ly, Christian, walk cheer - ful - ly through the fierce storm.
Christian, walk pray'rful - ly, Christian, walk pray'rful - ly, fear lest thou fall.
Christian, walk hope - ful - ly, Christian, walk hope - ful - ly, rest thou shalt gain.
No. 399. He Holds the Key.
"Casting all your care upon him, for he careth for you."—1 PET. 5: 7.
Rev. JOHN PARKER.
GEO. C. STEBBINS.
1. He holds the key of all un-known, And I am glad;
2. What if to - mor - row's cares were here With - out its rest?
3. The ver - y dim - ness of my sight Makes me se - cure;
4. I can - not read His fu - ture plans, But this I know:
5. E - nough; this cov - ers all my wants, And so I rest;
If oth - er hands should hold the key, Or, if He trust - ed
I'd rath - er He un - locked the day, And, as the hours swing
For, grop - ing in my mist - y way, I feel His hand; I
I have the smil - ing of His face, And all the ref - uge
For, what I can - not, He can see, And in His care I
it to me, I might be sad, I might be sad.
o - pen, say, "My will is best," "My will is best."
hear Him say, "My help is sure," "My help is sure."
of His grace, While here be - low, While here be - low.
safe shall be, For - ev - er blest, For - ev - er blest.
Copyright, 1887, by Ira. D. Sankey.

No. 400. Hallelujah for the Cross!

"God forbid that I should glory, save in the cross of our Lord Jesus Christ."—GAL. 6: 14.

DR. HORATIUS BONAR (arr.) JAMES MCGRANAHAN.

1. The cross it stand-eth fast, Hal-le-lu-jah! hal-le-lu-jah! Defy-ing ev-'ry blast, Hal-le-lu-jah! hal-le-lu-jah! The winds of hell have blown, The world its hate hath shown, Yet it is not o-ver-thrown, Hal-le-lu-jah for the cross!

2. It is the old cross still, Hal-le-lu-jah! hal-le-lu-jah! It's triumph let us tell, Hal-le-lu-jah! hal-le-lu-jah! The grace of God here shown, Thro' Christ the blessed Son, Who did for sin a-tone, Hal-le-lu-jah for the cross!

3. 'Twas here the debt was paid, Hal-le-lu-jah! hal-le-lu-jah! Our sins on Je-sus laid, Hal-le-lu-jah! hal-le-lu-jah! So round the cross we sing, Of Christ our of-fer-ing, Of Christ our liv-ing King, Hal-le-lu-jah for the cross!

cres. ... ff

*SOLO. SOP. OR TEN. OR DUET.

Hal-le-lu-jah, hal-le-lu-jah, hal-le-lu-jah for the cross, Hal-le-lu-jah,

SOPRANO AND ALTO.

CHO. *mp* Hal-le-lu-jah, hal-le-lu-jah, hal-le-lu-jah for the cross, hal-le-lu-jah for the cross, Hal-le-lu-jah,

TENOR AND BASS.

* If desired, the Soprano and Alto may sing the upper Staff, *omitting* the middle Staff.

Hal-le - lu - jah, it shall nev - er suf - fer loss.
Hal - le - lu - jah, it shall nev - er suf-fer, nev - er suf-fer loss.
f FULL CHORUS.
* Hal-le - lu - jah, hal - le - lu - jah, hal - le - lu - jah for the cross;
f
cres.
ff
Hal-le - lu - jah, hal - le - lu - jah, it shall nev - er suf - fer loss.
cres.
ff

* For a final ending, all the voices may sing the melody in unison through the last eight measures—the instrument playing the harmony.

No. 401. Have Courage, my Boy, to say No!

"Resist the devil and he will flee from you."—JAMES 4 : 7.

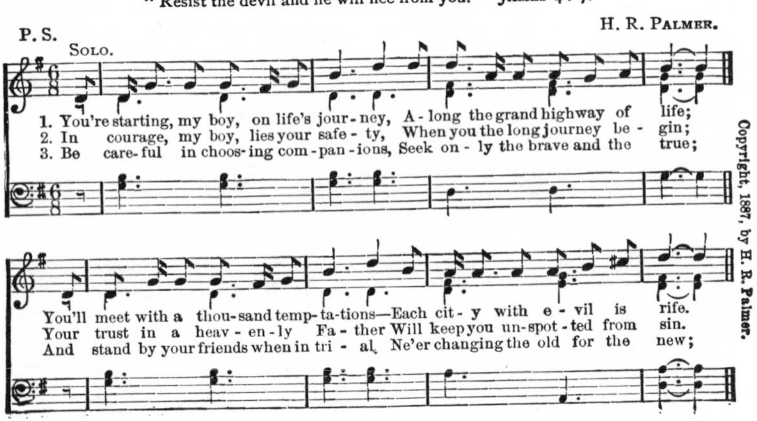
P. S.
H. R. PALMER.
SOLO.
1. You're starting, my boy, on life's jour - ney, A - long the grand highway of life;
2. In courage, my boy, lies your safe - ty, When you the long journey be - gin;
3. Be care - ful in choos - ing com - pan - ions, Seek on - ly the brave and the true;
You'll meet with a thou - sand temp - ta - tions—Each cit - y with e - vil is rife.
Your trust in a heav - en - ly Fa - ther Will keep you un - spot - ted from sin.
And stand by your friends when in tri - al, Ne'er changing the old for the new;

Have Courage, my Boy, to say No!

No. 402. God's Time Now.

"Behold, now is the accepted time."—2 Cor. 6: 2.

Joseph Cook, D.D. — Ira D. Sankey.

This world is a stage of ex - cite-ment, There's danger wher-ev-er you go;
Temp-ta- tions will go on in - creas - ing, As streams from a riv - u - let flow;
And when by false friends you are tempt-ed The taste of the winecup to know,
But if you are tempt-ed in weak-ness, Have courage, my boy, to say No!
But if you'd be true to your man-hood, Have courage, my boy, to say No!
With firm-ness, with pa-tience and kind-ness, Have courage, my boy, to say No!
Chorus.
Have courage, my boy, to say No! Have courage, my boy, to say No!
say No! say No!
Have courage, my boy, Have courage, my boy, Have courage, my boy, to say No!
Copyright, 1887, by Ira D. Sankey.
1. Choose I must, and soon must choose Hol - i - ness, or heav - en lose;
2. End - less sin means end - less woe; In - to end - less sin I go,
3. As the stream its chan - nel grooves, And with - in that chan - nel moves,
While what heav - en loves, I hate, Shut for me is heav - en's gate.
If my soul, from rea - son rent, Takes from sin its fi - nal bent.
So doth hab - it's deep - est tide Groove its bed, and there a - bide.

4 Light obeyed increaseth light;
Light resisted bringeth night;
Who shall give me will to choose,
If the love of light I lose?

5 Speed, my soul; this instant yield;
Let the Light its sceptre wield;
While thy God prolongeth grace,
Haste thee toward His holy face!

No. 403. O Morning Land.

"Until the day break and the shadows flee away."—CANT. 2: 17.

EBEN E. REXFORD. EDWARD H. PHELPS.

DUET.
1. "Some day," we say, and turn our eyes Tow'rd the fair hills of Par - a - dise; Some day, some
2. Some day our ears shall hear the song Of triumph o - ver sin and wrong; Some day, some
SOLO. Alto.
time, a sweet new rest Shall blossom, flower-like, in each breast; Some day, some time, our eyes shall
time, but oh! not yet; But we will wait and not for - get, That some day all these things shall
SOLO. Soprano.
see The fa - ces kept in mem - o - ry; Some day, some time, our eyes shall see
be, And rest be giv'n to you and me; That some day all these things shall be,
DUET. Slowly.
The fa ces kept in mem - o - ry; Some day their hands shall clasp our
And rest be giv - en you and me; So wait, my friends, tho' years move
Tempo.
hand, Just o - ver in the morning land, Just o - ver in the morning land; Some day their
slow, That happy time will come, we know, That happy time will come, we know, So wait, my
p rit. pp
hands shall clasp our hand, Just o - ver in the morning land; O morning land! O morning land!
friends, tho' years move slow, That happy time will come, we know, O morning land! O morning land!
Arranged by Geo. C. Stebbins and Copyright, 1887, by Ira D. Sankey.

No. 404. O What a Saviour.

"Come unto me."—MATT. 11 : 28.

J. L. STERLING. IRA D. SANKEY.

1. Come to the Sav-iour, hear His loving voice Nev-er will you find a Friend so true;
2. Blest words of com-fort, gently now they fall, Je - sus is the Life, the Truth, the Way;
3. Soft - ly the Spir - it whispers in the heart, Do not slight the Saviour's of-fered grace;
4. Light in the dark-ness, joy in a - ny pain, Ref-uge for the wea - ry and op-pressed;
Now He is wait - ing, trust Him and re - joice, Ten - der - ly He call - eth you.
Come to the fount-ain, there is room for all, Je - sus bids you come to - day.
Glad - ly re-ceive Him, let Him not de - part, Hap - py they who seek His face.
Still He is wait - ing, call-ing yet a - gain, Come and He will give you rest.
FINE.
Copyright, 1887, by Ira D. Sankey.
D.S.—Still He is wait-ing, grieve His love no more, Ten - der - ly He call - eth you.
O, what a Sav-iour standing at the door, Haste while He lin - gers, pardon now im-plore;
D.S.

No. 405. O Paradise!

"With me in Paradise."—LUKE 23 : 43.

G. M. J. JAMES McGRANAHAN.

1. O gold - en day, O day of God, When sin - less souls the gar - den trod! In bliss su - preme,
2. To Christ the Lord up - on the tree, A sin - ner cries:— "Re-mem-ber me!" "To-day shalt thou,"
3. O gold - en day when Christ de - scends, The curse re - moves and sor - row ends; All glo - ry - clad,
1. O gold - en day, &c.
Copyright, 1887, by James McGranahan.

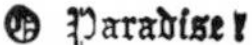

'neath sun-ny skies, In E-den fair, in Par-a - dise.
the Lord re - plies, "Be with me there in Par-a - dise."
the ransomed rise To reign with Him in Par-a - dise.

Chorus.

O Par - a - dise, sweet Par - a - dise, From scenes of earth we long to rise; O
Par - a - dise, bright Par - a - dise, Where Je - sus reigns.................... be-yond the skies.
be-yond the skies,

Fine.

2. The fa - tal fall, the sin, the shame, The death, the doom,
3. The bead-ed brow, the silvered hair, The ach-ing heart,

the sword a - flame, The curse, the crime be-yond dis -
the va - cant chair, The grass - y graves, the bro - ken

guise, The earth no more is Par - a - dise.
ties, Are not the scenes of Par - a - dise.

Go to Chorus.

No. 406. I Will Sing the Wondrous Story.

"I will sing of the mercies of the Lord forever."—Ps. 1: 89.

F. H. RAWLEY.
PETER BILHORN.
1. I will sing the wond-rous sto - ry, Of the Christ who died for me,
2. I was lost, but Je - sus found me, Found the sheep that went a - stray;
3. I was bruised, but Je - sus healed me, Faint was I from many a fall,
4. Days of dark - ness still come o'er me, Sor - row's paths I oft - en tread,
5. He will keep me till the riv - er Rolls its wa - ters at my feet;
How He left His home in glo - ry, For the cross on Cal - va - ry.
Threw His lov - ing arms a - round me, Drew me back in - to His way.
Sight was gone, and fears pos - sessed me, But He freed me from them all.
But the Sav - iour still is with me, By His hand I'm safe - ly led.
Then He'll bear me safe - ly o - ver, Where the loved ones I shall meet.
Copyright, 1887, by Ira D. Sankey.
CHORUS.
Yes' I'll sing.................. the won-drous sto - - ry Of the
Yes, I'll sing the won-drous sto - ry
Christ........... who died for me,.................... Sing it with........... the saints in
Of the Christ who died for me, Sing it with
glo - - ry, Gath-ered by.................. the crys - tal sea,
the saints in glo - ry, gath-ered by the the crys - tal sea.

No. 407. Loving Kindness. L. M.

Samuel Medley. Western Melody.

1. A - wake, my soul, to joy - ful lays, And sing thy great Re- deem-er's praise;
2. He saw me ru - ined by the fall, Yet loved me not - with- standing all;
3. Tho' num'rous hosts of might- y foes, Tho' earth and hell my way op - pose,
4. When trouble, like a gloom - y cloud, Has gath - er'd thick, and thunder'd loud,
He just - ly claims a song from me, His lov - ing - kind - ness, oh, how free!
He saved me from my lost es - tate, His lov - ing - kind - ness, oh, how great!
He safe - ly leads my soul a - long, His lov - ing - kind - ness, oh, how strong!
He near my soul has al- ways stood, His lov - ing - kind - ness, oh, how good!
Lov - ing - kindness, lov - ing - kindness, His lov - ing - kind - ness, oh, how free!
Lov - ing - kindness, lov - ing - kindness, His lov - ing - kind - ness, oh, how great!
Lov - ing - kindness, lov - ing - kindness, His lov - ing - kind - ness, oh, how strong!
Lov - ing - kindness, lov - ing - kindness, His lov- ing - kind - ness, oh, how good!
No. 408. The Model Church.
(Solo and Congregation.)
John H. Yates. Arr. by Ira D. Sankey.
1. Well, wife, I've found the mod - el church, And worshipp'd there to - day;
2. The sex - ton did not set me down, A - way back by the door;
3. I wish you'd heard the sing-ing, wife, It had the old - time ring;
It made me think of good old times, Be - fore my hair was gray:
He knew that I was old and deaf, And saw that I was poor;
The preach- er said with trump- et voice, Let all the peo - ple sing:

The Model Church.

The meet-ing house was fi-ner built, Than they were years a-go,
He must have been a Christ-ian man, He led me bold-ly through
"Old Cor-o-na-tion," was the tune; The mu-sic up-ward roll'd,
But then I found when I went in, It was not built for show.
The crowd-ed aisle of that grand church, To find a pleas-ant pew.
Un-til I thought the an-gel-choir Struck all their harps of gold.
Words used by per. Ph. Phillips. Arrangement Copyright, 1886, by Ira D. Sankey.
4.
My deafness seemed to melt away,
My spirit caught the fire;
I joined my feeble, trembling voice
With that melodious choir;
And sang as in my youthful days,
"Let angels prostrate fall;
*
Bring forth the roy-al di-a-dem,
And crown Him Lord of all; Bring
forth the roy-al di-a-dem,
And crown Him Lord of all;"
5.
I tell you, wife, it did me good
To sing that hymn once more;
I felt like some wrecked mariner
Who gets a glimpse of shore;
I almost want to lay aside
This weather-beaten form,
And anchor in the blessed port,
Forever from the storm.
6.
'Twas not a flowery sermon, wife,
But simple gospel truth;
It fitted humble men like me;
It suited hopeful youth;
To win immortal souls to Christ,
The earnest preacher tried;
He talked not of himself, or creed,
But Jesus crucified.
7.
Dear wife, the toil will soon be o'er,
The vic'try soon be won;
The shining land is just ahead,
Our race is nearly run:
We're nearing Canaan's happy shore,
Our home so bright and fair;
Thank God, we'll never sin again;
*
There'll be no sor-row there,
There'll be no sor-row there, In
heav'n a-bove Where all is love,
There'll be no sor-row there.

* All join in singing the old tunes.

No. 409. The Gospel Call.

"And the Spirit and the bride say, Come."—Rev. 22 : 17.

Arthur T. Pierson. Geo. C. Stebbins.

1. The Spir - it and the bride say, "Come!" And take the wa - ter of life!"
2. Let ev - 'ry one who hears, say "Come!" And joy - ful wit - ness give;
3. Ye souls who are a - thirst, for-sake Your bro - ken cis - terns first;
4. Yea, who - so - ev - er will may come, Your long - ings Christ can fill;
O bless - ed call! Good news to all Who tire of sin and strife.
I heard the sound, The stream I found, I drank, and now I live!
Then come, par-take, One draught will slake Your soul's con - sum - ing thirst.
The stream is free To you and me, And who - so - ev - er will.
Chorus.
The Spir - - it says, "Come!" The bride............ says, "Come!"
The Spir - it and the bride say, "Come!" The Spir - it and the bride say, "Come!"
And take............. of the wa - ter of life......................... free - ly.
And take the wa - ter of life, of life, The wa-ter of life free - ly.
The Spir - - it says, "Come!" The bride............... says, "Come!"
The Spir - it and the bride say, "Come!" The Spir - it and the bride say, "Come!"
And take............ of the wa - ter of life........................... free - ly.
And take the wa - ter of life, of life, The wa-ter of life free - ly.

No. 410. Come, Sinner, Come.

"Come unto me, all ye that labor and are heavy laden."—Matt. 11 : 28.

W. E. Witter. H. R. Palmer.

1. While Je - sus whis - pers to you, Come, sin - ner, come! While we are
2. Are you too heav - y lad - en? Come, sin - ner, come! Je - sus will
3. Oh, hear His ten - der plead - ing, Come, sin - ner, come! Come and re -

pray - ing for you, Come, sin - ner, come! Now is the time to own Him,
bear your bur - den, Come, sin - ner, come! Je - sus will not de - ceive you,
ceive the bless - ing, Come, sin - ner, come! While Je - sus whis - pers to you,

Come, sin - ner, come! Now is the time to know Him, Come, sin - ner, come!
Come, sin - ner, come! Je - sus will now re - ceive you, Come, sin - ner, come!
Come, sin - ner, come! While we are pray - ing for you, Come, sin - ner, come!

No. 411. When the Mists have Rolled Away.

"Until the day break and the shadows flee away."—Cant. 2 : 17.

Annie Herbert. Arr. Ira D. Sankey.

1. When the mists have rolled in splen - dor From the beau - ty of the hills,
2. Oft we tread the path be - fore us With a wea - ry bur - den'd heart,
3. We shall come with joy and glad - ness, We shall gath - er round the throne;
And the sun - light fall in glad - ness On the riv - er and the rills,
Oft we toil a - mid the shad - ows, And our fields are far a - part:
Face to face with those that love us, We shall know as we are known:
Copyright, 1883, by Ira D. Sankey.

When the Mists have Rolled Away.

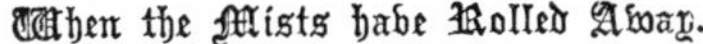

We re - call our Fa - ther's prom - ise In the rain - bow of the spray:
But the Sav - iour's "Come, ye bless - ed," All our la - bor will re - pay,
And the song of our re - demp - tion, Shall re - sound thro' end - less day,
rit.
We shall know each oth - er bet - ter When the mists have rolled a - way.
When we gath - er in the morn - ing Where the mists have rolled a - way.
When the shad - ows have de - part - ed, And the mists have rolled a - way.
Chorus.
known, as we are known,
We shall know......... as we are known,........... Nev - er - more........ to walk a -
We shall know as we are known, Nevermore to walk a -
lone,.................. In the dawning of the morning Of that bright and happy day:
lone, to walk a - lone,
rit.
We shall know each oth - er bet - ter, When the mists have rolled a - way.

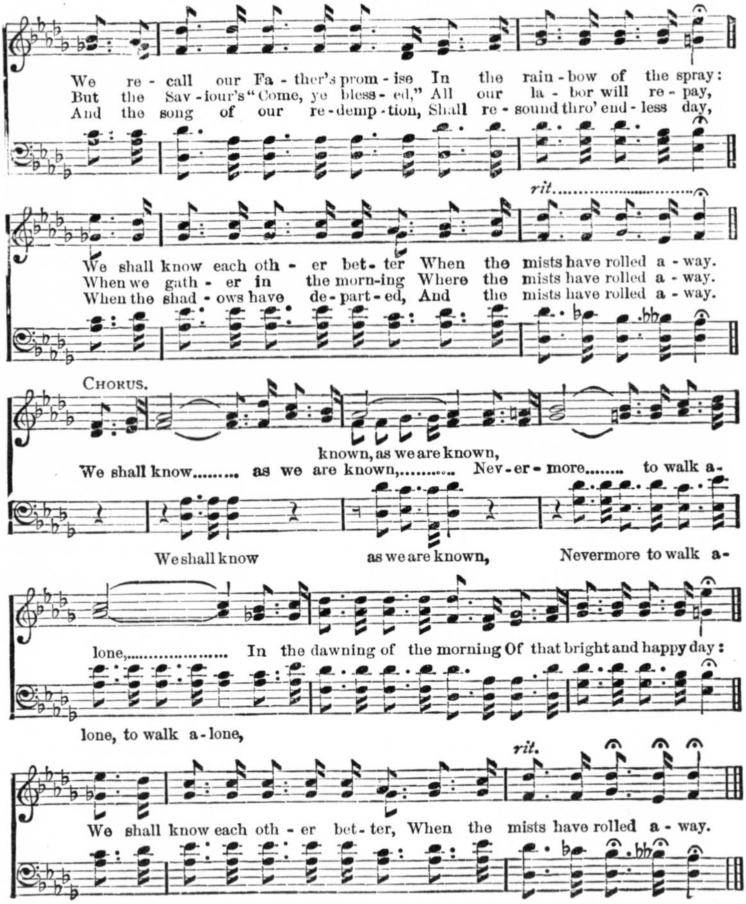

No. 412. Saviour, Again.

"The Lord will bless his people with peace."—Ps. 29 : 11.

John Ellerton. E. J. Hopkins.

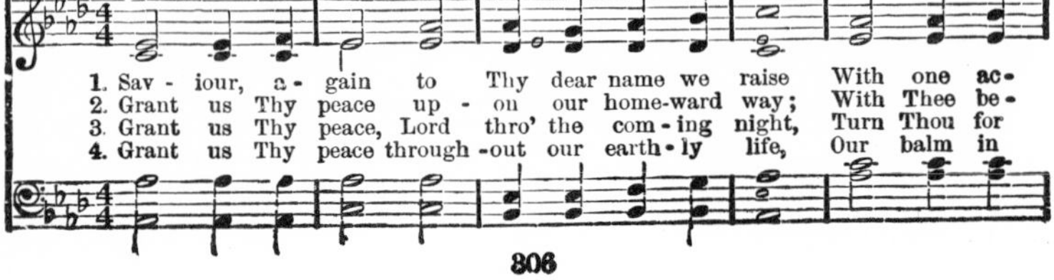

1. Sav - iour, a - gain to Thy dear name we raise With one ac -
2. Grant us Thy peace up - on our home-ward way; With Thee be -
3. Grant us Thy peace, Lord thro' the com - ing night, Turn Thou for
4. Grant us Thy peace through - out our earth - ly life, Our balm in

Saviour, Again.

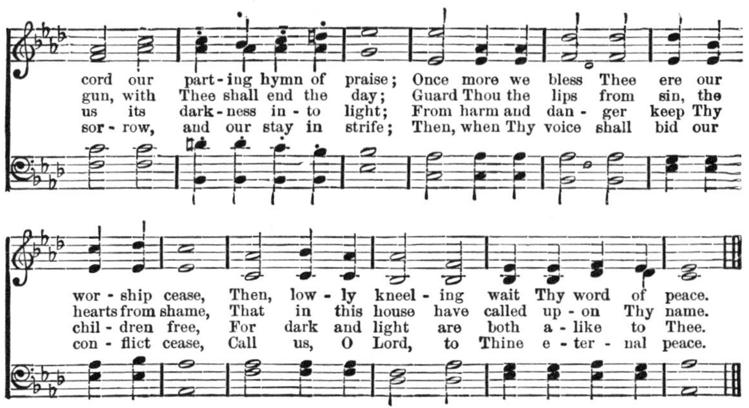
cord our parting hymn of praise; Once more we bless Thee ere our
gun, with Thee shall end the day; Guard Thou the lips from sin, the
us its darkness into light; From harm and danger keep Thy
sorrow, and our stay in strife; Then, when Thy voice shall bid our
worship cease, Then, lowly kneeling wait Thy word of peace.
hearts from shame, That in this house have called upon Thy name.
children free, For dark and light are both alike to Thee.
conflict cease, Call us, O Lord, to Thine eternal peace.

No. 413. What a Wonderful Saviour!

"And his name shall be called Wonderful."—Isa 9: 6.

E. A. H. — Elisha A. Hoffmann.

1. Christ has for sin atonement made, What a wonderful Saviour! We
2. I praise Him for the cleansing blood, What a wonderful Saviour! That
3. He cleansed my heart from all its sin, What a wonderful Saviour! And
4. He walks beside me all the way, What a wonderful Saviour! And

Chorus.
are redeemed! the price is paid! What a wonderful Saviour!
reconciled my soul to God; What a wonderful Saviour!
now He reigns and rules therein; What a wonderful Saviour!
keeps me faithful day by day; What a wonderful Saviour!
What a wonderful

Saviour is Jesus, my Jesus! What a wonderful Saviour is Jesus, my Lord!

5 He gives me overcoming power,
What a wonderful Saviour!
And triumph in each trying hour;
What a wonderful Saviour!

6 To Him I've given all my heart,
What a wonderful Saviour!
The world shall never share a part;
What a wonderful Saviour!

No. 414. A Mighty Fortress.

"The Lord is my rock and my fortress."—2 SAM. 22: 2.

F. H. HEDGE, tr. MARTIN LUTHER.

1. A might - y fort - ress is our God, A bul - wark nev - er fail - ing;
2. Did we in our own strength con - fide, Our striv - ing would be los - ing;
3. And tho' this world, with dev - ils filled, Should threaten to un - do us;

Our Help - er He, a - mid the flood Of mor - tal ills pre - vail - ing.
Were not the right man on our side, The man of God's own choos - ing.
We will not fear, for God hath will'd, His truth to tri - umph through us.

For still our an - cient foe Doth seek to work his woe: His craft and
Doth ask who that may be? Christ Je - sus, it is He! Lord Saba - oth
Let goods and kin - dred go, This mor - tal life al - so; The bod - y

pow'r are great, And armed with cru - el hate—On earth is not his e - qual.
is His name, From age to age the same; And He must win the bat - tle.
they may kill; God's truth a - bid - eth still, His king - dom is for - ev - er.

No. 415. O Glorious Fountain.

"A fountain opened for sin and for uncleanness."—ZEC. 13: 1.

Rev. F. BOTTOME. JAMES MCGRANAHAN.

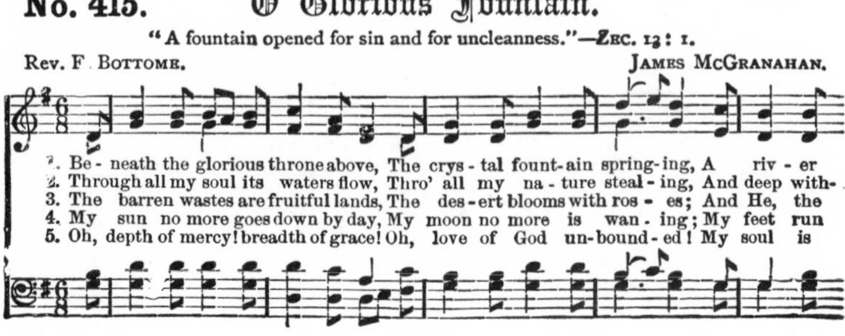

1. Be - neath the glorious throne above, The crys - tal fount - ain spring - ing, A riv - er
2. Through all my soul its waters flow, Thro' all my na - ture steal - ing, And deep with-
3. The barren wastes are fruitful lands, The des - ert blooms with ros - es; And He, the
4. My sun no more goes down by day, My moon no more is wan - ing; My feet run
5. Oh, depth of mercy! breadth of grace! Oh, love of God un - bound - ed! My soul is

O Glorious Fountain.

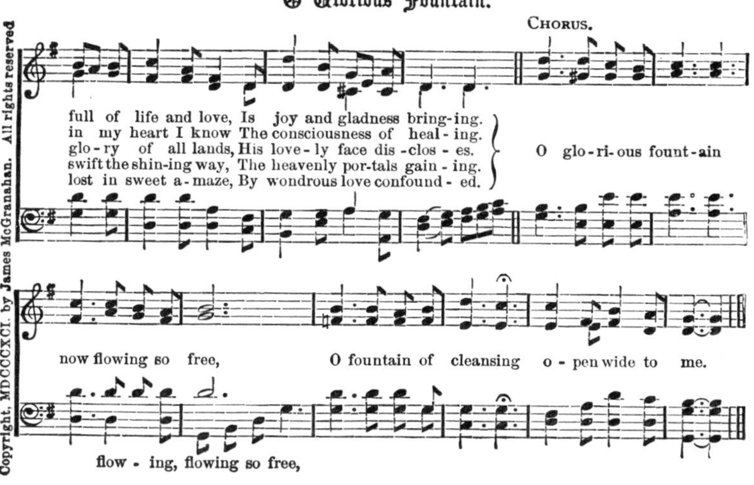
Chorus.
full of life and love, Is joy and gladness bring-ing.
in my heart I know The consciousness of heal-ing.
glo-ry of all lands, His love-ly face dis-clos-es.
swift the shin-ing way, The heavenly por-tals gain-ing.
lost in sweet a-maze, By wondrous love confound-ed.
O glo-ri-ous fount-ain
now flowing so free,
O fountain of cleansing o-pen wide to me.
flow-ing, flowing so free,

No. 416. Hear us, O Saviour.

"There shall be showers of blessing."—Ezek. 34: 26.

Charles Bruce. Ira D. Sankey.

1. Hear us, O Sav-iour, while we pray, Humbly our need con-fess-ing; Grant us the promised
2. Knowing Thy love, on Thee we call, Bold-ly Thy throne addressing; Pleading that show'rs of
3. Trusting Thy word that can-not fail, Master, we claim Thy promise; Oh that our faith may
Refrain.
show'rs to-day, Send them up-on us, O Lord.
grace may fall,—Send them up-on us, O Lord.
now pre-vail,—Send us the showers, O Lord.
Send show'rs of bless-ing;
Send show'rs re-fresh-ing; Send us show'rs of bless-ing; Send them, Lord, we pray.

No. 417. His Praises I Will Sing.

"I will sing praise to the Lord."—Judg. 5: 3.
J. B. Atchinson.
Geo. C. Stebbins.
1. I've learn'd to sing a glad new song Of praise un - to our King!
2. I've learn'd to sing the song of peace, 'Tis sweet - er ev - 'ry day,
3. I sing the song of per - fect love, It cast - eth out all fear!
4. I've learn'd to sing the song of joy, My cup is run - ning o'er
5. Soon I shall sing the new, new song Of Mo - ses and the Lamb,
And now with all my ran - som'd pow'rs His prais - es I will sing.
Since Je - sus calmed my troub - led soul, And bore my sins a - way.
O breadth, O length, O depth, O height! O love so full of cheer!
With bless - ings full of peace and love, And still there's more and more!
With all the saint - ed hosts a - bove, Be - fore the great I AM!
Chorus.
His prais - es I will sing, He is my Lord and King;
And now with all my ran-somed powers His prais - es I will sing.
Copyright, MDCCCXCI, by The Biglow & Main Co.
No. 418. Hope On.
"Happy is he whose hope is in the Lord."—Ps. 146: 5.
Robert Bruce.
J. H. Burke.
1. Hope on, hope on, O troubled heart; If doubts and fears o'ertake thee, Remember this—the
2. Hope on, hope on, tho' dark and deep The shadows gath - er o'er thee; Be not dismayed; thy
3. Hope on, hope on, go brave-ly forth Thro' tri - al and temp-ta - tion, Di - rect - ed by the

Hope On.

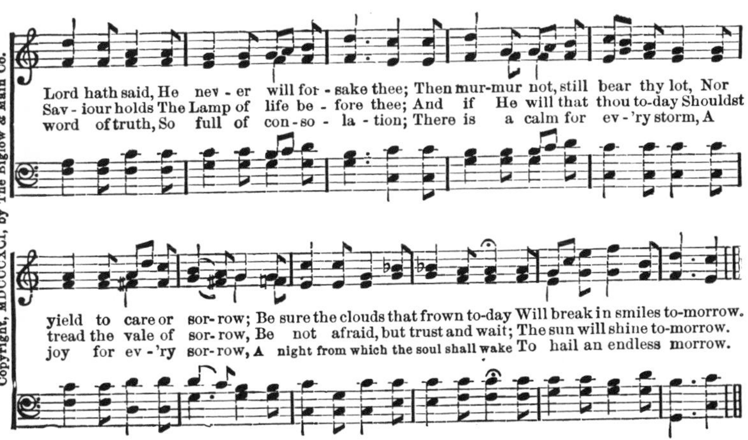
Lord hath said, He nev - er will for - sake thee; Then mur-mur not, still bear thy lot, Nor
Sav - iour holds The Lamp of life be - fore thee; And if He will that thou to-day Shouldst
word of truth, So full of con - so - la - tion; There is a calm for ev - 'ry storm, A
yield to care or sor - row; Be sure the clouds that frown to-day Will break in smiles to-morrow.
tread the vale of sor - row, Be not afraid, but trust and wait; The sun will shine to-morrow.
joy for ev - 'ry sor - row, A night from which the soul shall wake To hail an endless morrow.

No. 419. Narrow and Strait.

"Strait is the gate and narrow is the way."—Matt. 7: 14.

G. F. R. — Geo. F. Root.

1. Why do you lin - ger, Why do you stay In the broad road, that most
2. Do you find pleas - ures, Last - ing and pure, In the gay scenes that the
3. Come then, be - lov - ed, No long - er stay; Leave the broad high - way, O
dan - ger - ous way— While right be - fore you, Nar - row and strait, Is the bright
thoughtless al - lure— While your Re-deem - er With love so great, Points to the
leave it to - day; Make your de - cis - ion, Oh, do not wait; Take thou the
path - way to heav'n's pearl - y gate?
way that is nar - row and strait?
path - way so nar - row and strait.
Refrain.
Nar - row and strait,.............................
Nar - row and strait,

Narrow and Strait.

Nar-row and strait,.......................
Nar-row and strait, Is the bright pathway to heav'n's pearly gate.

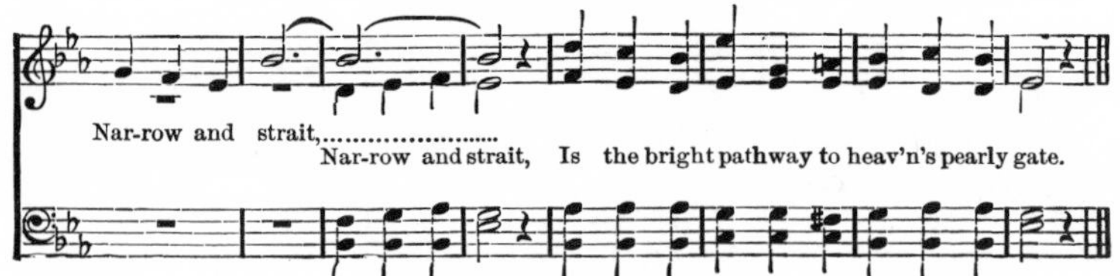

No. 420. O Rock of Ages.

"The Lord Jehovah is the Rock of Ages."—Isa. 26: 4.

Rev. H. L. Hastings. Hubert P. Main.

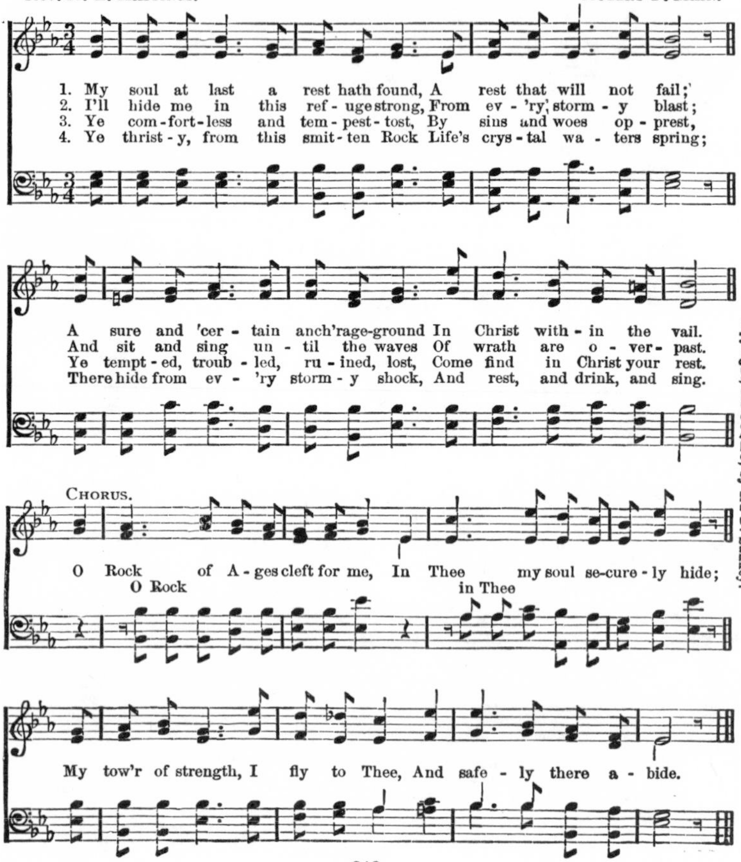

1. My soul at last a rest hath found, A rest that will not fail;
2. I'll hide me in this ref - uge strong, From ev - 'ry storm - y blast;
3. Ye com-fort-less and tem - pest - tost, By sins and woes op - prest,
4. Ye thrist - y, from this smit - ten Rock Life's crys - tal wa - ters spring;
A sure and 'cer - tain anch'rage-ground In Christ with - in the vail.
And sit and sing un - til the waves Of wrath are o - ver- past.
Ye tempt - ed, troub - led, ru - ined, lost, Come find in Christ your rest.
There hide from ev - 'ry storm - y shock, And rest, and drink, and sing.
Chorus.
O Rock of A - ges cleft for me, In Thee my soul se-cure - ly hide;
O Rock
in Thee
My tow'r of strength, I fly to Thee, And safe - ly there a - bide.

No. 421. Jesus Saves! O Blessed Story.

"He is able also to save them to the uttermost."—Heb. 7: 25.

Claudia May Ferrin. J. R. Murray.

1. Je-sus saves! O bless-ed sto - ry, Full of love and peace divine, Bursting from the realms of
2. Je-sus saves! O, who can fath-om All the ful-ness of His love? He once died for our re-
3. Je-sus saves! O sin-ner, hearken To the call of love to-day; There's no oth-er way to
glo - ry, Echoing thro' this world of time.
demption, Now He waits for us a - bove.
heav-en, Je - sus is the on - ly way.
Chorus.
Je-sus saves! O glo-ry! glo - ry! Shout the ti-dings o'er and o'er; Tell to all the earth the sto - ry, Je-sus saves for ev - er - more.

No. 422. Christ is my Redeemer.

"I the Lord am thy Saviour and thy Redeemer."—Isa. 49: 26.

El Nathan. James McGranahan.

Allegro.
1. How sweet the joy that fills my soul: Christ is my Re - deem - er;
2. Tho' Sa - tan oft my way op - pose, Christ is my Re - deem - er;
3. When tri - als come I still con - fess, Christ is my Re - deem - er;
4. The vic - to - ry by this I gain, Christ is my Re - deem - er:
His pre - cious blood has made me whole: Christ is my Re - deem - er;
With this I bold - ly meet my foes: Christ is my Re - deem - er;
He gives me grace each care to bless: Christ is my Re - deem - er;
By this I break sin's gall - ing chain: Christ is my Re - deem - er;

Christ is my Redeemer.
My sins were all up - on Him laid, A full a - tone-ment He hath made,
'Twas this that gave me life and light, 'Tis this that nerves me for the fight,
He guides and keeps me day by day, He clos - er comes when dark the way,
And if He tar - ry and I sleep, My dy - ing hour this hope shall keep,
For me He hath the ran - som paid: Christ is my Re - deem - er.
'Tis this my hope that shines so bright: Christ is my Re - deem - er.
He doth with this my fears al - lay; Christ is my Re - deem - er.
That when He comes the grave to reap, Christ is my Re - deem - er.
No. 423. The Shadow of the Rock.
" The shadow of a great rock in a weary land."—Isa. 32: 2.
F. J. Crosby.
Ira D. Sankey.
1. Lead to the shad-ow of the Rock of Ref - uge My wea - ry feet;
2. Lead to the shad-ow of the Rock E - ter - nal My heart op - pressed;
3. Lead to the shad-ow of the " Rock of A - ges," O keep thou me
Give me the wa - ter from the life stream flow - ing Clear, pure and sweet.
There in the se - cret of Thy ho - ly pres - ence, Calm shall I rest.
Safe from the ar - rows of the world's temp - ta - tions, Close, close to Thee.
Chorus.
There from the bil - lows and the tem - pest hid - ing, Un - der the shel - ter of Thy
love a - bid - ing, Safe in the shadow of the " Rock of A - ges," Joy shall be mine.
Copyright, MDCCCXCI, by The Biglow & Main Co.

No. 424. To Thee I Come.

"Come unto me."—MATT. 11 : 28.

Words arr. J. E. GOULD.

1. Je-sus, I come to Thee for light, Re-store to me my blind-ed sight, And from my soul dis-pel the night—Jesus, to Thee I come! Jesus, to Thee I come!
2. Je-sus, I come—I can-not stay From Thee an-oth-er pre-cious day; I would Thy word at once o-bey— Jesus, to Thee I come! Jesus, to Thee I come!
3. Je-sus, I come—"just as I am," To Thee, the ho-ly, spot-less Lamb; Thou wilt my troub-led spir-it calm— Jesus, to Thee I come! Jesus, to Thee I come!

No. 425. Ride on in Majesty.

"And in thy majesty ride prosperously."—Ps. 45 : 4.

H. H. MILMAN. GEO. C. STEBBINS.

1. Ride on! ride on in maj-es-ty! Hark! all the tribes hosan-na cry! O Saviour meek, pur-sue Thy road With palms and scatter'd garments strew'd.
2. Ride on! ride on in maj-es-ty! The an-gel ar-mies of the sky Look down with sad and wond'ring eyes To see the approaching Sac-ri-fice.
3. Ride on! ride on in maj-es-ty! The last and fiercest strife is nigh; The Father on His sapphire throne A-waits His own a-noint-ed Son.
4. Ride on! ride on in maj-es-ty! In low-ly pomp ride on to die; Bow Thy meek head to mor-tal pain, Then take, O God, Thy pow'r and reign.
CHORUS.
Ride on, ride on in maj-es-ty! In low-ly pomp, ride on to die.
Ride on, ride on, ride on, ride on in maj-es-ty, in maj-es-ty! In low-ly pomp, in low-ly pomp, ride on, ride on to die, to die.

No. 426. Raise high the Song.

"I will come again, and receive you unto myself."—John 14: 3.

Thos. Laurie. J. J. Lowe.

1. Our Sav-iour will descend a-gain, Earth's buried millions raising; With Him will come a glo-rious train, A - dor - ing Him and prais-ing.
2. And tho' these bod-ies lie in dust Be-fore that glad appear - ing, Yet shall they stand a - mong the just, Our Saviour's im - age wear- ing.
3. What, tho' earth's gath'ring tempests lower, And a- ges pass in sadness? Yet we may see that glo-rious hour, And hail the dawn with gladness.
4. Then, safe at last, this blessed throng, Set free from trib - u - la - tion, Shall ev - er praise in ho - ly song The God of their sal - va - tion.

Chorus.

Raise high the song that loud and long Be-fore Him ceaseth nev - er, Till, casting down each golden crown, We worship Him forev- er.

No. 427. O Glad and Glorious Gospel.

"God so loved the world that he gave his only begotten Son."—Jno. 3: 16.

M. Fraser. James McGranahan.

1. 'Tis a true and faithful say - ing, Je - sus died for sin - ful men; Tho' we've told the story oft - en, We must tell it o'er a - gain.
2. He has made a full a - tonement, Now His saving work is done; He has sat - is - fied the Fa - ther, Who accepts us in His Son.
3. Still upon His hands the nail prints, And the scars up-on His brow, Our Redeem-er, Lord and Sav - iour In the glo - ry stand-eth now.
4. But remem-ber this same Je - sus In the clouds will come again, And with Him His blood-bought peo - ple Ev - er-more shall live and reign.
Chorus.
O glad and glo- rious Gos - pel! With

O Glad and Glorious Gospel.

joy we now pro - claim A full and free sal - va - tion, Thro' faith in Je - sus' name.
we now proclaim

No. 428. Why Not Now?

"Behold, now is the accepted time."—2 Cor. 6: 2.

El Nathan. C. C. Case.

1. While we pray, and while we plead, While you see your soul's deep need,
While your Fa - ther calls you home, Will you not, my broth - er, come?

2. You have wan - dered far a - way, Do not risk an - oth - er day;
Do not turn from God your face, But to - day ac - cept His grace.

3. In the world you've fail'd to find Aught of peace for troub - led mind;
Come to Christ, on Him be - lieve, Peace and joy you shall re - ceive.

4. Come to Christ, con - fes - sion make; Come to Christ and par - don take;
Trust in Him from day to day, He will keep you all the way.

Chorus.

Why not now?........ why not now?....... Why not come to Je - sus now?
Why not now? Why not now?

Why not now?....... Why not now?....... Why not come to Je - sus now?
Why not now? Why not now?

No. 429. Victory Through Grace.

"He went forth conquering and to conquer."—Rev. 6: 2.

S. Martin. Jno. R. Sweney.

1. Con-quer-ing now and still to con-quer, Rid-eth a King in His might,
2. Con-quer-ing now and still to con-quer, Who is this won-der - ful King?
3. Con-quer-ing now and still to con-quer, Je - sus, Thou Rul - er of all,
Lead-ing the host of all the faith-ful In - to the midst of the fight;
Whence all the ar - mies which He lead - eth, While of His glo - ry they sing?
Thrones and their scepters all shall per - ish, Crowns and their splendor shall fall;
See them with cour-age ad - vanc-ing, Clad in their brill-iant ar - ray
He is our Lord and Re - deem - er, Sav-iour and Mon-arch di - vine,
Yet shall the arm - ies Thou lead - est, Faithful and true to the last,
Shout-ing the name of their Lead - er, Hear them ex - ult - ing - ly say:
They are the stars that for - ev - er Bright in His king-dom will shine.
Find in Thy mansions e - ter - nal, Rest when their war - fare is past.
Chorus.
"Not to the strong is the bat - tle, Not to the swift is the race,
Yet to the true and the faith - ful Vict' - ry is prom-ised through grace."

No. 430. Holy Ghost, with Light Divine.

"Lead me in thy truth, and teach me."—Ps. 25: 5.
Andrew Reed.
(Mercy. 7s.) L. M. Gottschalk, arr. by H. P. M.
1. Ho - ly Ghost, with light di - vine, Shine up - on this heart of mine;
2. Ho - ly Ghost, with pow'r di - vine, Cleanse this guilt - y heart of mine;
3. Ho - ly Ghost, with joy di - vine, Cheer this sad-dened heart of mine;
4. Ho - ly Spir - it, all di - vine, Dwell with - in this heart of mine;
Chase the shades of night a - way, Turn my dark - ness in - to day.
Long hath sin, with - out con - trol, Held do - min - ion o'er my soul.
Bid my ma - ny woes de - part, Heal my wounded, bleed - ing heart.
Cast down ev - 'ry i - dol - throne, Reign su - preme—and reign a - lone.
By per. O. Ditson Co., owners of copyright.
No. 431. Rejoice! Ye Saints.
"And again, I say, rejoice."—Phil. 4: 4.
C. R. H.
J. H. Burke.
1. Re-joice! ye saints, a - gain re-joice, And sing, with one ac - cord; Re - joice with all your heart and voice, In Christ your ris - en Lord.
2. Re-joice! re - joice! lift up your head, And praise the liv-ing God, That for your souls the Sav - iour shed His own most pre-cious blood.
3. Re-joice! re - joice! let praise a-bound Be - fore Je-hovah's throne, For dead ones raised, and lost ones found, And prod - i-gals brought home.
4. Re-joice! re - joice! the Lord will come, Ac - cord - ing to His word, And gath - er all His ransom'd home, "For ev - er with the Lord."
Chorus.
Rejoice, in the Lord, Re - joice in the Lord, Re-
joice in the Lord al-way; Re - joice, in the Lord, Rejoice in the Lord, And again I say, Re-joice.
Copyright, MDCCCX... by The Biglow & Main Co.

No. 432. Never Shone a Light so Fair.

"I am come a light into the world."—JOHN 12: 46.

F. J. CROSBY. Rev. ROBERT LOWRY.

1. Nev - er shone a light so fair, Nev - er fell so sweet a song, As the cho - rus in the air, Chant-ed by the an - gel-throng; Ev - ery star took up the sto - ry,
2. Still that Ju - bi - lee of song Breaks up - on the ris - ing morn; While the an-them rolls a - long, Floods of light the earth a - dorn; Old and young take up the sto - ry,
3. Wel-come now the bless-ed day When we praise the Lord our King; When we meet to praise and pray, And His love with glad-ness sing; Let the world take up the sto - ry,

"Christ has come, the Prince of glo - ry, Come in hum - ble hearts to dwell, God with us, God with us, God with us, Im - man - u - el."

No. 433. Hallelujah, Bless His Name.

"And again they said, Alleluia."—REV. 19: 3.

M. FRASER. JAMES MCGRANAHAN.

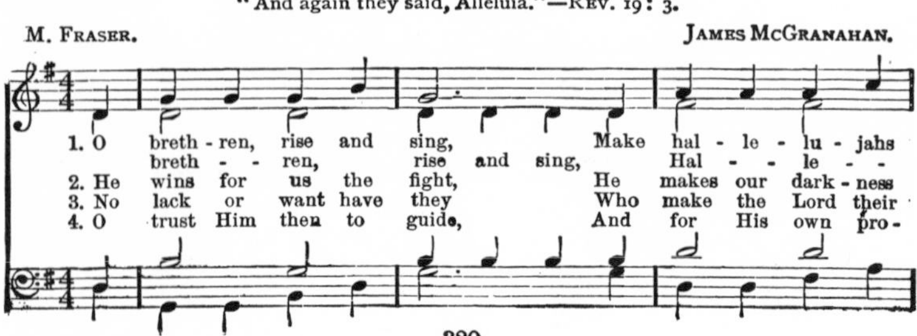
1. O breth - ren, rise and sing, Make hal - le - lu - jahs
breth - - ren, rise and sing, Hal - - le - -
2. He wins for us the fight, He makes our dark - ness
3. No lack or want have they Who make the Lord their
4. O trust Him then to guide, And for His own pro -

Hallelujah, Bless His Name.
ring To our Al-might-y King, And bless His name.
lu-jahs ring And bless His name.
light, All drear-y doubts take flight When He ap-pears.
stay; New strength for ev-'ry day His grace sup-plies.
vide; Should weal or woe be-tide, Trust to the end.
Chorus.
Hal-le-lu-jah, Hal-le-lu-jah, Hal-le-lu-jah, bless His name; Hal-le-
Hal-le-lu-jah, Hal-le-lu-jah. Hal-le-lu-jah,
Hal-le-lu-jah, Hal-le-lu-jah,
lu-jah, Hal-le-lu-jah, Hal-le-lu-jah, bless His name!
Hal-le-lu-jah, Hal-le-lu-jah, Hal-le-lu-jah,
Hal-le-lu-jah, Hal-le-lu-jah,
Copyright, MDCCCXCI, by James McGranahan. All rights reserved.
No. 434. Following Fully.
M. Fraser. "The Lord is my shepherd."—Psa. 23: 1. M. A. Sea.
1. One day the Shepherd passed, and turning, said, "Come, fol-low me;"
2. He led me through green pasture land, By wa-ters still;
3. From out no other eye had ever beamed Such love on me;
4. Black clouds were gathering on a blacker sky, the World all so drear;
5. Dear Lord, the darkness falls upon me, I can-not see;
6. And soon there came a loving call in answer, "Be not a-fraid;
7. None ever perished following Jesus fully, No, nev-er one;
What wonder that in haste I rose, So kind was He!
With such a Guide, who would not follow, Go where He will?
Good Shepherd, lead, and I will follow Hard aft-er Thee.
Upon the night wind rose the cry of One in great fear.
My feet are stumbling on the mountains; Oh! suc-cor me.
Mine eye shall guide the blind ones, and the weary Mine arm shall aid."
The weakest lambs are carried in His bosom, and Brought safe-ly home.
Copyright, MDCCCXCI, by James McGranahan. All rights reserved.

No. 435. Whosoever Will May Come.

"The Spirit and the bride say, Come."—Rev. 22 : 17.

A. Montieth. Ira D. Sankey.

1. O wand-'ring souls, why long - er roam A - way from God, a - way from home?
2. Be - hold His hands ex - tend -ed now, The dews of night are on His brow;
3. In sim - ple faith His word be - lieve, And His a - bun - dant grace re - ceive;
4. The "Spir - it and the Bride say, Come!" And find in Him sweet rest and home;

The Sav - iour calls, O hear Him say,—Who - ev - er will may come to - day.
He knocks, He calls, He wait - eth still; Oh, come to Him, who - ev - er will.
No love like His the heart can fill; Oh, come to Him, who - ev - er will.
Let Him that hear - eth ech - o still, The bless - ed *"who - so - ev - er will."*

Chorus.

All praise and glo - ry be un - to Je - sus, For He hath purchased a full sal - va - tion; Behold how wondrous the proc - la - ma - tion, "Who - so - ev - er will may come!"

No. 436. Hear Me, Blessed Jesus.

"Consider and hear me, O Lord my God."—Ps. 13 : 3.

Words arr. J. H. Burke.

1. Hear me, bless - ed Je - sus, Bid all fear de - part; Let Thy Spir - it
2. Let me ful - ly trust Thee, Rest - ing on Thy Word; Let me still with
3. Hid - ing in the shad - ow Of Thy shelt-'ring wings, I shall rest con -

Hear Me, Blessed Jesus.

Chorus.
whis - per Peace with - in my heart.
pa - tience Wait on Thee, O Lord.
fid - ing In the King of kings.
Then, what - e'er Thou send - est,
Hap - py shall I be, Je - sus, my Re-deem - er, Look-ing un - to Thee.

No. 437. Yes, We'll Meet in the Morning.

"Joy cometh in the morning."—Ps. 30: 5.

C. E. B, arr. GEO. F. ROOT.

Moderato.
1. Yes, we'll meet a - gain in the morn - ing, In the dawn of a fair - er day;
When the night of watch-ing and wait - ing, With its dark-ness has passed a - way.
2. Where our pre-cious ones now are dwell - ing, Free from toil and from ev - 'ry care;
With their garments spot-less and shin - ing, Like the robes that the an - gels wear.
3. O what joy when all shall be o - ver, And the jour - ney on earth we close,
And the an-gels homeward shall bear us, Where the life-stream for-ev - er flows.
Where no shad - ows veil the sun - shine, O - ver there in the heav'nly land,
When our pil - grim - age com - plet - ed, And our foot-steps no lon - ger roam,
We shall see the King of glo - ry, We shall praise Him with harp and voice;
And the crys - tal waves of the riv - er, Ev - er flow o'er the gold - en sand.
By the pearl - y gates glad-ly wait - ing, They will give us a wel - come home.
We shall sing the grace that re - deemed us, While our hearts in His love re - joice.

No. 438. Gird on the Sword and Armor.

"Put on the whole armor of God."—Eph. 6: 11.

C. H. Mann. J. H. Tenney.

1. Gird on the sword and ar - mor, Go raise the ban-ner high; The Cap-tain of Sal -
2. Gird on the sword and ar - mor, Let faith be thy strong shield; His prom-ise shall sus -
3. Gird on the sword and ar - mor, Press on the foe to fight; No en - e - my can
va - tion To Thee is ev - er nigh.
tain thee On ev - 'ry bat - tle field.
harm thee, For God sustains the right.
Chorus.
Then wave the glo-rious ban - ner, Press
for-ward in His name; And soon thy Guide and Cap - tain Will vic - to - ry proclaim.
His name;

No. 439. My Saviour tells me so.

"Him that cometh to me I will in nowise cast out."—Jno. 6: 37.

El. Nathan. James McGranahan.

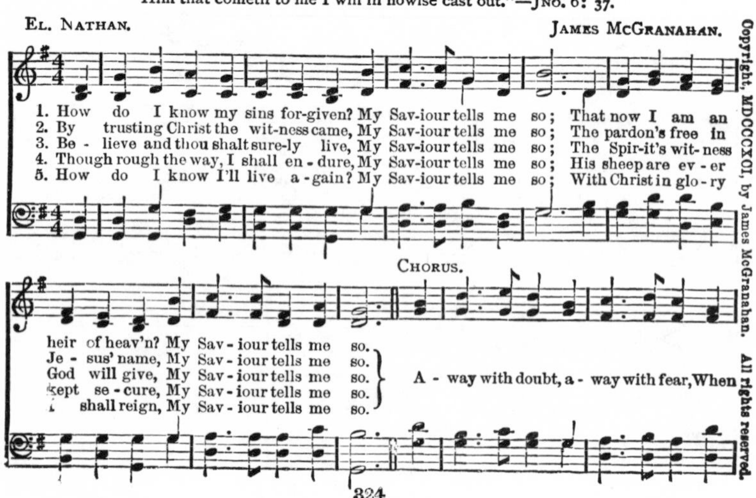

1. How do I know my sins for-given? My Sav-iour tells me so; That now I am an
2. By trusting Christ the wit-ness came, My Sav-iour tells me so; The pardon's free in
3. Be - lieve and thou shalt sure-ly live, My Sav-iour tells me so; The Spir-it's wit-ness
4. Though rough the way, I shall en - dure, My Sav-iour tells me so; His sheep are ev - er
5. How do I know I'll live a - gain? My Sav-iour tells me so; With Christ in glo - ry
heir of heav'n? My Sav - iour tells me so.
Je - sus' name, My Sav - iour tells me so.
God will give, My Sav - iour tells me so.
kept se - cure, My Sav - iour tells me so.
I shall reign, My Sav - iour tells me so.
Chorus.
A - way with doubt, a - way with fear, When

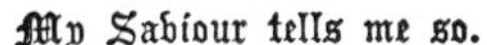

this by faith I know; God's word shall stand forev - er-more, My Saviour tells me so.

No. 440. Hide Me.

"He shall hide me."—Ps. 27: 5.

F. J. Crosby. W. H. Doane.

1. Hide me, O my Sav-iour, hide me In Thy ho - ly place; Resting there beneath Thy
2. Hide me, when the storm is rag - ing O'er life's troubled sea; Like a dove on o- cean's
3. Hide me, when my heart is break-ing With its weight of woe; When in tears I seek the

glo - ry, O let me see Thy face.
bil - lows, O let me fly to Thee.
com - fort Thou canst a-lone be - stow.

Refrain.

Hide me, hide me,
Hide me, hide me, safe - ly hide me,

O bless-ed Saviour, hide me; O Sav-iour, keep me Safe-ly, O Lord, with Thee.
O, my Saviour, keep Thou me.

No. 441. Throw out the Life-Line.

(May be sung as a Solo and Chorus.)

Rev. E. S. Ufford. E. S. Ufford. Arr. by Geo. C. Stebbins

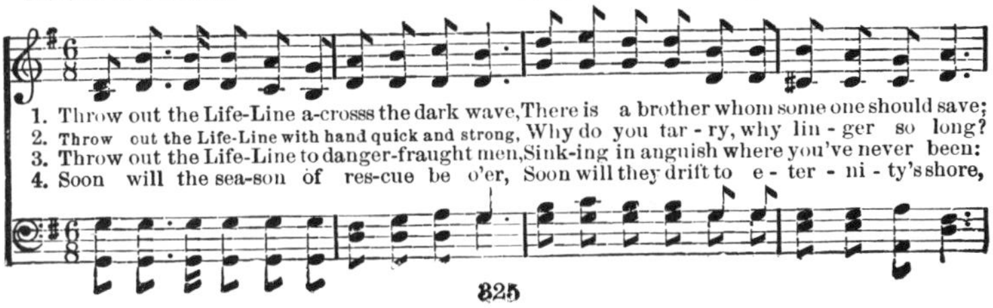

1. Throw out the Life-Line a-crosss the dark wave, There is a brother whom some one should save;
2. Throw out the Life-Line with hand quick and strong, Why do you tar - ry, why lin - ger so long?
3. Throw out the Life-Line to danger-fraught men, Sink-ing in anguish where you've never been:
4. Soon will the sea-son of res-cue be o'er, Soon will they drift to e - ter - ni - ty's shore,

Throw out the Life-Line.

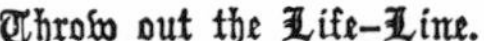

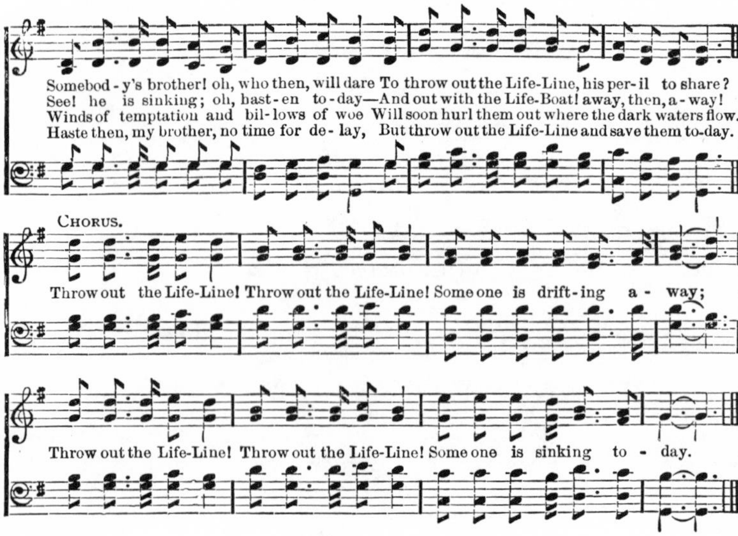

Somebod - y's brother! oh, who then, will dare To throw out the Life-Line, his per- il to share?
See! he is sinking; oh, hast- en to-day—And out with the Life-Boat! away, then, a-way!
Winds of temptation and bil- lows of woe Will soon hurl them out where the dark waters flow.
Haste then, my brother, no time for de- lay, But throw out the Life-Line and save them to-day.
Chorus.
Throw out the Life-Line! Throw out the Life-Line! Some one is drift- ing a - way;
Throw out the Life-Line! Throw out the Life-Line! Some one is sinking to - day.

No. 442. O Worship the King.

"All thy works shall praise thee, O Lord."—Psa. 145 : 10.

Robert Grant. F. J. Haydn.

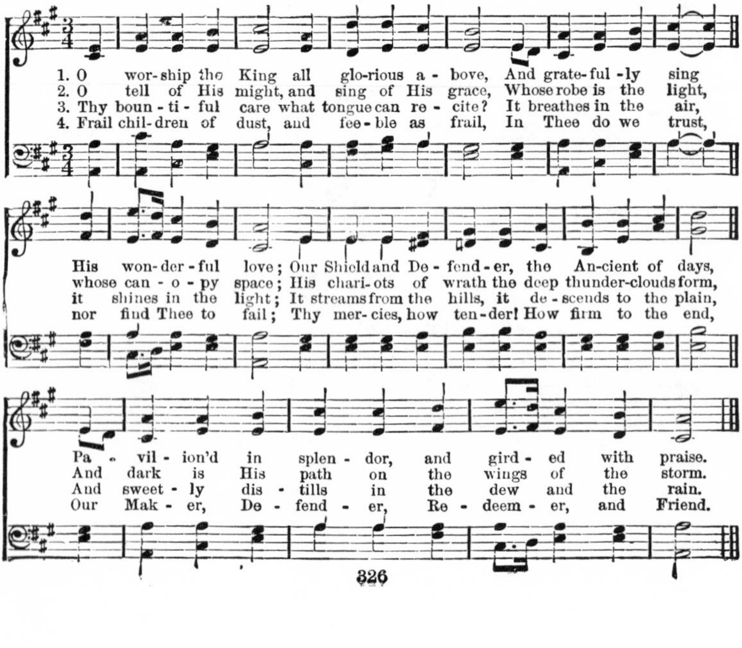

1. O wor-ship the King all glo-rious a - bove, And grate-ful - ly sing His won-der-ful love; Our Shield and De- fend- er, the An-cient of days, Pa - vil - ion'd in splen - dor, and gird - ed with praise.
2. O tell of His might, and sing of His grace, Whose robe is the light, whose can - o - py space; His chari- ots of wrath the deep thunder-clouds form, And dark is His path on the wings of the storm.
3. Thy boun - ti - ful care what tongue can re - cite? It breathes in the air, it shines in the light; It streams from the hills, it de - scends to the plain, And sweet - ly dis - tills in the dew and the rain.
4. Frail chil- dren of dust, and fee - ble as frail, In Thee do we trust, nor find Thee to fail; Thy mer- cies, how ten- der! How firm to the end, Our Mak - er, De - fend - er, Re - deem - er, and Friend.

No. 443. Holy Spirit, Teacher Thou.

"He shall teach you all things."—JOHN 14: 26.

L. W. MUNHALL. ROBERT LOWRY.

1. Ho - ly Spir - it, Teach-er Thou, At the throne of grace we bow; Come, perform Thine of - fice now, Teach us ev - er - more.
2. Comfort - er in-deed Thou art, Giv-ing strength to ev - 'ry heart; Let Thy pres-ence ne'er de - part, Com - fort ev - er - more.
3. Sent to be our Guide to - day, Keep us in the nar - row way; Grant that we may nev - er stray, Guide us ev - er - more.
4. Teacher, Com - fort - er, and Guide, In our hearts do Thou a - bide; And in life, what - e'er be - tide, Help us ev - er - more.
REFRAIN.
Ho - ly Spir - it, teach us ev - er,
Comfort, guide, and leave us never; Dwell within us, we im - plore, Now and ev - er - more.

No. 444. Preach the Gospel.

"Go ye into all the world and preach the gospel to every creature."—MARK 16: 15.

EL. NATHAN. JAMES MCGRANAHAN.

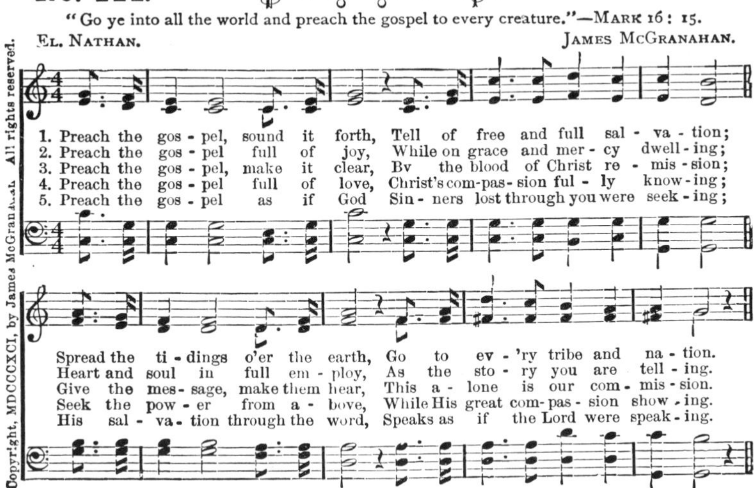
1. Preach the gos - pel, sound it forth, Tell of free and full sal - va - tion; Spread the ti - dings o'er the earth, Go to ev - 'ry tribe and na - tion.
2. Preach the gos - pel full of joy, While on grace and mer - cy dwell - ing; Heart and soul in full em - ploy, As the sto - ry you are tell - ing.
3. Preach the gos - pel, make it clear, By the blood of Christ re - mis - sion; Give the mes - sage, make them hear, This a - lone is our com - mis - sion.
4. Preach the gos - pel full of love, Christ's com - pas - sion ful - ly know - ing; Seek the pow - er from a - bove, While His great com - pas - sion show - ing.
5. Preach the gos - pel as if God Sin - ners lost through you were seek - ing; His sal - va - tion through the word, Speaks as if the Lord were speak - ing.

CHORUS.
Spread.............. the joy-ful ti - dings in an-them and sto-ry;
Spread the joy-ful ti - dings, spread the joy-ful ti-dings in
Je - - - - - sus hath redeemed us, O give Him the glo-ry.
Je-sus hath redeemed us, Je-sus hath redeemed us, O

No. 445. I am Trusting Thee, Lord Jesus.

"Trusting in the Lord."—Ps. 112: 7.

FRANCES R. HAVERGAL. J. H. BURKE.

1. I am trust-ing Thee, Lord Je-sus, Trust-ing on-ly Thee! Trust-ing Thee for full sal-va-tion, Great and free.
2. I am trust-ing Thee for par-don, At Thy feet I bow; For Thy grace and ten-der mer-cy, Trust-ing now.
3. I am trust-ing Thee for cleans-ing In the crim-son flood; Trust-ing Thee to make me ho-ly By Thy blood.
4. I am trust-ing Thee for pow-er, Thine can nev-er fail; Words which Thou Thy-self shalt give me, Must pre-vail.
5. I am trust-ing Thee, Lord Je-sus, Nev-er let me fall; I am trust-ing Thee for-ev-er, And for all.
CHORUS.
I am trust-ing,
I am trusting, I am trusting,
Trusting on-ly Thee! I am trust-ing, trust-ing, Trusting on-ly Thee.
trusting, trusting, I am trusting,
Copyright, MDCCCXCI, by The Biglow & Main Co.

No. 446. After.

"There remaineth therefore a rest for the people of God."—Heb. 4 : 9.

Words arr. Geo. C. Stebbins.

1. Aft - er the toil and troub-le, There cometh a day of rest; Aft-er the wea-ry
2. Aft - er the night of darkness, The shadows all flee a - way; Aft-er the day of
3. Aft - er the hours of chastening, The Spir - it made pure and bright; Aft-er the earth's dark
4. Aft - er the pain and sickness, The tears are all wiped a - way; Aft-er the flow'rs are
con - flict, Peace on the Sav - iour's breast; Aft - er the care and sor - row, The
sad - ness, Hope sheds her bright-est ray; Aft - er the strife and strug - gle, The
shad - ow, Clear in the light of Light; Aft - er the guid - ing coun - sel, Com-
gathered, No more of earth's de - cay; Aft - er the deep heart sor - row, An
glo - ry of light and love; After the wilderness journey, The Father's bright home above.
vic - to - ry is won; Aft - er the work is o - ver, The Master's own word, "Well done."
mun - ion full and sweet; Aft - er the will - ing service, All laid at the Saviour's feet.
end of ev - ery strife; Aft - er the dai - ly crosses, A glo - ri - ous crown of life.
Copyright, MDCCCXCI, by The Biglow & Main Co.
No. 447. Sin no More.
"Neither do I condemn thee; go, and sin no more."—Jno. 8 : 11.
M. A. B., arr. by El. Nathan. James McGranahan.
1. Sin no more, thy soul is free, Christ has died to ran - som thee;
2. Sin no more, but close - ly keep Near the Hand that guards the sheep;
3. Sin no more, His blood hath bought, Think on what His love hath wrought;
4. Sin no more, O sin no more, Je - sus lives to keep thee pure;
Now the power of sin is o'er, Je - sus bids thee "sin no more."
Shun the snares that lured be - fore, Trem - bling go, and sin no more.
Think of what for thee He bore, Weep - ing go, and sin no more.
If o'er - ta - ken He'll re - store, Say - ing, "Go, and sin no more."
Copyright, MDCCCXCI, by James McGranahan. All rights reserved.

Sin no More.

Chorus
Sin no more,............ thy soul is free, Christ has died............ to ransom
sin no more, thy soul is free, Christ has died
ritard.
thee; Sing the message o'er and o'er............Christ forgives thee, "sin no more."
to ransom thee;

No. 448. Take Time to be Holy.

"Be ye holy: for I am the Lord your God."—Lev. 20: 7.

W. D. Longstaff. Geo. C. Stebbins.

1. Take time to be ho - ly, Speak oft with thy Lord; A - bide in Him al - ways, And feed on His Word; Make friends of God's chil - dren, Help those who are weak, For - get - ing in noth - ing His bless - ing to seek.
2. Take time to be ho - ly, The world rush - es on; Spend much time in se - cret With Je - sus a - lone; By look - ing to Je - sus, Like Him thou shalt be; Thy friends in thy con - duct His like - ness shall see.
3. Take time to be ho - ly, Let Him be thy Guide, And run not be - fore Him, What - ev - er be - tide; In joy or in sor - row, Still fol - low the Lord, And, look - ing to Je - sus, Still trust in His Word.
4. Take time to be ho - ly, Be calm in thy soul, Each thought and each mo - tive Be - neath His con - trol; Thus led by His Spir - it, To fountains of love, Thou soon shalt be fit - ted For serv - ice a - bove.
Copyright, MDCCCXC, by Ira D. Sankey.

No. 449. The Lord is Coming.

"Behold the bridegroom cometh; go ye out to meet Him"—MATT. 25: 6.

E. A. H. — Rev. E. A. HOFFMANN.

1. The Lord is com - ing by and by, Be read - y when He comes;
He comes from His fair home on high, Be read - y when He comes;
He is the Lord our Righteous-ness, And comes His chos - en ones to bless,
And at His Fa - ther's throne con - fess; Be read - y when He comes.

2. He soon will come to earth a - gain, Be read - y when He comes;
Be - gin His u - ni - ver - sal reign, Be read - y when He comes;
With Hal - le - lu - jahs heav'n will ring, When Je - sus does re - demp - tion bring;
O trim your lamps to meet your King; Be read - y when He comes.

3. Be - hold! He comes to one and all, Be read - y when He comes;
He quick - ly comes with trum - pet call, Be read - y when He comes;
To judgment called at His command, Drawn thith - er by His might - y hand,
Be - fore His throne we all must stand; Be read - y when He comes.

CHORUS.

Will you be read - y when the Bride - groom comes? when He comes?
Will you be read - y when the Bridegroom comes? when He comes?
Will your lamps be trim'd and bright,
Be it morning, noon or night? Will you be read - y when the Bridegroom comes?

No. 450. Behold a Stranger.
" Behold, I stand at the door, and knock."—Rev. 3 : 20.
Rev. J. Grigg.
(Federal St. L. M.)
Henry K. Oliver.
1. Be - hold a Stran - ger at the door, He gen - tly knocks, has knocked be - fore;
2. O love - ly at - ti - tude! He stands With melting heart and la - den hands;
3. But will He prove a Friend in - deed? He will, the ver - y Friend you need;
4. Rise, touch'd with grati - tude di - vine; Turn out His en - e - my and thine,
Has wait - ed long,—is wait - ing still; You treat no oth - er friend so ill.
O matchless kindness! and He shows This matchless kindness to His foes.
The Friend of sin - ners, yes, 'tis He, With garments dyed on Cal - va - ry.
That soul-de-stroy - ing mon - ster, Sin; And let the heavenly Stran - ger in.
No. 451. We Praise Thee, we Bless Thee.
" We thank thee, and praise thy glorious name."—1 Chr. 29 : 13.
Fanny J. Crosby.
Koschat, arr. by Ira D. Sankey.
1. We praise Thee, we bless Thee, Our Sav - iour di - vine, All pow'r and do - min - ion For - ev - er be Thine; We sing of Thy mer - cy With joy - ful ac - claim; For Thou hast re - deemed us; All praise to Thy name; For Thou hast redeemed us; All praise to Thy name.
2. All hon - or and praise to Thine ex - cel - lent name; Thy love is un-changing, For - ev - er the same; We bless and a - dore Thee, O Saviour and King; With joy and thanks - giv - ing Thy prais - es we sing; With joy and thanksgiving Thy prais - es we sing.
3. The strength of the hills, and The depths of the sea, The earth and its full - ness, Be - long un - to Thee; And yet to the low - ly Thou bendest Thine ear, So read - y their hum - ble Pe - ti - tions to hear; So read - y their humble Pe - ti - tions to hear.
4. Thine in - fi - nite good - ness Our tongues shall employ; Thou giv - est us rich - ly All things to en - joy; We'll fol - low Thy footsteps, We'll rest in Thy love, And soon we shall praise Thee In mansions a - bove; And soon we shall praise Thee In mansions a - bove.
Words and Arr. Copyright, MDCCCXCI, by The Biglow & Main Co.

No. 452. What a Gospel!

"For I am not ashamed of the gospel of Christ."—Rom. 1: 16.

M. Fraser. James McGranahan.

1. It is fin-ished; what a gos-pel! Noth-ing has ‖: *been left :‖ to do,
2. It is fin-ished; what a gos-pel! Bringing news of ‖: vic - t'ry :‖ won,
3. It is fin-ished; what a gos-pel! Here each wea-ry ‖: la - den :‖ breast,
4. It is fin-ished; what a gos-pel! Je - sus died ‖: to save :‖ your soul;
But to take with grate-ful glad-ness What the Sav-iour did for you.
Tell-ing us of peace and par-don Thro' the blood of God's dear Son.
That ac-cepts God's gra-cious of-fer, En-ters in-to per-fect rest.
Have you tak-en His sal-va-tion? Have you let Him make you whole?
Chorus.
It is fin-ished; Hal-le-lu-jah! It is fin-ished Hal-le-lu-jah!
Christ the work has ful-ly done; Hal-le-lu-jah! All who will may
have their par-don Through the blood of God's own Son.

* Repeat for Alto and Tenor only.

No. 453. There is a Paradise of Rest.

"There remaineth therefore a rest."—Heb. 4: 9.
W. R. Lindsay.
Ira D. Sankey.
1. There is a Par-a-dise of rest On yon-der tran-quil shore; Be-yond the shad-ow and the gloom of night, Where toil and tears are o'er.
2. There is a Cit-y crown'd with light, Its joys no tongue can tell; For they who en-ter shall be-hold the King, And in His pres-ence dwell.
3. There is a crown laid up on high That Christ the Lord will give To those who pa-tient-ly His com-ing wait, And for His glo-ry live.
4. Oh, then be faith-ful un-to death, Press on the heaven-ly way, That we may en-ter thro' the Gates of Life To realms of end-less day.
Chorus.
Meet me there,......... oh, meet me there, At the dawning of the morning bright and fair;
meet me there, meet me there,
Meet me there,......... oh, meet me there, In the land beyond the river, meet me there.
meet me there, meet me there,
Copyright, MDCCCXC, by Ira D. Sankey.
No. 454. Lead, Kindly Light.
"Send thy light and truth, let them lead me."—Ps. 43: 3.
John H. Newman.
John B. Dykes.
1. Lead, kind-ly Light, a-mid th'encircling gloom, Lead Thou me on; The night is

Lead, Kindly Light.

dark, and I am far from home, Lead, Thou me on. Keep Thou my feet; I
do not ask to see........ The dis - tant scene; one step e - nough for me.

2 I was not ever thus, nor prayed that Thou
Shouldst lead me on;
I loved to choose and see my path; but now
Lead Thou me on.
I loved the garish day; and, spite of fears,
Pride ruled my will: remember not past years.

3 So long Thy power hath blest me, sure it still
Will lead me on
O'er moor and fen, o'er crag and torrent till
The night is gone,
And with the morn those angel faces smile,
Which I have loved long since, and lost awhile.

No. 455. I will Pass over You.

"When I see the blood, I will pass over you."—Ex. 12: 13.

El. Nathan. James McGranahan.

1. When God the way of life would teach And gath-er all His own, He placed them safe beyond the reach Of death, by blood a - lone.
2. By Christ, the sin-less Lamb of God, The precious blood was shed, When He fulfilled God's holy word, And suf-fered in our stead.
3. O soul, for thee sal-va-tion thus By God is free-ly giv'n; The blood of Christ atones for sin, And makes us meet for heav'n.
4. The wrath of God that was our due, Up-on the Lamb was laid; And by the shedding of His blood, The debt for us was paid.
5. How calm the judgment hour shall pass To all who do o - bey The word of God a-bout the blood, And make that word their stay.

Chorus.

It is His word, God's precious word, It stands for-ever true: When I, the Lord, shall see the blood, I will pass o-ver you.
It is His word, God's precious word, When I, the Lord, shall see the blood,

No. 456. Calling to Thee.

"Arise, he calleth thee."—MARK 10: 49.

GRACE J. FRANCES.
HUBERT P. MAIN.
1. Out on the mountain, sad and for-sak-en, Lost in its maz-es, no light can'st thou see;
2. Far on the mountain, why wilt thou wander? Deep-er in darkness thy path-way will be;
3. Flee from thy bond-age, Je-sus will help thee, On-ly believe Him, and thou shalt be free;
Yet in His mer-cy, full of com-pas-sion, Lo! the Good Shepherd is call-ing to thee.
Turn from thy roam-ing, fly from its dan-gers, While the Good Shepherd is call-ing to thee.
Won-der-ful mer-cy, boundless com-pas-sion, Still the Good Shepherd is call-ing to thee.
CHORUS.
Call-ing to thee, call-ing to thee; Je-sus is call-ing, "Come un-to me;"
Call-ing to thee, call-ing to thee. Hear the Good Shepherd call-ing to thee.
Copyright, MDCCCXCI, by The Biglow & Main Co.
No. 457. The Eye of Faith.
"Seekest thou great things for thyself? seek them not."—JER. 45: 5.
REV. J. J. MAXFIELD.
W. A. OGDEN.
1. I do not ask for earthly store Be-yond a day's sup-ply; I on-ly cov-et,
2. I care not for the emp-ty show That thoughtless worldlings see; I crave to do the
3. Whate'er the crosses mine shall be, I will not dare to shun; I on-ly ask to
4. And when at last, my la-bor o'er, I cross the nar-row sea, Grant, Lord, that on the

The Eye of Faith.

more and more, The clear and sin - gle eye, To see my du - ty face to face, And
best I know, And leave the rest with Thee;–Well sat - is-fied that sweet re - ward Is
live for Thee, And that Thy will be done; Thy will, O Lord, be mine each day, While
oth - er shore My soul may dwell with Thee; And learn what here I can - not know, Why
trust the Lord for dai - ly grace.
sure to those who trust the Lord.
press-ing on my homeward way.
Thou hast ev - er loved me so.
Chorus.
Then shall my heart keep sing - ing While to the cross I
singing, singing,
cling; For rest is sweet at Jesus' feet, While homeward faith keeps winging, While homeward faith keeps winging.
cling, I cling;
Copyright, MDCCCXCI, by The Biglow & Main Co.

No. 458. Lead Me On.

"For thy name's sake lead me, and guide me."—Ps. 31 : 3.

Words arr. IRA D. SANKEY.

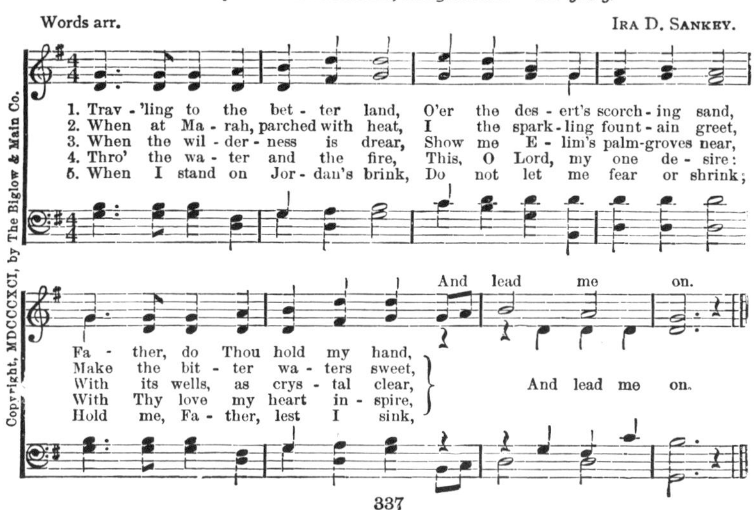
1. Trav - 'ling to the bet - ter land, O'er the des - ert's scorch - ing sand,
2. When at Ma - rah, parched with heat, I the spark - ling fount - ain greet,
3. When the wil - der - ness is drear, Show me E - lim's palm-groves near,
4. Thro' the wa - ter and the fire, This, O Lord, my one de - sire:
5. When I stand on Jor - dan's brink, Do not let me fear or shrink;
Fa - ther, do Thou hold my hand,
Make the bit - ter wa - ters sweet,
With its wells, as crys - tal clear,
With Thy love my heart in - spire,
Hold me, Fa - ther, lest I sink,
And lead me on.
And lead me on.
Copyright, MDCCCXCI, by The Biglow & Main Co.

No. 459. Only a Little Way.

"Make no tarrying, O my God."—Ps. 40: 17.

FANNY J. CROSBY.
W. H. DOANE.
1. 'Tis on - ly a lit-tle way on to my home, And there in its sunshine for-ev - er I'll
2. 'Tis on - ly a lit-tle way farther to go, O'er mountain and valley where dark waters
3. 'Tis on - ly a lit-tle way; there I shall see The friends that in glo - ry are waiting for
roam; While all the day long I journey with song, O beau-ti - ful Eden-land, thou art my home.
flow; My Saviour is near with blessings to cheer, His word is my guiding-star; why should I fear?
me; Their voices from home now float on the air, They're calling me tenderly, calling me there.
'Tis on - ly a little way, on-ly a little way, 'Tis on - ly a little way on to my home.
Copyright, MDCCCLXXXVI, by The Biglow & Main Co.
No. 460. I Will Praise Thee.
"Praise ye the Lord."—PSALM 148: 1.
EL. NATHAN.
JAMES MCGRANAHAN.
Allegretto.
1. I will praise the Lord my Glo - ry, I will praise the Lord my Light;
2. I will praise the Lord my Proph - et, Ho - ly Priest and Righteous King;
3. I will praise the Lord my Shepherd, Keep - er, Past - ure, Door and Fold;
4. I will praise the Lord my Fa - ther, Sav - iour, Broth - er, Guide and Friend;
5. I will love Him, I will trust Him, All the rem - nant of my days;
He my cloud by day to cov - er, He my fire to guide by night.
With the an - gels who a - dore Him, "Ho - ly, ho - ly," I will sing.
O'er the lone - ly hills He sought me, When the night was dark and cold.
He thus far in life hath led me, He will lead me to the end.
And will sing thro' end - less a - ges, On - ly my Re - deem - er's praise.
Copyright, MDCCCXC, by James McGranahan. All rights reserved.

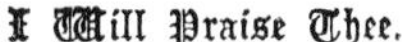
I Will Praise Thee.

Chorus.
I will praise Thee with my whole heart, will praise Thee, O Lord;
I will be glad and re - joice in Thee, O Thou most high.

No. 461. Not Try, but Trust.

"I will trust and not be afraid."—Isa. 12 : 2.

E. G. Taylor, D.D. Geo. C. Stebbins.

1. Not saved are we by try - ing, From self can come no aid; 'Tis on the blood re - ly - ing,
Once for our ran - som paid; 'Tis looking un - to Je - sus, The ho - ly One and Just;
'Tis His great work that saves us, It is not Try, but Trust.

2. 'Twas vain for Is - rael bit - ten By serpents on their way, To look to their own do - ing,
That aw - ful plague to stay; The on - ly way for heal - ing, When humbled in the dust;
Was of the Lord's re - veal - ing, It was not Try, but Trust.

3. No deeds of ours are need - ed To make Christ's merit more; No frames of mind, or feelings,
Can add to His great store; 'Tis sim - ply to re - ceive Him, The ho - ly One and Just;
'Tis on - ly to be - lieve Him, It is not Try, but Trust.

Chorus.

It is not Try, but Trust; It is not Try, but Trust; 'Tis His great work that saves us; It is not Try, but Trust.

No. 462. Come, Holy Spirit.
"I saw the Spirit descending from heaven like a dove."—John 1: 32.
Robert Bruce.
Ira D. Sankey.
1. Come, Ho-ly Spir-it, Like a dove descending, Rest Thou up-on us While we meet to pray;
2. Come, Ho-ly Spir-it, Ev'ry cloud dis-pel-ing, Fill us with gladness, Thro' the Master's name;
3. Come, Ho-ly Spir-it, Sent from God the Fa-ther— Thou Friend and Teacher, Comforter and Guide—
Show us the Sav-iour, All His love reveal-ing; Lead us to Him, The Life, the Truth, the Way.
Bring to our mem-'ry, Words that He hath spoken, Then shall our tongues His wondrous grace proclaim.
Our tho'ts di-rect-ing, Keep us close to Je-sus, And in our hearts For - ev-ermore a - bide.
Copyright, MDCCCXCI, by The Biglow & Main Co.
No. 463. Jesus of Nazareth.
"Jesus of Nazareth, a man approved of God among you."—Acts 2: 22.
El. Nathan.
James McGranahan.
1. "Je - sus of Naz - a-reth!" O what a name! Let us rejoice and His glo-ry proclaim;
2. Je - sus of Naz - a-reth, tru-ly a man, Low in His cra-dle His life He be-gan,
3. Je - sus of Naz - a-reth, nailed to the tree, Dy-ing that we by His death might be free,
4. Je - sus of Naz - areth, raised from the dead, Spotless and ho-ly, and still in our stead,
5. Je - sus of Naz - a-reth, seat-ed on high, Sending the Spir-it of grace to ap-ply
6. Je - sus of Naz - areth, earth's coming King, Peace to the warring world soon He shall bring,
Sav-iour and Keep-er for ev - er the same, Shepherd, Re - deem-er and Lord.
Lived before God, both in pat-tern and plan, Righteous, o - be-di-ent One.
Bearing the curse all for you and for me, Dy - ing a ran-som for all.
Made for us ev - er our glo - ri-fied Head, Rais'd from the dead for us all.
Life through the word unto men far and nigh, Off-'ring sal - va-tion to all.
Nations of saved ones His prais-es shall sing; All shall bow down at His name.
Chorus.
Je - sus of Naz - a-reth, once cru-ci-fied, Je - sus of Naz - a-reth, now glo-ri-fied,
Je - sus of Naz - a-reth, throned at God's side, Glo - ry and praise to His name.
Copyright, MDCCCXCI, by James McGranahan. All rights reserved.

No. 464. I Belong to Jesus.
"Whose I am and whom I serve."—Acts 27 : 23.
M. Fraser.
M. A. Sea.
Copyright, MDCCCXCI, by James McGranahan. All rights reserved.
1. I be-long to Je - sus; I am not my own; All I have and all I am, Shall be His a - lone.
2. I be-long to Je - sus; He is Lord and King, Reigning in my in - most heart, O - ver ev - 'ry - thing.
3. I be-long to Je - sus; What can hurt or harm, When He folds a - round my soul His al-might - y Arm?
4. I be-long to Je - sus; Bless - ed, bless-ed thought! With His own most pre-cious blood Has my soul been bought.
5 I belong to Jesus;
He has died for me;
I am His and He is mine,
Through eternity.
6 I belong to Jesus;
He will keep my soul,
When the deathly waters dark
Round about me roll.
7 I belong to Jesus;
And ere long I'll stand
With my precious Saviour there
In the glory land.
No. 465. O Come to the Saviour.
"Those that seek me early shall find me."—Prov. 8 : 17.
Words arr.
J. J. Lowe.
Copyright, MDCCCXCI, by The Biglow & Main Co.
1. O come to the Sav-iour while now He is call-ing, O come while there's mercy and par- don so free; O trust in His grace, He will keep thee from falling, And strength to o'er-come He of-fers to thee.
2. There's no oth- er name a-mong men that is giv-en, There's no oth-er way to be saved but His way; O trust in His mer-cy; too long hast thou striven With sin and with self; O come while you may.
3. The door of His mer-cy is now standing o-pen; O has-ten and en-ter, for "Yet there is room;" For if you re-ject Him, this word He hath spoken, That where He now is "Ye never can come."
4. And he that be-liev-eth, the prom-ise is writ-ten, Is saved thro' the blood of the Cru - ci-fied One; The Spir-it is pleading; O will you not has-ten, And find in his love a refuge and home.
Refrain.
O come, come to the Sav - iour, O come, come while you may;

O Come to the Saviour.

Rit.
O come, come to the Sav - iour, He's ten-der-ly call-ing to - day.

No. 466. Quiet, Lord, my froward Heart.

"My people shall dwell in quiet resting-places."—ISA. 32: 18.

J. NEWTON. (REPOSE. 7s, 61.) Arr. from F. KÜCKEN.

1. Qui - et, Lord, my fro - ward heart, Make me teach - a - ble and mild,
2. What Thou shalt to - day pro - vide, Let me as a child re - ceive;
3. As a lit - tle child re - lies On a care be - yond its own,
Up - right, sim - ple, free from art; Make me as a lit - tle child—
What to - mor - row may be - tide, Calm - ly to Thy wis - dom leave;
Be - ing nei - ther strong nor wise, Fears to take a step a - lone—
From dis - trust and en - vy free, Pleased with all that pleas - es Thee.
'Tis e - nough that Thou wilt care; Why should I the bur - den bear?
Let me thus with Thee a - bide, As my Fa - ther, Friend, and Guide.

Used by permission.

No. 467. Holy is the Lord.

"Let all the people praise thee, O God."—Ps. 67: 5.

F. J. C. WM. B. BRADBURY.

1. Ho - ly, ho - ly, ho - ly is the Lord! Sing, O ye peo - ple, glad - ly a - dore Him;
2. Praise Him, praise Him, shout aloud for joy, Watchman of Zi - on, her - ald the sto - ry;
3. King e - ter - nal, bless-ed be His name! So may His chil-dren glad - ly a - dore Him;

Holy is the Lord.
By per. The Biglow & Main Co., owners of Copyright.
Let the mountains trem-ble at His word, Let the hills be joy - ful be - fore Him;
Sin and death His kingdom shall destroy; All the earth shall sing of His glo - ry;
When in heav'n we join the hap- py strain, When we cast our bright crowns be- fore Him;
Might - y in wis - dom, boundless in mer - cy, Great is Je - ho - vah, King o - ver all.
Praise Him, ye an - gels, ye who be-hold Him Robed in His splendor, matchless, di- vine.
There in His like-ness joy - ful a-wak-ing, There we shall see Him, there we shall sing.
CHORUS.
Ho - ly, ho - ly ho - ly is the Lord! Let the hills be joy - ful be - fore Him.
No. 468. Praise, my Soul, the King of Heaven.
"Praise the Lord, O my soul."—Ps. 146: 1.
H. F. LYTE.
HENRY J. GAUNTLETT.
1. Praise, my soul, the King of heav - en; To His feet thy trib - ute bring;
2. Praise Him for His grace and fa - vor To our fa - thers in dis - tress;
3. An - gels, help us to a - dore Him, Ye be - hold Him face to face;
Ran - som'd, heal'd, re-stored, for - giv - en, Who like thee His praise shall sing?
Praise Him still, the same as ev - er, Slow to chide, and swift to bless;
Sun and moon, bow down be - fore Him, Dwell - ers all in time and space;
Praise Him! praise Him! praise Him! praise Him! Praise the ev - er - last - ing King!
Praise Him! praise Him! praise Him! praise Him! Glo - rious in His faith - ful - ness!
Praise Him! praise Him! praise Him! praise Him! Praise with us the God of grace!

No. 469. Christ, my All.

"Christ is all, and in all."—Col. 3: 11.

Horatius Bonar. Geo. C. Stebbins.

1. In the hour when guilt as - sails me, On His gra-cious name I call, Then I find the heavenly full-ness, Christ, my righteousness, my all.
2. In the night when sor-row clouds me, And the burn - ing tear-drops fall, Then I sing the song of patience, Christ, my Brother and my all.
3. In the day when this im - mor-tal Shall fling off its mor-tal thrall, Then my song of res-ur - rec-tion Shall be Christ, my all in all.

Chorus.

All my song when standing yon-der, Shall be Christ, my joy, my all, This shall ev - er be my anthem, "Christ my glo - ry, Christ my all;" This shall ev - er be my anthem, "Christ my glory, Christ my all."

Rit.

No. 470. O Wondrous Land.

"Thine eyes shall behold the land."—Isa. 33: 17.

Watts, arr. Ira D. Sankey.

1. There is a land of pure delight, Where saints immor-tal reign; E - ter - nal day ex -
2. There ev - er-last-ing spring abides, And nev - er-with'ring flow'rs; Death, like a nar - row
3. Sweet fields beyond the swelling flood Stand dress'd in liv-ing green; So to the Jews old
4. Could we but climb where Moses stood, And view the landscape o'er, Not Jordan's stream, nor

O Wondrous Land.

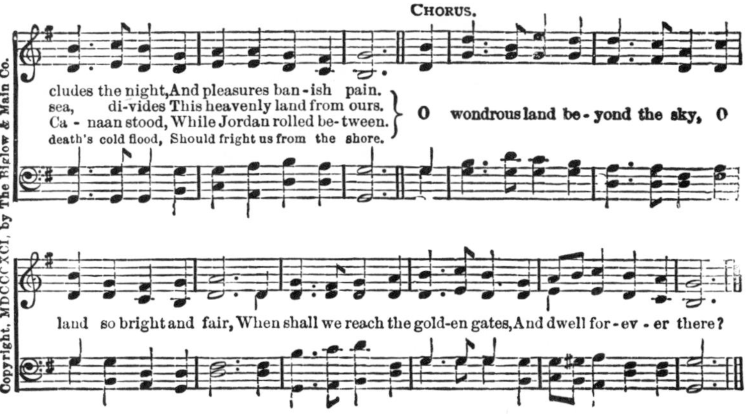

Chorus.
cludes the night, And pleasures ban-ish pain.
sea, di-vides This heavenly land from ours.
Ca - naan stood, While Jordan rolled be-tween.
death's cold flood, Should fright us from the shore.
O wondrous land be-yond the sky, O
land so bright and fair, When shall we reach the gold-en gates, And dwell for-ev-er there?
Copyright, MDCCCXCI, by The Biglow & Main Co.

No. 471. Christ Liveth in Me.

"Yet not I, but Christ liveth in me."—Gal. 2 : 20.

El. Nathan.
James McGranahan.
1. As lives the flow'r within the seed, As in the cone the tree, So, praise the God of truth and grace, His Spir-it dwelleth in me.
2. Once far from God and dead in sin, No light my heart could see; But in God's word the light I found, Now Christ liv-eth in me.
3. As rays of light from yon-der sun The flow'rs of earth set free, So life and light and love came forth From Christ liv-ing in me.
4. With longing all my heart is filled, That like Him I may be, As on the wondrous tho't I dwell, That Christ liv-eth in me.
Chorus.
Christ liv-eth in me, Christ liv-eth in me,
Christ liv-eth in me, Christ liv-eth in me, O
O what a sal-vation this, That Christ liveth in me!
Copyright, MDCCCXCI, by James McGranahan. All rights reserved.

No. 472. We Have Felt the Love of Jesus.

"I have loved thee with an everlasting love."—JER. 31: 3.

Rev. J. P. HUTCHINSON. Arr. by E. N. WILBUR A. CHRISTY.

1. We have felt the love of Je - sus In our hearts with rap - ture glow;
2. Chos - en not for our de - serv - ings, But that God His grace might show;
3. Will He leave when care en - croach - es? When we're tempt-ed will He go?

Will that love for - sake and leave us? Nev - er, no! oh, nev - er, no!
For our fail - ures will He leave us? Nev - er, no! oh, nev - er; no!
When the last dread hour ap - proach - es? Nev - er, no! oh, nev - er, no!

If on beds of pain we lan - guish, Earth - ly friends may light - ly go,
'Tis in Christ the Fa - ther sees us, To His Son the love doth flow;
And when safe - ly home in glo - ry, When sad tears no long - er flow,

Will He leave us in our an - guish? Never, no! oh, nev - er, no!
Will He turn a - way from Je - sus? Never, no! oh, nev - er, no!
Can we e'er for - get the sto - ry? Never, no! oh, nev - er, no!

No. 473. We'll Meet Each Other There.

"So shall we ever be with the Lord."—1 THESS. 4: 17.

R. L. ROBERT LOWRY.

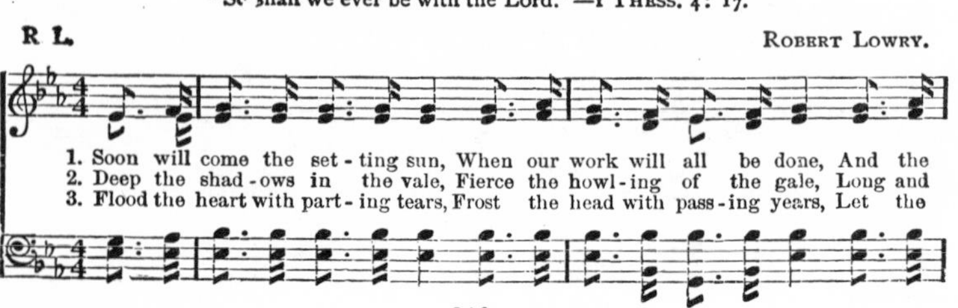
1. Soon will come the set - ting sun, When our work will all be done, And the
2. Deep the shad - ows in the vale, Fierce the howl - ing of the gale, Long and
3. Flood the heart with part - ing tears, Frost the head with pass - ing years, Let the

We'll Meet Each Other There.

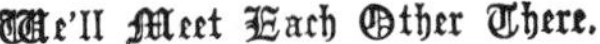

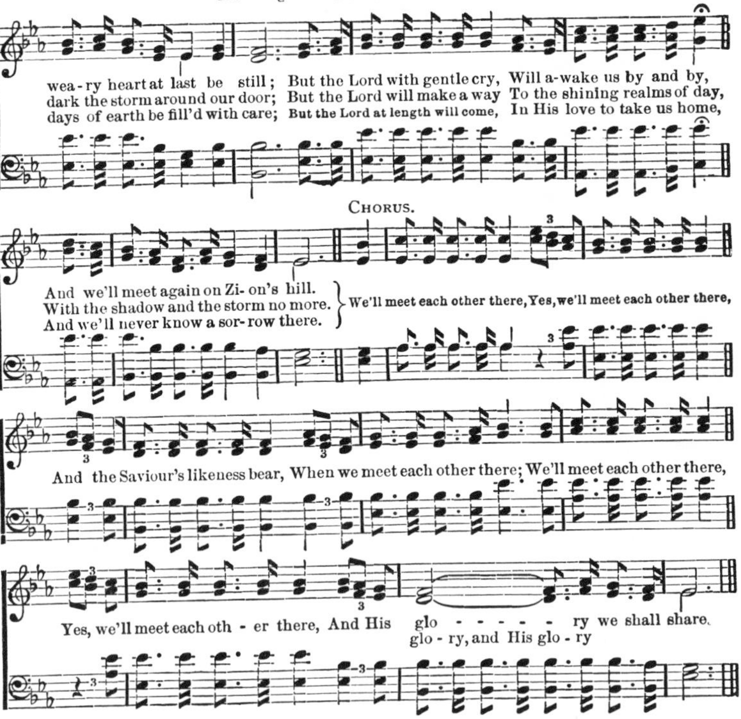

wea-ry heart at last be still; But the Lord with gentle cry, Will a-wake us by and by,
dark the storm around our door; But the Lord will make a way To the shining realms of day,
days of earth be fill'd with care; But the Lord at length will come, In His love to take us home,
CHORUS.
And we'll meet again on Zi-on's hill.
With the shadow and the storm no more.
And we'll never know a sor-row there.
We'll meet each other there, Yes, we'll meet each other there,
And the Saviour's likeness bear, When we meet each other there; We'll meet each other there,
Yes, we'll meet each oth - er there, And His glo - - - - - - ry we shall share.
glo - ry, and His glo - ry

Copyright, MDCCCXCI, by Robert Lowry.

No. 474. "'Tis Midnight."

"It is finished."—JOHN 19: 30.

WM. B. TAPPAN.

VIRGIL C. TAYLOR.

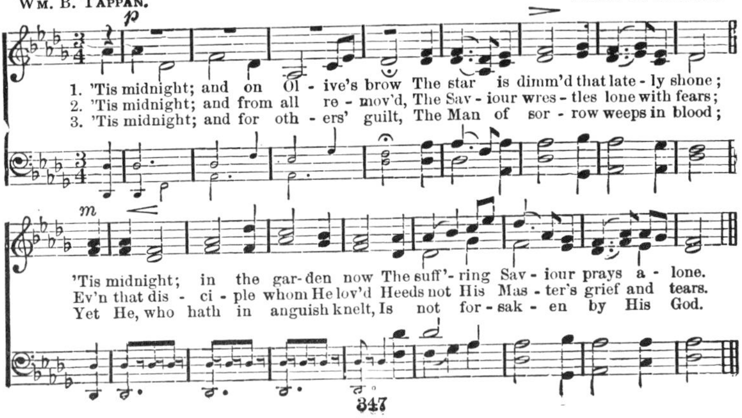

1. 'Tis midnight; and on Ol - ive's brow The star is dimm'd that late - ly shone;
2. 'Tis midnight; and from all re - mov'd, The Sav - iour wres - tles lone with fears;
3. 'Tis midnight; and for oth - ers' guilt, The Man of sor - row weeps in blood;
'Tis midnight; in the gar-den now The suff'-ring Sav-iour prays a - lone.
Ev'n that dis - ci - ple whom He lov'd Heeds not His Mas - ter's grief and tears.
Yet He, who hath in anguish knelt, Is not for-sak - en by His God.

No. 475. Blessed Saviour, Ever Nearer.

"Ye are made nigh by the blood of Christ."—EPH. 2: 13.

Furnished by MERTON SMITH.
Arr. by EL. NATHAN.

JAMES MCGRANAHAN.

1. Blessed Saviour, ev-er near-er, I am draw-ing to Thy feet; Thou hast borne my every
2. Blessed Saviour, I would never, Nev-er more Thy love reject; At Thy feet I learn the
3. Blessed Saviour, draw me nearer, Ev - er near-er to Thy heart, When I'm weary, heavy
4. Blessed Saviour, let me lin - ger Ev - er near Thy precious feet, Till I hear that welcome
sor-row, I am made in Thee complete; For Thy love my soul is yearn-ing, More and
les-son How Thine image to re - flect; There I go when all for-sake me, When by
la- den, And I feel the tempter's dart; Oft I stum-ble, oft I fal - ter, Oft I'm
summons, Come, thy loved ones now to greet; Oh, the joy that there a-waits me, While I
more its pow'r im-part; I have heard Thy tender pleading, Come and dwell within my heart.
foes I am oppressed; Then I hear Thy loved voice saying, Come to me, I'll give you rest.
toss'd on an-gry seas; But I know that Thou wilt guide me, Thro' the storm, to endless peace.
hope and watch and pray! For the morning light is dawning, Of the fair and endless day.
Copyright, MDCCCXCI, by James McGranahan. All rights reserved.
No. 476. Behold Him!
"Behold the Lamb of God."—JOHN 1: 29.
FANNY J. CROSBY.
GEO. C. STEBBINS.
1. Look up! look up! ye weary ones, Whose skies are veil'd in night, For He who knows the path you tread
2. The gifts ye bro't with loving hand Your Lord will not disown; Their odors sweet to heav'n shall rise
3. Rejoice, the grave is o-vercome, And lo! the an-gels sing; The grandest triumph ev - er known
Will yet restore the light; Look up! and hail the dawning Of hope's triumphant morning.
Like incense 'round His throne; Look up! and hail the dawning Of joy's transcendent morning.
Has come thro' Christ our King; All heav'n proclaims the dawning Of love's all-glorious morning.
Copyright, MDCCCXC, by Ira D. Sankey.

Behold Him!
Be - hold Him! be - hold Him! Your Sav - iour lives to - day;
Be - hold Him! be - hold Him! The clouds have roll'd a - way.
No. 477. Lead me, Saviour.
"For thy name's sake lead me and guide me."—Ps. 31: 3.
F. M. D.
FRANK M. DAVIS.
1. Saviour, lead me, lest I stray, (lest I stray,) Gen - tly lead me all the way; (all the way;)
2. Thou, the Refuge of my soul (of my soul) When life's stormy billows roll, (billows roll,)
3. Saviour, lead me, till at last, (till at last,) When the storm of life is past, (life is past,)
1. Sav - iour, lead me, lest I stray, Gen - tly lead me all the way;
I am safe when by Thy side, (by Thy side,) I would in Thy love a - bide. (love abide.)
I am safe when Thou art nigh, (Thou art nigh,) On Thy mer - cy I re - ly. (I re - ly.)
I shall reach the land of day, (land of day,) Where all tears are wip'd away. (wip'd away.)
I am safe when by Thy side, I would in Thy love abide.
Used by per. F. M. Davis, owner of copyright.
CHORUS.
Lead me, lead me, Sav - iour, lead me, lest I stray;..................
Saviour, lead me, lest I stray;
rit. e dim.
Gently down the stream of time, Lead me, Saviour, all the way.
stream of time, all the way.

No. 478. Return, O Wanderer!
"Return unto the Lord, and he will have mercy."—Isa. 55 : 7.
W. B. Collyer, arr.
Geo. F. Root.
1. Re-turn! re-turn! O wand'rer, now re-turn! Re-turn! re-turn! And seek thy Father's face;
2. Re-turn! re-turn! O wand'rer, now re-turn! Re-turn! re-turn! He hears thy humble sigh;
3. Re-turn! re-turn! O wand'rer, now re-turn! Re-turn! re-turn! Thy Saviour bids thee live;
Those new desires which in thee burn Were kindled by His grace, Were kindled by His grace.
He sees thy burden'd spirit mourn When no one else is nigh, When no one else is nigh.
Come hum-bly to His feet and learn How free-ly He'll for-give, How free-ly He'll for-give.
By per. The John Church Co., owners of copyright.
No. 479. Tenderly Calling.
"Turn ye, turn ye—for why will ye die."—Ezek. 33 : 11.
F. J. Crosby.
Ira D. Sankey.
1. Turn thee, O lost one, care-worn and weary, Lo! the Good Shepherd is call-ing to - day;
2. Still He is wait-ing, why wilt thou per-ish, Tho' thou hast wand'red so far from the fold?
3. List to His message, think of His mer - cy! Sin - less, yet bear-ing thy sins on the tree;
4. Come in the old way, come in the true way, En - ter thro' Je - sus, for He is the Door;
Seeking to save thee, waiting to cleanse thee, Haste to re-ceive Him, no lon-ger de - lay.
Yet, with His life-blood, He has redeem'd thee, Wondrous compassion that cannot be told!
Per-fect re-mis-sion, life ev - er - last-ing, Thro' His a - tone-ment, He of-fers to thee.
He is the Shep-herd, ten-der-ly call-ing, Come in thy weakness, and wander no more.
Chorus.
Ten-der-ly call - ing, pa-tient-ly call - ing, Hear the Good Shepherd call-ing to thee;
Ten-der-ly call - ing, pa-tient-ly call - ing, Lov-ing-ly say-ing, "Come unto me!"
Copyright, MDCCCXC, by Ira D. Sankey.

No. 480. Search me, O Lord.

"And know my heart."—Psa. 139: 23.

Grace J. Frances. Hubert P. Main.

1. Search me, O Lord, and try this heart of mine, Search me, and prove if I indeed am Thine; Test by Thy word, that never changed can be, My strength of hope and living faith in Thee.
2. Search me, O Lord, subdue each vain de-sire, And in my soul a deep-er love in-spire; Hide Thou my life, that I, supreme-ly blest, Beneath Thy wings in perfect peace may rest.
3. Search me, O Lord, and from the dross of sin, Re - fine as gold, and keep me pure within; Search Thou my tho'ts whose springs Thine eyes can see, From secret faults, O Saviour, cleanse Thou me.
4. Search me, O Lord, let faith thro' grace divine Thy - self re-flect in ev-'ry act of mine, Till at Thy call my waiting soul shall rise, Caught up with joy to meet Thee in the skies.

No. 481. Hear the Blessed Invitation.

"The Spirit and the bride say come."—Rev. 22: 17.

G. M. J. James McGranahan.

1. Hear the bless-ed in - vi - ta - tion, Come, come, come; To the fount-ain of sal - va - tion, Come, come, come; Healing streams are flow-ing still; Welcome, "who - so - ev - er will;
2. 'Tis the voice of Je - sus say - ing, Come, come, come; Now His blest command o - bey - ing, Come, come, come; He will cleanse from ev - 'ry ill; Welcome, "who - so - ev - er will;
3. 'Tis the Ho - ly Spir - it call - ing, Come, come, come; Ere the shades of death be fall - ing, Come, come, come; He the heart with peace will fill; Welcome, "who - so - ev - er will;
4. Lo! the Spir - it and the Bride say, Come, come, come; And let him that heareth now say, Come, come, come; And let him that is a - thirst Come, and "who - so - ev - er will;

Let him take the wa - ter of life free - ly."

Chorus.

Let him take,............... let him
Let him take,

Hear the Blessed Invitation.

No. 482. Up Yonder.

"Where I am, there ye may be also."—Jno. 14: 3.

M. Frazer. M. A. Sea.

1. Safe up - on the heav'n-ly shore, Done with pain for - ev - er-more, Wea - ri- ness and weak-ness o'er, Up yon - der; O the calm and qui - et rest On the lov - ing Saviour's breast; It is bet - ter than earth's best, Up yon - der.
2. Storms shall nev - er reach us there, No more sor - row, pain or care, No more cross for us to bear, Up yon - der; Gain for them that suf - fered loss, Crowns for them that bore the cross, And a calm for hearts that toss, Up yon - der.
3. Safe up - on the heav'n-ly shore, Done with sin for - ev - er-more, Wea - ri- ness and weak-ness o'er, Up yon - der; Nev - er more to know a fear, Nev - er - more to shed a tear, Bet - ter far than ev - er here, Up yon - der.

No. 483. In Heavenly Pastures.

"He maketh me to lie down in green pastures."—Ps. 23: 2.

Mrs. M. A. Whitaker.
Geo. F. Root.
1. In the heav'n-ly past-ures fair, 'Neath the ten-der Shepherd's care, Let us rest be-side the liv-ing stream to - day; Calm-ly there in peace recline, Drink-ing in the truth di-vine, As His lov-ing call we now with joy o - bey (with joy obey).
2. Far from all the noise and strife That dis - turb our dai - ly life, Let us pause a-while in si-lence and a - dore; Then the sound of His dear voice Will our wait-ing souls re-joice, As He nam-eth us His own for ev-er-more (for ever-more).
3. O how good and true and kind, Seek-ing His stray sheep to find, If they wan-der in - to dan-ger from His side; Ev - er close-ly may we tread Where His ho - ly feet have led, So at last with Him in heav'n we may a - bide (we may abide).
Chorus.
Glorious stream of life e - ter - nal, Beauteous fields of liv - ing green (living green),
Tho' re - vealed with - in the word Of our Shep - herd and our Lord,
rit.
By the pure in heart a - lone can they be seen (ev - er seen).

No. 484. I'm Going Home.

"In my Father's house are many mansions."—Jno. 14: 2.

Rev. Wm. Hunter. Wm. Miller.

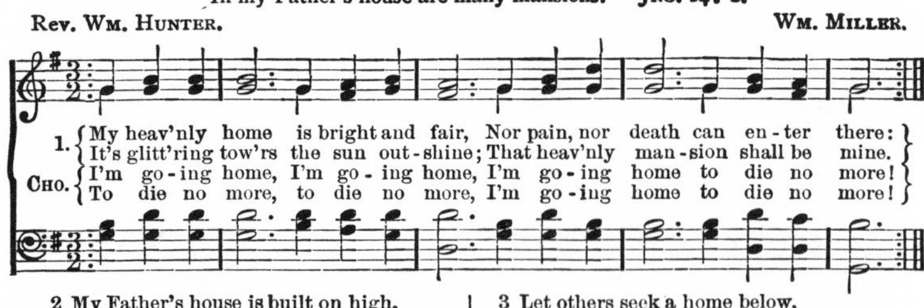

2 My Father's house is built on high,
Far, far above the starry sky;
When from this earthly prison free,
That heavenly mansion mine shall be.

3 Let others seek a home below,
Which flames devour, or waves o'erflow;
Be mine a happier lot to own
A heavenly mansion near the throne.

No. 485. Satisfied.

"I shall be satisfied, when I wake with thy likeness."—Ps. 17: 15.

Horatius Bonar. Geo. C. Stebbins.

1. When I shall wake in that fair morn of morns, Aft - er whose dawn - ing nev - er night re - turns, And with whose glo - ry day e - ter - nal burns,
2. When I shall see Thy glo - ry face to face, When in Thine arms Thou wilt Thy child em - brace, When Thou shalt o - pen all Thy store of grace,
3. When I shall meet with those that I have loved, Clasp in my arms the dear ones long re - moved, And find how faith - ful Thou to me hast prov'd,
4. When I shall gaze up - on the face of Him Who died for me, with eyes no long - er dim, And praise Him with the ev - er - last - ing hymn,

I shall be sat - is - fied, be sat - is - fied.

Refrain.

I shall be sat - is - fied, (I shall be) I shall be sat - is - fied, (I shall be) When I shall (When I shall) wake in

Satisfied.

that fair morn of morns; I shall be sat - is - fied, shall be
I shall be I shall be
sat - is - fied, When I shall wake in that fair morn of morns.
When I shall

No. 486. Take Thou My Hand.

"I the Lord thy God will hold thy right hand."—ISA. 41 : 13.

JULIA STERLING. IRA D. SANKEY.

1. Take Thou my hand, and lead me—Choose Thou my way; "Not as I
2. Take Thou my hand, and lead me—Lord, I am Thine; Fill with Thy
3. Take Thou my hand, and lead me, Lord, as I go; In - to Thy
will," O Fa-ther, Teach me to say; What though the storms may gath - er?
Ho - ly Spir - it This heart of mine; Then in the hour of tri - al
per - fect im - age Help me to grow; Still in Thine own pa - vil - ion
Thou know-est best; Safe in Thy ho - ly keep-ing, There would I rest.
Strong shall I be— Read - y to do, or suf - fer, Dear Lord, for Thee.
Shel - ter Thou me; Keep me, O Fa-ther, keep me, Close, close to Thee.
Copyright, MDCCCLXXXVII, by Ira D. Sankey.

No. 487. Waiting at the Door.

"I will come again, and receive you unto myself."—John 14: 3.

Mrs. K. M. Reasoner.
T. C. O'Kane.
1. I am wait-ing for the Mas-ter, Who will bid me rise and come
2. Many a wea-ry path I've trav-eled, In the dark-est storm and strife,
3. Ma-ny friends that trav-eled with me Reached that por-tal long a-go;
4. Yes, their pil-grim-age was short-er, And their tri-umphs soon-er won;
To the glo-ry of His pres-ence, To the glad-ness of His home.
Bear-ing many a heav-y bur-den, Oft-en strug-gling for my life.
One by one they left me bat-tling With the dark and craft-y foe.
Oh, how lov-ing-ly they'll greet me When the toils of life are done.
Chorus.
They are watch - - ing at the port-al, They are wait - - ing at the door;
They are watching, they are watching at the portal, They are waiting, they are waiting at the door;
Wait-ing on - - ly for my coming, All the loved................ ones gone be-fore.
Wait-ing only, waiting on-ly for my coming, All the loved ones, all the loved ones gone before.
By per. T. C. O'Kane, owner of copyright.
No. 488. They Crucified Him.
"—and parted his garments."—Matt. 27: 35.
Mrs. M. B. C. Slade.
Reverently.
Geo. F. Root.
1. From the Bethlehem man-ger-home, Walk-ing His dear form be-side, We to
2. Scorn-ful words the sol-diers fling; Wick-ed rul-ers Him de-ride, Say-ing,
3. Won-drous love for sin-ful men, Of the sin-less One that died! May we

They Crucified Him.

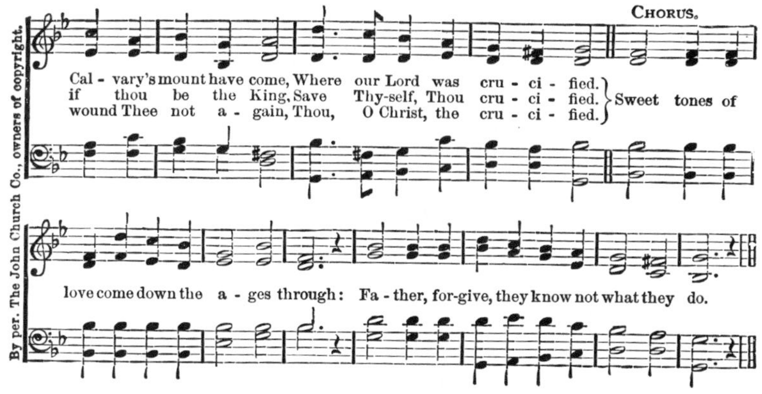

CHORUS.
Cal - vary's mount have come, Where our Lord was cru - ci - fied.
if thou be the King, Save Thy-self, Thou cru - ci - fied.
wound Thee not a - gain, Thou, O Christ, the cru - ci - fied.
Sweet tones of
love come down the a - ges through: Fa - ther, for-give, they know not what they do.

No. 489. Pass it On.

"Preach the word; be instant in season, out of season."—2 Tim 4: 2.

M. FRAZER. JAMES MCGRANAHAN.

Allegretto moderato.

1. Pass a - long the in - vi - ta - tion, Who - so - ev - er will may come;
2. Pass a - long the cup of com - fort That the Lord has giv - en you;
3. Pass a - long each boon and bless - ing That may come to you through life;
4. Pass a - long the watchword, "Courage;" Soon the dark - ness will be o'er;

Pass it on, pass it on,

Pass it on, pass it on,

Pass a - long the lov - ing mes - sage Un - to ev - 'ry thirst - y one; Pass it on,............ pass it on.

Oth - er wea - ry, troubled spir - its Need to taste its sweetness too; Pass it on,............ pass it on.

You may help the wea - ry - heart - ed Who are faint a - mid the strife; Pass it on,............ pass it on.

See, al - read - y dawn is break - ing On the bright ce - les - tial shore; Pass it on,............ pass it on.

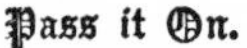
Pass it On.

CHORUS.
Pass a - long the in - vi - ta - tion, Pass a - long the word of God,
Un - til ev - 'ry tribe and na - tion Shall have heard of Christ the Lord, Shall have
heard Shall have heard, Shall have heard of Christ the Lord.
of Christ the Lord, of Christ the Lord,

No. 490. More of Jesus.

"Grace and peace be multiplied unto you through the knowledge of God, and of Jesus our Lord."—2 PETER 1 : 2.

M. FRASER.
M. A. SEA.
1. More of Je - sus, More of Je - sus, 'Tis the Chris-tian's yearn-ing cry;
2. More of Je - sus, More of Je - sus, While I tread earth's wea - ry ways;
3. More of Je - sus, More of Je - sus, O to feel His love each hour!
4. More of Je - sus, More of Je - sus, In my weak-ness and my pain;
5. More of Je - sus, More of Je - sus, Sore - ly do I need His grace;
More of Je - sus, More of Je - sus, On - ly He can sat - is - fy.
More of Je - sus, More of Je - sus, Till in Heav'n I hymn His praise.
More of Je - sus, More of Je - sus, O to re - al - ize His power!
More of Je - sus, More of Je - sus, He can turn my loss to gain.
More of Je - sus, Bless - ed Je - sus, When shall I be - hold His face?
Copyright, MDCCCXCI, by James McGranahan. All rights reserved.

No. 491. The Wondrous Cross.

"The Cross of our Lord Jesus Christ."—GAL. 6: 14.

ISAAC WATTS, arr.
IRA D. SANKEY.
1. When I sur - vey........................ the wondrous cross,.................. On which the Prince.................. of glo - ry died,...................... My rich - est gain..................... I count but loss,..................... And pour con - tempt.................. on all my pride.
2. For - bid it, Lord,................... that I should boast,.................. Save in the death................... of Christ, my Lord;................... All earth-ly things.................... that charm me most,.................. I sac - ri - fice........................ them to His blood.
3. See, from His head,.................. His hands, His feet,.................... Sor - row and love..................... flow min-gled down;.................. Did e'er such love...................... and sor-row meet,.................. Or thorns com - pose.................... so rich a crown?
4. Were all the realm.................. of na - ture mine,.................. That were a gift...................... by far too small;.................. A love so great...................... and so di - vine,.................. De-mands my soul,...................... my life, my all.
1. When I sur-vey the wondrous cross, On which the Prince of glo - ry died, My rich - est gain I count but loss, and pour contempt
CHORUS.
O wondrous cross where Je - sus died, And for my sins was cru - ci - fied;
My long-ing eyes look up to Thee, Thou blessed Lamb of Cal - va - ry.
Copyright, MDCCCXCI, by The Biglow & Main Co.

No. 492. Our Refuge.

"God is our refuge and strength."—Ps. 46: 1.
Mrs. C. Warren.
Hubert P. Main.
1. Je - sus, Thou Ref - uge of the soul, To Thy dear arms I flee;
2. Tho' clouds may rise, tho' tem - pests rage, Thou wilt my shel - ter be,
3. No power on earth, or power be - low, Can tear me from Thy side,
4. Not death it - self, that last dread foe, Can hold me with his chain;
From Sa-tan's wiles, from self and sin, O make and keep me free.
While with a stead - fast heart and true, My trust is stayed on Thee.
If 'neath Thy shel - t'ring wings of love, Dear Ref - uge, I a - bide.
Thro' Christ, who con - quered Death, I rise, And life e - ter - nal gain.
Copyright, MDCCCXCI, by The Biglow & Main Co.
No. 493. In Me ye shall have Peace.
"In me ye might have peace."—John 16: 33.
Mrs. E. W. Chapman.
J. H. Tenney.
1. In times of sor - row, God is near, His vig - ils nev - er cease,—
2. Tho' long and wea - ry is the night, And morn brings no re - lief,
3. His love we may not un - der - stand, While tri - als here in - crease,
4. Soon shall our eyes the land be - hold Where pain and care shall cease;
His ten - der, lov - ing voice I hear, "In me ye shall have peace."
Yet faith the prom - ise still be - lieves, "In me ye shall have peace."
But yet we know His word is sure, "In me ye shall have peace."
Till then we'll trust the prom - ise sweet, "In me ye shall have peace."
Chorus.
O bless - - ed peace! sweet boon of heav'n! That
O bless-ed peace! O bless-ed peace! sweet boon of heav'n! sweet boon of heav'n! That
Copyright, MDCCCXCI, by The Biglow & Main Co.

In Me ye shall have Peace.

bids our troub-le cease; O precious word, divine-ly giv'n, "In me ye shall have peace!"

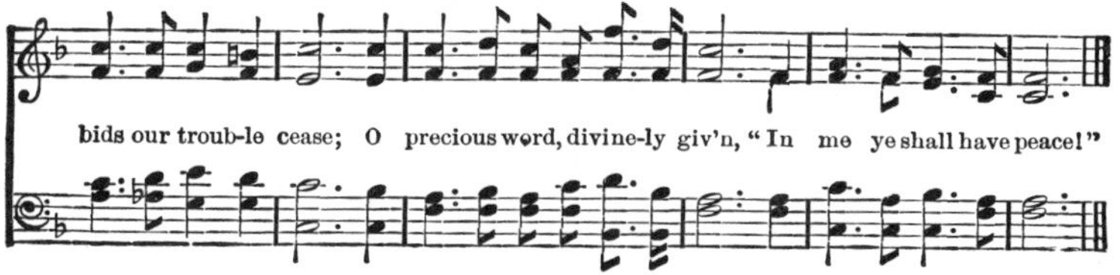

No. 494. A Soldier of the Cross.

"A good soldier of Jesus Christ."—2 Tim. 2: 3.

Isaac Watts. Ira D. Sankey.

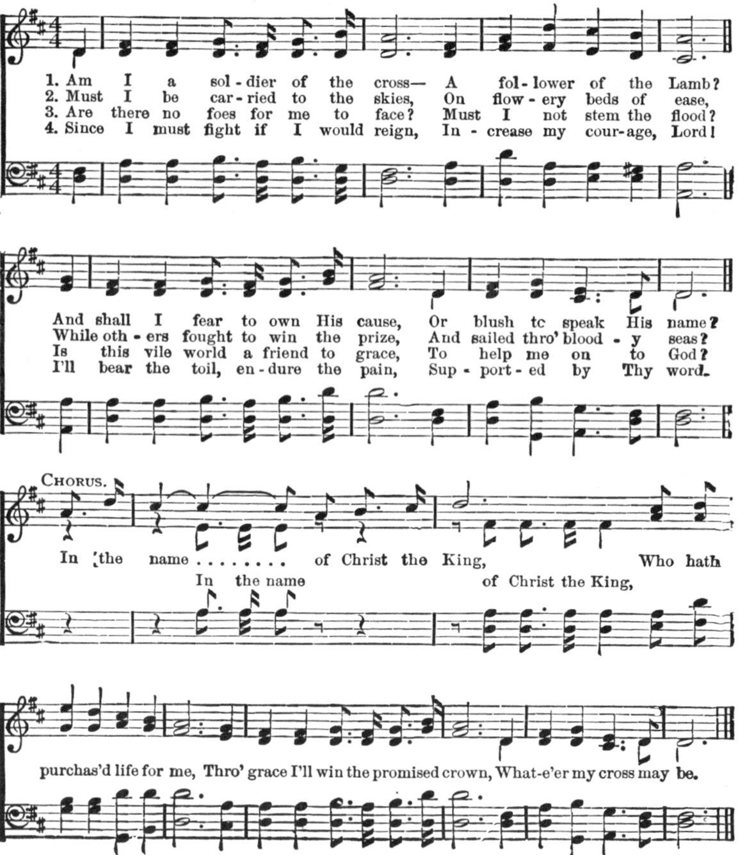

1. Am I a sol-dier of the cross— A fol-lower of the Lamb?
2. Must I be car-ried to the skies, On flow-ery beds of ease,
3. Are there no foes for me to face? Must I not stem the flood?
4. Since I must fight if I would reign, In-crease my cour-age, Lord!
And shall I fear to own His cause, Or blush tc speak His name?
While oth-ers fought to win the prize, And sailed thro' blood-y seas?
Is this vile world a friend to grace, To help me on to God?
I'll bear the toil, en-dure the pain, Sup-port-ed by Thy word.
Chorus.
In the name . . . . of Christ the King, Who hath
In the name of Christ the King,
purchas'd life for me, Thro' grace I'll win the promised crown, What-e'er my cross may be.

No. 495. My God and my All.

"Behold, God is mine helper."—Ps. 54: 4.

Wm. Young.
J. R. Murray.
1. While Thou, O my God, art my help and de-fend - er, No cares can o'er -
2. Yes, Thou art my ref - uge in sor - row and dan - ger, My strength when I
3. And when Thou de-mand - est the life Thou hast giv - en, With joy will I
whelm me, no ter-rors ap-pall; The wiles and the snares of the world will but ren - der
suf - fer, my hope when I fall; My com-fort and joy in this land of the stran-ger,
an - swer Thy mer - ci - ful call, And quit this poor earth but to find Thee in heav-en,
More live - ly my hope in my God and my all.
My treas - ure, my glo - ry, my God and my all.
My por - tion for - ev - er, my God and my all.
Refrain.
My God and my all, My
My God, my all,
God and my all,
My God, my all, My treas - ure, my glo - ry, My God and my all.
Copyright, MDCCCXCI, by The John Church Co.
No. 496. O I Love to Talk with Jesus.
"Let me talk with thee."—Jer. 12: 1.
Words arr.
W. G. Fischer.
1. O I love to talk with Je - sus, for it smooths the rug - ged road;
And it seems to help me on - ward, when I faint be-neath my load;
2. Oft I tell Him I am wea - ry, and I fain would be at rest;
That I'm dai - ly, hour - ly, long - ing to re - pose up - on His breast;

O I Love to Talk with Jesus.

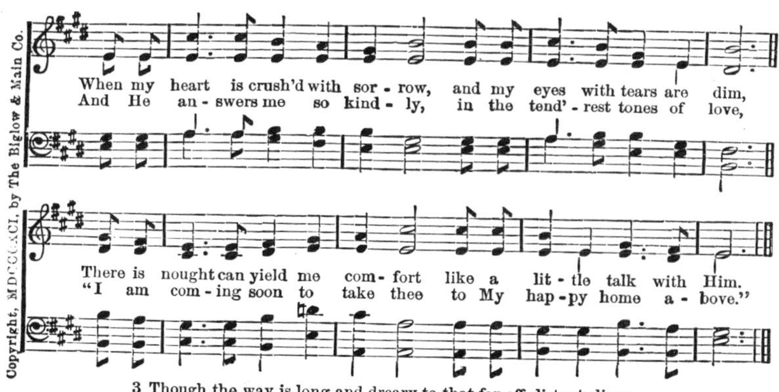

When my heart is crush'd with sor - row, and my eyes with tears are dim,
And He an - swers me so kind - ly, in the tend' - rest tones of love,
There is nought can yield me com- fort like a lit - tle talk with Him.
"I am com - ing soon to take thee to My hap - py home a - bove."
Copyright, MDCCCXCI, by The Biglow & Main Co.

3 Though the way is long and dreary to that far-off distant clime,
Yet I know that my Redeemer journeys with me all the time;
And the more I come to know Him, and His wondrous grace explore,
How my longing groweth stronger still to know Him more and more.

4 So I'll wait a little longer, till my Lord's appointed time,
And along the upward pathway still my pilgrim feet shall climb;
Soon within my Father's dwelling, where the many mansions be,
I shall see my blessed Saviour, and He then will talk with me.

No. 497. Sing unto the Lord.

"Give thanks at the remembrance of his holiness."—Ps. 30: 4.

J. H. Johnston.
James McGranahan.
"Sing un- to the Lord, O ye saints of His, sing, sing, Sing un- to the Lord,
And at the remembrance of His ho - li- ness, O give thanks un- to the Lord."
Fine.
1. O Lord, Thy lov -ing kind- ness Doth com-pass all our ways, And "Thy compass- ions
2. Thy goodness we re - mem - ber, We praise Thy ho - li - ness, We look to Thee, O
3. Let saints recount His mer - cies, And fill His courts with praise; Let all who know His
Copyright, MDCCCXCI, by James McGranahan. All rights reserved.

Sing unto the Lord.
fail not," Thro' all the pass - ing days; To Thee, O great Je - ho - vah, In
Sav - iour, To save, and heal, and bless; 'Tis by Thy lov - ing fa - vor Thy
goodness, Their hal - le - lu - jahs raise; Praise God, the lov - ing Fa - ther, And
D.C.
"time of need" we cry; And all who call up - on Thee Shall find Thee ev - er nigh.
trust - ing children stand, Up - held, and kept, and guid - ed, By Thy protect - ing hand.
Je - sus Christ His Son, With God the Ho - ly Spir - it, The glorious Three in One.
No. 498. I wait for Thee, O Lord.
"My soul waiteth for the Lord."—Ps. 130 : 8.
E. B.
M. A. Sea.
1. I wait for Thee, O Lord! Thy glo - rious face to see,
2. I wait for Thee, O Lord! Be - fore Thy feet to fall,
3. I wait for Thee, O Lord! Thy lov - ing hand to feel,
4. I wait for Thee, O Lord! Thy rapt - ure deep to know,
5. I wait for Thee, O Lord! But for a lit - tle while;
That ho - ly face that once was marred, Was marred, O Lord, for me.
To wor - ship low - ly and a - dore My Sav - iour, all in all.
Whose ten - der touch can e - ven now The wound - ed spir - it heal.
Of liv - ing ev - er - more with Thee; Love can - not more be - stow.
This night my long - ing eyes may meet Thy joy - ful, wel - come smile.
Copyright, MDCCCXCI, by James McGranahan. All rights reserved.
No. 499. The Many Mansions.
"Let not your heart be troubled."—John 14 : 1.
Charles Bruce.
Ira D. Sankey.
1. How oft our souls are lift - ed up, When clouds are dark and drear,
2. How oft a - mid our dai - ly toil, With anx - ious care op - pressed,
3. O may our faith in Him be strong, Who feels our ev - 'ry care,
4. Then let us work, and watch and pray, Re - ly - ing on the love

The Many Mansions.
For Je - sus comes, and kind - ly speaks These lov - ing words of cheer.
We hear a - gain the pre - cious word That tells of joy and rest.
And will for us, as He hath said, A place in heaven pre - pare.
Of Him who now pre - pares a place For us in heav'n a - bove.
CHORUS. JOHN 14: 2.
"In my Father's house are many mansions; If it were not so I would have told you;
In my Father's house are ma - ny mansions," "I go to prepare a place for you."
ritard.
Copyright, MDCCCXCI, by The Biglow & Main Co.
No. 500. We would see Jesus.
"Sir, we would see Jesus."—JOHN 12: 21.
Anon.
F. MENDELSSOHN. Arr.
1. We would see Je - sus— for the shadows length - en A - cross this lit - tle land-scape of our life; We would see Je - sus, our weak faith to strength-en For the last wea - ri - ness—the fi - nal strife.
2. We would see Je - sus— the great Rock-foun - da - tion, Where - on our feet were set with sov'reign grace; Not life, nor death, with all their ag - i - ta - tion, Can thence re - move us, if we see His face.
3. We would see Je - sus— oth - er lights are pal - ing, Which for long years we have re - joiced to see; The bless - ings of our pil - grim - age are fail - ing; We would not mourn them, for we go to Thee.
4. We would see Je - sus— this is all we're need - ing, Strength, joy, and will - ing - ness come with the sight; We would see Je - sus, dy - ing, ris - en, plead - ing; Then wel-come, day! and fare - well, mor - tal night!

No. 501. 

Pray, Brethren, Pray!

"Watch and pray."—Mark 13: 33.

Dr. Horatius Bonar. Philip Phillips.

Moderato.
1. Pray, brethren! pray! The sands are fall-ing; Pray, brethren, pray! God's voice is call-ing,
2. Praise, brethren, praise! The skies are rend-ing; Praise, brethren, praise! The fight is end-ing.
3. Watch, brethren, watch! The years are dy-ing; Watch, brethren, watch! Old time is fly-ing!
4. Look, brethren, look! The day is breaking; Hark, brethren, hark! The dead are wak-ing,
Allegro.
Yon tur-ret strikes the dy-ing chime; We kneel up-on the verge of time:
Be-hold, the glo-ry draw-eth near The King Him-self will soon ap-pear:
Watch as men watch the part-ing breath, Watch as men watch for life or death:
With gird-ed loins all read-y stand; Be-hold, the Bridegroom is at hand!
Refrain. Slow. ritard. After last verse only. Adagio.
E-ter-ni-ty is drawing nigh! E-ter-ni-ty is drawing nigh! is drawing nigh!

No. 502. Young Men in Christ the Lord.

Dedicated to the Young Men's Christian Associations of the World.

Robert Weidensall. Geo. C. Stebbins.

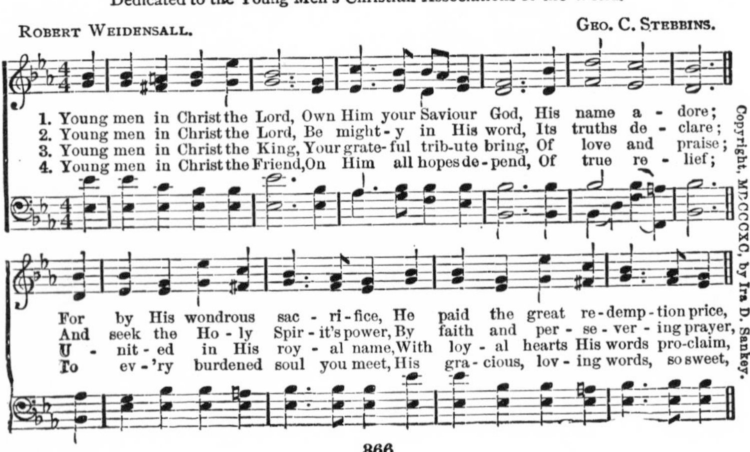
1. Young men in Christ the Lord, Own Him your Saviour God, His name a-dore;
2. Young men in Christ the Lord, Be might-y in His word, Its truths de-clare;
3. Young men in Christ the King, Your grate-ful trib-ute bring, Of love and praise;
4. Young men in Christ the Friend, On Him all hopes de-pend, Of true re-lief;
For by His wondrous sac-ri-fice, He paid the great re-demp-tion price,
And seek the Ho-ly Spir-it's power, By faith and per-se-ver-ing prayer,
U-nit-ed in His roy-al name, With loy-al hearts His words pro-claim,
To ev-'ry burdened soul you meet, His gra-cious, lov-ing words, so sweet,

Young Men in Christ the Lord.
That all might have e - ter - nal life, That come to God thro' Him.
That ye may wit - ness a - ny - where, That sin - ful men are found.
Throughout the world to all Young Men, "Ye must be born a - gain."
"Come un - to me," with love re - peat, "And I will give you rest."
5 Young men in Christ, arise,
The world before you lies,
Enslaved in sin;
Make haste to swell the mission band,
Prepared to go at His command,
To save lost men in every land,
At any sacrifice
6 Young men in Christ the Son,
In Him we all are one;
For this He prayed;
Then let us join the heavenly throng,
To sound His praise in endless song,
For all we have and are belong
To Christ, our Lord Divine.
No. 503. Coming Home To-Night.
"Him that cometh to me I will in no wise cast out."—John 6: 37.
Fanny J. Crosby.
Robert Lowry.
1. We are coming home to Je - sus, We have heard His wel-come voice; We are
2. We are coming home to Je - sus, For He died that we might live; He is
3. We are coming home to Je - sus, By the cross, our on - ly way; There He
trust-ing in His goodness, In His mer-cy we re-joice.
will - ing to receive us, He is wait-ing to for-give.
fin - ished our redemption, And we can no more de - lay.
Refrain.
We are com-ing home, we are
coming, coming
com-ing home, We are coming from the darkness to the light;............... We are
com-ing, com-ing
light, to the light;
com-ing home, We are com-ing home, We are com-ing home to - night.
coming, coming
coming, coming
coming, coming
Copyright, MDCCCXCI, by The Biglow & Main Co.

No. 504. At Even, ere the Sun was Set.

"He healed them that had need of healing."—LUKE 9: 11.

Rev. HENRY TWELLS. TIMOTHY B. MASON.

1. At e - ven, ere the sun was set, The sick, O Lord, a-round Thee lay;
2. Once more 'tis e - ven-tide; and we, Op - press'd with var - ious ills, draw near;
3. O Sav - iour Christ, our woes dis-pel; For some are sick and some are sad,
Oh, in what di - vers pains they met! Oh, with what joy they went a - way!
What if Thy form we can - not see! We know and feel that Thou art here.
And some have nev - er loved Thee well, And some have lost the love they had.

4 And all, O Lord, crave perfect rest,
And to be wholly free from sin;
And they who fain would serve Thee best,
Are conscious most of sin within.

5 Thy touch has still its ancient power;
No word from Thee can fruitless fall;
Here in this solemn evening hour,
Lord, in Thy mercy heal us all.

No. 505. Beseechings of Jesus.

"As though God did beseech you by us."—2 COR. 5: 20.

EL. NATHAN. JAMES McGRANAHAN.

Moderato.

1. O ten - der beseech-ings of Je - sus! How sweet-ly they fall on the ear!
2. Be - seech-ing in love for our Sav - iour, Un - wor - thy we pray in His stead;
3. Be - seech-ing His blood-bought, His ransom'd, Your bod - ies to Him glad - ly yield,
4. Be - seech-ing the saints to be ho - ly, Fill'd al - ways with meekness and love;
5. Be - seech-ing that all for His com - ing Un - shak-en may ev - er re - main,

O gos - pel of grace and of kind - ness, God's love and com-pas-sion bro't near!
Be - lieve in the word of for-give - ness, Ac - cept of the ran-som He made.
That, in you, and thro' you, and by you, His grace may be ful - ly re - vealed.
Like Je - sus so gen - tle and low - ly, Re - flect-ing the light from a - bove.
And stand with the sav'd and the chos - en, With Him in His glo - ri - ous reign.

CHORUS.

Is the Spir - it of Je - sus now striv - ing? His warn-ing, my brother, o - bey;

Beseechings of Jesus.

cres - cen - do.
Rit.
Re - sist not His gra-cious be - seech - ing, O grieve not the Sav - iour a - way.
1. Troub-led heart, thy God is call - ing! He is draw - ing ver - y near;
2. Come, the Spir - it still is plead-ing, Come to Him, the meek and mild;
3. Art thou wait - ing till the mor-row? Thou may'st nev - er see its light;
4. Let the an - gels bear the ti-dings Up - ward to the courts of heav'n!
Do not hide thy deep e - mo-tion, Do not check that fall-ing tear.
He is wait-ing now to save you, Wilt thou not be rec- on-ciled?
Come at once! ac - cept His mer-cy; He is wait-ing—come to-night.
Let them sing with ho - ly rapture, O'er an-oth - er soul forgiv'n!
CHORUS.
O be saved, His grace is free! O, be saved, He died for thee! O, be saved, He died for thee!
rit.
By per. The Biglow & Main Co., owners of Copyright.
1. O Lord, my soul re - joic - eth in Thee, My tongue Thy mer - cy is tell - ing;
2. I came to Thee o'er-burdened with care, My guilt with sor - row con - fess - ing;
3. To Thee, my hope and ref - uge di - vine, My faith is fer - vent-ly cling - ing;
4. I look be - yond this val - ley of tears, Where Thou, a man - sion pre - par - ing;

No. 506. He Died for Thee.

"The Son of man is come to save."—MATT. 18: 11.

F. J. CROSBY. S. J. VAIL.

No. 507. Wonderful Love!

"As the Father loved me, so have I loved you."—JOHN 15: 9.

GRACE J. FRANCES. HUBERT P. MAIN.

Wonderful Love!

I've found Thy love so precious to me, My heart with its rap-ture is swell-ing.
'Twas love, Thy love, that banished my fear, And gave me for sadness a bless-ing.
And ev-'ry hour some to-ken of love New joy to my spir-it is bring-ing.
Wilt call me home for-ev-er with Thee, The bliss of the glo-ri-fied shar-ing.
Refrain.
Won-der-ful love! O won-der-ful love! I'll sing of its ful-ness for-ev-er;
I've found the way that lead-eth a-bove, The way to the life-giv-ing riv-er.
Copyright, MDCCCXC, by Ira D. Sankey.
No. 508.
O Blessed Word.
"The sword of the Spirit, which is the word of God."—Eph. 6: 17.
L. W. Munhall.
Ira D. Sankey.
1. E-ter-nal life God's word proclaims To lost and dy-ing men;
2. God's grace is in His Ho-ly Word; We need it ev-'ry day;
3. By this same Word we know our work, And how it should be done;
Fine.
By it a-lone we know the Lord, Un-seen by mor-tal ken.
In all our con-flicts, this the sword, Our ev-'ry foe to slay.
How we should live, and how thro' grace The prom-ised crown is won.
D.S.—O may it be our Strength and Sword, Till earth-ly strife is o'er.
Chorus.
D.S.
O bless-ed Word, O gra-cious Word, We love it more and more;
Copyright, MDCCCXCI, by The Biglow & Main Co.

No. 509. O Come to the Merciful Saviour.

"Come unto me all ye that labor."—MATT. 11: 28.
F. W. FABER, arr.
IRA D. SANKEY.
Moderato.
1. O come to the mer-ci-ful Sav-iour who calls you, O come to the Lord who for-gives and for-gets; Tho' dark be the fortune on earth that be-falls you, A bright home a-waits you whose sun never sets.
2. O come then to Je-sus whose arms are ex-tend-ed To fold His dear children in clos-est em-brace; O come, and your ex-ile shall short-ly be end-ed, And Je-sus will show you the light of His face.
3. Then come to the Sav-iour, whose mercy grows brighter The long-er you look at the depths of His love; O fear not, 'tis Je-sus, and life's cares grow lighter While thinking of home and the glo-ry a-bove.
CHORUS.
Come home,...... come home,......
Come home, come home, In darkness no longer to roam, 'Tis Je-sus who tender-ly calls you to-day, Oh brother, my brother, come home.
Copyright, MDCCCXCI, by The Biglow & Main Co.
No. 510. My Saviour.
"My Refuge, my Saviour."—2 SAM. 22: 3.
DORA GREENWELL.
WM. J. KIRKPATRICK
1. I am not skill'd to un-derstand What God hath will'd, what God hath plann'd;
2. I take Him at His word indeed: "Christ died for sin-ners," this I read;
3. That He should leave His place on high, And come for sin-ful man to die,
4. And O that He ful-filled may see The tra-vail of His soul in me,
5. Yea, liv-ing, dy-ing, let me bring My strength, my so-lace from this spring,
Copyright, MDCCCLXXXV, by W. J. Kirkpatrick, used by per.

My Saviour.

I only know at His right hand Is One who is my Saviour!
For in my heart I find a need Of Him to be my Saviour!
You count it strange?—so once did I, Before I knew my Saviour!
And with His work contented be, As I with my dear Saviour!
That He who lives to be my King Once died to be my Saviour!

No. 511. Christ the Fountain.

"The blood of Jesus Christ his Son cleanseth us from all sin."—1 Jno. 1: 7.

Newman Hall. C. C. Case.

1. Fount-ain of pur - i - ty opened for sin, Here may the pen - i - tent wash and be clean;
Je - sus, Thou blessed Re-deem-er from woe, Wash me and I shall be whit-er than snow.

2. Though I have la-bored a - gain and a - gain, All my self-cleansing is ut - ter - ly vain;
Je - sus, Re-deem-er from sor-row and woe, Wash me and I shall be whit-er than snow.

3. Cleanse Thou the tho'ts of my heart, I implore, Help me Thy light to re-flect more and more;
Dai - ly in lov - ing o - bedience to grow, Wash me and I shall be whit-er than snow.

4. Whit-er than snow! nothing further I need, Christ is the Fountain; this on - ly I plead;
Je - sus my Sav - iour, to Thee will I go, Wash me and I shall be whit-er than snow.

Chorus.

Whit - er than snow,............ whit - er than snow,........... Wash me, Re - deem - - - er, And I shall be whit - er than snow.................
Whiter than snow, whiter than snow, Wash me, Re-deem-er, whit-er than snow.

No. 512. My Offering.
"Create in me a clean heart, O God."—Ps. 51: 10.
J. H. Johnston.
James McGranahan.
1. I bring to Thee, O Mas - ter, My bur - den and my grief;
2. I bring my guilt - y nat - ure, For cleans - ing and for cure;
3. Thy mer - cy reach - es low - er Than all the depths of sin;
4. My fal - tering faith I bring Thee, My weak and wavering will;
I do be - lieve Thy prom - ise, Help Thou mine un - be - lief.
Oh, heal my sore dis - eas - es, Re - store and make me pure.
As Thy com - pas - sions fail not, Oh, give me peace with - in.
My spir - it fails and fal - ters; Thy prom - is - es ful - fill.
Copyright, MDCCCXCI, by James McGranahan. All rights reserved.
No. 513. Coming To-Day.
"Rise, he calleth thee."—Mark 10: 49.
F. J. Crosby.
Jno. R. Sweney.
1. Out on the des - ert, seek - ing, seek - ing, Sin - ner, 'tis Je - sus seek - ing for thee;
2. Still He is wait - ing, wait - ing, wait - ing; O what com - pas - sion beams in His eye!
3. Lov - ing - ly plead - ing, plead - ing, plead - ing, Mer - cy, tho' slight - ed, bears with thee yet;
Ten - der - ly call - ing, call - ing, call - ing, Hith - er, thou lost one, O come un - to Me.
Hear Him re - peat - ing, gent - ly, gent - ly, Come to thy Sav - iour, O why wilt thou die?
Thou canst be hap - py, hap - py, hap - py; Come ere the life - star for - ev - er shall set.
Refrain.
Je - sus is call - ing, Je - sus is call - ing; Why dost thou lin - ger? why tar - ry a - way?
Come to Him quick - ly, say to Him glad - ly, Lord, I am com - ing, com - ing to - day.
Copyright, MDCCCLXXX, by John J. Hood. Used by per.

No. 514. God Bless You.

"God, even our Father, comfort your hearts."—2 THESS. 2 : 16, 17.

EL. NATHAN.
JAMES McGRANAHAN.
1. "God bless you!" from the heart we sing, God give to ev - 'ry one His grace,
2. God bless you on your pil- grim way, Thro' storm and sun - shine guid - ing still;
3. God bless you in this world of strife, When oft the soul would homeward fly,
4. God bless you, and the patience give To walk thro' life by Je - sus' side;
5. God bless us all, and give us rest When Christ shall come and glo - ry dawn;
Till He on high His ransomed bring To dwell with Him in end - less peace.
His pres - ence guard you day by day, And keep you safe from ev - 'ry ill.
And give the sweet - ness to your life, Of wait - ing for the rest on high.
For Him to bear, for Him to live, And then with Him be glo - ri - fied.
Our sun is swing - ing toward the west, Life's lit - tle day will soon be gone.
CHORUS.
God bless you! God bless you! Bless and keep us all in Je - sus' love,
And, when our part - ings here are o - ver, Take us to the joys a - bove.
when our part - ings
Copyright, MDCCCXCI, by James McGranahan. All rights reserved.
No. 515. Is Thy Cruse of Comfort Failing?
"Neither did the cruse of oil fail."—1 KING 17 : 16.
Mrs. E. R. CHARLES, arr.
IRA D. SANKEY.
1. Is thy cruse of com - fort fail - ing? Rise and share it with a friend, And thro'
2. For the heart grows rich in giv - ing; All its wealth is liv - ing grain; Seeds, which
3. Lost and wea - ry on the mountains, Wouldst thou sleep amidst the snow? Chafe that
4. Is thy heart a well left emp - ty? None but God its void can fill; Noth - ing

Is Thy Cruse of Comfort Failing?
all the years of fam-ine It shall serve thee to the end. Love di-vine will fill thy
mil-dew in the gar-ner, Scattered, fill with gold the plain. Is thy bur-den hard and
froz-en form be-side thee, And to-geth-er both shall glow. Art thou wound-ed in life's
but a cease-less fountain Can its ceaseless longings still. Is thy heart a liv-ing
storehouse, Or thy hand-ful still re-new; Scant-y fare for one will oft-en Make a
heav-y? Do thy steps drag wea-ri-ly? Help to lift thy brother's bur-den, God will
bat-tle? Ma-ny stricken round thee moan; Give to them thy precious ointment, And that
pow-er? Self-entwined, its strength sinks low; It can on-ly live by lov-ing, And by
roy-al feast for two; Scanty fare for one will oft-en Make a roy-al feast for two.
bear both it and thee; Help to lift thy brother's burden, God will bear both it and thee.
balm shall heal thine own; Give to them thy precious ointment, And that balm shall heal thine own.
serving, love will grow; It can on-ly live by lov-ing, And by serv-ing love will grow.
Copyright, MDCCCLXXXIX, by Ira D. Sankey.
No. 516.
Jesus, my All.
"Christ is all and in all."—Col. 3: 11.
F. J. Crosby.
Anon.
rit.
1. Lord, at Thy mer-cy-seat Hum-bly I fall; Plead-ing Thy
2. Tears of re-pent-ant grief Si-lent-ly fall; Help Thou my
3. Still at Thy mer-cy-seat Sav-iour, I fall; Trust-ing Thy
rit.
prom-ise sweet, Lord, hear my call; Now let Thy work be-gin,
un-be-lief, Hear Thou my call; Oh, how I pine for Thee!
prom-ise sweet, Heard is my call; Faith wings my soul to Thee;
rit.
Oh, make me pure with-in, Cleanse me from ev-'ry sin, Je-sus, my all.
'Tis all my hope and plea: Je-sus has died for me, Je-sus, my all.
This all my song shall be, Je-sus has died for me, Je-sus, my all.
Used by permission.

No. 517. Singing with Grace to the Lord.

"Singing with grace in your hearts to the Lord."—Col. 3: 16.

J. H. Johnston.
James McGranahan.
1. Come in - to His presence with sing - ing, O wor-ship the Lord with a song;
2. Not yet, as the an-gels in heav - en, May mortals their grat - i - tude sing;
3. Then come to His courts with re-joic - ing, And join in the cho - rus of praise;
A trib - ute of grat - i - tude bring-ing, To Him to whom prais-es be - long;
Not here up - on earth is it giv - en, Per - fect - ion of serv - ice to bring;
The pray'r and the an - them but voic - ing The thanks which your loving hearts raise;
But oh, while you join in thanksgiv - ing, With voi - ces in tune - ful ac - cord,
But ear - nest and true ad - o - ra - tion, The heart in the hymn and the pray'r,
With grace in your hearts e - ven du - ty Will change in - to pleas - ure ere long,
Re-mem-ber, He watch-es your *liv - ing*, And sing with your hearts to the Lord.
Will be an ac - cept - ed ob - la - tion, And light - en life's bur - den and care.
And see - ing the King in His beau - ty, Your life shall then be as a song.
Chorus.
Sing-ing,........................ sing - ing,............ This is true wor - ship and love;
Sing - ing with grace in your heart to the Lord,
Liv - ing,........................ sing - ing,............ This is ac - cept - ed a - bove.
Liv - ing and sing - ing in sweet - est ac - cord,
Copyright, MDCCCXCI, by James McGranahan. All rights reserved.

No. 518. True-Hearted, Whole-Hearted.

" I will praise Thee, O Lord, with my whole heart."—Ps. 9: 1.

FRANCES R. HAVERGAL.
GEO. C. STEBBINS.
1. True-heart-ed, whole-heart-ed, faith - ful and loy - al, King of our lives, by Thy
2. True-heart-ed, whole-heart-ed, full - est al - le-giance Yield - ing henceforth to our
3. True-heart-ed, whole-heart-ed, Sav - iour all-glo-rious! Take Thy great pow - er and
grace we will be; Un - der the stan-dard ex - alt - ed and roy - al, Strong in Thy
glo - ri-ous King; Val - iant en-deav - or and lov - ing o - be-dience, Free - ly and
reign there a - lone, O - ver our wills and af - fec - tions vic - to - rious, Free - ly sur -
strength we will bat - tle for Thee.
joy - ous-ly now would we bring.
ren - dered and wholly Thine own.
CHORUS.
Peal out the watchword! si - lence it nev - er!
Peal si-lence
Song of our spir - it's re - joic - ing and free; Peal out the watchword!
Song re-joic-ing and free; Peal
loy - al for - ev - er! King of our lives, By thy grace we will be.
loy - al King

No. 519. Blest Jesus, Grant us Strength.

"Give thy strength unto thy servant."—Ps. 86: 16.

Rev. W. W. How. G. J. Elvey.

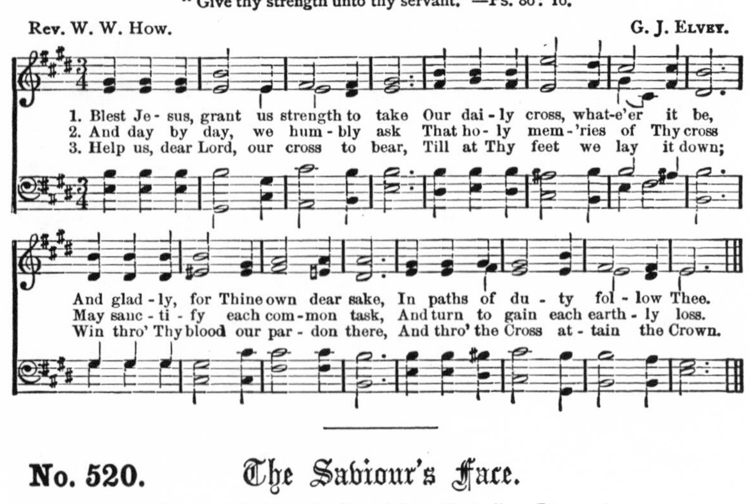
1. Blest Je - sus, grant us strength to take Our dai - ly cross, what-e'er it be,
2. And day by day, we hum - bly ask That ho - ly mem - 'ries of Thy cross
3. Help us, dear Lord, our cross to bear, Till at Thy feet we lay it down;
And glad - ly, for Thine own dear sake, In paths of du - ty fol - low Thee.
May sanc - ti - fy each com - mon task, And turn to gain each earth - ly loss.
Win thro' Thy blood our par - don there, And thro' the Cross at - tain the Crown.

No. 520. The Saviour's Face.

"The glory of God in the face of Jesus Christ."—2 Cor. 4: 6.

Edw. A. Collier, D.D. Geo. F. Root.

Reverently.
1. How sweet, O Lord, Thy word of grace Which bids a sin - ner seek Thy face, And
2. Thy visage, marred and crowned with thorn, Thou didst not hide from grief and scorn, Nor
3. The heavens de-clare Thy power and love; In all Thy works, be - low, a - bove, Thy
4. The bright - ness of Thy glo - ry, Lord, Fills heaven and earth and writ - ten Word With
nev - er seek in vain, And nev - er seek in vain; That face, once set so stead - fast - ly To
from the dews of night, Nor from the dews of night; Yet, in that face a love appears Which
maj - es - ty I trace, Thy maj - es - ty I trace, But mer - cy shines not in the skies, And
beams of heavenly grace, With beams of heaven - ly grace; But all the hosts of Heaven shine With
meet Thy cross of ag - o - ny, Can nev - er me dis - dain, Can nev - er me dis - dain.
scat - ters all my gloom - y fears, And fills my soul with light, And fills my soul with light.
hope with - in my spir - it dies, Un - til I see Thy face, Un - til I see Thy face.
no such ra - di - ance di - vine As Thy most bless - ed face, As Thy most bless - ed face.

No. 521. Hallowed Hour of Prayer.

"My house shall be called the house of prayer."—Isa. 56: 7.

E. A. Hoffman. J. H. Tenney.

1. 'Tis the hal-lowed hour of pray'r, And we trust-ing-ly bring All our
2. 'Tis the pre-cious hour of pray'r, And we hum-bly en-treat: Fa-ther,
3. 'Tis the sa-cred hour of pray'r, Calm as heav-en a-bove; Soul to

doubt-ings and our fears To our Sav-iour and King; For we know that He de-
breathe the Spir-it now, As we bow at Thy feet; Touch our lips with pow'r of
soul is breathing here The com-mun-ion of love; Ev-'ry heart is sweet-ly

lights A glad wel-come to give, And the bless-ings that we ask for
song; Fill our souls with Thy love; And be-stow the ben-e-dic-tion
filled With a peace most pro-found; Oh, the place is like to heav-en

We shall ful-ly re-ceive.
Of Thy peace from a-bove.
Where such true joys abound.

CHORUS.

Pre-cious hour of pray'r! Hallowed hour of pray'r!
Sa-cred sea-son of com-mun-ion, It is sweet to be there!

No. 522. Thou shalt be Saved.

"If thou shalt confess.........the Lord Jesus."—Rom. 10: 9.

El. Nathan. James McGranahan.

1. Be-hold how plain the truth is made; Since Christ the ran-som price has paid,
2. The death of Christ up-on the tree Was for the judg-ment due to thee;
3. By rais-ing Je-sus from the dead Our bless-ed God has sure-ly said,
4. And now to God as sons brought nigh We come and "Ab-ba Fa-ther" cry,

Thou shalt be Saved.

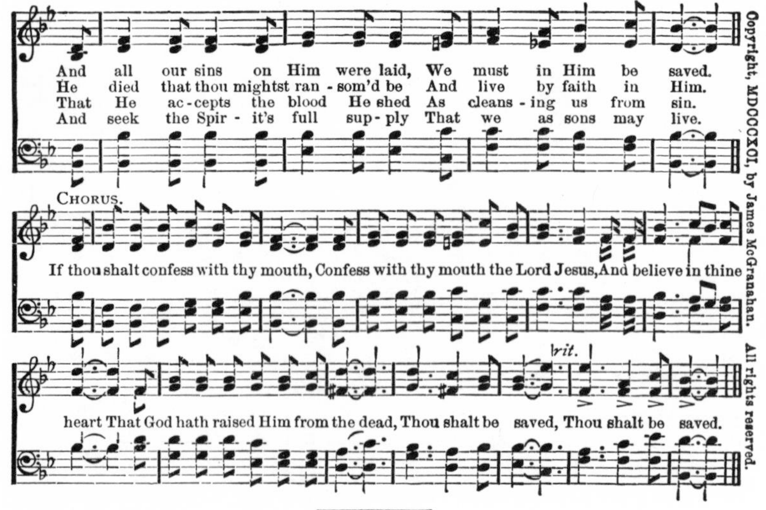
And all our sins on Him were laid, We must in Him be saved.
He died that thou mightst ran - som'd be And live by faith in Him.
That He ac-cepts the blood He shed As cleans - ing us from sin.
And seek the Spir - it's full sup-ply That we as sons may live.
Chorus.
If thou shalt confess with thy mouth, Confess with thy mouth the Lord Jesus, And believe in thine
heart That God hath raised Him from the dead, Thou shalt be saved, Thou shalt be saved.
rit.

No. 523. The Lord Keep Watch Between Us.

"Mizpah; * * * The Lord watch between me and thee, when we are absent one from another."—Gen. 31: 49.

J. H. Johnston. James McGranahan.

Allegro.
1. The Lord keep watch between us, The ev - er pres- ent Friend; No love like His so might - y, To keep and to de - fend.
2. Though ab- sent from each oth - er, We are not far from Him; Let not our courage fal - ter, Let not our faith grow dim.
3. Though time and space may sev - er The Mas-ter's serv-ants here, 'Tis on - ly for a sea - son, The meet - ing-time draws near.
4. The Lord Himself is watch-ing, In ten-der-ness and love; Let prais-es meet and min - gle A - round the throne a - bove.
Chorus.
Miz-pah! Miz-pah!
The Lord keep watch be-tween us, Keep watch in tend'rest love, Un - til our prais- es min - gle A-round the throne a - bove.

No. 524. Faith is the Victory.

"The victory that overcometh the world, even our faith."—1 John 5: 4.

John H. Yates. Ira D. Sankey.

1. Encamped a-long the hills of light, Ye Chris-tian sol-diers, rise, And press the
2. His ban-ner o-ver us is love, Our sword the word of God; We tread the
3. On ev-'ry hand the foe we find Drawn up in dread ar-ray; Let tents of
4. To Him that o-ver-comes the foe, White raiment shall be giv'n; Be-fore the
bat-tle ere the night Shall veil the glow-ing skies; A-gainst the foe in
road the saints a-bove With shouts of tri-umph trod; By faith, they like a
ease be left be-hind, And on-ward to the fray; Sal-va-tion's hel-met
an-gels he shall know His name con-fessed in heaven; Then on-ward from the
vales be-low, Let all our strength be hurled; Faith is the vic-to-
whirlwind's breath, Swept on o'er ev-'ry field; The faith by which they
on each head, With truth all girt a-bout, The earth shall trem-ble
hills of light, Our hearts with love a-flame; We'll van-quish all the
ry, we know, That o-vercomes the world.
conquered Death Is still our shin-ing shield.
'neath our tread, And ech-o with our shout.
hosts of night, In Je-sus' conquering name.
Chorus.
Faith is the vic-to-ry!
Faith is the vic-to-ry!
Faith is the vic-to-ry! Oh, glo-ri-ous vic-to-ry, That o-vercomes the world.
Faith is the vic-to-ry!
Copyright, MDCCCXCI, by The Biglow & Main Co.

No. 525. Mission Hymn.

"All nations shall come and worship before thee."—Rev. 15: 4.

F. J. Crosby. Ira D. Sankey.

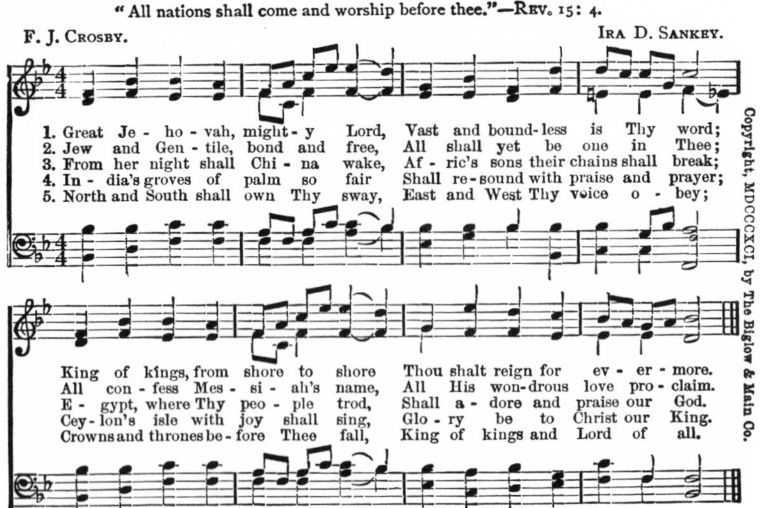

1. Great Je - ho - vah, might - y Lord, Vast and bound- less is Thy word;
2. Jew and Gen - tile, bond and free, All shall yet be one in Thee;
3. From her night shall Chi - na wake, Af - ric's sons their chains shall break;
4. In - dia's groves of palm so fair Shall re - sound with praise and prayer;
5. North and South shall own Thy sway, East and West Thy voice o - bey;
King of kings, from shore to shore Thou shalt reign for ev - er - more.
All con - fess Mes - si - ah's name, All His won-drous love pro - claim.
E - gypt, where Thy peo - ple trod, Shall a - dore and praise our God.
Cey- lon's isle with joy shall sing, Glo - ry be to Christ our King.
Crowns and thrones be - fore Thee fall, King of kings and Lord of all.
Copyright, MDCCCXCI, by The Biglow & Main Co.

No. 526. The Christian's "Good-Night."

It is said: The early Christians were accustomed to bid their dying friends Good-night, so sure were they of their awakening on the Resurrection Morning.

Sarah Doudney. Ira D. Sankey.

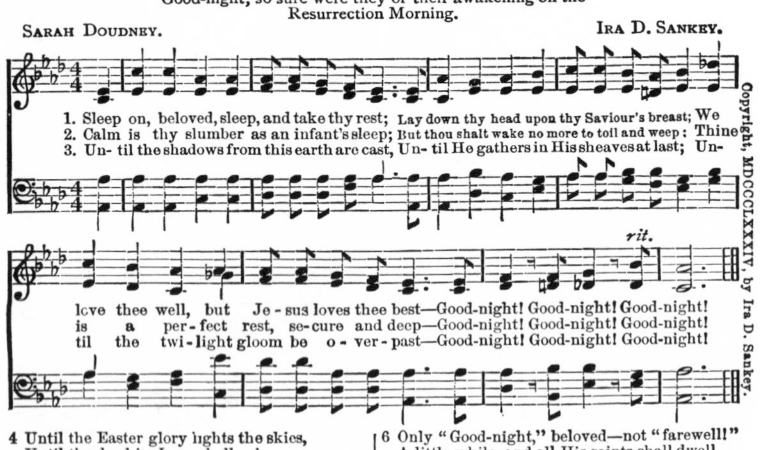

1. Sleep on, beloved, sleep, and take thy rest; Lay down thy head upon thy Saviour's breast; We
2. Calm is thy slumber as an infant's sleep; But thou shalt wake no more to toil and weep: Thine
3. Un- til the shadows from this earth are cast, Un- til He gathers in His sheaves at last; Un-
rit.
love thee well, but Je - sus loves thee best—Good-night! Good-night! Good-night!
is a per- fect rest, se-cure and deep—Good-night! Good-night! Good-night!
til the twi - light gloom be o - ver - past—Good-night! Good-night! Good-night!
Copyright, MDCCCLXXXIV, by Ira D. Sankey.

4 Until the Easter glory lights the skies,
Until the dead in Jesus shall arise,
And He shall come, but not in lowly guise—
Good-night!

5 Until, made beautiful by Love Divine,
Thou, in the likeness of thy Lord shalt shine,
And He shall bring that golden crown of thine—
Good-night!

6 Only "Good-night," beloved—not "farewell!"
A little while, and all His saints shall dwell
In hallowed union indivisible—
Good-night!

7 Until we meet again before His throne,
Clothed in the spotless robe He gives His own,
Until we know even as we are known—
Good-night!

No. 527.
Christ is Risen.
Fanny J. Crosby.
"For he is risen, as he said."—Matt. 28 : 6.
Geo. C. Stebbins.
1. Christ hath ris-en! Hal-le-lu-jah! Blessed morn of life and light; Lo, the grave is rent a-sun-der, Death is conquered thro' His might.
2. Christ hath ris-en! Hal-le-lu-jah! Friends of Jesus, dry your tears; Thro' the vail of gloom and darkness, Lo, the Son of God appears.
3. Christ hath ris-en! Hal-le-lu-jah! He hath ris-en, as He said; He is now the King of glo-ry, And our great ex-alt-ed Head.
Refrain.
Christ is ris-en! Hal-le-lu-jah! Gladness fills the world to-day; From the tomb that could not hold Him, See, the stone is rolled a-way.
Copyright, MDCCCXCI, by The Biglow & Main Co.
No. 528.
In Jesus' Face.
"The light of the knowledge of the glory of God in the face of Jesus Christ."—2 Cor. 4 : 6.
El. Nathan.
James McGranahan.
1. The liv-ing God, who by His might Spake but the word and there was light, Hath promised now to show His grace To sin-ful men, in Je-sus' face.
2. This mighty Christ, so strong and true, Has come from God, His work to do; He comes with power the soul to save, To give the vict'ry o'er the grave.
3. In Je-sus' face our God we know, And trust in Him to bear us through; He will not leave us to de-feat, But make our victo-ry com-plete.
4. When darkness gives the soul distress, When sorrows on our pathway press, One look at Him will clouds displace, While comfort beams from Je-sus' face.
5. Then come, ye wea-ry ones, and rest; Come, sinful souls, and here be blessed; With-in your heart give Christ His place, And see God's love in Je-sus' face.
Chorus.
In Je-sus' face! in Je-sus' face! O wondrous sight! O wondrous grace! The living God thro' sin concealed, In Jesus' face is now revealed.
Copyright, MDCCCXCI, by James McGranahan. All rights reserved.

No. 529. O Saviour, Precious Saviour.

"He shall save his people from their sins."—MATT. 1: 21.

FRANCES R. HAVERGAL. J. H. BURKE.

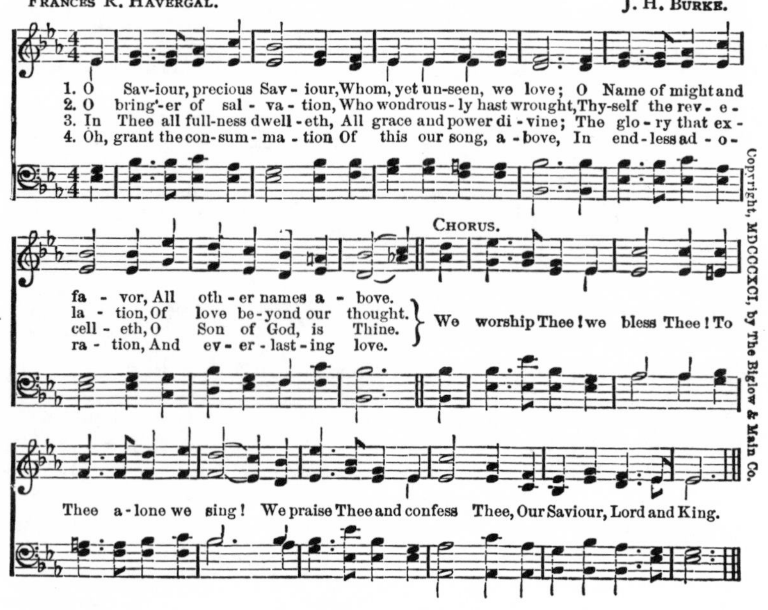

1. O Sav-iour, precious Sav - iour, Whom, yet un-seen, we love; O Name of might and fa - vor, All oth - er names a - bove.
2. O bring-er of sal - va - tion, Who wondrous - ly hast wrought, Thy-self the rev - e - la - tion, Of love be-yond our thought.
3. In Thee all full-ness dwell - eth, All grace and power di - vine; The glo - ry that ex - cell - eth, O Son of God, is Thine.
4. Oh, grant the con-sum - ma - tion Of this our song, a - bove, In end-less ad - o - ra - tion, And ev - er - last - ing love.
CHORUS.
We worship Thee! we bless Thee! To Thee a - lone we sing! We praise Thee and confess Thee, Our Saviour, Lord and King.
Copyright, MDCCCXCI, by The Biglow & Main Co.

No. 530. A Home on High.

"That where I am, there ye may be also."—JOHN 14: 3.

L. W. MANSFIELD. GEO. C. STEBBINS.

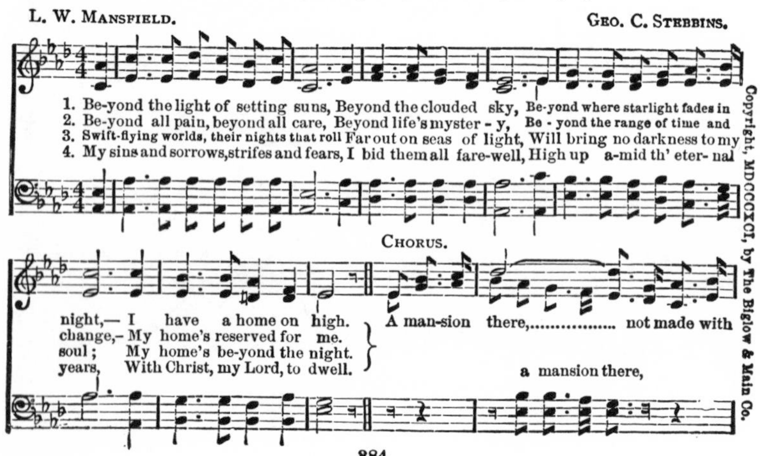

1. Be-yond the light of setting suns, Beyond the clouded sky, Be-yond where starlight fades in night,— I have a home on high.
2. Be-yond all pain, beyond all care, Beyond life's myster - y, Be - yond the range of time and change,– My home's reserved for me.
3. Swift-flying worlds, their nights that roll Far out on seas of light, Will bring no darkness to my soul; My home's be-yond the night.
4. My sins and sorrows, strifes and fears, I bid them all fare-well, High up a-mid th' eter- nal years, With Christ, my Lord, to dwell.
CHORUS.
A man-sion there,................ not made with
a mansion there,
Copyright, MDCCCXCI, by The Biglow & Main Co.

A Home on High.
hands,.................... A place................ prepared for me;...................
not made with hands, a place prepared for me;
And while God lives, and angels sing........... That home..... my home shall be....................
an-gels sing, that home my home shall be.
ritard.
No. 531. O Day of Rest and Gladness.
"The rest of the holy Sabbath."—Ex. 16: 23.
C. Wordsworth.
German Melody.
1. { O day of rest and gladness, O day of joy and light; }
{ O balm of care and sadness, Most beauti-ful, most bright; } On thee the high and low-ly,
Thro' a-ges joined in tune, Sing "Ho-ly, ho-ly, ho-ly," To the great God Tri-une.
2 On thee, at the creation,
The light first had its birth;
On thee, for our salvation,
Christ rose from depths of earth;
On thee our Lord victorious,
The Spirit sent from heaven;
And thus on thee, most glorious,
A triple light was given.
3 New graces ever gaining
From this our day of rest,
We reach the rest remaining
To spirits of the blest;
To Holy Ghost be praises,
To Father, and to Son;
The Church her voice upraises
To Thee, blest Three in One.
No. 532. Stretch Forth Thy Hand.
"And it was restored whole, like as the other."—Matt. 12: 13.
El. Nathan.
H. H. McGranahan.
1. "Stretch forth thy hand," thy pal-sied hand, Fear not, it is the Lord's com-mand;
2. "Stretch forth thy hand," thy emp-ty hand, No gift of thine will God com-mend;
3. "Stretch forth thy hand," thy help-less hand, Up-held by God, thy soul shall stand;
4. "Stretch forth thy hand," thy dy-ing hand, When thou shalt come to Jor-dan's strand;

Stretch Forth Thy Hand.

Seek not from Him to hide thy sin, Con-fess, and ask to be made clean.
The emp - ty hand that shows thy need, Of this a - lone will He take heed.
Fight not in thine own strength the foe, But trust-ing Je - sus, on - ward go.
Thro' all the bil - lows Christ shall guide, And bring them safe to Ca - naan's side.
CHORUS.
"Stretch forth thy hand," on Christ be - lieve, "Stretch forth thy hand," the pow'r re - ceive;
He of - fers grace so full and free, "Stretch forth thy hand," He speaks to thee.
Copyright, MDCCCXCI, by James McGranahan. All rights reserved.

No. 533. Sometime We'll Understand.

"What I do thou knowest not now; but thou shalt know hereafter."—JOHN 13 : 7.

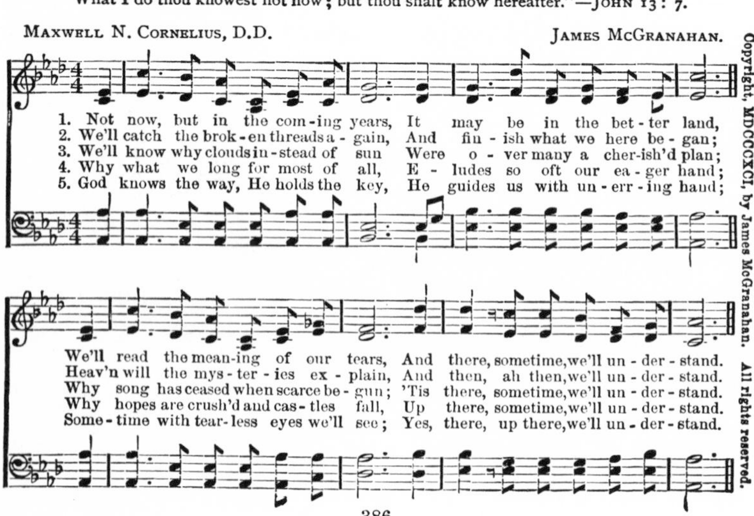

MAXWELL N. CORNELIUS, D.D.
JAMES MCGRANAHAN.
1. Not now, but in the com-ing years, It may be in the bet - ter land,
2. We'll catch the brok - en threads a - gain, And fin - ish what we here be - gan;
3. We'll know why clouds in - stead of sun Were o - ver many a cher-ish'd plan;
4. Why what we long for most of all, E - ludes so oft our ea - ger hand;
5. God knows the way, He holds the key, He guides us with un - err - ing hand;
We'll read the mean-ing of our tears, And there, sometime, we'll un - der - stand.
Heav'n will the mys - ter - ies ex - plain, And then, ah then, we'll un - der - stand.
Why song has ceased when scarce be - gun; 'Tis there, sometime, we'll un - der - stand.
Why hopes are crush'd and cas - tles fall, Up there, sometime, we'll un - der - stand.
Some - time with tear - less eyes we'll see; Yes, there, up there, we'll un - der - stand.
Copyright, MDCCCXCI, by James McGranahan. All rights reserved.

Sometime we'll Understand.
Chorus.
A little faster.
* doth hold thy hand;
Then trust in God thro' all thy days; Fear not, for He ‖: doth hold :‖ thy hand;
a tempo primo.
cres.
ad lib.
Tho' dark thy way, still sing and praise; Sometime, sometime, we'll un-der-stand.
* Repeat for alto only.
No. 534. Only Remembered.
"I will make thy name remembered."—Ps. 45 : 17.
Horatius Bonar, (alt.)
Ira D. Sankey.
1. Fad - ing a-way like the stars of the morning, Los-ing their light in the glo - ri - ous sun—
2. Shall we be miss'd tho' by oth-ers suc-ceed-ed, Reap-ing the fields we in spring-time have sown?
3. On - ly the truth that in life we have spoken, On - ly the seed that on earth we have sown;
4. Oh, when the Saviour shall make up His jewels, When the bright crowns of rejoicing are won,
Thus would we pass from the earth and its toiling, On - ly remembered by what we have done.
No, for the sowers may pass from their labors, On - ly remembered by what they have done.
These shall pass onward when we are for-got-ten, Fruits of the harvest and what we have done.
Then shall His wea - ry and faith-ful dis - ci - ples, All be remember'd by what they have done.
Refrain.
On - ly remembered, on - ly remembered, On - ly remembered by what we have done;
Thus would we pass from the earth and its toiling, On - ly remembered by what we have done.
Copyright, MDCCCXCI, by The Biglow & Main Co.

No. 535. Work for Time is Flying.
"Remember how short my time is."—Ps. 89: 47.
Horatius Bonar.
Geo. C. Stebbins.
1. Work, for time is fly-ing, Work with hearts sincere; Work, for souls are dying, Work, for night is near;
2 In this glorious call-ing, Work till day is o'er; Work, till evening falling, You can work no more;
3. There where saints adore Him, Where the ransom'd meet, Joy they show before Him, Bowing at His feet;
In the Master's vineyard, Go and work to-day; Be no useless sluggard Standing in the way.
Then your labor bringing To the King of kings, Borne with joy and singing Home on angels' wings.
Hear the Master say-ing, From His heav'nly throne, When thy toil rewarding, "Laborer, well done!"
Copyright, MDCCCXCI, by The Biglow & Main Co.
No. 536. Have You Sought?
"My sheep wandered through all the mountains."—Ezk. 34: 6.
F. J. C.
Ira D. Sankey.
1. Have you sought for the sheep that have wandered, Far a-way on the dark mountains cold?
2. Have you been to the sad and the lone-ly Whose burdens are heav-y to bear?
3. Have you knelt by the sick and the dy-ing, The mes-sage of mer-cy to tell?
4. If to Je-sus you an-swer these questions, And to Him have been faithful and true,
Have you gone, like the ten-der Shep-herd, To bring them a-gain to the fold?
Have you car-ried the name of Je-sus, And ten-der-ly breathed it in prayer?
Have you stood by the tremb'ling cap-tive A-lone in his dark pris-on cell?
Then be-hold, in the mansions yon-der Are crowns of re-joic-ing for you;
Have you followed their wea-ry foot-steps? And the wild des-ert waste have you crossed,
Have you told of the great sal-va-tion He died on the cross to se-cure?
Have you pointed the lost to Je-sus, And urged them on Him to be-lieve?
And there from the King e-ter-nal Your wel-come and greeting shall be,
Copyright, MDCCCXCI, by The Biglow & Main Co.

Have You Sought?

Nor lingered till safe home re-turn-ing, You have gathered the sheep that were lost?
Have you asked them to trust in the Sav-iour Whose love shall for-ev-er en-dure?
Have you told of the life ev-er-last-ing That all, if they will, may re-ceive?
"In-as-much" as 'twas done for "my brethren," E-ven so it was done "un-to me."

No. 537. When Morning Gilds the Skies.

"I will praise thy name, O Lord."—Ps. 54: 6.

Rev. E. Caswall. J. Barnby.

1. When morning gilds the skies, My heart a-wak-ing cries, May Je-sus Christ be prais'd; A-like at work and prayer, To Je-sus I re-pair; May Je-sus Christ be prais'd.
2. Does sad-ness fill my mind? A so-lace here I find, May Je-sus Christ be prais'd; Or fades my earth-ly bliss? My comfort still is this, May Je-sus Christ be prais'd.
3. Be this, while life is mine, My can-ti-cle di-vine, May Je-sus Christ be prais'd; Be this th'e-ter-nal song, Thro' all the a-ges long, May Je-sus Christ be prais'd.

No. 538. Let us go Forth.

"Let us go forth unto him."—Heb. 13: 13.

El. Nathan. James McGranahan.

1. The call of God is sounding clear, O Christian let it reach thine ear; Endeav-or now of souls to bring A band to love and serve the King.
2. Let us go forth, as call'd of God, Redeem'd by Je-sus' precious blood; His love to show, His life to live, His message speak, His mer-cy give.
3. Let "Christ a-lone" our watchword be— The Son of God who made us free; He bore our sins, He makes us pure, For His name's sake we all en-dure.
4. The Christ of God to glo-ri-fy, His grace in us to mag-ni-fy,— His word of life to all make known, Be this our work, and this a-lone.

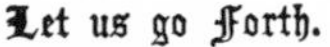
Let us go Forth.

CHORUS.
Let us go forth,.................. the call is clear,.................. Let us go
Let us go forth, the call is clear,
forth,............ no tar-ry-ing here;............. For Him to live,.............. the Christ, the
Let us go forth, no tarrying here; For Him to live,
Lord,.................. A crown from Him,.................. our high re - ward.
the Christ, the Lord, A crown from Him,

No. 539. I Will Lift up Mine Eyes.

PSALM 121.

G. F. ROOT.

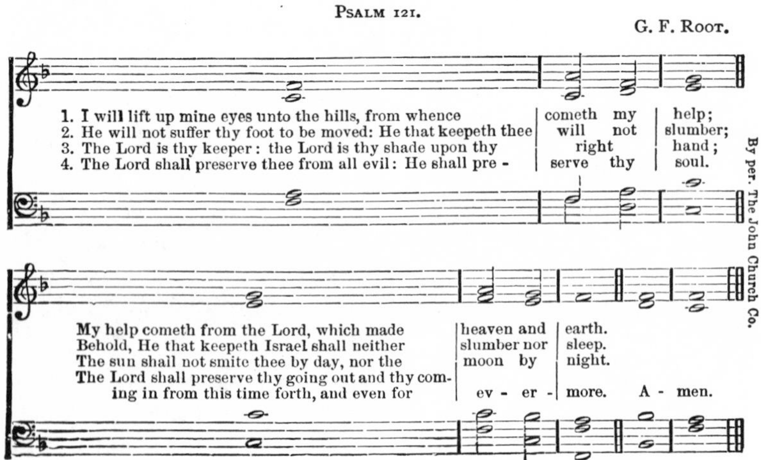
1. I will lift up mine eyes unto the hills, from whence | cometh my | help;
2. He will not suffer thy foot to be moved: He that keepeth thee | will not | slumber;
3. The Lord is thy keeper: the Lord is thy shade upon thy | right | hand;
4. The Lord shall preserve thee from all evil: He shall pre - | serve thy | soul.
My help cometh from the Lord, which made | heaven and | earth.
Behold, He that keepeth Israel shall neither | slumber nor | sleep.
The sun shall not smite thee by day, nor the | moon by | night.
The Lord shall preserve thy going out and thy coming in from this time forth, and even for | ev - er - | more. A - men.

By per. The John Church Co.

No. 540. Press On.
F. J. C.
"Ye shall be gathered one by one."—Isa. 27: 12.
Ira D. Sankey.
1. Press on, press on, O pilgrim, Re - joicing in the Lord, Be- lieving in His prom- ise,
2. Press on, press on, O pilgrim, A - long the heav'nly way; Remember God commands us
3. Press on, press on, O pilgrim, Tho' clouds and storms may rise; The Light that never faileth
And trusting in His word; Fear not, for He is with us, Whate'er the cross we bear;
To watch and work and pray; He bids us all be faith - ful, And cast on Him our care;
Shines brightly in the skies; Press on where crowns await us, In yonder mansions fair;
Refrain.
And soon, beyond the swelling tide, We'll gather o - ver there. Gather o - ver there,
Gather o - ver there; And soon, beyond the swelling tide, We'll gather o - ver there.
Copyright, MDCCCXCI, by The Biglow & Main Co.
No. 541. There's a Wideness in God's Mercy.
Ps. 136: 1–26.
Frederick W. Faber.
Lizzie S. Tourjèe.
1. There's a wide- ness in God's mer - cy, Like the wide - ness of the sea:
2. There is wel- come for the sin - ner, And more grac - es for the good;
3. For the love of God is broad - er Than the meas - ure of man's mind;
4. If our love were but more sim - ple, We should take Him at His word;
There's a kind - ness in His jus - tice, Which is more than lib - er - ty.
There is mer - cy with the Sav - iour; There is heal - ing in His blood.
And the heart of the E - ter - nal Is most won - der - ful - ly kind.
And our lives would be all sun-shine In the sweet - ness of our Lord.
Used by permission.

No. 542. The Palace of the King.
Psalm 45: 10–17.
Dr. J. B. Herbert.
1. { O daughter take good heed, In-cline, and give good ear; Thou must for-get thy kin-dred all, And father's house most dear.
Thy beau-ty to the King, Shall then de-light-ful be: And do thou hum-bly worship Him, Be-cause thy Lord is He. }
2. { The daughter then of Tyre There with a gift shall be, And all the wealth-y of the land Shall make their suit to thee.
The daughter of the King All glo-rious is with-in; And with em-broi-der-ies of gold Her garments wrought have been. }
Chorus.
With gladness and with joy, Thou all of them shalt bring, And they to-geth-er en-ter shall The palace of the King, The pal-ace of the King, The pal-ace of the King; And they togeth-er enter shall, The palace of the King.
rit.
Copyright, MDCCCXC, by United Pres. Board of Publication. Used by permission.
3 She cometh to the King
In robes with needle wrought;
The virgins that do follow her
Shall unto thee be brought.
With gladness and with joy,
Thou all of them shalt bring,
And they together enter shall
The palace of the King.
Cho.—With gladness, etc.
4 And in thy fathers' stead,
Thy children thou shalt take,
And in all places of the earth
Them noble princes make.
I will show forth thy name
To generations all:
The people therefore evermore
To Thee give praises shall.
Cho.—With gladness, etc.
No. 543. Happy Day.
"Happy is that people whose God is the Lord."—Psa. 144: 15.
P. Doddridge.
From E. F. Rimbault.
Chorus.
1. { O happy day that fixed my choice On Thee, my Saviour, and my God!
Well may this glowing heart rejoice, And tell its raptures all a-broad. }
D.S. Happy day, hap-py day,

Happy Day.

FINE.
D.S.
When Jesus washed my sins away; He taught me how to watch and pray, And live rejoicing ev'ry day;

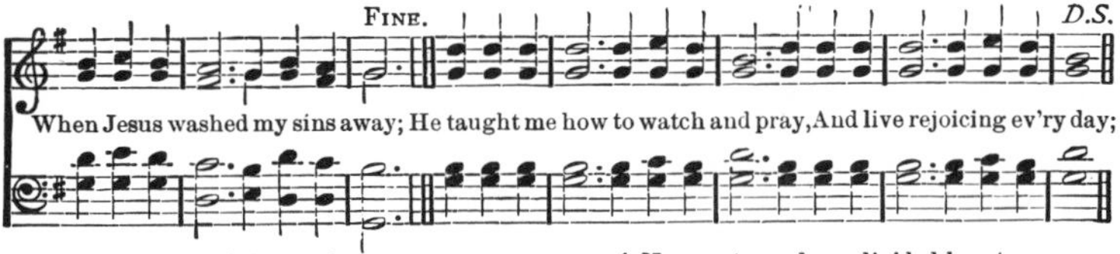

2 O happy bond that seals my vows
To Him who merits all my love;
Let cheerful anthems fill His house,
While to that sacred shrine I move.

3 'Tis done, the great transaction's done;
I am my Lord's and He is mine;
He drew me, and I follow'd on,
Charm'd to confess the voice divine.

4 Now rest, my long-divided heart,
Fix'd on this blissful centre, rest;
Nor ever from thy Lord depart,
With Him of every good possess'd.

5 High heaven, that heard the solemn vow,
That vow renew'd shall daily hear,
Till in life's latest hour I bow,
And bless in death a bond so dear.

No. 544. Speed Away.

"Go ye into all the world and preach the gospel."—MATT. 16: 15.

F. J. CROSBY. I. B. WOODBURY, arr.

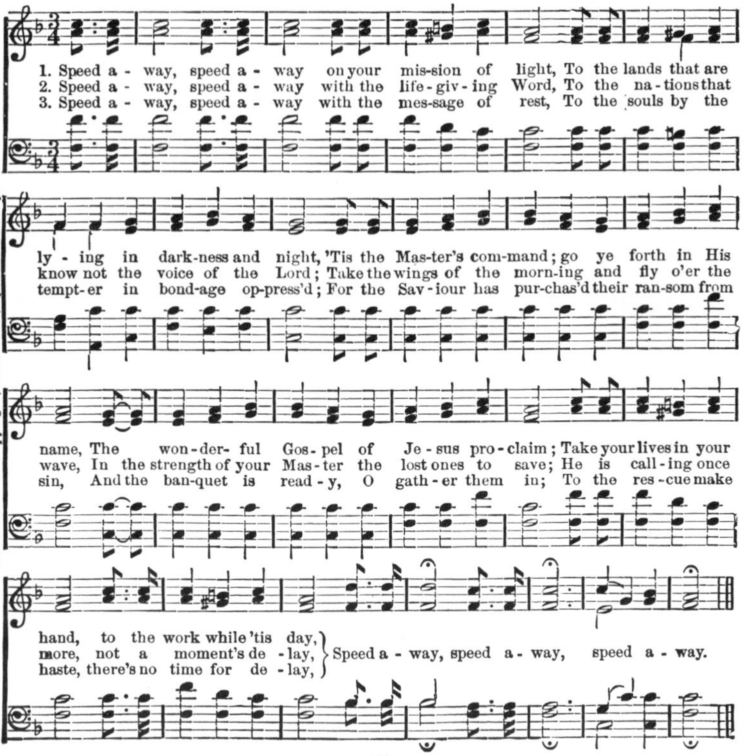

1. Speed a - way, speed a - way on your mis-sion of light, To the lands that are
2. Speed a - way, speed a - way with the life-giv - ing Word, To the na - tions that
3. Speed a - way, speed a - way with the mes-sage of rest, To the souls by the
ly - ing in dark-ness and night, 'Tis the Mas-ter's com-mand; go ye forth in His
know not the voice of the Lord; Take the wings of the morn-ing and fly o'er the
tempt-er in bond-age op-press'd; For the Sav - iour has pur-chas'd their ran-som from
name, The won-der- ful Gos- pel of Je - sus pro - claim; Take your lives in your
wave, In the strength of your Mas - ter the lost ones to save; He is call - ing once
sin, And the ban-quet is read - y, O gath - er them in; To the res - cue make
hand, to the work while 'tis day,
more, not a moment's de - lay,
haste, there's no time for de - lay,
Speed a - way, speed a - way, speed a - way.

No. 545. Hallelujah! Christ is Risen.

"Who according to his abundant mercy hath begotten us again."—1 Pet. 1 : 3.

Bishop Wordsworth, alt. | James McGranahan.

1. Hal - le - lu - jah! Hal - le - lu - jah! Hearts to heav'n and voic - es raise;
2. Christ is ris - en, Christ the first fruits Of the ho - ly har-vest field,
3. Hal - le - lu - jah! Hal - le - lu - jah! Glo - ry be to God a - bove!

Hearts to heav'n and voic - es raise;

Sing to God a hymn of glad-ness, Sing to God a hymn of praise;
Which will all its full a-bund-ance, At His glo-rious ad-vent, yield;
Hal - le - lu - jah to the Sav - iour, Fount of life and source of love;

Sing to God a hymn of praise;

He who on the cross a vic - tim For the world's sal - va - tion bled,
Then the gold - en ears of har - vest Will be - fore His pres - ence wave,
Hal - le - lu - jah to the Spir - it; Let our high as - crip - tions be,

Je - sus Christ the King of glo - ry, Now is ris - en from the dead.
Ris - ing in His sun-shine joy - ous, From the fur - rows of the grave.
Hal - le - lu - jah, now and ev - er, To the bless - ed Trin - i - ty.

No. 546. Cast thy Bread upon the Waters.

"For thou shall find it after many days."—Eccl. 11 : 1.

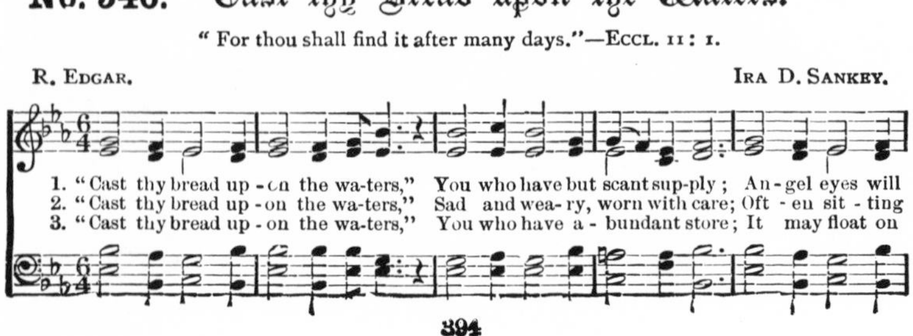
R. Edgar.
Ira D. Sankey.
1. "Cast thy bread up - on the wa-ters," You who have but scant sup-ply; An - gel eyes will
2. "Cast thy bread up - on the wa-ters," Sad and wea - ry, worn with care; Oft - en sit - ting
3. "Cast thy bread up - on the wa-ters," You who have a - bundant store; It may float on

Cast thy Bread upon the Waters.

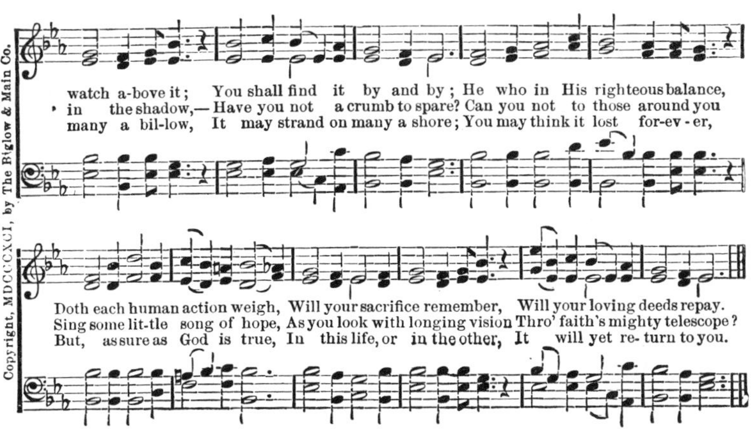

watch a-bove it; You shall find it by and by; He who in His righteous balance,
in the shadow,—Have you not a crumb to spare? Can you not to those around you
many a bil-low, It may strand on many a shore; You may think it lost for-ev - er,
Doth each human action weigh, Will your sacrifice remember, Will your loving deeds repay.
Sing some lit-tle song of hope, As you look with longing vision Thro' faith's mighty telescope?
But, as sure as God is true, In this life, or in the other, It will yet re- turn to you.

No. 547. Come, Come Away.

"All things are ready, come."—MATT. 22: 4.

F. J. CROSBY. GEO. C. STEBBINS.

1. Oh, list to the watch-man cry - ing, Come, come a - way; The
2. The Spir - it of God is plead - ing, Come, come a - way; The
3. The mer - cy of God is call - ing, Come, come a - way; How
4. The an - gels of God en - treat you, Come, come a - way; The
ar - rows of death are fly - ing, Come, come to - day.
Sav - iour is in - ter - ced - ing, Come, come to - day.
sweet-ly the words are fall - ing, Come, come to - day.
Fa - ther Him-self will meet you, Come, come to - day.
CHORUS.
Come, come a - way;
Come, come a - way; Je - sus is gen - tly call - ing, Come, come to - day.

No. 548. Whosoever Calleth.

Julia Sterling. Ira D. Sankey.

1. Oh, hear the joy-ful mes-sage, 'Tis sounding far and wide; Good news of full sal-va-tion, Thro' Him, the Cru-ci-fied; God's Word is truth e-ter-nal; Its prom-ise all may claim, Who look by faith to Je-sus, And call up-on His name.

2. Ye souls that long in dark-ness The path of sin have trod, Be-hold, the light of mer-cy! Be-hold the Lamb of God; With all your heart be-lieve Him, And now the prom-ise claim, That none shall ev-er per-ish, Who call up-on His name.

3. Ye wea-ry, heav-y la-den, Oppressed with toil and care, He waits to bid you wel-come, And all your bur-dens bear; A pre-cious gift He of-fers, A gift that all may claim, Who look to Him be-liev-ing, And call up-on His name.

Chorus.

"Who-so-ev-er call-eth, Who-so-ev-er call-eth, Who-so-ev-er call-eth on His name shall be saved! Who-so-ev-er call-eth, Who-so-ev-er call-eth, Who-so-ev-er call-eth on the Lord shall be saved!"

No. 549. Though your Sins be as Scarlet.

F. J. CROSBY. W. H. DOANE.

DUET. *Gently.*

1. "Tho' your sins be as scar - let, They shall be as white as snow; as snow;
2. Hear the voice that en - treats you, Oh, re - turn ye un - to God! to God!
3. He'll for - give your trans - gressions, And re - mem - ber them no more! no more;

QUARTET.

Tho' they be red........................ like crim - son, They shall be as wool;"
He is of great........................ com - pas - sion, And of won - drous love;
"Look un - to me........................ ye peo - ple," Saith the Lord your God;

Tho' they be red

DUET. *p* QUARTET. *f*

"Tho' your sins be as scar - let, Tho' your sins be as scar - let,
Hear the voice that en - treats you, Hear the voice that en - treats you,
He'll for - give your trans - gres - sions, He'll for - give your trans - gres - sions,

p ritard.

They shall be as white as snow, They shall be as white as snow."
Oh, re - turn ye un - to God! Oh, re - turn ye un - to God!
And re - mem - ber them no more, And re - mem - ber them no more.

No. 550. They that Wait upon the Lord.

G. M. J. JAMES MCGRANAHAN.

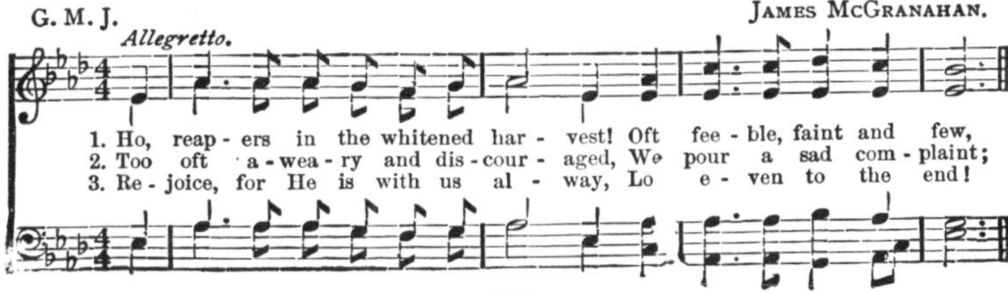
Allegretto.
1. Ho, reap - ers in the whitened har - vest! Oft fee - ble, faint and few,
2. Too oft a - wea - ry and dis - cour - aged, We pour a sad com - plaint;
3. Re - joice, for He is with us al - way, Lo e - ven to the end!

They that Wait upon the Lord.

Come wait up - on the bless-ed Mas - ter, Our strength He will re - new.
Be - liev - ing in a liv-ing Sav - iour, Why should we ev - er faint?
Look up, take cour-age and go for - ward, All need - ed grace He'll send.
CHORUS. ISA. 40: 31.
"For they that wait up-on the Lord........................ shall re - new........... their
that wait up- on the Lord shall re - new,......... shall re-
strength, they shall mount up with wings, they shall mount up with wings as ea-gles;
new their strength, they shall mount........up with wings,
they shall mount up, shall mount up with wings,
rit.
a tempo.
They shall run.......... and not be wea - ry, they shall walk and not faint;
They shall run and not be weary, They shall walk, shall walk and not faint;
They shall run................ and not be wea - - - ry, they shall walk and not
They shall run and not be wea-ry, they shall walk, shall
faint; They shall run and not be wea - ry, shall walk and not faint."
walk and not faint;
Copyright, 1887, by James McGranahan.

No. 551. Neither do I Condemn Thee.
El. Nathan.
James McGranahan.
1. "Neither do I condemn thee,"—O words of wondrous grace; Thy sins were borne up-
2. "Neither do I condemn thee,"—For there is there-fore now No con-dem-na-tion
3. "Neither do I condemn thee,"—I came not to con-demn; I came from God to
4. "Neither do I condemn thee,"—O praise the God of grace; O praise His Son our
on the cross, Be-lieve, and go in peace.
for thee, As at the cross you bow.
save thee, And turn thee from thy sin.
Sav-iour, For this His word of peace.
Chorus.
"Nei-ther do I con-demn thee," O
sing it o'er and o'er; "Neither do I condemn thee, Go and sin no more."
Copyright, 1885, by James McGranahan.
No. 552. Our Saviour King.
"His mercy endureth forever."—Ps. 136: 1.
J. H. Johnston.
James McGranahan.
1. He lives and loves, our Sav-iour King; With joy-ful lips your trib-ute bring;
2. His Hand is strong, His word en-dures, His sac-ri-fice our peace se-cures;
3. Each day re-veals His constant love, With "mercies new" from heav'n a-bove;
Re-peat His praise, ex-alt His name, Whose grace and truth are still the same.
From sin and death He doth re-deem, His changeless love be all our theme.
Thro' a-ges past His word has stood; Oh, taste and see that He is good.
Copyright, MDCCCXCI, by James McGranahan. All rights reserved.

Our Saviour King.

CHORUS.
His mer - cy flows, an end- less stream, To all e - ter - ni - ty the same;
To all e - ter - ni - ty, to all e - ter - ni - ty, To all e - ter - ni - ty the same.

No. 553. His Mercy Flows.

1 O thank the Lord, the Lord of love,
O thank the God all gods above;
O thank the mighty King of kings,
Whose arm hath done such wondrous things.

2 Whose wisdom gave the heav'ns their birth,
And on the waters spread the earth;
Who taught yon glorious lights their way,
The radiant sun to rule the day.

3 The moon and stars to rule the night,
With radiance of a milder light;
Who smote the Egyptians' stubborn pride,
When in His wrath, their first-born died.

4 Who thought on us amidst our woes,
And rescued us from all our foes;
Who daily feeds each living thing;
O thank the heaven's Almighty King.

By permission.

No. 554. Morning Lights.

(Metrical Version.)

PSALM 143. WILL H. YOUNG.

1. When morn - ing lights the east - ern skies, Thy mer - cy, Lord, dis - close;
2. Teach me the way where I should go; I lift my soul to Thee;
3. Be - cause Thou art my God, I pray, Teach me to do Thy will;
4. Re - vive me, Lord, for Thy great name, And, for Thy judgment's sake,
And let Thy lov - ing kind - ness rise; On Thee my hopes re - pose.
Re - deem me from the rag - ing foe; To Thee, O Lord, I flee.
O lead me in the per - fect way By Thy good Spir - it still.
From all my woes; O Lord, re - claim, My soul from troub - le take.
REFRAIN.
On Thee............ my hopes re - pose, On Thee............ my hopes re - pose;
On Thee, on Thee my On Thee, on Thee

Used by per. of the United Board of Pres. Publication.

Morning Lights.
And let Thy lov - ing kind - ness rise; On Thee my hopes re - pose.
No. 555. Bless the Lord.
Psalm 103.
(Metrical Version.)
James McGranahan.
Not too slow.
1. O thou my soul, bless God the Lord, And all that in me is;
2. Bless, O my soul, the Lord thy God, And not for - get - ful be
3. All thy in - iq - ui - ties who doth Most gra - cious - ly for - give;
4. Who doth re - deem thy life, that thou To death may'st not go down;
Be lift - ed up His ho - ly name, To mag - ni - fy and bless.
Of all His gra - cious ben - e - fits He hath be - stowed on thee.
Who thy dis - eas - es all and pains Doth heal, and thee re - lieve.
Who thee with lov - ing - kind - ness doth And ten - der mer - cies crown.
Copyright, MDCCCXC, by James McGranahan.
Chorus.
"Bless the Lord, Bless the Lord, Bless the Lord, O my soul,
Bless the Lord, Bless the Lord,
And all that is with - in me, Bless His ho - - - ly name."
Bless His ho - ly

No. 556. I'll Thee Exalt.

1 I'll Thee exalt, my God, O King,
Thy name I will adore;
I'll bless Thee every day, and praise
Thy name forevermore.

2 The Lord is great, much to be praised,
His greatness search exceeds;
Race unto race shall praise Thy works,
And show Thy mighty deeds.

By permission.

3 I of Thy glorious majesty
The honor will record;
I'll speak of all Thy mighty works,
Which wondrous are, O Lord.

4 Men, of Thine acts the might shall show,
Thine acts that dreadful are;
And I, Thy glory to advance,
Thy greatness will declare.

No. 557.
I Cried to God.
Psalm 77.
(Metrical Version.)
W. S. Marshall.
1. I cried to God, I cried, He heard; In day of grief I sought the Lord;
2. I thought of God, and was distressed; Complained, yet trouble round me pressed;
3. The days of old I called to mind, The ancient years when God was kind;
4. Will God cast off for ev - er-more? His fa - vor will He ne'er re - store?
All night with hands stretch'd out I wept, My soul no com - fort would ac - cept.
Thou hold - est, Lord, my eyes a-wake; So great my grief I can - not speak.
I called to mind my song by night; My mus - ing spir - it sought for light.
Has grace for ev - er passed a - way? Or, doth His prom - ise fail for aye?
Used by permission.
Chorus.
Hath God for - got - ten to be kind? His ten - der love in wrath confined?
My weakness this, yet faith doth stand Re - call - ing years of God's right hand.
No. 558.
Whiter than Snow.
Psalm 51.
(Metrical Version.)
J. B. Herbert.
1. In Thy great lov - ing kind - ness, Lord, Be mer - ci - ful to me;
2. O wash me thor - ough - ly from sin; From all my guilt me cleanse;
3. 'Gainst Thee, Thee on - ly have I sinned, Done e - vil in Thy sight,
4. Be - hold, I in in - iq - ui - ty My be - ing first re - ceived;
In Thy com - pass - ions great blot out All my in - iq - ui - ty.
For my trans - gres - sions I con - fess; I ev - er see my sins.
That when Thou speak'st Thou may'st be just, And in Thy judg - ing right.
And with a na - ture all cor - rupt My moth - er me con - ceived.
Copyright, MDCCCXC, by United Pres. Board of Publication.

Whiter than Snow.
Chorus.
Wash............... Thou me, yes, wash............... Thou me, And
Wash Thou me, yea, wash Thou me, Wash Thou me, yea, wash Thou me,
then I shall be whit-er than the snow,.......... I shall be whit-er than the snow.
snow, the snow,
No. 559. Thee will I Love.
Psalm 18.
(Metrical Version.)
James McGranahan.
Allegretto.
1. Thee will I love, O Lord, my strength, My fort - ress is the Lord;
2. The Lord is wor - thy to be prais'd, Up - on His name I'll call;
3. In my dis - tress I call'd on God, Cry to my God did I;
4. I there-fore will to Thee, O Lord, In songs my thanks pro - claim;
My rock, and He that doth to me De - liv - er - ance af - ford.
And He from all my en - e - mies Pre - serve me safe - ly shall.
He from His tem - ple heard my voice, To His ears came my cry.
And I a - mong the hea - then will Sing prais - es to Thy name.
Copyright, MDCCCXC, by James McGranahan.
Chorus.
My God whom I will trust, A buck-ler un - to me,........
My God, my strength,
cres.
The horn of my sal - va - tion, too, And my high tow'r is He.

No. 560. As Pants the Hart.
Psalm 42.
(Metrical Version.)
James McGranahan.
1. Far from Thy sa - cred courts my tears Have been my food by night and day,
2. These things I'll call to mind, and cry, When I shall tread the sa - cred way
3. O why art thou cast down, my soul? And what should so dis - qui - et thee?
While con-stant - ly, with bit - ter sneers, "Where is thy God?" the scof - fers say.
To Zi - on, prais - ing God on high, With throngs who keep the ho - ly day.
Still hope in God, and Him ex - tol, Whose face brings saving health to me.
Chorus.
rit.
As pants the hart for wa-ter brooks, So pants my soul, O God, for
As pants the hart for wa-ter brooks, So pants my soul, O
a tempo.
Thee: For Thee it thirsts, to Thee it looks, And longs the liv-ing God to see.
God, for Thee:
Copyright, MDCCCLXXXIX, by James McGranahan. All rights reserved.
No. 561. For Jehovah I am Waiting.
Psalm 130.
(Metrical Version.)
Wilbur A. Christy.
1. From the depths do I in - voke Thee, O Je - ho - vah, give an ear;
2. Lord, if Thou shouldst mark transgressions, Who be - fore Thee, Lord, shall stand?
3. Is - rael, hope thou in Je - ho - vah, Mer-cies great are found with Him;
To my voice be Thou at - ten - tive, And my sup - pli - ca - tions hear.
But with Thee there is for - give - ness, That Thy name may fear com - mand.
He, a - bound - ing in re - demp - tion, Is - rael will from sin re - deem.
Copyright, MDCCCXCI, by James McGranahan. All rights reserved.

For Jehovah I am Waiting.
Chorus.
I am wait-ing,... I am wait-ing,.......... And my hope is in His word;
For Je-ho-vah I am wait-ing, wait-ing, My hope is in His word;
I am wait-ing,...... ev-er wait-ing,............ Yea, my soul waits for the Lord........
In His word of prom-ise, my hope is in His word, Yea, my soul.......... waits for the Lord.
No. 562. O Praise Him.
Psalm 150. (Metrical Version.) James McGranahan.
Allegretto.
1. O praise our Lord, where rich in grace His pres-ence fills His ho - ly place;
2. O praise Him for His deeds of fame, O praise the great-ness of His name;
3. O praise Him with the notes of joy, And ev - 'ry harp in praise em-ploy;
Praise Him in yon ce - les- tial arch, Where holds His pow'r its glorious march, Where holds His pow'r its glo - rious march.
O praise Him with the trumpet's sound, With harp and psaltery answering round, With harp and psal - tery answering round.
On cym-bals loud, Je- hovah praise, On cymbals high His glo - ry raise, On cym - bals high His glo - ry raise.
Copyright, MCCCDXC, by James McGranahan.
Chorus.
O praise Him, O praise Him for all His deeds of fame; O praise Him, O praise Him, O praise His might-y name; Let all that
Let all

O Praise Him.
Lift up their voice,
breathe with glad accord, Lift up their voice, their voice, and praise, and praise the Lord.
that breathe
No. 563.
Remember Me.
Psalm 25.
(Metrical Version.)
C. E. Pollock.
Chorus.
1. To Thee I lift my soul, O Lord; My God, I trust in Thee;
O let me nev - er be a-shamed, Nor foes ex - ult o'er me.
2. O Lord, let none be put to shame, Up-on Thee who at-tend;
But make all those to be a-shamed, Who causeless-ly of-fend.
3. Thy ways, Lord, show; teach me Thy paths; Lead me in truth, teach me;
For of my safe - ty Thou art God; All day I wait on Thee.
4. Let not the er - rors of my youth, Nor sins re-mem-bered be;
In mer - cy, for Thy good-ness' sake, O Lord, re - mem - ber me.
Re-mem-ber me, re-
member me, O Lord, re-member me; In mer-cy for Thy goodness' sake, O Lord, remember me.
Used by permission of Pres. Board of Publication.
No. 564.
Follow On!
W. O. Cushing.
Robert Lowry.
1. Down in the val - ley, with my Sav - iour I would go, Where the flow'rs are
2. Down in the val - ley, with my Sav - iour I would go, Where the storms are
3. Down in the val - ley, or up - on the mount-ain steep, Close be - side my
bloom - ing and the sweet wa - ters flow; Ev - 'ry-where He leads me I would
sweep - ing and the dark wa - ters flow; With His hand to lead me I will
Sav - iour would my soul ev - er keep; He will lead me safe - ly, in the
Copyright, 1880, by Biglow & Main.

Follow On!

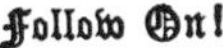

fol - low, fol - low on, Walk-ing in His foot-steps till the crown be won.
nev - er, nev - er fear, Dan-gers can-not fright me if my Lord is near.
path that He has trod, Up to where they gath-er on the hills of God.
REFRAIN.
Fol - low! fol - low! I would follow Je - sus! Anywhere, ev'rywhere, I would follow on!
Fol - low! fol - low! I would follow Je - sus! Ev'rywhere, He leads me I would follow on!

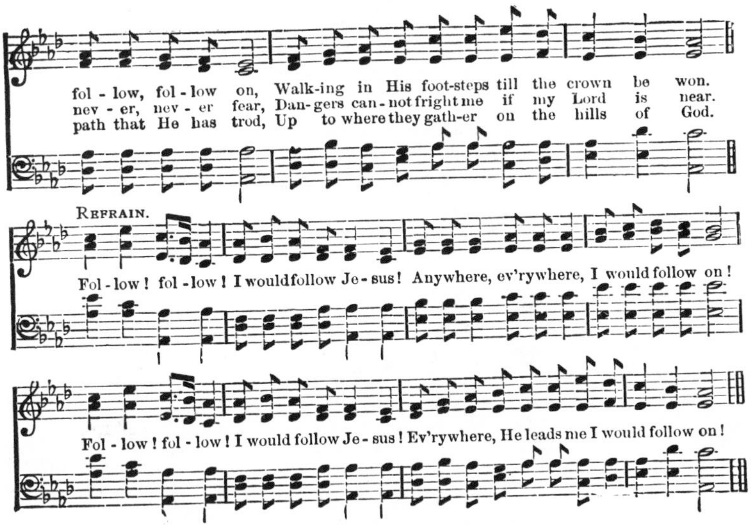

No. 565. Jesus Knows thy Sorrow.

W. O. Cushing. Ira D. Sankey.

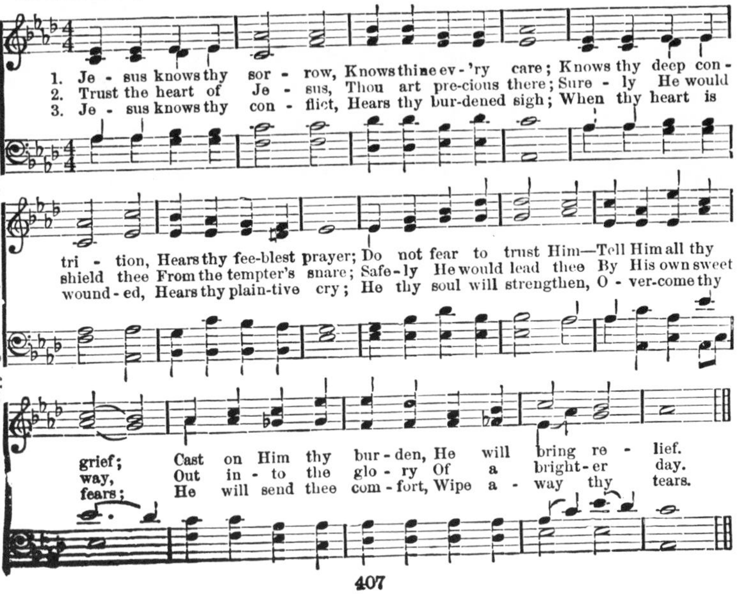

1. Je - sus knows thy sor - row, Knows thine ev - 'ry care; Knows thy deep con - tri - tion, Hears thy fee-blest prayer; Do not fear to trust Him—Tell Him all thy grief; Cast on Him thy bur-den, He will bring re - lief.
2. Trust the heart of Je - sus, Thou art pre-cious there; Sure - ly He would shield thee From the tempter's snare; Safe-ly He would lead thee By His own sweet way, Out in - to the glo - ry Of a bright-er day.
3. Je - sus knows thy con - flict, Hears thy bur-dened sigh; When thy heart is wound - ed, Hears thy plain-tive cry; He thy soul will strengthen, O - ver-come thy fears; He will send thee com - fort, Wipe a - way thy tears.

No. 566.
Gather Them In.
F. J. Van Alstyne.
Geo. C. Stebbins.
1. Gath-er them in! for yet there is room At the feast that the King has spread;
2. Gath-er them in! for yet there is room; But our hearts—how they throb with pain,
3. Gath-er them in! for yet there is room; 'Tis a mes-sage from God a-bove;
Oh, gath-er them in!—let His house be filled, And the hun-gry and poor be fed.
To think of the ma-ny who slight the call That may nev-er be heard a-gain!
Oh, gath-er them in-to the fold of grace, And the arms of the Saviour's love!
Copyright, 1883, by Geo. C. Stebbins.
Refrain.
Out in the high-way, out in the by-way, Out in the dark paths of sin,
Go forth, go forth, with a lov-ing heart, And gath-er the wand'rers in!
No. 567.
We're Marching to Zion.
Isaac Watts.
Rev. R. Lowry.
Spirited.
1. Come, ye that love the Lord, And let your joys be known, Join in a song with
2. Let those re-fuse to sing Who nev-er knew our God; But children of the
3. The hill of Zi-on yields A thousand sa-cred sweets, Be-fore we reach the
4. Then let our songs a-bound, And ev-'ry tear be dry; We're marching thro' Im-
sweet ac-cord, Join in a song with sweet accord, And thus sur-round the throne, And
heav'n-ly King, But children of the heav'nly King, May speak their joys a-broad, May
heav'n-ly fields, Be-fore we reach the heav'nly field, Or walk the gold-en streets, Or
manuel's ground, We're marching thro' Immanuel's ground, To fair-er world's on high, To
Copyright, 1867, by Rev. R. Lowry.

thus surround the throne, And thus sur-

We're Marching to Zion.
CHORUS.
thus surround the throne.
speak their joys a - broad.
walk the gold - en streets.
fair - er worlds on high.
We're march - ing to Zi - on, Beau - ti-ful, beau-ti - ful
round the throne. We're marching on to Zi - on,
Zi - on; We're marching upward to Zi - on, The beau - ti-ful cit - y of God.
Zi - on, Zi-on,
No. 568. Have you any Room for Jesus?
Arr. by W. W. D. from L. W. M.
C. C. WILLIAMS.
1. Have you a - ny room for Je - sus, He who bore your load of sin;
2. Room for pleas-ure, room for business, But for Christ the cru - ci - fied;
3. Have you a - ny room for Je - sus, As in grace He calls a - gain?
4. Room and time now give to Je - sus, Soon will pass God's day of grace;
As He knocks and asks ad - mis - sion, Sin - ner will you let Him in?
Not a place that He can en - ter, In the heart for which He died?
O to - day is time ac - cept - ed, To - mor - row you may call in vain.
Soon thy heart left cold and si - lent, And thy Saviour's plead-ing cease.
Copyright, 1878, by James McGranahan.
CHORUS.
Room for Je - sus, King of glo - ry! Has - ten now His word o - bey!
Swing the heart's door wide - ly o - pen, Bid Him en - ter while you may.

No. 569.

Almost Persuaded.

P. P. Bliss. P. P. Bliss.

1. "Al- most per - suad - ed," Now to be - lieve; "Al- most per - suad - ed,"
2. "Al - most per - suad - ed," Come, come to - day; "Al- most per - suad - ed,"
3. "Al - most per - suad - ed," Har- vest is past! "Al - most per - suad - ed,"
Christ to re - ceive; Seems now some soul to say, "Go, Spir - it,
Turn not a - way; Je - sus in - vites you here, An - gels are
Doom comes at last! "Al - most" can not a - vail; "Al - most" is
go Thy way, Some more con - ven - ient day On Thee I'll call."
linger- ing near, Pray'rs rise from hearts so dear: O wan - d'rer come.
but to fail! Sad, sad, that bit - ter wail— "Al - most—but lost!"

No. 570. The Ninety and Nine.

To be sung only as a Solo.

E. C. Clephane. Ira D. Sankey.

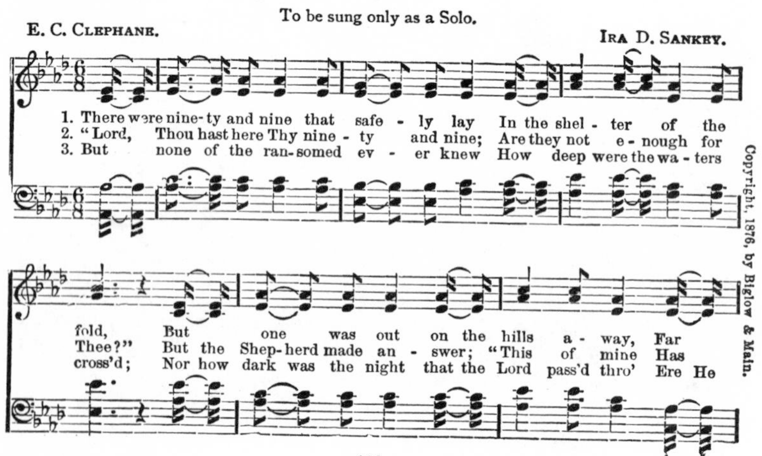

1. There were nine- ty and nine that safe - ly lay In the shel - ter of the
2. "Lord, Thou hast here Thy nine - ty and nine; Are they not e - nough for
3. But none of the ran- somed ev - er knew How deep were the wa - ters
fold, But one was out on the hills a - way, Far
Thee?" But the Shep- herd made an - swer; "This of mine Has
cross'd; Nor how dark was the night that the Lord pass'd thro' Ere He

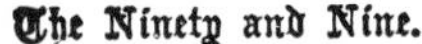
The Ninety and Nine.

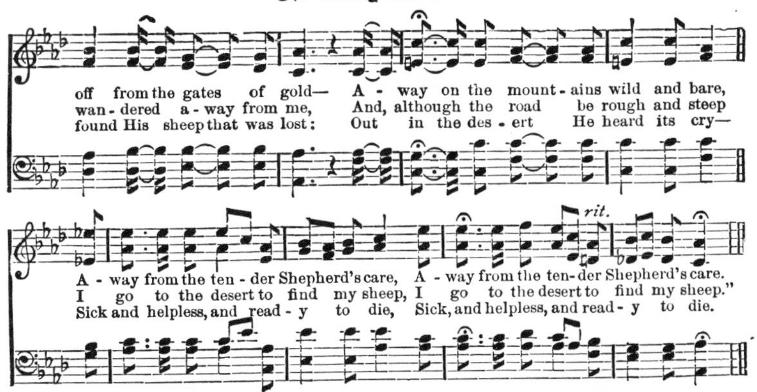
off from the gates of gold— A - way on the mount - ains wild and bare,
wan - dered a - way from me, And, although the road be rough and steep
found His sheep that was lost: Out in the des - ert He heard its cry—
A - way from the ten - der Shepherd's care, A - way from the ten - der Shepherd's care.
I go to the desert to find my sheep, I go to the desert to find my sheep."
Sick and helpless, and read - y to die, Sick, and helpless, and read - y to die.
rit.

4 "Lord, whence are those blood-drops all the way
That mark out the mountain's track?"
"They were shed for one who had gone astray
Ere the Shepherd could bring him back:"
"Lord, whence are Thy hands so rent and torn?"
"They are pierced to-night by many a thorn."

5 But all thro' the mountains, thunder-riven,
And up from the rocky steep,
There arose a glad cry to the gate of heaven,
"Rejoice! I have found my sheep!"
And the Angels echoed around the throne,
"Rejoice! for the Lord brings back His own!"

No. 571. Revive Thy Work.

Albert Midlane. James McGranahan.

1. Re - vive Thy work, O Lord! Thy mighty arm make bare; Speak with the voice that wakes the dead, And make Thy peo - ple hear.
2. Re - vive Thy work, O Lord! Dis - turb this sleep of death; Quick - en the smould'ring em - bers now By Thine Almight - y breath.
3. Re - vive Thy work, O Lord! Cre - ate soul-thirst for Thee; But hung'ring for the bread of life, Oh, may our spir - its be!
4. Re - vive Thy work, O Lord! Ex - alt Thy precious name; And, by the Ho - ly Ghost, our love For Thee and Thine in - flame.

Chorus.

Re - vive!........ re - vive!......... And give re - freshing showers; The glo - ry shall be all Thine own; The blessing shall be ours.

Re - vive Thy work! re - vive Thy work! And give, oh, give, refreshing showers;

No. 572. I am Thine, O Lord.

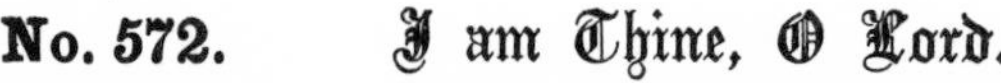

F. J. Crosby. W. H. Doane.

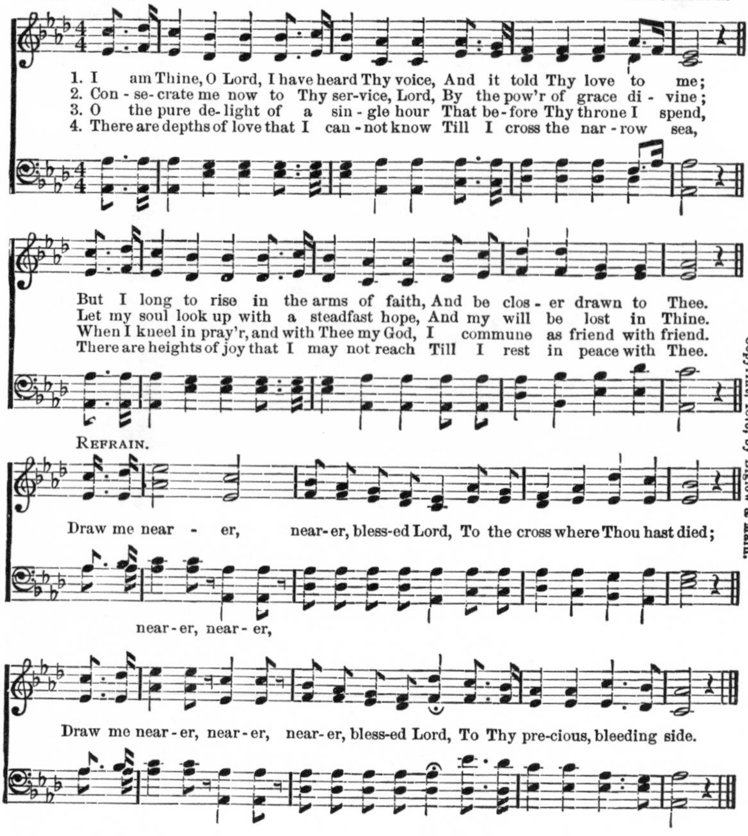

1. I am Thine, O Lord, I have heard Thy voice, And it told Thy love to me;
2. Con - se- crate me now to Thy ser-vice, Lord, By the pow'r of grace di - vine;
3. O the pure de- light of a sin - gle hour That be-fore Thy throne I spend,
4. There are depths of love that I can - not know Till I cross the nar - row sea,
But I long to rise in the arms of faith, And be clos - er drawn to Thee.
Let my soul look up with a steadfast hope, And my will be lost in Thine.
When I kneel in pray'r, and with Thee my God, I commune as friend with friend.
There are heights of joy that I may not reach Till I rest in peace with Thee.
Refrain.
Draw me near - er, near-er, bless-ed Lord, To the cross where Thou hast died;
near-er, near-er,
Draw me near-er, near-er, near-er, bless-ed Lord, To Thy pre-cious, bleeding side.

No. 573. It is Well with My Soul.

H. G. Stafford. P. P. Bliss.

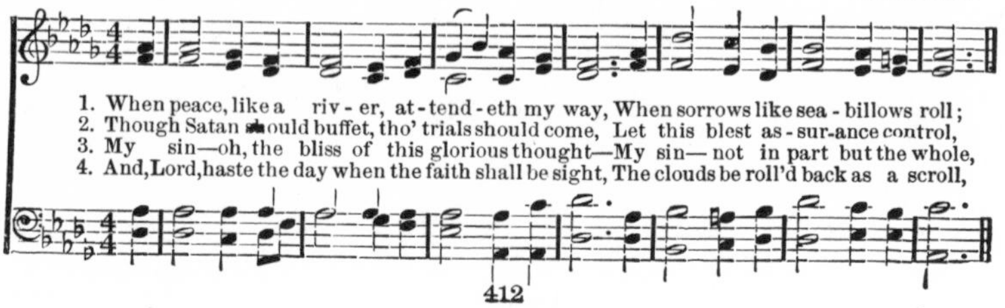

1. When peace, like a riv - er, at - tend - eth my way, When sorrows like sea - billows roll;
2. Though Satan should buffet, tho' trials should come, Let this blest as - sur-ance control,
3. My sin—oh, the bliss of this glorious thought—My sin— not in part but the whole,
4. And, Lord, haste the day when the faith shall be sight, The clouds be roll'd back as a scroll,

It is Well with My Soul.
What-ev-er my lot, Thou hast taught me to say, It is well, it is well with my soul.
That Christ hath regard-ed my help-less es-tate, And hath shed His own blood for my soul.
Is nailed to His cross and I bear it no more, Praise the Lord, praise the Lord, oh, my soul!
The trump shall resound, and the Lord shall de-scend, "Even so"—it is well with my soul.
Copyright, 1876, by The John Church Co.
CHORUS.
It is well............ with my soul,............
It is well with my soul, It is well, it is well with my soul.
No. 574.
Hiding in Thee.
WILLIAM O. CUSHING.
IRA D. SANKEY.
1. O safe to the Rock that is high-er than I, My soul in its con-flicts and sor-rows would fly; So sin-ful, so wea-ry, Thine, Thine would I be; Thou blest "Rock of A-ges," I'm hid-ing in Thee.
2. In the calm of the noon-tide, in sor-row's lone hour, In times when temp-ta-tion casts o'er me its pow'r; In the tem-pests of life, on its wide, heav-ing sea, Thou blest "Rock of A-ges," I'm hid-ing in Thee.
3. How oft in the con-flict, when press'd by the foe, I have fled to my Ref-uge and breathed out my woe; How oft-en when tri-als, like sea-bil-lows roll, Have I hid-den in Thee, O Thou Rock of my soul.
Copyright, 1877, by Biglow & Main.
CHORUS.
Hid-ing in Thee, Hid-ing in Thee, Thou blest "Rock of A-ges," I'm hid-ing in Thee.

No. 575. Oh, Where are the Reapers.

EBEN E. REXFORD. GEO. F. ROOT.

1. Oh, where are the reap-ers that gar-ner in The sheaves of the good from the fields of sin;
2. Go out in the by-ways and search them all; The wheat may be there, tho' the weeds are tall;
3. The fields all are ripening, and far and wide The world now is waiting the har-vest tide:
4. So come with your sickles, ye sons of men, And gather togeth - er the gold-en grain;
With sick-les of truth must the work be done, And no one may rest till the "harvest home."
Then search in the highway, and pass none by, But gath-er from all for the home on high.
But reap-ers are few, and the work is great, And much will be lost should the harvest wait.
Toil on till the Lord of the har-vest come, Then share ye His joy in the "harvest home."
CHORUS.
Where are the reapers! Oh, who will come And share in the glo-ry of the "harvest home?"
Oh, who will help us to gar-ner in The sheaves of good from the fields of sin.
By permission J. Church & Co., owners of Copyright.
No. 576. To the Work.
F. J. CROSBY. W. H. DOANE.
1. To the work! to the work! we are ser - vants of God, Let us
2. To the work! to the work! let the hun - gry be fed; To the
3. To the work! to the work! there is la - bor for all, For the
4. To the work! to the work! in the strength of the Lord, And a

fol - low the path that our Mas - ter has trod; With the balm of His coun - sel our
fount-ain of Life let the wea - ry be led; In the cross and its ban - ner our
king-dom of dark- ness and er - ror shall fall; And the name of Je - ho - vah ex -
robe and a crown shall our la - bor re-ward; When the home of the faith - ful our

strength to re - new, Let us do with our might what our hands find to do.
glo - ry shall be, While we her - ald the tid - ings, "*Sal - va - tion is free!*
alt - ed shall be In the loud swell-ing cho - rus, "*Sal - va - tion is free!*
dwell - ing shall be, And we shout with the ransom'd, "*Sal - va - tion is free!*

CHORUS.

Toil - ing on, Toil - ing on, Toil - ing on, Toil - ing
Toil - ing on, Toil - ing on, Toil - ing on,

on, Let us hope, Let us watch, And la - bor till the Mas - ter comes.
Toiling on, and trust, and pray,

No. 577. My Redeemer.

P. P. BLISS. JAMES MCGRANAHAN.

1. I will sing of my Re - deem - er And His won - drous love to me;
2. I will tell the wondrous sto - ry, How my lost es - tate to save,
3. I will praise my dear Re - deem - er, His tri - umph - ant pow'r I'll tell,
4. I will sing of my Re - deem - er, And His heav'n - ly love to me;

On the cru - el cross He suf - fered, From the curse to set me free.
In His boundless love and mer - cy, He the ran - som free ly gave.
How the vic - to - ry He giv - eth O - ver sin, and death, and hell.
He from death to life hath brought me, Son of God, with Him to be.

My Redeemer.
Chorus.
Sing, oh! sing,.......................... of my Re-deem - er, With His
Sing, oh! sing of my Re-deem-er, Sing, oh! sing of my Re-deem-er, With His
blood.........................
blood He pur-chased me, He pur-chased me,.................................. On the
blood............................ He pur-chased me,
blood He pur-chased me, With His blood He pur-chased me; On the
cross............................ He sealed my par - don, Paid the
cross, He sealed my par-don, On the cross He sealed my par-don, Paid the
Repeat pp after last verse.
debt, and made me free, And made me free, and made me free.
debt, and made me free,
Used by per. The John Church Co., owners of the Copyright.
No. 578. While the Days are going By.
George Cooper.
Ira D. Sankey.
1. There are lone-ly hearts to cher-ish, While the days are go-ing by;
There are wea-ry souls who per-ish, While the days are go-ing by;
2. There's no time for i-dle scorn-ing, While the days are go-ing by;
Let your face be like the morn-ing, While the days are go-ing by;
3. All the lov-ing links that bind us, While the days are go-ing by;
One by one we leave be-hind us, While the days are go-ing by;
If a smile we can re-new, As our jour-ney we pur-sue, Oh, the
Oh, the world is full of sighs, Full of sad and weep-ing eyes; Help your
But the seeds of good we sow, Both in shade and shine will grow, And will
Copyright, 1881, by Ira D. Sankey.

While the Days are going By.

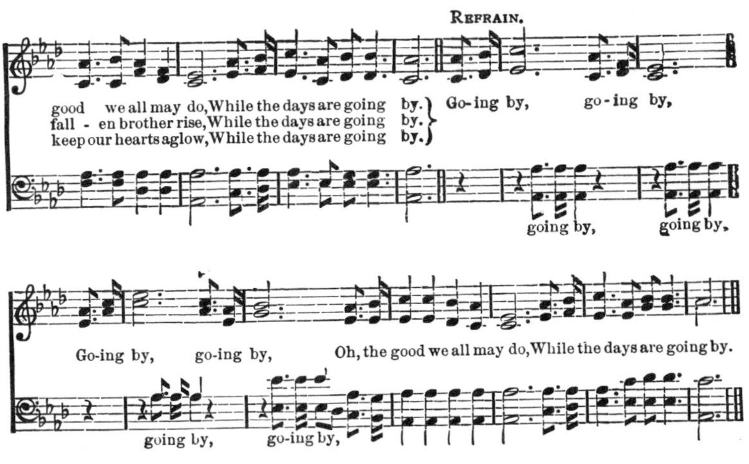
Refrain.
good we all may do, While the days are going by.
fall - en brother rise, While the days are going by.
keep our hearts aglow, While the days are going by.
Go-ing by, go-ing by,
going by, going by,
Go-ing by, go-ing by, Oh, the good we all may do, While the days are going by.
going by, go-ing by,

No. 579. Wonderful Words of Life.

P. P. B.
P. P. Bliss.
1. Sing them o - ver a - gain to me, Won-derful words of Life, Let me more of their
2. Christ, the blessed One gives to all, Won-derful words of Life, Sin - ner, list to the
3. Sweet- ly ech - o the gos - pel call, Won-derful words of Life, Of - fer pardon and
beau - ty see, Wonderful words of Life. Words of life and beauty, Teach me faith and du-ty;
lov - ing call, Wonderful words of Life. All so free-ly giv-en, Woo-ing us to heav-en.
peace to all, Wonderful words of Life. Je - sus, on - ly Saviour, Sanc - ti - fy for - ev - er.
Beau - ti - ful words, won - der - ful words, Wonder - ful words of Life, Life.

No. 580. Behold, what Love!

M. S. S.

JAMES MCGRANAHAN.

1. Be - hold, what love, what boundless love, The Fa - ther hath be - stowed On sin-ners lost, that we should be Now called the sons of God!
2. No long - er far from Him, but now By "precious blood" made nigh; Ac - cept - ed in the "Well-beloved," Near to God's heart we lie.
3. What we in glo - ry soon shall be, It doth not yet ap - pear; But when our pre - cious Lord we see, We shall His im - age bear.
4. With such a bless - ed hope in view, We would more ho - ly be, More like our ris - en, glo-rious Lord, Whose face we soon shall see.
CHORUS.
Be - hold, what manner of love!..................What manner of love the Fa - ther hath bestowed up - on us,
What manner of love,
That we,......that we should be call'd,.................. Should be call'd the sons of God.
the sons of God,
Copyright, 1879, by James McGranahan.

No. 581. Trusting Jesus, That is All.

E. P. STITES.

IRA D. SANKEY.

1. Simp - ly trust - ing ev - 'ry day, Trust-ing thro' a storm-y way; E - ven when my
2. Bright-ly doth His Spir - it shine In - to this poor heart of mine; While He leads I
3. Sing - ing, if my way is clear; Pray-ing, if the path is drear; If in dan-ger,
4. Trust - ing Him while life shall last, Trusting Him till earth is past; Till with-in the

Trusting Jesus, That is All.

CHORUS.
faith is small, Trusting Je - sus, that is all.
can - not fall, Trusting Je - sus, that is all.
for Him call, Trusting Je - sus, that is all.
jas - per wall, Trusting Je - sus, that is all.
Trust-ing as the mo-ments fly,
Trust-ing as the days go by; Trusting Him whate'er befall, Trusting Je-sus, that is all.
Copyright, 1876, by Biglow & Main.
No. 582. Yield Not to Temptation.
H. R. PALMER.
H. R. PALMER.
1. Yield not to temp-ta - tion, For yield-ing is sin, Each vic-t'ry will help you
2. Shun e - vil com-pan - ions, Bad language dis - dain, God's name hold in rev-'rence,
3. To him that o'er-com - eth God giv - eth a crown, Thro' faith we shall con-quer,
Some oth - er to win; Fight man-ful - ly on - ward, Dark passions sub - due,
Nor take it in vain; Be thoughtful and earn - est, Kind-hearted and true,
Though oft - en cast down; He who is our Sav - iour, Our strength will re-new,
Look ev - er to Je - sus, He'll car-ry you through.
CHORUS.
Ask the Saviour to help you,
Comfort, strengthen, and keep you; He is will-ing to aid you, He will car-ry you through.
Copyright, 1868, by H. R. Palmer.

No. 583. What a Friend We have in Jesus.

JOSEPH SCRIVEN. Alt.
CHARLES C. CONVERSE.
1. What a friend we have in Je - sus, All our sins and griefs to bear; What a priv-i-lege to carry Ev-'ry thing to God in prayer. Oh, what peace we oft - en for - feit, Oh, what needless pain we bear—All because we do not car - ry Ev'ry thing to God in prayer.
2. Have we tri-als and tempta- tions? Is there trouble an - y-where? We should never be dis - cour - aged, Take it to the Lord in prayer. Can we find a Friend so faith - ful, Who will all our sorrows share? Jesus knows our ev'ry weakness, Take it to the Lord in prayer.
3. Are we weak and heavy - la - den, Cumbered with a load of care? Pre-cious Saviour, still our Ref - uge,—Take it to the Lord in prayer. Do thy friends de-spise, for - sake thee? Take it to the Lord in prayer; In His arms He'll take and shield thee, Thou wilt find a solace there.
Used by per.
No. 584. I've Found a Friend.
Rev. J. G. SMALL.
GEO. C. STEBBINS.
1. I've found a Friend; oh, such a Friend! He loved me ere I knew Him; He drew me with the cords of love, And thus He bound me to Him. And 'round my heart still closely twine Those
2. I've found a Friend; oh, such a Friend! He bled, He died to save me; And not a-lone the gift of life, But His own self He gave me. Nought that I have my own I call, I
3. I've found a Friend; oh, such a Friend! All power to Him is giv - en; To guard me on my onward course, And bring me safe to heav - en. Th' e - ter - nal glo-ries gleam a - far, To
4. I've found a Friend; oh, such a Friend! So kind, and true, and ten-der, So wise a Coun-sel - lor and Guide, So might - y a De-fend - er! From Him, who loves me now so well, What
Used by per. The John Church Co., owners of the Copyright.

I've Found a Friend.

ties which naught can sever, For I am His, and He is mine, For-ev - er and for-ev-er.
hold it for the Giv - er; My heart, my strength, my life, my all, Are His, and His for-ev-er.
nerve my faint endeav - or: So now to watch, to work, to war, And then to rest for-ev-er.
power my soul can sev - er? Shall life or death, or earth or hell? No; I am His for-ev-er.
No. 585. Pass Me Not.
Fanny J. Crosby.
W. H. Doane.
1. Pass me not, O gen - tle Sav - iour, Hear my hum - ble cry;
2. Let me at a throne of mer - cy Find a sweet re - lief;
3. Trust - ing on - ly in Thy mer - it, Would I seek Thy face;
4. Thou the Spring of all my com - fort More than life to me,
While on oth - ers Thou art smil - ing, Do not pass me by.
Kneel - ing there in deep con - tri - tion, Help my un - be - lief:
Heal my wounded, broken spir - it, Save me by Thy grace.
Whom have I on earth be - side Thee? Whom in heav'n but Thee?
Chorus.
Sav - iour, Sav - iour, hear my hum - ble cry, While on others Thou art call - ing, Do not pass me by.
Copyright, 1870, by W. H. Doane.
No. 586. My Jesus, I Love Thee.
A. J. Gordon.
Used by per.
1. My Je - sus, I love Thee, I know Thou art mine,
2. I love Thee, be - cause Thou hast first lov - ed me,
3. I will love Thee in life, I will love Thee in death,
4. In man - sions of glo - ry and end - less de - light,

My Jesus, I Love Thee.

For Thee all the fol - lies of sin I re - sign; My gra-cious Re - deem - er, my
And pur-chased my par - don on Cal - va-ry's tree; I love Thee for wear - ing the
And praise Thee as long as Thou lend-est me breath; And say when the death-dew lies
I'll ev - er a - dore Thee in heav-en so bright; I'll sing with the glit - ter - ing
Sav - iour art Thou, If ev - er I loved Thee, my Je - sus, 'tis now.
thorns on Thy brow; If ev - er I loved Thee, my Je - sus, 'tis now.
cold on my brow, If ev - er I loved Thee, my Je - sus, 'tis now.
crown on my brow, If ev - er I loved Thee, my Je - sus, 'tis now.
No. 587. Only Trust Him.
J. H. S.
J. H. Stockton.
1. Come, ev - 'ry soul by sin oppressed, There's mercy with the Lord, And He will sure-ly
2. For Je - sus shed His precious blood Rich blessings to be - stow; Plunge now in - to the
3. Yes, Je - sus is the Truth, the Way, That leads you in - to rest; Be - lieve in Him with-
4. Come then, and join this ho - ly band, And on to glo - ry go, To dwell in that ce -
give you rest, By trust-ing in His word.
crim - son flood That wash - es white as snow.
out de - lay, And you are ful - ly blest.
les - tial land, Where joys im - mor - tal flow.
Chorus.
On - ly trust Him, on - ly trust Him,
On-ly trust Him now; He will save you, He will save you, He will save you now.
Used by per.

No. 588. All to Christ I Owe.

Elvina M. Hall. John T. Grape.

1. I hear the Sav-iour say, Thy strength in-deed is small;
2. Lord, now in-deed I find Thy pow'r, and Thine a-lone,
3. For noth-ing good have I Where-by Thy grace to claim—
4. When from my dy-ing bed My ran-somed soul shall rise,
5. And when be-fore the throne I stand in Him com-plete,
Child of weak-ness, watch and pray, Find in Me thine all in all.
Can change the lep-er's spots, And melt the heart of stone.
I'll wash my gar-ments white In the blood of Calvary's Lamb.
Then "Je-sus paid it all" Shall rend the vault-ed skies.
I'll lay my tro-phies down, All down at Je-sus' feet.
Used by per.
Chorus.
Je-sus, paid it all, All to Him I owe;
Sin had left a crim-son stain: He washed it white as snow.

No. 589. I Am Praying for You.

S. O'Maley Cluff. Ira D. Sankey.

1. I have a Sav-iour, He's pleading in glo-ry, A dear, lov-ing Sav-iour tho'
2. I have a Fa-ther: to me He has giv-en A hope for e-ter-ni-ty,
3. I have a robe: 'tis re-splendent in whiteness, A-wait-ing in glo-ry my
4. I have a peace: it is calm as a riv-er—A peace that the friends of this
5. When Je-sus has found you, tell others the sto-ry, That my lov-ing Sav-iour is

I Am Praying for You.

earth-friends be few; And now He is watch-ing in ten-derness o'er me, But
bless-ed and true; And soon will He call me to meet Him in heav-en, But
won-der-ing view; Oh, when I re-ceive it all shin-ing in brightness, Dear
world nev-er knew; My Sav-iour a-lone is its Au-thor and Giv-er, And
your Sav-iour too; Then pray that your Sav-iour may bring them to glo-ry, And
Copyright property of The Biglow & Main Co.
CHORUS.
oh, that my Sav-iour were your Sav-iour too.
oh, that He'd let me bring you with me too!
friends, could I see you re-ceiv-ing one too!
oh, could I know it was giv-en to you!
pray'r will be answered—'twas an-swered for you!
For you I am pray-ing, For
p
f
pp
rall.
you I am pray-ing, For you I am pray-ing, I'm pray-ing for you.
No. 590.
I shall be Satisfied.
El. Nathan.
James McGranahan.
1. Soul of mine, in earth-ly tem-ple, Why not here con-tent a-bide?
2. Soul of mine, my heart is cling-ing To the earth's fair pomp and pride;
3. Soul of mine, must I sur-ren-der, See my-self as cru-ci-fied;
4. Soul of mine, con-tin-ue plead-ing; Sin re-buke, and fol-ly chide;
Why art thou for-ev-er plead-ing? Why art thou not sat-is-fied?
Ah, why dost thou thus re-prove me? Why art thou not sat-is-fied?
Turn from all of earth's am-bi-tion, That thou may'st be sat-is-fied?
I ac-cept the cross of Je-sus, That thou may'st be sat-is-fied.
Copyright, 1879, by James McGranahan.

I shall be Satisfied.
CHORUS.
I .... shall be sat-is-fied, I .... shall be sat-is-fied,
I shall be sat-is-fied, I shall be sat-is-fied, I shall be sat-is-fied,
When I a-wake in His like-ness, I .... shall be sat-is-fied,
I shall be sat-is-fied,
I .... shall be sat-is-fied, When I a-wake in His like-ness.
I shall be sat-is-fied, I shall be sat-is-fied,
No. 591. Something for Jesus.
S. D. PHELPS.
ROBERT LOWRY.
1. Sav-iour! Thy dy-ing love Thou gav-est me, Nor should I aught with-hold, Dear Lord, from Thee; In love my soul would bow, My heart ful-fill its vow, Some offering bring Thee now, Something for Thee.
2. O'er the blest mer-cy-seat, Plead-ing for me, My fee-ble faith looks up, Je-sus, to Thee: Help me the cross to bear, Thy won-drous love de-clare, Some song to raise, or prayer, Something for Thee.
3. Give me a faith-ful heart— Like-ness to Thee— That each de-part-ing day Hence-forth may see Some work of love be-gun, Some deed of kind-ness done, Some wand'rer sought and won, Something for Thee.
4. All that I am and have— Thy gifts so free— In joy, in grief, through life, Dear Lord, for Thee! And when Thy face I see, My ransomed soul shall be, Through all e-ter-ni-ty, Something for Thee.
Copyright, 1871, by Biglow & Main.

No. 592. Rescue the Perishing.
F. J. Crosby.
W. H. Doane.
1. Res - cue the per - ish - ing, Care for the dy - ing, Snatch them in pit - y from
2. Tho' they are slighting Him, Still He is wait - ing, Wait - ing the pen - i - tent
3. Down in the hu-man heart, Crush'd by the tempt - er, Feel - ings lie bur - ied that
4. Res - cue the per - ish - ing, Du - ty de - mands it; Strength for thy la - bor the
sin and the grave; Weep o'er the err - ing one, Lift up the fall - en,
child to re - ceive; Plead with them ear - nest - ly, Plead with them gent - ly:
grace can re - store: Touched by a lov - ing heart, Wak - ened by kind - ness,
Lord will pro - vide: Back to the nar - row way Pa - tient - ly win them;
Copyright, 1870, by W. H. Doane.
Tell them of Je - sus the migh - ty to save.
He will for - give if they on - ly be - lieve.
Chords that were bro - ken will vi - brate once more.
Tell the poor wan - d'rer a Sav - iour has died.
Chorus.
Res - cue the per - ish - ing,
Care for the dy - ing; Je - sus is mer - ci - ful, Je - sus will save.
No. 593. Saviour, More than Life.
Fanny J. Crosby.
W. H. Doane.
1. Sav - iour, more than life to me, I am clinging, clinging close to Thee;
2. Thro' this chang - ing world be - low, Lead me gent - ly, gent - ly as I go;
3. Let me love Thee more and more, Till this fleeting, fleeting life is o'er;

Saviour, More than Life.
Let Thy pre-cious blood ap-plied, Keep me ev-er, ev-er near Thy side.
Trust-ing Thee, I can-not stray, I can nev-er, nev-er lose my way.
Till my soul is lost in love, In a brighter, brighter world a-bove.
Refrain.
Ev-'ry day, ev-'ry hour, Let me feel Thy cleansing pow'r;
Ev-'ry day and hour, ev-'ry day and hour,
May Thy ten-der love to me Bind me clos-er, clos-er, Lord, to Thee.
Copyright, 1875, by Biglow & Main.
No. 594.
My Prayer.
P. P. Bliss.
P. P. Bliss.
1. More ho-li-ness give me, More striv-ings with-in;
2. More grat-i-tude give me, More trust in the Lord;
3. More pu-ri-ty give me, More strength to o'er-come;
More patience in suff-'ring, More sor-row for sin; More faith in my Sav-iour,
More pride in His glo-ry, More hope in His word; More tears for His sor-rows,
More freedom from earth-stains, More longings for home; More fit for the king-dom,
rit.
More sense of His care; More joy in His ser-vice, More pur-pose in prayer.
More pain at His grief; More meekness in tri-al, More praise for re-lief.
More used would I be; More bless-ed and ho-ly, More, Saviour, like Thee.
Used by per. The John Church Co., owners of the Copyright.

No. 595. I Hear Thy Welcome Voice.

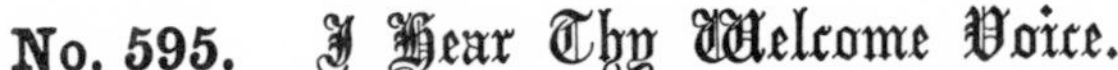

L. H. Lewis Hartsough.

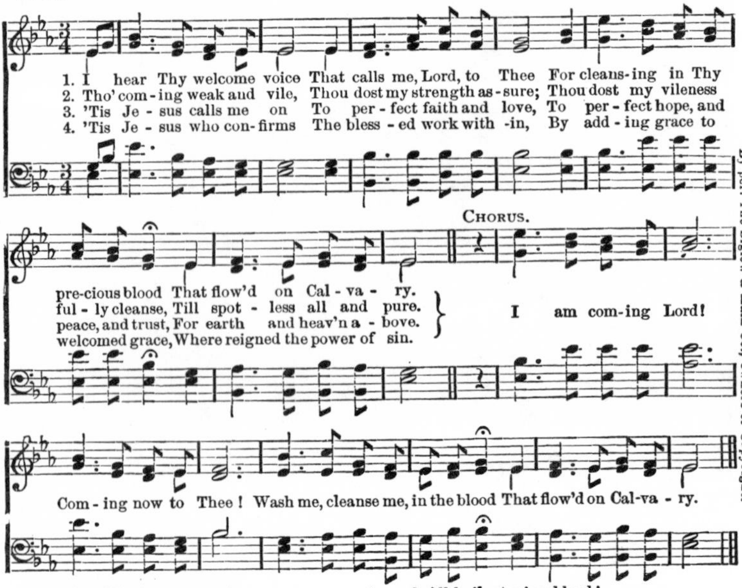

1. I hear Thy welcome voice That calls me, Lord, to Thee For cleans-ing in Thy pre-cious blood That flow'd on Cal - va - ry.
2. Tho' com - ing weak and vile, Thou dost my strength as - sure; Thou dost my vileness ful - ly cleanse, Till spot - less all and pure.
3. 'Tis Je - sus calls me on To per - fect faith and love, To per - fect hope, and peace, and trust, For earth and heav'n a - bove.
4. 'Tis Je - sus who con - firms The bless - ed work with - in, By add - ing grace to welcomed grace, Where reigned the power of sin.
Chorus.
I am com-ing Lord! Com - ing now to Thee! Wash me, cleanse me, in the blood That flow'd on Cal-va - ry.

5 And He the witness gives
To loyal hearts and free,
That every promise is fulfilled,
If faith but brings the plea.

6 All hail, atoning blood!
All hail, redeeming grace!
All hail, the Gift of Christ, our Lord,
Our Strength and Righteousness!

No. 596. 'Tis the Blessed Hour of Prayer.

F. J. Crosby. W. H. Doane.

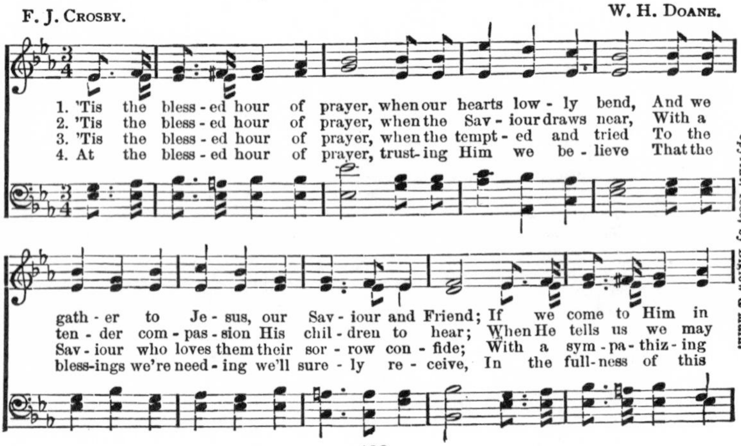

1. 'Tis the bless - ed hour of prayer, when our hearts low - ly bend, And we gath - er to Je - sus, our Sav - iour and Friend; If we come to Him in
2. 'Tis the bless - ed hour of prayer, when the Sav - iour draws near, With a ten - der com - pas - sion His chil - dren to hear; When He tells us we may
3. 'Tis the bless - ed hour of prayer, when the tempt - ed and tried To the Sav - iour who loves them their sor - row con - fide; With a sym - pa - thiz - ing
4. At the bless - ed hour of prayer, trust - ing Him we be - lieve That the bless-ings we're need - ing we'll sure - ly re - ceive, In the full - ness of this

'Tis the Blessed Hour of Prayer.
faith, His pro-tec-tion to share;
cast at His feet ev-'ry care;
heart He re-moves ev-'ry care;
trust we shall lose ev-'ry care;
What a balm for the wea-ry! O how
D.S.—What a balm for the wea-ry! O how
Fine. Chorus.
D.S
sweet to be there! Bless-ed hour of pray'r, Bless-ed hour of pray'r;
sweet to be there!
No. 597. I Need Thee Every Hour.
Annie S. Hawks.
Robert Lowry.
1. I need Thee ev-'ry hour, Most gra-cious Lord; No ten-der voice like Thine Can peace af-ford.
2. I need Thee ev-'ry hour; Stay Thou near by; Temp-ta-tions lose their pow'r When Thou art nigh.
3. I need Thee ev-'ry hour, In joy or pain; Come quick-ly and a-bide, Or life is vain.
4. I need Thee ev-'ry hour; Teach me Thy will; And Thy rich prom-is-es In me ful-fil.
5. I need Thee ev-'ry hour, Most Ho-ly One; Oh, make me Thine in-deed, Thou bless-ed Son.
Copyright, 1872, by R. Lowry.
Refrain.
I need Thee, oh! I need Thee; Ev-'ry hour I need Thee; O bless me now, my Sav-iour! I come to Thee.

No. 598. Near the Cross.
F. J. Crosby.
W. H. Doane.
1. Je - sus, keep me near the Cross, There a pre- cious fount - ain Free to all— a heal - ing stream, Flows from Cal- vary's mountain.
2. Near the Cross, a trembling soul, Love and mer - cy found me; There the Bright and Morn- ing Star Shed its beams a - round me.
3. Near the Cross! O Lamb of God, Bring its scenes be - fore me; Help me walk from day to day, With its shad-ows o'er me.
4. Near the Cross I'll watch and wait, Hop- ing, trust - ing ev - er, Till I reach the gold - en strand, Just be - yond the riv - er.
Chorus.
In the Cross, in the Cross, Be my glo - ry ev - er; Till my raptured soul shall find Rest beyond the riv - er.
Copyright, 1869, by Biglow & Main.
No. 599. Close to Thee.
F. J. Crosby.
S. J. Vail.
1. Thou my ev - er - last - ing por - tion, More than friend or life to me, All a - long my pil-grim journey, Saviour, let me walk with Thee.
2. Not for ease or world- ly pleasure, Nor for fame my prayer shall be; Glad- ly will I toil and suf- fer, On - ly let me walk with Thee.
3. Lead me thro' the vale of shadows, Bear me o'er life's fit - ful sea: Then the gate of life e - ter - nal, May I enter, Lord, with Thee.
Refrain.
Close to Thee, close to Thee, Close to Thee, close to Thee; All a- long my pil-grim journey, Saviour, let me walk with Thee.
Close to Thee, close to Thee, Close to Thee, close to Thee; Glad- ly will I toil and suf- fer, On - ly let me walk with Thee.
Close to Thee, close to Thee, Close to Thee, close to Thee; Then the gate of life e - ter - nal, May I en - ter, Lord, with Thee.
By per. Biglow & Main, owners of the Copyright.

No. 600. I Gave My Life for Thee.

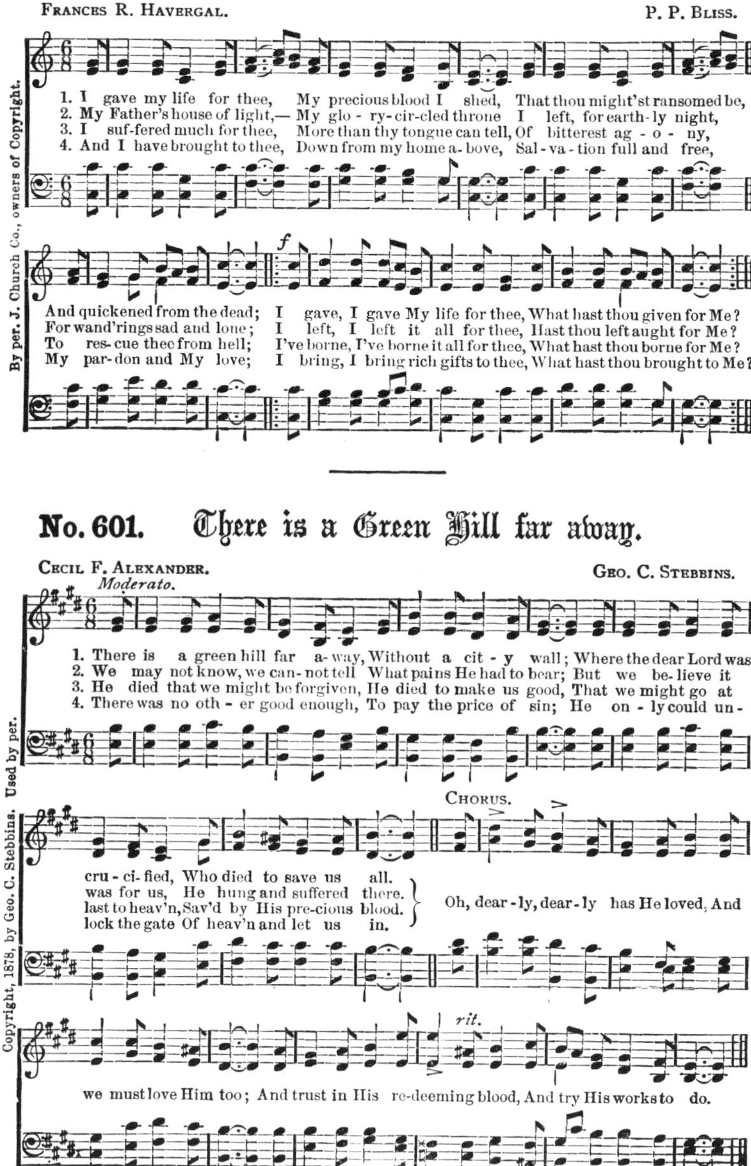

Frances R. Havergal.
P. P. Bliss.
1. I gave my life for thee, My precious blood I shed, That thou might'st ransomed be, And quickened from the dead;
2. My Father's house of light,— My glo - ry-cir-cled throne I left, for earth-ly night, For wand'rings sad and lone;
3. I suf-fered much for thee, More than thy tongue can tell, Of bitterest ag - o - ny, To res-cue thee from hell;
4. And I have brought to thee, Down from my home a-bove, Sal-va-tion full and free, My par-don and My love;
f
I gave, I gave My life for thee, What hast thou given for Me?
I left, I left it all for thee, Hast thou left aught for Me?
I've borne, I've borne it all for thee, What hast thou borne for Me?
I bring, I bring rich gifts to thee, What hast thou brought to Me?
By per. J. Church Co., owners of Copyright.
No. 601. There is a Green Hill far away.
Cecil F. Alexander.
Geo. C. Stebbins.
Moderato.
1. There is a green hill far a-way, Without a cit - y wall; Where the dear Lord was cru-ci-fied, Who died to save us all.
2. We may not know, we can-not tell What pains He had to bear; But we be-lieve it was for us, He hung and suffered there.
3. He died that we might be forgiven, He died to make us good, That we might go at last to heav'n, Sav'd by His pre-cious blood.
4. There was no oth - er good enough, To pay the price of sin; He on - ly could un-lock the gate Of heav'n and let us in.
Chorus.
Oh, dear-ly, dear-ly has He loved, And we must love Him too; And trust in His re-deeming blood, And try His works to do.
rit.
Copyright, 1878, by Geo. C. Stebbins. Used by per.

No. 602. Beyond the Smiling and the Weeping.

HORATIUS BONAR.
GEO. C. STEBBINS.
1. Be-yond the smil-ing and the weep-ing, I shall be soon, I shall be soon; Be-yond the waking and the sleeping, Beyond the sowing and the reap-ing, I shall be soon,
2. Be-yond the blooming and the fad-ing, I shall be soon, I shall be soon; Be-yond the shining and the shading, Beyond the hoping and the dreading, I shall be soon,
3. Be-yond the part-ing and the meet-ing, I shall be soon, I shall be soon; Be-yond the farewell and the greeting, Beyond the pulse's fe-ver beat-ing, I shall be soon,
4. Be-yond the frost-chain and the fe-ver, I shall be soon, I shall be soon; Be-yond the rock-waste and the river, Beyond the ev-er and the nev-er, I shall be soon,
REFRAIN.
I shall be soon. Love, rest and home! Sweet, sweet home! Lord, tarry not, Lord tarry not, but come.
Copyright, 1880, by Geo. C. Stebbins.
No. 603. Eternity.
ELLEN M. H. GATES.
P. P. BLISS.
1. Oh, the clang-ing bells of Time! Night and day they nev-er cease; We are wea-ried with their chime, For they do not bring us peace;
2. Oh, the clang-ing bells of Time! How their chang-es rise and fall, But in un-der-tone sub-lime, Sounding clear-ly through them all,
3. Oh, the clang-ing bells of Time! To their voic-es, loud and low, In a long, un-rest-ing line We are march-ing to and fro;
4. Oh, the clang-ing bells of Time! Soon their notes will all be dumb, And in joy and peace sub-lime, We shall feel the si-lence come;
Used by per. The John Church Co., owners of the Copyright.
432

And we hush our breath to hear, And we strain our eyes to see
Is a voice that must be heard, As our mo - ments on - ward flee,
And we yearn for sight or sound, Of the life that is to be,
And our souls their thirst will slake, And our eyes the King will see,

Rit. *Rallentando.*

If thy shores are draw - ing near,— E - ter - ni - ty! E - ter - ni - ty!
And it speak - eth, aye, one word,— E - ter - ni - ty! E - ter - ni - ty!
For thy breath doth wrap us round,— E - ter - ni - ty! E - ter - ni - ty!
When thy glo - rious morn shall break,— E - ter - ni - ty! E - ter - ni - ty!

No. 604. We Shall Meet, By and By.

JOHN ATKINSON. HUBERT P. MAIN.

ff *pp*

1. We shall meet be - yond the riv - er, By and by, by and by; And the dark - ness
2. We shall strike the harps of glo - ry, By and by, by and by; We shall sing re -
3. We shall see and be like Je - sus, By and by, by and by; Who a crown of
4. There our tears shall all cease flowing, By and by, by and by; And with sweetest

ff *pp*

shall be o - ver, By and by, By and by; With the toil - some jour - ney done,
demption's sto - ry, By and by, By and by; And the strains for ev - er - more
life will give us, By and by, By and by; And the an - gels who ful - fil
rap - ture knowing, By and by, By and by; All the blest ones, who have gone

ff *pp*

And the glorious bat - tle won, We shall shine forth as the sun, By and by, by and by.
Shall resound in sweetness o'er Yonder ev - er - last - ing shore, By and by, by and by.
All the mandates of His will Shall attend, and love us still, By and by, by and by.
To the land of life and song, - We with shoutings shall rejoin, By and by, by and by.

No. 605. Christ is Coming.

J. R. MACDUFF. GEO. C. STEBBINS.

1. Christ is com - ing! let cre - a - tion From her groans and tra - vail cease;
2. Earth can now but tell the sto - ry Of Thy bit - ter cross and pain;
3. Though once cra - dled in a man - ger, Oft no pil - low but the sod;
4. Long Thy ex - iles have been pin - ing, Far from rest, and home, and Thee;
5. With that "bless - ed hope" be - fore us, Let no harp re - main un - strung;
Let the glo - rious proc - la - ma - tion Hope re - store and faith in - crease:
She shall yet be - hold Thy glo - ry, When Thou com - est back to reign.
Here an a - lien and a stran - ger, Mock'd of men, dis - own'd of God.
But, in heaven - ly ves - ture shin - ing, Soon they shall Thy glo - ry see.
Let the might - y ran - som'd cho - rus On - ward roll from tongue to tongue.
CHORUS.
Christ is com - ing! Christ is com - ing! Come, Thou bless - ed Prince of peace!
Christ is com - ing! Christ is com - ing! Come, Thou bless - ed Prince of peace!

Copyright, 1871, by Geo. C. Stebbins.

No. 606. Joy to the World.

I. WATTS. (ANTIOCH. C. M.) Arr. fr. GEO. F. HANDEL.

1. Joy to the world! the Lord is come; Let earth re - ceive her King; Let
2. Joy to the world! the Sav - iour reigns; Let men their songs em - ploy; While
3. He rules the world with truth and grace, And makes the na - tions prove The
ev - 'ry heart pre - pare Him room, And heav'n and na - ture sing, And
fields and floods, rocks, hills, and plains, Re - peat the sound - ing joy, Re -
glo - ries of His right - eous - ness, And won - ders of His love, And
And heav'n, And heav'n and nature

heav'n and na - ture sing, And heav'n, And heav'n and na - ture sing.
peat the ound-ing joy, Re - peat, Re - peat the sound-ing joy.
won - ders of His love, And wonders, And won - ders of His love.
sing,............ And heav'n and na - ture sing.

No. 607. My Ain Countrie.

M. L. Demarest, 1860–1881. Mrs. I. T. Hanna. Har. by H. P. Main.

1. { I am far frae my hame, an' I'm wea - ry aft - en whiles, For the langed-for hame-bringin', an' my Faither's welcome smiles }
{ An' I'll ne'er be fu' con - tent, un - til mine een do see The gow - den gates o' heav'n an' my .... } ain coun - trie.

D.C.—But these sights an' these soun's will as naething be to me, When I hear the an - gels singin' in my .... ain coun - trie.

Fine.

{ The earth is fleck'd wi' flow - ers, mon - y - tint - ed, fresh an' gay. }
{ The bird - ies war - ble blithe-ly, for my Faither made them sae: }

D.C.

2 I've His gude word o' promise that some gladsome day the King
To His ain royal palace His banished hame will bring;
Wi' een an' wi' hert rinnin' owre, we shall see
The King in His beauty, in oor ain countrie.
My sins hae been mony, an' my sorrows hae been sair;
But there they'll never vex me, nor be remembered mair
For His bluid has made me white, an' His han' shall dry my e'e,
When He brings me hame at last, to my ain countrie.

3 Sae little noo I ken, o' yon blessed, bonnie place,
I only ken it's Hame, whaur we shall see His face;
It wad surely be eneuch for ever mair to be
In the glory o' His presence, in oor ain countrie.
Like a bairn to its mither, a wee birdie to its nest,
I wad fain be gangin' noo, unto my Saviour's breast,
For He gathers in His bosom witless, worthless lambs like me,
An' carries them Himsel', to His ain countrie.

4 He is faithfu' that hath promised, an' He'll surely come again,
He'll keep His tryst wi' me, at what 'oor I dinna ken;
But He bids me still to wait, an' ready aye to be,
To gang at ony moment to my ain countrie.
Sae I'm watching aye, and singin' o' my hame, as I wait
For the soun'in' o' His fitfa' this side the gowden gate:
God gie His grace to ilka ane wha' listens noo to me,
That we a' may gang in gladness to oor ain countrie.

No. 608. Beulah Land.
E. P. Stites.
Jno. R. Sweney.
1. I've reach'd the land of corn and wine, And all its rich - es free - ly mine;
2. The Sav-iour comes and walks with me, And sweet com-mun - ion here have we;
3. A sweet per-fume up - on the breeze Is borne from ev - er ver - nal trees,
4 The zeph - yrs seem to float to me, Sweet sounds of heav - en's mel - o - dy,
Here shines undimm'd one bliss - ful day, For all my night has pass'd a - way.
He gent - ly leads me with His hand, For this is heav - en's bor - der-land.
And flow'rs that nev - er fad - ing grow Where streams of life for - ev - er-flow.
As an - gels, with the white-robed throng, Join in the sweet re - demp - tion song.
Chorus.
O Beu - lah land, sweet Beu - lah land, As on thy high - est mount I stand,
I look a - way a - cross the sea, Where man-sions are pre - pared for me,
And view the shin - ing glo - ry shore, My heav'n, my home for - ev - er-more.
From "Goodly Pearls," by per. John J. Hood.
No. 609. Bringing in the Sheaves.
Knowles Shaw.
George A. Minor.
1. Sow - ing in the morn - ing, sow - ing seeds of kind - ness, Sow - ing in the noon - tide
2. Sow - ing in the sun - shine, sow - ing in the shad - ows, Fearing nei - ther clouds nor
3. Go - ing forth with weeping, sow - ing for the Mas - ter, Tho' the loss sustain'd our
Used by per.

Bringing in the Sheaves.
and the dew - y eve; Wait-ing for the har - vest, and the time of reap - ing,
win-ter's chill-ing breeze; By and by the har - vest, and the la - bor end - ed,
spir - it oft - en grieves; When our weep-ing's o - ver, He will bid us wel - come,
We shall come, re - joic - ing, Bring-ing in the sheaves.
CHORUS.
Bring-ing in the sheaves,
bring-ing in the sheaves, We shall come, re - joic - ing, Bring-ing in the sheaves,
Bringing in the sheaves,
Bringing in the sheaves,
We shall come, rejoicing,
Bringing in the sheaves.
No. 610. Depth of Mercy.
C. Wesley.
F. W. Kücken. Arr. H. P. Main.
Arr. copyright, 1887, by Ira. D. Sankey.
1. Depth of mer-cy! can there be Mer - cy still re - served for me? Can my God His
2. I have long with-stood His grace; Long provoked Him to His face; Would not hearken
3. Now, in-cline me to re - pent; Let me now my sins la - ment; Now my foul re -
wrath for-bear? Me, the chief of sin-ners, spare? Me, the chief of sin-ners, spare?
to His calls, Grieved Him by a thousand falls, Grieved Him by a thousand falls.
volt de-plore, Look, be-lieve, and sin no more, Look, be-lieve, and sin no more.

No. 611. The Crowning Day.

EL. NATHAN. JAMES MCGRANAHAN.

1. Our Lord is now re - ject - ed, And by the world dis-owned,
2. The heav'ns shall glow with splen - dor, But bright - er far than they
3. Our pain shall then be o - ver, We'll sin and sigh no more,
4. Let all that look for, has - ten The com - ing joy - ful day,
By the ma - ny still ne - glect - ed, And by the few en-throned,
The saints shall shine in glo - ry, As Christ shall them ar - ray,
Be - hind us all of sor - row, And naught but joy be - fore,
By ear - nest con - se - cra - tion, To walk the nar - row way,
But soon He'll come in glo - ry, The hour is draw - ing nigh, For the
The beau - ty of the Sav - iour, Shall daz - zle ev - 'ry eye, In the
A joy in our Re - deem - er, As we to Him are nigh, In the
By gath - 'ring in the lost ones, For whom our Lord did die, For the
crown-ing day is coming by and by.
crown-ing day that's coming by and by.
crown-ing day that's coming by and by.
crown-ing day that's coming by and by.
CHORUS.
Oh, the crown-ing day is com-ing,
Is com - ing by and by, When our Lord shall come in "pow - er,"
And "glo - ry" from on high. Oh, the glo - rious sight will glad - den, Each
Copyright, 1881, by James McGranahan.

The Crowning Day.

wait-ing, watch-ful eye, In the crown-ing day that's coming by and by.
No. 612.
Over the Line.
Ellen K. Bradford.
E. H. Phelps.
1. Oh, ten-der and sweet was the Mas-ter's voice, As He lov-ing-ly call'd to me,
2. But my sins are ma-ny, my faith is small, Lo! the answer came quick and clear;
3. But my flesh is weak, I tear-ful-ly said, And the way I can-not see;
4. Ah, the world is cold, and I can-not go back, Press for-ward I sure-ly must;
"Come o-ver the line, it is on-ly a step—I am waiting, My child, for thee."
"Thou needest not trust in thy-self at all, Step o-ver the line, I am here."
I fear if I try I may sad-ly fail, And thus may dis-hon-or Thee.
I will place my hand in His wound-ed palm, Step o-ver the line, and *trust.*
Refrain.
"O-ver the line," hear the sweet refrain, An-gels are chant-ing the heav-en-ly strain;
"O-ver the line,"—Why should I re-main With a step between me and Je-sus.
4th v. "O-ver the line,"—I *will not* re-main, I'll cross it and go to Je-sus.
Copyright, 1878, by Biglow & Main.

No. 613. How Firm a Foundation.

(PORTUGUESE HYMN. 11s.)

G. KEITH. M. PORTOGALLO.

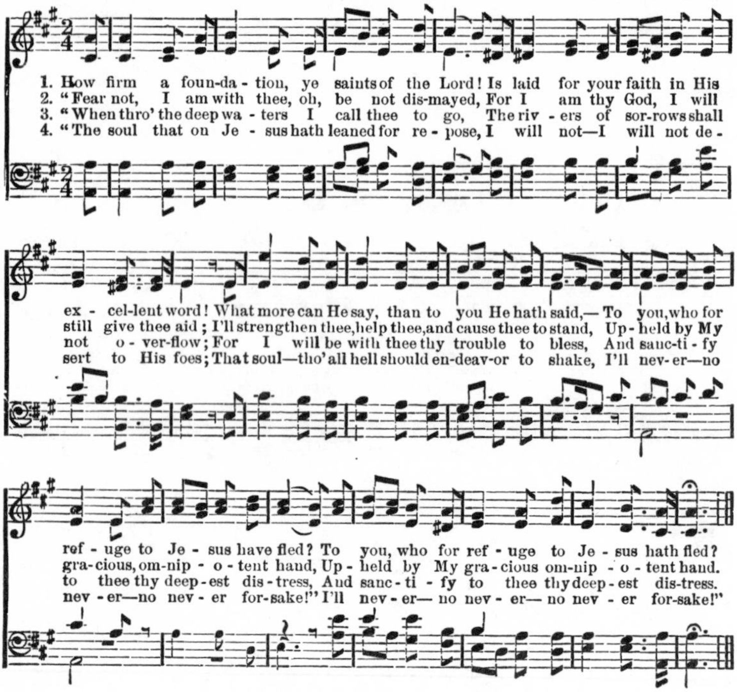

1. How firm a foun-da - tion, ye saints of the Lord! Is laid for your faith in His
2. "Fear not, I am with thee, oh, be not dis-mayed, For I am thy God, I will
3. "When thro' the deep wa - ters I call thee to go, The riv - ers of sor-rows shall
4. "The soul that on Je - sus hath leaned for re - pose, I will not—I will not de -
ex - cel-lent word! What more can He say, than to you He hath said,— To you, who for
still give thee aid; I'll strengthen thee, help thee, and cause thee to stand, Up - held by My
not o - ver-flow; For I will be with thee thy trouble to bless, And sanc-ti - fy
sert to His foes; That soul—tho' all hell should en-deav-or to shake, I'll nev-er—no
ref - uge to Je - sus have fled? To you, who for ref - uge to Je - sus hath fled?
gra-cious, om-nip - o - tent hand, Up - held by My gra-cious om-nip - o - tent hand.
to thee thy deep-est dis-tress, And sanc-ti - fy to thee thy deep-est dis-tress.
nev - er—no nev - er for-sake!" I'll nev - er—no nev - er—no nev - er for-sake!"

No. 614. Glory be to the Father.

H. W. GREATOREX.

Glo - ry be to the Fa - ther, and to the Son, and to the Ho - ly Ghost; As it
was in the be-ginning, is now, and ever shall be, world without end: A - men, A - men.

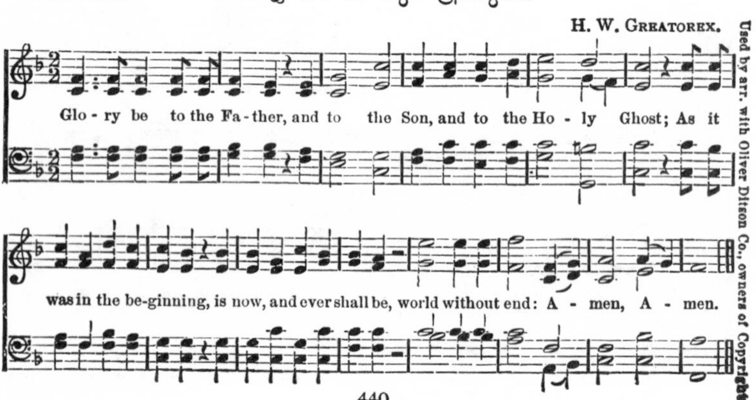

No. 615. Stand up for Jesus.

(WEBB. 7s. 6s.)

G. DUFFIELD. G. J. WEBB.

2 Stand up!—stand up for Jesus!
The trumpet call obey;
Forth to the mighty conflict,
In this His glorious day:
"Ye that are men, now serve Him,"
Against unnumbered foes;
Let courage rise with danger,
And strength to strength oppose.

3 Stand up!—stand up for Jesus!
Stand in His strength alone;
The arm of flesh will fail you—
Ye dare not trust your own:
Put on the gospel armor,
And, watching unto prayer,
Where duty calls, or danger,
Be never wanting there.

4 Stand up!—stand up for Jesus!
The strife will not be long;
This day, the noise of battle,
The next, the victor's song:
To him that overcometh,
A crown of life shall be;
He with the King of glory
Shall reign eternally!

No. 616.

The Morning Light. 7s. 6s.

1 The morning light is breaking;
The darkness disappears!
The sons of earth are waking
To penitential tears;
Each breeze that sweeps the ocean
Brings tidings from afar,
Of nations in commotion,
Prepared for Zion's war.

2 See heathen nations bending
Before the God we love,
And thousand hearts ascending
In gratitude above;
While sinners, now confessing,
The gospel call obey,
And seek the Saviour's blessing—
A nation in a day.

3 Blest river of salvation!
Pursue thine onward way;
Flow thou to every nation,
Nor in thy richness stay:
Stay not till all the lowly
Triumphant reach their home:
Stay not till all the holy
Proclaim—"The Lord is come!"

S. F. Smith.

No. 617.

Sometimes a Light Surprises.

1 Sometimes a light surprises
The Christian while he sings;
It is the Lord who rises
With healing in His wings:
When comforts are declining,
He grants the soul again
A season of clear shining,
To cheer it after rain.

2 In holy contemplation,
We sweetly then pursue
The theme of God's salvation,
And find it ever new;
Set free from present sorrow,
We cheerfully can say,
Let the unknown to-morrow
Bring with it what it may.

3 It can bring with it nothing,
But He will bring us through;
Who gives the lilies clothing,
Will clothe His people too:
Beneath the spreading heavens,
No creature but is fed;
And He who feeds the ravens,
Will give His children bread.

4 Though vine nor fig-tree neither,
Their wonted fruit should bear,
Though all the fields should wither,
Nor flocks, nor herds be there;
Yet God the same abiding,
His praise shall tune my voice,
For while in Him confiding,
I cannot but rejoice.

W. Cowper.

No. 618. "Whosoever Will."
P. P. B.
P. P. Bliss.
Joyfully.
1. "Who - so - ev - er hear - eth." shout, shout the sound! Send the bless- ed tid - ings
2. "Who - so - ev - er com - eth need not de - lay, Nor the door is o - pen,
3. "Who - so - ev - er will," the prom - ise se - cure, "Who-so - ev - er will," for
all the world a - round; Spread the joy - ful news wher - ev - er man is found:
en - ter while you may; Je - sus is the true, the on - ly Liv - ing Way:
ev - er must en - dure; "Who - so - ev - er will," 'tis life for - ev - er-more;
Chorus.
"Who - so - ev - er will, may come." "Who - so - ev - er will, who - so - ev - er will,"
Send the proc - la - ma - tion o - ver vale and hill; 'Tis a lov - ing
Fa - ther calls the wand - 'rer home!" "Who - so - ev - er will, may come."
By per. The John Church Co., owners of Copyright.
No. 619. Crown Him.
Rev. Thos. Kelly.
Arr. by Geo. C. Stebbins.
1. Look, ye saints, the sight is glo - rious; See the "Man of sor - rows" now;
2. Crown the Sav - iour, an - gels, crown Him; Rich the tro-phies Je - sus brings;
3. Sin - ners in de - ri - son crown'd Him; Mock-ing thus the Sav-iour's claim;
4. Hark! the bursts of ac - cla - ma - tion! Hark! these loud tri-umph- ant chords;

Crown Him.

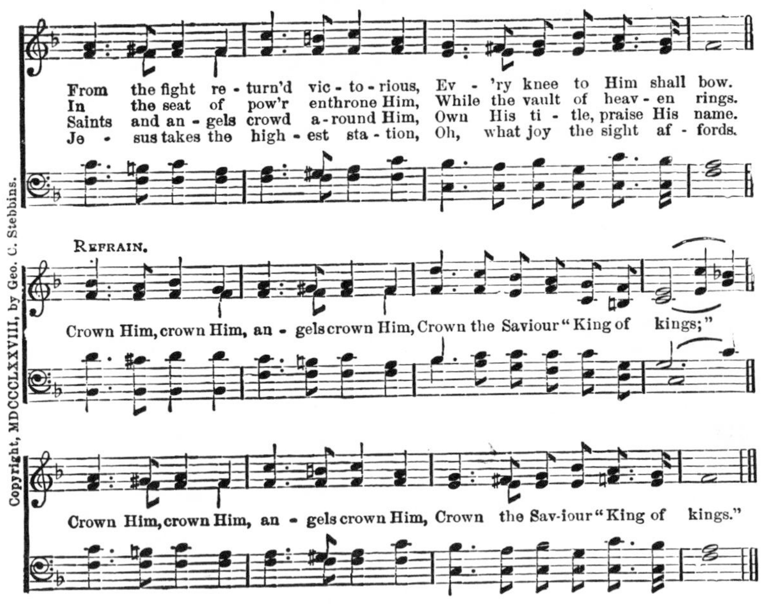

From the fight re - turn'd vic - to - rious, Ev - 'ry knee to Him shall bow.
In the seat of pow'r enthrone Him, While the vault of heav - en rings.
Saints and an - gels crowd a - round Him, Own His ti - tle, praise His name.
Je - sus takes the high - est sta - tion, Oh, what joy the sight af - fords.
Refrain.
Crown Him, crown Him, an - gels crown Him, Crown the Saviour "King of kings;"
Crown Him, crown Him, an - gels crown Him, Crown the Sav-iour "King of kings."
Copyright, MDCCCLXXVIII, by Geo. C. Stebbins.

No. 620. Jesus Christ is Passing By.

J. Denham Smith. Mrs. Jos. F. Knapp.

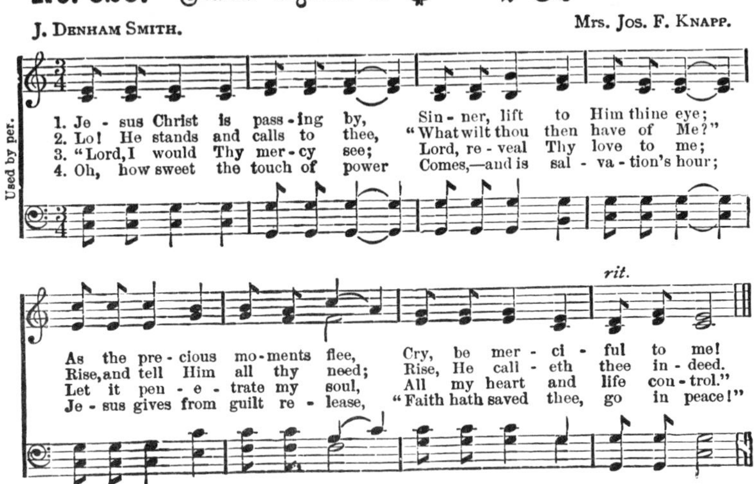

1. Je - sus Christ is pass - ing by, Sin - ner, lift to Him thine eye;
2. Lo! He stands and calls to thee, "What wilt thou then have of Me?"
3. "Lord, I would Thy mer - cy see; Lord, re - veal Thy love to me;
4. Oh, how sweet the touch of power Comes,—and is sal - va - tion's hour;
Used by per.
rit.
As the pre - cious mo - ments flee, Cry, be mer - ci - ful to me!
Rise, and tell Him all thy need; Rise, He call - eth thee in - deed.
Let it pen - e - trate my soul, All my heart and life con - trol."
Je - sus gives from guilt re - lease, "Faith hath saved thee, go in peace!"

No. 621. That will be Heaven for Me.
P. P. Bliss.
James McGranahan.
1. I know not the hour when my Lord will come To take me a-way to His own dear home;
2. I know not the song that the an - gels sing, I know not the sound of the harps' glad ring;
3. I know not the form of my man-sion fair, I know not the name that I then shall bear;
But I know that His presence will lighten the gloom, And that will be glo-ry for me.
But I know there'll be mention of Je-sus our King, And that will be mu-sic for me.
But I know that my Sav-iour will welcome me there, And that will be heav-en for me.
Chorus.
And that will be glo-ry for me,............ Oh, that will be glo-ry for me;
And that will be mu-sic for me,............ Oh, that will be mu-sic for me;
And that will be heav-en for me,............ Oh, that will be heav-en for me;
Yes, that will be glo-ry, oh, that will be glo-ry for me;
Yes, that will be mu-sic, oh, that will be mu-sic for me;
Yes, that will be heaven, oh, that will be heav-en for me;
Ritard.
But I know that His presence will lighten the gloom, And that will be glo-ry for me.
But I know there'll be mention of Je-sus our King, And that will be mu-sic for me.
But I know that my Sav-iour will welcome me there, And that will be heaven for me.
By per. The John Church Co., owners of copyright.
No. 622. Ring the Bells of Heaven.
Rev. Wm. O. Cushing.
Geo. F. Root.
1. Ring the bells of heav - en! there is joy to-day, For a soul, re-
2. Ring the bells of heav - en! there is joy to-day, For the wanderer
3. Ring the bells of heav - en! spread the feast to-day, An - gels, swell the
D.C.—'Tis the ran-somed ar - my, like a might-y sea, Peal-ing forth the
Fine.
turn-ing from the wild; See! the Fa-ther meets him out up-on the way,
now is rec-on-ciled; Yes, a soul is res-cued from his sin-ful way,
glad tri-umphant strain! Tell the joy-ful ti-dings! bear it far a-way!
an-them of the free.
By per. The John Church Co., owners of copyright.

Ring the Bells.
CHORUS.
Wel - com-ing His wea - ry, wand'ring child.
And is born a - new a ran-somed child.
For a pre - cious soul is born a - gain.
Glo - ry! glo - ry! how the an - gels sing; Glo - ry! glo - ry! how the loud harps ring;
D.C.
No. 623. Wondrous Love.
Mrs. M. Stockton.
Wm. G. Fischer.
1. God loved the world of sin - ners lost And ru - ined by the fall; Sal - va - tion full, at high - est cost, He of - fers free to all.
2. E'en now by faith I claim Him mine, The ris - en Son of God; Re - demption by His death I find, And cleansing thro' the blood.
3. Love brings the glo - rious ful - ness in, And to His saints makes known The bless-ed rest from in - bred sin, Thro' faith in Christ a - lone.
4. Be - liev - ing souls, re - joic - ing go; There shall to you be given A glo-rious fore-taste, here be - low, Of end - less life in heaven.
5. Of vic - tory now o'er Sa - tan's power Let all the ran - somed sing, And tri-umph in the dy - ing hour Thro' Christ the Lord our King.
By per. W. G. Fischer, owner of copyright.
CHORUS.
Oh, 'twas love, 'twas won-drous love! The love of God to me; It brought my Sav - iour from a - bove, To die on Cal - va - ry.

No. 624. Jesus Shall Reign.

ISAAC WATTS. (DUKE STREET. L. M.) JOHN HATTON.

1. Je - sus shall reign wher - e'er the sun Does his suc- ces - sive jour-neys run,
2. To Him shall end - less pray'r be made, And prais-es throng to crown His head:
3. Peo - ple and realms of ev - 'ry tongue, Dwell on His love with sweet-est song;
His kingdom spread from shore to shore, Till moons shall wax and wane no more.
His name, like sweet per - fume shall rise With ev-'ry morn - ing sac - ri - fice.
And in-fant voic - es shall pro - claim Their ear-ly bless - ings on His Name.

4 Blessings abound where'er He reigns
The prisoner leaps to loose his chains;
The weary find eternal rest,
And all the sons of want are blest.

5 Let every creature rise, and bring
Peculiar honors to our King:
Angels descend with songs again,
And earth repeat the loud amen.

No. 625. Tune—DUKE STREET. L. M.

1 So let our lips and lives express
The holy gospel we profess;
So let our works and virtues shine;
To prove the doctrine all divine.

2 Thus shall we best proclaim abroad
The honors of our Saviour God;
When His salvation reigns within,
And grace subdues the power of sin.

3 Religion bears our spirits up,
While we expect that blessed hope,—
The bright appearance of the Lord:
And faith stands leaning on His word.

Isaac Watts.

No. 626. The Light of the World is Jesus.

P. P. B. P. P. BLISS.

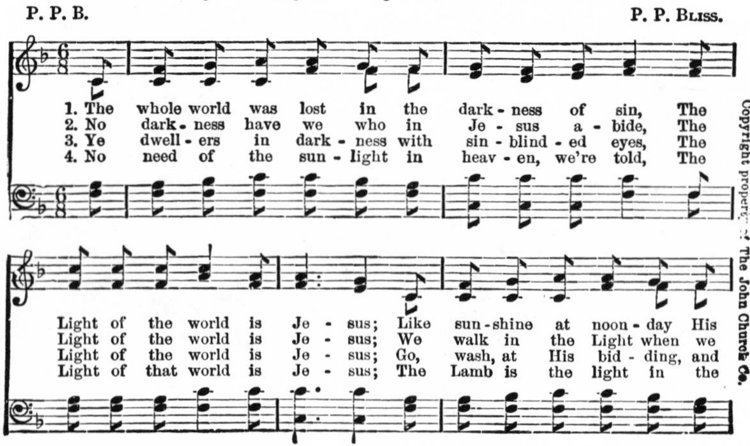
1. The whole world was lost in the dark - ness of sin, The
2. No dark - ness have we who in Je - sus a - bide, The
3. Ye dwell - ers in dark - ness with sin - blind - ed eyes, The
4. No need of the sun - light in heav - en, we're told, The
Light of the world is Je - sus; Like sun - shine at noon - day His
Light of the world is Je - sus; We walk in the Light when we
Light of the world is Je - sus; Go, wash, at His bid - ding, and
Light of that world is Je - sus; The Lamb is the light in the

The Light of the World.
glo - ry shone in, The Light of the world is Je - sus.
fol - low our Guide, The Light of the world is Je - sus.
light will a - rise, The Light of the world is Je - sus.
Cit - y of Gold, The Light of that world is Je - sus.
CHORUS.
Come to the Light, 'tis shin-ing for thee: Sweet-ly the Light has dawn'd up-on me,
Once I was blind, but now I can see: The Light of the world is Je - sus.
No. 627. The Prodigal Child.
Mrs. ELLEN H. GATES.
W. H. DOANE.
Used by per. The Biglow & Main Co., owners of copyright.
1. Come home! come home! You are wea - ry at heart, For the way has been dark, And so lone - ly and wild; O prod - i - gal child! Come home! oh, come home!
2. Come home! come home! For we watch and we wait, And we stand at the gate, While the shad - ows are piled; O prod - i - gal child! Come home! oh, come home!
CHORUS.
Come home! Come, oh, come home!
Come home! Come, oh, come home, come home!
Come home, come home!
rit.

3 Come home! come home!
From the sorrow and blame,
From the sin and the shame,
And the tempter that smiled,
O prodigal child!
Come home, oh, come home!

4 Come home! come home!
There is bread and to spare,
And a warm welcome there;
Then, to friends reconciled,
O prodigal child!
Come home, oh, come home!

No. 628. Not Now, My Child.

Mrs. PENNEFATHER. IRA D. SANKEY.

Slow, and with expression.
1. Not now, my child,— a lit - tle more rough toss - ing, A lit - tle long - er on the bil - lows' foam; A few more journeyings in the des - ert dark - ness, And then, the sunshine of thy Fa - ther's Home!
2. Not now; for I have wan - d'rers in the dis - tance, And thou must call them in with pa - tient love; Not now; for I have sheep up - on the mountains, And thou must fol - low them wher - e'er they rove.
3. Not now; for I have loved ones sad and wea - ry; Wilt thou not cheer them with a kind - ly smile? Sick ones, who need thee in their lone - ly sor - row; Wilt thou not tend them yet a lit - tle while?
By per. The Biglow & Main Co., owners of copyright.

4 Not now; for wounded hearts are sorely bleeding,
 And thou must teach those widowed hearts to sing:
Not now; for orphans' tears are quickly falling,
 They must be gathered 'neath some sheltering wing.

5 Go, with the name of Jesus, to the dying,
 And speak that Name in all its living power;
Why should thy fainting heart grow chill and weary?
 Canst thou not watch with Me one little hour?

6 One little hour! and then the glorious crowning,
 The golden harp-strings, and the victor's palm;
One little hour! and then the hallelujah!
 Eternity's long, deep, thanksgiving psalm!

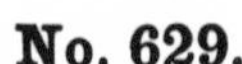

No. 629. The Great Physician.

Rev. WM. HUNTER. Arr. by Rev. J. H. STOCKTON.

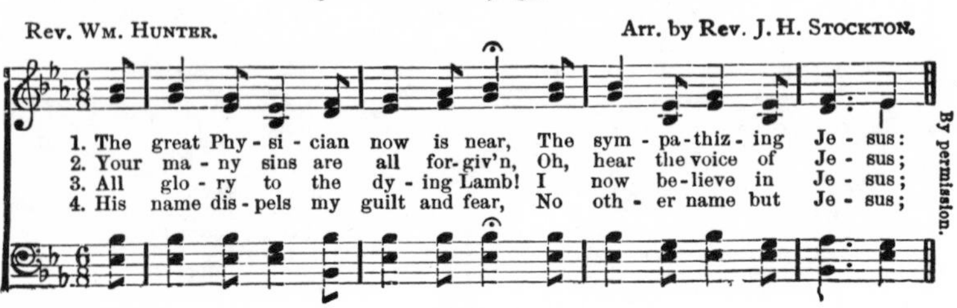
1. The great Phy - si - cian now is near, The sym - pa - thiz - ing Je - sus:
2. Your ma - ny sins are all for - giv'n, Oh, hear the voice of Je - sus;
3. All glo - ry to the dy - ing Lamb! I now be - lieve in Je - sus;
4. His name dis - pels my guilt and fear, No oth - er name but Je - sus;
By permission.

The Great Physician.

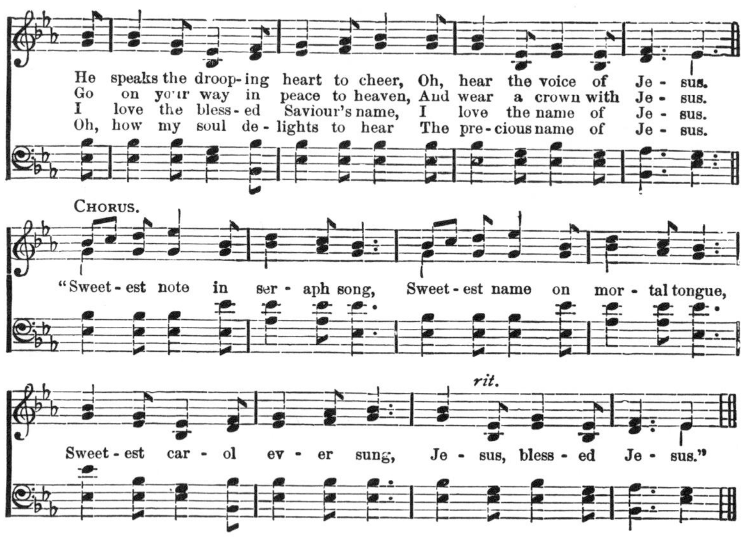
He speaks the droop-ing heart to cheer, Oh, hear the voice of Je - sus.
Go on your way in peace to heaven, And wear a crown with Je - sus.
I love the bless-ed Saviour's name, I love the name of Je - sus.
Oh, how my soul de-lights to hear The pre-cious name of Je - sus.
CHORUS.
"Sweet-est note in ser - aph song, Sweet-est name on mor - tal tongue,
rit.
Sweet-est car - ol ev - er sung, Je - sus, bless - ed Je - sus."

No. 630. To-Day the Saviour Calls.

S. F. SMITH, D.D.

LOWELL MASON.

1. To - day the Sav-iour calls; Ye wand'rers, come; O ye be-night-ed souls, Why long-er roam?
2. To - day the Sav-iour calls; O hear Him now; With-in these sa-cred walls To Je-sus bow.
3. To - day the Sav-iour calls; For ref - uge fly; The storm of jus-tice falls, And death is nigh.
4. The Spir-it calls to - day; Yield to His pow'r; O grieve Him not a - way, 'Tis mer-cy's hour.
CODA.
Come home, come home, The Sav-iour calls, come home,
Come home, come home,
Come home, come home, The Sav - iour calls, come home,
Come home, come home, come home.
rit.

No. 631. Where is my Boy to-night?

R. L.
Rev. R. Lowry.
With tenderness.
1. Where is my wand'ring boy to-night—The boy of my tenderest care, The boy that was once my joy and light, The child of my love and prayer?
2. Once he was pure as morn-ing dew, As he knelt at his moth-er's knee; No face was so bright, no heart more true, And none was so sweet as he.
3. O could I see you now, my boy, As fair as in old-en time, When prat-tle and smile made home a joy, And life was a mer-ry chime!
4. Go for my wand'ring boy to-night; Go, search for him where you will; But bring him to me with all his blight, And tell him I love him still.
Chorus. Not too fast.
O where is my boy to-night? O where is my boy to-night? My heart o'erflows, for I love him he knows; O where is my boy to-night?
Copyright, MDCCCLXXVII, by The Biglow & Main Co.
No. 632. It Passeth Knowledge.
Mary Shekleton.
Ira D. Sankey.
1. It pass-eth know-ledge, that dear love of Thine! My Je-sus! Sav-iour!
2. It pass-eth tell-ing! that dear love of Thine! My Je-sus! Sav-iour!
3. It pass-eth prais-es! that dear love of Thine! My Je-sus! Sav-iour!

It Passeth Knowledge.

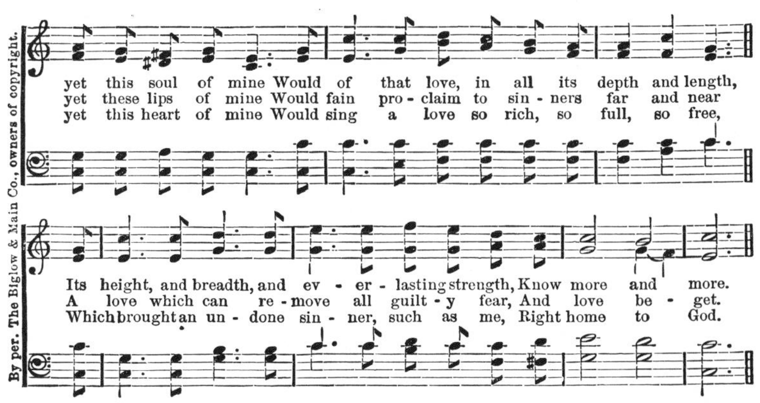
By per. The Biglow & Main Co., owners of copyright.
yet this soul of mine Would of that love, in all its depth and length,
yet these lips of mine Would fain pro - claim to sin - ners far and near
yet this heart of mine Would sing a love so rich, so full, so free,
Its height, and breadth, and ev - er - lasting strength, Know more and more.
A love which can re - move all guilt - y fear, And love be - get.
Which brought an un - done sin - ner, such as me, Right home to God.

4 But ah! I cannot tell, or sing, or know,
The fullness of that love whilst here below;
Yet my poor vessel I may freely bring;
O Thou who art of love the living spring,
My vessel fill.

5 I *am* an empty vessel! scarce one thought
Or look of love to Thee I've ever brought;
Yet, I *may* come, and come again to Thee
With this—the contrite sinner's truthful plea—
"*Thou lovest me.*"

6 Oh, *fill* me, Jesus, Saviour, with Thy love!
May woes but drive me to the fount above;
Thither may I in childlike faith draw nigh,
And never to another fountain fly
But unto Thee!

7 And when, my Jesus! Thy dear face I see,
When at the lofty throne I bend the knee,
Then of Thy love—in all its breadth and length,
Its height, and depth, and everlasting strength—
My soul shall sing.

No. 633. Come, Thou Fount.

Rev. R. Robinson. John Wyeth.

Fine.
1. Come, Thou Fount of ev - 'ry bless - ing, Tune my heart to sing Thy grace;
Streams of mer - cy, nev - er ceas - ing, Call for songs of loud - est praise;
D.C.—Praise the mount—I'm fixed up - on it! Mount of Thy re - deem - ing love.
D.C.
Teach me some mel - o - dious son - net, Sung by flam - ing tongues a - bove;

2 Here I'll raise my Ebenezer,
Hither by Thy help I'm come;
And I hope, by Thy good pleasure,
Safely to arrive at home;
Jesus sought me when a stranger,
Wandering from the fold of God;
He, to rescue me from danger,
Interposed His precious blood.

3 Oh, to grace how great a debtor,
Daily I'm constrained to be!
Let Thy goodness, as a fetter,
Bind my wandering heart to Thee;
Prone to wander, Lord, I feel it—
Prone to leave the God I love—
Here's my heart, oh, take and seal it,
Seal it for Thy courts above.

No. 634. Sweet Hour of Prayer.

W. W. Walford. Wm. B. Bradbury.

Slow.

1. Sweet hour of prayer! sweet hour of prayer! That calls me from a world of care, And bids me at my Fa - ther's throne Make all my wants and wish - es known: *Fine.* In sea - sons of dis - tress and grief, My soul has oft - en found re - lief; *D.C.*

D.C.—And oft es - caped the temp - ter's snare, By thy re - turn, sweet hour of prayer; And oft es - caped the temp - ter's snare, By thy re - turn, sweet hour of prayer.

2 Sweet hour of prayer! sweet hour of prayer!
Thy wings shall my petition bear
To Him whose truth and faithfulness
Engage the waiting soul to bless:
And since He bids me seek His face,
Believe His word, and trust His grace,
‖: I'll cast on Him my every care,
And wait for thee, sweet hour of prayer! :‖

3 Sweet hour of prayer! sweet hour of prayer!
May I thy consolation share,
Till, from Mount Pisgah's lofty height,
I view my home and take my flight;
This robe of flesh I'll drop, and rise
To seize the everlasting prize;
‖: And shout, while passing through the air,
Farewell, farewell, sweet hour of prayer! :‖

No. 635. There is Life for a Look.

Amelia M. Hull. Rev. E. G. Taylor.

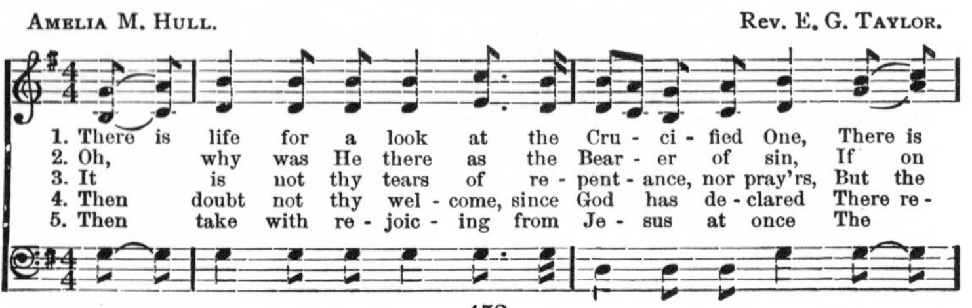
1. There is life for a look at the Cru - ci - fied One, There is
2. Oh, why was He there as the Bear - er of sin, If on
3. It is not thy tears of re - pent - ance, nor pray'rs, But the
4. Then doubt not thy wel - come, since God has de - clared There re -
5. Then take with re - joic - ing from Je - sus at once The

There is Life for a Look.
life at this mo-ment for thee; Then look, sin-ner, look un-to Him and be saved,
Je-sus thy guilt was not laid? Oh, why from His side flowed the sin-cleansing blood,
Blood, that a-tones for the soul; On Him, then, who shed it, thou may-est at once
main-eth no more to be done; That once in the end of the world He appeared,
life ev-er-last-ing He gives; And know with as-sur-ance thou nev-er canst die,
Un-to Him who was nailed to the tree.
If His dy-ing thy debt has not paid?
Thy weight of in-iq-ui-ties roll.
And com-plet-ed the work He be-gun.
Since Je-sus thy right-eous-ness, lives.
Refrain.
Look! look! look and live! There is
life for a look at the Cru-ci-fied One, There is life at this mo-ment for thee.
By per. The Biglow & Main Co., owners of copyright.
No. 636. Come to the Saviour.
G. F. R.
Geo. F. Root.
1. Come to the Sav-iour, make no de-lay; Here in His word He's shown us the way;
2. "Suf-fer the chil-dren!" Oh, hear His voice, Let ev-'ry heart leap forth and re-joice,
3. Think once a-gain, He's with us to-day; Heed now His blest com-mands, and o-bey;
Fine.
Here in our midst He's stand-ing to-day, Ten-der-ly say-ing, "Come!"
And let us free-ly make Him our choice; Do not de-lay, but come.
Hear now His ac-cents ten-der-ly say, "Will you, my chil-dren, come?"
D.S.—And we shall gath-er, Sav-iour, with Thee, In our e-ter-nal home.
Chorus.
D.S.
Joy-ful, joy-ful will the meet-ing be, When from sin our hearts are pure and free;
By per. The John Church Co., owners of copyright.

No. 637. He Leadeth Me.
Jos. H. Gilmore.
Wm. B. Bradbury.
1. He lead - eth me! oh! bless-ed thought, Oh! words with heav'nly com-fort fraught;
2. Some- times 'mid scenes of deep - est gloom, Sometimes where E - den's bow - ers bloom,
3. Lord, I would clasp Thy hand in mine, Nor ev - er mur - mur nor re - pine—
4. And when my task on earth is done, When, by Thy grace, the vic- tr'y's won,
What - e'er I do, wher - e'er I be, Still 'tis God's hand that lead - eth me.
By wa - ters still, o'er troub - led see, Still 'tis God's hand that lead - eth me.
Con - tent, what-ev - er lot I see, Since 'tis my God that lead - eth me.
E'en death's cold wave I will not flee, Since God through Jor - dan lead - eth me.
Refrain.
He lead - eth me! He lead - eth me! By His own hand He lead- eth me;
His faith - ful follower I would be, For by His hand He lead - eth me.
By per. The Biglow & Main Co., owners of copyright.
No. 638. Jewels.
Rev. W. O. Cushing.
Geo. F. Root.
Moderato.
1. When He com - eth, when He com - eth To make up His jew - els, All His
2. He will gath - er, He will gath - er The gems for His king - dom: All the
3. Lit - tle chil - dren, lit - tle chil - dren, Who love their Re - deem - er, Are the
jew - els, pre-cious jew - els, His lov'd and His own.
pure ones, all the bright ones, His lov'd and His own.
jew - els, pre-cious jew - els, His lov'd and His own.
Chorus.
Like the stars of the
By per. The John Church Co., owners of copyright.

Jewels.
morning, His bright crown adorning, They shall shine in their beauty, Bright gems for His crown.
No. 639.
Even Me.
Mrs. Eliz. Codner.
Wm. B. Bradbury.
1. Lord, I hear of show'rs of blessing Thou art scatt'ring full and free—Show'rs the thirsty land re-
2. Pass me not, O gracious Father, Sin - ful tho' my heart may be; Thou might st leave me, but the
3. Pass me not, O tender Saviour! Let me love and cling to Thee; I am longing for Thy
4. Pass me not, O might-y Spir-it Thou canst make the blind to see; Wit-ness-er of Je-sus'
freshing; Let some droopings fall on me-
rath - er Let Thy mer-cy fall on me—
fav - or; Whilst Thou'rt calling, oh, call me—
mer - it, Speak the word of pow'r to me—
E-ven me, E-ven me, Let Thy blessing fall on me.
By per. The Biglow & Main Co., owners of c.
5 Love of God, so pure and changeless;
Blood of Christ, so rich and free;
Grace of God, so strong and boundless;—
Magnify them all in me—
6 Pass me not! Thy lost one bringing,
Bind my heart, O Lord, to Thee;
While the streams of life are springing,
Blessing others, oh, bless me—
No. 640.
Here am I; Send Me
Dan'l. March.
S. M. Grannis.
1. Hark! the voice of Je - sus cry-ing—"Who will go and work to - day? Fields are
2. If you can-not cross the o-cean, And the hea-then lands ex - plore, You can
3. If you can-not speak like an-gels, If you can - not preach like Paul, You can
4. If you can-not be the watchman, Stand-ing high on Zi - on's wall, Point-ing
5. If a - mong the old - er peo-ple, You may not be apt to teach, "Feed my
6. Let none hear you i - dly say-ing, "There is noth - ing I can do." While the
white, and har - vest wait-ing; Who will bear the sheaves a - way?" Loud and strong the
find the hea-then near - er, You can help them at your door, If you can - not
tell the love of Je - sus, You can say He died for all. If you can - not
out the path to heav - en, Offering life and peace to all;—With your pray'rs and
lambs," said Christ, our Shepherd, "Place the food with - in their reach." And it may be
souls of men are dy - ing, And the Mas - ter calls for you. Take the task He
By per. S. Brainard's Sons, owners of copyright.

Here am I; Send Me.

Mas - ter call-eth, Rich re - ward He of - fers thee; Who will an - swer, glad - ly
give your thousands, You can give the wid - ow's mite; And the least you do for
rouse the wick - ed With the judgment's dread a - larms, You can lead the lit - tle
with your bounties You can do what heav'n demands; You can be like faith - ful
that the chil-dren You have led with trembling hand, Will be found a - mong your
gives you glad - ly, Let His work your pleas - ure be; An - swer quick - ly when He
say - ing, "Here am I; send me, send me!" "Here am I; send me, send me!"
Je - sus, Will be pre - cious in His sight, Will be pre - cious in His sight.
chil-dren To the Sav - iour's wait - ing arms, To the Sav-iour's wait - ing arms.
Aa - ron, Hold - ing up the proph - et's hands, Hold - ing up the proph - et's hands.
jew - els, When you reach the bet - ter land, When you reach the bet - ter land.
call - eth, "Here am I; send me, send me!" "Here am I; send me, send me!"
No. 641. Nothing but Leaves.
L. E. Akerman, alt.
Silas J. Vail.
1. Noth-ing but leaves! The Spir - it grieves O'er years of wast - ed life; O'er
2. Noth-ing but leaves! No gathered sheaves Of life's fair rip - 'ning grain: We
3. Noth-ing but leaves! Sad mem-'ry weaves No veil to hide the past: And
4. Ah, who shall thus the Mas - ter meet, And bring but with - ered leaves? Ah,
sins indulged while conscience slept, O'er vows and prom - is - es un - kept, And
sow our seeds; lo! tares and weeds,—Words, i - dle words, for earn-est deeds—Then
as we trace our wea - ry way, And count each lost and mis - spent day, We
who shall, at the Sav - iour's feet, Be - fore the aw - ful judg-ment-seat, Lay
reap from years of strife— Nothing but leaves! Nothing but leaves!
reap, with toil and pain, Nothing but leaves! Nothing but leaves!
sad - ly find at last— Nothing but leaves! Nothing but leaves!
down for, gold - en sheaves,— Nothing but leaves? Nothing but leaves?

No. 642. Yet There is Room.

Dr. Horatius Bonar. Ira D. Sankey.

Slow, with expression.

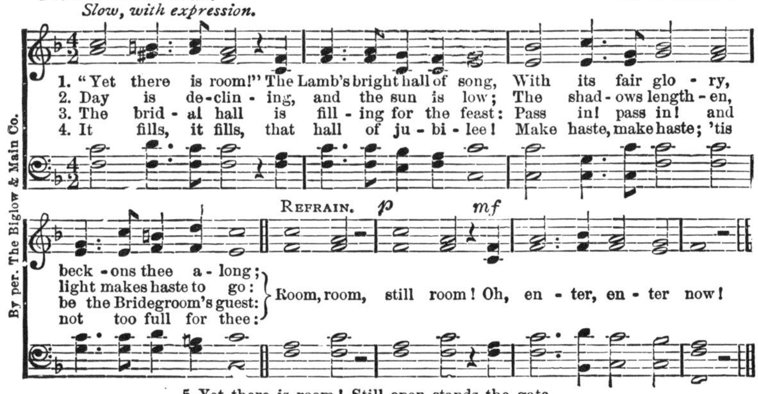

1. "Yet there is room!" The Lamb's bright hall of song, With its fair glo - ry, beck - ons thee a - long;
2. Day is de-clin - ing, and the sun is low; The shad - ows length - en, light makes haste to go:
3. The brid - al hall is fill - ing for the feast: Pass in! pass in! and be the Bridegroom's guest:
4. It fills, it fills, that hall of ju - bi - lee! Make haste, make haste; 'tis not too full for thee:
Refrain.
p
mf
Room, room, still room! Oh, en - ter, en - ter now!

By per. The Biglow & Main Co.

5 Yet there is room! Still open stands the gate,
The gate of love; it is not yet too late:
Room, room, still room! oh, enter, enter now!

6 Pass in, pass in! That banquet is for thee;
That cup of everlasting love is free:
Room, room, still room! oh, enter, enter now!

7 All heaven is there, all joy! Go in, go in;
The angels beckon thee the prize to win:
Room, room, still room! oh, enter, enter now!

8 Ere night that gate may close, and seal thy doom:
Then the last, low, long cry:—"No room, no room!"
No room, no room:—oh, woful cry, "No room!"

No. 643. Windows open toward Jerusalem.

P. P. B. P. P. Bliss.

1. Do you see the Hebrew cap-tive kneel-ing, At morning, noon and night, to pray? In his chamber he re-mem-bers Zi - on, Tho' in ex - ile far a - way.
2. Do not fear to tread the fie - ry fur-nace, Nor shrink the lion's den to share; For the God of Dan-iel will de - liv - er, He will send His an - gel there
3. Children of the liv-ing God, take cour - age; Your great deliv'rance sweet - ly sing: Set your fac - es toward the hill of Zi - on, Thence to hail your com - ing King
Chorus.
Are your windows open toward Jeru - sa-lem, Tho' as captives here a "little while" we stay?

By per. The John Church Co., owners of copyright.

Windows open toward Jerusalem.

For the coming of the King in His glo - ry, Are you watching day by day?
No. 644. The Glorious Morning.
Rev. Wm. Hunter.
Wm. B. Bradbury.
1. Soon shall we see the glo - rious morn-ing, Saints a - rise! Saints a - rise!
2. Hear ye the trump of God re - sound-ing, Saints a - rise! Saints a - rise!
3. The Saints who sleep, with joy a - wak - en, All a - rise! all a - rise!
4. Fast by the throne of God be - hold them Crown'd at last! crown'd at last!
Sin - ners, at - tend the notes of warn - ing; Saints a - rise! Saints a - rise!
Thro' all the vaults of death re - bound - ing; Saints a - rise! Saints a - rise!
Their beds of death are quick for - sak - en; All a - rise! all a - rise!
See in His arms the Sav - iour folds them, Crown'd at last! crown'd at last!
The res - ur - rec - tion day draws near, The King of Saints shall soon ap - pear,
To meet the Bridegroom, haste, prepare, Put on your bri - dal garments fair,
Not one of all the faith - ful few Who here on earth the Sav - iour knew,
With wreaths of glo - ry round their head, No tears of sor - row now are shed,
And high His roy - al stand - ard rear; Saints a - rise! Saints a - rise!
And hail your Sav - iour in the air; Saints a - rise! Saints a - rise!
But starts with bliss His Lord to view; All a - rise! all a - rise!
To joy's full fount - ain all are led, Crown'd at last! crown'd at last!
Copyright, MDCCCLXXXI, by The Biglow & Main Co.

No. 645. Hallelujah, What a Saviour!

P. P. B. — P. P. Bliss.

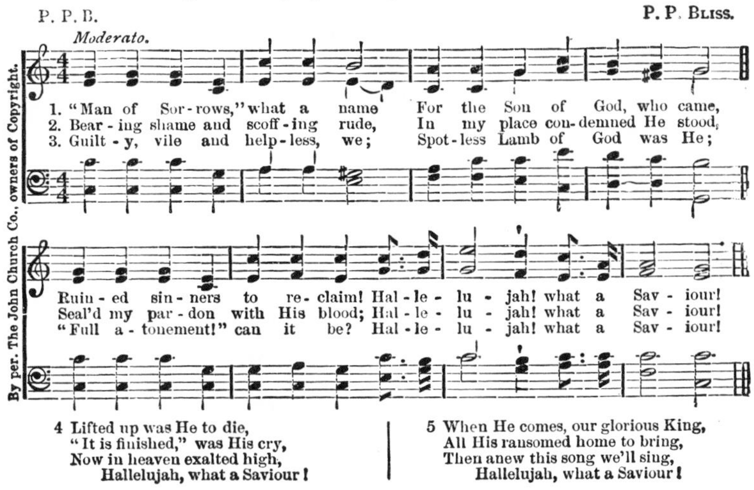
Moderato.
1. "Man of Sor-rows," what a name For the Son of God, who came,
2. Bear-ing shame and scoff-ing rude, In my place con-demned He stood,
3. Guilt-y, vile and help-less, we; Spot-less Lamb of God was He;
Ruin-ed sin-ners to re-claim! Hal-le-lu-jah! what a Sav-iour!
Seal'd my par-don with His blood; Hal-le-lu-jah! what a Sav-iour!
"Full a-tonement!" can it be? Hal-le-lu-jah! what a Sav-iour!
By per. The John Church Co., owners of Copyright.

4 Lifted up was He to die,
"It is finished," was His cry,
Now in heaven exalted high,
Hallelujah, what a Saviour!

5 When He comes, our glorious King,
All His ransomed home to bring,
Then anew this song we'll sing,
Hallelujah, what a Saviour!

No. 646. Ho! Reapers of Life's Harvest.

I. B. W. — I. B. Woodbury.

Spirited.
1. Ho! reap-ers of life's har-vest, Why stand with rust-ed blade, Un-til the night draws round thee, And day be-gins to fade? Why stand ye i-dle, wait-ing For reap-ers more to come? The gold-en morn is pass-ing, Why sit ye i-dle, dumb?
2. Thrust in your sharpened sick-le, And gath-er in the grain, The night is fast ap-proaching, And soon will come a-gain; The Mas-ter calls for reap-ers, And shall He call in vain? Shall sheaves lie there ungathered, And waste up-on the plain?
3. Mount up the heights of Wisdom, And crush each er-ror low; Keep back no words of knowledge That hu-man hearts should know. Be faith-ful to thy mis-sion, In serv-ice of thy Lord, And then a gold-en chap-let Shall be thy just re-ward.
By per. O. Ditson Co., owners of copyright.

No. 647. Jesus is Mine.

Mrs. C. J. Bonar.
T. E. Perkins.
1. Fade, fade, each earthly joy; Jesus is mine! Break, ev'ry ten-der tie; Je - sus is mine!
2. Tempt not my soul away; Jesus is mine! Here would I ev- er stay; Je - sus is mine!
3. Farewell, ye dreams of night; Jesus is mine! Lost in this dawning light; Je - sus is mine!
4. Farewell, mor- tal - i - ty; Jesus is mine! Welcome, e - ter- ni - ty; Je - sus is mine!
Dark is the wilderness, Earth has no resting place, Jesus a- lone can bless, Je- sus is mine!
Perishing things of clay, Born but for one brief day, Pass from my heart away, Je- sus is mine!
All that my soul has tried, Left but a dismal void, Jesus has sat-is - fied, Je- sus is mine!
Welcome, O loved and blest, Welcome, sweet scenes of rest, Welcome, my Saviour's breast, Jesus is mine!
By per. T. E. Perkins, owner of copyright.
No. 648. Knocking, Knocking.
Mrs. H. B. Stowe, arr.
Geo. F. Root.
1. Knocking, knocking, who is there? Wait-ing, wait-ing, oh, how fair!
2. Knocking, knooking, still He's there? Wait-ing, wait-ing, wondrous fair!
3. Knocking, knocking,—what! still there? Wait-ing, wait-ing, grand and fair!
'Tis a Pil - grim, strange and king - ly, Nev- er such was seen be - fore;
But the door is hard to o - pen, For the weeds and i - vy - vine,
Yes, the pierc - ed hand still knock-eth, And be-neath the crown-ed hair
Ah! my soul, for such a won - der Wilt thou not un - do the door?
With their dark and cling-ing ten - drils, Ev - er round the hing - es twine.
Beam with pa - tient eyes, so ten - der, Of thy Sav - iour, wait-ing there.
By per. The John Church Co., owners of copyright.

No. 649. I Heard the Voice of Jesus Say.

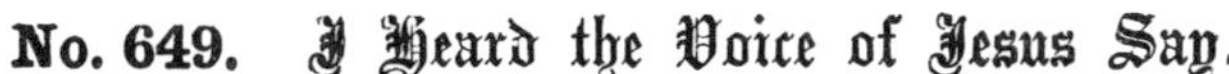

H. Bonar, D.D. (Evan. C. M.) Wm. H. Havergal.

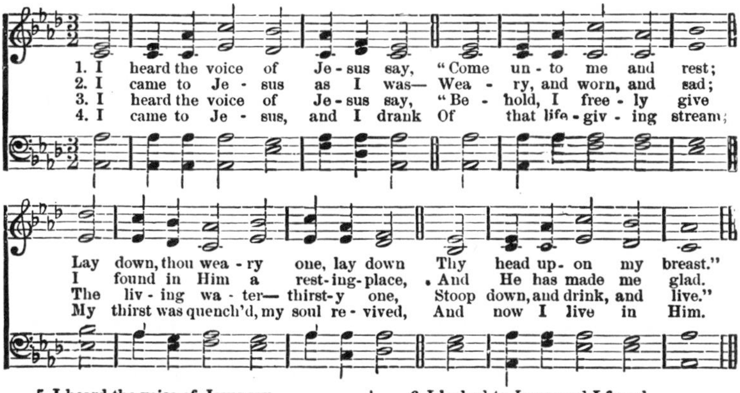

1. I heard the voice of Je - sus say, "Come un - to me and rest;
2. I came to Je - sus as I was— Wea - ry, and worn, and sad;
3. I heard the voice of Je - sus say, "Be - hold, I free - ly give
4. I came to Je - sus, and I drank Of that life - giv - ing stream;
Lay down, thou wea - ry one, lay down Thy head up - on my breast."
I found in Him a rest - ing - place, And He has made me glad.
The liv - ing wa - ter— thirst - y one, Stoop down, and drink, and live."
My thirst was quench'd, my soul re - vived, And now I live in Him.

5 I heard the voice of Jesus say,
"I am this dark world's Light;
Look unto me, thy morn shall rise,
And all thy day be bright."

6 I looked to Jesus, and I found
In Him my Star, my Sun;
And in that light of life I'll walk
'Till trav'ling days are done.

No. 650. The Half was Never Told.

P. P. B. P. P. Bliss.

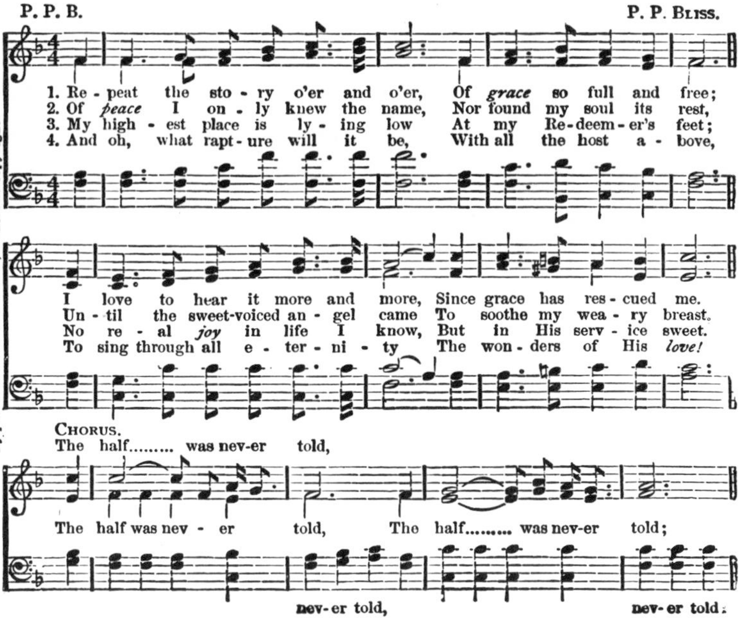

1. Re - peat the sto - ry o'er and o'er, Of *grace* so full and free;
2. Of *peace* I on - ly knew the name, Nor found my soul its rest,
3. My high - est place is ly - ing low At my Re - deem - er's feet;
4. And oh, what rapt - ure will it be, With all the host a - bove,
I love to hear it more and more, Since grace has res - cued me.
Un - til the sweet-voiced an - gel came To soothe my wea - ry breast.
No re - al *joy* in life I know, But in His serv - ice sweet.
To sing through all e - ter - ni - ty The won - ders of His *love!*
Chorus.
The half......... was nev-er told,
The half was nev - er told, The half......... was nev-er told;
nev - er told, nev - er told.

The Half was Never Told.
The half........ was nev-er told;
1. Of grace di-vine, so won-der-ful, The half was nev - er told.
2. Of peace, etc. nev-er told.
3. Of joy, etc.
4. Of love, etc.
No. 651. Christ Returneth.
H. L. Turner.
James McGranahan.
1. It may be at morn, when the day is a - wak-ing, When sun-light thro' dark - ness and shad - ow is break - ing, That Je - sus will come in the full - ness of glo - ry, To re - ceive from the world "His own."
2. It may be at mid - day, it may be at twi-light, It may be, per-chance, that the black-ness of mid - night Will burst in - to light in the blaze of His glo - ry, When Je - sus re - ceives "His own."
3. While its hosts cry Ho - san - na, from heaven de-scending, With glo - ri - fied saints and the an - gels at - tend - ing, With grace on His brow, like a ha - lo of glo - ry, Will Je - sus re - ceive "His own."
4. Oh, joy! oh, de - light! should we go with-out dy - ing, No sick-ness, no sad - ness, no dread and no cry - ing, Caught up thro' the clouds with our Lord in - to glo - ry, When Je - sus re - ceives "His own."
Chorus.
O Lord Je - sus, how long? how long Ere we shout the glad song? Christ re-turn-eth; Hal-le - lu - jah! hal-le - lu - jah! A - men, Hal - le - lu - jah! A - men.
rit.
Copyright, MDCCCLXXVII, by James McGranahan, used by per.

No. 652. Dare to be a Daniel.

P. P. B.
P. P. Bliss.
By per. The John Church Co., owners of copyright.
1. Standing by a purpose true, Heeding God's command,
2. Many mighty men are lost, Daring not to stand,
3. Many giants, great and tall, Stalking thro' the land,
4. Hold the gospel banner high! On to vict'ry grand!
Honor them, the faithful few! All hail to Daniel's Band!
Who for God had been a host, By joining Daniel's Band!
Headlong to the earth would fall, If met by Daniel's Band!
Satan and his hosts defy, And shout for Daniel's Band!
Chorus.
Dare to be a Daniel, Dare to stand alone! Dare to have a purpose firm! Dare to make it known!
No. 653. Arise, my Soul, Arise.
Ch. Wesley.
(Lenox. 6s, 8s.)
Lewis Edson.
1. Arise, my soul, arise; Shake off thy guilty fears; The bleeding sacrifice
2. He ever lives above, For me to intercede; His all redeeming love,
3. Five bleeding wounds He bears, Received on Calvary; They pour effectual prayers,
4. My God is reconciled; His pard'ning voice I hear; He owns me for His child;
In my behalf appears; Before the throne my Surety stands,
His precious blood to plead; His blood atoned for all our race,
They strongly plead for me; Forgive him, oh, forgive they cry,
I can no longer fear; With confidence I now draw nigh,
Before the throne my Surety stands, My name is written on His hands.
His blood atoned for all our race, And sprinkles now the throne of grace.
Forgive him, oh, forgive, they cry, Nor let that ransomed sinner die.
With confidence I now draw nigh, And "Father, Abba, Father," cry.

No. 654. The Solid Rock.
Rev. Edward Mote.
Wm. B. Bradbury.
1. My hope is built on noth-ing less Than Je-sus' blood and righteousness;
2. When darkness veils His love-ly face, I rest on His un-changing grace;
3. His oath, His cov-e-nant, His blood, Sup-port me in the whelming flood;
4. When He shall come with trump-et sound, O, may I then in Him be found;
I dare not trust the sweet-est frame, But whol-ly lean on Je-sus' name.
In ev-'ry high and storm-y gale, My anch-or holds with-in the vail.
When all a-round my soul gives way, He then is all my hope and stay.
Cloth'd in His righteous-ness a-lone, Fault-less to stand be-fore the throne!
Chorus.
On Christ, the Solid Rock, I stand; All other ground is sinking sand, All other ground is sinking sand.
By per. The Biglow & Main Co., owners of copyright.
No. 655. The Beautiful Land on High.
James Nicholson.
Wm. U. Butcher.
1. There's a beau-ti-ful land on high, To its glo-ries I fain would fly,
2. There's a beau-ti-ful land on high, I shall en-ter it by and by;
3. There's a beau-ti-ful land on high; Then why should I fear to die,
When by sorrows press'd down, I long for a crown In that beauti-ful land on high.
There with friends hand in hand, I shall walk on the strand, In that beauti-ful land on high.
When death is the way To the realms of day, In that beauti-ful land on high.
Chorus.
In that beau-ti-ful land I'll be, From earth and its cares set free;
Used by permission.

The Beautiful Land on High.

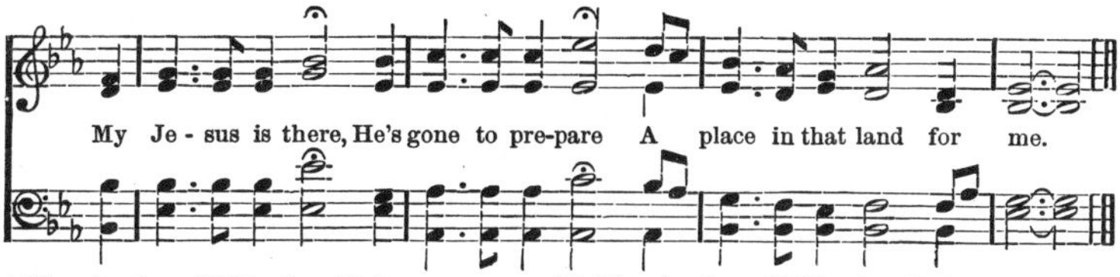

My Je - sus is there, He's gone to pre-pare A place in that land for me.

4 There's a beautiful land on high,
And my kindred its bliss enjoy;
And methinks I now see how they're waiting for me,
In that beautiful land on high.

5 There's a beautiful land on high,
Where we never shall say "good-bye;"
Where the righteous will sing, and their chorus will ring
In that beautiful land on high.

No. 656. Why not To-night?

Eliza Reed. Ira D. Sankey.

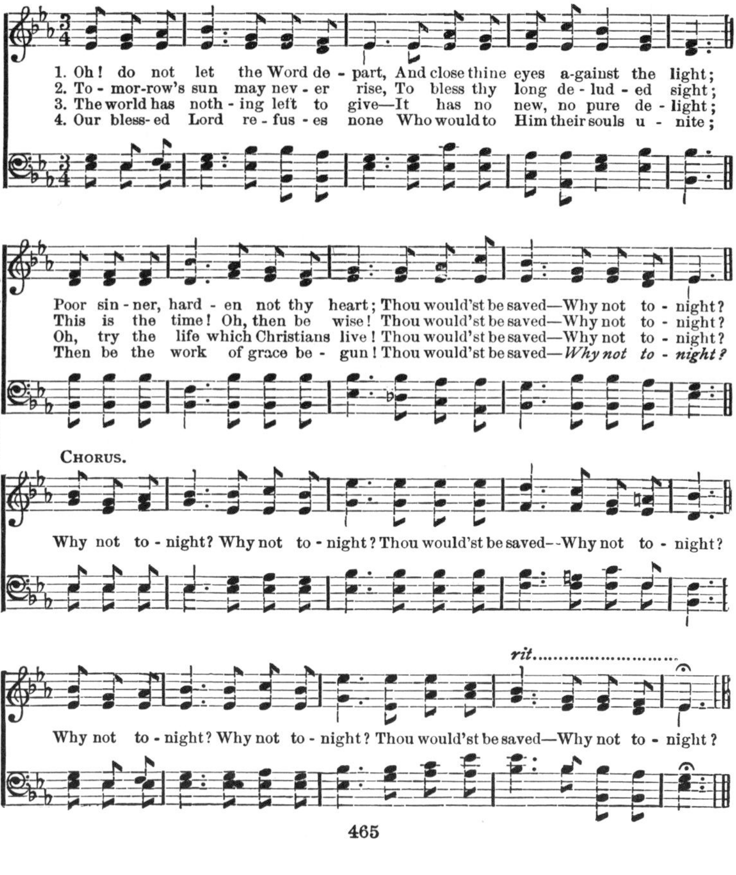

1. Oh! do not let the Word de - part, And close thine eyes a-gainst the light;
2. To - mor-row's sun may nev - er rise, To bless thy long de - lud - ed sight;
3. The world has noth - ing left to give—It has no new, no pure de - light;
4. Our bless-ed Lord re - fus - es none Who would to Him their souls u - nite;

Poor sin - ner, hard - en not thy heart; Thou would'st be saved—Why not to - night?
This is the time! Oh, then be wise! Thou would'st be saved—Why not to - night?
Oh, try the life which Christians live! Thou would'st be saved—Why not to - night?
Then be the work of grace be - gun! Thou would'st be saved—*Why not to - night?*

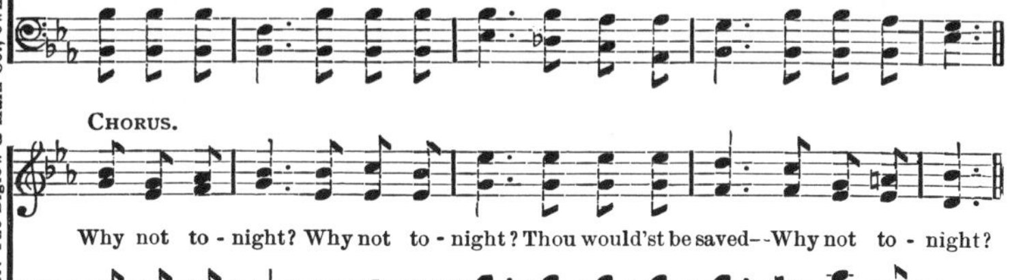

No. 657. The Hem of His Garment.
G. F. R.
Geo. F. Root.
1. She on - ly touch'd the hem of His gar-ment As to His side she stole,
2. She came in fear and trembling be-fore Him, She knew her Lord had come;
3. He turn'd with "Daughter, be of good com-fort, Thy faith hath made thee whole;"
A - mid the crowd that gath-er'd around Him, And straightway she was whole.
She felt that from Him vir-tue had healed her, The might - y deed was done.
And peace that pass- eth all un - der-stand-ing With glad - ness filled her soul.
Chorus.
Oh, touch the hem of His gar - ment! And thou, too, shalt be free;
His sav - ing pow'r this ver - y hour Shall give new life to thee.
By per. The John Church Co., owners of copyright.
No. 658. I am Coming to the Cross.
Rev. Wm. McDonald.
Wm. G. Fischer.
1. I am com - ing to the cross; I am poor, and weak, and blind; I am
2. Long my heart has sighed for Thee, Long has e - vil reigned with-in; Je - sus
3. Here I give my all to Thee, Friends, and time, and earth - ly store; Soul and
Cho.—I am trust - ing, Lord, in Thee, Bless-ed Lamb of Cal - va - ry; Hum-bly
D.C. Chorus.
count - ing all but dross, I shall full sal - va - tion find.
sweet - ly speaks to me,— "I will cleanse you from all sin.
bod - y Thine to be,— Whol - ly Thine for ev - er - more.
at Thy cross I bow, Save me, Je - sus, save me now.
Copyright, MDCCCLXIX, by Wm. G. Fischer, used by per.

4 In the promises I trust,
Now I feel the blood applied:
I am prostrate in the dust,
I with Christ am crucified.

5 Jesus comes! He fills my soul!
Perfected in Him I am;
I am every whit made whole:
Glory, glory to the Lamb.

No. 659. Will Jesus Find us Watching?

FANNY J. CROSBY.
W. H. DOANE.
1. When Je-sus comes to re-ward His servants, Whether it be noon or night,
2. If at the dawn of the ear-ly morn-ing, He shall call us one by one,
3. Have we been true to the trust He left us? Do we seek to do our best?
4. Bless-ed are those whom the Lord finds watching, In His glo-ry they shall share;
rit.
Faith-ful to Him will He find us watching, With our lamps all trimm'd and bright?
When to the Lord we re-store our tal-ents, Will He answer thee—"Well done?"
If in our hearts there is naught con-demns us, We shall have a glo-rious rest.
If He shall come at the dawn or midnight, Will He find us watch-ing there?
REFRAIN.
Oh, can we say we are read-y, broth-er?—Read-y for the soul's bright home?
Say, will He find you and me still watching, Waiting, waiting when the Lord shall come?
Copyright, MDCCCLXXVI, by W. H. Doane. Used by per.

No. 660. Saviour, Like a Shepherd.

DOROTHY A. THRUPP.
WM. B. BRADBURY

1. {Sav-iour, like a shep-herd lead us, Much we need Thy tend'rest care;}
{In Thy pleas-ant pas-tures feed us, For our use Thy folds pre-pare.}
2. {We are Thine, do Thou be-friend us, Be the Guardian of our way;}
{Keep Thy flock, from sin de-fend us, Seek us when we go a-stray.}
3. {Thou hast prom-ised to re-ceive us, Poor and sin-ful tho' we be;}
{Thou hast mer-cy to re-lieve us, Grace to cleanse, and power to free.}

Saviour, Like a Shepherd.

Bless-ed Je - sus, Bless-ed Je - sus, Thou hast bought us, Thine we are;
Bless-ed Je - sus, Bless-ed Je - sus, Hear, O hear us, when we pray;
Bless-ed Je sus, Bless-ed Je - sus, We will ear - ly turn to Thee;
Bless-ed Je - sus, Bless-ed Je - sus, Thou hast bought us, Thine we are.
Bless-ed Je - sus, Bless-ed Je - sus, Hear, O hear us, when we pray.
Bless-ed Je - sus, Bless-ed Je - sus, We will ear - ly turn to Thee.
By per. The Biglow & Main Co., owners of copyright.
No. 661. Come, ye Disconsolate.
Thos. Moore, alt.
Samuel Webbe.
1. Come, ye dis - con - so - late! wher - e'er ye lan - guish, Come to the
2. Joy of the des - o - late! light of the stray - ing, Hope of the
3. Here see the bread of life: see wa - ters flow - ing Forth from the
mer - cy - seat, fer - vent - ly kneel: Here bring your wound - ed hearts,
pen - i - tent, fade - less and pure! Here speaks the Com - fort - er,
throne of God, pure from a - bove: Come to the feast of love;
here tell your an - guish; Earth has no sor - row that heav'n can - not heal.
ten - der - ly say - ing, Earth has no sor - row that heav'n can - not cure.
come, ev - er know-ing, Earth has no sor - rows but heav'n can re - move

No. 662. What Shall the Harvest Be?

Miss Emily S. Oakey. P. P. Bliss.

1. Sow-ing the seed by the day-light fair, Sow-ing the seed by the noon-day glare,
2. Sow-ing the seed by the way-side high, Sow-ing the seed on the rocks to die,
3. Sow-ing the seed of a lingering pain, Sow-ing the seed of a maddened brain,
4. Sow-ing the seed with an ach-ing heart Sow-ing the seed while the tear-drops start,
Sow-ing the seed by the fad-ing light, Sow-ing the seed in the sol-emn night;
Sow-ing the seed where the thorns will spoil, Sow-ing the seed in the fer-tile soil;
Sow-ing the seed of a tarnished name, Sow-ing the seed of e-ter-nal shame;
Sow-ing in hope till the reap-ers come Glad-ly to gath-er the har-vest home:
Oh, what shall the har-vest be?......... Oh, what shall the har-vest be?.........
Chorus.
Sown.................. in the dark - - ness or sown.............. in the
Sown in the dark-ness or sown in the light, Sown in the dark-ness or
light,.................. Sown.................. in our weak - - ness or
sown in the light, Sown in our weak-ness or sown in our might,
By per. The John Church Co., owners of copyright.

No. 663. Take My Life and Let it Be.

FRANCES R. HAVERGAL. W. A. MOZART, arr. by H. P. MAIN.

No. 664. "Come."

MRS. JAS. G. JOHNSON. JAMES MCGRANAHAN.

sown............... in our might,............ Gath - er'd in time or e-
Sown in our weakness or sown in our might, Gath - er'd in - time or e-
ter - ni - ty, Sure, ah, sure will the har - vest be.........
ter - ni - ty, Sure, ah, sure will the har - vest, har-vest be.
1. Take my life and let it be Con - se - cra - ted, Lord, to Thee;
2. Take my feet and let them be Swift and beau - ti - ful for Thee;
3. Take my mo - ments and my days, Let them flow in end - less praise;
4. Take my will and make it Thine, It shall be no long - er mine;
5. Take my love, my God, I pour At Thy feet its treas - ure - store;
Take my hands and let them move At the im - pulse of Thy love.
Take my voice and let me sing Al - ways— on - ly— for my King.
Take my in - tel - lect, and use Ev - 'ry pow'r as Thou shalt choose.
Take my heart, it is Thine own, It shall be Thy roy - al throne.
Take my - self, and I will be Ev - er, on - ly, all for Thee.
Copyright, MDCCCXC, by The Biglow & Main Co.
Voices in Unison.
1. O word of words the sweet - est, Oh words, in which there lie
2. O soul! why shouldst thou wan - der From such a lov - ing Friend?
3. O, each time draw me near - er, That soon the "Come" may be

All prom - ise, all ful - fill - ment, And end of mys - ter - y;
Cling clos - er, clos - er to Him, Stay with Him to the end;
Naught but a gen - tle whis - per, To one close, close to Thee;

La - ment - ing or re - joic - ing, With doubt or ter - ror nigh,
A - las! I am so help - less, So ver - y full of sin,
Then, o - ver sea and mount - ain, Far from or near my home,

I hear the "Come!" of Je - sus, And to His cross I fly.
For I am ev - er wand'ring, And com - ing back a - gain.
I'll take Thy hand and fol - low, At that sweet whis - per "Come!"

REFRAIN.

Come, oh, come to me,......... Come, oh, come to me,......... Wea - ry, heav - y
Come, come, come, come, come, come, come, come, Come, come,

la - den, Come, oh, come to me, Come, oh, come to me,............
me, Oh come, come, come, come, come,

Come, oh, come to me,.......... Wea - ry, heav - y la - den, come, oh, come to me.
rit............
Come, come, come, come, come.

No. 665. The Shining Shore.
Rev. David Nelson.
Geo. F. Root.
1. My days are glid - ing swift - ly by, And I, a pil - grim stran - ger,
Would not de - tain them as they fly, Those hours of toil and dan - ger.
Fine.
D.S.—just be - fore, the shin - ing shore We may al - most dis - cov - er.
Chorus.
For, oh! we stand on Jor - dan's strand; Our friends are pass - ing o - ver; And,
D.S.
By per. Geo. F. Root, owner of copyright.
2 Should coming days be cold and dark,
We need not cease our singing;
That perfect rest naught can molest,
Where golden harps are ringing.
For, oh! we stand, etc.
3 Let sorrow's rudest tempest blow,
Each cord on earth to sever;
Our King says—"Come!"—and there's our [home,
For ever, oh! for ever!
For, oh! we stand, etc.
No. 666. I am Sweeping Thro' the Gate.
Rev. John Parker.
Philip Phillips.
1. I am now a child of God, For I'm wash'd in Je - sus' blood; I am
2. Oh! the bless - ed Lord of light, He up - holds me by His might: And His
3. I am sweeping thro' the gate Where the bless - ed for me wait: Where the
4. Burst are all my pris - on bars; And I soar be - yond the stars, To my
watch - ing and I'm long - ing while I wait. Soon on wings of love I'll fly,
arms en - fold, and com - fort while I wait. I am lean - ing on His breast,
wea - ry work - ers rest for - ev - er - more; Where the strife of earth is done,
Fa - ther's house, the bright and blest es - tate, Lo! the morn e - ter - nal breaks,
Copyright property of The Biglow & Main Co.

I am Sweeping Thro' the Gate.
To my home be-yond the sky, To my welcome, as I'm sweeping thro' the gate.
Oh! the sweetness of His rest, Hal-le-lu-jah, I am sweeping thro' the gate.
And the crown of life is won: Oh, the glo-ry of that cit-y just be-fore!
And the song im-mor-tal wakes, Rob'd in whiteness I am sweeping thro' the gate.
Refrain.
In the blood of yon-der Lamb, Wash'd from ev-'ry stain I am;
rit.
Repeat pp.
Rob'd in white-ness, clad in bright-ness, I am sweeping thro' the gate.
No. 667. Pardon, Peace and Power.
El. Nathan.
James McGranahan.
1. Would we be joy-ful in the Lord? Then count the rich-es o'er,
2. For ev-'ry sin, by grace di-vine A par-don free be-stowed;
3. Of grace to break the pow'r of sin, He gives a full sup-ply;
4. The power to win a soul to God, The Spir-it, too im-parts;
5. These bless-ings we by faith re-ceive, By sim-ple child-like trust;
Re-vealed to faith with-in His word, And note the bound-less store.
And with the par-don peace is mine, The peace in Je-sus' blood.
The Ho-ly Ghost, the heart with-in, From sin doth pu-ri-fy.
And He, the gift of Christ our Lord, Dwells now in all our hearts.
In Christ, 'tis God's de-light to give; He prom-ised, and He must.
Chorus.
There is par-don, peace and pow'r,........ And pu-ri-
pardon, peace, and pow'r, pardon, peace and pow'r,
Copyright, 1883, by James McGranahan.

Pardon, Peace and Power.
ty.................... and Par - a - dise;................. With all of these.................. in
And pur - i - ty, and Par - a- dise; With all of these in
Christ for me........................ Let joy - ful songs of praise to Him a - rise!
in Christ for me,
No. 668. Come now saith the Lord.
W. W. D.
James McGranahan.
1. Come souls that are long-ing for pleas-ure, Our Sav-iour has pleasures to give;
2. The pleas-ures of sin are de-ceiv-ing, They've nothing for yes- ter-day's pain,
3. The pleas-ures of sin are all fleet-ing, They van-ish with life's pass-ing morn;
4. Then all who are long-ing for pleas-ure, Ye wea-ry, and all who are worn;
5. Of Je - sus, thy choice be now mak-ing, Re-deem-er, and Sav-iour, and Lord;
Come find in His love the rare treasure, That makes ev-'ry true pleasure live.
But hope of to-mor-row re-ceiv-ing, And then, its—To-morrow—a - gain.
Like dew-drops the morning sun greet-ing, They glist-en and then they are gone.
Come find in the Lord a sure treasure, That from you shall nev- er be torn.
And soon in the glo - ry a - wak-ing, You'll share in the Saint's blest re - ward,
Copyright, 1878, by James McGranahan.
Chorus.
Come now saith the Lord, let us rea - son, Come now and your pur-pose de - clare;
Is it pleasures of sin for a sea - son, Or pleasures the glo - ri - fied share?

No. 669. Beautiful River.

R. Lowry.
Rev. Robert Lowry.
Cheerful.
1. Shall we gather at the riv - er Where bright angel feet have trod; With its crystal tide for ev - er Flowing by the throne of God?
2. On the margin of the riv - er, Wash-ing up its sil- ver spray, We will walk and worship ev - er, All the hap-py, gold- en day.
3. Ere we reach the shining river, Lay we ev-'ry burden down; Grace our spirits will de- liv - er, And provide a robe and crown.
Chorus.
Yes, we'll gather at the riv - er; The beautiful, the beau-ti - ful riv - er— Gather with the saints at the riv - er, That flows by the throne of God.
From "Bright Jewels," by permission.
4 At the smiling of the river,
Mirror of the Saviour's face,
Saints, whom death will never sever,
Lift their songs of saving grace.
5 Soon we'll reach the silver river,
Soon our pilgrimage will cease;
Soon our happy hearts will quiver,
With the melody of peace.
No. 670. Come, Ye Sinners.
Rev. John Newton.
(Zion. 8s. 7s. & 4.)
Dr. Thos. Hastings.
1. Come, ye sin-ners, poor and need-y, Weak and wounded, sick and sore; Je - sus read - y stands to save you, Full of pit - y, love and pow'r; He is a - ble, He is will-ing: doubt no more; He is a - ble, He is will-ing: doubt no more.
2. Now, ye need - y, come and welcome; God's free bounty glo - ri - fy; True be- lief, and true repentance,—Ev'ry grace that brings you nigh,— Without mon- ey, Come to Je- sus Christ and buy; Without mon-ey, Come to Je- sus Christ and buy.
3 Let not conscience make you linger;
Nor of fitness fondly dream:
All the fitness He requireth
Is to feel your need of Him:
This He gives you,—
'Tis the Spirit's glimm'ring beam.
4 Come, ye weary, heavy-laden,
Bruised and mangled by the fall;
If you tarry 'till you're better,
You will never come at all;
Not the righteous,—
Sinners, Jesus came to call.

No. 671. God is Love.

Sir John Bowring. (Wilmot. 8s. 7s.) C. M. Von Weber.

1. God is love; His mer - cy bright - ens All the path in which we rove;
2. Time and change are bus - y ev - er; Man de - cays, and a - ges move;
3. E'en the hour that dark - est seem - eth Will His change-less good-ness prove;
4. He with earth - ly cares en - twin - eth Hope and com - fort from a - bove;
Bliss He wakes, and woe He light - ens, God is wis - dom, God is love.
But His mer - cy wan - eth nev - er; God is wis - dom, God is love.
From the gloom His bright-ness streameth, God is wis - dom, God is love.
Ev - 'ry - where His glo - ry shin - eth, God is wis - dom, God is love.

No. 672. Tune—Duke St. L. M. No. 624.

1 From all that dwell below the skies,
Let the Creator's praise arise;
Let the Redeemer's name be sung,
Through every land, by every tongue.

2 Eternal are Thy mercies, Lord;
Eternal truth attends Thy word:
Thy praise shall sound from shore to shore,
Till suns shall rise and set no more.

Isaac Watts.

No. 673. Rest for the Weary.

Rev. S. Y. Harmer. Rev. Wm. McDonald.

1. {In the Christ-ian's home in glo - ry, There re - mains a land of rest;
{There my Sav - iour's gone be - fore me, [Omit.]
To ful - fil my soul's re - quest,
Chorus.
{There is rest for the wea - ry, There is rest for the wea - ry, There is rest for the wea - ry, There is rest for you.
{On the oth - er side of Jor - dan, In the sweet fields of E - den, Where the tree of life is blooming, There is rest for you.

2 He is fitting up my mansion,
Which eternally shall stand,
For my stay shall not be transient,
In that holy, happy land.
There is rest, etc.

3 Sing, Oh! sing, ye heirs of glory!
Shout your triumph as you go!
Zion's gate will open for you,
You shall find an entrance through.
There is rest, etc.

No. 674. Sun of My Soul.
J. Keble.
Peter Ritter.
1. Sun of my soul, Thou Sav - iour dear, It is not night if Thou be near;
2. When the soft dews of kind - ly sleep My wearied eye - lids gent - ly steep,
3. A - bide with me from morn till eve, For without Thee I can - not live;
4. If some poor wandering child of Thine Have spurned to-day the voice di - vine
Oh, may no earth - born cloud a - rise, To hide Thee from Thy serv - ant's eyes.
Be my last thought, how sweet to rest For - ev - er on my Sav - iour's breast.
A - bide with me when night is nigh, For without Thee I dare not die.
Now, Lord, the gra - cious work be - gin; Let him no more lie down in sin.

No. 675. Tune—Lenox. 6s. 8s. No. 653.

1 Come every joyful heart,
That loves the Saviour's name!
Your noblest powers exert,
To celebrate His fame;
Tell all above, and all below,
The debt of love to Him you owe.

2 He left His starry crown,
And laid His robes aside;
On wings of love come down,
And wept, and bled, and died;
What He endured no tongue can tell,
To save our souls from death and hell.

3 From the dark grave He rose—
The mansion of the dead;
And thence His mighty foes
In glorious triumph led;
Up thro' the sky the Conqueror rode
And reigns on high the Saviour God.

4 From thence He'll quickly come—
His chariot will not stay—
And bear our spirits home
To realms of endless day;
There shall we see His lovely face,
And ever be in His embrace.

Samuel Stennet.

No. 676. Laban. S. M.
Geo. Heath.
Dr. Lowell Mason.
1. My soul, be on thy guard, Ten thou - sand foes a - rise;
2. O watch, and fight, and pray; The bat - tle ne'er give o'er;
3. Ne'er think the vict - 'ry won, Nor lay thine arm - or down:
The hosts of sin are press - ing hard, To draw Thee from the skies.
Re - new it bold - ly ev - 'ry day, And help di - vine im - plore.
The work of faith will not be done, Till thou ob - tain the crown.

No. 677. Tune—Christmas. C. M. No. 693.

1 Awake, my soul, stretch every nerve,
And press with vigor on;
A heavenly race demands thy zeal,
And an immortal crown.

2 A cloud of witnesses around
Hold thee in full survey;
Forget the steps already trod,
And onward urge thy way.

3 'Tis God's all-animating voice,
That calls thee from on high,
'Tis His own hand presents the prize
To thine aspiring eye.

4 Blest Saviour, introduced by Thee
Have I my race begun;
And, crowned with victory, at Thy feet
I'll lay my honors down.

P. Doddridge.

No. 678. The Lord's My Shepherd.
Psalm 23.
(Belmont. C. M.)
Wm. Gardiner.
1. The Lord's my Shep-herd, I'll not want: He makes me down to lie
2. My soul He doth re - store a - gain; And me to walk doth make
3. Yea, tho' I walk in death's dark vale, Yet I will fear none ill;
In pas - tures green: He lead - eth me The qui - et wa - ters by.
With - in the paths of right - eous-ness, E'en for His own name's sake.
For Thou art with me; and Thy rod And staff me com - fort still.
4 My table Thou hast furnished
In presence of my foes;
My head Thou dost with oil anoint,
And my cup overflows.
5 Goodness and mercy all my life
Shall surely follow me;
And in God's house for evermore
My dwelling-place shall be.
No. 679. Tune—Belmont. C. M.
1 Majestic sweetness sits enthroned
Upon the Saviour's brow;
His head with radiant glories crowned,
His lips with grace o'erflow.
2 He saw me plunged in deep distress,
And flew to my relief;
For me He bore the shameful cross,
And carried all my grief.
3 To heaven, the place of His abode,
He brings my weary feet;
Shows me the glories of my God,
And makes my joys complete.
4 Since from Thy bounty I receive
Such proofs of love divine,
Had I a thousand hearts to give,
Lord! they should all be Thine.
Samuel Stennett.
No. 680. Warwick. C. M.
Rev. John Newton.
Samuel Stanley.
1. A - maz - ing grace, how sweet the sound, That saved a wretch like me!
2. 'Twas grace that taught my heart to fear, And grace my fears re - lieved;
3. Thro' ma - ny dan - gers, toils, and snares, I have al - read - y come;
I once was lost, but now am found; Was blind, but now I see.
How pre - cious did that grace ap - pear, The hour I first be - lieved.
'Tis grace that brought me safe thus far, And grace will lead me home.
4 Yes, when this heart and flesh shall fail,
And mortal life shall cease,
I shall possess, within the vail,
A life of joy and peace.
No. 681. Tune—Marlow. C. M. Key G.
1 Come, Holy Spirit, Heavenly Dove!
With all Thy quickening powers;
Kindle a flame of sacred love
In these cold hearts of ours.
2 Dear Lord! and shall we ever live
At this poor dying rate?
Our love so faint, so cold to Thee,
And Thine to us so great?
3 Come, Holy Spirit, Heavenly Dove,
With all Thy quickening powers;
Come, shed abroad a Saviour's love,
And that shall kindle ours.
Isaac Watts.

No. 682. Just as I Am.

CHARLOTTE ELLIOTT. (WOODWORTH. L. M.) WM. B. BRADBURY.

Used by per.

1. Just as I am, with-out one plea, But that Thy blood was shed for me,
2. Just as I am, and wait-ing not To rid my soul of one dark blot,
3. Just as I am, though tossed a-bout, With many a con-flict, many a doubt,
And that Thou bidd'st me come to Thee, O Lamb of God! I come, I come!
To Thee, whose blood can cleanse each spot, O Lamb of God! I come, I come!
Fightings and fears with-in, with-out, O Lamb of God! I come, I come!

4 Just as I am, poor, wretched, blind,
Sight, riches, healing of the mind,
Yea, all I need, in Thee to find,
O Lamb of God! I come, I come!

5 Just as I am; Thou wilt receive,
Wilt welcome, pardon, cleanse, relieve;
Because Thy promise I believe,
O Lamb of God! I come, I come!

No. 683. Tune—HENDON. 7s. No. 731.

1 Come, said Jesus' sacred voice
Come, and make My paths your choice;
I will guide you to your home,
Weary pilgrim, hither come!

2 Thou who, homeless, sole, forlorn,
Long hast borne the proud world's scorn,
Long hast roamed the barren waste,
Weary pilgrim, hither haste.

3 Ye who, tossed on beds of pain,
Seek for ease, but seek in vain;
Ye, by fiercer anguish torn,
In remorse for guilt who mourn;—

4 Hither come! for here is found
Balm that flows for every wound,
Peace that ever shall endure,
Rest eternal, sacred, sure.

Ann L. Barbauld.

No. 684. Hebron. L. M.

TIMOTHY DWIGHT, D. D. DR. LOWELL MASON.

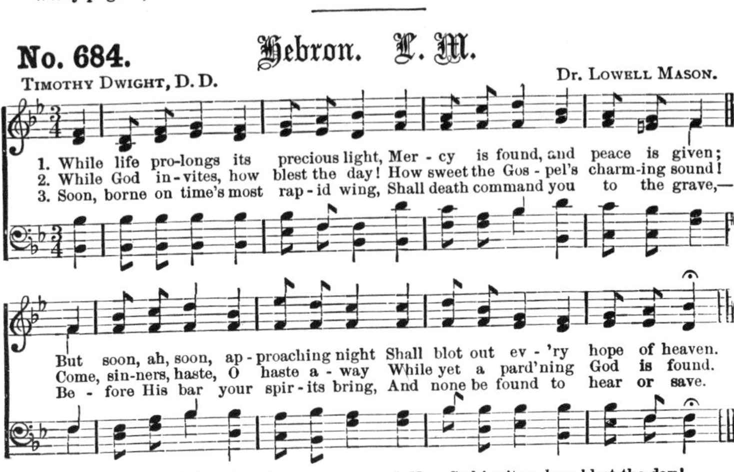
1. While life pro-longs its precious light, Mer-cy is found, and peace is given;
2. While God in-vites, how blest the day! How sweet the Gos-pel's charm-ing sound!
3. Soon, borne on time's most rap-id wing, Shall death command you to the grave,—
But soon, ah, soon, ap-proaching night Shall blot out ev-'ry hope of heaven.
Come, sin-ners, haste, O haste a-way While yet a pard'ning God is found.
Be-fore His bar your spir-its bring, And none be found to hear or save.

4 In that lone land of deep despair,
No Sabbath's heavenly light shall rise,—
No God regard your bitter prayer,
No Saviour call you to the skies.

5 Now God invites; how blest the day!
How sweet the Gospel's charming sound!
Come, sinners, haste, O haste away,
While yet a pard'ning God is found.

No. 685. Olive's Brow. L. M.

Rev. Hugh Stowell. Wm. B. Bradbury.

1. From ev - 'ry storm-y wind that blows, From ev - 'ry swelling tide of woes,
2. There is a place, where Je - sus sheds The oil of gladness on our heads;
3. There is a scene where spir - its blend, Where friend holds fellowship with friend:
Used by per.
There is a calm, a sure re - treat; 'Tis found be-neath the mer - cy - seat.
A place than all be - sides more sweet,—It is the blood-bought mer - cy - seat.
Though sunder'd far, by faith we meet, A - round one com-mon mer - cy - seat.

No. 686. Tune—No. 600.

1 Once I was dead in sin,
And hope within me died;
But now I'm dead to sin—
With Jesus crucified.

Cho.—And can it be that "He loved me,
And gave Himself for me?"

2 Oh height I cannot reach,
Oh depth I cannot sound,
Oh love, O boundless love,
In my Redeemer found!

3 O cold, ungrateful heart
That can from Jesus turn,
When living fires of love
Should on His altar burn.

4 I live—and yet, not I,
But Christ that lives in me;
Who from the law of sin
And death hath made me free.

Rev. A. T. Pierson.

No. 687. Tune—St. Thomas. S. M. No. 692.

1 O Holy Spirit, come,
And Jesus' love declare;
Oh, tell us of our heavenly home,
And guide us safely there.

2 Our unbelief remove
By Thine almighty breath;
Oh, work the wondrous work of love,
The mighty work of faith.

3 Come with resistless power,
Come with almighty grace,
Come with the long-expected shower,
And fall upon this place.

Oswald Allen.

No. 688. Shirland. S. M.

Timothy Dwight, D. D. Samuel Stanley.

1. I love Thy king - dom, Lord, The house of Thine a - bode,
2. I love Thy Church, O God! Her walls be - fore Thee stand,
3. For her my tears shall fall; For her my prayers as - cend;
The Church our blest Re deem-er saved With His own pre-cious blood.
Dear as the ap - ple of Thine eye, And grav - en on Thy hand.
To her my cares and toils be given, Till toils and cares shall end.

4 Beyond my highest joy
I prize her heavenly ways;
Her sweet communion, solemn vows
Her hymns of love and praise.

5 Sure as Thy truth shall last,
To Zion shall be given
The brightest glories earth can yield,
And brighter bliss of heaven.

No. 689. Boylston. S. M.

Isaac Watts. Dr. Lowell Mason.

1. Not all the blood of beasts On Jew - ish al - tars slain,
2. But Christ, the heav'n - ly Lamb, Takes all our sins a - way;
3. My faith would lay her hand On that dear head of Thine,
4. My soul looks back to see The bur - den thou didst bear,
Could give the guilt - y con-science peace, Or wash a - way the stain.
A sac - ri - fice of no - bler name And rich - er blood than they.
While like a pen - i - tent I stand, And there con - fess my sin.
While hang - ing on th'ac - curs - ed tree, And knows her guilt was there.

No. 690. Tune—Boylston. S. M.

1 How solemn are the words,
And yet to faith how plain,
Which Jesus uttered while on earth—
"*Ye must be born again!*"

2 "*Ye must be born again!*"
For so hath God decreed;
Nor reformation will suffice—
'Tis *life* poor sinners need.

3 "*Ye must be born again!*"
And life *in Christ* must have;
In vain the soul may elsewhere go—
'Tis He *alone* can save.

4. "*Ye must be born again!*"
Or never enter heaven;
'Tis only blood-washed ones are there,
The ransomed and forgiven.

Anon.

No. 691. Tune—Boylston. S. M.

1 Lord, bless and pity us,
Shine on us with Thy face:
That th' earth Thy way, and nations all
May know Thy saving grace.

2 Let people praise Thee, Lord!
Let people all Thee praise!
Oh, let the nations all be glad,
In songs their voices raise!

3 Thou'lt justly people judge,
On earth rule nations all;
Let people praise Thee, Lord! let them
Praise Thee, both great and small!

4 The earth her fruit shall yield,
Our God shall blessing send;
God shall us bless: men shall Him fear
Unto earth's utmost end.

Psalm 67.

No. 692. St. Thomas. S. M.

Rev. Wm. Hammond. G. F. Handel.

1. A - wake, and sing the song Of Mo - ses and the Lamb;
2. Sing of His dy - ing love; Sing of His ris - en power;
3. Ye pil - grims, on the road To Zi - on's cit - y sing;
4. There shall each rap - tured tongue Hts end - less praise pro - claim;
Wake, ev - 'ry heart and ev - 'ry tongue, To praise the Sav - iour's name.
Sing how He in - ter - cedes a - bove For those whose sins He bore.
Re - joice ye in the Lamb of God— In Christ, th'e - ter - nal King.
And sweet - er voic - es tune the song Of Mo - ses and the Lamb.

No. 693. While Shepherds Watched.

N. Tate. (Christmas. C. M.) G. F. Handel.

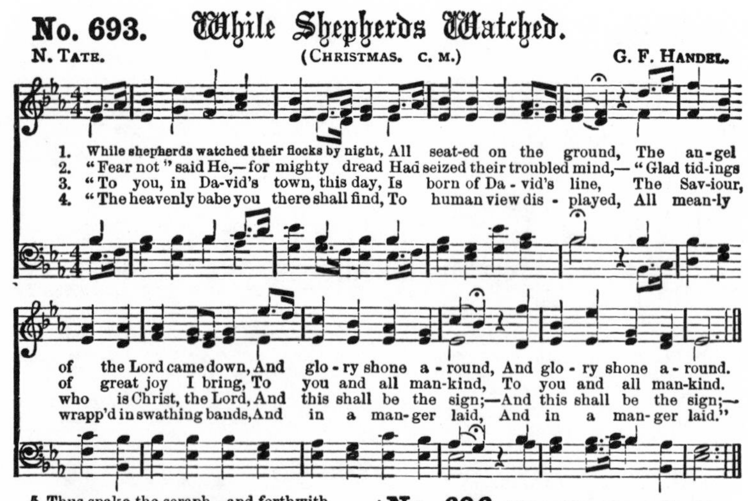

1. While shepherds watched their flocks by night, All seat-ed on the ground, The an-gel
2. "Fear not" said He,—for mighty dread Had seized their troubled mind,—"Glad tid-ings
3. "To you, in Da-vid's town, this day, Is born of Da-vid's line, The Sav-iour,
4. "The heavenly babe you there shall find, To human view dis-played, All mean-ly
of the Lord came down, And glo-ry shone a-round, And glo-ry shone a-round.
of great joy I bring, To you and all man-kind, To you and all man-kind.
who is Christ, the Lord, And this shall be the sign;—And this shall be the sign;—
wrapp'd in swathing bands, And in a man-ger laid, And in a man-ger laid."

5 Thus spake the seraph—and forthwith
Appeared a shining throng
Of angels, praising God, who thus
Addressed their joyful song:—

6 "All glory be to God on high,
And to the earth be peace;
Good-will henceforth from heaven to men
Begin, and never cease!"

No. 694. Tune—Azmon. C. M. Key A.

1 Salvation! O the joyful sound!
What pleasure to our ears;
A sovereign balm for every wound
A cordial for our fears.

2 Salvation! let the echo fly
The spacious earth around,
While all the armies of the sky
Conspire to raise the sound.

3 Salvation! O Thou bleeding Lamb!
To Thee the praise belongs:
Salvation shall inspire our hearts,
And dwell upon our tongues.

Isaac Watts.

No. 695. Tune—Mear. C. M. Key F.

1 Spirit of truth, O let me know
The love of Christ to me;
Its conquering, quickening power bestow,
To set me wholly free.

2 I long to know its depth and height,
To scan its breadth and length;
Drink in its ocean of delight,
And triumph in its strength.

3 It is Thine office to reveal
My Saviour's wond'rous love;
Oh, deepen on my heart Thy seal,
And bless me from above.

4 Thy quickening power to me impart,
And be my constant Guide;
With richer gladness fill my heart;
Be Jesus glorified.

Anon.

No. 696. Tune—Rathbun. No. 698.

1 O my soul, bless thou Jehovah,
And within me, bless His name;
Bless Jehovah, and forget not
All His mercies to proclaim.

2 Who forgives all thy transgressions,
Thy diseases all who heals;
Who redeems thee from destruction,
Who with thee so kindly deals.

3 Who with tender mercies crowns thee,
Who with good-things fills thy mouth,
So that even like the eagle
Thou hast been restored to youth.

4 In His righteousness, Jehovah
Will deliver those distressed;
He will execute just judgment
In the cause of all oppressed.

Psalm 103.

No. 697. Tune—Wilmot. 8s. 7s. No. 671.

1 Jesus only, when the morning
Beams upon the path I tread;
Jesus only when the darkness
Gathers round my weary head.

2 Jesus only, when the billows
Cold and sullen o'er me roll;
Jesus only, when the trumpet
Rends the tomb and wakes the soul.

3 Jesus only, when in judgment
Boding fears my heart appall:
Jesus only, when the wretched
On the rocks and mountains call.

4 Jesus only, when adoring,
Saints their crown before Him bring;
Jesus only, I will, joyous,
Through eternal ages sing.

Rev. Elias Nason.

No. 698. In the Cross of Christ.

Sir John Bowring. (Rathbun. 8s. 7s.) Ithamar Conkey.

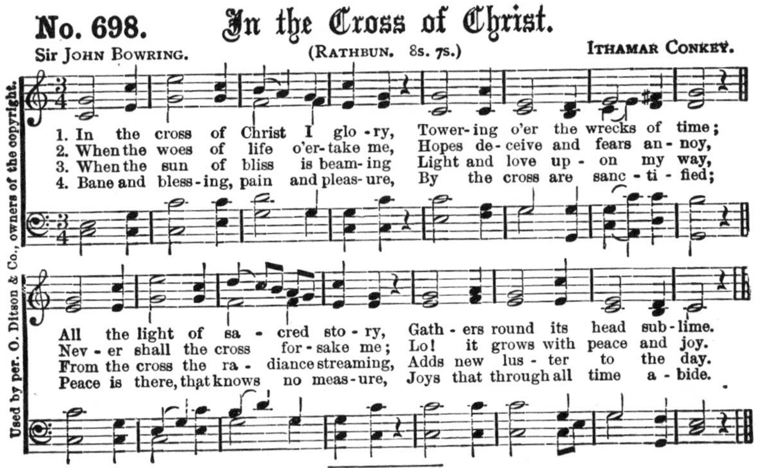
Used by per. O. Ditson & Co., owners of the copyright.
1. In the cross of Christ I glo - ry, Tower- ing o'er the wrecks of time;
2. When the woes of life o'er- take me, Hopes de - ceive and fears an - noy,
3. When the sun of bliss is beam- ing Light and love up - on my way,
4. Bane and bless - ing, pain and pleas- ure, By the cross are sanc - ti - fied;
All the light of sa - cred sto - ry, Gath - ers round its head sub - lime.
Nev - er shall the cross for - sake me; Lo! it grows with peace and joy.
From the cross the ra - diance streaming, Adds new lus - ter to the day.
Peace is there, that knows no meas- ure, Joys that through all time a - bide.

No. 699. Tune—Rathbun. 8s. 7s.

1 We are waiting by the river,
We are watching by the shore,
Only waiting for the boatman,
Soon he'll come to bear us o'er.

2 Though the mist hang o'er the river,
And its billows loudly roar,
Yet we hear the song of angels,
Wafted from the other shore.

3 And the bright celestial city,—
We have caught such radiant gleams
Of its towers like dazzling sunlight,
With its sweet and peaceful streams.

4 He has called for many a loved one,
We have seen them leave our side;
With our Saviour we shall meet them
When we too, have crossed the tide.

5 When we've passed the vale of shadows,
With its dark and chilling tide,
In that bright and glorious city
We shall evermore abide.

Miss Mary P. Griffin.

No. 700. Tune—Rathbun. 8s. 7s.

1 Saviour! visit Thy plantation;
Grant us, Lord, a gracious rain;
All will come to desolation,
Unless Thou return again.

2 Keep no longer at a distance;—
Shine upon us from on high,
Lest for want of Thine assistance,
Every plant should droop and die.

3 Let our mutual love be fervent,
Make us prevalent in prayers;
Let each one, esteemed Thy servant,
Shun the world's enticing snares.

4 Break the tempter's fatal power;
Turn the stony heart to flesh;
And begin from this good hour,
To revive Thy work afresh.

Rev. John Newton.

No. 701. Tune—Rathbun. 8s. 7s.

1 Jesus, hail! enthroned in glory
There for ever to abide;
All the heavenly hosts adore Thee,
Seated at Thy Father's side.

2 There for sinnere thou art pleading,
There Thou dost our place prepare;
Ever for us interceding,
Till in glory we appear.

3 Worship, honor, power and blessing
Thou art worthy to receive:
Loudest praises, without ceasing,
Meet it is for us to give.

4 Help, ye bright angelic spirits!
Bring your sweetest, noblest lays;
Help to sing our Saviour's merits—
Help to chant Immanuel's praise.

Rev. John Bakewell.

No. 702. Tune—Autumn. 8s. 7s. No. 263.

1 Jesus wept! those tears are over
But His heart is still the same,
Kinsman, Friend, and Elder Brother,
Is His everlasting name.
Saviour, who can love like Thee,
Gracious One of Bethany.

2 When the pangs of trial seize us,
When the waves of sorrow roll,
I will lay my head on Jesus,
Pillow of the troubled soul.
Surely, none can feel like Thee,
Weeping One of Bethany.

3 Jesus wept! and still in glory,
He can mark each mourner's tears;
Living to retrace the story
Of the hearts He solaced here.
Lord, when I am called to die,
Let me think of Bethany.

4 Jesus wept! those tears of sorrow
Are a legacy of love;
Yesterday, to day, to-morrow,
He the same doth ever prove,
Thou art all in all to me
Living One of Bethany.

Sir Edward Denny.

No. 703. I Waited for the Lord.

40th Psalm. (Dundee. C. M.) Andro Hart's Psalter.

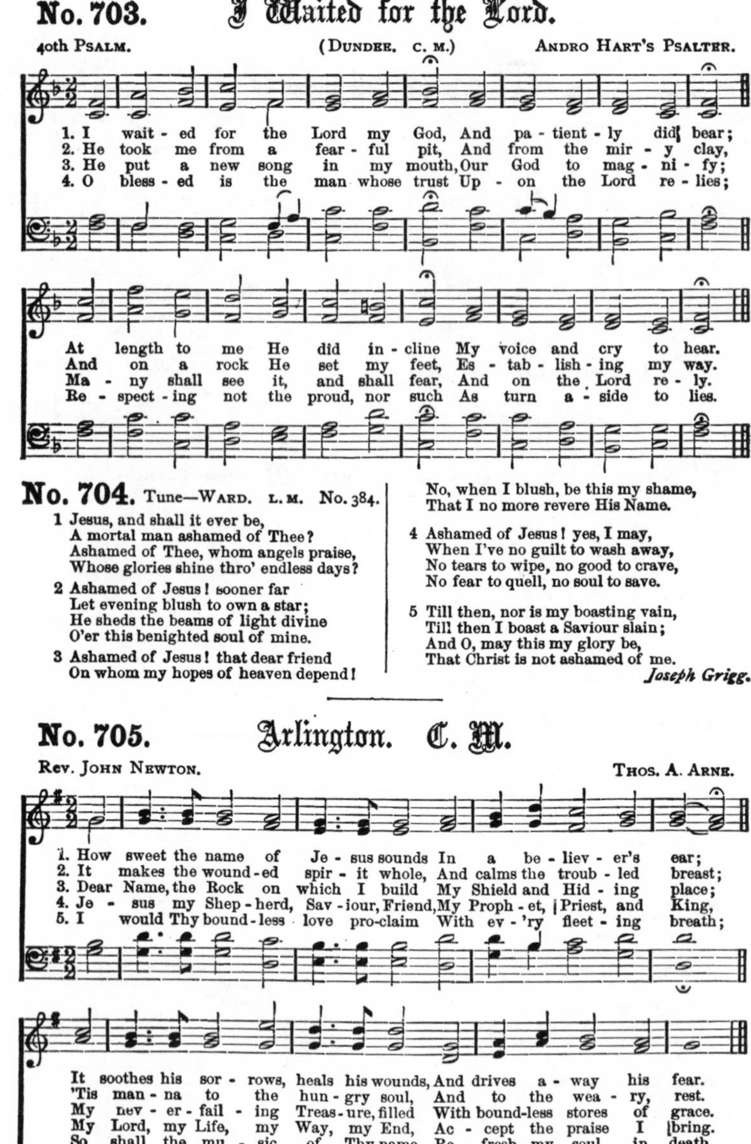
1. I wait - ed for the Lord my God, And pa - tient - ly did bear;
2. He took me from a fear - ful pit, And from the mir - y clay,
3. He put a new song in my mouth, Our God to mag - ni - fy;
4. O bless - ed is the man whose trust Up - on the Lord re - lies;
At length to me He did in - cline My voice and cry to hear.
And on a rock He set my feet, Es - tab - lish - ing my way.
Ma - ny shall see it, and shall fear, And on the Lord re - ly.
Re - spect - ing not the proud, nor such As turn a - side to lies.

No. 704. Tune—Ward. L. M. No. 384.

1 Jesus, and shall it ever be,
A mortal man ashamed of Thee?
Ashamed of Thee, whom angels praise,
Whose glories shine thro' endless days?

2 Ashamed of Jesus! sooner far
Let evening blush to own a star;
He sheds the beams of light divine
O'er this benighted soul of mine.

3 Ashamed of Jesus! that dear friend
On whom my hopes of heaven depend!
No, when I blush, be this my shame,
That I no more revere His Name.

4 Ashamed of Jesus! yes, I may,
When I've no guilt to wash away,
No tears to wipe, no good to crave,
No fear to quell, no soul to save.

5 Till then, nor is my boasting vain,
Till then I boast a Saviour slain;
And O, may this my glory be,
That Christ is not ashamed of me.

Joseph Grigg.

No. 705. Arlington. C. M.

Rev. John Newton. Thos. A. Arne.

1. How sweet the name of Je - sus sounds In a be - liev - er's ear;
2. It makes the wound - ed spir - it whole, And calms the troub - led breast;
3. Dear Name, the Rock on which I build My Shield and Hid - ing place;
4. Je - sus my Shep - herd, Sav - iour, Friend, My Proph - et, Priest, and King,
5. I would Thy bound - less love pro - claim With ev - 'ry fleet - ing breath;
It soothes his sor - rows, heals his wounds, And drives a - way his fear.
'Tis man - na to the hun - gry soul, And to the wea - ry, rest.
My nev - er - fail - ing Treas - ure, filled With bound - less stores of grace.
My Lord, my Life, my Way, my End, Ac - cept the praise I bring.
So shall the mu - sic of Thy name, Re - fresh my soul in death.

No. 706. Save, Jesus, Save!

Anon. GEO. C. STEBBINS.

Used by per.
1. Save, Je - sus, save! Thy blessing now we crave; For ev - 'ry anx- ious sin - ner here,
2. Save, Je - sus, save! Thy ban - ner o'er us wave, Of love e - ter - nal and di - vine;
3. Save, Je - sus, save! Thou conqueror o'er the grave, Give ev - 'ry fet - tered soul re - lease,
4. Save, Je - sus, save! And Thou a - lone shalt have The glo - ry of the work di - vine,
Oh, let Thy mer - cy now ap - pear, Lord Je - sus, save, Lord Je - sus, save.
O Lord, let each one here be Thine, Lord Je - sus, save, Lord Je - sus, save.
And to the troub - led, whisper "Peace." Lord Je - sus, save, Lord Je - sus, save.
Yea, end - less prais - es shall be Thine! Lord Je - sus, save, Lord Je - sus, save.

No. 707. Tune—ARLINGTON. C. M. No. 705.

1 O for a faith that will not shrink,
Though pressed by every foe,
That will not tremble on the brink
Of any earthly woe.

2 That will not murmur or complain
Beneath the chast'ning rod,
But, in the hour of grief or pain,
Will lean upon its God;—

3 A faith that shines more bright and clear
When tempests rage without;
And when in danger knows no fear,
In darkness feels no doubt.

4 Lord, give us such a faith as this,
And then, whate'er may come,
We'll taste e'en here the hallowed bliss
Of an eternal home.

Rev. W. H. Bathurst.

No. 708. "Looking Home."

K. J. T. SPITTA. WM. B. BRADBURY.

Used by per.
1. Ah, this heart is void and chill, 'Mid earth's nois-y throng-ing; For my Fa-ther's man - sion, still Ear - nest - ly I'm long - ing.
2. Soon the glo-rious day will dawn, Heav'nly pleasures bring - ing; Night will be ex - changed for morn, Sighs give place to sing - ing.
REFRAIN.
Look - ing home, look - ing home,
T'ward the heav'nly man-sion, Je - sus hath prepared for me, In His Fa-ther's kingdom.

3 Oh, to be at home, and gain,
All for which we're sighing,
From all earthly want and pain
To be swiftly flying.—

4 Blessed home! oh, blessed home!
There no more to sever;
Soon we'll meet around the throne
Praising God forever.

No. 709.
Hamburg. L. M.
Isaac Watts.
Ad. by Lowell Mason.
1. When I sur-vey the won-drous cross On which the Prince of Glo-ry died,
2. For-bid it, Lord, that I should boast, Save in the death of Christ my God:
My richest gain I count but loss, And pour contempt on all my pride.
All the vain things that charm me most, I sac-ri-fice them to His blood.
3 See! from His head, His hands, His feet,
Sorrow and love flow mingled down!
Did e'er such love and sorrow meet,
Or thorns compose so rich a crown?
4 Were the whole realm of nature mine,
That were an offering far too small:
Love so amazing, so divine,
Demands my soul, my life, my all.
No. 710.
Rockingham. L. M.
Wm. Cowper.
Dr. Lowell Mason.
1. What vari-ous hin-dran-ces we meet, In com-ing to the mer-cy-seat!
2. Pray'r makes the dark-ened clouds withdraw; Pray'r climbs the lad-der Ja-cob saw,
3. Re-strain-ing pray'r, we cease to fight; Pray'r makes the Christian's ar-mor bright;
Yet who that knows the worth of pray'r, But wish-es to be oft-en there?
Gives ex-er-cise to faith and love, Brings ev-'ry bless-ing from a-bove.
And Sa-tan trem-bles when he sees The weak-est saint up-on his knees.
No. 711.
Sessions. L. M.
A. D. 1531.
L. O. Emerson.
1. Faith is a liv-ing pow'er from heaven Which grasps the prom-ise God has giv'n;
2. Faith finds in Christ what-e'er we need To save and strengthen, guide and feed;
3. Faith to the conscience whis-pers peace; And bids the mourn-er's sigh-ing cease;
4. Such faith in us, O God, im-plant, And to our pray'rs Thy fav-or grant.

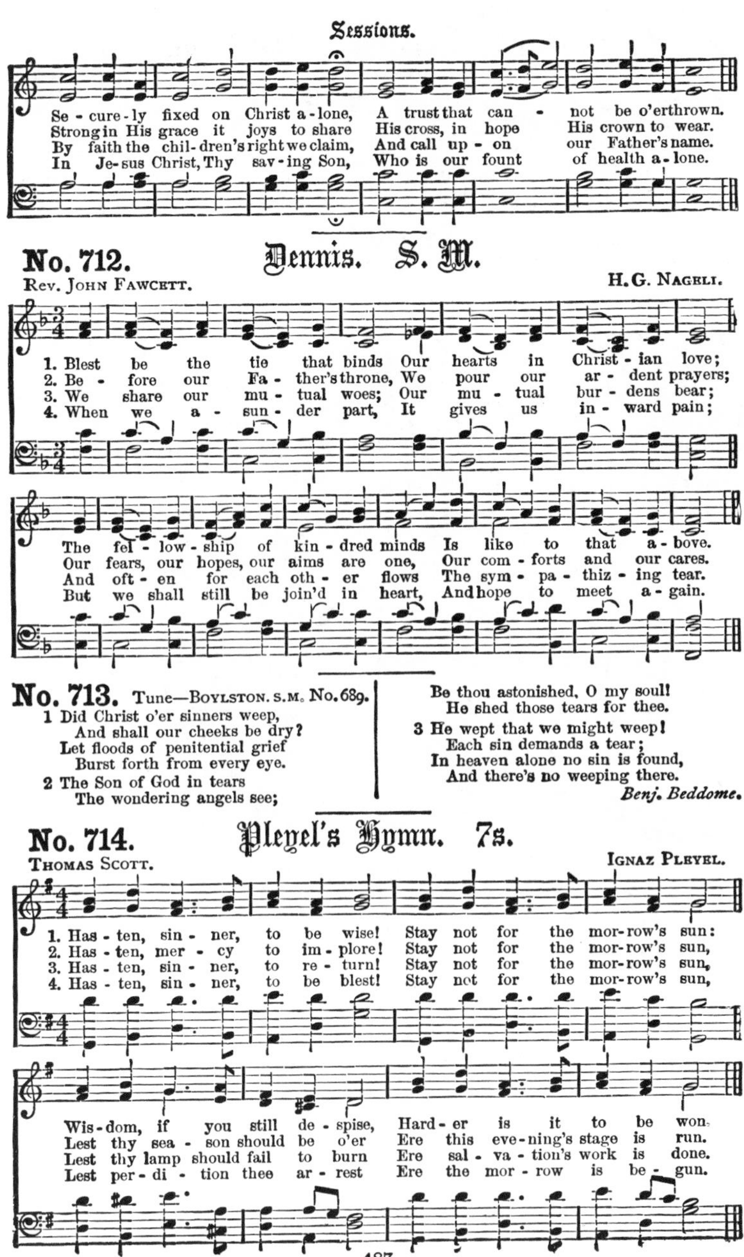
Sessions.
Se-cure-ly fixed on Christ a-lone, A trust that can - not be o'erthrown.
Strong in His grace it joys to share His cross, in hope His crown to wear.
By faith the chil-dren's right we claim, And call up-on our Father's name.
In Je-sus Christ, Thy sav-ing Son, Who is our fount of health a-lone.
No. 712. Dennis. S. M.
Rev. John Fawcett.
H. G. Nageli.
1. Blest be the tie that binds Our hearts in Christ-ian love;
2. Be-fore our Fa-ther's throne, We pour our ar-dent prayers;
3. We share our mu-tual woes; Our mu-tual bur-dens bear;
4. When we a-sun-der part, It gives us in-ward pain;
The fel-low-ship of kin-dred minds Is like to that a-bove.
Our fears, our hopes, our aims are one, Our com-forts and our cares.
And oft-en for each oth-er flows The sym-pa-thiz-ing tear.
But we shall still be join'd in heart, And hope to meet a-gain.
No. 713. Tune—Boylston. s.m. No. 689.
1 Did Christ o'er sinners weep,
And shall our cheeks be dry?
Let floods of penitential grief
Burst forth from every eye.
2 The Son of God in tears
The wondering angels see;
Be thou astonished, O my soul!
He shed those tears for thee.
3 He wept that we might weep!
Each sin demands a tear;
In heaven alone no sin is found,
And there's no weeping there.
Benj. Beddome.
No. 714. Pleyel's Hymn. 7s.
Thomas Scott.
Ignaz Pleyel.
1. Has-ten, sin-ner, to be wise! Stay not for the mor-row's sun:
2. Has-ten, mer-cy to im-plore! Stay not for the mor-row's sun,
3. Has-ten, sin-ner, to re-turn! Stay not for the mor-row's sun,
4. Has-ten, sin-ner, to be blest! Stay not for the mor-row's sun,
Wis-dom, if you still de-spise, Hard-er is it to be won.
Lest thy sea-son should be o'er Ere this eve-ning's stage is run.
Lest thy lamp should fail to burn Ere sal-va-tion's work is done.
Lest per-di-tion thee ar-rest Ere the mor-row is be-gun.

No. 715. Come, Thou Almighty King.

CHARLES WESLEY. (ITALIAN HYMN. 6s. 4s.) FELICE GIARDINI.

1. Come, Thou almight-y King, Help us Thy name to sing, Help us to praise: Fa-ther! all-glo-ri-ous, O'er all vic-to-ri-ous, Come, and reign o-ver us, An-cient of Days!
2. Come, Thou in-carnate Word, Gird on Thy might-y sword; Our pray'r attend: Come, and Thy peo-ple bless, And give Thy word success: Spir-it of ho-li-ness! On us de-scend.
3. Come, ho-ly Com-fort-er! Thy sa-cred wit-ness bear, In this glad hour: Thou, who al-might-y art, Now rule in ev-'ry heart, And ne'er from us de-part, Spir-it of pow'r!
4. To the great One in Three, The highest prais-es be, Hence ever-more! His sov'reign ma-jes-ty May we in glo-ry see, And to e-ter-ni-ty Love and a-dore.

No. 716. Tune—ITALIAN HYMN. 6s. 4s.

1 Sound, sound the truth abroad,
Bear ye the word of God
Through the wide world:
Tell what our Lord has done,
Tell how the day is won,
And from His lofty throne
Satan is hurled.

2 Speed on the wings of love,
Jesus, who reigns above,
Bids us to fly;
They who His message bear
Should neither doubt nor fear,
He will their Friend appear,
He will be nigh.

3 Ye, who forsaking all,
At your loved Master's call,
Comforts resign;
Soon will your work be done;
Soon will the prize be won;
Brighter than yonder sun
Then shall ye shine.

Thos. Kelly.

No. 717. Tune—ITALIAN HYMN. 6s. 4s.

1 Rise, glorious Conqueror, rise
Into Thy native skies,—
Assume Thy right;
And where in many a fold
The clouds are backward rolled—
Pass through those gates of gold,
And reign in light!

2 Victor o'er death and hell!
Cherubic legions swell
Thy radiant train:
Praises all heaven inspire;
Each angel sweeps his lyre,
And waves his wings of fire,—
Thou Lamb once slain!

3 Enter, incarnate God!—
No feet but Thine, have trod
The serpent down
Blow the full trumpets, blow!
Wider yon portals throw!
Saviour triumphant—go,
And take Thy crown!

4 Lion of Judah—Hail!
And let Thy name prevail
From age to age;
Lord of the rolling years!
Claim for Thine own the spheres,
For Thou hast bought with tears
Thy heritage.

5 And then was heard afar
Star answering to star—
"Lo! these have come
Followers of Him who gave
His life their lives to save;
And now their palms they wave,
Brought safely home."

Matthew Bridges

No. 718. My Faith Looks up to Thee.

RAY PALMER, D.D. (OLIVET. 6s. 4s.) DR. LOWELL MASON.

1. My faith looks up to Thee, Thou Lamb of Cal-va-ry, Sav-iour di-vine! Now hear me
2. May Thy rich grace impart Strength to my fainting heart, My zeal inspire; As thou hast
3. While life's dark maze I tread, And griefs around me spread, Be Thou my Guide; Bid darkness
4. When ends life's transient dream, When death's cold, sullen stream Shall o'er me roll, Blest Saviour!

My Faith Looks up to Thee.
while I pray, Take all my guilt a-way, Oh, let me from this day Be whol-ly Thine.
died for me, Oh, may my love to Thee Pure, warm, and changeless be A liv-ing fire!
turn to day, Wipe sorrow's tears a-way, Nor let me ev-er stray From Thee a-side.
then, in love, Fear and distrust remove; Oh, bear me safe a-bove, A ransomed soul!
No. 719. Nearer, My God to Thee.
Sarah F. Adams.
(Bethany. 6s. 4s.)
Dr. Lowell Mason.
1. Near-er, my God, to Thee, Near-er to Thee; E'en though it be a cross
2. Tho' like the wan-der-er, The sun gone down, Dark-ness be o-ver me,
3. There let the way ap-pear Steps un-to heaven; All that Thou send-est me,
4. Then with my wak-ing tho'ts, Bright with Thy praise, Out of my sto-ny griefs,
5. Or if, on joy-ful wing, Cleav-ing the sky, Sun, moon, and stars for-got,
D.S.—Near-er, my God, to Thee!
Fine.
D.S.
That rais-eth me, Still all my song shall be— Near-er, my God, to Thee!
My rest a stone, Yet in my dreams I'd be Near-er, my God, to Thee!
In mer-cy given: An-gels to beck-on me Near-er, my God, to Thee!
Beth-el I'll raise; So by my woes to be Near-er, my God, to Thee!
Up-ward I fly, Still all my song shall be Near-er, my God, to Thee!
Near-er to Thee!
Used by per. O. Ditson & Co., owners of copyright.
No. 720. Come to Jesus Just Now.
E. P. Hammond.
J. Fawcett.
1. Come to Je-sus, Come to Je-sus, Come to Je-sus just now,
2. He will save you, He will save you, He will save you just now,
Just now come to Je-sus, Come to Je-sus just now.
Just now He will save you, He will save you just now.

3 He is able, etc.
4 He is willing, etc.
5 He is waiting, etc.
6 He will hear you, etc.
7 He will cleanse you, etc.
8 He'll renew you, etc.
9 He'll forgive you, etc.
10 If you'll trust Him, etc.
11 He will save you, etc.

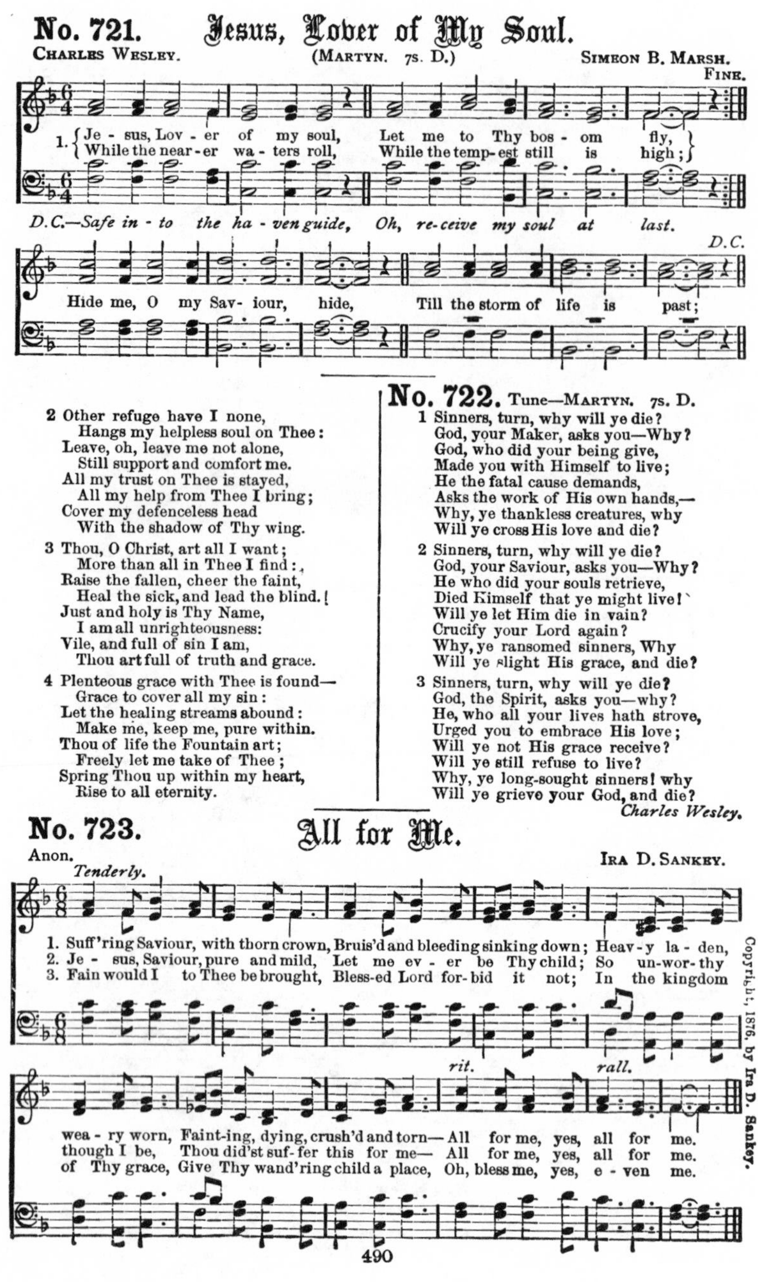
No. 721. Jesus, Lover of My Soul.
Charles Wesley.
(Martyn. 7s. D.)
Simeon B. Marsh.
Fine.
1. { Je - sus, Lov - er of my soul, Let me to Thy bos - om fly, }
{ While the near - er wa - ters roll, While the temp - est still is high; }
D.C.—Safe in - to the ha - ven guide, Oh, re - ceive my soul at last.
D.C.
Hide me, O my Sav - iour, hide, Till the storm of life is past;

2 Other refuge have I none,
Hangs my helpless soul on Thee:
Leave, oh, leave me not alone,
Still support and comfort me.
All my trust on Thee is stayed,
All my help from Thee I bring;
Cover my defenceless head
With the shadow of Thy wing.

3 Thou, O Christ, art all I want;
More than all in Thee I find:
Raise the fallen, cheer the faint,
Heal the sick, and lead the blind.
Just and holy is Thy Name,
I am all unrighteousness:
Vile, and full of sin I am,
Thou art full of truth and grace.

4 Plenteous grace with Thee is found—
Grace to cover all my sin:
Let the healing streams abound:
Make me, keep me, pure within.
Thou of life the Fountain art;
Freely let me take of Thee;
Spring Thou up within my heart,
Rise to all eternity.

No. 722. Tune—Martyn. 7s. D.

1 Sinners, turn, why will ye die?
God, your Maker, asks you—Why?
God, who did your being give,
Made you with Himself to live;
He the fatal cause demands,
Asks the work of His own hands,—
Why, ye thankless creatures, why
Will ye cross His love and die?

2 Sinners, turn, why will ye die?
God, your Saviour, asks you—Why?
He who did your souls retrieve,
Died Himself that ye might live!
Will ye let Him die in vain?
Crucify your Lord again?
Why, ye ransomed sinners, Why
Will ye slight His grace, and die?

3 Sinners, turn, why will ye die?
God, the Spirit, asks you—why?
He, who all your lives hath strove,
Urged you to embrace His love;
Will ye not His grace receive?
Will ye still refuse to live?
Why, ye long-sought sinners! why
Will ye grieve your God, and die?

Charles Wesley.

No. 723. All for Me.
Anon.
Ira D. Sankey.
Tenderly.
1. Suff'ring Saviour, with thorn crown, Bruis'd and bleeding sinking down; Heav - y la - den,
2. Je - sus, Saviour, pure and mild, Let me ev - er be Thy child; So un - wor - thy
3. Fain would I to Thee be brought, Bless - ed Lord for - bid it not; In the kingdom
rit. rall.
wea - ry worn, Faint - ing, dying, crush'd and torn— All for me, yes, all for me.
though I be, Thou did'st suf - fer this for me— All for me, yes, all for me.
of Thy grace, Give Thy wand'ring child a place, Oh, bless me, yes, e - ven me.
Copyright, 1876, by Ira D. Sankey.

No. 724. Jesus Loves Me!

Anna B. Warner. Wm. B. Bradbury.

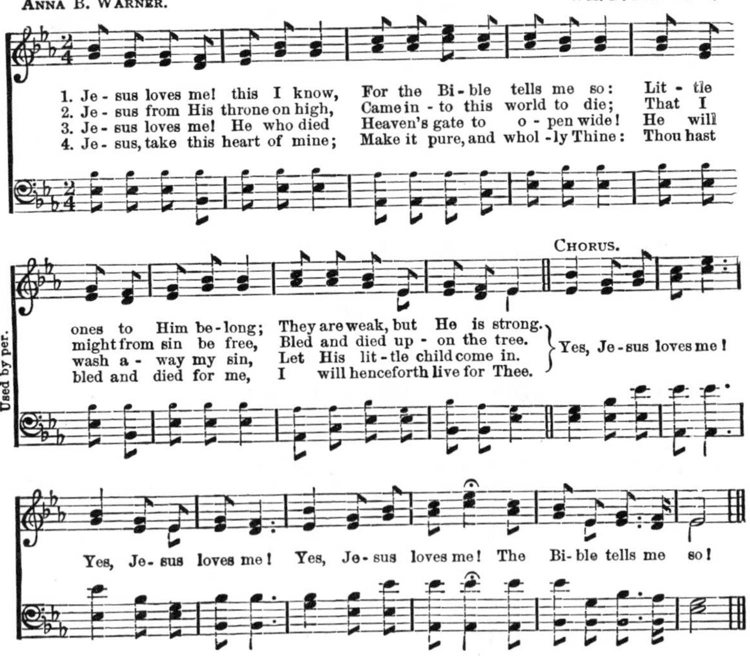
1. Je - sus loves me! this I know, For the Bi - ble tells me so: Lit - tle
2. Je - sus from His throne on high, Came in - to this world to die; That I
3. Je - sus loves me! He who died Heaven's gate to o - pen wide! He will
4. Je - sus, take this heart of mine; Make it pure, and whol - ly Thine: Thou hast
Chorus.
ones to Him be - long; They are weak, but He is strong.
might from sin be free, Bled and died up - on the tree.
wash a - way my sin, Let His lit - tle child come in.
bled and died for me, I will henceforth live for Thee.
Yes, Je - sus loves me!
Used by per.
Yes, Je - sus loves me! Yes, Je - sus loves me! The Bi - ble tells me so!

No. 725. Tune—Italian Hymn. No. 715.

1 Glory to God on high!
Let heaven and earth reply,
"Praise ye His name!"
His love and grace adore,
Who all our sorrows bore;
Sing loud for evermore,
"Worthy the Lamb."

2 While they around the throne
Cheerfully join in one,
Praising His name—
Ye who have felt His blood,
Sealing your peace with God,
Sound His dear name abroad,
"Worthy the Lamb!"

3 Join, all ye ransomed race,
Our Lord and God to bless;
Praise ye His name—
In Him we will rejoice,
And make a joyful noise,
Shouting with heart and voice,
"Worthy the Lamb!"

4 Soon must we change our place,
Yet will we never cease
Praising His name;
To Him our songs we bring;
Hail Him our gracious King;
And, through all ages sing,
"Worthy the Lamb!"

J. Allen, alt.

No. 726. (Tune, No. 19.)

1 My God I have found
The thrice blessed ground,
Where life and where joy, and true comfort abound.

Cho.—Hallelujah! Thine the glory!
Hallelujah! Amen!
Hallelujah! Thine the glory!
Revive us again.

2 'Tis found in the blood
Of Him who once stood
My refuge and safety, my surety with God.

3 He bore on the tree
The sentence for me,
And now both the surety and sinner are free.

4 And though here below
'Mid sorrow and woe,
My place is in heaven with Jesus, I know.

5 And this I shall find
For such is his mind,
"He'll not be in glory and leave me behind."

Rev. John Gambold

No. 727. Jesus, Lover of My Soul.

CHARLES WESLEY. (REFUGE. 7s. D.) JOS. P. HOLBROOK.

1. Je - sus, Lov - er of my soul, Let me to Thy bo - som fly, While the near - er
2. Oth - er ref - uge have I none, Hangs my helpless soul on Thee; Leave, oh, leave me
3. Thou, O Christ, art all I want; More than all in Thee I find: Raise the fall - en
4. Plenteous grace with Thee is found–Grace to cov - er all my sin: Let the heal-ing

wa - ters roll, While the tem - pest still is high; Hide me, oh my Saviour hide, Till the
not a - lone Still sup - port and comfort me: All my trust on Thee is stayed, All my
cheer the faint Heal the sick and lead the blind: Just and ho - ly is Thy name, I am
streams abound; Make me, keep me, pure with - in, Thou of life the Fountain art, Free-ly

storm of life is past; Safe in - to the ha - ven guide, Oh, re - ceive my soul at last.
help from Thee I bring; Cov - er my defenceless head With the shad - ow of Thy wing.
all unrighteous - ness; Vile and full of sin I am, Thou art full of truth and grace.
let me take of Thee; Spring Thou up within my heart, Rise to all e - ter - ni - ty.

Used by per.

No. 728. Windham. L. M.

CHARLES WESLEY. DANIEL READ.

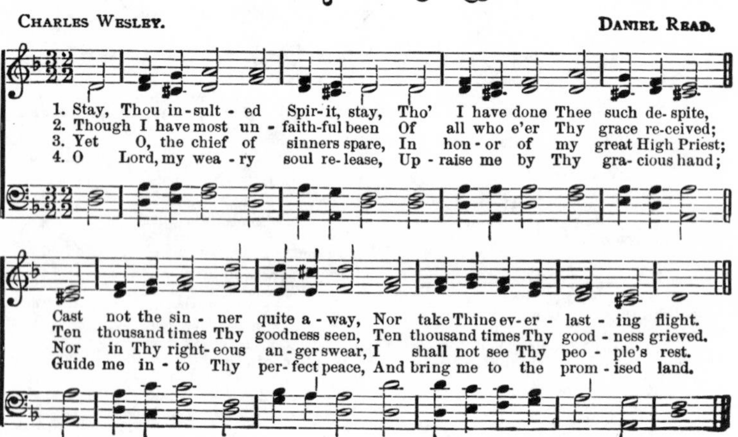
1. Stay, Thou in - sult - ed Spir - it, stay, Tho' I have done Thee such de - spite,
2. Though I have most un - faith - ful been Of all who e'er Thy grace re - ceived;
3. Yet O, the chief of sinners spare, In hon - or of my great High Priest;
4. O Lord, my wea - ry soul re - lease, Up - raise me by Thy gra - cious hand;
Cast not the sin - ner quite a - way, Nor take Thine ev - er - last - ing flight.
Ten thousand times Thy goodness seen, Ten thousand times Thy good - ness grieved.
Nor in Thy right - eous an - ger swear, I shall not see Thy peo - ple's rest.
Guide me in - to Thy per - fect peace, And bring me to the prom - ised land.

No. 729. All Hail the Power.
E. Perronet.
(Coronation. C. M.)
Oliver Holden.
1. All hail the power of Je - sus' name! Let an - gels pros - trate fall;
2. Let ev - 'ry kin - dred, ev - 'ry tribe, On this ter - res - trial ball,
3. Oh, that with yon - der sa - cred throng We at His feet may fall;
Bring forth the roy - al di - a - dem, And crown Him Lord of all;
To Him all maj - es - ty as - cribe, And crown Him Lord of all;
We'll join the ev - er - last - ing song, And crown Him Lord of all;
Bring forth the roy - al di - a - dem, And crown Him Lord...... of all.
To Him all maj - es - ty as - cribe, And crown Him Lord...... of all.
We'll join the ev - er - last - ing song, And crown Him Lord...... of all.
No. 730. Tune—Coronation. C. M.
1 O for a thousand tongues to sing
My great Redeemer's praise;
The glories of my God and king,
The triumphs of His grace.
2 My gracious Master, and my God,
Assist me to proclaim,—
To spread, thro' all the earth abroad,
The honors of Thy Name.
3 Jesus!—the Name that charms our fears,
That bids our sorrows cease;
'Tis music in the sinner's ears,
'Tis life, and health, and peace.
4 He breaks the power of cancell'd sin,
He sets the pris'ner free;
His blood can make the foulest clean;
His blood avail'd for me.
Charles Wesley.
No. 731. Hendon. 7s.
Rev. J. S. B. Monsell.
C. H. A. Malan.
1. Ask ye what great thing I know That de - lights and stirs me so? What the high re - ward I win? Whose the name I glo - ry in? Je - sus Christ, the Cru - ci - fied.
2. What is faith's foun - dation strong! What a - wakes my lips to song? He who bore my sin - ful load, Pur - chased for me peace with God, Je - sus Christ, the Cru - ci - fied.
3. Who de - feats my fierc - est foes? Who con - soles my sad - dest woes? Who re - vives my faint - ing heart, Heal - ing all its hid - den smart? Je - sus Christ, the Cru - ci - fied.
4 Who is life in life to me?
Who the death of death will be?
Who will place me on His right
With the countless hosts of light?
Jesus Christ, the Crucified.
5 This is that great thing I know;
This delights and stirs me so;
Faith in Him who died to save,
Him who triumphed o'er the grave,
Jesus Christ, the Crucified.
498

No. 732. Lord, Dismiss Us.

John Fawcett, D. D. (Greenville. 8s. 7s. & 4.) J. J. Rosseau.

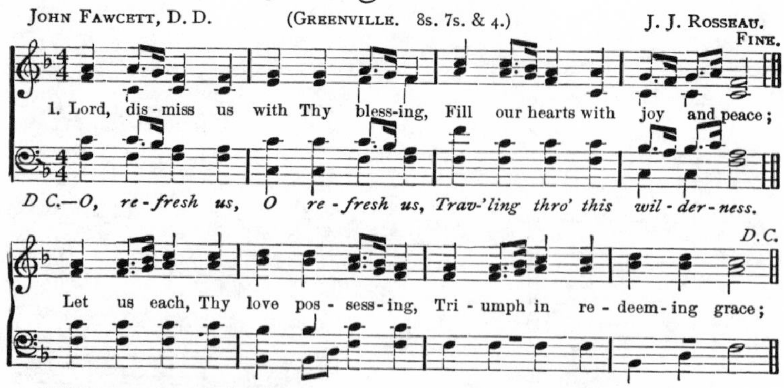
Fine.
1. Lord, dis-miss us with Thy bless-ing, Fill our hearts with joy and peace;
D C.—O, re-fresh us, O re-fresh us, Trav-'ling thro' this wil-der-ness.
D.C.
Let us each, Thy love pos-sess-ing, Tri-umph in re-deem-ing grace;

2 Thanks we give and adoration,
For Thy gospel's joyful sound:
May the fruits of Thy salvation
In our hearts and lives abound;
Ever faithful, Ever faithful,
To the truth may we be found.

3 So, whene'er the signal's given
Us from earth to call away,
Borne on angel's wings to heaven,
Glad the summons to obey,
May we ever, May we ever
Reign with Christ in endless day!

No. 733. There is a Fountain.

Rev. William Cowper. (Cowper. C. M) Dr. Lowell Mason.

1. There is a fount-ain filled with blood, Drawn from Im-man-uel's veins;
Fine.
And sin-ners plunged be-neath that flood, Lose all their guilt-y stains.
D.S.
Lose all their guilt-y stains, Lose all their guilt-y stains.

2 The dying thief rejoiced to see
That fountain in his day,
And there may I, though vile as he,
Wash all my sins away.

3 Dear dying Lamb, Thy precious blood
Shall never lose its power,
Till all the ransomed church of God
Be saved to sin no more.

4 E'er since, by faith I saw the stream
Thy flowing wounds supply,
Redeeming love has been my theme,
And shall be, till I die.

5 Then in a nobler, sweeter song,
I'll sing Thy power to save,
When this poor lisping, stammering tongue
Lies silent in the grave.

No. 734. Mercy's Free.

RICHARD JUKES. From D. F. E. AUBER.

1. { By faith I view my Sav-iour dy - ing, On the tree, On the tree: }
{ To ev - 'ry na - tion He is cry - ing, Look to me, Look to me; }
2. { Did Christ, when I was sin pur - su - ing, Pit - y me, Pit - y me? }
{ And did He snatch my soul from ru - in, Can it be, Can it be? }
He bids the guilt - y now draw near, Re - pent, be - lieve, dis - miss their fear:
Oh, yes! He did sal - va - tion bring; He is my Proph - et, Priest and King;
Hark, hark what pre - cious words I hear, Mer - cy's free, Mer - cy's free.
And now my hap - py soul can sing, Mer - cy's free, Mer - cy's free.

3 Jesus my weary soul refreshes:
Mercy's free, Mercy's free,
And every moment Christ is precious
Unto me, Unto me;
None can describe the bliss I prove,
While through this wilderness I rove,
All may enjov the Saviour's love,
Mercy's free, Mercy's free.

4 Long as I live, I'll still be crying,
Mercy's free, Mercy's free,
And this shall be my theme when dying,
Mercy's free, Mercy's free,
And when the vale of death I've passed,
When lodged above the stormy blast,
I'll sing while endless ages last,
Mercy's free, Mercy's free.

No. 735. Tune—BELMONT. C. M. No. 678.

1 O for a heart to praise my God,
A heart from sin set free;—
A heart that always feels Thy blood,
So freely shed for me:—

2 A heart resigned, submissive, meek,
My great Redeemer's throne;
Where only Christ is heard to speak,—
Where Jesus reigns alone.

3 O for a lowly, contrite heart,
Believing, true, and clean;
Which neither life nor death can part
From Him that dwells within:—

4 A heart in every thought renewed,
And full of love divine;
Perfect, and right, and pure, and good,
A copy, Lord, of Thine.

Charles Wesley.

No. 736. Tune—HENDON. 7s. No. 731.

1 Wait, my soul, upon the Lord,
To His gracious promise flee,
Laying hold upon His word
‖: "As thy days thy strength shall be." :‖

2 If the sorrows of thy case,
Seem peculiar still to Thee,
God has promised needful grace
‖: "As thy days thy strength shall be." ‖

3 Days of trial, days of grief
In succession thou may'st see,
This is still thy sweet relief
‖: "As thy days thy strength shall be." :‖

4 Rock of Ages, I'm secure,
With Thy promise full and free,
Faithful, positive, and sure—
‖: "As thy days thy strength shall be." ‖

Wm. F. Lloyd.

No. 737. Tune—HENDON. 7s. No. 731.

1 Come, my soul, thy suit prepare,
Jesus loves to answer prayer.
He Himself has bid thee pray,
Therefore will not say thee nay.

2 Thou art coming to a King,
Large petitions with thee bring,
For His grace and power are such,
None can ever ask too much.

3 With my burden I begin,
Lord, remove this load of sin;
Let Thy blood for sinners spilt,
Set my conscience free from guilt.

4 Lord, I come to Thee for rest,
Take possession of my breast,
There Thy blood-bought right maintain,
And without a rival reign.

Rev. John Newton.

No. 738. My Country, 'tis of Thee.
S. F. Smith, D.D.
(America. 6s. 4s.)
H. Carey.
1. My coun-try, 'tis of thee, Sweet land of lib - er - ty, Of thee I sing; Land where my fa - thers died Land of the pilgrim's pride, From ev - 'ry mountain side, Let free-dom ring.
2. My na - tive country, thee, Land of the no - ble free, Thy name I love; I love thy rocks and rills, Thy woods and templed hills, My heart with rapture thrills, Like that a - bove.
3. Let music swell the breeze, And ring from all the trees Sweet freedom's song; Let mor - tal tongues awake, Let all that breathe partake, Let rocks their silence break, The sound prolong.
4. Our fa - thers' God, to thee, Au - thor of lib - er - ty, To Thee we sing; Long may our land be bright, With freedom's ho - ly light, Protect us by Thy might, Great God, our King!
cres.
No. 739. The Lord Bless thee and Keep thee.
(Written for Mr. Moody's Schools at Northfield, Mass.)
Num. 6: 24-26.
Lucy Rider Meyer.
The Lord bless thee, and keep thee! The Lord make his face shine up - on thee, and be gra - cious un - to thee: And be gra - cious un - to thee: The Lord lift up his countenance, his countenance up - on thee, and give thee peace.
and give thee peace..............................
dim.................
Copyright, 1891, by Lucy Rider Meyer. Used by per. The Biglow & Main Co., owners of Copyright.
496

TOPICAL INDEX.

GOSPEL HYMNS, 1 TO 6 COMPLETE.

ADOPTION.

ASSURANCE.

BLOOD of CHRIST (The).

CHILDREN.

CHRIST A FRIEND.

CHRIST SEEKING.

CHRIST SOUGHT BY THE SINNER.

CROSS of CHRIST (The).

CHRIST, THE SHEPHERD.

COMING of CHRIST (The).

CONFESSION.

COMMUNION, or THE LORD'S SUPPER.

GRACE.

CONSECRATION.

ETERNITY.

FAITH.

FEAR NOT.

FELLOWSHIP WITH CHRIST.

FUNERAL and BURIAL.

GOD'S WORD.

GUIDANCE.

HEAVEN.

"ALMOST THERE."

HEAVEN.

HOLY SPIRIT.

INVITATION.

JOY.

LOVE.

MISCELLANEOUS.

MISSIONARY.

PARTING HYMNS.

PEACE AND REST.

PRAISE.

PRAYER.

PRECIOUS PROMISES.

REFUGE.

REPENTANCE.

RESURRECTION.

SALVATION.

SORROW.

SUFFERINGS OF CHRIST.

TEMPERANCE.

TEMPTATION.

TRUST.

GOSPEL HYMNS, NOS. 1 to 6 COMPLETE.—*Concluded.*

WARNING.

WORK.

WORSHIP.

INDEX.

Titles in Small Capitals; *First Lines in* Roman.

Index.

INDEX.

Index.

Index.

Index.

Index.